C. HUBERT H. PARRY

Parry at *c*.35

C. Hubert H. Parry

His Life and Music

৯৬

JEREMY DIBBLE

'The mission of democracy is to convert the
false estimate of art as an appanage of luxury'
Notebook

CLARENDON PRESS · OXFORD
1992

Oxford University Press, Walton Street, Oxford OX2 6DP
Oxford New York Toronto
Delhi Bombay Calcutta Madras Karachi
Petaling Jaya Singapore Hong Kong Tokyo
Nairobi Dar es Salaam Cape Town
Melbourne Auckland
and associated companies in
Berlin Ibadan

Oxford is a trade mark of Oxford University Press

Published in the United States
by Oxford University Press, New York

British Library Cataloguing in Publication Data
Data available
ISBN 0–19–315330–0

Library of Congress Cataloging in Publication Data
Dibble, Jeremy.
C. Hubert H. Parry/Jeremy Dibble.
Includes bibliographical references and index.
1. Parry, C. Hubert H. (Charles Hubert Hastings), 1848–1918.
2. Composers—England—Biography.   I. Title.
ML410.P173D5   1992
780'.92—dc20
[B]
ISBN 0–19–315330–0

Set by Hope Services (Abingdon) Ltd.
Printed in Great Britain by
Biddles Ltd., Guildford and King's Lynn

For my wife, Alison

PREFACE AND
ACKNOWLEDGEMENTS

IT was while an undergraduate at Cambridge University in the late 1970s that I became interested in the music of Sir Hubert Parry, though it was not until the end of my first degree that I began to contemplate the serious proposition of doing research initially into his music and later into his life. Perhaps the most important catalyst in my decision to pursue research was Sir Adrian Boult's recording of the *Symphonic Fantasia, '1912'* (Fifth Symphony), the *Elegy for Brahms*, and the Symphonic Variations made in October 1978 and issued by EMI the following year. Wishing to find out more I wrote to Sir Adrian expressing my intentions and his reply was full of the most inspiring encouragement. 'Yes I am pleased,' he wrote, 'that my recording "swan song" has given old Parry a good boost—he was a splendid musician and an enthusiast could do a great deal for him.' The quality of the orchestral material confirmed a curiosity already aroused by Sir Adrian's earlier recording of the *Overture to an Unwritten Tragedy*, the *Lady Radnor* Suite and the *English* Suite which I had been introduced to during my late teens, and as a result I began to scour the libraries for information. It was only then that I realized that very little in the form of substantial musicological enquiry had been made into Parry's considerable output: a few short articles, obituaries, centenary lectures, a brief summation in general historical primers on the late nineteenth century, and transcripts of the odd broadcast; these and a two-volume biography of Parry by Charles Larcom Graves published by Macmillan in 1926.

The manner in which Graves organized his biography, devoting ten chapters to the life, and only one to Parry as a musician, immediately spurred me into an analytical study of the composer's music for a doctoral thesis. But when it came to the matter of considering a new 'life and works' study of the man, it became clear to me that a quite different treatment of the available material was necessary. Graves, who was himself more a man of letters than a musician (being assistant editor of the *Spectator* and on the staff of *Punch* magazine), was inclined to see Parry primarily in biographical terms in which the composer's musical existence could be divorced from his day-to-day existence. In this respect Graves was not alone, for it was widely accepted in the past that biography could be so conveniently divided; life and works could be viewed as separate entities without much cross-reference. Today such an approach has seemed puzzling to many musical commentators including myself who are of the opinion that the two phenomena are largely insignificant when observed alone, but when seen together show a cross-fertilization across a broad spectrum of musicological, historical, sociological, and psychological planes. Above all it is this approach that I have tried to take with regard to Parry's creative life. I have attempted to give as full a picture of his spiritual growth, the influence of personal relationships, the music he heard, the men he met and from whom he learnt, what he read, and what he shunned through the use of diaries and letters, and in turn I have used this documentation to give perspective to an examination of his large creative output.

Although Graves undertook the task of writing the biography in the early 1920s, it was inevitable that he should have had his hands largely tied. Too many people closely related or associated with Parry were still alive so soon after the composer's death which prevented the publication of any controversial material. It is clear from correspondence between Graves and Dorothea Ponsonby (Parry's elder daughter) in 1921 that Lady Maude Parry harboured severe reservations about the use of the diaries, but was reassured after an undertaking from the author that nothing of a private matter would be included about her. Consequently Maude's role in Graves's biography is conspicuous by its very absence. Likewise it is evident from the same correspondence that Parry's half-sisters were also unhappy about other aspects of his life being brought out into the open. So as to avoid wounding their feelings, Graves found it necessary to soften comments made about Thomas Gambier Parry's unwillingness to allow his son to adopt music as a profession. The sisters were also inclined to suppress the facts regarding Parry's penchant for melancholy and religious unorthodoxy, and though Graves was unwilling to expurgate all the passages concerning these issues, some of them were undoubtedly negotiated away. Similarly there is little mention of Clinton, Parry's gifted yet tragic elder brother who left a legacy of disgrace, despair, and devastation on his family. Neither is there any hint of the terrible and irrevocable rift that opened up between Parry and his eldest half-brother, Ernest Gambier Parry, in the 1890s. Last but not least, the difficulties regarding Parry's forty-year relationship with Stanford and his attitude towards the Irishman's music were left out, first because Lady Stanford was still alive, and secondly because Graves himself was counted amongst Stanford's closest friends.

From this point of view I have found myself in a much more advantageous position than my predecessor. With the cushion of seventy years since Parry's death I have not been trammelled by such personal restrictions, and the descendants of Parry's family, to whom I am eternally grateful, have not imposed any conditions on what material could or could not be used. In this respect therefore I have been free to illuminate the nature of Parry's relationship with his wife from the many surviving letters before and after their marriage. I have been able to piece together the circumstances surrounding the decline of Clinton Parry and its detrimental effect on his younger brother. I have been able to assess something of the relationships between Parry and his father, his mother-in-law, his half-brother Ernest, with Dannreuther, Stanford, Bridges, Jaeger, and other friends and associates. This may, I suspect, help to debunk a good many popular misconceptions of the composer's image reinforced by tradition.

In the writing of this study I am grateful to a large number of people and institutions for their guidance, advice, help, and assistance. With regard to financial assistance I must mention the generous help of *Music and Letters* and the Finzi Trust. I am grateful also to Lord Bridges who allowed me to publish extracts from his grandfather's letters. My thanks go to Christopher Bornet, Celia Clarke, and Peter Horton at the Royal College of Music for their help with the extensive Parry archive. Similarly I am indebted to the staff of the Music Reading Room and Manuscript Reading Room of the British Library; the Bodleian Library, Oxford; Cambridge University Library; Bristol University Library; the Brotherton Library (University of Leeds); the Reid Library (University of Edinburgh); Reading University Library (with special thanks to Margaret Laurie and Christopher Kent); the University of London Library; the Library, Trinity College, Dublin; the Mills Memorial Library, McMaster University, Hamilton, Ontario; the Rowe Library, King's College, Cambridge; the Wren Library, Trinity College, Cambridge; the library of Exeter College, Oxford; the Fitzwilliam Museum, Cambridge; Eton College Library; Gloucester City Library; Norwich Central Library; and Brighton Central Library. I am also grateful to the Hereford and Worcester Record Office and the Elgar Birthplace Museum as I am to the Royal Archive at Windsor; the Royal Institution of Great Britain; and to the National Portrait Gallery.
  The following people have all generously and willingly plied me with information and on numerous occasions they have also munificently provided me with their hospitality: Michael Allis, Stephen Banfield, Robin Bowman, David Brown, Peter Burman, Michael Darke, Tom Fenton, Christopher Fifield, Joy Finzi, Lewis Foreman, David Frendo, Richard Hall, Michael Hurd, Captain Robert Lowry, Carmel MacCallum Barry, Christopher Mark, Michael Pope, Peter Scott, and Geoffrey Spratt. Moreover it would be remiss of me if I did not mention Frank Donaldson, and my cousins Jane and Victor Sullivan who made it possible for me to see many of Parry's favourite haunts on the west coast

of Ireland. I remember in particular a quite memorable visit to the Skelligs.

There are a number of colleagues and friends to whom I owe a great debt of gratitude. I should thank John Rippin, for it was he who sowed the first seeds of my interest in British music of the late nineteenth and early twentieth centuries. I should mention Richard Marlow who persistently encouraged me and Peter Evans who patiently supervised me. But perhaps most of all I am indebted to the help, support, humour, and untiring interest of Kate and Ian Russell and Laura Ponsonby at Shulbrede Priory. Their kindness over the years, and especially their culinary imagination, has made the toil of research infinitely pleasurable! My thanks go to the editorial team at Oxford University Press, and to my colleague, Paul Everett, for helping me so expertly with the music examples. Finally, I must thank my parents and, above all, my wife Alison, to whom this work is dedicated.

J.D.

Cork
1991

CONTENTS

LIST OF PLATES
(between pp. 272 and 273)

ABBREVIATIONS

BL	British Library
BLUL	Brotherton Library, University of Leeds
Bod.	Bodleian Library, Oxford
BPL	Boston Public Library
BUL	Bristol University Library
CUL	Cambridge University Library
ECO	Exeter College Library, Oxford
FzMC	Fitzwilliam Museum, Cambridge
HWRO	Hereford and Worcester Public Records Office
McUL	Mills Memorial Library, McMaster University, Hamilton, Ontario
NYPL	New York Public Library
ORHG	Old Rectory, Highnam, Gloucester
OUDS	Oxford University Dramatic Society
PRONI	Public Records Office, Northern Ireland
RAA	Royal Academy of Art
RAWC	Royal Archive, Windsor Castle
RCM	Royal College of Music
RCO	Royal College of Organists
RHBNC	Royal Holloway and Bedford New College, London University
RUL	Reading University Library
ShP	Shulbrede Priory, Lynchmere, Sussex
TCC	Trinity College, Cambridge

NOTE

As this book went to press, the manuscript of Parry's String Quartet in G major, for which I have been searching for many years, emerged. As it has now transpired, the manuscript was indeed in the possession of Gerald Finzi (as anticipated in the text, p. 179) when he was given the task of sorting and depositing many of Parry's manuscripts in the Bodleian in the 1950s. It still remains something of a mystery, however, why this work did not reach the Bodleian along with many of its chamber-music counterparts, since Finzi was punctilious in his working habits. The story of its disappearance is a rather tortuous, complicated, and not entirely clear one, but, in short, it became mixed up with many of Finzi's remaining papers and manuscripts after his death and was consequently overlooked. In 1983, Philip Thomas, who was then currently working on Finzi, was asked to take care of and examine some papers by the composer's widow, amongst which was the Parry quartet. To compound the problem further, there was no name on the manuscript, and so, with no one able to identify the handwriting, a conclusion was eventually drawn that it was probably an early work by Finzi's most significant teacher, Ernest Farrar. Only this year (April 1992) was it recognized to be Parry's lost string quartet by Dr Stephen Banfield in the course of his own work on Gerald Finzi. To Dr Banfield, Philip Thomas, and to Michael Allis I am grateful for drawing this manuscript to my attention.

Parry's String Quartet in G belongs to the composer's feverishly productive period of creativity at the end of the 1870s when his interests were focused on the composition of instrumental works, and most notably on chamber music. To confirm Colles's impression of the work (see pp. 179–80), the quartet reveals the thirty-year-old composer prepared to take structural risks, and the thematic material has the same energy and fertile invention as the contemporary Fantasie Sonate and later Piano Quartet. Besides the unconventional recapitulatory process and a continued predilection for thematic displacement in the first movement (as mentioned by Colles), the last movement, a modified sonata-rondo is also extremely intriguing, particularly in the manner in which Parry reverses the order of recapitulation, but also allows the restatement of the second-group material to begin outside the tonic (on V of E major). Furthermore, there is great subtlety in the two variegated allusions to the rondo theme that recur thereafter.

In addition to the structural imagination of the work, the quality of melodic and harmonic material is also of a high standard. Much of the

thematic vitality of the finale foreshadows the outer movements of the
First Symphony, a feeling reinforced by the contrapuntal intensity,
while the first movement, somewhat more inchoate stylistically, has a
similar rhythmic momentum to the first movement of the Nonet. Just as
in the later Piano Quartet, the strongest material is to be found in the
slow movement and Scherzo. The former in many ways prefigures the
extended melodic writing of the 'Cambridge' Symphony, particularly in
the nature of its accompaniment, the spacious writing for the first violin,
and some of the arresting modulations that all seem reminiscent of
Dvořák. For sheer excitement, however, the 'death's head Scherzo' is
undoubtedly the most successful movement. Rhythmically dynamic and
in the same driving compound duple time as its counterpart in the Piano
Quartet, there is a combination of Beethovenian compulsion (established
by the almost sinister sounds of the tritone that characterise both the
opening idea on the viola and the ensuing harmony) and Brahmsian
tranquillity in the trio which derives its thematic material directly from
the Scherzo.

The manuscript of the String Quartet is to be deposited in the
Bodleian Library, Oxford.

June 1992

PART I

1848–1872
The Early Years

I

Antecedents and Childhood

THE next morning I went by Railroad to Bournemouth, which I reached at about half past five. This is my little Hubert's Birthday—this day three years ago he was born in this place. This is a sweet place. There is a wild nature about the surrounding heathy plains studded here and there with dark groves of pinasters, which is quite different to anything I know in England. The high cliffs commanding an immensely wide seaview and not bare and barren. As the evening grew dusky I wandered out upon the open heath above the house where I last looked upon the beloved form of my incomparable Isabel. It was a beautiful evening, warm as June and bright with stars. Long and deep were the prayers I made on that wide open heath for my three children and myself. I called all to my recollection since that too happy day, just at this period of the year in 1839, (12 years ago) when I first made the acquaintance with my loved and now lost wife. How miserably ungrateful man's blindness and infirmities make him!—me in particular.

The house we had, No. 2 Richmond Terrace, is occupied. I looked long at that window—that room where I last nursed and watched that beloved being.

As it grew dark I went to the churchyard. All was silence—not a breath of air stirred the dark Pine wood around that sacred spot. By the bright star light I read and reread the inscription on her grave. I need not write more—I want no memoranda of what is indelible in memory. Some kind hand has planted crocus and snowdrop and other flowers about her grave. . . . I sent a snowdrop from that sacred place to dear Lucy, and to dear Mrs Clinton . . . I wandered about the walks once trodden by dear feet—and returned late to the hotel.[1]

Thomas Gambier Parry wrote these heart-rending words in his diary on 27 February 1851, marking the third birthday of his youngest son, Charles Hubert Hastings. Early in 1848 his wife Isabella had travelled to Bournemouth on medical advice in a vain attempt to alleviate her failing health. Consumption was in its final terrible stages, and she was also heavily pregnant with her sixth child. Sadly but inevitably the strains and exertions of Hubert's birth in February sapped any remaining strength she had held in reserve, so that twelve days later, on 11 March, she died at the tender age of 32, and was buried in the churchyard of St Peter's, Bournemouth. For Thomas Gambier Parry the event was

---

[1] Diaries in the possession of Mr Tom Fenton, the Old Rectory, Highnam, Gloucester.

devastating. Besides the emotional shock of finding himself a widower after only nine years of marriage, he had been left to raise three young children: Clinton who was 8, Lucy who was 7, and now baby Hubert. The prospects for the future seemed decidedly bleak and uncertain.

To a large extent tragedy had overshadowed Thomas Gambier Parry's early life. Born in 1816, the son of Richard and Mary Parry, he had been orphaned at the age of 5. His father had enjoyed a distinguished career in the civil service spending much of his professional life in India. Two years after returning to England in 1813 his election to a Directorship of the East India Company assured him of greater wealth. Yet he was hardly able to enjoy his new position or his new son for he died in 1817. Mary Parry came from a family saturated in naval history and distinction, her father being a Commissioner of Her Majesty's Navy and her uncle, Lord Gambier, Admiral of the Fleet. When in 1821 Mary Parry died, her son's upbringing became her mother's responsibility. Consequently it was Thomas Gambier Parry's association with his mother's family which induced him to appropriate 'Gambier' as part of his surname in later life. His Christian name almost certainly came from his grandfather, Thomas Parry, who also enjoyed an illustrious career in the navy. Of Thomas Parry we know relatively little since, according to Thomas Gambier Parry, he had all his papers destroyed. Fortunately the painting by Zoffany made between 1762 and 1764 has survived in which we at least have a view of him appearing along with Admiral Samuel Cornish and his flag-captain Captain Richard Kempenfelt after being appointed to HMS *Norfolk* as secretary to the Admiral.[2] Although Thomas Parry accrued some wealth from his numerous appointments within the navy, much of his affluence arose from being elected a Director of the East India Company in 1783, a situation he used to the advantage of his sons. In 1816, at the grand age of 85, he died, leaving much of his wealth to his namesake and only grandson, who was born two months before his death.

At the instigation of the Gambiers, Thomas Gambier Parry was educated at Eton where, under William Evans (who instituted Evans's House at the college), he studied watercolour painting. Moreover, his not insignificant talent for music led him to become proficient on the piano and the French horn as well as in the study of composition. From Eton he went up to Trinity College, Cambridge in 1834 where his interests in art and religion appear to have been instantly recognized. During his years at Cambridge he travelled abroad making one extensive tour in 1836 through Belgium, France, Germany, and Switzerland purely to view and absorb the styles of continental architecture

---

[2] In possession of Mr Tom Fenton, the Old Rectory, Highnam, Gloucester.

(particularly of the ecclesiastical type), sculpture, and especially painting. The money he was due to inherit from his grandfather on coming of age in 1837 had been wisely invested, for it enabled him to purchase a country seat. With the considerable fortune that remained it was not only possible to maintain and develop the estate, but also to continue his studies and accumulation of paintings and *objets d'art*, and to pursue his own interest in water-colour painting. Furthermore he at last had the opportunity to settle and create the sort of stable family environment which he had lacked in his youth and for which he must have craved.

Highnam Court, a seventeenth-century house close to the River Severn about two miles west of Gloucester, provided the ideal site; it included extensive woodlands, a mill, a river wharf, and a substantial area of good farm land tilled by a number of tenants. The potential was enormous both creatively and socially. With the help of James Pulham, well known for his artificial rock-work, the gardens were planned and laid out with exotic specification. One of the lasting creations on the estate was a pinetum—among the earliest in Britain—which he planned with the help of his friend and relation by marriage, William Robert Baker, the ardent arboriculturalist. But perhaps most important of all, he was free to realize his ambition to travel and to cultivate a passion for the continent, in particular for the Mediterranean. It was here that his keen insights into the merits of Italian Renaissance and Quattrocento art led to the making of a unique collection of sculptures, paintings, ivories, enamels, china, and glass. Much of it is now on public view in the Courtauld Institute Gallery, Somerset House.[3]

In 1839 Gambier Parry married Anna Maria Isabella Fynes Clinton, the second daughter of Henry Fynes Clinton. Although his father-in-law could boast of aristocratic lineage and his experience as a one-time Member of Parliament for Aldborough, Yorkshire, it was surely the flair and energy shown by Mr Fynes Clinton for classical scholarship and the arts which produced an empathy between the two men. Marriage also meant the introduction to Mrs Katherine Fynes Clinton's family which was no less eminent than her husband's. Her background conjures up the Trollopian vision of clerical well-being. As the third of nine daughters of Dr Henry William Majendie, Bishop of Bangor, her whole life had been immersed in the society of the Established Church, and with her father's elevated position she was accustomed to the wealth that went with such a status. However, it would appear from contemporary family writings that, owing to her husband's preference for scholarship, she was forced to embrace a humbler life-style. The attraction of clericalism within the Majendie family continued to remain strong, for

[3] Bequeathed by his grandson Mark Gambier Parry in 1967.

her younger sister, Isabella Mary, married the Reverend Francis Lear who, after periods as Rector of Downton-Chilmark and Bishopstone, became Dean of Salisbury in 1846. The connection with the Lears was to have great significance for Thomas Gambier Parry in later life.

Indeed, Mrs Lear's diaries provide a number of fascinating and unreserved comments about her niece Isabella Fynes Clinton. Two months before their marriage in June 1839 Isabella and her future husband paid a visit to her home in Welwyn:

Isabel the bride elect and her father arrived . . . and the following morning Tom Parry, my future nephew made his appearance while we were at church—his first visit to Welwyn and most affectionately was he welcomed by the whole family. They are so lately returned from France that the establishment is still quite in disorder . . . Isabel struck me as less handsome than when I saw her last, and I fear that her disposition is not calculated to contribute to Mr Parry's happiness, who appears one of the most pleasing and superior young men I almost ever saw. I cannot help from my private observation entertaining some fears respecting the result of this engagement.[4]

Mrs Lear's opinion of Thomas Gambier Parry was unquestionably enhanced by his financial situation as is revealed by her somewhat abrupt remarks on the day of the couple's wedding on 13 August:

Poor Isabel felt the parting with her father more deeply than anything else . . . and tho' Mr Clinton and dear Kate were affected as parents must be at parting with a beloved child, they could only rejoice in placing her in such hands, for without a single exception, Tom Parry does certainly appear to be one of the most delightful and superior young men possible with a fortune of £10,000 a year while she has not a farthing. I suppose few girls under these circumstances marry as she and Anna have [Anna Fynes Clinton, Isabella's eldest sister, had married William Robert Baker, a wealthy Hertfordshire gentleman, who owned a large mansion near Hertford called Bayfordbury], and I earnestly pray to the Lord who has ordered both events to give his blessing to them.

Yet, contrary to Mrs Lear's scepticism, the match appears to have been a happy one, for the couple shared a mutual love of travel, and Isabella's energetic personality appears to have had a positive effect upon her husband.

The years after their marriage were largely spent abroad pursuing art treasures. There were also swift additions to the family; Charles Clinton was born in October 1840 and Lucy in 1841. Yet Isabella did not possess a strong constitution, for the constant and arduous journeys in carriages

---

[4] 22 June 1839, ShP.

across Europe (railways still being something of a novelty), together with the stresses of childbirth, must have told on her health. In April 1841 Mrs Lear noted in her diary: 'The Gambier Parrys who had not been seen since the day of their marriage [visited us] . . . Isabel still retaining great beauty tho' rather thin and flinched and I suspect from nursing, greatly softened and improved in manners, and her husband one of the most fascinating and agreeable creatures.'[5] Sure enough, as the years passed, Isabella's fragile constitution began to fail. Francis Gambier, born in Naples in March 1843, died in Messina, Sicily in June the same year and was subsequently buried there. Edward Clement Hervey, born in London in November 1844 lived until July 1845, dying at Highnam. Henry was born at Bayfordbury in 1846 and died there, living no more than an hour. Finally, stricken with consumption, she gave birth to Charles Hubert Hastings on 27 February 1848. He, perhaps miraculously, survived, but this final exertion killed her.

During their short marriage the improvements to the estate at Highnam had been the subject of lengthy discussion. Thomas Gambier Parry was of an intensely religious disposition, and in the spirit of many nineteenth-century Victorian landed gentry, to fulfil his deeply held convictions he viewed his wealth as a means of benevolence. Before her death Isabella had suggested the possibility of building a church in the grounds of the estate for the residents, many of whom were forced to walk long distances to their local parish church. As a result, on returning to Highnam in 1848 Thomas Gambier Parry was seized with the idea of constructing a church which would be a memorial to his wife and to the three children they had lost. By October the outline had been devised for a church, a school, a house for the sacristan, and a Parsonage. By 29 April 1851 the church was ready for consecration. The same year he married again, this time to Ethelinda Lear, second daughter of the Reverend Francis Lear who had been Dean of Salisbury until his death in March 1850; and we may well infer from those glowing yet intriguing remarks in Mrs Lear's earlier diaries about her new son-in-law that she was quite delighted with the match! However, according to Thomas Gambier Parry's granddaughter, Lady Ponsonby (née Dorothea Parry), Ethelinda's influence had a stultifying effect upon her husband. With Isabella he had shared a zest for life and a certain degree of artistic abandon, but his new wife's sterner clerical background led to a hardening of his religious and moral convictions to the point of intransigence.

The marriage of Thomas and Ethelinda Gambier Parry produced another six children, Linda (b. 1852), Ernest (b. 1853), (Mary) Beatrice

[5] 23 Apr. 1841, ShP.

(b. 1855), Ethel Geraldine (b. 1857), Sidney (b. 1859) and Hilda (b. 1866), and we may presume that, in order to distinguish between the 'Fynes Clinton' and the 'Lear' progeny, the second family adopted the double surname, while Clinton, Lucy, and Hubert simply took the name 'Parry'. It is also fascinating to observe, as an example of the high degree of inbreeding that often took place amongst the upper classes, the relationship between these two sets of children. For since Isabella Fynes Clinton and Ethelinda Lear were first cousins, we are faced with the curious result that the children of each marriage, sharing the same father, were not only half-brothers and sisters but also second cousins.

It is evident from Thomas Gambier Parry's own chronicles that he was a man of prodigious energy, his character being described as emanating 'straight out of the pages of Trollope, the best brand of amateur'.[6] Yet, although he was strictly an amateur, his art collection has continued to be a source of amazement owing to the remarkably high quality of his purchases. His earliest acquisitions were conventional, being drawn entirely from the Italian seicento with painters such as Giovanni Lanfranco, Salvator Rosa, and Albertinelli. But in the 1850s his interests turned to Florentine art of the trecento and quattrocento which led to the purchase of works by artists such as Bernardo Daddi, Lorenzo Monaco, and Pesellino, an enthusiasm which soon brought him to the forefront of modern art collectors. His love of the Middle Ages also brought about the acquisition of numerous *objets d'art* including finely selected Limoges enamels and ivories, and in Venice he collected several fine specimens of mid-thirteenth-century Islamic metalwork. Yet probably the most striking consequence of his passion for medieval and renaissance art was his detailed study of painting techniques of this period. The result was an invention which he called 'Spirit Fresco' which he claimed could be used in the damp English climate for wall painting. The validity of his methods was proved by the wall paintings with which he subsequently began to decorate the church at Highnam; especially noteworthy is the depiction of the *Last Judgement* over the chancel arch commenced in 1859. Such was the reputation of his invention that various artists sought his advice after being commissioned to provide extensive mural paintings for buildings such as the Houses of Parliament, Westminster Hall, and St Paul's Cathedral. The crowning achievement of Thomas Gambier Parry's own exploits in this medium was the completion of the nave roof of Ely Cathedral begun in 1859 by his friend Henry Styleman Le Strange. Le Strange died in 1862, at which point Gambier Parry offered to complete the roof at his own expense which he did in 1864. Later, as a

---

[6] D. Trelford, '£750,000 paintings come out of hiding', *Observer* (5 Mar. 1967), quoting Sir Anthony Blunt, Director of the Courtauld Institute.

characteristic gesture of his munificence, he also decorated the octagon at Ely and the St Andrew's Chapel at Gloucester Cathedral.

Inevitably Thomas Gambier Parry's circle of friends and acquaintances consisted of the most eminent artists, writers, and architects of his day. He was known to Landseer and Thackeray, and was a personal friend of Sir Frederick Leighton (whose 'Nazarene' tendencies undoubtedly influenced him). In March 1853 he wrote in his diary of the satisfaction he gained from a visit to London where he mentions meeting his 'old friends . . . Le Strange . . . and Ruskin,—and having made acquaintance with Dyce, Hunt, and Millais'. Ruskin, whom he had met on numerous occasions in the past, some of them on his continental tours, was almost certainly the means by which Gambier Parry secured an introduction to the major figures of the Pre-Raphaelite Brotherhood. Ruskin also thought highly of Gambier Parry's own talents as a water-colourist; moreover, the two men shared an admiration for Turner at a time when that artist had undergone savage attacks from reviewers.

Music also played a central role in Gambier Parry's busy life which stemmed from a keen pursuit of the subject in his youth. Yet, although his attitude to painting evinces an appetite for modern trends, in music he was a true conservative with conventional Victorian tastes. Fortunately the Three Choirs Festivals provided congenial programmes, largely orientated around the English choral staple diet of Mendelssohn's *Elijah*, Handel's *Messiah*, Haydn's *Creation*, and Spohr's *Last Judgement*. Well known in the elevated circles of Gloucester society through his benefactions, as a magistrate, as High Sheriff of the County in 1850, and as Deputy Lieutenant in 1853, Gambier Parry also occupied a prominent position amongst those stewards who undertook the financial risks of the music Festival. He was also conspicuous in his efforts to save the Festivals when they were under serious threat of cessation from the puritanical obsessions of the Dean of Worcester between 1874 and 1875.[7]

The art of musical composition in Britain in the early and mid-nineteenth century has often provoked derision from both native and foreign commentators. It could be fairly summarized 'as a time of missed opportunities . . . and of craven subordination to foreign influences (Mendelssohn, Gounod), as well as of sheer incompatability between the ethics of Victorianism and the aesthetics of Romanticism'.[8] Yet the great tide of optimism in the country, expressed in such forward-looking bills as the Public Health Act of 1848, the moves towards greater suffrage in

[7] Revd D. Lysons, J. Amott, C. Lee Williams, H. Godwin Chance, *Origins and Progress of the Meeting of the Three Choirs of Gloucester, Worcester, and Hereford and of the Charity connected with it, commenced by the Revd Daniel Lysons, carried on to 1864 by John Amott (organist of Gloucester Cathedral), and continued to 1894 by C. Lee Williams and H. Godwin Chance* (Gloucester, 1895), 253–61.

[8] A. Whittall, *Romantic Music* (London, 1987), 152–4.

the Reform Acts of 1832, 1867, and 1884, and the entrepreneurial spirit epitomized by the Great Exhibition of 1851 undoubtedly exerted some influence on music and music-making in this country. Likewise, those born with musical talent in the 1840s and 1850s were able, perhaps more than any others for at least a century, to avail themselves of the greater opportunities that were arising out of the rapidly developing social attitudes towards the subject. Music was slowly but surely entering the school curriculum through the stalwart work of John Hullah and John Curwen. Singing, viewed as a vehicle of moral rectitude, assumed an important role in the life of the population; a role facilitated by an emphasis on new and comparatively simple systems of notation such as tonic sol-fa. Choral societies underwent a period of expansion, particularly in Yorkshire and the Pottery towns—an enthusiasm subsequently reflected in the plethora of competitive festivals. It was also a time when those in the higher echelons of London's musical society began to re-examine the state of the art in the capital. The improved standard of instrumental playing was in part due to the numbers of disenchanted immigrant musicians from Germany and France who flocked here after the 1848 revolutions, and to the forceful, though conservative personality of Sir Michael Costa, conductor of the Royal Italian Opera and from 1846 to 1854 the Philharmonic Society. The Philharmonic Society had dominated London's concert platforms since its institution in 1813, but its concert programmes rarely strayed from the music of Mendelssohn, and it was governed by a fraternity of wealthy amateurs. To counteract the exclusivity and prohibitive expense of the Philharmonic Society concerts, the New Philharmonic Society was formed in 1852 to promote contemporary music, performing initially in the Exeter Hall. So began a phase of expansion in London's concert life. To popularize the new St James's Hall, finished in 1858, the Monday Popular Concerts were instituted. Such was their success that regular Saturday concerts were introduced from 1865. The Crystal Palace became a platform for more ambitious musical ventures after its removal from Hyde Park and reconstruction at Sydenham in 1852, notably under the direction of August Manns who was appointed chief conductor in 1855. It was also the era of a series of idiosyncratic though enormously popular concerts given by the extrovert Louis Antoine Jullien and his orchestra. Despite much contemporary criticism of his grandiose, not to say ostentatious approach to performance, Jullien must certainly be credited with the raising of standards, not to mention the success he had in persuading Berlioz to come to England. With the increased number of concerts came the expansion of musical criticism with such prominent names as J. W. Davison of *The Times* and H. F. Chorley of the *Athenaeum*. Musical journals also began to multiply as did the number of publishing houses;

there was, in fact, an explosion in the dissemination of printed music, aided particularly by the enterprising publications of Vincent Novello.

This evidence might by itself suggest that music in Britain was in a more healthy condition than it had been for some time. Yet from the creative angle the country had driven itself into a corner from which there seemed little prospect of escape, for it was here that the most distasteful aspects of Victorianism found voice. Moral puritanism was championed by the Anglican Establishment and no institution whether political, educational, or artistic was free of its influence. Cathedral cities provided the stage for the country's major musical festivals, and the clergy, suspicious of continental innovations, had the power to reject performances of new music which they considered unsuitable for the sacred environment. This approach was largely reinforced by the ancient universities whose attitudes had hardened under a series of moribund professors. There was a steady movement towards archaism led by such figures as Professor William Crotch of Oxford who fervently advocated a return to the 'pure' language of the sixteenth and seventeenth centuries. The Revd Sir Frederick Arthur Gore Ouseley continued this trend with the 'model' foundation of St Michael's College, Tenbury in 1854, and then proceeded to build on Crotch's legacy on becoming Professor of Oxford in 1855. Ouseley was clear and stern about the best models for students: for instrumental music he prescribed the study of Mozart; for oratorio, Handel; and for cathedral music, the seventeenth-century masters. In the case of secular vocal music, composers had to look no further than the part-song, an idiom whose popularity had been consolidated by Mendelssohn's insipid contributions to the repertoire. Mendelssohn, of course, was lauded not only as the successor to Handel and Old Testament oratorio, but also as the paragon of virtue (a view crystallized in Elizabeth S. Sheppard's extraordinary novel *Charles Auchester* of 1853). In itself society's veneration of Mendelssohn highlighted the blinkered attitude of the British concert-goer who was not able to divorce the composer, his life, and morality, from his work. In writing about the now little-known German composer, Schachner, Hubert Parry complained that such an attitude was a peculiar failing of the Englishman: 'As an artist he [Schachner] feels more rightly about music than *Englishmen* generally do, as their tenets are so miserably wrong. They forget the music in their prejudice for or against the individual connected with it, and look upon the composer as the *man* to be opposed, rather than upon the talents he possesses (separate from his individuality) as the thing to be fostered.'[9] Out of this very prejudice there evolved an unwritten moral code in the art of composition which

---

[9] Diary, 21 Sept. 1868.

was fostered by Walmisley, Sterndale Bennett, and Macfarren, all
Professors at Cambridge, as it was also in the almost exclusively sacred
output of S. S. Wesley. This 'style of composition' soon established a set
of banal characteristics and criteria in which the 'harmonized melody',
unrelenting homophony, trite verse, and simple tonality were the most
predominant features.

Such a combination of banality, archaism, and Mendelssohnian
enslavement was consolidated in the submissions necessary for those
supplicating for the degrees of B.Mus. or D.Mus. As evidence
of a composer's proficiency and reputation, these 'Exercises' quickly
conformed to the techniques required to produce standard Cantata or
Oratorio forms. Ouseley, with his election to the chair in Oxford and
after being made D.Mus. the previous year with his oratorio *The
Martyrdom of St Polycarp*, set about reforming the Oxford degrees. The
rather superficial method of submitting the Exercise was supplemented
with written examinations which specified fluency in certain techniques:
five-part vocal writing, an aria, an accompanied quartet, and a five-part
fugue, as well as the rigours of species counterpoint. Undoubtedly
Ouseley's aim was to sift out those students who were less able to master
the more exacting musical procedures; but because the specifications
were so inflexible in their demands, many students were able to treat the
examination as a series of mechanical problems in which they could
devise formulas, and have their degrees virtually guaranteed. The
inevitable result was a system where technical correctness was no longer
the servant but the master; and consequently the new examination
system gave rise to a standardization of selected skills which stressed
above all the furtherance of a contrapuntal stringency which seemed
hardly relevant to the development of an original musical style.
Moreover, virtually the whole of the English musical pedagogy was
dominated by church musicians who ultimately expected their pupils to
become church organists, believing this to be the worthiest cause.

The ecclesiastical orientation of the university degrees also throws into
relief the rift that existed between music in and out of church. Henry
Hugo Pierson found the bias in academia in favour of sacred music
intolerable. After being elected Reid Professor of Music at Edinburgh
University he soon resigned the post to seek voluntary exile in Germany.
As a friend of Mendelssohn, Schumann, Spohr, and an admirer of
Berlioz (an admiration which led to the production of a series of
Shakespeare-influenced overtures: *Macbeth*, *As You Like It*, and *Romeo
and Juliet*), Pierson revelled in the eulogies of an appreciative German
Press, enjoying success with his opera *Leila* in Hamburg in 1848 and
wide acclaim for his setting of the second part of Goethe's *Faust* in 1854.
His inclination towards German tastes and attitudes articulated a

contempt for the British musical scene which was later vindicated when Davison launched a scathing attack on his oratorio *Jerusalem* written for the Norwich Festival in 1852, and thus deterred him from writing any more music for English audiences. Pierson's interests were essentially for dramatic music which was quite antipathetical to current British sentiments. 'The widespread distrust of opera derived from a certain amount of anti-Romanist feeling as well as from a largely unformulated xenophobia. It was also associated with a recurrent zeal for purity'.[10] This response was reinforced by the public condemnations made by Carlyle and Ruskin. The years surrounding 1860 not only helped to accentuate this country's suspicion of opera but were also witness to the chasm that was gradually forming between Britain and the rest of Europe. *Tristan und Isolde* had been completed in 1859 while Ouseley and Stainer were in the process of forming the first edition of *Hymns Ancient and Modern* which appeared in print in 1861.

This was the musical world into which Charles Hubert Hastings Parry was born. In his childhood, music must have been a familiar part of domestic life at Highnam. His father not only played and composed, but, as has already been mentioned, was actively involved on an executive level in the organization of the Gloucester Three Choirs Festival. His brother Clinton played the piano and the cello and seems to have shown exceptional musical talent; and his sister Lucy played the piano a little. It is uncertain when Hubert commenced music lessons but it was probably quite early. Yet paradoxically his father, in spite of a willingness to stimulate music in Gloucester, tended to discourage the serious attitude that both Clinton and Hubert revealed for the subject. In Victorian England, and particularly amongst the upper classes, professional status was accorded to the painter but not to the musician. There were many reasons for this. The view was commonly held that the life of a musician was beset with financial risks, an existence unbecoming to the sons of country squires who were set to inherit and manage the estates or enter respectable professions such as the army (with an automatic commission) or the church (with the guarantee of preferment). Furthermore, music was not infrequently associated both with the immorality of continentals and with a sense of unmanliness; hence there was a determined attempt to dampen enthusiasm for music beyond its pursuit as a genteel pastime. At Highnam artistic discrimination may have been cultivated as part of the children's upbringing, but this was tempered by the prudent instruction in the established religion. The latter was seen to by Thomas Gambier Parry personally, for his diaries speak of occasions when the children were brought together on Sundays to study the Bible

---

[10] E. D. Mackerness, *A Social History of English Music* (London, 1964), 187.

or other religious literature. In performing this duty he expected that his family would follow loyally in the same religious mould. Initially this seems to have been the case, but eventually religion was to become a source of friction and division for both Clinton and Hubert.

Thomas Gambier Parry did his best to create a happy and loving household when he was at Highnam. But it is evident that he spent much of his time away from home during Hubert's childhood. His diaries show that he was often only home for brief interludes from his exploits on the continent. Indeed the longest single period he spent at Highnam may well have been during the building of the church after Isabella's death. After marrying Ethelinda in 1851, however, foreign tours began again with a keenness perhaps even greater than before, and Hubert being too young was left at Highnam with a governess. Since Clinton was at school and Lucy was seven years his senior, these years were undeniably lonely for him, which he apparently combated by creating imaginary companions, a fact he later intimated to his elder daughter Dorothea.[11] When he was not receiving lessons from his governess, much of his time was spent in vigorous outdoor pursuits which mainly consisted of riding either around the estate or longer distances to May Hill, Elmore, or Frampton, often with his brother when he was home from school. This love of physical exertion was a feature of his character that remained with him to the end. It was also indicative of the nervous, hyperactive tendency he was to show later in professional life, though paradoxically it was to aggravate his somewhat fragile health caused by a weak heart condition which began to emerge during his teens.

Highnam may have been quiet in his father's absence but when he was home it evidently provided a lively centre for visits by numerous eminent personages who were all part of the elevated strata of society to which Thomas Gambier Parry belonged. One connection which later proved to have significant consequences was that of the aristocratic Herbert family of Wilton House, Salisbury, seat of the Earls of Pembroke. Their acquaintance appears to have been made through Ethelinda's family, for her father Francis Lear had at one time been Rector at Downton-Chilmark and Bishopstone, parishes patronized by the Herbert family, and had also been employed as a private tutor to Sidney Herbert. Hubert was introduced to Maude Herbert in May 1858 at Bishopstone.[12] Beyond the record of their meeting there are no details, but we may be certain that they forged a close friendship and soon became childhood sweethearts.

Having become accustomed to a rather solitary existence at Highnam, it was with some excitement that he had accepted the prospect of

[11] Charles L. Graves, *Hubert Parry* (London, 1926), i. 12. [12] Ibid. 13.

preparatory school and the chance of mixing with boys of his own age. In January 1856 he was sent to Malvern where he stayed until the summer of 1858. Probably on the advice and recommendation of Gambier Parry's neighbours, the Guises of Elmore, he was transferred to a preparatory school at Twyford near Winchester, then under the care of the young Revd George William Kitchin. Here Hubert's academic achievements appear to have blossomed, and his appetite for music met with approval.

Twyford was a small preparatory institution but it reflected the more futuristic attitudes of its headmaster. Kitchin, who was only at the school until 1861, was in many ways an educational pioneer. After inheriting a typically severe curriculum from his predecessors, he immediately set about its modification, introducing more unusual subjects to the 'table of hours' such as music and drawing. He also encouraged the masters to develop the characters of the boys, particularly in their out-of-school hobbies and pursuits. In fact so different was the atmosphere of school life at Twyford that C. L. Dodgson (better known as Lewis Carroll) was forced to comment in his diary after a visit to the school:

I like very much the system of freedom and intimacy which prevails here between masters and boys; though there must often be a risk of the boys passing over the bounds of respect due to their masters. It is quite the system of ruling by love, and with a master like Kitchin seems to answer well, but I should doubt if there are many in whose hands it would succeed.[13]

According to Hubert's half-sister Linda Gambier Parry, 'he [Kitchin] always spoke with pride of him and of having fostered his music in his private school days—no doubt there was a music master there, but we never heard him mentioned—anyhow Kitchin kept his eye on him . . .'.[14] In fact it is quite unlikely that the school would have employed a music master, for such a post was rare in mid-nineteenth-century preparatory schools. Kitchin was, however, a keen musician who appears to have been solely responsible for the organization of school concerts. These grew too large to be accommodated in the nearby parish church, so in 1858, the year in which Hubert entered the school, they were moved to the New School Room. In the inaugural concert for this new venue, Hubert's name is mentioned amongst those who contributed to the programme of sacred and secular vocal items—an indication that his musical abilities were recognized soon after his

[13] R. G. Wickham, *Shades of the Prison-House* (Winchester, 1986), 50.
[14] Letter from Beatrice Gambier Parry to Dorothea Ponsonby, 14 Jan. 1920, ShP.

arrival. In 1898 Parry recalled in a feature article for the *Musical Times*[15] the circumstances surrounding his musical activities at Twyford:

There was no piano in the school, but Dr Kitchin who was sympathetic to music, allowed strumming at certain rare hours on the cottage pianoforte in his drawing-room. I took pianoforte lessons from a parochial organist in the neighbourhood. He was the composer of a large quantity of parish anthems, and, by way of doing a little extra business, supplied them to me *seriatim*. He actually attempted to teach me the instrument by making me play the accompaniments to those anthems, which were a kind of feeble four-part harmony. Did you ever see such stuff?

Besides the instruction he obtained at Twyford, there were frequent opportunities to visit Winchester close by, and to make the acquaintance of Samuel Sebastian Wesley who was presently organist at the Cathedral. Wesley responded immediately to Parry's innate musicianship and permitted him to sit in the organ loft during services. 'There I used to sit,' Parry recollected, 'while old Wesley, with his eyebrows raised and his chin sticking out, ruminated on the organ. He was awfully kind to me. A sympathetic under-master showed me the "48", which very soon surpassed everything in my affections.'[16]

During the school holidays Hubert elicited the help of Edward Brind who took up the post of organist at Highnam church in 1860. In addition to piano lessons, Brind taught him the basics of harmony and counterpoint and gave him the chance to accompany the singing in the services. Practice was eagerly devoted to the learning of Bach's 48 Preludes and Fugues and elementary composition was encouraged in the form of chants and hymn tunes, the results of which he was able to hear sung by the Highnam choir.[17] Brind also strove to broaden his pupil's musical experiences taking him to the Hereford Festival in 1861. The atmosphere of the occasion, the sound and sight of massed choirs and orchestra together with the music of Handel, Mendelssohn, and Spohr, undoubtedly made a lasting impression on the 13-year-old. Moreover, and perhaps most significantly, Brind's positive attitude must have been considerably heartening to the young Parry in contrast to the general posture of dissuasion adopted by his father. Hubert must have also sensed that the artistic world was at last beginning to unveil itself to him. As a relief from the preoccupations of music, he found time to acquaint himself with the London theatres, museums, and galleries which kindled his lifelong interest in literature and the visual arts. He was also of the

[15] 'Hubert Parry', *Musical Times* (July 1898), 441–2.   [16] Ibid.
[17] These early chants have been preserved in the so-called 'Eton Books' which have survived and are now housed at Shulbrede Priory. Dr Emily Daymond also copied out many of these youthful pieces (Bod. MS Mus. d.229, Earliest Compositions 1862–5) which were later the basis of an article: 'On an Early Manuscript Book of Sir Hubert Parry's', *RCM Magazine*, 19/2: 75–9.

age where the Victorian aspirations of continental travel became a reality, joining his parents for the first time in Menton during the Easter holidays of 1861.

Yet all was not happiness and tranquillity in the family at this time. In a letter to Hubert from Genoa, his elder sister Lucy, who had largely assumed a maternal role towards her younger brother, alluded to her fragile condition regarding the family's journey home and her doctor's advice against their taking the route through the Alps.[18] Evidently Lucy had inherited her mother's poor health and was an object of constant worry to those around her. However, it was not Lucy but Clinton who was the focus of their parents' immediate concern. At Eton he appears to have led a comparatively normal existence, promising well academically and showing a considerable talent for music. But his diaries reveal that the seeds of religious doubt had already been sown. This, combined with a passion for music dampened by his father's disfavour, brought on severe depression. After going up to Christ Church, Oxford in 1859 these feelings had crystallized into an emotional state bordering on schizophrenia. On the other hand he began his university career auspiciously by performing several times before the Prince of Wales, the programmes of his recitals including some of his own works. Thoughts subsequently entered his mind of introducing orchestral music to the then unambitious Oxford Amateur Musical Society. He was also determined to obtain both his B.Mus. and a first-class degree in modern history. Sadly, all his good intentions came to nothing. Preyed on by a circle of dubious friends, his weak personality yielded to a riotous life of womanizing, drinking, and opium which culminated in his being sent down in disgrace. To make matters worse his father also became aware of his rejection of the Christian faith. While at Twyford Hubert was to an appreciable extent both physically and emotionally removed from the humiliation brought on the family by Clinton's actions. But as he grew older and more aware of the increasing unpredictability of his brother's character, it became impossible to shield him from terrible scenes of distress and confrontation.

The reasons for Clinton's flawed personality are unclear but the absence of any mechanism in Victorian society either to understand or accommodate the nature of his mental problems undoubtedly exacerbated them. Today we might well consider the experience of his mother's death, at an impressionable age, a disturbing factor—an emotional crisis his younger brother fortunately avoided. The fact that, in his later diaries, he recorded his mother's premature death with anguish suggests that the bond was close. Hence, if the relationship had been an intimate

---

[18] Letter from Lucy Parry, 15 May 1861, ShP.

one, it is also probable that Clinton inherited the refractory element of his mother's contumacious spirit. It is quite plausible therefore, that, with the material freedom that Oxford provided, his outlandish behaviour was simply a reaction against his father's oppressive and socially conventional attitudes. However, Thomas Gambier Parry was more concerned to save face by negotiating Clinton's return to Oxford than to confront the reality of his mental problems. Meanwhile, amid this series of turbulent domestic episodes, Hubert was preparing to enter Eton.

2

Eton

FOR Parry's first three years at Eton we have comparatively little documentary material. What has come down to us is mainly in the form of personal reminiscences and a few letters, one of which Parry himself provided for the purposes of his half-brother Ernest Gambier Parry's book *Annals of an Eton House* published in 1907. However, in 1864 he began to keep a diary of day-to-day events, a habit that lasted a lifetime. So detailed are the accounts of his life at Eton that substantial extracts of the diaries from 1864 to 1866 were published in the school's magazine,[1] partly as a tribute to an old boy, but also as an invaluable insight into life at Eton in the mid-nineteenth century.

His school career began solemnly. Besides the tense atmosphere at Highnam over Clinton's disgrace and his father's efforts to pacify the authorities at Christ Church, a shadow had been cast over the year by the loss of Maude Herbert's father, Sidney, 1st Lord Herbert of Lea, who, exhausted by his humanitarian efforts during the Crimean War, had died of pleurisy at Wilton on 2 August 1861. But a more immediate tragedy was to follow. On 16 November Lucy Parry died from consumption. She was 19. His sister's death evidently affected Hubert severely for a long period, for the end of his 1864 diary contains a touching lament of an adolescent youth still experiencing an acute sense of loss. Nevertheless, although impressionable, at 13 he was able to throw himself into the life at Eton with characteristic energy.

In some respects he was fortunate to enter the school at this time, for reform in the English public school system was gathering momentum. With the setting up of the Clarendon Commission that same year, Palmerston's government was seeking to investigate the alleged abuses of huge endowments enjoyed by the schools for centuries; and, having uncovered a catalogue of irregularities, the Commission then suggested other reforms such as the organization of a curriculum and the setting up of governing bodies.

But Eton was slow to acknowledge criticism, either of its curriculum or its internal social structure. It remained a world in which the system of houses, colours, ties, caps, the hierarchy of the upper years,

[1] 'An Eton Boy's Diary, 1864–1866', *Etoniana*, 103 (1946), 33–40; 104 (1947), 49–57.

prefectorial privileges, and 'fagging' were vigorously pursued, and this was reinforced by the Victorian educational ideology of games and athleticism which was becoming an obsession. Such ethics as team spirit, leadership, self-abnegation, and earnestness were enthusiastically embraced by the headmaster, pupils, masters, and parents alike, for not only did these bolster the underlying Christian foundations of the school, but also strengthened the Victorian ideals of strong character and manliness. However, such a system of social priorities and moral values could not hide the level of academic apathy and philistinism which existed at Eton in the 1860s, and was to undergo little change for the rest of the century.

Evans's House had become a tradition for Parry's family. His older brother had been in the House during his own career at Eton, while Ernest and Sidney Gambier Parry were due to follow. Parry's first impressions were recorded much later in the letter written to Ernest for his book. Of his housemaster he recalled:

I remember 'Beeves', as we used to call William Evans, very well, and he was especially kind to me on account of having known our father for many years, being somewhat of a personality in the artistic world. He used to have a big, comfortable room looking out into the garden, where he used to lounge in a sort of Olympic grandeur. I used to visit him there occasionally, and I think he must have been of a very kindly disposition. I was too small and too much impressed by the immense world of Eton to get into the sort of mischief that would bring me into collision with him.[2]

Ernest's book is perhaps only of limited interest today in that it concentrates on the events and deeds of cameraderie in a rarified world of privilege. However, notwithstanding the air of self-glorification, what it does convey indirectly is the powerful advantage gained by moving in 'Eton society'. Parry's circle of friends all came from influential backgrounds, and many proved to be significant contacts in later life. There were the Lyttelton brothers (sons of the fourth Baron Lyttelton), notably Arthur, Spencer, and Robert; Julian Sturgis the novelist; J. R. Selwyn of clerical fame and Master of the Cambridge college; Robert Bridges the poet; Martin Le Marchant Gosselin, First Secretary to the British Legation in Paris; Edward W. Hamilton, a future Permanent Financial Secretary to the Treasury, private secretary to Gladstone, and Parry's cousin; and last but not least, George Herbert, Maude Herbert's brother, by then the 13th Earl of Pembroke.

The athletic orientation of Eton evidently suited Parry's temperament well, for most of the written recollections of his school activities concentrate on his success at football, cricket, and Fives, which were all

[2] E. Gambier Parry, *Annals of an Eton House* (London, 1907), 166.

the more heroic on the grounds of a temperamental heart condition. The list of his sporting achievements is, even by nineteenth-century standards, impressive. In this sense, therefore, he was a model schoolboy and the epitome of Victorian manliness. Much space in his diaries is taken up with fastidious reports of house matches, scores, strategy, depression in losing, and euphoria in winning. Parry himself apparently later criticized his Eton diaries as 'nothing but records of the prowess of individuals in various matches and daily games of Fives, with debates in "Pop" [the Eton debating society], and accounts of wildly foolish boyish escapades'.[3] While there is some truth in this disparaging comment, there is much also in these early diaries that refers to intellectual and musical development.

It is questionable whether Parry genuinely found favour academically at Eton owing to his preference for subjects that lay outside the traditional curriculum, namely music and literature. His friend Robert Lyttelton wrote:

In one respect Hubert was unfortunate at Eton. For some reason or other his father had chosen Russell Day to be his Tutor. Hubert was an average scholar, but, speaking from memory, I should say that his tastes did not lie in the way of mathematics or classics, which in those days formed the backbone of Public School Education. He loved poetry, and very likely would have taken to history or some subject not then taught, and of course was a born musician. But his Tutor was a fine Classical scholar of a sardonic type of wit, and as far as I can remember, utterly unsympathetic to music, and to him Hubert owed nothing. This was very unfortunate, as any Etonian would admit, who knows what great opportunities an understanding Tutor has who is able to appreciate and encourage a pupil like Parry.[4]

Such conservatism, not to say philistinism, was prevalent at most of the great public schools. Moreover, the choice of the unsympathetic Russell Day as Tutor was surely a deliberate ploy on the part of Thomas Gambier Parry to divert his son's attention away from the pursuit of music. Likewise the study and absorption of literature outside the prescribed diet of classical texts was largely of his own volition. His diaries provide fascinating evidence of his literary explorations, which are often represented by comments (sometimes at length) on the text, and at the end by a comprehensive list of books read during the year. The latter became routine for the rest of his life.

Academic progress at Eton was steady though not especially out-standing.[5] It was, however, a happy and stable existence, for at Highnam there was still a mood of unrest and anxiety as Clinton's second attempt at an honourable Oxford career began to deteriorate. Though his

[3] Ibid. 165. [4] Charles L. Graves, *Hubert Parry* (London, 1926), i. 18n.
[5] Ibid. i. 19.

brother's 1862 diary commences with numerous promises and maxims for hard work and self-improvement,[6] these had quickly dissolved by July when Clinton wrote proudly of 'enjoying life with friends and drinking a little and making *love much*'. Further on he recorded his amorous exploits with an air of casual bravado: 'Sweetest Georgie *what* moments we *have* passed together! with your little innocent head on my shoulder and your burning cheek against mine. Why was it that poor ill-dressed Clinton should be preferred to the regular "Lady Killers" of Oxford in all their Swelldom? Why was it that the "Lily of Godstow" should prefer him and treat him as a hero of Romance?'[7] But this fecklessness is accompanied typically by a sense of guilt and remorse: 'I may literally be said to have not opened a book this last term . . . Life certainly was very enjoyable and careless, but not profitable. I really regret immensely my folly, and hope to do something this vacation.'[8]

This was the pattern of his life at Oxford until the spring of 1863 when he was sent down 'for helping a friend in difficulties for the rest of the term by the injustice of the dons'.[9] Injustice or not, he evidently did little to enhance his reputation, for after briefly returning to Oxford at the end of April, he was sent down again, but this time permanently 'as a natural consequence of not working'.[10] The situation now being irrevocable, Clinton hastily left for Paris under a cloud.

The family at Highnam must have been plunged into emotional turmoil with the disgrace of the eldest son. Though Hubert never expressed any sense of pressure, it is clear that his father now looked to him to restore the family's reputation. Such a position must have created a dilemma for him. On the one hand he must have been particularly anxious to perform well academically, but on the other hand his interest in music had grown to such a point where it could no longer be ignored or thrown away. Yet with the knowledge of his father's opposition to a musical career, and having seen how such a denial had contributed to the rebellious nature of his brother's character, the burden of expectation must have seemed enormous.

The very lack of music during Parry's early years at the school provided the incentive to generate fresh interest. In 1861 there had been attempts to initiate a musical society. In reality this was merely a singing class, but it quickly foundered owing to financial difficulties, in particular, through the failure to pay the singing master. The following year a new society was formed and an organ was purchased. This was placed in one of the large rooms of the New Schools where the society could also practise. Rehearsals were also improved by the employment of a lay clerk from Westminster Abbey and the Chapel Royal, John Foster,

[6] Diary of Clinton Parry, 26 Jan. 1862, ShP.   [7] Ibid. 20 July 1862, ShP.
[8] Ibid.   [9] Ibid. [Apr.] 1863, ShP.   [10] Ibid. 4 May 1863.

who was eventually appointed as singing master. Thereafter the Eton Musical Society began to crystallize. Parry's cousin, Eddie Hamilton, became President in 1863 by which time the society had grown to forty members. Parry, Eddie Hamilton, Spencer Lyttelton, and Martin Le M. Gosselin now took the opportunity to organize annual concerts. Parry later wrote of the Society's achievement:

I can't remember what was the origin of the Musical Society. There were a lot of boys who liked music heartily, and Masters like Cornish and Browning and Snow encouraged them. My diary shows that there was a lot going on, and boys used to come and sit in my room for me to play to them, and really preferred Bach and Handel and Mendelssohn and such. The Musical Society was a singularly casual sort of affair at first. They were allowed to meet in some room or other under the supervision of a master, but it consisted in little more than spending an evening in an irregular manner. Some boys played the pianoforte and sang, and we had a try at a simple part-song or two. Then, by some one's advice, 'Johnnie' Foster, as we used to call him, was appointed to get things into some sort of order, but the order didn't amount to much . . . However, by degrees, the Society got plenty of members, and we worked away at part-songs and Madrigals and Handel Choruses and Mendelssohn's psalms, and gave concerts . . . As time went on they took things more seriously, and our Concerts were quite decent, and nearly always made up of quite good things . . . I and Eddie Hamilton used to play duets, and Spencer sang . . . [11]

These musical activities may have been small in scale and the standard of performance no more than average, but the concerts provided the all-important platform for Parry's growing list of compositions.

The nature of Parry's musical environment is clearly reflected in the limited range of genres of these pieces. Under the tuition of Brind his attention was focused primarily on the composition of functional sacred works for the Anglican liturgy: hymns, chants, Kyries, and an attempt at a service. Consequently instrumental music was given little consideration except for a few miniatures composed for domestic music-making at Highnam. Lessons continued with Brind during the school holidays until the end of 1862. He then began to search in earnest for more advanced tuition. Eton itself was unable to provide him with what he required. John Mitchell, the chapel organist since 1831, was quite unsuitable, for, as an incompetent performer, he appears to have shown equal inadequacy in his abilities to run the chapel choir. Parry's contempt for his 'bungling' was unreserved. A diary entry from 1865 records the chaos that was a regular part of worship:

We had a most extraordinary exhibition in the music line in Chapel this afternoon I ever heard in my life. First in the Psalms old Mitchell began wandering about on the keys, as if he had lost his place, and played the chant

[11] Gambier Parry, *Annals of an Eton House*, 166–7.

wrong all the way through. Then when the *Magnificat* began it seemed as if he was gone quite mad. He began to play seemingly just whatever came into his head. The choir began to sing snatches of the *Magnificat* at intervals, trying to make out what he was doing; this went on in the most hopeful manner for full three minutes, till one of the choirmen (Adams) went and stopped him, and made him play a chant. The whole chapel was convulsed, it was useless to try and prevent it.[12]

It was therefore necessary to look further afield. Fortunately he did not have to look far, for in close proximity to the school was St George's Chapel, Windsor whose organist was Dr George Elvey.

Elvey was very much a product of ancient university training. Initially he had received his musical education from his brother Stephen Elvey who was organist of New College, Oxford. At the Royal Academy of Music his conservative approach, combined with a certain proficiency, found favour with the teachers of composition who awarded him the Gresham prize in 1834 for his anthem 'Bow thine ear' in preference to S. S. Wesley's comparatively more adventurous 'The Wilderness'. In 1835 Elvey was again destined to be preferred to Wesley (a coup for which Wesley never forgave him) this time as organist at St George's Chapel, Windsor, a post in which he was to remain until his retirement in 1882. As a composer his style has been described as depressingly conservative, if not anachronistic, though the label 'Handelian' has been vehemently disputed. The words of Dr Arnold, in a letter to Lady Elvey after her husband's death, are an indignant example: 'I do not consider your late husband was only a Handelian; he was a continuation of the school of English musicians who have a *style of their own*, based upon the Church and madrigal writers.'[13] Yet even if Elvey admired those composers he considered more progressive, such as Schumann or Chopin, they never formed part of his teaching methods. In spite of Dr Arnold's auspicious evaluation of the 'English' style, the musical language of Elvey's anthems is, if anything, the most concise example of the inward-looking, creative sterility that had blighted indigenous composition. His predilection for Handel over Mendelssohn is clearly shown in his Oxford B.Mus. exercise *The Resurrection and Ascension* of 1837, the oratorio *Mount Carmel*, and the music he provided for the Prince Consort's funeral in 1861. Today he is perhaps best known for his hymn-tunes such as *Diademata* ('Crown him with many crowns') and *St George* ('Come, ye faithful people, come'), and a handful of Anglican chants. But though his compositions may be of limited value, his achievements at St George's Chapel, Windsor are notable. Just as Stainer and Wesley protested loudly about the depths to which the standards of

[12] Diary, 11 Feb. 1865.
[13] Lady Elvey, *The Life and Reminiscences of Sir George Elvey Knt* (London, 1894), 142n.

church music had plummeted, Elvey voiced his own disapproval, subsequently improving the choir, enlarging the meagre repertoire, and redesigning the organ. He was knighted in 1871 for his services to music and to the royal foundation.

Parry began lessons with Elvey sometime in 1863. It is clear from the list of works at the end of his 1864 diary that, besides the usual production of small-scale church pieces, he was subjected to the first stages of the well-established contrapuntal disciplines. His exercises were primarily orientated around canon and fugue, and when permitted to indulge in 'free' composition his studies were devoted almost exclusively to standard anthem settings of psalm texts modelled on those of his teacher. This is evident from a comment Parry included in his diary during the composition of his anthem 'O sing unto the Lord a new song': 'I scribbled away at my anthem "Sing unto the Lord" in the morning. I have got a large number of subjects in the first piece; almost too many. And it begins rather too like Elvey's service.'[14] The relationship between master and student appears to have been a good one; Elvey responded to the enthusiasm and appetite for work shown by his young pupil while Parry initially viewed his teacher as something of an idol: 'To St George's, and there they had Cook in C and Elvey's "When Israel", which I think is almost the finest anthem ever written.'[15] The organ loft at St George's Chapel was a frequent haunt and the venue for much of his tuition and formative musical experiences. This is emphatically portrayed in a number of early entries in his diary such as: 'After dinner, Day came to me and we went to the organ together and talked about music etc., and after Chapel I went with him to St George's, where they had Elvey's service, and Mozart's Twelfth Mass. I never saw such a squash in the organ loft before. There was hardly room to move about.'[16] The habit of hearing regular services at St George's Chapel naturally prompted Parry to compose music for the choir's repertoire. In this way he was able to gain first-hand practical experience which was not available at Eton. Elvey's guidance was unswervingly orthodox and there can be little doubt that he had already made up his mind that his budding young pupil, with perhaps a further two years' study, should be encouraged to supplicate for the Oxford B.Mus. degree.

1864 was much more industrious and serious in intent than previous years. Parry completed four anthems: 'In my distress' (begun in 1863), 'My God, my God', 'O sing unto the Lord', and 'Fear thou not' together with an Evening Service in A. Three other anthems were begun— 'Blessed is He', 'Why boastest thou thyself', and 'Prevent us O Lord', and a 'Madrigal' on Shakespeare's words "Tell me where is fancy bred'

<hr />

[14] Diary, 20 June 1864.   [15] Ibid. 19 June 1864.   [16] Ibid. 5 June 1864.

from *The Merchant of Venice*, rewritten in July 1865. His main concern in these exercises was, in the best traditions of Victorian musical 'correctness', the attainment of an assured fugal technique. Indeed, his obsession for fugue reflected the ancient universities' fetishistic attitude to contrapuntal proficiency. Many of Parry's comments in his diary mention his quest for suitable fugue subjects. His study was extremely thorough. In 1862 he had been given W. T. Best's edition of Bach's '48' as a present which he then frequently annotated. A typical example can be found above the F minor fugue in Book I: 'In this fugue there is no stretto, but the beauty of this fugue lies in its rhythmic parts, and the sort of second subject, which makes the accompaniment to the first subject.'[17] In January he 'finished reading the fugues through'[18] which was followed by a similar dissection of those for the organ. The result was an ambitious Bachian 'Grand Fugue on 3 Subjects' for organ which he completed at the end of 1864, but was not performed until February 1865 when it was played by Elvey in St George's Chapel.

Elvey was inevitably instrumental in shaping Parry's early musical tastes and criteria. Since the organ loft was the main venue for musical instruction, the organ itself became a focal point for exploration. Each visit to a church or cathedral was accompanied by an assessment of its organ. All this was essential to the 'organist' mentality. His musical library echoed Elvey's conservative palette in which Handel dominated a noticeably smaller number of works, mostly sacred, by Haydn, Mozart, Beethoven, Mendelssohn, Spohr, and Costa. There was also the diet of liturgical music by Attwood, Cook, Nares, Elvey, Smart, and Crotch, and he may have become familiar with a number of operatic arias and choruses adapted to sacred texts, for this was common practice. Secular music was limited primarily to the most sanctimonious of Victorian idioms, the part-song, whose chief exponent was Mendelssohn, though Parry's library also contained examples by Macfarren and Balfe.

Moral conservatism, a more deep-seated characteristic of the Victorian musical pedagogy, was very much a part of Elvey's personality, and its influence on Parry is evident from a number of remarks made in his diary. Elvey disapproved of dramatic effects which he felt had infiltrated into contemporary church music. Parry wrote: 'He [Elvey] talked long also about modern church music. He said "the improvement of organs has been the destruction of real church music" having led to separate and flourishy accompaniments. Beware to too many diatonic successions; and Spohrry chords in peaceful music.'[19] One may presume therefore that Elvey would not have recommended the study of S. S. Wesley who freely imbibed Spohr's chromaticisms, or Walmisley, who successfully

---

[17] Parry's copy of Bach's '48', ShP.   [18] Ibid.
[19] Diary, 26 Oct. 1864.

demonstrated the effect of the independent organ part in his Evening Service in D minor. Initially Parry appears to subscribe to his teacher's views, for after hearing Mendelssohn's 'Why rage furiously' in Chapel he recorded: 'I don't think there is any word in the English language which perfectly expresses the excess of *beauty* of this anthem. It is *quite* perfection in the *beauty* line, but a little dramatic for church use.'[20] However, Elvey's influence can be seen more clearly in Parry's response to works by Spohr and Rossini performed at the Hereford Three Choirs Festival. It is also interesting to observe how fugue lay at the heart of Parry's critical acumen:

It began with Spohr's *Tale of Babylon*. I think he is rather extraneous in his keys. There can be no possible reason for beginning in 4 sharps and changing suddenly to 5 flats . . . The orchestration in the overture is very fine, but the writing too chromatic. It begins in 6 flats. There is a very Mendelssohnian subject at the beginning, 'To thee O Jehovah thy children are in trouble.' It is most beautiful. Rossini's *Stabat Mater* I was thoroughly disgusted with. It is no more fit to be played in a sacred building than a quadrille. The 'quando corpus' and last chorus are fine. The last chorus particularly so. But it is not a good *fugue*. The Handel part of the performance was of course magnificent. It began with the Occasional Overture. I had never heard it performed in an orchestra before. It is exceedingly fine, though not a strict fugue. It is thorough 'Handel'.[21]

This last entry is most revealing, for, even though its manner is that of a naïve and impressionable teenager, it contains the seeds of intolerance, religious bigotry, and insidious puritanism so prevalent in British musical circles. Though in one sense Parry was to develop and move away substantially from such a constricted frame of mind in the future, the nature of his early training was to have much greater significance on a subconscious compositional level, and its effect can be observed in works of a later date.

With his musical activities underpinned by a firm and disciplined training, the possibility of realizing a musical career must have seemed more of a reality to Parry. His happiness was further increased by the invitation to spend the summer at Wilton House. After one delirious holiday there during the summer of 1863 with his cousin Eddie Hamilton, Lady Herbert invited them to spend the first two weeks of August 1864 on the estate. Though Wilton with its idyllic grandeur and extensive grounds afforded the opportunity to indulge in the aristocratic pastimes of hunting, fishing, and shooting, the ulterior motive for spending time at Wilton was Maude. It is evident from the brief remarks made at regular intervals in his diary that his friendship with her had

[20] Ibid. 26 June 1864.   [21] Ibid. 1 Sept. 1864.

steadily turned to pubescent infatuation. George Pembroke, Maude's brother, was often used as a go-between for obtaining snippets of information about her, as one entry reveals: 'I found Georgie Pembroke . . . at last come back from abroad. I sat in my room all the evening, and he told me his adventures and journeys in Egypt, and Syria, and Jerusalem; and he told me a great deal about Maudie.'[22] Had Lady Herbert got wind of the fact that the friendship between her daughter and this young man from Gloucestershire was gradually assuming a new complexion, it is certain she would have put an end to their meetings and to any further visits to Wilton. She was, however, completely unaware of any such sentiments. This may be partly attributed to her obsession with foreign travel and religion, the latter of which had preoccupied her since her husband's premature death. In fact, during their time in the Middle East in the first half of 1864 George had written to Parry with the disturbing news that Lady Herbert was about to embrace Catholicism:

I hope you are happier and better now than when I last saw you. Perhaps you would like to hear something about Syria. We are at Jerusalem and tomorrow start for Damascus. Maudie is very well and happy . . . But there is something else I want to talk to you about, but don't tell *anyone anything about it*. That is about Mamma. I do feel very wretched. I am so afraid she is really going to become a Roman Catholick [*sic*]. In fact she hardly tries to hide it. She has been in the Church of the Holy Sepulchre the whole of the holy week even sometimes staying there the whole night. I am very much afraid she will become a Roman Catholick. You can't think what a curious feeling I have about it. Somehow it makes me feel uncommonly wretched. But I trust you will tell this to no-one at all.[23]

George's anxieties were well founded. The stigma of conversion to Catholicism, particularly amongst the aristocracy who were looked upon as the social foundation of the Established Church, was considerable. Yet Lady Herbert remained doggedly determined and her piety remained a source of constant irritation to all concerned. However, it is intriguing to note that her new-found faith did not humble her at all. She remained highly conscious of her social position and tended to patronize the young Parry who, although from wealthy landowning stock, was nevertheless of a lower social stratum. In his turn Parry, single-minded as ever, ignored Lady Herbert's condescension as he became more and more absorbed with Maude. His most private thoughts were written in code ($\Box < \rho\delta - \oint\ \lambda\ \partial < \wedge\Box - \times =$ 'Darling Maudie'), as if, even in his diary, he feared he might be discovered.

[22] Ibid. 23 June 1864.
[23] Letter from George Herbert, 13th Earl of Pembroke, Easter Monday 1864, ShP.

The idyllic summer days at Wilton were for Parry a paradise: 'I think of all the days I ever spent in my life', he wrote, 'this was nearly or quite the happiest. With $\partial < \wedge \square - \times$ all day.'[24] Leaving Wilton was an emotional strain: 'And now again I must leave Wilton; packing and preparing to leave a place which I am sorry to confess I love more than my home.'[25] He knew that it would be some time before he would see Maude again and therefore confided in his friend Eddie Hamilton who, as a more regular visitor at Wilton (as the son of the Bishop of Salisbury), acted as a secret messenger.

Back at Highnam he was cheered by the return of his brother, though during his time away Clinton had done little to make reparation for his infamous behaviour at Oxford. If anything, matters had been made worse by his falling in love with a woman deemed to be from a lower class and of whom his father vehemently disapproved. Hubert's private thoughts about Clinton, with whom he largely sympathized, were committed to code, suggesting again that he did not wish others to know of his true sentiments. In particular he had no intention of revealing his sympathies to his father. Since Clinton's emotional estrangement from the family, Hubert's relationship with his father had grown somewhat stronger—a fact emphasized by a rapturous visit to Ely at the end of the summer holidays where he spent much time admiring the progress of the cathedral roof-paintings which were nearing completion.

The Michaelmas term of 1864 was taken up with the composition of motets under the watchful eye of Elvey. The preoccupation with fugue persisted, but one senses occasionally that Parry was becoming mildly impatient with the strictures placed upon him by his teacher. In October he had set to work on a short introit 'Prevent us O Lord'. By today's standards it is very much a sterile, unimaginative, four-part exercise but he was annoyed when Elvey 'corrected' it: 'Had a middling lesson. He changed my "Prevent us O Lord" a good deal—more than I liked.'[26] His energies were also directed towards organizing a programme of glees, Handel choruses, and piano solos for the first Musical Society concert which took place on 13 December. This was, however, to some extent interrupted by a number of severe recurrences of heart trouble almost certainly brought on by excessive mental and physical exertion. Several attacks occurred on the football field, but one was the result of mental strain during a visit from his brother in November who, now showing signs of alcoholism, broke the news that he was to leave Highnam in order to pursue his intention of marrying Florence Hinde, the woman with whom he had fallen in love.

[24] Diary, 16 Aug. 1864.　　[25] Ibid. 23 Aug. 1864.
[26] Ibid. 2 Nov. 1864.

Clinton was in fact potentially suicidal at this time for his dipsomania had reached the point of no return. His wedding in August 1865 was a pathetic, solitary affair which none of his family was permitted to attend, and his marriage was almost certainly the final nail in the coffin so far as inheritance of his father's estate was concerned. To counteract this disturbing sequence of events, Hubert befriended an older cousin, Lewis Majendie, who in many ways assumed the position of elder brother, and with whom Hubert felt happier seeking advice or discussing more personal matters. Most important of all perhaps, it was Lewis Majendie who provided Hubert with the essential encouragement to continue his musical studies. On his birthday in February, Lewis had come down to Eton, bringing with him a fine volume of Tennyson's poems which provided Hubert with a much-needed interlude from the exasperations of school work. In a letter to Lewis, written later in March, he expressed his annoyance with academic routine which he felt was impeding his studies for his B.Mus. degree as well as his aspirations to take up music as a profession. Under the influence of Elizabeth Sheppard's novel *Charles Auchester*, he dreamed of leading a musical life in imitation of Mendelssohn's 'noble example', though he also alluded to an inescapable tendency towards melancholy brought on by emotional confusion and frustration.[27] Lewis's reply, sympathetic though somewhat didactic in tone, attempted to console him:

> Hedingham Castle,
> Halstead,
> Essex.

My dear Hubert,

You will have expected to hear from me sooner, but I could not attempt to answer your letter at all satisfactorily until I was quiet at home and had time to think of what I could best say. Your letter is very dear to me for I delight to think that you can write freely to me and tell me what you think and what you feel— and that you treat me as a brother; I do hope that you will always do so, for I love to share your thoughts and if I ever can to help you in any trouble. I can quite understand what you say about a growing vilesomeness towards school work: it is not at all unnatural and is what I have often feared might sooner or later be one of your trials, but I would say meet it as a trial sent for your good and do not give way to the feeling. I cannot help thinking that the more you stick to schoolwork and try to do your best in it, the better it will be for your music, because the work in itself will strengthen your mind and so make you a more able man, as time goes on, and the very struggle against this feeling and the determination to do your school work, which is *in reality your main duty now*, will

---

[27] See Graves, *Hubert Parry*, i. 48.

help you towards the struggle and battle of life which must come to all of us as time goes on . . . I am afraid you will think this poor comfort, but still I believe it to be the best—and I feel it all the more to be true, first because I can most thoroughly sympathise with your feeling. So too can I understand what you say about wishing that music could be your profession—but as to this I would quote your favourite text—'Commit thy ways unto the Lord'—go on now with your school work and afterwards with Oxford work, with music for your pleasure and relief too, and depend upon it, He will reward you by ordering that which is in truth best for you. Sometimes it is hard to feel this but one must try.

Do not think me hard or unsympathising, dear Hubert, for indeed I do not mean to be so, only to try to help you if I can.

I should like to read this life of Mendelssohn of which you speak for I do not know enough about him,—I certainly do not think it wrong to try to imitate a man—up to a certain point at least—unless it in any way leads one to forget, or even not to have constantly before one, *the Great Example,*—but short of this it cannot be wrong to try to imitate the good life of any really good man—who has framed his life after the Great Example of all—the chief danger is making a sort of idol of a man and imitating more details in his character and so losing one's own individuality—I think you know what I mean.[28]

Lewis's response to Hubert's talk of melancholy was, with good reason, one of alarm, for he feared that it was this very tendency that signalled Clinton's emotional decline at Oxford:

And now as to melancholy . . . It is very difficult to write exactly what I mean and I wish I could talk instead—but to tell the truth I think that feeling about melancholy, which I have often felt, rather dangerous. It is no doubt a sort of happiness and it does seem to raise one's soul and lead one to higher thoughts— but its very seductiveness is the danger—it is apt to lead one to seek it for its own sake and to indulge in it as a sort of luxury . . . .

There is another danger too in indulging in melancholy freely—it almost always leads to *unreality*—a very great danger. I think you may see this in Clinton, many of whose faults I think I can trace to the influence of cultivating melancholy as a sort of necessity—and so becoming by degrees unreal, and then at last what he is now.

For all its over simplification and religious panacea, Hubert evidently valued the advice, above all because, in Lewis Majendie, he at last had an ally. This is clear in his reply:

I can assure you that however much I have been inclined to be lazy in my school work, as I told you, I have not in the least yielded to it, as you will understand if I tell you that the number of verses we are obliged to do is 24, and last week I

[28] Letter from Lewis Majendie, 28 Mar. 1865, ShP.

did 56. And you must have heard me say that verses is the part of my work at Eton that I dislike most of all; but I always find that the best way to get through anything one dislikes is to take as much interest in it as possible; and I really believe that by that means one can even make a punishment pleasant—I mean the common punishment of writing out so many lines. And so I find it the best way to try and do my best in verses and in every other school work I especially dislike, more than even in that part of my work which I like. I was rather afraid of the issue of my Trials at first, but I have heard rather pleasant reports from different masters, to make me think that I have not done so remarkably badly.

. . . I don't think you would take any interest to speak of in the book I spoke of as containing a sort of life of Mendelssohn. The name of it is *Charles Auchester*, and it is really a very strange book, and has left the sort of impression on my mind of its being the sort of book a person would have written in a musical dream . . . I will always remember what you quoted about 'cheerfulness', and will not allow melancholy to have the slightest influence over me, though it may be a struggle. It never at all unfits me for work, but rather gives me another opinion of it at the time, which I cannot define except in speaking.[29]

Fortunately, vital reassurance also came from other quarters. During the Easter vacation of 1865 he was invited to sing in a concert of choral music in Gloucester cathedral which was to include a performance of his setting of Shakespeare's 'Take, O take those lips away' for four-part male-voice choir, written in February for his father's birthday. After the dress rehearsal on 17 April Parry noted in his diary: 'We had a full dress rehearsal in the evening conducted by Sterndale Bennett and Wesley. The things which we rehearsed were Professor Sterndale Bennett's "May Queen", Dr Wesley's "Ode", Mendelssohn's "Lorelei" and some part songs. I had to conduct my own. Sterndale Bennett I think is one of the most kind and delightful men I ever met. He was very kind to me.' S. S. Wesley, who had succeeded Amott as the organist of Gloucester, also took the young Parry under his wing, boosting his confidence by participating in the performance of his part-song, as well as allowing him the freedom of the cathedral organ:

Had rehearsal again at 12. The 'Ode' was the chief thing we had to practise. I had luncheon at the Palace, and went afterwards to the Cathedral and played the out voluntary. Dr Wesley gave me leave to play there whenever I like . . . In the evening we had the concert . . . with the following additions: Bishop's 'Merry Boys', a most horrible thing, and Pearsall's 'In dulci jubilo' which is most glorious. Some parts of Wesley's ode are quite magnificent, especially the first bass solo. The fugue is good . . . The last chorus is rather strange, with some very novel ideas in it, very fast. Wesley takes it all *very* fast. The great beauties of Bennett's May Queen are many . . . My little part song went very badly through not having enough rehearsal . . . Dr Wesley positively sang bass in it.

[29] Graves, *Hubert Parry*, i. 49.

The Lorelei was quite glorious, such music!! It is quite strange how it shows the hand of a perfect master in *some* parts in comparison to the other things of the evening, even against Wesley and Bennett.[30]

His devotion to the music of Mendelssohn remained fervent and was romantically fortified through the reading of *Charles Auchester* and volumes of the composer's letters. His enthusiasm for the 'dramatic' anthem *Why rage furiously*, heard at St George's the previous year, provoked him into modelling a setting of Psalm 52 'Why boastest thou thyself' on the piece. Moreover, his devotion was reinforced by the profusion of Mendelssohn's choral works in the 1865 Gloucester Festival which included *St Paul*, *Elijah*, the *Lobgesang*, and *Die Erste Walpurgisnacht* which was 'so fine that it soon drove all the rest of the concert out of my head'. Indeed the excitement of Goethe's preternatural text provoked Parry into making more penetrating criticisms of his musical idol: 'The whole Walpurgis Night is well worthy of Mendelssohn and I think contains some of the sublimest ideas of all his thoughts—It has not so much melody as one might expect, but the general outline is of a deeper character than is usual in his works.'[31] His response to Beethoven at the Gloucester Festival was somewhat guarded. He found the Eighth Symphony intellectually challenging and the structural experimentation of the Choral Fantasia he described reticently as 'a sort of dream which no-one but Beethoven is allowed to indulge'; while his assessment of Spohr's *Die Letzten Dinge* was still coloured by a distaste for superfluous chromaticism.

Parry's production of vocal music in 1865 was remarkable. In addition to the verse anthem 'Why boastest thou thyself', he completed an Evening Service in B flat, and part-song settings of Horace's 'Persicos odi' (written as a New Year's present for his stepmother) and Herrick's 'Fair Daffodils' (categorized by Parry as a madrigal, reflecting his continuing fascination for the Elizabethans) which was later performed at the Royal Glee and Madrigal Union on 12 February 1866 and at the Eton College Musical Society's spring concert on 22 March 1866. He produced three songs: 'Love not me for comely grace' (written initially for his stepmother though later dedicated to Eddie Hamilton), 'Autumn' to words by Hood for Lewis Majendie (which appears to have begun life as a song for voice and orchestra, being rewritten for voice and piano in March 1866), and 'When stars are in the quiet skies', written for Carrie Somerset during the Easter vacation, though not completed until August. Two anthems were also revised and performed: 'Prevent us O Lord' was sung at Salisbury Cathedral and formed part of the Eton Musical Society's winter programme, while 'Blessed is He' was sung at

[30] Diary, 18 Apr. 1865.　　　[31] Ibid. 6 Sept. 1865.

St George's on several occasions, which, at Elvey's instigation, was subsequently published by Novello later that year. This voracious appetite for work fuelled largely by nervous energy resulted in a further breakdown in health at the end of the summer term. In August Elvey wrote to his pupil at Highnam anxious that he should enjoy some rest away from the rigours of study:

I was indeed worried to hear your leaving so ill before you left Eton and disappointed that I did not see you, . . . We did your anthem 'Blessed is the man' and it went off very well . . . As regards your studies during the holidays if you can find the time for writing, compose another anthem [and] an organ fugue after the style of the one in E major [by] Bach. Then write an Air with [variations] for 4 violins after the style of Haydn's 'God preserve the Emperor' which I suppose you are acquainted with. Now I think I have given you *enough* to do (more than I should like myself) and the best advice I can give you now, is to refrain from working *altogether* unless you *are quite well*. I hope the holidays will set you up, and trust when you return to Eton I shall see you looking quite *jolly*.[32]

Elvey's correspondence also reveals that increasing attention was being given to instrumental music, though the course of training was inevitably conservative. Elvey vociferously applauded the maxims of Ouseley, suggesting that Parry should acquire and study the quartets of Haydn and Mozart, though it is also evident that Parry, through his own initiative, was already becoming familiar with the orchestral scores of Beethoven, Weber, and, of course, Mendelssohn. In February the Provost of Eton had arranged a concert of instrumental music in the College Hall in which a reduced 'orchestra' of two violins, viola, cello, double bass, flute, and piano delivered a programme of Rossini's *Semiramide* Overture, Weber's *Der Freischütz* Overture, and selected movements of Beethoven's First and Second Symphonies. Even with such modest resources, these performances must have been enormously instructive, for the luxury of hearing a full-size orchestra was as yet restricted to the Three Choirs Festival which came only once a year.

Having been mainly restricted to the world of the organ and its repertoire, Parry's response to the intellectual dimensions of more extensive instrumental forms was rapid. During the Michaelmas term of 1865 he produced two works for piano duet in less than six weeks. Having been knocked virtually unconscious during a football match, and being laid up in the sanatorium in the latter part of October, he first completed a sonata in F minor which was tentative, structurally unambitious, and extremely Mendelssohnian. More substantial than this, however, was an Overture in B minor composed for Eddie

---

[32] Letter from Sir George Elvey, 5 Aug. 1865, ShP.

Hamilton and himself to play at the Musical Society concert on 9 December. Perhaps the most striking feature of this piece, especially in comparison with the earlier sonata, is the competence shown in handling structure on a larger scale—a facility he had gained more through private study rather than from his teacher. The piece, which consists of no fewer than 455 bars, clearly reflects the influence of the *Hebrides* Overture, not only in the choice of key, but also in the contrast of first- and second-group ideas (Exx. 1*a* and 1*b*), their registral similarities, and the 'scoring' suggested by the various piano textures. The internal organization also displays a degree of imagination over and above the conventional requirements of sonata form. It is interesting to see for example how Parry avoids the expositional repeat and how the rather naïve, though extensive developmental treatment grows out of the consequent material to his second-group idea. A central feature of the development is the introduction of a new thematic figure in A major (Ex. 1*c*) which is later redeployed in the recapitulation. The recapitulation itself is subject to thematic displacement. The second group is restated first in B major over a dominant pedal which, as it undergoes further development, reveals Parry experimenting with more adventurous harmonic progressions

Ex. 1. Overture in B minor (1865). *a* first-group idea; *b* second-group idea; *c* new thematic figure in development.

cont. over/

Ex. 1. cont.

(bars 234–59). This paragraph initially cadences into B minor, but a third cadential repetition gives way unexpectedly to a prolonged submediant pedal over which the new idea of the development returns (bars 259–74). Finally the first idea reappears (bars 275–359), though the balance of Parry's structure is perhaps weakened here by too much literal repetition. The coda (bar 359) is also over-long, too insistent on its Neapolitan deflections (bars 387 and 399), and almost too overtly indebted to the *Hebrides* in its final bars—a fact Parry must have recognized, since he subsequently revised bars 425 to the end.

In the latter part of 1865 it is clear that Parry's admiration for S. S. Wesley began to eclipse that of his present teacher. Elvey's conservatism was becoming a source of frustration, while Wesley's greater skill as organist and conductor, combined with his more adventurous harmonic idiom, provided a greater stimulus. The exasperation with Elvey's inability to interpret Wesley's anthems at St George's was recorded in plain terms: 'Went to St George's after 4. We had Wesley's "Blessed be God". Elvey abused it a great deal and played it so as to spoil nearly all its beauties.'[33] Moreover, as a close acquaintance of Thomas Gambier Parry, Wesley also became a regular visitor at Highnam which provided ample opportunity for Parry to quiz him, particularly on the subject of instrumentation. After a visit in early January 1866, Parry recalled his attitudes and advice in some detail:

Dr Wesley (& Mrs) came to dinner tonight. We got some very interesting conversation out of him. He said that he thought that the reason why Beethoven and more especially Spohr were sometimes (frequently) so unsatisfactory was because [they] lacked the necessary and beneficial basis of hard work at counterpoint; and he said that he considered that the reason why Mendelssohn so excelled was entirely because he had that instruction, and went through that preparation thoroughly. I had a short talk with him over the Full Score of the Hymn of Praise. He told me that the reason why Spohr so excelled was because he could bring such a marvellous tone out of his orchestra. Mendelssohn could not be sure of it . . . He played some of Bach's Preludes and Fugues and Mendelssohn's 'Lieder ohne Wörte'. I played the E major fugue—He says it will be impossible for me to get on well in orchestration without lessons from a London master.[34]

On his return to Eton the frequency of lessons with Elvey was intensified. The madrigal, 'Fair Daffodils', and the Overture were scrutinized, as was the anthem, 'Why boastest thou'; all were given a clean bill of health. Tuition in instrumentation was begun, much to Parry's delight. Elvey's sights were now firmly fixed on preparing his young pupil for the Oxford degree and this meant that he required some rudimentary training in orchestration for the exercise. For this Bach's '48' formed the basis, though he also attempted to score some of his own fugues, one of which, in C minor, was described as 'for free Orchestral Overture style'.[35]

The production of songs, as shown by a setting of 'Love the Tyrant', continued unabated and this was mainly due to his growing awareness of lyrical poetry. Besides his interest in the seventeenth-century lyricists and his continuing enthusiasm for Spenser (which had incidentally initiated an interest in Tudor music and literature and led him to introduce madrigals to the Eton Musical Society), his tastes were rapidly expanding in the direction of nineteenth-century poetry. He had already discovered the poems of Hood whom he found 'remarkable' and 'deliciously fresh' in its wit. But his attention was soon diverted when

[33] Diary, 1 Oct. 1865. [34] Ibid. 5 Jan. 1866.
[35] E. Daymond, 'On an Early Manuscript Book of Sir Hubert Parry's', *RCM Magazine*, 19/3: 76.

Lewis Majendie presented him with a volume of Keats on his birthday in February. 'They are mostly very delightful. Very dreamy generally speaking . . .', wrote Parry the following day.[36] The simple lyrics of Thomas Moore had also attracted him, which is reflected in the rather sentimental, though touchingly naïve 'Why does azure deck the sky', written for his friend Cecil Ricardo, who sang it at the Eton Musical Society concert in March. It was also his first published song, being taken up by Lamborn Cock the same year. Another of his closest friends, Spencer Lyttelton, who had recently gone up to Trinity College, Cambridge, was the dedicatee of a setting of Lord Francis Hervey's poem, 'Angel hosts, sweet love, befriend thee', which Lamborn Cock agreed to publish the following year. The Society concert on 22 March was a great success considering its lack of rehearsal. The programme, conservative as ever, shows Parry dominating the proceedings, displaying his versatility as singer, pianist, accompanist, organist, and composer:

Part 1

Chorus	'O Father whose Almighty Power'	Handel
Solo	'With thee the Unsheltered Moor'	Handel
Organ solo	Andante (CHHP)	Smart
Chorus	'Come gentle Spring' (The Seasons)	Haydn
Song	'Why does azure deck the sky' (Ricardo and CHHP)	C. Hubert H. Parry
Madrigal	'Flow O my tears'	Bennett
Song	'Nazareth' (sung by CHHP)	Gounod

Part 2

Chorus	'Christmas Pastorale'	Schachner
Organ solo	Sonata No. 2 (CHHP)	Mendelssohn
Chorus	'See what love' (St Paul)	Mendelssohn
Madrigal	'Fair Daffodils'	C. Hubert H. Parry
Solo	'O God have mercy' (St Paul)	Mendelssohn
Psalm	'By Babylon's waves'	Gounod

By the end of the term, under Elvey's guidance, Parry had already begun to draw up an outline for his B.Mus. exercise—a cantata, setting numerous well-known passages from the Old Testament, entitled *O Lord, Thou hast cast us out*. The work soon took shape, its format adhering strictly to the examination rubric. The Overture, scored for string orchestra and piano duet, and obviously modelled on the Handelian bipartite design (such as one finds in *Messiah*), opens with solemn Largo replete with pathetic chromaticisms, followed by a fugue which studiously attempts to incorporate several countersubjects to the one fugal subject—a scheme far too ambitious for the movement's mere

---

[36] Diary, 28 Feb. 1866.

54 bars. This flaw, however, would probably not have worried the examiners, since they were looking primarily for contrapuntal proficiency. The six choral movements are equally conventional and consist of three five-part choruses interspersed by three solos. The first chorus is, predictably, a fugue setting the text from which the cantata finds its title. A central chorus, 'O Lord why hast Thou cast us out for ever', is of a traditional 'chorale' design, commonly found in Handel and Bach, as well as Mendelssohn's *St Paul*; while the final chorus, in B flat, begins with triumphal Handelian declamation followed by the inevitable fugue. The solos are equally derivative. The bass aria, 'O Israel return', is, if anything, more reminiscent of a similar movement, 'Be not very sure O Lord' in S. S. Wesley's 'Let us lift up our heart'. The tenor solo, 'I will pour out my spirit on thy seed' (which includes the lines 'Drop down ye heavens from above' set much more imaginatively by Stainer the very same year), is a 'song without words'; likewise, the movement for soprano that succeeds it is also clearly indebted to Mendelssohn and clearly shows the influence of *Elijah* and the *Lobgesang*.

Most of the exercise was composed at Highnam in April. In between times he gained useful experience conducting the Highnam Choral Society and hearing various new works by Haydn, Beethoven (which included the acquisition of the score of the Choral Symphony), Spohr, Rossini, Verdi, and Donizetti at concerts in Gloucester. He also found time to compose another song, 'Go lovely rose' to words by Edmund Waller, dated 12 April. One visitor to Highnam was the young Charles Harford Lloyd, who, though Parry's junior by one year, was already making a name for himself as an organist in Gloucester, and was strongly tipped to succeed S. S. Wesley (which he eventually did in June 1876). Together they stayed up until the small hours singing and playing in the drawing-room. As part of his recollection of their profound and lasting friendship Lloyd wrote later: 'It was while he was still an Eton boy that I first met him at Highnam, his beautiful home in Gloucestershire, where his handsome artistic father had invited me to spend a few days in order to make his son's acquaintance. I remember the vigour he displayed in various ways, and especially the boyish pranks in which he indulged when he rowed me in a boat on the lake.'[37] Although music occupied him for most of the day, Parry's domestic responsibilities were also increasing, for now he was called upon, as a more senior member of the family, to be godfather to his youngest half-sister, Hilda, who was christened in Highnam church on 15 April. Only days later he travelled to Bayfordbury, home of William Baker and his aunt Anna (his mother's sister) to stand godfather to a cousin.

[37] C. H. Lloyd, 'Parry at Play', *RCM Magazine*, 15/1: 18.

On his return to Highnam discussion was already under way regarding the path of his future education. There was still debate as to whether he would follow in his father's footsteps and go to Cambridge, or whether his father and tutor would again favour Oxford. It was in fact, early in May, through the intervention of Lewis Majendie, that the suggestion to attempt an Exhibition at New College, Oxford was made and subsequently endorsed. Though enthusiastic about the prospect, for some reason Hubert did not succeed in the matriculation. However, he did use his week in Oxford constructively. In addition to meeting Dr G. W. Kitchin, his old Twyford headmaster, at Christ Church, and calling on Eddie Hamilton who had recently moved up to Oxford from Eton, he took the opportunity to renew the acquaintance of John Stainer whom he had met briefly at the Gloucester Festival the previous year. He was a regular visitor to Magdalen Chapel to hear Stainer play the organ as an entry of 20 May recalls: 'Went to Magdalen to 5 o'clock service . . . We had S. Elvey in A and "The Lord spake the word." Stainer played the last 3 movements of the Sonata in B flat (Mendelssohn) afterwards most gloriously; and brought out the "Tuba mirabilis" tremendously in the last strain.' Besides showing Parry the organ, Stainer, who had only the previous year successfully received his Doctorate, was also able to offer him advice about his forthcoming degree examination: 'Went to Magdalen Chapel at 12. Met Stainer and tried the organ. Stainer was very kind and told me also about my musical degree and how I am to take it. And what I am to write.'[38]

The rest of the term at Eton was spent preparing for Collections in which he gained a second class. Otherwise much of his time was absorbed in socializing in the customary Eton fashion of water parties, inter-school cricket matches, and late-night festivities which included a welcome complement of the opposite sex. It was inevitable therefore that musical activities would take second place, though to some extent his enthusiasm for the Musical Society had been tempered by the breaking up of the original fraternity, for Eddie Hamilton had gone up to Oxford, and Spencer Lyttelton to Cambridge. However, he was able to fit in a visit to Covent Garden with Lewis Majendie to hear Meyerbeer's *Les Huguenots*. His reaction was not favourable: 'I was very much disappointed. There is a frightful amount of row and a great deal of bosh in it. The noise is perfectly awful . . .'.[39] Meyerbeer also featured at a concert of music given by the Canonbury Union on 24 July. His operatically conceived 'Pater Noster' and Psalm 91 provoked an even more indignant outburst in which the moral tone of Parry's education surfaced once again: '[Meyerbeer's *Pater Noster*] was rather good in

---

[38] Diary, 22 May 1866.   [39] Diary, 13 July 1866.

parts. But somewhat too wild and eccentric to please me much . . . Meyerbeer's Psalm XCI has some of the most utterly absurd passages for voices I have ever heard, or conceived. He introduces horn passages and violin passages quite promiscuously in the voices . . .'.

On returning to Highnam he found his father hard at work providing the wall frescos for the St Andrew's Chapel in Gloucester Cathedral. There was also a measure of reconciliation between his father and Clinton who returned briefly to Highnam for the christening of his first child, a daughter Isabel Clinton, in the church. From a musical point of view however, Parry must have sensed for the first time that he had outgrown the environment of his home. With the one interlude of the Worcester Festival in September, to which he went principally for the *Lobgesang*, and another visit to Bayfordbury, all his time was spent working at the cantata with his sights towards its submission in October and the written examinations in December. Consequently he was impatient to return to Eton.

During his final term at Eton Parry shared a room with his brother Ernest who had just entered Evans's House. The term also marked a peak in his athletic achievements at the school for which he was given his 'Wall Shirt' playing for the Oppidans. He suffered numerous injuries, some of which prevented him from making further appearances as captain of the side. In one incident 'he was carried off the field on a sheep-hurdle in an unconscious condition, straw subsequently laid down in Keate's Lane'[40] where he was given urgent attention by the doctor. But in being laid up with badly sprained ankles or cut shins, he was able to finish his exercise. His half-brother, Ernest, wrote later:

I realized nothing of it then, but have often wondered since how he got through that half. He was Keeper of the Field, in other words, captain of the School football eleven; he was Second Keeper of the Wall, no one being allowed to hold the captaincy of both; he was captain of my Dame's school eleven; he was of course in 'Pop'; and there was besides his work to be done. Added to this, he was working with Elvey in preparation for the examination for the Bachelor's degree in music at Oxford, and he was writing his exercise for this—'O Lord, Thou hast cast us out'. His room was always thronged with friends, and the piano there was always to be heard.[41]

The cantata was eventually completed on 22 October. Elvey advised a few alterations before the fair copy was drawn up, and finally, on 30 October it was dispatched. 'It is all copied and looks immense.' Parry wrote, 'I gave it a last touch and sent it off in the evening for its awful inspection.'[42]

[40] Gambier Parry, *Annals of an Eton House*, 136.
[41] Graves, *Hubert Parry*, i. 66.   [42] Diary, 30 Oct. 1866.

News came from Sir Frederick Ouseley on 4 November informing Parry that the results would be delayed for a week or two. Elvey augured well from the tone of the letter, and when instructions arrived for him to attend the written examinations in Oxford, it was obvious that his cantata had been accepted, though it still had to be performed as a further requirement of the degree rubric. Parry was given leave to go up to Oxford in early December, where on his first day there he was delighted to be invited to attend a musical party at the home of Professor Donkin, himself a proficient amateur violinist. There, for the first time, he was more officially introduced to the leading figures in Oxford's musical life. 'Sir Frederick Ouseley and Stainer were both there. The Donkins performed a quartett of Sir Frederick's which he had composed for them',[43] Parry recorded, and he also made the acquaintance of James Taylor, organist of New College and a capable pianist.

The written examinations took place in the *Schola Musicae* on the morning of 6 December. In his diary Parry included an account of the questions that he attempted, giving us a fascinating insight into the rudimentary nature of the B.Mus. degree and of the obsessive contrapuntal stringency imposed on candidates as a result of Ouseley's archaic attitudes:

The first paper I had was, 1st question, to find the roots of some rum chords, which were all exactly the same but were written differently, and consequently had different roots. I did that question. The second I didn't go at because I thought it would take me too long. A long bass with figures to harmonize in 5 parts. The 3rd question. Put a counterpoint (one part only added) to the following canto fermo, in each species.

4th question: Add 2 parts in each species of counterpoint to the preceding canto fermo. I did all the 3rd and part of the fourth. Then I did the 6th question which was 'Write a correct stretto of the following subject:

i) In Canon, ii) By Inversion, iii) By Augmentation, iv) By Diminution, v) Write a Stretto on a Pedal.'

I then did the 5th question which was 'Add 4 parts to the following bass.'

---

[43] Diary, 4 Dec. 1866.

I found that rather stiff.
They then gave me another paper to do, which was questions of every kind. Such as 'Give the form of a Sonata in 1) the Major and 2) Minor keys.' 'What is the meaning of Rhythm, Enharmonic, Root, Discord, Harmonic etc.' 'Give the parts of a fugue' and lots of other questions. However when I had got about a quarter of the way through the paper they told me I need not do any more. And let me go. Sir Frederick was very kind and when they [Ouseley, Corfe, and Stainer] came out about a quarter of an hour afterwards I heard that . . . I had got my testamur. Glorious! Sir Frederick Ouseley asked me to come and stay with him at Tenbury.[44]

From the last comment in Parry's diary entry it is evident that Ouseley was more than impressed with the 18-year-old's technical assurance, and hoped perhaps to entice him to Tenbury as he had done successfully with Stainer in 1857. This was not to be, however, for, still conscious that his father would be suspicious of such a move, Parry's sights remained firmly fixed towards Oxford where he hoped to matriculate early the following year. As far as his B.Mus. was concerned he had only now to arrange the public performance of his exercise to be the youngest successful candidate ever of the degree. The examination rules stipulated that this should take place in Oxford, but Parry, anxious that all should go well, organized a dress-rehearsal at Eton on 8 December. The performance was apparently successful, meeting with the approval of the somewhat pious critic of the *Eton College Chronicle*,[45] whose plaudits demonstrate generally the level of moral satisfaction and stylistic complacency pervading English musical criticism during the mid-nineteenth century:

On Saturday, December 8, was held a performance which ought to be, and doubtless will be, long remembered by the fortunate audience, of a Sacred Cantata of Mr C. Hubert Parry, which he wrote for his Musical Degree at Oxford. We may say that he passed this examination most successfully. With regard to the Cantata itself, it is made up chiefly of passages from the Old Testament; bearing first on the subject of Forgiveness, secondly of Repentance, and lastly of Thanksgiving. It is written for four stringed instruments, and the Chorus is throughout in five vocal parts.

The Overture commences with a slow Minor movement, and is followed by an extremely fine fugue, which is most ably marked; this, if we may criticize it at all, we should say, if anything, is rather too short. The first Chorus, 'O Lord, Thou hast scattered us abroad', consists also of a fugue, equally well worked out, and very creditably sung, with the exception of a slight hitch at the commencement. The Bass Solo that follows was carefully rendered by Mr Peach, with a flowing and original melody in the Mendelssohnian style, the Recitative of which is unusually fine and impressive. The next Chorus, which is

[44] Ibid. 6 Dec. 1866.   [45] Graves, *Hubert Parry*, i. 68–70.

of a serene and massive style, was hardly enough appreciated by the audience, though there are some remarkably fine 'fugal' passages in it.

The Tenor solo which next follows was to have been sung by Mr Gibbons, who, however, owing to unavoidable circumstances, was unable to appear; but a most able and efficient substitute was found in Mr Snow, who most kindly consented to sing the Air, and this most difficult task he performed admirably, and was greeted with uproarious and lengthened applause. This Air, which, on the whole, we think perhaps to be the best of the three Solos, has a lovely running accompaniment . . . Then came the grand Finale, which is, in our estimation, by far the finest composition. It commences with the Old Hundredth Psalm, which is most exquisitely arranged for five voices, the Air of which is afterwards worked up with a brilliant fugue in a most masterly manner. It is needless to say that the whole Cantata was loudly encored. Dr Elvey most kindly consented to play the part of first Violin, the composer himself conducting . . . We must also tender our best thanks to Mr C. H. Parry himself, for the great honour he has conferred upon the School by obtaining his Musical Degree; and it is with the deepest regret that we have to announce his departure from the School, and the loss the Musical Society has sustained in being deprived of so able and energetic a President.

After the performance all that remained for Hubert at Eton was the academic chore of Collections and a final appearance at the Musical Society concert on 11 December at which a new madrigal, 'Oft in the stilly night', was given with moderate success. Perhaps the greatest benefit for Parry on leaving Eton was the tradition of 'leaving books' in which masters and pupils provided those leaving the school with money to purchase a handsome collection of volumes. The gift was intended as the basis of a library which would be useful, if not essential, to study at university. A portion of those titles selected by Parry reflect the current Victorian tastes for Mediterranean travel and general histories, but the majority of texts reflect his rapidly developing interest in English poetry, a subject once again that would not fall within the confines of his degree. Established names are represented by Milton, Byron, and Herbert, but the presence of nineteenth-century works by Browning, Keats, Words-worth, Longfellow, Coleridge, and Shelley is much more noticeable. Volumes devoted to musical studies formed very little part of the gift, though the complete Beethoven symphonies and Mendelssohn's *Elijah* were particularly welcome, as was the score of Spohr's Fourth Symphony, Op. 86 *The Consecration of Sound* bought in London with funds from his father and stepmother who must have been well satisfied with the commendatory letter from the senior mathematical master, Stephen Hawtrey:

I am glad of the opportunity of saying how affecting and interesting was your son's final farewell of us. I shall never forget his conducting his own Cantata— having just passed so honourable an examination at Oxford. His whole manner was so simple, manly, unconscious, perfect, that taking all the circumstances into account one must have been hard of heart not to have been moved deeply. My kindest and best wishes accompany him. His success confers great honour on the school where he was educated. I can only hope, and I do fully, that his heart will cling in kindly recollection to a place where he will be long remembered with pride and affection.[46]

The success of his cantata, albeit one tempered by his cloistered Etonian environment, must have strengthened Parry's resolve to continue his musical studies, even though he was aware that, after leaving Eton, there would be no regular supervision in composition from an established teacher. Furthermore, he knew full well that, on entering either Oxford or Cambridge, he was embarking on the next stage of the traditional gentleman's education which would almost certainly set him up on the path of a respectable career in accordance with his father's wishes. Consequently his musical instruction would be largely his own responsibility and, ostensibly, would still have to be pursued as a serious pastime rather than as a means of earning his living.

His farewell to Eton on 14 December, in the company of George Pembroke, was recorded in his diary with a tinge of regret: 'Came away with George at 3. I watched the old place from the train till I couldn't see it any more; and so now I have done with the happiness of school life. I don't at all comprehend it, and I think it's a good thing I don't.'[47] There may be something of the teenage philosopher in these comments, yet one senses that, having enjoyed a modicum of stability at Eton where his musical preoccupations had been given structure and discipline, he realized that his life at university would be entirely different and fears that the lack of technical guidance and reassurance might impair his motivation. His dejection was counteracted, however, by spending the following week with his confidant, Lewis Majendie, at the latter's country home at Hedingham in the north-Essex countryside. Then it was back to Highnam for Christmas as it had been decided that he should attempt matriculation for Exeter College, Oxford in January.

---

[46] Ibid. 70.   [47] Diary, 14 Dec. 1866.

3

Oxford

IT appears that the choice of Oxford college was very much a last minute decision. Many of Parry's friends went to Christ Church, a college whose links with Eton were well known and long established. But since Clinton's exploits and disgrace were still fresh in the minds of the Christ Church dons, Thomas Gambier Parry no doubt wished to avoid reviving the memory. Robert Bridges suggested that he might apply to Corpus Christi, but eventually Exeter was selected because of its ties with the Majendie family. January 1867 was largely devoted to study for the matriculation exams, and for these his father had arranged for him to be tutored by a local Gloucester clergyman, the Revd Washbourne, who, being well versed in classical literature was well suited to the traditional thrust of a matriculation examination which prescribed three well-worn texts: the *Bacchae*, the *Hippolytus*, and the *Georgics*. Parry went up to Oxford on 24 January to sit papers in Arithmetic, Euclid, and Latin prose. He then had the trying experience of a *viva voce* examination on the Latin set texts, whereafter he was informed that he had passed satisfactorily. He then remained in Oxford for a further two days to acquaint himself with the college, and wasted no time in introducing himself to F. Scotson Clark, the chapel organist. On 26 January, having been notified that he should take up residence immediately, he matriculated that same morning, chose his rooms, and spent the rest of the day with Kitchin at Christ Church. He was then obliged to hurry back to Highnam, pack, and return to Oxford within a week, so that by 2 February he was able to rejoice in the fact that he was now 'in the strange and novel position of an Oxford Freshman'.[1]

In many ways Oxford was merely a social and educational extension of life at Eton. Even before arriving in college his reputation both as a musician and sportsman had already spread around the university—with the result that the demands on his time were destined to be particularly exacting. His circle of friends included many familiar Etonians who were to be found mainly at Christ Church. Two of them, Eddie Hamilton and Martin Gosselin, had worked closely with him in the Eton Musical Society, but other friendships blossomed, notably with such keen

[1] Diary, 2 Feb. 1867.

performers as Frank Pownall of his own college, and Hugh de Fellenberg Montgomery (of Blessingbourne, County Tyrone) who, according to Parry's recollections, had a fine baritone voice. But Oxford was not only attractive because of the musical potential and the sporting facilities it offered. The city was also a magnet for prominent members of the Anglican clergy who regularly preached sermons in the college chapels and university church that were intended to provide moral directives to the students. This environment suited the 18-year-old Parry, for, having largely avoided the influence of his older brother, his Christian faith was still firmly moulded on the unshakeable beliefs of his father—a frame of mind confirmed by a fervent affirmation written at the end of the year: 'It is a mystery which we must believe implicitly before we even venture to reason about it; and we must not expect to understand it altogether. It is a mystery. Faith would lose its value if we saw or understood everything we had to believe. We must believe the things because we have been told them by God, not because we understand them.'[2] He found the variety of preachers spiritually fortifying as well as intellectually stimulating; besides which, as a frequent guest of the Liddells at the Christ Church Deanery, he was accustomed to the company and conversation of the country's leading theologians. Eton's 'Pop' was replaced by vigorous discussion in the forum of the Canning Club, while the more revelous, not to say drunken, escapades took place in the 'Adelphi' (the Exeter College wine club). But perhaps Oxford's most seductive attraction was the congenial style and pace of its life. The three daily mealtimes, as the traditional pretext for socializing, were quintessential to the student's manner of sophisticated living, and Parry's existence was no exception to this rule. His diary entries, notably in his first year of study, bear this out conclusively: 'Played tennis for an hour and a half in the morning with Moffat. Lunched with him without changing and then went to the gymnasium, where we boxed and fenced and single-sticked and gymnasticized for another one and a half hour[s] and then went and played rackets for yet another one and a half hour[s]. Dined with Moffat.'[3] His list of social engagements was enormous; indeed, it was a miracle that he ever found room for the academic considerations of law and history which he had chosen as the basis of his degree.

During his first term the catalogue of breakfast, lunch, and dinner parties, both with Fellows of the college and friends, seemed endless, as was the list of sporting activities. His involvement in Oxford's musical life was immediate. Musical societies had begun to flourish through the efforts of Stainer and Taylor. Within the colleges individually, enthusiasm

[2] Ibid. 1867 [Memoranda].   [3] Ibid. 29 Mar. 1867.

for choral music in particular was spreading. Stainer, for example, had accepted the conductorship of the Magdalen College Musical Society which was in many ways a natural extension of his duties as organist at that college; but he was also asked to undertake the running of the Exeter College Musical Society and the University Amateur Musical Society—tasks which were much more onerous owing to the generally poor standard. Larger, more public bodies also benefited from Stainer's baton. The Oxford Philharmonic Society, which Stainer had founded in 1865, was soon capable of performing the large-scale repertoire such as *Elijah* which Stainer conducted at the Society's first concert in 1866. He also gave new life to the ailing Oxford Choral Society (founded by Crotch in 1819), after which a natural rivalry evolved between itself and the Philharmonic Society. In addition there was the Oxford Orpheus Society, again exclusively choral in orientation, which Stainer founded in 1865. James Taylor, of New College, whom Parry had met at the Donkins' while doing the written section of his B.Mus. during the previous December, was also extremely active, succeeding Stainer as the conductor of the Oxford Philharmonic in 1866. Taylor's ability as a pianist, one which Parry regarded as more significant than his powers as an organist, was also conspicuous in the development and cultivation of chamber music in the university. One further society, the Christ Church Philharmonic, Parry joined soon after his arrival, chiefly because most of his musical friends from Eton were already members. And, as if this was not enough to distract him from his academic duties, he also felt obliged to join the chapel choir at Exeter, though the competence of F. S. Clark apparently left much to be desired.

To add to these extra-curricular undertakings, news arrived on 17 February from Ouseley that he was to take his B.Mus. degree four days later, and so, at very short notice, he was faced with the task of gathering singers and instrumentalists together for a performance of his cantata. His colleagues at Christ Church volunteered to provide the lower voices and Taylor promised the services of his boys from New College. The rehearsal on 20 February, which could only be described as chaotic, left Parry in some doubt as to whether the performance, which was to follow soon afterwards, would be viable. Judging by his remarks, the rather cavalier attitude shown by those taking part must have given little more than a rough impression of the piece: '[the performance] went off pretty well, though hardly any of our instruments or chorus appeared till the beginning of the first chorus.'[4] This also suggests that, to fulfil the requirements of the degree, the technical expectations and polish of these public performances were purely nominal.

⁴ Diary, 20 Feb. 1867.

Although Parry received no formal compositional training in Oxford, there can be no doubt that, with his music degree now behind him, he had the freedom and opportunity to widen his horizons, in particular that of the instrumental repertoire. The production of vocal music still continued as usual for the moment. Work on various anthems (nearly all of them aborted) and a Morning Service in D (later dedicated to Stainer) occupied him during the early months of 1867, and a part-song setting, for which Parry chose William Cullen Bryant's poem 'Dost thou idly ask', was commissioned by the Exeter Musical Society and completed in June. The grip of the ecclesiastical idiom was, however, steadily diminishing in favour of chamber music which had yet to achieve popularity in the university. Parry had been introduced to the intimacy of the genre at the home of Professor W. F. Donkin (the Savilian Professor of Astronomy) during his visit to Oxford the previous year. The Donkin family, who were all proficient string players, had gained a reputation for their performances of chamber works and their home had become a frequent meeting-place for Oxford's most prominent musicians. Ouseley and Stainer both wrote quartets for them, and Taylor often stood in as pianist in the performances of piano trios and piano quartets. Chamber music was also a regular part of the Taylor household as Parry soon discovered: 'At Taylors. Quartetts. When I got there they were playing one of Mendelssohn's. We had Duos and quartetts and solos and songs. They played for me Mendelssohn's Quartett No.1 for Pianforte, Violin, Viola, and Cello.'[5] This was an exciting departure for Parry, for these new experiences rapidly encouraged him to explore the repertoire. With Taylor he soon became familiar with Mendelssohn's piano trios in D and C minor, and at the Donkins' his string quartets and piano quartets were invariably part of their chamber-music evenings. In Gloucester he managed to hear Weber's Clarinet Quintet,[6] and, at the end of the year, he had his first taste of the Monday 'Pop' series of concerts at the St James's Hall where he heard Beethoven's Quintet for piano and wind, a violin sonata by Mozart, and a quartet by Haydn.[7] Chamber music at the ancient universities was a rare phenomenon and had received little attention during the first half of the nineteenth century. Yet, judging from the response shown in both Oxford and Cambridge to the prospect of regular performances overseen by dedicated and forward-looking groups of students, the interest had always been there, but had remained unharnessed. For example, Stanford's recollections of his years at Cambridge from 1870 produced an identical impression:

Music in Cambridge was then in a disorganized state. There was plenty of talent, but no means of concentrating it for useful purposes. The University

[5] Ibid. 8 Feb. 1867.   [6] Ibid. 22 Apr. 1867.   [7] Ibid. 16 Dec. 1867.

Musical Society, which was one of the most ancient in England, was at low ebb . . . Chamber music was also well to the fore, and the public performances of quartets and concerted pieces by finished players gave a speedy impulse to the music-loving undergraduates, who formed a string quartet of their own. This devoted four used to practise assiduously, often into the small hours of the morning, in rooms in the great court tower of Trinity facing the chapel. They played steadily through all the quartets of Haydn, and many of those of other great masters; . . . later Mr Abdy Williams, the musical historian, eventually founded a series of weekly concerts in connection with the University Musical Society, called 'The Wednesday Pops', which gave abundant opportunities for talented students to be heard both in vocal and instrumental works.[8]

As a natural consequence of the students' newly found enthusiasm for chamber music at Oxford, Parry's rooms in Exeter College were soon established as a popular venue for informal recitals. Such gatherings were often regarded as the first inception of the Oxford Musical Club,[9] whose actual foundation was in fact the work of his friend Charles Harford Lloyd of Magdalen Hall (now Hertford College) who became its first president in 1872 after Parry had left the university. Parry later confirmed this in a letter to Lloyd:

I certainly never had anything to do with the founding of it. It did not come into existence till after my time. The founding of a Club of some sort was discussed in my rooms in the Turl after we had been having occasional orgies of erratic attempts at quartets and singing. I remember Charles Stuart Wortley came and discussed the founding of some Musical Club in my rooms with a few of us, and that is the utmost extent of my liability. As far as I know, the Club owes its existence to you, and a great glory it is to have been the founder.[10]

Parry soon found the atmosphere and conviviality of these informal gatherings conducive to composition and it was not long before he began to try his hand at string quartets. Initially he sketched two movements, an Allegro in D (dated 20 May) and an Andante in E flat (dated 12 June), and these were almost certainly tried over at a meeting of friends in Christ Church. As Parry wrote: 'It was suggested to me to have my quartett tried this evening, so at 1 I set to work . . . I managed to get the two 1st movements finished . . . They tried them in the evening in Gosselin's rooms. I think the slow movement is best.' Although Mendelssohn's grip on Parry's stylistic horizons was still profound, it is evident from his diary that he was steadily becoming aware of that composer's expressive limitations, and so consequently his attentions were seeking a new path. His appreciation of Beethoven, whose music

    [8] Sir Charles Villiers Stanford, *Pages from an Unwritten Diary* (London, 1914), 112–16.
    [9] 'Charles Harford Lloyd', *Musical Times* (Apr. 1899), 372.
    [10] Letter to Charles Harford Lloyd. Now missing. See Charles L. Graves, *Hubert Parry* (London, 1926), i. 78n.

initially he found to be too much of an intellectual challenge, suddenly erupted. At the end of 1866 he began to explore Beethoven's piano sonatas, in particular, the Sonata in F, Op. 10 No. 2.[11] These works immediately cast a powerful spell, so that by April, diary entries such as 'Practised the whole morning. Beethoven mostly.' summarized his musical preoccupations. Moreover, aware that his technique had many shortcomings, he took piano lessons from Taylor who soon had him tackling the Op. 57 Sonata (the 'Appassionata'). Then, on 1 July, he heard the Fifth Symphony at a Philharmonic Society concert. The effect was devastating: 'words cannot express the hopeless gloriousness of this old ruffian . . . so tremendously massive . . .' Wagner was also represented in the same programme by his Overture *Tannhäuser*. 'I couldn't understand the *reason* of a great deal of it,' he wrote, 'some of it was very fine. Somewhat giving the sensation of Chaos with creation and form beginning to be perceptible.' His impression of these works was almost certainly strengthened by their juxtaposition to Sterndale Bennet's familiar Symphony in G minor and Weber's *Jubilee* Overture, both of which must have seemed tame by comparison.

At the end of the summer term Parry received news from his father that arrangements had been made for him to travel to Paris to meet the composer Henry Hugo Pierson and from there to continue on to Stuttgart to spend the whole summer vacation with Pierson and his family. Here again the elevated circle of friends cultivated by Parry's father paid off to his advantage. Thomas Gambier Parry had known Pearson (as he then used to spell his name) at Trinity College, Cambridge, and later they occasionally met at the Deanery in Salisbury which between 1823 and 1846 was the home of Pearson's father, Dr Hugh Nicholas Pearson. After leaving Cambridge, Pearson toured Europe and won the admiration of Schumann and Spohr. But, like many before as well as after him, Pearson's choice of career was met with concerted opposition by his family, and, to compound his parents' disapproval he entered into an unacceptable love-affair which eventually caused him to Germanize his surname to mitigate his family's embarrassment. Germany also proved to be more artistically accommodating for him and he settled there soon after resigning the Reid Professorship of Edinburgh University. At this time Pierson (or 'Edgar Mannsfeldt' which he adopted as a suitably Teutonic *nom de plume*) was at the height of his creative powers; but by 1867, engaged in the compostion of his last major work, the opera *Contarini*, his reputation was on the decline. On his death in January 1873 a Leipzig journal provided the

[11] Diary, 27 Dec. 1866.

following obituary which captured the nature of his peculiarly veiled character:

Holding no musical appointment and consequently without influence; highly educated, but, after the fashion of a true genius, somewhat of a recluse, and withal unpractical, he did not know how to make his glorious works valued. He showed himself seldom, though his appearance was poetic and imposing; and he was such a player on both organ and pianoforte as is rarely met with.[12]

On 9 July Parry met Pierson at the Gare du Nord and was at once taken with his imposing countenance. '[He was] exceedingly kind', Parry recalled,[13] 'most wonderfully jolly . . . German in appearance . . . with long dark hair, grayish eyes, tallish, and slightly Beethovenish altogether. Not quite what I expected I must say.' They travelled on the same day to Stuttgart where Parry contentedly spent the next two months in the rural calm of Pierson's comfortable villa.

This short séjour in Germany to study with Pierson has long been over-emphasized in that it has been labelled too readily as Parry's 'continental musical education', placed in the same category as the experience of those others (such as Sullivan, Cowen, Stanford, and even Delius) who took the opportunity to spend three whole years under German tutelage. Moreover, although Parry's time with Pierson was used to further his musical interests, the secondary, and equally important purpose of his stay was to learn German and imbibe the country's culture as much as possible. '[It is] rather a change from England', he wrote, 'However, I must Germanize myself for the present, as much as I can.' The method used whereby Parry learnt German would nowadays be described as 'immersion therapy', for Pierson's wife (née Caroline Leonhardt) was a native and their children were all German-speaking. Consequently German was spoken in all domestic situations; English was reserved only for music lessons, if, as he described, 'lessons they can be called'.[14]

Acting on the advice of S. S. Wesley, his main reason for travelling to Stuttgart, from a musical standpoint, was to study instrumentation, though he did also receive some compositional instruction. As Parry later recalled, '[Pierson] chiefly occupied the time of my lessons by trying to disabuse me of Bach and Mendelssohn'.[15] The first few weeks were entirely absorbed with the exploration of instrumental technicalities, capabilities, and timbres—matters which were undoubtedly elucidated by Berlioz's famous treatise, a work for which Pierson had a profound respect. 'We sit with weeds in our mouths', Parry wrote, 'while Dr

---

[12] Revd H. Pearson, S. V. 'Pierson, Henry Hugo', *Grove's Dictionary of Music and Musicians*, 1st edn. (London, 1879), ii. 752–3.
[13] Diary, 9 July 1867.   [14] Ibid. 11 July 1867.
[15] 'Hubert Parry', *Musical Times* (July 1898), 444.

Pierson descants on the peculiarities of different instruments for nearly two hours before luncheon. After luncheon we smoke and have coffee. Then I practise, and after that we go for a walk.'[16] Pierson's approach may have been informal, but as a taskmaster he was severe. When the theoretical material had been sufficiently covered, Parry was put to work on several well-known pieces including Weber's Overture *Der Freischütz*, parts of Rossini's *William Tell*, the Entr'acte from Beethoven's incidental music to *Egmont*, and the March from Pierson's *Faust*. He also attempted to score three of his own compositions: his setting of 'Autumn', the Overture from his cantata, and the *Intermezzo religioso* (slow movement) from his sonata for piano duet in F minor. These exercises he found highly instructive, in particular the instrumentation of 'Autumn', since this song had already been scored somewhat basically in 1865, and Pierson therefore deliberately chose it to illustrate more imaginative and colourful possibilities, most notably in the woodwind.

With his studies centred on orchestration (which also managed to incorporate some rudimentary viola lessons with a local teacher, Huhn), it is not surprising that the impetus to compose instrumental music was strengthened. Sketches were made of a Piano Trio in D minor of which only a first movement was completed.[17] In the middle of August, under Pierson's influence, he read *Hamlet* and *King Lear* which kindled an interest in the possibilities of incidental music, and led to his writing an Entr'acte for *As You Like It*.[18] He then commenced its instrumentation:

Worked very hard at the instrumentation of the so-called Entracte which has been considerably changed in form from the first idea and will now probably make the middle movement of a Symphony; if I can manage to write one. It was finished . . . to Dr Pierson's satisfaction.[19]

Indeed the symphonic context of this movement prevailed, for by the beginning of September he was no longer referring to it as an Entr'acte but as an *Allegretto Scherzando*, deftly scored for small orchestra (and triangle!). The Symphony in question never fully materialized, though sketches of an introduction to a first movement (dated Highnam 13 October) and a Finale entitled *Träume Sinfonie* made in August 1868 (and which continued to preoccupy him in the September[20]) suggest that he was still contemplating a large-scale orchestral work. His 1867 'Manuscript Book' includes the outlines of a string quartet in C major (sketched during a short stay at Hedingham with Lewis Majendie in December), but this work did not finally take shape until 1868. However, the first movement (dated 'Stuttgart' August–October 'Oxford' 1867) of a quartet in G minor was completed. The thematic orientation

[16] Diary, 11 July 1867. [17] Ibid. 12 Aug. 1867. [18] Ibid. 16 Aug. 1867.
[19] Ibid. 19 Aug. 1867. [20] Ibid. 21 Sept. 1868.

of this movement is Mendelssohnian through and through but the internal proportions of the individual movements are generally slighter, having more in common with Mozart and Haydn. In terms of structure it is evident that Parry sought to continue his experiments in thematic and tonal integration from where he left off in the earlier Overture in B minor. It was also a tendency with which Pierson, himself something of a musical maverick, thoroughly sympathized. The organization of thematic material is extremely unconventional, particularly in a comparison of the exposition and restatement (see Ex. 2*a*). The interesting divergencies of this movement lie not only in the additional theme introduced at the outset of the development (Ex. 2*d*) in the key of the second group (B flat major), but in the recapitulation, where two restatements (the first very much truncated) of Theme 1 (Ex. 2*b*) flank the repetitions of a telescoped Theme 3 (itself an unexpected return) and Theme 2 (Ex. 2*c*), again in the relative. Precedents for this type of procedure are rare, though it is quite likely that Parry developed the technique from a close study of Mozart's quartets (e.g. the first movement of K. 458) which sometimes introduce a new thematic idea at the beginning of the first movement's development, but subsequently do not incorporate it into the restatement. It is possible that Parry, under Pierson's guidance, was familiar with Mendelssohn's 'Italian' Symphony which presents new material at the same stage of the piece (i.e. the fugato episode from bar 202 onwards) and redeploys it in the recapitulation (bars 453–64).

The quartet consists, unusually, of only two other movements. The second movement, a gentle Andante in 2/4, completed at Oxford (dated 5 November), is purely a revision of the Andante in E flat major written in Oxford during the previous June, while the last movement in G major, an Allegro vivace in 4/4, was composed hastily at Highnam in early October and scored in Oxford. Tuition with Pierson regrettably only lasted until 11 September, but his teacher at least made the offer of a further vacation in 1868 which raised Parry's hopes, though of course the financing of a second trip rested entirely with his father. The cultural jolt of returning to England left him uneasy for several days for he immediately felt the absence of the continent's vibrancy, of Pierson's stimulating mind, and, perhaps most of all, his lack of artistic inhibition. His experiences filled a letter to Spencer Lyttelton whose reply confirmed a considerable shift of opinion away from the English pedagogical approaches of Ouseley and Elvey. No longer is fugue venerated; instead, through the discovery of Beethoven, there is a shift towards the need for melodic profundity. It was a change of heart that Lyttelton found hard to comprehend:

Fugal writing and counterpoint is [*sic*] certainly produced to a great degree by study and learning; at the same time so much of what is first-rate and full of

Ex. 2. String Quartet in G minor (1867), first movement. *a* tonal and thematic structure; *b* theme 1; *c* theme 2; *d* theme 3.

genius has been produced by men whose predominant feature is in that line, that I have always supposed the two went together to a great degree in most instances (not in the case of Ouseley certainly, not much original genius there; in Elvey there is more I imagine, but not enough, and certainly not enough originality of mind) . . . Of course, as coming from Germany, you are full of Beethoven, as indeed all real musicians are; but don't let his gigantic genius allow you no room for a little quiet love for the non-aesthetic, inferior as it is in every way. Perhaps it is hardly fair to name Ouseley as the chief representative of English music; remember S. Bennett (whose last Cantata was however entirely of the pedantic school), Wesley, one of the most exceptional of composers, and others though certainly few in numbers, have I hope, some real genius in them, which will uphold the honour of English music, both at the present time, and in the future. It is quite true what you say of its being regarded as the proper thing in musical amateurs to admire a grand fugal chorus more than a divine melody; and I must plead guilty to have so regarded it; but in point of fact, a grand choric fugue does (in my case at least) supply a kind of longing in the mind, and a sense of such wonderful satisfaction, which a melody hardly does, though that gives pleasure enough in all conscience but of a different kind.[21]

In the Michaelmas term of 1867 Parry was elected on to the committee of the Exeter College Musical Society where he was able to work closely with John Stainer, the Society's honorary conductor. Stainer's principal duty, with Parry acting as repetiteur, was to train the Society's modest choir which comprised approximately thirty singers of which the alto, tenor, and bass voices were provided by members of the college and the top line by a contingent of boys from New College and a few from the Exeter Chapel choir. The chief aim of the Society was to give concerts at the end of each term, though this was not always possible owing to the constant variation in ability and numbers caused by those leaving and those coming up for the first time. However, the Society rallied for the Winter concert on 11 December, and evidently grew sufficiently in confidence for the Commemoration concert in the Trinity (summer) term when they performed Mendelssohn's *Athalie*:

thanks to Dr Stainer's great energy the whole Chorus were well up in their parts and all passed off in the most satisfactory manner. The applications for tickets were more numerous than ever, partly because so few entertainments were being given . . . and partly for the reputation the E.C.M.S. has acquired of late for producing an entire work at their Commemoration Concert, instead of performing a variety of selections.[22]

For the second half of the programme Parry composed another part-song ('Pure spirit; oh where art thou now') which pleased its critic, though 'it

[21] Letter from Spencer Lyttleton, 29 Oct. 1867, ShP.
[22] Minutes of the Exeter College Musical Society, Michaelmas Term 1867, ECO.

suffered from being rather too high for the executants'.[23] Piano duets were also a popular feature of these concerts for it was the only means whereby performers and audience could regularly gain access to orchestral works. The Exeter College concerts always began with a popular overture such as Beethoven's *Egmont* or Spohr's *Jessonda*, though Parry attempted to include lesser-known symphonic works as well. In this way the Scherzo from Mendelssohn's 'Reformation' Symphony got its first hearing in Oxford.

Although Mendelssohn's style continued to influence the language and genres of Parry's work (epitomized by the composition of his first set of *Sonnets and Songs without Words*), it is quite clear that Mendelssohn did not occupy centre stage after his studies in Stuttgart. Indeed his prolonged sessions with Pierson acted as a significant catalyst in turning his attentions seriously to the music of others. Indeed, it soon generated more acetic comments. On 16 January 1868 he attended a recital given by the Bristol Madrigal Society where the audience's automatic plaudits for two part-songs by their German idol irritated him. 'Two rotten partsongs by Mendelssohn . . . were of course encored,' he wrote in his diary. Similarly, he had occasion to hear Mendelssohn's little-known *Concertstück* for clarinet and corno di bassetto in a concert whose sole aim was to revive neglected concertos. 'Mendelssohn's [concerto]', he wrote, 'has never before been heard in London (and if Mendelssohn lovers are wise, should never be heard again).'[24] His appetite for orchestral music drew him to the Philharmonic concerts, and more especially to the Crystal Palace where, for the first time, he was able to enjoy orchestral playing of a higher standard and programmes of greater variety than those he was accustomed to in the provinces. On 29 February he heard Wagner's *Tannhäuser* Overture again together with Beethoven's familiar Overture to *Egmont* and the totally unfamiliar 'Tragic' Symphony by Schubert which he described as 'magnificent'. A second concert in March included a performance of Schumann's Symphony No. 2, of which the slow movement's exploratory harmony and luscious instrumentation proved to be a revelation:

Went to the Crystal Palace concert at which we had a symphony of Schumann's—which surpassed everything *almost* I have heard lately. The Scherzo was wildly glorious. The slow movement was very fine, and contains a most wonderful bit of modulation, in which the chief feature is a very long passage in shakes for the 1st violins, which had the most delicious effect. I'll never go to hear anything of Mendelssohn's in preference to Schumann's C major Symphony if I can help it. Madame Schumann played Mendelssohn's Concerto in D after magnificently, but it fell very flat after Schumann's Symphony . . .[25]

[23] Ibid.   [24] Diary, [July] 1868.   [25] Ibid. Mar. 1868.

Schumann's brazen Romanticism was one source of rapture. Another was Beethoven, whose Sixth and Eighth Symphonies, heard during the Philharmonic's season, caused Parry's criticism of Mendelssohn to intensify to the point of aversion: 'I can hardly bear to hear or smell a large work by Mendelssohn in the same week as a great work of dear old Beet.'[26]

Yet, though his chronicles tell of his captivation with the works of Beethoven and Schumann, his own compositions persisted in their conservative allegiance to Mendelssohn. This restraint is clear from the 'Zweite Quartette in C Dur'[27] which, notwithstanding its slightly larger canvas of four movements, shows no linguistic advance on its G minor predecessor. Nevertheless, consistent with the unusual structural schemes of the Overture and earlier quartet, it shows a willingness to manipulate sonata form. The first movement, with its subdominant recapitulation, suggests that Parry must have learned a number of useful lessons from Mozart (who surely lies behind the grave introduction in the tonic minor), Beethoven, and Schubert in their attempted syntheses of 'rounded binary' and sonata principles. In addition he had also learned to avoid the pitfalls of such a scheme, the most obvious one being a mechanical tonal and thematic repetition of the exposition (i.e. I–V) in the restatement (i.e. IV–I) as one finds for example in the Finale of Schubert's 'Trout' Quintet. The subdominant key plays a significant though bizarre role in the Finale, for, running quite contrary to the sonata principles of tonal dialectics, Parry deploys it as the second-group key resulting in a movement with an extraordinarily lopsided tonal plan.

The quartet in C major proved to be the only ambitious work to come to fruition in 1868. This was largely owing to the academic pressure of Mods., and from a packed social life absorbed in cricket, croquet parties, various societies musical and non-musical (some of the latter of questionable repute), and so-called 'Festive luncheons' in his own rooms at Exeter. Hours spent in composition were largely replaced by concert-going, visiting the opera to hear Mozart's *Le nozze di Figaro* (whose scoring, structure, and melodic writing impressed him enormously), Meyerbeer's *L'Africaine*, and Gounod's new *Roméo et Juliette*. Much time was devoted to reading Longfellow's *Hyperion*, Byron's *Childe Harold*, and poetry by Keats and Browning. These literary interludes often provided material for new song-texts, though only one song came from his pen during the whole year. Instead, following the example of Pierson, whose impulse to compose orchestral music arose essentially

[26] Diary, 3 Apr. 1868.
[27] Ibid. 9 Apr. 1868. Parry often referred to this quartet in C *minor*, owing to the introduction in that key. Barring the sketches made in 1867, it was begun in earnest in April 1868 and completed in October the same year.

from literary influences, Parry began to consider the notion of attempting an orchestral overture on the subject of Vivien, drawing on his impressions of Tennyson's legendary world of *Idylls of the King*. Work commenced on the overture in October with the sketch taking little more than two days to complete,[28] though the final form of the overture had to wait another five years before work was resumed. Indeed, a further period of study with Pierson was uppermost in Parry's mind as the summer term at Oxford drew to a close. A letter, dated 16 June,[29] confirms that Pierson was also anxious that his budding young pupil should spend another summer in Stuttgart:

> Paris
> Hotel de Calais,
> Rue neuve des capucines

My best Uberto,

I leave this for Stuttgart *on the 20th* (by rights), having done my work here for the present. Please send me a line and let me know whether you wish to have another *go* with me, or not; if such be your intention you might as well rattle over here and return with me to Stuttgart, i.e. that if you could join me by Monday morning (22nd) *at latest*,—in that case I would wait for you (as you said you could not leave Oxford before the 20th); otherwise I leave this on Saturday the 20th so pray write *instanter*, that I may make my arrangements

. . . Now just send me a line *prestissimo*, there's a dear boy, and tell me what are your plans or wishes. Wilshere (quoting some passages from a letter of your father's, not complimentary to the musical vocation) said he did not know whether you are coming to me or no.

What have you been a writin' of? I send you a Paris journal with a notice @ my opera. There is a lot more @ it in 'L'art musical', latest number. It is awfully hot here and I am impatient to get away.

> Ever your affectionate
> Padre della musica.

Pierson's passing allusion to the attitude of Parry's father accentuated the unremitting disapproval of which Hubert was only too aware, for a second opportunity to travel to Stuttgart was turned down. His disappointment was considerable, and it almost certainly caused him to lose heart. Demoralized, he passed some of his time at Bayfordbury where he immersed himself in literature. He was revived, however, by an invitation to spend a week at Wilton at the end of August where he would once again see his sweetheart Maude. In the intervening years, since he had last seen her in the summer of 1864, Maude had grown into a beautiful, educated young woman. It was a transformation which

---

[28] Ibid. 8 and 9 Oct. 1868.   [29] Letter from H. H. Pierson, 16 June 1868, ShP.

caused Parry's youthful affection to turn swiftly into passionate love. He
was totally smitten:

Wilton is quite the same as it used to be when I was there last, only the people
are more kind, more affectionate, and more delightful than ever . . . Maudie and
I were like brother and sister, always together. I should never be tired of being
with her. Both she and Mary [her sister] are the most wonderfully well read, and
well informed girls you could find anywhere . . . Dear Lady Herbert is as
fascinating and impulsive as ever . . . Sandie (Lady Adine) and Maudie and I
were photographed together, to cement the bond of unity between us . . .[30]

Little did Parry realize that the air of pleasantness at Wilton was
nothing more than a façade, for Lady Herbert, astute in her own peculiar
way, soon became aware of their increasing empathy. Undoubtedly she
harboured plans for her daughter's well-being and financial security
which would be guaranteed by marriage within aristocratic circles. Parry
came from landed gentry, which, though privileged and relatively
wealthy, was not of the same social stratum as the noble house of
Pembroke. His presence, therefore, had rapidly become an intrusion, so
that it was a great relief to Lady Herbert when he was forced to leave
Wilton at the beginning of September to attend the Gloucester Festival.
On the other hand, she did not anticipate that the parting of Hubert and
Maude would provoke a protracted and sustained correspondence which
she could do little to stem.

The 1868 Gloucester Festival did much to relieve the depression
brought on by his departure from Wilton, for Wesley had agreed to
include his *Intermezzo Religioso* in the same programme as Haydn's
Creation and Samuel Wesley's *Confitebor* on 8 September. Though Parry
was already familiar to the Gloucester public through a performance
during the Easter vacation in 1867 of his B.Mus. cantata, this appearance
at the Three Choirs meeting was of much greater kudos. The rehearsal
proved to be an exasperating affair and the performance elicited only a
muted response from the audience. From one London daily newspaper,
the *Standard*, it provoked some unexpected invective:

No key to the composer's intentions was published in the programme. It may be
assumed that between Haydn and Samuel Wesley there is some intermediate
stage, and that between the *Creation* and the Psalm it was necessary that the
mind should be relieved by a kind of voluntary executed by full orchestra. If it
had been a playing out of a congregation any intermezzo would suffice, and that
of Hubert Parry would have received as much attention as is ordinarily paid to
voluntaries after long sermons. The movement of the intermezzo itself has the
character of a dirge; it opens with a grave strain from the strings, and the ear
catches for a moment some Spohrish characters in the sound, the oboe having a

[30] Diary, 24 Aug. 1868.

prominent place therein, and then a kind of Mendelssohnian subject, languid and undulating, winds up the piece, the workmanship of which is creditable, but the invention of which is not exciting, and the whole had the sin of being thrust in the programme where it was not wanted.

Such harsh criticism gave rise to over-defensive reaction. Graves, for example, in his biography attempted to vindicate the *Intermezzo* on the grounds of prejudice, that Parry was 'an interloping amateur' and the victim of 'a fairly typical specimen of mid-Victorian musical criticism, obscurantist and obstructionist, and as obstinately distrustful of all novelty as the neo-Georgian critics are effusively idolatrous thereof'.[31] Wesley maintained that the attack was the result of a grudge borne by the critic against the festival,[32] while Grove (to whom Parry was introduced for the first time through the efforts of Sullivan) attempted to console him with the advice that abuse was 'a good sign'.[33] Superficially he may have acknowledged the counsels of Wesley and Grove and the congratulations of the many attending musicians, but in fact beneath the surface the seeds of determination to change and progress had been sown. He was at last becoming aware of his own immaturity.

After the excitement of the festival week, his spirits were raised by a letter from Maude whom he affectionately nicknamed his 'little Faerie Queene' after Spenser's poem. Her letter immediately initiated a long series of impassioned letters from Parry that seem almost Schumannesque in their Romanticism. He impetuously replied the same day:

My dear little Faerie Queene,

Thank you so very much for your most delightful letter; I can't tell you how delighted I was when it came. I never thought before that little Maudie cared for me enough to write me such a glorious long letter. You may be sure I shall always keep it as a great treasure in a very safe place, and I hope some day I may have another like it. I waited for some time for the dream of St Gerontius thinking I had better not write till it came, but I am sorry to say that at last instead of the little book there came the intelligence that it is out of print, and cannot be had for any trouble. I may find it for you some day, and then I shall send it. I am very glad you have got a Keats, though I don't expect you really to like it for some time. You must read the Ode to the Nightingale and those sort of things many times before you get accustomed to the style, and to his peculiarities of expression which sometimes are rather difficult.

The Festival was altogether successful; some of the music went better than ever, and the singers sang sometimes almost better than they perhaps thought themselves capable of doing . . . I was complimented on my little Intermezzo a good deal by all the swell musicians who were down here, and some of them congratulated me more especially on its not being very highly approved of by

---

[31] C. L. Graves, *Hubert Parry* (London, 1926), i. 103.
[32] Diary, 19 Sept. 1868.   [33] Ibid. [?] Sept. 1868.

some of the newspaper critics, as that is always said to be a good sign. I believe the 'Guardian' critic will be kind to me, but his criticism will not come out till next week; if you see it ever, look and see if he abuses me . . . And when are the other photos coming; I have been longing for them day after day, as they are such a pleasant remembrance of that delightful time. I do hope still that such a time may yet come again, though chances seem so against it. I don't think 'coming out' will much change the little Faerie Queene, and if the spies don't put on too much pressure, the little brother and sister may still gallop on the downs together again.

Do you think I may be allowed to write to you sometimes, to tell you if ever I come across . . . anything you should read? I should like to very much, and it would serve to remind you of me sometimes. . . .

Ever your most affectionate
C. Hubert H. Parry.[34]

Behind the brave face of Festival news and their mutual love of literature, it is clear from the depressed tone of this letter that already Lady Herbert and her confederates had begun to exert their authority. Maude was 17 years old and due to 'come out' into society the following year, and consequently she was only too well aware that her mother would plan a suitable match when she was of age. The constraints placed upon her are confirmed in a reply to a second letter Parry received a week later:

My dear little Faerie Queene,

I was so very glad to get your letter this morning, as I have been thinking of you very much, and quite longed for some pretext for writing to you.

I, like you, have been having solitary rides, which would be somewhat dismal if I didn't sometimes almost forget my solitude in thinking of you . . . Don't say that Lady Herbert will never let us be together again; I can't believe she would be so cruel; we must meet at all events sometimes, and in the interim, we can keep our minds together by the medium of letters . . . I hope these lengthy epistles don't bore you Maudie, but for the first time in my life I find a pleasure in letter writing, and I can't help giving way to it a little . . .[35]

But Lady Herbert's word was final. Parry was not only refused any visits to Wilton but he was also forbidden to see Maude at any time. Only one slender ray of hope remained in Maude's elder sister, Mary, who was sympathetic to their cause. She offered to act as a go-between.

At Highnam his despair manifested itself in a second set of *Lieder ohne Wörte,* the three pieces, *Resignation, L'Allegro,* and *Il Penseroso* (from Milton's poem) reflecting his state of mind as does the dedication 'In Memoriam, Sept. 1868'. In sketching his Overture *Vivien* and two Duettinos for Donkin at Oxford he sought refuge from his frustration.

[34] Letter to Lady Maude Herbert, 17 Sept. 1868, ShP.
[35] Letter to Lady Maude Herbert, [?] Sept. 1868, ShP.

Then came several letters from Mary Herbert encouraging Hubert not to abandon hope for there was no doubting Maude's faith, for while that persisted their aspirations remained alive; only, he would have to be patient and tenacious to mollify Lady Herbert's obstinacy. 'Hope first dawned upon me,' he wrote, 'and an object in life I never felt before.'[36] The response to her second letter was more hopeful:

Dear Mary,

I really don't know how to thank you for your two intensely kind letters. I am perfectly wild with happiness after reading the one which made its appearance last night. I am sure that to have given such happiness to any mortal even for a single moment as that letter did to me must be a deed worthy of everlasting remembrance; and it certainly is one which I hope I shall be indebted to you for to the day of my death. It could have roused me at the brink of the grave giving me something to live for. I hope you won't laugh at me for speaking so strongly for I can't help it after reading a letter which gave me more pleasure than almost any other I ever received.

I must explain to you why, or you may wonder at the vehemence of the feelings you roused in me. It is no use concealing what you know already that Maudie is to me more than all the world besides, and that I love Wilton more than home, and for some inconceivable reason everybody connected with it more than brothers and sisters (which sounds a humiliating confession, but it is not really). But with all this I never felt that I had any right to expect a return, much less in the way you spoke of, for though I confess the fulfilment of my affection had often taken the form of a happy but quickly fading dream, it never took the form of a hope till your letter came and then for a moment it was like the long subdued fire bursting into a brilliant flame. Such a glorious feeling of hope and relief . . . My happiness however soon trembled a little when I thought how soon Maudie might find somebody worthier of her, or someone of the young fashionables she will meet in such multitudes when she comes out next year whom she may like better. And then of course I thought how rash it would be to think that you could never change your mind, and think me (wh. you well might) a very bad bargain for a brother. But still you had given my affection a definite shape which it cannot lose till it is wrenched from me. I will bide my time as you say and patiently, while such a goal is before me. And I hope Maude may not change her mind, and you may not change yours. I promise to act up to your advice if I am allowed to come to Wilton again, and be very careful and be as civil to Maudie as a Town mouse when anybody is watching us. Do let me keep your letter. It is so very precious [and] I will keep it tight locked up where nobody can possibly get at it but myself. It will be such a talisman to me, greater than the power of a very Savonarola. Please forgive me for writing such a long, mad, and selfish letter. But you dipped so deep into my heart, that it was natural that all the pent up fire in me should burst out headlong. You know 'love is always selfish' so I never considered for a moment whether or no you would take no trouble to wade all through my ravings. But why should Maude be sad as you

[36] Diary, 6 Oct. 1868.

say. I can't be when you have given me such hope. Don't be angry with me for writing this long letter. Like you, it does me a world of good to speak out.

I shall be everlastingly grateful to you for your last letter and I hope you may never repent having written it. There! my tale is told and you are the only created being in the whole world who knows my whole heart.[37]

The distraction of the Mods. examinations at Oxford during the Michaelmas term temporarily directed his attention away from despondency, as did the composition of an Ode of Anacreon, 'Away, away, you men of rules', written for Frank Pownall and sung at the college's winter concert on 8 December. The bluster of this rather vulgar, melodramatic, drinking song, reminiscent of Sullivan's parodies, nevertheless maintained the jovial exterior with which his colleagues were so familiar. But his closest friends, Eddie Hamilton and his trusted confidant Lewis Majendie, with whom he sought solace at Hedingham after term was over, were the only ones privy to his emotional predicament. Not long after he had returned to Oxford, Maude began to show signs of capitulating to her mother's dictates as she insisted that he should not write any further letters. Persistent as ever, Parry could not accede to her wishes, and instead, in a passionate outburst, fowardly declared his love:

My dearest little Maudie,

I have just come back from our midnight celebration which we always have here at the birth of the New Year, and I cannot resist the temptation to disobey your wish, that I should not write to you any more, and write my first letter in the year to my little Faerie Queene. The year is scarcely an hour old; I am afraid I did not welcome him as I usually do; I was so sorry to lose the old year. It has been such an extraordinarily memorable year to me, that I felt a little misgiving as I passed from the old to the New. Wilton and you made 1868 a sacred year in my life—I hope you won't think this all rubbish, for I am as in earnest as ever mortal was; and if I wish you a happy new year, it will not be as the common compliment every man pays to his friend, but rather an earnest prayer such as can only be made by those who know all the intensity of a pure love. Don't be startled, Maudie, you have used the word yourself in another shape . . . You must not be angry with me for writing to you again. I have been obedient so long—so long without a word to you or from you . . . Goodbye my most dear little Fairie Queene (Do you still put an interminable veto on my writing to you? Must I be silent again for months?).

your loving Hubert.[38]

A week later he received a letter from Mary which included a note from Maude. The frankness of its contents plunged him into the depths of despair: 'I had a memorable letter from Mary this morning; warning me of my position with regard to Maudie; and showing me clearly how

[37] Letter to Lady Mary Herbert, [Oct.] 1868, ShP.
[38] Letter to Lady Maude Herbert, 1 Jan. 1869, ShP.

difficult my path would be. Also a precious, hopeful letter from Maudie herself which made me happy in my very misery. Nevertheless, I was very wretched all day at the thought of being cut off from Wilton . . .'.[39] Since visits to Wilton were prohibited, their only recourse was to arrange clandestine meetings in London while Maude was staying at the Herberts' London residence in Chesham Place, Knightsbridge, and Parry was in the capital to hear concerts at the St James's Hall or the Crystal Palace. But their main concern always was secrecy, as Maude's letter of 28 January confirms:

My dear Hubert,

After leaving you I had a distracting conversation with Mrs Doyle on various deep subjects . . . Talking was a bore, as I felt both sleepy and melancholy. How did you get on with Lizzie . . .? She told Mary that she was certain I cared for you, and that you were much too charming etc. Is it not a nuisance? I am in fear and trembling of her telling Mama . . . Do you think we shall see each other again on your way back from Oxford? I daresay we shall be in London then . . .[40]

But the pressure exerted by Lady Herbert soon became too much for Maude. On Hubert's birthday, she resorted to writing in a manner so muted and cold as to deter him. Formalities were imposed on their correspondence. Letters were to be exchanged at specific times in the year: at Christmas, New Year, Easter, birthdays, and Whit Sunday. His reaction was at once one of bewilderment, and yet the tone of his reply was pathetically obsequious in its apology for being outspoken, hotheaded, and outwardly emotional:

My dearest little Faerie Queen,

I have two very precious letters of yours to answer, so I must answer them one at a time, as they are so very different in character . . . Now please remember Maudie that I am going to answer one letter at a time. Now for your Christmas one.

I can't tell you how happy I was [on] reading it, because it made me hope more than I ever did before, and your love seemed then at least as if it would never desert me. I thanked you for your prayers, and for that one word before your signature which I thought would always be my great consolation. Your letter was indeed an angel's visit, and seemed to tell me I might hope more than I did before. Not for any fulfilment, but for the lasting confirmation of such a love as angels bear to each other, which looks for no reward beyond itself.

I must excuse my strong expressions in the plea that this is an answer to a letter which contained nothing but the same feelings, and that in one of . . . Mary's letters, she expressed a sentiment that between two people whose affection was so decided, the formalities of the world whatever they are, had no real right to [throw] the veil of prosaicism.

[39] Diary, 11 Jan. 1869.
[40] Letter from Lady Maude Herbert, 28 Jan. 1869, ShP.

After such a letter as yours I was always looking forward to the next. Hoping for the same kindness and openness and almost picturing to myself what it would be. Alas! the dream is gone.

I must read the dear, precious Xmas letter over once again, for perhaps the last time, before I begin to answer the withering birthday letter.I have read it again Maudie, and pray now that some one else who is more worthy of your love, (as it cannot be otherwise) may someday write such a letter to you and give you as divine a sensation of happiness as that letter once gave me.

I do not agree with you entirely Maudie, that we are bound to write to each other as mere friends . . . You are a very wise little lady, Maudie, but what made you think that you could cure any human being of his misery by telling him to forget the only thing that could give him happiness; and that is indeed what you did; and you did more—you taught me, that you being my only physician, had trained yourself to forget the only remedy that existed, by hardening the kindness of your words; I think you will see that your advice did not admit of much examination. But I am too bitter for wisdom; and *will* not see that my earnestness has any need to be restrained . . .

I am very very glad that you are happy now, even though it be by forgetting, or almost forgetting me. It is very wise and just you should do so. Yet there are words of consolation,—little bits of kindness here and there in your second letter, which seem yet like a little reflection of the happy past; and as if you did not wish to forget me yet. . . .

Since I may not think of the hope of a consummation of wordly love, I ask that one prayer may always be each others, that our love, though we may be obliged to be silent from henceforward, may not die, and that we may be divided without forgetting each other, because our spirits shall always be together.

Please write to me first on Easter day because it will be no use my writing again till I know whether you are angry with me for writing so madly.You will easily understand why from this. You know that while we were together I never said one word to you about my love; I thought you far too much above me to be even nearer than a good angel. But the world with its formalities and fooleries of etiquette drove me to write more than my greatest impudence could ever have said. So that by trying to crush me it effected the opposite result, and my heart spoke where my mouth would otherwise have been silent.

Forgive me Maudie, for my violence, and believe me when I tell you that your writing to me does me no earthly harm; but what made me write like this was that the change from your Christmas letter to your birthday letter so verified the change of your way of signing yourself that my only hope was to write you one last earnest letter; the last I mean in which I will speak my entire heart, and will hereafter learn resignation, or at least obey your command to fight against my sadness of heart; on condition; that you keep your promise to write to me as you suggest, on Easter, Xmas, New Year's day, our birthdays, *and* Whit Sunday . . . and that you write to me first at Easter to tell me whether or no you are angry with me for this wild letter. Please tear it up and forget it all but the requests, at once . . .

I am afraid you must be wearied as well as angry with this long letter. The peculiarity of the emergency called it out of my thoughts. I cannot write any commonplace now; but when I answer your promised Easter letter, it shall be all correct, proper and matter of fact, unless you permit me one word of what I feel.

Goodbye dear Maudie.

I will never write again like this. It seemed so much like the last word of earnestness I might write, that I could not help speaking out. Do forgive me,

your ever loving,
Hubert.[41]

Maude soon succumbed to the passionate exhortation of Parry's letter, responding with the suggestion that they should try to continue their meetings in London. Their most popular venues were Westminster Abbey and St Paul's, Knightsbridge, before the services, while the congregation was going into church. Frequently Maude and her sister 'were in great trepidation lest a spy should appear'[42] so they would resort to taking walks in Constitution Hill which, for Parry, soon became a haunt infused with romantic associations though, inevitably, tinged with sadness: 'I left them after a delicious half hour at the corner of Belgrave Square. Constitution Hill becomes an enchanted place—It was sad to part with them; it may be so long before we meet again, while these miserable formalities of the world separate us so hopelessly.'[43]

Eddie Hamilton and a new ally, Mary Gladstone (daughter of W. E. Gladstone), a close friend of Mary Herbert's and a fine amateur pianist, urged Parry to 'hope on' even though they reported Lady Herbert's increasing ire after their own visits to Wilton. Eddie Hamilton frequently found himself in an uncomfortable position. Lady Herbert would write letters to him about Parry in confidence, but his loyalty to Parry was greater. In a letter of 27 March to Maude, having received word from his friend, Parry related Lady Herbert's hurtful attitude in which she seemed as far away as ever from agreeing to an engagement:

My dearest Maude,

I found it was no good to attempt to go down by the same train with you from London, as I should not have got home at all by it that day, unless at some unearthly hour in the night, which would have made my people very uncomfortable. And to tell the truth I was rather afraid of meeting Lady Herbert under the circumstances; partly through fear of betraying anything which might put her yet more on her guard against me, and partly through the feeling that I should be in an odd position with her. Eddie sent me the letter which she had written to him about me. It was most kind and affectionate, but horribly determined as you can understand from a passage like this: 'I think nothing so cruel and unfair as to awaken feelings which cannot be gratified. It might lay up a store of lasting misery for them both,—and that as a mother I am

[41] Letter to Lady Maude Herbert, n.d. [? 28 Feb.] 1869, ShP.
[42] Diary, 15 Mar. 1869.   [43] Ibid. 16 Mar. 1869.

bound to consider and avert in spite of my own feelings etc.' These are very bitter words—and she puts it now in as plain a light as possible—no longer veiling it under the principle that people *will* talk. Nothing could be more kind than the way in which she put it all—But you see it is too late to talk about averting a malady when it is fairly grown in the system, and this malady of love is one of the hardest to cure I know of. However I shall not despair while I have that last precious letter you wrote to me at Oxford.[44]

Certainly his 'malady of love' was beyond curing. On the evidence of the intimate outpourings of his Easter letter, it seemed that he lived for Maude and nothing else:

My own dearest little Maudie,

your letter has made me most intensely happy. I am answering it directly before the first glow of pleasure has faded.

I thank you Maudie with all my heart—while I have this precious letter in my memory I never can be unhappy again as I was before. The intense longing may come again to see your dear face and hear your voice, but unhappy I cannot be, while I feel that I may give you my whole love and never fear that such a love should be unacceptable to you—I cannot write what I feel Maudie, perhaps it would not be right of me to do so. So I shall make my letter very short.

I shall be always content now while our love is such as it is. Always praying for you, and that however long we are separated, the frailty of our human nature may not alter my heart one shade from the intensity of the feeling I now bear towards you.[45]

The secret meetings at the theatre and in the Herbert's box at the opera continued unabated for several more months. Shortly after the summer term was over, a message came from George Pembroke and Maude, pressing him to come to Cowes for a few days yachting. In this Parry saw an opportunity to see Maude for longer than those agonizingly fleeting glimpses in London, but in the knowledge that he would be under the watchful eye of Lady Herbert, he went in the company of Eddie Hamilton. The days were precious for it would be several months before he would see Maude again.

It had been arranged that, during the summer months, Parry should go abroad to Liège in Belgium to learn and practise French. Thomas Gambier Parry, through his continental travels, had made the acquaintance of a cultured Protestant pastor, Monsieur Pradez, who had duly agreed to act as host and tutor for his son. Pradez was educated and well-read, introducing Hubert to the works of Hugo, de Musset, and Chénier, but he was not especially musical. Consequently, the attractions of Liège were not destined to be those of Stuttgart. The city itself he found dirty with the grime of industry, and the company of Pradez's family was kind

[44] Letter to Lady Maude Herbert, 27 Mar. 1869, ShP.
[45] Letter to Lady Maude Herbert, [Easter] 1869, ShP.

but wearisome. A letter to Maude, intended to greet her on her birthday, reveals his dissatisfaction and boredom:

I have nothing to tell you about myself except that I am dragging on a very weary existence, which I make endurable by working and reading all day long. My chief sufferings arise from the daughters of the old Pasteur, who weary my life out. One of them 'rubs me up the wrong way' so much that I can hardly endure being in the room with her. She intends to be very kind, so I do my best to like her, but my endeavours are not very successful.I have got a pianoforte over my head, another under my feet, and another at my side. The lady over my head practises from 9.30 till 1.30 in the morning which is delightful; the piano underneath me is practised on by 3 young ladies in succession, morning and noon; and in the next house are two other young ladies who practise vocal scales and vocal exercises (which to my ears represent a series of violent screams of a person in real suffering) for more than an hour at a time . . .

About my coming back to England soon, I am afraid there rests a considerable difficulty. I am not my own master in this case. My father managed everything for me on the condition that I stayed two months good; and it was his intention I know to come abroad at the end of that period, and meet me here, and go about Holland and Belgium with me to see the [curious] old towns and churches. I must try and put that out of his mind—but as you see that anyhow I shall be obliged to stay here till the beginning of September.[46]

The purpose of his stay in Liège was to prepare for a career in business for which his father already had plans. Parry himself had little or no idea of which profession he might enter, though in the same letter to Maude it is clear that he had considered the traditional careers open to younger sons of gentry—the Church and the Army:

You seem very horrified at the idea of my being ordained. You may think me very unfit, as much as Mary thinks that the life would not suit me.It is probably very true that I should not be fit, though at least I should try to make myself as much so as I could. As to its not suiting me in the manner of life etc. to me that would be no question. I can only explain that by telling you that I never looked upon it as a profession . . . and though it has been opposed by everybody including my father, and Lady Herbert, it has clung to me for years, though I have rarely mentioned it to anybody. It begins to take the dimensions of impossibility nowadays, and I am very glad you guessed right as I know all your feelings on the subject. As to the Army, I know that would suit me even worse. The species 'army man' is unutterably distasteful to me. The idiotic contempt for intellectual pursuits which generally characterises the younger officers and their selfish sporting tendencies always disgust me.[47]

With the preoccupations of choosing a career and the uncertainty of the future regarding his relationship with Maude, it is perhaps not surprising that Parry found little time nor the inclination to compose

---

[46] Letter to Lady Maude Herbert, 27 July 1869, ShP.   [47] Ibid.

much during 1869. However, he did use the occasions of his frequent visits to London to attend the Crystal Palace and St James's Hall which proved to be highly formative. Mann's performances of Beethoven's Third and Fourth Symphonies, the Overture *Leonora No. 1*, and parts of Schubert's *Rosamunde* took priority in concert series that were still largely saturated with Mendelssohn's works, while in March the Monday 'Pops' were notably enhanced by the appearance of Madame Schumann and Joachim who gave several performances of the *Kreutzer* Sonata. The interpretations of Schubert's A minor quartet and Beethoven's F minor quartet Op. 95 by Joachim's quartet were also a powerful attraction, though Parry still had to confess that 'parts of the Beethoven were fairly beyond [him] at the first hearing'.[48] But superseding his interest in Beethoven was his appetite for Schumann. The piano works such as *Carnaval*, the *Romanzen*, *Faschingsschwank aus Wien*, and *Phantasiestücke* Op. 12 (from which he copied out 'Warum') dominated the short recitals he gave as soloist in the Exeter College Musical Society concerts, and he was intrigued by the Society's enterprising *pièce de résistance*—the cantata *Das Glück von Edenhall*—which Stainer adapted for its first performance in this country, in English, for the college's Commemoration concert on 8 June.

As 1869 progressed his situation and emotional predicament led him to identify even more closely with the circumstances of Schumann's love for Clara as he became ever more engrossed in that composer's Lieder and piano literature. But he still lacked the necessary courage to break free from the confines of Mendelssohn's language, a fact evidenced by the insipidly sentimental setting of George Pembroke's poem 'A River of Life', dedicated to Maude. However, in Liège, his friendship with Kayser, a talented pianist and ardent follower of both Schumann and Chopin, induced him to sketch some ideas for a piano concerto in G minor which certainly shows a departure from the unambitious piano style of the *Songs and Sonnets*. The concerto appears to have been commenced in the last days of July and by 21 August he had finished copying the first movement, though it is not clear from his diary whether this was in full or short score. All that now remains of the work are eight pages of full score, and the rest of the movement, which is incomplete, exists only as a sketched short score. The fully scored material begins with a grave andante introduction followed by an allegro which includes a full orchestral ritornello and piano solo (marked 'risoluto'), the latter of which modulates to the dominant. At this juncture there are only four and a half further bars of orchestral material in full score before the manuscript breaks off into sketch. Although the structure of this

---

[48] Diary, 13 Mar. 1869.

material bears little resemblance to the shared sonata plan of the first movement of Mendelssohn's G minor piano concerto (indeed, the andante—allegro plan seems more outwardly akin to that of Schumann's late Introduction and Allegro in D minor, Op. 134 for piano and orchestra infused with the piano style of Sterndale Bennett's Concerto in F minor), it is clear from Parry's ideas that Mendelssohn's work was at the back of his mind. The gesture of the opening orchestral phrase, with its quasi-dramatic swell from p to f, is one striking similarity (though not the final unexpected modulation to the Neapolitan) as is the rhetoric of the piano's 'come recitativo' which brings to mind Mendelssohn's expressive transition from the first movement to his central andante (Ex. 3).

On his return from Liège Parry went first to Hedingham and then to Bayfordbury before going on to Highnam. There he had a brief but sad encounter with his brother Clinton who had agreed to make an appearance for the sake of a family reunion. The signs of continual deterioration in his personality, caused by dipsomania, were tragically evident, and the irrevocability of the situation was enormously distressing as was the strained atmosphere until he departed. Then a letter arrived from Maude summoning him and Eddie Hamilton to Cowes for another week on Lord Pembroke's yacht. It was a pleasant time spent idly in walks or gentle excursions around the island, but it was never possible to be alone with Maude for one moment.

Academic pressures at Oxford during the Michaelmas term were at their peak, for the following year he would have to sit for his 'Schools' examinations. Consequently composition was neglected, but his musical activities in college continued unabated. On 23 October, having been nominated by Pownall and another member of the Exeter College Musical Society's standing committee, J. S. Hardy, he was elected President. A further boost to his morale came with the news that Lamborn Cock had agreed to publish 'A River of Life' and Novello had taken on his Evening Service in D. This success was nevertheless tempered by the uncertainty of events at Wilton. The tone of Maude's letters became increasingly nervous and urgent as more and more trusted friends were taken into confidence. George Pembroke believed that already too many people had wind of their secret meetings, and that it must eventually come out. So that the lovers could gain a glimpse of each other, Mary Gladstone invited Hubert to a house party at Hawarden where Lady Herbert, Mary, and Maude were also guests. There was a brief respite when Lady Herbert went abroad for part of the winter and they were able to meet in London a little more regularly. However, in the knowledge that their relationship would be discovered sooner rather than later, they decided to get engaged in the spring of 1870 but to keep

Ex. 3. Opening of Piano Concerto in G minor (1869).

it a secret for as long as possible. For George Pembroke this situation was intolerable as is clear from the agitated mood of Maude's letter of 25 May:

My dear Hubert,

I have received a most disagreeable letter from George this mail obliging me to tell Mama of our engagement.

There is no other course left open, as if we don't he'll take sides against us. And unless he helps us I don't see how we are to get out. I think that I had better tell her, as being on the spot it would be easier.

It is a horrid bore—rather like cutting one's own throat. Though fortunately Mama as good as knows it already, only now of course she will be obliged to take decisive steps one way or the other.

If she writes to you—*mind* make no promises, and don't get put on your honour about writing, or anything.

Please answer by return of post, and say if you approve of my decision, and then I'll speak at once.

Till then I shall be quiet. I am so sorry this should happen just when you are up to your ears in work. But I am all for getting over a disagreeable thing quick. We must make up our minds for a row, but I hope we have both courage enough to see it out.—Don't be downhearted whatever happens as really opposition can make no *earthly* difference to me. Let us look hopefully on the bright side and not despond. It will all come right some day, though the clouds are very heavy just at present . . .[49]

It was indeed dispiriting news for Parry knew that it would mean the end of all communication, but none the less he reluctantly consented to the announcement. Having heard from Maude that the news had been broken he wrote to her on 12 June to assure her of his steadfastness:

My darling Maudie,

thank you very much for your precious though sad letter. Of course I am not angry. It was very generous of you to undertake so disagreeable a duty; and perhaps I ought not to be sorry that the first step has been so soon taken. It is very grievous to think that I shall have no more of your dear letters—They have become so much a part of my life that there will be a terrible blank now to look forward to. I am not the least afraid of meeting Lady Herbert personally or by letter. It will be of course sufficiently trying that I should seem the chief opponent of the wishes of one who has always been as kind as a mother to me— But necessity knows no law.

. . . I hope you won't be unhappy Maudie. I shall always pray for you—and that I may be true [to] you. I have got 'Steps to the Altar'; a copy which once belonged to my only sister—the only person in the world whose loss I still regret . . .

[49] Letter from Lady Maude Herbert, 25 May 1870, ShP.

My Schools are not over till next Wednesday. I hope I shall get through, as it will be such a burden off my mind; and will leave me much more free for my other difficulties . . .[50]

By mid-June he had taken his final examinations and obtained his degree with a Second Class. Then, as he recorded in his 1870 diary, 'the crash came, correspondence and loving converse were stopped, and for a short time all was black. But the people concerned were still kind, and my sorrow was soon dispelled by the assurance of a faithful heart yet left to me in all the changings of fortune.'

The so-called 'crash' was a long letter of 20 June from Lady Herbert in which, besides unleashing her anger in a furious and sometimes bitter diatribe, she made plain the real reasons for her complete objection to the engagement:

38, Chesham Place S.W.

My dear Hubert,

I am very much grieved to have to write to you on the subject of Maude. But you have left me no alternative but to write or speak—and I prefer the former.

I am sure you will do me the justice to say that I have never for one single moment led you to suppose that I could sanction an engagement between you which would result in utter ruin and misery to both. From the very first moment when gossip coupled your names together and I saw there was a danger that your boy and girl friendship would ripen into Love I spoke to Eddie and forbid [*sic*] your meeting. When you were invited to Cowes it was done by Pembroke without my knowledge. And when I remonstrated with him, he positively assured me that there was nothing between you but brother and sister feelings such as the girls have for Eddie, and he added that the way to create the sentiments I dreaded was to separate you entirely. I foolishly yielded and did not take Maude away when you arrived, which now I feel I ought to have done. When you met at Hawarden, I was extremely annoyed and told Mrs Gladstone that had I known you were to be there, I should not have brought Maude at all. She was vexed and said she 'quite saw it all—but that it had been managed by the "two Marys" and she knew nothing of it'.

I go over all this to show you that I have never varied in my opposition to your wishes. And now for a practical businesslike view of the case. Owing to Lord Herbert's having given his name to the Duke of Newcastle for a newspaper speculation some years ago, which failed, I became liable after his death to the whole debt and had to pay £130,000. That took away the whole of my younger children's fortunes as well as my own, so that Maude will have next to nothing. Pembroke himself will never have more that £40,000 a year from the heavy charges on his estate. Supposing that he gives his sister £20,000 which is more than he could well afford in justice to the others, that would give her £600 a year. How is it possible that she could live upon that? Your father says that first and last you can never have more than £10,000 and after his death. That would

[50] Letter to Lady Maude Herbert, 12 June 1870, ShP.

give you £300 a year. So that your joint income would be £900 a year. Now I ask you plainly if you think it *possible* for Maude to live upon that, educated as she has been and brought up in every luxury and comfort? Can you love her and wish to expose her to such utter misery? And should children come, would you like to see yourself unable to bring them up as gentlemen or send them to school or college? I put it to you so plainly because you seem to have got a most marvellous misconception of the state of things. Pembroke himself wrote to me to say 'he had never undertaken to provide you the means of marrying'. But what he, in his boyish ignorance, does *not* know, is that *he has not the means of doing so*, even if he would!! I cannot understand any honourable man either, liking to be dependent on the charity of a Brother-in-law, and the chance kindness of any future wife he may have. My Brother-in-law, Lord Clanwilliam, wrote to me on this wretched business a fortnight ago and said 'Before many months have rolled over his head, I will answer for it that Pembroke will see the utter madness of such a proposal as strongly as we do. The thing is so thoroughly inadmissable that I hope you will make your "no" so emphatic that there shall be no loophole for future hope. Turn it which way you will, there is nothing but misery in store for poor Maude in such an alliance to which no parent or guardian of hers could *ever* give a consent.'

I confess I am lost in astonishment when I think how you could have the courage to entangle Maude into an engagement when you have no home to offer her nor any prospect of one. I cannot but feel that you took advantage of George's inexperience and of my widowhood; for had her father lived you would never have ventured to take so cruel a course. I say *cruel* deliberately, for you have brought terrible suffering on Maude and on me. It breaks my heart to be the cause of making her so unhappy; but I feel I must be firm now to save her from an amount of future misery which I really cannot contemplate.

I must also say that I think your corresponding with her as you have done without my knowledge and knowing what my feelings were on the subject, is utterly unjustifiable. I am very sorry to speak so harshly; but when I see how my darling Maude's life is wrecked for the time, you cannot expect me to be patient with the cause of all this misery. What I want you to understand clearly is, that the thing must be altogether at an end; that I can allow *no* correspondence between you, and that you must release Maude from any engagement implied or otherwise. She told me herself that she 'considered herself so completely bound to you that she could no more receive the attentions of others than if she were married.'—Now, as an honourable man, I must charge you to release her from this tacit engagement. *It never can be.* So that to ruin all prospects of her being well settled and having a happy home by a folly of this sort is sheer madness on your part. You cannot wish to drag her down to misery and ruin if you care for her, and yet you have selfishly engaged her affections to such an extent as altogether to compromise her future! She will not give you up. Therefore I can only hope you will have sufficient right feeling to give her up yourself and tell her that you have done so. I know it will cost you both a great deal. But if you will once believe that the thing is *utterly hopeless*, you will, I am sure, be generous enough to help her to give it up.—Dear Hubert. If I have written severely it is not that I do not care for you, but that for both your sakes, I feel and see the utter madness of such a marriage to an extent of which you can have no idea. After all, Maude and you would never get on if you had even the means of living. She hates music except for your sake, and you have a passion for it, and she is thoroughly unbusinesslike and would make the worst poor man's wife in the world! Then, as Clanwilliam says, 'not one woman in 10 marries her first love and certainly not one man in a thousand!'

So, for the love of God and of Maude, dearest Hubert, be generous and honourable in this matter and try for once to see it and judge it fairly. I will not say all the pain this letter has cost me to write. But I love Maude dearer than my life and I feel that she will thank me hereafter for having been what she and you may think hard and cruel now.

yours affectionately,

M. E. Herbert[51]

Such an odious letter would have deterred many a determined suitor, but to someone of Parry's single-minded, tenacious character, Lady Herbert's interdict, couched in so vehement and frank, not to say hurtful terms, served only to increase his mood of defiance. He stood fast in his intentions, but was forced to comply with conditions laid down by Lady Herbert. To convince his future mother-in-law that he was capable of supporting Maude, he agreed to find a respectable career outside music, a decision, incidentally, which was altogether pleasing to his father who had never strayed in his opposition to his son's musical aspirations.

Indeed, while he was seeing out his last weeks at Oxford, his father had been hard at work making provision for his entry into the City. A career in insurance at Lloyd's Register of Shipping had been suggested both by Thomas Gambier Parry (who put up the £5,000 demanded as guarantee) and Lewis Majendie. Hubert had accepted it with apparent equanimity. It was intended that he should begin in late September, but owing to the dilatoriness of his father's lawyer in drawing up the deeds, this had to be deferred until the middle of November. A partner for his business exploits, Aeneas Ranald McDonnell (son of Aeneas Ranald McDonnell, Chief of Glengarry), had also been secured and a weekend meeting was arranged at Hedingham in early October for them to make each other's acquaintance. McDonnell proved to be an amiable companion with a healthy interest in the arts, but it was yet to be seen whether he possessed the confidence and necessary business acumen to make the partnership a success, for there can be no doubt that Parry, with no experience of the financial world, took on his responsibilities with some trepidation.

---

[51] Letter from Lady M. Elizabeth Herbert, 20 June 1870, ShP.

4

London and Marriage

I FELT the parting from Oxford most bitterly. There is much to treasure in its remembrance: with all the follies and recklessness of that youthful common-wealth, there is much that is lovely and lovable, much that is true and generous, much even that is high and noble. Farewell cherished reminiscences! Happy Deanery evenings—social 'Adelphis'—merry unambitious lodging-house dinner parties—football matches—and happiest of all, the many intertwinings of youthful loving souls in music and pure conversation—ye are of the irrevocable. Farewell!

From thence I passed to a fit scene to drown my earthly sorrows, and entered on the latter part of a rushing London season—a time which made the days seem as though they were not, and whose nights were as the restlessness of troubled spirits which seek the unattainable.[1]

So reads Parry's account of his painful wrench from university. Such nostalgic valediction was perhaps typical of someone who had been so bound up in Oxford life both socially and musically. But what may be also inferred from this statement is the fear that his departure from the university environment for the capital would bring to an abrupt end his creative aspirations, either through want of time or lack of motivation. With the modest exception of two unambitious pieces of church music 'Blessed are they who dwell in thy house' (dated September 1870) and 'Lord, I have loved the habitation of thy house' (probably written for Wesley at Gloucester), and a song 'Fairest dreams may be forgotten' to his own words,[2] composition had all but ceased. It appears that, according to Parry's later recollections,[3] he took a few lessons with Sir William Sterndale Bennett at this time. This is corroborated in the biography of Bennett,[4] but since Parry's diary is so sketchy between 1870 and the middle of 1873, it is difficult to pinpoint an exact date for these lessons. What we do know is that Bennett proved to be unsuitable, for, as Parry stated, 'he was extremely kind and sympathetic, but he was

[1] Diary, 1870.
[2] The words of this song were later published as 'A Sequence of Analogies' in *Macmillan's Magazine*, May 1875.
[3] 'Hubert Parry', *Musical Times* (July 1898), 444. This is also confirmed in an article written by Parry himself presumably for *Grove's Dictionary of Music and Musicians* written c.1884 (see Bod. MS Eng. Letters e 117)
[4] J. R. Sterndale Bennett, *The Life of Sir William Sterndale Bennett* (Cambridge, 1907), 399.

too sensitive ever to criticize'. Furthermore, there was the anxiety that his new occupation would soon isolate him from the maelstrom of new ideas, both political and artistic, that were being aired at Oxford during the three years of his residence. For Parry, university education had increasingly proved to be a valuable formative experience, for besides the musical stimuli provided by friends such as Stainer, Taylor, the Donkins, Pownall, and Montgomery, he took full advantage of lecture courses connected with other realms of the humanities. Above all we should acknowledge one of the principal influences which left its mark on him—the lectures and personage of Ruskin, who was appointed Slade Professor of Fine Art. The interpretations of paintings and architecture declared at the beginning of Ruskin's career had been met with overwhelming and enduring success in Victorian society. The belief that art contained issues relevant to morality preached with the earnestness of a Victorian evangelical were undoubtedly words that Ruskin's contemporaries wanted to hear, though the later political dimensions he construed in art contained in such works as *Unto This Last* (1862) left his audience confused, not to say uncomfortable; and there were those who dismissed his last volumes of *Modern Painters* as palpably 'mad' if not dangerous. But Ruskin's power of argument, underpinned by the rejection of orthodox Christianity and the Bible, impressed Parry deeply. In 1870 he attended Ruskin's first lectures at the university ('Lectures on Art') which paraded the old scholar's moral approach, and shortly after leaving Oxford, he took up *The Queen of the Air* which forcefully postulated the theory of virtue and good art:

Great art is the expression of the mind of a great man, and mean art, that of the want of mind of a weak man. A foolish person builds foolishly, and a wise one, sensibly; a virtuous one, beautifully; and a vicious one, basely. If stone work is well put together, it means that a thoughtful man planned it, and a careful man cut it, and an honest man cemented it. If it has too much ornament, it means that its carver was too greedy of pleasure; if too little, that he was rude, or insensitive, or stupid, and the like. So that when you have learned how to spell these most precious of all legends,—pictures and buildings,—you may read the characters of men, and of nations, in their art, as in a mirror; . . .[5]

Parry completed his study of *The Queen of the Air* in October at Highnam, concluding that though as a thesis it lacked coherence, it was 'a thoroughly remarkable book and most wonderfully well written . . . He harps much on his hobby of the connection between art and morality of which he gave us such a dose in the Oxford lectures . . . it is well worth study; and it must be confessed that he makes a good case for his art-and-morality doctrine . . .'.[6] Indeed, the case for 'morality' in art was one

    [5] J. Ruskin, from Lecture III, *The Queen of the Air* (1869), 102.
    [6] Diary, Oct. 1870.

which Parry readily confronted. Ruskin's doctrines concerning the visual arts, and posing such questions of colour, content, intellect, message, and purpose, suggested strong musical parallels. These were to have far-reaching consequences in Parry's future stylistic decisions and were to surface time and again in his approaches to composition and those of other composers. Equally important, however, was the way in which Ruskin's ideas seemed to be founded on much wider moral issues which were no longer based on the immutable wisdom of Scripture or theistic imagery. The seeds of disbelief in conventional religion had already begun to take root in Parry's mind, and there can be little doubt that Ruskin's wholesale repudiation of Christianity must have served in part to accelerate his increasing scepticism. Such sentiments, however, were kept absolutely private, for had his father got wind of them, it would have inevitably caused a storm in the Parry household and only exacerbated the delicate predicament at Wilton.

On 22 November, after a short stay at Bayfordbury, Parry moved into lodgings at 5 Chapel Street off Grosvenor Place. From here he began to commute to the City. Within a few weeks, however, the eternal clamour of financial dealings began to irritate him. The blasé attitude of Lloyd's, which had been prevalent during the era of the Regency, had undergone a radical transformation as a new sense of commercial morality had swept through London's financial houses. The City had experienced something of a revival as the country moved from the economic misery and political ferment of the 1840s to a period of Victorian prosperity. Yet the air of seriousness, which was now the fashion, seemed to Parry to be totally irreconcilable to his conception of artistic sensibility. Dislike of his work soon gave rise to the long-term vision to escape from it entirely. But for the moment this was impractical. The purpose of his employment was to prove a point as he was reminded in a letter from George Pembroke in December:

Dear Hubert,

Thank you very much for your letter—I think you have behaved very well and done the right thing. All you can do now is to be patient and *work hard*. I know you will agree with me that it would be wrong to marry a girl before you could support her. And girls are very expensive animals. If you can only manage to earn enough to support a wife, no-one can or will stand in your way.[7]

Acquiescence was, for the time being, the best form of diplomacy, but it was a bitter pill to swallow. Some relief was gained by London's celebration of the Beethoven Centenary organized by Grove and Manns. As Parry recorded with some excitement in November: 'All the concerts in London are now devoted to Beethoven'.

[7] Letter from George Pembroke, 6 Dec. 1870, ShP.

Parry's efforts at Lloyd's with McDonnell had already gone some way in placating Lady Herbert. Early in the new year he was invited to Wilton for a few days where he found the more senior Herberts better disposed towards him. Encouraged by the favourable change in his fortunes, he returned to London with a new zest. Writing to Lady Herbert who was away on another of her Mediterranean tours, this time in north Africa, he spoke of the greater challenges posed by his insurance enterprises: 'My work gets a little harder by degrees. I have had one or two days of it by myself and found it quite enough at a time. We get on pretty well, and hope to make something the first year to give us larger capital insurances in the second.'[8] Yet though the progress in business seemed promising, the real advances occurred in his introduction into the higher echelons of London's musical society as he recorded in the summary of his 1871 diary:

The three months in question have been conspicuous to me in as much as I have therein made the acquaintance of Joachim and the exceedingly kind and agreeable Walter Broadwood and Stockhausen; and Madame Schumann and her daughters whom I revere highly as the wife and children of one of the highest of my ideal composers. Joachim is one of the most charming of men, a genius of the highest order. I spent a most agreeable afternoon with him at Broadwood's, and sat with him while young Hallé was painting, to help to keep him awake. Madame Schumann I met first at Lady Goldschmidt's.[9]

The acquaintance of Walter Broadwood (which had been assisted by the latter's friendship with Parry's father), a partner in the famous London firm of piano builders, was a highly advantageous contact. Walter Broadwood's circle of friends included an impressive array of international composers, performers, technicians, and artists which to Parry opened up a new world of opportunity. His home at 3 Queen's Gate Gardens, South Kensington, not far from Parry's own lodgings, was a regular meeting-place where private concerts were held. Joachim and Clara Schumann were frequent visitors, but others such as the pianists William Coenen, Ferdinand Hiller, Lubeck, and Pauer were seen there from time to time as were the singers Viardot-Garcia and the baritone much favoured by Brahms, Julius Stockhausen.

It was through Clara Schumann, Joachim, and Stockhausen that Parry first learned of Brahms whose music was relatively unknown in Britain. Contemporary music in London was still a scarce commodity. Reports in the *Musical Times* on concerts in the capital during the early 1870s clearly show that they remained doggedly conservative. The prospectus for the 'Oratorio Season' issued in February 1871 lists only one truly ambitious work—Beethoven's *Missa Solemnis*; the rest of the season ventured no

[8] Letter to Lady M. Elizabeth Herbert, 19 Mar. 1871, ShP.   [9] Diary, [early] 1871.

further than Benedict's *St Peter* (lauded by the British press as having caused a 'sensation' at the Birmingham Festival in 1870), J. F. Barnett's *Paradise and the Peri*, and *Nala and Damayanti* by Dr Ferdinand Hiller. Attention given to chamber music had certainly increased, but the choice of works was lamentably restricted. Just occasionally there would be the odd ray of light such as the concert given at the St George's Hall on 26 January 1871 by an ensemble led by the prominent native violinist, Henry Holmes. The programme included a rare performance of Brahms's Sextet in B flat, Op. 18, which was received enthusiastically by its reviewer who believed that the work ought 'to excite considerable attention, even amongst those who are least disposed to admit the claims of "Young Germany"'.[10] The latter remark, however, reflected the widespread reservations felt by the public and those in academia for modern German music. One of the more forward-looking musicians resident in London at this time was the Dutch pianist, William Coenen. His interest in new chamber works resulted in a series of three concerts at the Hanover Square Rooms where works by Volckman, Reinecke, Rubinstein, and Brahms were given a hearing. Billed by the *Musical Times* as 'Mr Coenen's Chamber Concerts of Modern Music', the performances had a mixed reception. Brahms's Piano Quintet, which had received its first performance in Paris in 1868, was among the works played. Though it received a moderately favourable critique from the reviewer, the somewhat sycophantic plaudits for the Trio in D by Reinecke (who was in London for the season) show that London was still not accustomed to the severe intellectualism of Brahms's style:

J. Brahms and Reinecke are creative artists of whom we have a right to be proud, although the clear and musicianlike writing of the latter is in our judgement infinitely superior to the somewhat forced and exaggerated style of the former. At the last concert, on the 21st ult. Rubinstein's dreary and uninteresting Quartett in B flat, which was placed before Reinecke's Trio in D, depressed the audience to such an extent that nothing but the brightness of the succeeding piece, coupled with the composer's charming playing of the pianoforte part, could have induced many to remain. The Quintett in F minor, by Brahms, which concluded the concert, is an unequal work, but contains much clever writing, the first movement and Scherzo being especially worthy of commendation.[11]

After attending this concert Parry wrote in his diary: 'I heard some of his [Brahms] music at one of Coenen's concerts. A quintett. Frightfully difficult. Some of it rather crude at first hearing. But wonderfully vigorous in treatment.'[12] The quintet's recommendation had come

[10] *Musical Times* (1 Mar. 1871), 11.
[11] 'Mr Coenen's Chamber Concerts of Modern Music', *Musical Times* (1 May 1871), 76.
[12] Diary, [? Apr.] 1871.

largely from Clara Schumann whose involvement with the work, particularly its gestation, was second to none. She was able to give Parry a first-hand account of Brahms's devotion to early music (notably Bach) and to classical precepts of form. Lubeck, on the other hand, from whom Parry took eight piano lessons, was more reticent in his opinion. For Lubeck the issue remained one of balance between 'beauty' and structure, the latter of which he felt had often eluded Schumann, and the former Brahms.[13] Much to Parry's disappointment Lubeck soon returned to Germany so that once again Parry found himself without a teacher who could provide him with the reassurance he so badly needed. 'It was very sad for me', he wrote, 'that Lubeck left England so soon, as it was very delightful working with him; a few more lessons might have enabled me to attain a certain degree of excellence, which I altogether despair of without help. However, he has taught me at least how to practise, if I can find the time for it.'[14]

As far as his relations with the Herberts were concerned, things improved markedly. 'I was allowed to go frequently to Chesham Place', he recorded, 'and spent some delightful days at Wilton, and on the night (ever memorable to me) of Tuesday June 20th I received the news that it was to be no more a secret. Oh! the fever of happiness when the cloud cleared away.'[15] Lady Herbert was evidently convinced both by Parry's persistence, and of his steadfast pecuniary efforts to see that Maude would be assured of an acceptable standard of living. The engagement, therefore, was allowed to become public knowledge. Relief from the burden was tremendous, but no sooner had his spirits been raised when Lady Herbert, with her obsession for the Mediterranean, decreed that Maude was to go abroad with her for four months. Parry naturally protested at such a lengthy period of absence, and, reading between the lines, the slightly nervous tone in his letter suggests that he feared that Lady Herbert might at any time renege on her earlier decision. In consequence this caused Parry bitterness, which resulted in an impatience with Lady Herbert's quixotic behaviour and doubt about her sincerity:

I am so glad you refused stoutly the offer to take you abroad. The very idea of your going abroad for four months makes me quite ill. Why, I thought if you went at all it would only be for a short time, but really four months is absurd. It's the very hyperbole of iniquity and cruelty. What *should* I do. And besides it would not do you any good I am quite sure . . . Don't go please. Surely Lady Herbert doesn't want to break it off after all? However I shall hope for the best. Why does she want to go for such a long time? If she had asked for a short time I should have thought it a duty of generosity and unselfishness to bear your absence; but 4 months is too exorbitant a demand. Such a thing can't be

[13] Charles L. Graves, *Hubert Parry* (London, 1926), i. 130.
[14] Diary, [? June] 1871.   [15] Ibid.

endured, particularly when for a long time being constantly with you has become a necessity of my existence. Don't go Maudie dear. It is too much to demand even of the generosity of Francis d'Assisi if he were in existence.[16]

On a more optimistic note the letter also mentions his father's approval of the match and of a brief meeting with Lady Herbert who had decided on the date of the forthcoming marriage:

I am very glad too that Lady Herbert likes Possie [Thomas Gambier Parry]. That is a decidedly good thing. He told me this morning he had had a talk with Lady Herbert about us. And she said she intended it to come off about the middle of next year. I'm so glad. I do hope she means it. And that dear Possie says he is going to furnish our house for us. Of course I mustn't let him do it all, as I don't think he could afford it, but I know he will do a great deal. Isn't it good of him. And I was so pleased too at what he said about you. It made me proud and quite happy. He quite understands that I have found my pearl of great price. My little angel. Oh! I am so glad he loves her. Because [too] it is something to relieve the bitterness of the memory of sorrows that have gone before.

In the early summer Maude made her first visit to Highnam, but her stay was destined to be short, for she was obliged to accompany her mother to Mount Merrion, Lord Pembroke's Irish estate in Booterstown near Dublin,[17] where the whole Herbert family was to spend the rest of July. The estate of Mount Merrion, which passed to the Pembrokes from the 7th Viscount Fitzwilliam in 1816, was indeed a substantial estate. It commanded a panoramic view of the mountains together with the whole city of Dublin and right across the bay beyond to Howth. The grounds were particularly spectacular consisting of orchards, decoy ponds, woods, sunken gardens, a deer park, and an impressive drive lined with sycamores leading up to the house. The house itself (judging from the water colours made by William Ashford towards the end of the eighteenth century[18]) was not especially grand in comparison with its surroundings, but it had provided a splendid retreat for several generations of the Pembroke dynasty and was to do so in the future for Hubert and Maude after their marriage. Parry in his turn was unable to travel to Ireland owing to an expedition he and McDonnell had already booked to Caen, Rouen, and Lisieux. But they were reunited in August at Wilton when plans were made for a formal meeting of the parents which subsequently took place in early October. This finally sealed the

[16] Letter to Lady Maude Herbert, [July] 1871, ShP.
[17] The estate of Mount Merrion no longer exists. Soon after the Pembrokes' departure [in the 1920s?] the house was converted into a church (St Teresa, Dundrum). By 1926 extensive building began in the grounds and now only the new Deer Park and part of the woods remain as city parkland in a much expanded Dublin.
[18] Fitzwilliam Museum, Cambridge.

reality of their engagement and though they were not able to spend Christmas together, Parry was reassured by a letter from his future mother-in-law on 24 December:

God bless you, dear old boy and give you many, many happy Xmases. This is the last, please God, you will spend without her.

You will have a good deal to do to fill up all the love she has had in her home, but I trust you to make her happy and not to let all the deep love evaporate (as I see in so many married people) after the first Xmas or two! *Ours* (Sidney's and mine) went on *crescendo* to the end! God grant yours may too, for my little darling's sake.

My heart is full to the brim when I think this is the last Xmas she will be with us, so you must forgive all the fears which crop up in my mother's heart.

> God bless and keep you ever in His Holy Love.
> yours ever affectionately,
> M. E. Herbert.[19]

The 'deep love' described in Lady Herbert's letter indeed perfectly summarized the intensity of Parry's feeling for Maude. It was to fuel his undying devotion to her, at least outwardly. Yet, when they exchanged letters at Christmas, Maude seemed suddenly cold and indifferent, as if now that their wedding arrangements had been finalized, there was no need of their former passions. The letter so disconcerted Parry that, in his reply, he urged Maude to shake off her inhibitions and (perhaps conscious of the conventions in aristocratic marriages) he reminded her that their relationship was not 'arranged', nor was it simply a matter of convenience:

Though you are the biggest darling in the world my precious Maudie, I declare you are very funny. Your letters are so matter of fact that they very often act as a positive damper to the intensity of my affection. I daresay it is very good for me; for yesterday I really felt quite ill for lack of you; . . . I looked forward with fierce eagerness for your letter, and when I got it there was such an amount of philosophical indifference displayed in it that I think an ordinary looker on would have thought with Sidney Meade that the engagement was only a sort of mutual agreement which we had entered upon for some fancied convenience which the general public were incapable of appreciating. The signature being a matter of courtesy, and all that approached to affection in the letter being just the sort of commonplace that a pair of French fiancées made for the sake of mutual social advantage, might enter upon. It makes me quite ashamed of the impulse I have to pour out the burning love I feel, which is so chilled by matter-of-factness. When I think of the difference between your Xmas letter and mine I can only wonder; but I must confess to you Maudie that I should be utterly miserable if I felt it necessary to write to you as you do to me. I don't know whether you like me to write as my nature dictates, or whether you like cold

---

[19] Letter from Lady M. Elizabeth Herbert, 24 Dec. 1871. ShP.

matter of fact better. I think I understand the reason of your letters being what they are pretty well. Do you understand mine? tell me.

What you say about my thinking of you is quite absurd. My darling I can't think of you more on Xmas day than any other day. All day long I am thinking of you and praying for your happiness, and all night I think of you and dream of you . . . This is not a happy Xmas day. My love for my own family is only half real and full, for there is a vacant place of yearning love between me and them. Yesterday was positively hateful. Oh Maudie if there is anything disagreeable in this letter it is only the bitterness which pervades my mind for your absence. I couldn't love you so intensely if you were anything but what you are . . .

God grant we may spend next Xmas together . . . Don't be shy, *please.*[20]

Maude complained that she could not express her own feelings in a letter, but in fact her reticence was the first indication of the marked differences in their personalities, which gradually were to become more and more accentuated as they grew older. Besotted, however, by youthful love, Parry was blind to such realities and longed only for the time when there would be no more enforced separation.

Through pressure of work at Lloyd's, the constant journeys backwards and forwards to Wilton, and feverish letter-writing, Parry found no time to continue his diary in 1872. Nevertheless, we can safely assume that he continued to be involved in the London musical scene, regularly attending concerts with an especially keen interest in new works.

Curiosity for new music, though still tentative amongst the general public, was gaining momentum. In February the Crystal Palace included two novelties, Hiller's Schumannesque *Symphonische Phantasie*, Op. 67 subtitled *Es muss doch Frühling werden* and Rubinstein's *Don Quixote, musical pictures after Cervantes* completed in 1870. More momentous was a performance of Brahms's Piano Concerto in D minor on 9 March which again 'caused a divided opinion on the merits of this exponent of the music of "Young Germany"'.[21] The Philharmonic, on the other hand, was satisfied with the promulgation of orchestral and vocal works of Gounod who, having fled to England during the Franco-Prussian war, had rapidly become a favourite of the concert-going public. Only in June, at the persuasion of the Danish virtuoso pianist, Frits Hartvigson, did they stage a performance of Liszt's E flat major concerto, which failed to elicit any significant reaction from the critics. Most of the enterprising concerts, however, were of the chamber variety. William Coenen's 'Three Concerts of Modern Music' at the Hanover Square Rooms featured prominently, the first of which introduced Brahms's Piano Quartet in G minor, and the second, the Piano Trio, Op. 8 in B together with Schumann's string quartet, Op. 41 No. 3 and Chopin's

---

[20] Letter to Lady Maude Herbert, 25 Dec. 1871, ShP.
[21] Review, 'Crystal Palace', *Musical Times* (1 Apr. 1872), 434.

Cello sonata in G minor, Op. 65. The impression left by Coenen's choice of works provoked the critic of the *Musical Times* to complain that 'Mr Coenen [had] strictly limited himself to the presentation of modern German compositions.' It was a comment to which Coenen, with his pioneering energy, took great exception, for it raised to consciousness the vital question concerning the dearth of contemporary English chamber music. Coenen's indignant reply[22] to the *Musical Times* articulated this very point:

Dear Sir,

In the criticisms in your valuable paper upon the concerts of Modern Chamber Music, I find myself repeatedly reproached for confining my choice of music to that of German composers, and consequently neglecting English works. It certainly would be difficult to compile three programmes of chamber music without drawing largely on the works of German composers. But I can at once refute the charge of partiality and exclusiveness, which your able critic brings against me, by drawing attention to three composers who were originally included in my programmes, viz., Gade, a Dane, Rubinstein, a Russian, and Chopin, a Pole, not to mention the songs by authors of various nationalities. But, he says, 'Why not have works of English composers?' I answer, Where are they?? I am fully aware that Sir S. Bennett and Mr Macfarren have written important works of chamber music, but, as my concerts are given for the purpose of introducing music not generally known to a London audience, I have, as a matter of course, omitted their well-known compositions from my programmes. I must confess I know of no other English composers whose works of chamber music can rank with those of Sir S. Bennett and Mr Macfarren, and with those I selected for my concerts; and I shall be only too thankful to your critic if he can mention any. I can do no more than carefully study the catalogue of printed chamber music issued by the principal music-sellers of Europe, and select from the works named in them those which, in my humble opinion, are the most important. It is strange that, for instance, in the catalogue of Messrs. Novello, Ewer and Co., I find no mention of these numerous English compositions your critic speaks of. Such works may exist, for aught I know, in manuscript; but in that case, if they are not known and performed, the blame would seem to attach rather to the editors who do not publish them than to myself. I beg that, in justice to me, you will insert these few remarks in your valuable paper, and oblige

> Yours very truly,
> William Coenen

This letter encapsulated the essential flaws in British chamber music: native composers were more interested in producing choral works which were both more lucrative and more expedient in gaining a wider

---

[22] Letter from William Coenen to the Editor *Musical Times* (1 May 1872), 478–9.

audience; furthermore, publishers such as Novello, Lamborn Cock, or Stanley Lucas, were understandably not interested in publishing music for an extremely limited market.

Much of the pioneering groundwork in the dissemination of contemporary chamber and orchestral music in Britain must be attributed to European emigrés such as Coenen, who were awake to continental developments (such as the forming of the Société Nationale de Musique chiefly founded by Saint-Saëns in 1871 for the propagation of modern chamber music). More often than not, their most valuable work was done in private, at the performers' own residences and consequently went unnoticed by the critics. Of these gatherings one of the most important was a group who dubbed themselves 'The Working Men's Society'. In their midst were four virtuoso pianists: Frits Hartvigson, known for his performances of the Liszt piano concertos; Walter Bache, a pupil of Liszt; Edward Dannreuther, a pupil of Hauptmann and Moscheles, and an ardent champion of Wagner; last but not least, in the role of mentor was the pianist, teacher, and conductor, Karl Klindworth, who also applauded the achievements of Wagner. Meetings of the society had begun in July 1867 in which performances of orchestral music were given in arrangements for two pianos. At the first meeting (held in Klindworth's home at 74 Cambridge Street, Pimlico), the programme consisted of Liszt's arrangement of the first three movements of Beethoven's Ninth Symphony (played by Klindworth and Dannreuther), Klindworth's arrangement of Berlioz's *Fête chez Capulet* for two pianos and eight hands (played by Klindworth, Dannreuther, Hartvigson, and Bache), and Rubinstein's recent Fourth Piano Concerto in D minor (played by Hartvigson and Bache). Of particular significance, however, were a series of gatherings which began on 18 January 1868, when Klindworth (who was later entrusted by Wagner to prepare the vocal scores of *The Ring*) played through *Das Rheingold* and *Die Walküre*. The spirit of exploration continued even after Klindworth had left England to join the staff of the newly formed Moscow Conservatory, for Dannreuther introduced the rest of the society to *Tristan und Isolde*. With enthusiasm for Wagner at high pitch, Bache then began to introduce Liszt's piano and orchestral works. Bache, who had struck up a close friendship with Dannreuther after his return to London in 1865, set about arranging many of Liszt's symphonic poems for two pianos, performing 'Les Préludes' with Dannreuther in July, 1865. After the voluntary disbanding of the Working Men's Society, Bache continued his Lisztian crusade, eventually initiating annual orchestral concerts in 1871 with the support of Dannreuther. The concerts were, at least at the outset, a labour of love, for they were received somewhat cynically by the critics as the patronizing tone of the following review exemplifies. One thing was certain, however—Bache and Dannreuther had firmly established a reputation as exponents of new music:

At the annual concert of Mr Walter Bache a programme of conventional pieces is so little expected that no surprise is created when the selection does not include a single composition either of Beethoven, Mozart, or any other of the honoured names of those who have advanced the art to its present high position. The performance of Friday evening the 26th May, given at the Hanover Square Rooms, was no exception to the rule. Liszt's Piano Concerto in E flat, and the same composer's 'Les Préludes' (Poème symphonique d'après Lamartine) were the works in which the orchestra were engaged; and although we can scarcely believe that Mr Bache converted any of his audience to the worship of the eccentric German [*sic*] composer, there can be no doubt that the performance was highly satisfactory to those who are already his disciples, and exceedingly interesting to those who heard the preaching of his musical doctrines for the first time.[23]

Bache's annual Liszt concerts continued until 1886 during which time he introduced to the London public at least five of the symphonic poems together with the *Faust* and *Dante* Symphonies. Fired by his colleague's energy, Dannreuther inaugurated the Wagner Society in 1872 and made plans to re-establish the atmosphere of the Working Men's Society, though his vision did not in fact materialize until the following year.

Owing to Parry's failure to keep a diary during 1872 we have no concrete documentary evidence to confirm that his attentions were pointing in this direction. Nevertheless, it is clear from the events and sentiments expressed in 1873 that he was actively looking for both a piano teacher to fill the gap left by Lubeck and a teacher of composition who emanated from 'modernist' circles. That he eventually sought lessons from Dannreuther in 1873 suggests strongly that he was fully aware of the trends they were setting, and that he was, albeit shyly, attempting to introduce himself into their circles. However, exacerbated by the lack of professional guidance, confidence in his own musical abilities had reached crisis point, as a letter to Maude in April bears out:

It is very nice of Miss Froude to come and read to you and tell you to rest yourself. Please give her any message she will take from me. I like her so much. She looks so cheery always, and so kind. What she says about my music is all humbug I am afraid. It is just those things which distress me. Well meaning people who know nothing about me are apparently always talking about my musical abilities behind my back and it distresses me particularly to think that I am altogether unworthy of their praise. They take their opinion on hearsay. I know perfectly well that if an opportunity was ever afforded them of testing what they say, they would be ashamed of themselves for praising me without due consideration, and would make me the more distressed for being the innocent cause of their disappointment. I am sorry Miss Froude has been led

[23] Review, *Musical Times* (1 July 1871), 147.

into such extravagant anticipations, and I heartily wish she could be undeceived.[24]

Time given to composition had been, to say the least, sporadic. During 1871 Parry had spent most of his free time copying and revising earlier works. This could also be said for the first part of 1872 with the exception of three songs, 'The poet's song' (Tennyson), 'More fond than cushat dove' (Ingoldsby), and 'Music' (Shelley). The technique and vocabulary of these pieces show an advance well beyond the limited scope of his earlier vocal music, reflecting, especially in the setting of Shelley's 'Music', his growing preoccupation with Schumann. After completing them in May, Parry decided to submit them to Novello where they were looked over by the firm's adviser, Joseph Barnby. Barnby's opinion of the songs was positive, but a recommendation to publish them was not forthcoming:

1, Berners St
W.

My dear Sir,

I fear your three songs had slipped my memory—for which I must apologize. I have however now carefully looked over them and have come to the conclusion that I could not well recommend them to Messrs. Novello and Co. Not that they are deficient in musicianly qualities—quite the reverse—but they are not the kind of thing the public would look at for a moment. 'They are too full of [meat]'. The publication of such music could only benefit you and at the expense of publishing them at your own cost and giving away the copies in every direction. Forgive me speaking so plainly. Even Sir Sterndale Bennett's classical works are in a business point of view almost worthless when compared with Brinley Richards and Blumenthal.[25]

In the event, Parry made up his mind to withhold them from publication until 1873 when Lamborn Cock agreed to take them. To them he also added dedications—the first to Lady Alexandrina Murray (a cousin of Maude's) and the other two to his wife.

By comparison with contemporary German or French achievements, Parry's three songs seem on the whole rather tame. 'More fond than cushat dove' is excessively sentimental and stereotyped, more reminiscent of a Sullivanesque parlour song. 'A poet's song' displays a little more harmonic invention in the brief sidestep into the flattened mediant (at the words 'That made the wild swan pause on her cloud'), but the second verse fails to capitalize on this move, and Parry opts instead for a harmonically trite conclusion which enfeebles the modicum of imagination shown in the first verse. By far the most successful of the three, in terms of design and content, is 'Music' (Example 4). Here one can sense

---

[24] Letter to Lady Maude Herbert, 9 Apr. 1872, ShP.
[25] Letter from Joseph Barnby, 21 May 1872, ShP.

Ex. 4. 'Music' (1872).

the influence of Schumann, particularly in the nature of the harmonic language and the more overt role of the piano (which, in Parry's previous songs had been totally subordinate to the voice). Regarding the latter, one is not only conscious of the consistent use of countermelody in the right hand, but also in the more sophisticated integration of the piano's opening material which begins obliquely on the dominant. It is to this dominant that the last line of the first verse ('Live within the sense they quicken') phrases, avoiding the cliché of cadencing into the tonic and neatly ushering in the return of the piano. Similarly, the cadence is held in abeyance at the end of the second verse ('Love itself shall slumber on') where the voice is left suspended above the supporting dominant pedal. Moreover, the subsequent resolution to the tonic, again left in the main to the piano, is itself somewhat relaxed by the subdominant inflection. The more advanced technique of 'Music', with its more extensively modified verse structure, raises it well above the banal strophic forms of the two other songs (and it may well be that it was the song's more serious constructional approach that deterred Barnby). In addition, it is evident that, through his experience of new music and its devotees, Parry was beginning, albeit very tentatively, to summon the courage to move beyond the blinkered stylistic frontiers established by his forebears. Nevertheless, he would require a more potent catalyst in the form of a forward-looking teacher to provide him with sufficient self-confidence to make such a move.

The disappointment of Barnby's rejection did not distract him from the great happiness brought about by his marriage to Maude which took place on 25 June at St Paul's, Knightsbridge, the venue of so many of their clandestine meetings. '[It was] the supreme event of my life,' he wrote, 'I remember I was not a bit nervous at the marriage, only absorbed in utter happiness. It was rather like a dream.'[26] So euphoric was his mood that he resorted to writing passionate love poetry. While it could in no way be described as artistic, his verses certainly embodied the profound devotion that endured throughout his marriage. It was very much the memory of 'first love' that sustained his relationship, for outwardly his affection for Maude remained unchanged, epitomizing the characteristically unswervable moral stance for which he later became known. Yet, as regards Maude's love for him, there remains a question mark; for as Parry's fame and mastery grew, her interest in his achievements waned, and to maintain her husband's attention she developed valetudinarian tendencies designed effectively to divide his loyalty between her and his work. Seen in this perspective, Lady Herbert's remarks concerning their incompatibility, made initially to bolster her own opposition to the engagement, were to become ominously true.

[26] Diary, May 1873.

PART II

1872–1886
Years of Struggle

5

Dannreuther
Emancipation

THE honeymoon was passed at Wilton. Thereafter visits were paid first to the family at Highnam and later to Lady Herbert at Chesham Place who was especially anxious over the matter of their accommodation in London since Parry had given up his bachelor rooms in Chapel Street. For the moment nothing 'suitable' had been found, so eventually help was secured from one of the Gambier family, who placed at their disposal a house 'St Holme' in the village of Bengeo not far from Hertford which they rented until July 1873. Its location had advantages and disadvantages, however. On the positive side it was a wonderfully peaceful place to live. On the negative side it meant long daily journeys by rail to London which not only prevented him from attending concerts but also affected his health which began to deteriorate alarmingly. His financial situation was also undoubtedly a constant worry. Business at Lloyd's was not proving to be profitable, and, though there was the cushion of Maude's allowance, he was forced to accept a gift of £400 from George Pembroke. His father, who had promised a modest yearly allowance, was unable to help him beyond that, for the Highnam coffers were low and the estate's outlook for the first time seemed uncertain. This Thomas Gambier Parry confessed in a letter to his son in November:

About your Lloyds affairs I am indeed sorry to hear. I had hoped better things, but I had also always hoped that your association with city work would lead to other opportunities—and they may come e'er long. Our family means need replenishing. I cannot blame myself for what I have spent. I know that the establishment of our family, in a way worthy of it, could best be done by all the means I have employed. They have been costly. The only misfortune was that I could not receive better advice when I was very young—but I had no confidence in what little advice was given me, because I knew that it was not based on any real knowledge or personal experience in those who gave it. But indeed it amounted to next to none at all. No-one told me the awful expenses entailed by Landed property—no-one hinted to me that Highnam was simply a ruin. Every farm, every cottage was little better than a ruin—and young as I was, I knew more of farmhouses as things to sketch than things to build!—and when I had got deeply into the mud here, it was too late to withdraw. So I had but one course—to go on, and to [plant] a family in good repute—and with some influence for good—the only end worth living or dying for.

—As for the works of art here, they are not to be thought of in the expenditure—for £3,000 *spread over* all the purchases of a *long series* of years would pay for them—and they have more *than repaid* themselves by the wide interest they have thrown around our home, and the *influence they* have insensibly produced on our family and very many people far beyond it. I have but little regret of what the work of establishing a family, as I have been permitted to do, has cost me—but it has to a certain degree injured the resources of our family income.[1]

Overshadowing this, however, was the news of Clinton who had gone to Natal in South Africa in an attempt to establish himself in business. Initially, believing that the venture might restore him to his senses, Thomas Gambier Parry agreed to provide the necessary capital, only to learn that Clinton had squandered everything and planned to return to England. Still worse was the misery of his wife and children who were regularly subjected to his fits of madness, often violent, brought on by chronic dipsomania:

—And now other things press upon me—I mean especially Clinton's affairs. What is to be done about or for his family I cannot conceive. He simply does nothing—or rather worse than nothing. He said at first that everything was so cheap that we were to advise all poor people to come there—£200 a year was a fortune—of course irrespective of capital to establish any business—but he has got through his £500 a year and two thirds of the *capital* sum of £5,000 which I placed at his disposal to establish his family for their future existence.

I enclose a letter from poor little Florence. What on earth is to be done with Clinton if he comes home in this state? I have told you, as I felt my duty to his next brother, all that has occurred. If Natal is so injurious a climate, why not sell off—and try healthy New Zealand where many gentlemen and ladies are to be found . . . I wrote a reply to Florence's first letter . . . saying what madness it would be to come to England, unless for some extraordinary reason it were *forced* on them. What on earth could Clinton do?—*Here* he would simply drop into intensest idleness, diffuseness—if not worse—unless, if it may have pleased God, which is my only hope and incessant prayer, he be utterly and altogether a changed being. I wish in all that is done or proposed with respect to him and his to have your confidence—and counsel.[2]

The prospect of Clinton's return was indeed a disturbing one since his dipsomania had become so acute that no profession would hold him. In January 1873 Parry received an even more pressing confidential letter from his father:

Do not leave the enclosed about but return them
Dearest Hubert,

The letter wh[ich] I enclose will show you how things stand with poor Clinton. Nothing can be worse. He is in a hospital under the charge of men—because

[1] Letter from Thomas Gambier Parry, 3 Nov. 1872, ShP.   [2] Ibid.

poor Florence can manage him no more. She has been a good and faithful wife to him—hiding all from us as much as possible. He is simply frantic from delirium tremens—with lucid quiet intervals . . . Florence's letter . . . says that he knows his state and desires to place himself under some control, for recovery, when he comes to England—that is what he means—though, as usual, he does not say so in words. He may now be on his way home—and arrive any day. I lose no time to prepare for him. Dr Wood is much interested in our family—and I have felt that it is absolutely necessary to *make a friend* of someone. So I have been for a long time this afternoon with Dr Wood. He enters most kindly and interestedly into the whole case. Of course Fisherton, the place mentioned by Florence, as chosen by Clinton, would be undesirable—close to the Lears, Hamiltons, and Herberts . . . It would be desirable to keep the matter most private—and therefore at a distance. Dr Wood recommended 2 places—and will think it all over and enquire and let me know . . .

But our conversation went far beyond all that. He says that as for Clinton's idea of a 'cruise' home—and back—it is worse than absurd. Finally he said that such cases were incurable—on my expression of anxious remonstrance, he replied 'When did you ever hear of such a case recovering?—He can never go back. It would take several years' discipline to produce any lasting effect—and as for that, suppose he were to return to Natal, he would be sure to go off again—for the only hope is entire tea totalism and that wants such resolution in those cases as you rarely find. The *craving* for alcohol is such as we have no idea of—it is a mania—and is tantamount to incurable.'—Such is the pith, and so far as memory serves, very much the words of what Dr Wood said. He offered to do anything—indeed far more than I would hear of. He will fully enquire and report—the object being to find a fit place for Clinton to go to immediately he sets foot in England . . .[3]

It is clear that Thomas Gambier Parry was now convinced that Clinton's predicament was irrevocable and that he was lost to the family. As a result, the issue of Clinton's rights of inheritance to the estate through primogeniture began to be questioned seriously, for Hubert was now seen as the most natural and responsible heir. When the matter finally surfaced at the end of 1873 it caused Hubert a great deal of heart-searching. For although Clinton's misbehaviour had done much to accelerate their father's decision, it was his outright rejection of Christianity that had clinched matters—and it was on account of this that Parry was forced eventually to declare his own position and thus create an uncomfortable barrier between himself and his father.

Clinton's return was an unwelcome ruction to the relative peace enjoyed at Bengeo. Now that the traumas and uncertainties that had preceded his marriage were over, the weekends could be spent composing and practising the piano. In September he began a series of Schumannesque pieces for violin and piano named *Freundschaftslieder*.

[3] Letter from Thomas Gambier Parry, 7 Jan. 1873, ShP.

An Andante in E major (No. 1) subtitled 'The confidence of Love' and a Nocturne in G minor (No. 3) were completed by the end of October. The Ballade in D minor (No. 4), which under the title bears the inscription 'The poet telleth unto the people a ballad with a somewhat tragical ending', was written at Chesham Place along with an Andante in F (No. 5) in November. The last piece, an Allegro in C minor, was composed shortly afterwards at Bengeo (No. 2, an Allegro in C major may be from the same time, though since the manuscript has not yet been found, it cannot be dated exactly). These, it appears, were written initially for his half-brother Ernest to play. 'The confidence of Love' and the Nocturne were met with great approval from Thomas Gambier Parry: 'I delight in your violin duets—only one bit of one of them I should like *you* to reconsider—we can go through them. Ernest really begins to play very well.'[4] In a similar Schumannesque vein were seven *Charakterbilder* for the piano written for, and dedicated to, Miss Susan Stephenson, an able pianist whom Parry had befriended in London before his marriage, and who had introduced him to Lubeck. The *Charakterbilder*, subtitled 'Seven Ages of Mind' (published by Augener in 1872) show a definite advance in piano technique. The first piece, 'Prelude' (also subtitled 'Dreaming'), in G flat, immediately recalls Schumann's Romance in F sharp, Op. 28 No. 2 both in its choice of key and in the similar inner-voice duet played principally by the two thumbs. No. 2, 'Con energia' (Ex. 5) and No. 3, 'Passion' are reminiscent of Schumann's *Novelletten* while No. 4 and No. 6, which are much more substantial, bring to mind respectively the march rhythms of *Davids-bündler* and the Finale of *Carnaval*. No. 5, 'Espressivo', the shortest of the set, attempts to capture the wistful nature of Schumann's 'innig' style, though Parry's less adventurous harmonic language and phraseology barely raise it above the banal.

During the early part of 1873, with business at Lloyd's proving so uneventful, it is evident that Parry was more impatient than ever to find a teacher both for the piano and for composition. Fixed within his sights was the time when he could abandon his work at Lloyd's altogether, yet it seems that he lacked the courage to approach those teachers whom he thought sympathetic and who might eventually provide him with sufficient opportunities in the musical world from which he could earn a modest living. Brahms's music continued to impress him enormously; the Crystal Palace orchestra and the Philharmonic Society were at last beginning to perform the German's music more regularly, notably the Serenades, Opp. 11 and 16, the Piano Concerto in D minor, and the *Requiem*. The notion then came to Parry that, if he were bold enough,

---

[4] Letter from Thomas Gambier Parry, 3 Nov. 1872, ShP.

Ex. 5. Opening of No. 2 of the *Charakterbilder*; 'Con Energia' (1873).

and if Brahms, or someone of similar stature, took pupils, he could go to Vienna for a period. But whom should he approach and was the idea preposterous? While cogitating on this problem he also continued to take a lively interest in the Wagner Society's newly established series of concerts which began on 19 February with Dannreuther at the helm. As Parry was too shy to confront him, it was left to his two exasperated half-sisters, Beatrice and Linda, to approach the renowned pianist. After their meeting Beatrice wrote to her half-brother hardly able to contain her excitement:

22 Mansfield St

Here goes to tell you (that in my excitement) old boy what ought to please you much!—We have shown your 'Philosopher' as I call it [probably one of the *Charakterbilder*] to Dannreuther. The little man seated himself and looked quietly at the first page, whilst Linda and I almost stopped breathing—then he began. He *did* begin! and played the prelude quite through and then said 'that's good'—then he played the next thing (Linda swares [*sic*] his eyes glistened but I could not see his face) and said 'your brother must be a great pianist: these are very difficult' etc . . . When he came to 'Triumphing' he went at it in great excitement and said in the middle 'this is splendid!' The last thing we told him you had written long ago. When he had played it he said 'very poetical'. I then ventured to tell him that you hope he will give you some lessons as you are coming to live in London: he said 'I could not teach a man who can write this.' He misunderstood me and thought I meant the science of music, but I informed him it was more playing you want. 'Yes I might help his fingers' said he: and then 'there is not a spark of the amateur in this. I shall certainly get them!' So you see how he pooh poohed them!

> Love to Maudie.
> From your affectionate and rejoicing sister,
> M. Beatrice Parry[5]

Parry's reply was naturally exultant:

Sweet Little B.

—I was quite wild with delight over your letter. I never had such encouragement or any so worth having in my life before. I was crazy all day Saturday after it came. And what ducks you and Linda are to take such an interest in my music. It is so nice of you both to be so eager for a good opinion from Dannreuther. I hope he meant what he said and that you did not exaggerate through your dear willingness to make me happy. You need not have any qualms about learning any of them now, need you? after having such an opinion, and I hope you won't find them very hard . . . Was Possie pleased at Dannreuther's opinion?[6]

Dannreuther's positive response straightway provided Parry with the motivation to pursue his goal of taking lessons with Brahms, and it was to Walter Broadwood that he initially made inquiries. Broadwood suggested that Joachim would probably be a useful judge of his compositions and would himself be able to suggest an appropriate teacher in either Vienna or Leipzig with whom Parry might work for a

---

[5] Letter from M. Beatrice Parry, 18 Apr. 1873, ShP.
[6] Letter to M. Beatrice Parry, 21 Apr. 1873; Charles L. Graves, *Hubert Parry* (London, 1926), i. 140.

period. Parry agreed and the latest songs and piano works were promptly dispatched to Joachim—a fact confirmed by Broadwood's reply:

> 3 Queens Gate Gardens
> South Kensington.

My dear Parry,

I don't know whether my hurried note lately was intelligible. What I meant to say was, that Joachim did receive your music—and did look it over. He told me that he was so occupied that he could not find time to get through all his correspondence, but hoped to write to you after again looking through what you sent.

He thought he should do so on the morning of the day he was starting . . . and he was to charge his brother to send back your music after he (Joseph) should have left.

What about the compositions? I said—'Well, they are clever, but Mr Parry should work for a time with a man like for instance Brahms—a first rate man—from what I see I should suppose he has studied with men less familiar with the resources of harmony.—His thoughts are not yet quite free but he has talent'—Words to that effect—You know Joachim is a very sincere man —above paying mere compliments, and speaking his mind unreservedly, because he believes you to be in earnest. I am sure you know too much to believe in unassisted genius—inspiration which is independent of rules, and all that nonsense. Else I should simply refer you to your father and his first conversations with De Wint—which he related to me, last Highnam visit, in such language as no-one else commands—but I suppose all *real* workers have recognized, that only those who have penetrated far—very far—into an art or science, can tell you what are the bye roads to be shunned by those who wish to save precious time—that time during which imagination is still fresh.—Joachim, I am sure, does not doubt but that you would work out the problem for yourself, but he thinks that the quickest way would be to work for a while with one of the big men.—That is the impression I gleaned from what he said.[7]

The very fact that Joachim volunteered the name of Brahms as a potential teacher immediately galvanized Parry into action. He wrote back to Broadwood the same day, urging him to find out whether Brahms took pupils. He received an answer without delay:

My dear Parry,

I will gladly make inquiries of those to whom Brahms is known as to whether he takes pupils. He lives at Vienna or did not long since.

I will first ask Pauer, himself a Viennese—or Straus, who comes here to teach (accompaniment lessons) my two girls. He also is from Vienna and will know Brahms—and then eventually, if you really think anything of the matter, Joachim will, I make no doubt, introduce and recommend you to Brahms. I won't lose more time than I can help, but all this will take some little time if it

---

[7] Letter from Walter Broadwood, 21 Apr. [1873], ShP.

involves a correspondence with Joachim who must now be in Berlin. Straus was here today playing Bach and Schubert with his pupils—and is away for some days at Manchester. Pauer I may find—or I will write to him. He lives close to you (Onslow Square). Anything I can do, I will—Yes, it must be a fine thing to have nothing between your thought and its expression—no mechanical trammels—and you *have* thoughts so I can understand your yearnings after complete freedom.

> Ever truly yours,
> W. S. Broadwood

P.S. Have just written to Pauer without naming you.[8]

Broadwood's closing comments confirmed Parry's restlessness and hunger for the technique he knew was lacking in his present work. In early April he composed two songs, 'An evening cloud' and 'A shadow'. These were not published but during their composition he was planning a 'Lieder cyclus of old-fashioned songs'[9] to be dedicated to McDonnell. The cycle was completed by the beginning of June though the songs had to wait until 1874 before they were published by Lamborn Cock under the title *A Garland of Shakespearian and Other Old-Fashioned Songs* (originally entitled *A Garland of Shakespeare and Other Old-Fashioned Lyrics*). The style of the cycle reflects the growing popularity of ballads and songs written, to quote Parry's own words, 'in old style'.[10] It was a style that was to gain greater currency at the turn of the century in the theatre music of Edward German and most notably in the now forgotten H. Lane Wilson and his *Old English Melodies*. Such a penchant for the bogus-Baroque was often combined with Shakespearian or other 'old' Elizabethan verse as one finds, for example, in Sullivan's Shakespeare songs of 1866 published by Metzler. These songs would have been extremely familiar to Parry, as would the 'mock archaisms' in Sullivan's incidental music to *The Tempest* (1861–4) and *The Merchant of Venice* (1871). The second song of Parry's cycle, 'A Spring Song', sketched in 1872, is pure Sullivan with its cadential clichés and 'quasi-Handelian' language and could easily have formed part of an incidental score or operetta.

Composition in 'the old style' also provoked Parry into the production of a *Suite de Pièces* which reflected his continuing interest in Bach and, more particularly, the Baroque Suite. Certainly this work was sent on to Joachim in Germany together with the latest songs, but news from Joachim was slow in coming and the anticipation brought Parry to breaking-point as he made call after call to Broadwood's home only to

---

[8] Letter from Walter Broadwood, 22 Apr. [1873], ShP.
[9] Diary, 1 June 1873.   [10] Diary, 19 May 1873.

find that no letter had arrived. Joachim's inattention also began to anger Broadwood:

My dear Parry,

I came back just after you had called—sorry to miss you, but heard your song in the evening, sung by Spencer Lyttelton—the *Eton* song I think—very nice. Some of those later ones that I heard at Highnam dwell in my memory.—I am getting savage—no word or line from Joachim—I will fire an arrow that shall 'fetch' the giant.—Joachim though he be, he ought to be ashamed of himself— and *shall*! . . . When I shall have drawn Joachim I will come and see you.

—I feel as did David when adjusting the stone to his sling—I know a vulnerable spot—Only fancy (don't tell) that vast musician prides himself on being—Genteel!! . . .[11]

It was not, however, until nearly the end of June before Joachim finally replied to Broadwood:

> 3, Beethovenstrasse, N.W.
> Thiergarten.
> [Berlin]

My dear Mr Broadwood,

I have asked Miss Arnold [daughter of the Revd Arnold of Rugby and pupil of the Berlin Hochschule] to take the music of Parry to London, and she herewith brings it to you. I like a good deal in it, especially in the Suite, which I think was also composed latest, and though I should not publish it in its present state, as there are weak, and even faulty points amongst many fine ones, Parry ought decidedly to go on writing but—under a master of authority over him, not under a friend who corrects a few errors and tells him that the rest is beautiful. I mean, he ought to have somebody to improve his whole style, and raise his standard altogether, because I think it is worthwhile. I asked Brahms whether he would give lessons to a talented, distinguished amateur, but he declined doing so; still he might (*I* think) take an interest in Mr Parry if he made his acquaintance, and if your friend went to Switzerland this summer, it would be just a good thing to look him up there, or to pay him a visit next winter in Vienna.

Miss Arnold wishes to ask you a question concerning her piano, which you must answer quite independently from you and her being both friends of mine; it has merely to do with the great chieftain of the race of Pianomakers. I mention the question, because I think it will make her less shy of stating her case to know that I wrote about it already. She wishes to know whether by giving back her old Broadwood and paying a certain sum, which you would have to name, she might get a *new* one? Is this feasible?

Excuse the trouble I gave you by keeping Mr Parry's music so long;

[11] Letter from Walter Broadwood, Friday [? May/June 1873], ShP.

remember me to him and especially most kindly to Mrs Broadwood and the two musical daughters, and believe me to be ever faithfully

> yours,
> Joseph Joachim[12]

Brahms's refusal was a source of great disappointment to Broadwood, and the ulterior motive for Joachim's reply also embittered him:

Here at last is Joachim and when put through a strainer the residuum is exactly equivalent to that of my first conversation with him—only that Brahms' refusal is superadded—and alack! our sad mortality. Miss Arnold's desire to get a piano cheap proves to be a motive power stronger than any friendship for me or for you!

But for this, we never should have got an answer; albeit I had latterly aimed my shafts *au défaut de la cuirasse* of the Giant. Well, I am an ignorant outsider, still I am of the stuff of which audiences are made, and I still remember certain songs and the way in which, having first written, you accompanied them—so that I hold strongly that there is music both in your soul and in your fingers.

I suppose I have no sort of right to say anything—but I wonder whether Mozart was *taught* all he knew . . . but may not a careful analysis of the way in which great effects are produced—as seen in the works of great artists—have sufficed to him?

Might it not suffice for you?

Ask your father—he is *my* oracle on all these points—my conviction is, that if you are neither elated nor discouraged by praise or by criticism, you will succeed.[13]

Since his endeavours to secure tuition from Brahms came to nothing, Parry's attentions turned from Vienna towards home and the possibility of obtaining instruction from Dannreuther. All this had to be suspended, however, in order to find time to move house, for on 15 July he and Maude left Bengeo for their new home at 7 Cranley Place in South Kensington. It was a trying ordeal, for prior to their moving in, Lady Herbert had intervened with her own ideas of interior decoration and had irritated Parry greatly: 'Lady Herbert has evidently made a gratuitous muddle of our house arrangements, as she has taken the furnishing etc. into her own hands without any authority from us, and is of course doing it much too grandly for our notions . . . And there is no stopping her.'[14] Lady Herbert's interference was to be a constant source of annoyance. At the same time as the house was being bedecked with, as Parry viewed it, ostentatious furniture and fittings, Lady Herbert was also playing an influential role in steering Mary Herbert towards Romanism and marriage to Friedrich von Hügel, later a prominent

---

[12] Letter from Joseph Joachim to Walter Broadwood, 25 June [1873], ShP.
[13] Letter from Walter Broadwood, 30 June [1873], ShP.
[14] Diary, 20 May, 1873.

Catholic essayist. 'Lady Herbert professes to have no hand in it at all',[15] he wrote sarcastically in his diary and was devastated and not a little angry when he heard the news from George Pembroke that his sister-in-law had at last 'gone over'. Matters were no better at Highnam at the end of July for Clinton and his family had arrived home from South Africa. As Thomas Gambier Parry had predicted, Clinton's fits of drunkenness had increased in his environment of idleness. There were frightening scenes of wildness where, as Parry stated in his diary, he was 'only partially under control',[16] and with the insatiable need for more and more alcohol he resorted increasingly to devious means of procuring it so that those around him found it impossible to stop him. Within a few days the situation had become so intolerable that he had to be sent away to an asylum in Scotland. Relief came in a holiday to north Devon and a few days at Wilton where he befriended the Countess of Radnor, a keen and able amateur musician whose unpretentiousness Parry found a welcome tonic. This friendship was to blossom in 1894 when Lady Radnor persuaded Parry to compose a suite for her amateur string orchestra.

By the end of August Parry was back in London to feast on the new music of which he had been largely deprived since his installation at Bengeo. In his absence the Crystal Palace had celebrated the 45th anniversary of Schubert's death with performances of the Symphony No. 5 (unearthed by George Grove) as well as the little-known overture to *Rosamunde*. Yet more auspicious was the Wagner Society's first concert on 19 February with a programme featuring the Prelude to *Die Meistersinger*, the Prelude and several extracts from *Lohengrin* and Siegmund's 'Liebeslied' from *Die Walküre*. Walter Bache, in his quest to perform Liszt's major works, gave a performance of *Psalm 13* on 28 February which elicited, perhaps surprisingly, a warm reception from the public. Wagner's overtures to *Der Fliegende Holländer* and *Tannhäuser* were also beginning to gain a wider currency in orchestral programmes and the New Philharmonic Society went as far as to give a full concert performance of *Lohengrin*, but the societies had not yet ventured to include any music from *Tristan und Isolde*. The Introduction and *Liebestod* from Act III of *Tristan* formed part of the last Wagner Society concert on 9 May which was conducted from memory by Hans von Bülow who was already attracting vast crowds to his piano recitals and concerto performances with the Philharmonic Society.

Early in November Parry took the opportunity to contact Dannreuther who was in the process of organizing the Wagner Society's new series of concerts. A reply was soon forthcoming:

[15] Diary, 20 May, 1873.   [16] Diary, 21 July, 1873.

12, Orme Square

Dear Mr Parry,

I would have given myself the pleasure of calling upon you if I would have found the time.

May I expect you here at four o'clock on *Tuesday next* (11th next)?

We are old friends from your 'Characterstücke' [*Charakterbilder*]—I shall be delighted to see you—If I can be of any use to you as a pianist I shall be happy— as a writer you do not want any help as far as I can see.

> Believe me
> most truly yours,
> Edward Dannreuther.[17]

Accordingly, Parry went to his first lesson with Dannreuther on 11 November. They concentrated exclusively on piano technique and Parry was overwhelmed by Dannreuther's progressive attitudes:

He is a decided Radical in music, and goes in for the most advanced style and the most liberal interpretation of the old style. He teaches the pianoforte in a thoroughly radical way and dispenses with all the old dogmas of playing with the intention of obtaining the finest effect by any means. He goes to work thoroughly and has set me to work at Tausig's hideous mechanical exercises, and one sonata to work at at a time. If the former don't drive me mad or kill me, I should think he will do me a wonderful lot of good.[18]

Dannreuther's reputation as a performer was perhaps even greater than as a champion of new music. His interpretations of the late Beethoven sonatas were vociferously applauded by Chorley and J. W. Davison, and he was especially well known for his introduction to the English public of new piano concertos at the Crystal Palace including those by Chopin (in F minor) on 11 April 1863, Grieg on 18 April 1874, Liszt (in A) on 21 November 1874, Tchaikovsky (in B flat minor) on 11 March 1876, and by Xaver Scharwenka (in B flat minor) on 27 October 1877. The initiative witnessed in the ambitious programmes of the Wagner Society was also experienced on a more private level with the institution of chamber concerts at his home at 12 Orme Square, Bayswater. These soon became renowned for their progressive programmes in which many new works by contemporary composers (such as Brahms, Scharwenka, Rheinberger, Richard Strauss, and Stanford) were heard in England for the first time. 'There are probably no concerts given in London at which so many novelties are to be heard as at these performances' wrote one critic for the *Musical Times* in 1878. Subsequently they were to provide the ideal platform for an impressive catalogue of chamber works that Parry was to produce over the next seventeen years.

[17] Letter from Edward Dannreuther, 8 Nov. 1873, ShP.
[18] Diary, 11 Nov. 1873.

Many years later Dannreuther was to recall these early lessons with the brightest of his pupils:

Parry has the quickest brain I have ever met with. It works with lightning rapidity. He can do two or three things at the same time. His mental horizon is as vast as the keenness of his intellect. He grasps a thing at once. It becomes imprinted on his brain in a moment and remains there. All his music is conceived this way. The complete design of the composition is fixed in his mind before he puts anything on paper. In this respect he resembles J. S. Bach and Wagner. For him to do anything slowly is out of the question. He writes rapidly: but, be it observed, he revises with the utmost care . . . I was glad to give him that ready encouragement and personal sympathy which he seemed to need. He used to come to my house every Sunday afternoon at two, and stay till four or five—the happiest hours of my life.

From 1872 [actually meaning 1873] I gave Sir Hubert pianoforte lessons for several, I believe seven years. We worked right through Beethoven—not exclusively from a technical standpoint, but rather more as an intellectual study in music. He can play an *Adagio* of Beethoven's very beautifully, his accent is so good and true. As you may imagine, he came to grief now and then in the allegros, when his impetuosity literally outran his technical facility.

. . . Whenever he wants anything from me he thinks nothing of flying over here on his bicycle, and if it were possible I believe that he would ride upstairs right into this room! . . . Once, when calling to see Grove at Macmillan's, he rushed into the Bedford Street shop, shouting, 'Is Mr Gage disengroved?'.[19]

Lessons with Dannreuther continued with fortnightly regularity and soon began to enrich Parry's musical awareness as well as make available new opportunities. Immediately he became more involved in the Wagner Society's activities, enjoying the November concert of the year immensely which consisted of Berlioz's overture *King Lear*, Liszt's *Fantasia on Hungarian Airs*, and excerpts from *Die Meistersinger*. This also facilitated an introduction to Hans von Bülow who was soloist in a performance of Raff's new C minor concerto. The 'Pops' concerts, in which Bülow figured prominently, continued to be a major attraction, particularly for Piano Trios by Beethoven, Schumann's Sonata in A and Trio in F, and especially Brahms's Piano Quartet in A. At the Crystal Palace the novelties mainly consisted of new works by Sterndale Bennett (his overture *A Winter's Tale* and a piano sonata *The Maid of Orleans*), but Bülow's interpretation of Liszt's E flat concerto generated considerable excitement as Parry noted: '[It] was the most astounding exhibition of playing I ever saw or heard.'[20]

Although much of the time spent with Dannreuther was devoted to improving his piano technique, Parry was not prevented from bringing his own works to the lessons, and these were frequently left with his

[19] 'Hubert Parry', *Musical Times* (1 July 1898), 445.   [20] Diary, 12 Dec. 1873.

teacher for more extensive scrutiny. By the beginning of September
Parry had completed a new set of variations on an aria of Bach, playing
them over to Ranald McDonnell. This work, along with an overture,
Vivien, inspired by the second volume of Tennyson's *Idylls of the King* (a
book with which he had been familiar since his early days at Oxford),
were subsequently shown to Dannreuther who used his influence to
persuade Sir August Manns to give the overture a hearing in rehearsal on
21 November at the Crystal Palace. This was a chance to test out various
experiments in orchestration, since it was the first time Parry had tried
his hand at instrumentation for a full-size Romantic orchestra. Later the
same day he recorded his impressions:

I was very nervous lest my want of practice in writing for the orchestra should
make me do something ridiculous, but was rather agreeably surprised at the
effect of the orchestration. The Coda, however, seems too long and not so
effective as I hoped in detail. The performance was rather rough, and neither
Manns nor his band seemed to take much trouble about it . . . My companion at
the rehearsal was Davison the critic, who was voluble with funny stories and
rhymes on well-known professionals and literary men: altogether good fun. He
was very kind about my overture and spoke well to Grove about it.[21]

In spite of Davison's encouragement, Parry did not follow up the
rehearsal with a request for its inclusion in a concert programme, and
since no trace remains of the work, it is quite likely that he destroyed it
sometime later.

Zeal for composition was, however, overshadowed at the end of the
year by the uneasiness of his political conscience. This was initially
thrown into relief during a visit to Wilton in early December where, after
a few pleasant days in the company of Lady Radnor, he found himself
short of patience amongst George Pembroke's aristocratic 'sporting
friends'. 'They despise anything intellectual', he wrote angrily, 'and
spend all their time in shooting, hunting, rabbiting, smoking, and
billiards. Music is naturally utterly condemned.'[22] It was one of the first
indications of his aversion to the indolence, arrogance, and self-
satisfaction paraded by those who enjoyed the privileges of aristocratic
life. Their behaviour eventually provoked a ferocious outburst in his
diary which, one imagines, must have provided an invaluable outlet for
his indignation:

All aristocrats, specimens of the Upper Ten, Society's ornaments! It is enough
to make one a bitter democrat to be long in the company of people brought up in
luxury, utterly without aspirations of any kind, without education of mind, and
as uselessly ornamental and as injuriously bigoted about their 'rights' and
'position' as it is possible to be. Certainly one of the prime conditions of a better-

[21] Ibid. 21 Nov. 1873.   [22] Ibid. [?] Dec. 1873.

constituted Society must be a better and more equal distribution of the luxuries of life and the questionable advantages of wealth and opportunities of pleasure.[23]

This was one of the first occasions when Parry began to express a sympathy for egalitarianism and political reform. There can be no doubt that his distaste of aristocratic imperiousness helped to accelerate his rejection of the Toryism to which both his own family and that of his wife's swore undying allegiance. Disraeli, above all, was the target of one of his most vitriolic attacks—one expressed with an anti-semitic vehemence and sarcasm that were very much a preoccupation of the period:

If ever the gods had occasion to make the heavens reverberate with thunderous laughter, it was when the party of English country gentlemen grovelled in obeisance before this utterly fortuitous fetish—the Semitic Disraeli. He was everything that the typical country gentleman holds most pernicious; everything that the atmosphere of simple honesty, which is the greatest asset of this class, would repudiate. He was cunning, crafty, mean, unscrupulous, artificial, a poser, a juggler with words, a fantastic braggart, a worshipper of tinsel and pasteboard, superficial, vulgar, insincere, venomous when he thought it was safe to bully, glossy and fawning when he thought it served his shallow aims. He had the Semitic gift of mere technique in the fullest measure, and he used it to hoodwink and cajole the unintelligent, the simpletons, the party folks who were glad of a man with such supreme facility of diction to express their shibboleths, their hatreds and their interests. He could pretend to be moved by the most exalted sentiments; he could present the shallowest fallacies in terms that sounded like noble truths; he could bewilder adverse experts in the subjects he discussed by the appearance of deep conviction, and dazzle the minds of the ignorant with high-flown rhetoric.

Aversion to Disraeli, however, was only one of several catalysts on the way to radicalism. Acquaintance with recent provocative texts such as Arnold's *Literature and Dogma*, Strauss's *Das Leben Jesu*, Samuel Butler's *Erewhon* (inspired by the evolutionary theories of Darwin), a number of George Eliot's 'evolutionist' novels, and the writings of Swinburne also undoubtedly strengthened his objections to conventional Victorian values and religion. This force of argument drew him rapidly towards Liberalism, and, caught up in the tide of Victorian progressive thinking, he found it necessary, perhaps inevitably, to renounce orthodox Christian beliefs.

As much a part of this rejection of Christianity was his increasing repugnance for organized religion *per se*. It is no surprise therefore that, with regard to the latter, he developed a violent loathing for Romanism. But Romanism was not the only source of irritation, for the intransigence

[23] Diary, [?] Dec. 1873.

and pedantry of High Church advocates infuriated him in a similar way. Lady Herbert's pious behaviour frequently roused his ire on the subject:

She [Lady Herbert] makes enough fuss about religion and goes to church enough to do for a dozen people . . . For my part I think a man more likely to have a really high moral standard and to be less tainted with the meaner vices of the age if he doesn't go to church or make a fuss about his religion. However, the said High Church enthusiasts are saturated with religious sentimentalism and the theory that nothing is worth doing though even so heroic or unselfish an action if it is not done "through Jesus Christ" (whatever that may mean) that they are impregnable to the most commonplace arguments.[24]

Romanism proved to be a constant barrier in Parry's relationship with his mother-in-law, but he was also aware that a similar barrier might exist between himself and his father should he break the news of his repudiation of the family religion. Yet soon the situation demanded such a declaration as Parry explained in his diary:

A few days before I left London I sent Possie [his father] a statement (as short as I could make it) of my opinions, and history of them; explaining how I had come by them and reminding him that it was not of wilfulness or carelessness as he himself might know if he would. My reason for doing so was that he had often hinted to me his intention of leaving Highnam to me because Clin had 'thrown overboard his religion etc.' So I told him that I had done the same, as gently as I could, in order that he might not do Clin an injustice through a false impression of me.[25]

The statement of his beliefs took many pages of detailed argument and explanation in an attempt to convince his father that his decision had been a gradual one, formed over several years. Its tone was fervent and courageous, and outlines for us in more concrete terms the nature of his unorthodoxy, and, moreover, his own profound sense of justice and morality:

I fear that without an explanation from me on the subject you might act upon your suppositions and thereby do Clin an injustice. There are other reasons which need not be mentioned, one of the least of them is my own feeling that it is better and healthier to be abused for what one really is than praised for what one is not. You know very well, and I think there is none that will deny it that as a boy I was of a very religious turn of mind. I say as a boy because I think that at that period my religion was of a kind to be more generally recognized, and not because I became less so in reality as I grew older. I think that even you yourself could hardly have wished me to be more High Church, more 'full of faith', or more of a church-goer than I was. I believed everything I was told, and was really very deeply impressed with the exercises of religion, and with all which I believed of my earnestness . . . However, by accident I suppose (if it was by design it was the more honourable to those who educated me) a part of religious

---

[24] Diary, Dec. 1873.　　　[25] Ibid.

training, which is [here] so generally impressed upon young minds in religious families, was left out. I mean the indoctrination of the idea that in all points when reason proved one thing and revelation said another, the former was seen to be leading astray, and it would be wicked to doubt the so called revelation. I consequently brought my reason to bear upon questions of faith very early, though at first only in a modified form and without any idea that my faith would thereby be in any degree changed: for I remember well thinking on the contrary that my faith would thereby be strengthened and made more worthy. It was in this manner and without any idea of heterodoxy that I ceased to believe in the theory that we are all punished for the sin of our first progenitors, as altogether contradictory to the theory that God was good and beautiful; as I conceived very early that no being called good would punish other beings whom he himself brought into existence for sins they had nothing to do with. Along with this naturally went the idea of Hell—which I early thought an unfit conception for any rational being.[26]

Hand in hand with his rejection of Hell went that of the Creation and, as he described it, Genesis's 'early history of mankind' which he dismissed as interesting, but nevertheless, the 'poetical conceptions of a barbaric people in a very early stage of development'. He further argued that the source of his disbelief emanated from science (from his knowledge of Darwin) and most importantly through the application of Reason (an approach affirmed through his reading of Butler's *The Fair Haven*—an elaborate and cynical attack on the dogma of the Resurrection). Parry then turned his attention from the divinity of scripture to questions of organized religion, the power of the Church, and the formation of dogma:

It was not till I was reading history at Oxford and had done what logic was required . . . that I began to consider the value of modern dogmas and theology. I was struck first with the history of the wrangling and fighting which went on in the earliest ages of the Church. The very unsaintly and acrimonious bitterness which the fathers used to one another in discussing dogmas. And the extraordinary and often questionable manner in which such dogmas were fixed, and how often they changed, and how much it seemed a matter of chance what we hold now.

This historical knowledge of doctrinal evolution subsequently resulted in a total evaporation of trust in those who originally imparted the bases of Christian teaching to him, not least because they attempted to instil in him a sense of hatred for those who did not subscribe to their theology. 'And you will readily appreciate', he wrote, 'that when my former respect for them was gone, and when those whom I looked upon as my Popes in matters of doctrine and trusted to for real religious truth had lost their hold on me, my belief was left face to face with my reason.' The

[26] Letter to Thomas Gambier Parry, 15 Dec. 1873, ShP.

last part of the letter contains the very heart of Parry's religious belief in which he declares his essentially humanitarian position with regard to the nature of God, organized religion, and the Eucharist, his total abhorrence of dogmatic theory, and, perhaps most important of all, the absolute necessity of personal integrity:

No-one can be the exclusive depository of infallible truth . . . Some there are who have been so brought up and are so constituted that they could not think otherwise than as they have been educated. I cannot blame them. Let them not blame me. I have done what I earnestly believe to be right and no-one has either reason or even right to be unhappy that my conclusions are not the same as theirs. Here is the sum of them.

  I believe in religion, but one so pure and simple that its chiefest maxim is 'strive after virtue for itself'. I believe that the theological part of Christianity and all dogmas connected with it are a mistake. I believe in Communion as one of the best formalities of religion possible—because it is the 'Eucharist'—that which reminds us of our mutual dependence on one another and our mutual duties of love and affection to one another. And I think that if people had that idea when they went instead of some dogmatic theory or some extravagant feeling of sentiment, there would be less sorrow and distress in the world. I believe in God, and I believe that he is good, and I think that is the one form of 'faith' that will always stick to me. Beyond that I believe we can know nothing of him . . . The path I have chosen is a harder one to tread than the paths of those who live in the bosom of the Church, and think without reflection or examination the same as do most of those they love. Perhaps too it is easier to be good and virtuous in the Church than out of it, for ordinary mortals. I cannot help that. I cannot believe a thing because I should live easier for believing it. What is truth to me is truth for itself and for no other reason.

In spite of Parry's honourable scruples with regard to his brother— qualities which, in fairness, his father duly recognized—it was inevitable that Thomas Gambier Parry's reaction would be one of complete astonishment and dismay. The reply when it came, was an anguished one mixed with feelings of grief, despair, anger, and some hurtful accusations. 'My eldest son has from early days led a life too grievous to bear exposure . . .', he wrote dolefully, 'I had therefore set my heart— and based my hopes on you—and now even *you* appear to fail me. It is too deep a grief—you, my loved Hubert, cast off the Lord who bought you!'[27] For Thomas Gambier Parry there was also the horror of his son's action becoming public knowledge: 'I am sure that on second thoughts you could not wish *me* (by the circulation of that painful letter) to be the instrument employed by you to publish to our relations and friends that my loved son Hubert is an Infidel!' Parry was also charged with the duty of withholding his beliefs from his brothers and sisters lest he should

---

[27] Letter from Thomas Gambier Parry, 19 Dec. 1873, ShP.

'disturb their pure and holy principles of "the Faith"', and more invidiously, his father hoped that 'this deadliest Poison of the Pride of modern life' might somehow be kept from Maude. Parry's reaction was one of pain and resentment for it was not only irrational but antirational that his father, through the excesses of his own creed, should ascribe such disbelief to pride and intellect. But the reality that his position as a sceptic would be one of hopeless antagonism towards his father was one that had to be faced with regret and equanimity.

Though Dannreuther's musical companionship proved edifying and rewarding in the first few months of 1874, the new year failed to bring any financial breakthrough at Lloyd's. On returning to the city Parry 'found Ranald very melancholy . . . our money is at a very low ebb,'[28] and he was obliged to resort to his wife's income to keep body and soul together. Their home in Cranley Place was expensive to run and largely maintained at the whim of Lady Herbert who wanted to ensure that Maude was not suffering a cut in living standards. But by May the financial situation had worsened to the point where anxiety, overwork, and heart trouble forced him to write to his father in the hope of a small allowance. His father's response raised doubts about the incompatability of his son's marriage and the attitudes of his in-laws:

I am grieved at your heart trouble, in the family reflections on you and your position—I always, as soon as I first heard of your engagement, dreaded this as inevitable. Your most sweet and precious wife is true and unswerving. She made her resolve, and but girl as she was, she knew that she had resolved to abide by any circumstances, though the perfect luxury of life, ease, freedom, means, and all else that she was educated, or not educated in, little fitted her to realize the future—but the family is not Maude—Pembroke is a noble fellow—and has the making of a still nobler one—but he cannot realize your or our position. By plunging into such a family you have accepted great difficulties, humiliations, and great pains. They will and *must* come—I always felt it. I am greatly against such marriages as yours in general. The family is sure to be hard—vexed that one of its members should be brought into a sphere of anxieties to which she was not born . . . How you get on in that pet play thing baby house of yours I cannot imagine. Things must cost money—and where yours comes from I know not.[29]

Money, or rather the lack of it, proved to be source of bitterness which the Herberts had no reservations in expressing. Maude's health remained a cause for concern and the London climate, particularly during the winter, did not suit her which frequently resulted in visits to Wilton or to other parts of the country to escape the city atmosphere.

Only the Crystal Palace and Wagner Society concerts seemed to help Parry overcome periods of both depression and, in the absence of his

---

[28] Diary, 14 Jan. 1874.   [29] Letter from Thomas Gambier Parry, 18 May 1874, ShP.

wife, severe loneliness. Memories of his former teacher, Pierson (who had died in Leipzig the previous year), were recalled when Manns conducted the first London performance of the Shakespearian overture *As You Like It*, but it failed to make any impression. Other interesting novelties included new symphonies by Prout and Macfarren, Brahms's *Variations on a Theme of Haydn* and the first performance in England of his *Schicksalslied* which, though indifferently performed at the Crystal Palace, was cordially received. Dannreuther continued to conduct extracts from *Die Meistersinger*, *Lohengrin*, *Der Fliegende Holländer*, Gluck's overture to *Iphigénie en Aulide* (to which Wagner had provided a new coda to replace the one already supplied by Mozart), and in the last concert on 13 May, as a climax to the series, music from *Tristan und Isolde* dominated the programme. As a pianist Dannreuther's talent and enterprise were given over to the first performance in England of Grieg's Piano Concerto, and he was already in the process of preparing the solo part of Liszt's Concerto in A for a Crystal Palace concert in November which was the focus of attention during lessons with Parry in May and June. In the latter part of May, in order to gain some relief from the demoralizingly 'low exchequer' at Lloyd's, he and McDonnell took a holiday to the Channel Islands (though without Maude who would not travel by sea for health reasons). This restored his energy and morale. Refreshed he resumed lessons with Dannreuther who, conscious that his pupil's understanding of the mainstream German symphonic and operatic repertoire needed to be increased, advised him to study German with the distinguished scholar Friedrich Althaus. This acquaintance later proved useful during the preparation of the libretto of Parry's abortive opera *Guenever*, when, to assist Stanford's attempts to secure its performance in Germany, Althaus agreed to provide a German translation.

The climax of this period of concert-going occurred at the end of June when, at a Philharmonic concert, he heard Brahms's Serenade in A, Op. 16. 'I never was so delighted with anything at first hearing as at the Serenade',[30] he wrote in his diary. The unusual scoring for wind and lower strings (a combination which baffled the critics) thrilled him and he immediately set about obtaining a score. Much in the same way as Bach had gained a knowledge of contemporary music, Parry learnt to appreciate Brahms's Serenade by copying out every detail of the score meticulously. From July until September he and Maude passed the time at Mount Merrion. Here he continued to copy out Brahms and also extended his study of works to Mozart's *Don Giovanni* and Cherubini's *Médée*. Yet though he may have learnt from the theatrical immediacy of

[30] Diary, [29 June] 1874.

both Mozart and Cherubini, not to mention the ravishing orchestration contained in both works, it was ultimately to the new intellectualism of Brahms that Parry was drawn. In August his former Oxford friend, Hugh Montgomery, came down to Mount Merrion for a few days. Montgomery was a fine amateur singer who had introduced Schumann's *Lieder* to Parry in the late 1860s. On this occasion however, Parry insisted that they play through a number of Brahms's songs which he had become acquainted with earlier in the year. He had been greatly impressed by Brahms's elusive simplicity combined with a strong intellectual tonal construction and progressive sense of phraseology, with the result that he was moved to compose two settings (with Montgomery in mind) of Shakespeare's Sonnets. Parry did not state in his diary the titles of these two songs, but we know that one of them was a setting of Sonnet XXXII, 'If thou survive my well-contented day', a version whose manuscript is dated 'Mount Merrion, Aug. 1 1874', and the second was an early version of Sonnet LXXI, 'No longer mourn for me when I am dead', which was subject to extensive alterations in 1875 after he began lessons with Sir George Macfarren.

In September Parry returned to England in order to attend the Gloucester Festival where he met Grove and Stainer. But perhaps the most memorable experience was a brief meeting with Herbert Spencer, the founder of evolutionary philosophy. Spencer's first really controversial work, *First Principles*, written after reading Darwin, had left a profound affect on Parry which strengthened after reading *The Study of Sociology* published in 1873. According to Parry's diary, Spencer also succeeded in provoking anger from those around him by refusing to stand during the 'Hallelujah' chorus which was the common custom. From Highnam they were obliged to make a short visit to Wilton to pay their respects to George Pembroke and his new wife, Lady Gertrude (née Talbot). By all accounts, the marriage had caused widespread distress since Gertrude was ten years older than her husband and there was talk of congenital madness in her family.

After the trials of Wilton society, Parry was eager to get back to London in order to resume his lessons with Dannreuther and for the new concert season. Business at Lloyd's was, as usual, uneventful, but the productive work carried out in Ireland had renewed his desire to compose again. Shakespeare's Sonnets continued to attract him and, with his head already brimming with Schumann and Brahms *Lieder*, he became interested in the possibility of setting them in German. At the end of September he wrote to his friend Gosselin, who now worked in the British Embassy in Berlin, asking him to send a copy of the German translation. Gosselin obliged with the recent translations by Bodenstedt:

British Embassy
Berlin

My dear Hubert,

Herewith come the Sonnets in German dress. I have not had time to look into them, but they tell me the translation is the best yet published. Anyhow, from the preface I see that the man admires the great Shakespeare which is more than can be said of all his compatriots. A certain school of ultra Teutons have lately been running him down . . . All this of course makes me very angry, and long to punch their heads. For the present it seems impossible for them to find any limits for their self-glorification or for their love of running down everything not 'ächtes [*sic*] Deutsch'—drunk with success—that's what they are.[31]

By mid-November Parry was at work on a setting of Sonnet XXIX in the German ('Wenn ich, von Gott und Menschen übersehn'), 'as I found I could get along better with the German than the English words "When in disgrace". Wrote it mostly very fast. Finished it on Friday', he wrote.[32] As yet Parry's song-writing efforts had been inauspicious, and, largely for financial reasons and at the instigation of Lamborn Cock, his artistic parameters had been confined to the sentimental gestures of the 'drawing-room style', even though some of the results, such as *Music*, had been moderately sophisticated. It was a frame of mind still very much in evidence in *Twilight*, a setting of another text by his brother-in-law. The three Shakespeare Sonnets, however, marked a decisive departure away from stylistic inertia for it is clear from 'When in disgrace' and 'No longer mourn for me' that, though they show a degree of linguistic indecision (the former to Schumann, the latter to Brahms), Parry had at last decided to forsake the whims of his publishers.

That Parry found the German text more congenial in 'When in disgrace' (Ex. 6) is apparent from the vocal line which, being essentially independent of the syncopated accompaniment, is certainly more motivically unified than its English counterpart. This can be observed in the way Parry maintains the motive of bars 3–4 at the beginning of line three (bars 11–12). Similarly the motive and rhythm at the beginning of line two is maintained in line five (cf. bars 7 and 19). These two ideas are then neatly conflated at the climax of the central section (bar 30), before they are once more separated with the return of the opening material. It is particularly with the move to E major (bar 39) that the motivic workings of the English version are noticeably less sufficient. Having already restated the material of line one, Parry reiterates the opening of line two, music shared note for note by both versions. But whereas we are already familiar with this motive from previous material in the German vocal line (i.e. lines two and five), it is less emphatic in the

---

[31] Letter from Martin Le M. Gosselin, 3 Oct. 1874, ShP.
[32] Diary, 19 Nov. 1874.

Ex. 6. Opening of 'When in disgrace' ('*Wenn ich von Gott*') (1874).

English version, where, in both cases, Parry has altered the essential rhythm. One also senses a greater ease with the German in the frequency of feminine cadences which are well suited to words such as 'erscheine' (bars 9–10), 'beweine' (bars 17–18), 'hochgeboren' (bars 24–25), and 'erkoren' (bars 32–33), and which are less satisfactory when sung in single English syllables (e.g. 'fate'—bar 18, and 'least'—bar 33). At the beginning of the final E major section there is evidence that Parry made an effort to lend pathos to the change of mood by introducing textual repetition for the first time ('Doch denk ich Dein, ist aller Gram besiegt'), and in the resulting musical sequence added poignance is lent to the repetition of 'Dein' (bar 44) with the D ♮. This exact transposition is not included as part of the English vocal line, though the effect persists with the repeat in the piano at the higher registral level (a particularly Schumannesque effect). The repetition of line ten is then mirrored in the similar treatment of the last line of the song.

The Sonnet also provides an example of an unusual poetical form (i.e. twelve lines rhyming *abab cdcd efef* with a final rhyming couplet) being manipulated into a well-modified ternary structure in which, as already stated, line nine is used to restate material from the opening before a transformed line ten is taken up in the tonic major as the beginning of an extended coda (A 1–18; B 19–34; A + coda 35–end)—this form was emulated in a much later setting of Sonnet CIX, 'O never say that I was false of heart' (English Lyrics Set VII).

At some time after receiving the German translation of the Sonnets from Gosselin, Parry evidently considered the notion of a dual text for 'No longer mourn for me', since the manuscript clearly shows a 'sketched' German text either above or below the vocal staff. What is clear from this, however, is that the song was initially conceived for the English text, unlike 'When in disgrace'. The predominant influence is unequivocally Brahms, not only in the beautifully projected vocal phrases (e.g. bars 7–11 'Then you shall hear the surly sullen bell Give warning to the world that I am fled') but also in the manner in which Parry deliberately delays the cadence into F minor until the very end (bar 70), a technique prevalent in many of Brahms's finest songs such as 'Die Mainacht', Op. 43 No. 2. Parry's assimilation of this technique is particularly evident at the end of the fourth line of text where a perfect cadence seems the obvious platitude, but in true Brahmsian fashion, he prolongs the dominant, neatly returning to the introductory material which was itself characterized by an extended dominant pedal (cf. bars 1–5). Thereafter each section of text, which involves a fresh tonal deviation, phrases to the dominant to be followed by the persistent opening figure. Most telling of all is the last, more agitated phrase ('Lest the wise world should look into your moan'), which, temporarily shifting to duple metre and the major mode, enigmatically concludes as the last words are chillingly imbued with a sense of uncertainty as the voice is left suspended above the dominant pedal. The piano subsequently is left with the final cadence in which memories of the main thematic ideas are incorporated—a device Parry surely gleaned from Schumann.

In the last months of 1874 Parry's attendance of concerts in London reached fever pitch. At the Crystal Palace Manns continued to explore Pierson's little-known orchestral music with a performance of *Romeo and Juliet* which Parry, somewhat disorientated by his former teacher's idiosyncracies, described as 'thoroughly original but utterly without form and consequently puzzling at first hearing. But certainly a fine work and to me preferable to the "As you like it" we had last year [*sic*].'[33] Bülow continued to give recitals at the 'Pops' concerts which primarily featured the sonatas and chamber works of Beethoven. But many other compositions by Schubert, Schumann, Mendelssohn, Raff, and Rheinberger contributed to wide and varied programmes which, together with the commencement of Dannreuther's Orme Square gatherings, renewed his fascination for chamber music so that by the end of November he was sketching ideas for a violin sonata in D minor. Most of his time, however, was devoted to piano practice. Liszt's Piano Concerto in A, which received its first English performance with Dannreuther on 21 November, was the first of several major concertos which Parry was made to learn. Yet for all Dannreuther's enthusiasm he found Liszt's work disagreeable mainly because he felt that the musical content in no way matched the high degree of histrionic gestures, though its cyclic structure intrigued him greatly. Parry was subsequently much heartened by Dannreuther's compliments concerning his progress as a pianist. The process of learning was not merely practical for some lessons were passed entirely in analytical discussion which shed an invaluable light on questions of formal and tonal organization. These were the first significant steps towards the emancipation from the limited horizons of his formative musical education and they affirm the claim that Parry later made that Dannreuther taught him more about the art of composition than anyone else.

The positive influence of Dannreuther's teaching methods soon led Parry to neglect his duties at Lloyd's. Less and less time was spent in the city and little regard was given to the already depressed state of finances which McDonnell was in the habit of reporting. More pressing, however, was his wife's constitution which had been progressively deteriorating since settling in London the year before: 'Poor little Maudie is very low. It is heartbreaking to see her. She is always so tired . . . and sad. And so dreadfully depressed about herself. I don't know what to do. It has been going on so long that I am beginning to get frightened.'[34] Yet Maude's poor health cannot be reconciled with the periods of considerable activity generated by her enthusiasm for the 'Women's Rights' movement. During November both she and her

[33] Diary, 7 Nov. 1874. Here Parry actually refers to Pierson's *As You Like It* which he heard in early 1874, and not in 1873.
[34] Diary, 5 Dec. 1874.

husband had dined regularly with Rhoda and Agnes Garrett who, besides being renowned for their skills in interior decoration, were both fervent advocates of the cause. Parry, in particular, much enjoyed their company, for he responded to their lack of affectation, their humour, and their genuine interest in the humanities. Maude's delicate condition appeared to evaporate as she became more politically motivated. She was always able to summon the energy to attend the meetings of 'Women's Rights' in order to hear speeches made by the Garretts. But without such a stimulus she became restive, depressed, and, as was so often the case with many unoccupied aristocratic Victorian women, she became obsessed with her own health. This had the added effect of feeding Parry's natural concern for her welfare and consequently made her the centre of his attention. Furthermore, the misrepresentations and misinterpretations of Maude's condition by Lady Herbert led to the surfacing of old recriminations from Lord Pembroke:

Two long conversations with George, in which he pointed out to me as mildly as he could that he considered me a pauper and dependent on him. That I never took any trouble to make money and had deceived the family by the expectations I had raised before we married. That . . . I was indolent and lived upon Maude's money instead of making it as he said I ought . . . He thinks it would be very easy to make money and considers that it is merely my laziness which prevents my doing so. He thinks Lloyds is no work at all, and very dangerous—indeed mere gambling.[35]

In a desperate attempt to resolve the situation, Parry seriously considered the prospect of leaving London and building a house in rural surroundings where his ailing wife could escape from the oppressive climate of the capital. His father's reply was not encouraging for the state of finances at Highnam was at a low ebb; besides which, Thomas Gambier Parry was anxious that his son should continue to weather the storm at Lloyd's:

I do not see any way to assist you in any such scheme as you propose. I am indeed sorry to hear that dear Maude's health requires you seriously to think of leaving London—but as for buying land and building a house, you write as one of a very far larger range of means than our family possesses. I have not £5000 available anyhow for you—and indeed if I had, I shd. need to be very far better informed of the scheme before I could at all feel justified in aiding you towards it. Your plan has many sides to it. You only present the sunny one of a charming little earthly paradise. I wish you could—or could have—got more into the acquaintance of some of the leading men in the city, with whom . . . your introduction would most assuredly have opened ways to the improvement of your finances.[36]

---

[35] Ibid. Diary, [Jan.] 1875.
[36] Letter from Thomas Gambier Parry, 1 Apr. 1875, ShP.

If only as a temporary measure, Parry decided to let the house at Cranley Place and rent a house in Ottershaw (belonging to his friend Robert Oldham), not far north of Woking, where he and his wife resided between March and October. It was far enough away from London's unhealthy air, but near enough to make regular visits for concerts, Dannreuther, and his nucleus of close friends. Furthermore, being removed from the vicissitudes of city life, Maude could take every opportunity to rest since by May she was one month pregnant with their first child.

In spite of the onerous domestic pressures, Parry remained doggedly determined in his efforts to improve his technique and to maintain contact with contemporary thinking. With regard to the latter, Hugh Montgomery invited him to his home in Bayswater together with other old Oxford companions, Eddie Hamilton, Frank Pownall, William Hoare, and the artist Pepys Cockerell to participate in the informal 'Essay and Discussion Club' which, over dinner, concentrated on modern questions of morality, politics, and philosophy. Meetings also took place in Hoare's rooms in Clarges Street and here Lord Pembroke, Robin Benson, and Spencer Lyttelton also participated in animated debates on Bentham's utilitarianism, art, psychology, and sociology— topics for whom their great high priest was Herbert Spencer. As Pepys Cockerell recalled, the gatherings created an enduring intimacy and all members of the club remained close friends throughout their lives and subsequently wrote to each other with a personal frankness and candour. 'Hubert', Cockerell recollected, 'was well informed, impetuous, hardly calm enough to express himself with balance.'[37] But serious debate did not absorb all their time together. Invariably the meetings concluded with music, Parry improvising at the piano, and Montgomery singing Parry's Shakespeare Sonnets and Lieder by Schumann and Brahms.

The popularity of Brahms in London, particularly through his orchestral music, was growing rapidly, as is borne out by the more regular appearance of his works in the Crystal Palace programmes. On 29 January the *Variations on a Theme of Haydn* left a deep impression: 'There is in them a dignity and depth, individuality and ingenuity, earnestness and fine beauty, with discretion and wonderfully calculated effectiveness of the different kinds of sentiment and feeling set off against one another.'[38] Parry had been to the concert with his friend, the art connoisseur Robin Benson, who, in mentioning the fortunes of a number of British composers fortunate enough to continue their studies abroad, rudely reminded him of the lost opportunity of studying with Brahms in Vienna. 'He told me a great deal about rising men in the art,

[37] Graves, *Hubert Parry*, i. 152.   [38] Diary, 29 Jan. 1875.

whom I had not heard of,' Parry wrote in his diary, 'especially the new organist of Trinity College, Cambridge, called I think Stanford, who according to him must be a tip-top man and is studying energetically in Germany with Reinecke.'[39] Parry's study of Beethoven's C minor concerto soon prompted Dannreuther to suggest a closer scrutiny of Mozart's works for piano: 'He is going to put me in a straitjacket', Parry wrote, 'and make me play some Mozart, as he says the elements of that style have been altogether neglected in my education—which is certainly true.'[40] Dannreuther much approved of the Sonnet 'When in disgrace', but though he was encouraged by his pupil's progress, he felt uneasy in the role of compositional advisor and recommended Parry to seek the opinions of a more established composer. Trusting Dannreuther's counsel, Parry decided to dispatch his three Shakespeare Sonnets to George Macfarren who, as a longstanding professor at the Royal Academy of Music, commanded a healthy respect from his contemporaries as one of the country's most distinguished composer–teachers.

While awaiting Macfarren's verdict he took the chance to hear Mlle Krebs play Brahms's Piano Concerto in D minor at the Crystal Palace on 20 February. The experience was overwhelming:

quite an astonishing performance. It is horribly difficult and she played it with perfect mastery and the most unflagging vigour. It is quite extraordinary to see so slight a creature go through such an amount of muscular exertion with such ease. It is a superb work. Fierce and vehement. Joachim told us that Brahms wrote it when they were living together—and he thought that the reason of its peculiarly angry and passionate character was mostly that Brahms was so much upset by the news of Schumann's madness which came to them just about that time.[41]

His elation was, however, abated by a visit from Hugh Montgomery who came the following day with word of Macfarren's reactions to the Sonnets. The news was not good: 'what distressed me very much', he wrote, '[was] that Macfarren finds great fault with my 3 Shakespearean Sonnets on the score of unwarrantable progressions and unauthenticated treatment of form. I hope to get at him to make him explain.'[42] On 7 March Parry took his first lesson from Macfarren; it was to be a stormy relationship for Macfarren was a disciple of Beethoven and Mendelssohn and therefore failed to share his pupil's interest in Schumann and Wagner, though he did warm to the classical aspirations of Brahms. Parry's opinion of Macfarren as a composer varied from praise of his oratorio *John the Baptist* to more disparaging criticism of the instrumental works such as the Violin Concerto, which, in spite of its 'exceptionally good workmanship', was 'not very interesting'.[43] Their early sessions

[39] Ibid.   [40] Ibid. [Jan.] 1875.   [41] Ibid. [20] Feb. 1875.
[42] Ibid. [21] Feb. 1875.   [43] Ibid. 3 Apr. 1875.

were confined to strict counterpoint and the study of Ouseley's primer *Musical Form and Composition*. By the beginning of April, however, they had moved on to Parry's Shakespeare Sonnets and the Bach variations. To the latter were added a new variation (bringing the total to fifteen) and a finale of which Macfarren highly approved; the whole work was subsequently dedicated to him. But the Sonnets were the source of more serious disagreement as they came to blows over matters of style and harmonic syntax: 'He was very liberal about the "If thou survive" sonnet. I fought about one passage he thought wrong, and we went back to it over and over again, and at least he confessed he had misunderstood it.'[44] But Macfarren's doctrinaire attitude to harmony could not be reconciled to the more experimental language of 'When in disgrace':[45]

We fought about a progression which he held to be inadmissible. I could see he was very angry; but he was wonderfully patient. I held that a chord which was made up of notes which are in the minor scale is always legitimate. He said that the common chord of the minor third (i.e. of the relative major) was inadmissable in a progression from the key to its dominant e.g.

The offending passage was between bars 5 and 10 (see Ex. 6), though it appears from the published edition that Parry eventually acceded to Macfarren's demands since the bass note D (bar 8) is made to form part of a diminished seventh and not a chord of IIIc. Changes were also made to 'No longer mourn for me' with some reluctance, and gradually Parry became more and more impatient with his teacher's inability to suggest more inventive alternatives; yet he also admired the 'kind old man's' intuition. This curious mixture of respect and frustration persisted as is evident from comments made after Macfarren had looked at the Violin Sonata in D minor: 'His criticisms are wonderfully acute,' he wrote, 'but the alterations he suggests are equally or more dry and unimaginative.'[46]

The first movement of the Violin Sonata in D minor clearly shows a dilemma between the traditionalist approach favoured by Macfarren and the more contemporary attitude of Dannreuther. The final version of the first movement exists in a manuscript separate from that of the whole work, necessitated by an entire revision of its tonal and internal proportions. Originally a form comparable with those of his two early quartets had been contemplated: the modest exposition of 59 bars has a conventional I (D minor)—III (F major) plan; the development,

[44] Diary, 7 Apr. 1875.   [45] Ibid. 20 Apr. 1875.   [46] Ibid. 6 May 1875.

comprising a mere 37 bars, derives its material from the short falling
melodic cell of the two-bar 'adagio' introduction (Ex. 7*a*), accompanied
by a syncopation (Ex. 7*b*), the combination of which sounds strikingly
reminiscent of Schumann's Piano Quintet which Parry had heard in
February. The development's obsession with the above-mentioned
melodic fragment is directed towards its final bars which are themselves
a more forceful repetition of the 'adagio' opening. This in turn heralds
the recapitulation. Parry's dissatisfaction with the movement in this state
is emphasized by the pages of superfluous developmental sketches that
are crossed out in the manuscript. Evidently his initial conception was of
a small movement of classical proportions, with a noticeably short
development. The revised version, however, breaks new ground by
using a third relationship for the first time: D minor/B flat major.
Unquestionably aware of the use and potential of similar relationships in

Ex. 7. Violin Sonata in D minor (1875), first movement. *a* opening;
b development of introductory figure.

Schubert and Brahms, Parry attempted at last to expand his tonal horizons. In addition he extended the exposition, adding a new codetta for the expositional repeat; more significantly, a larger part of the sketch material, formerly discarded, was incorporated into an enormously protracted development of 121 bars.

If the first movement of the D minor sonata shows an advance through its expansion of a tonal and structural plan, then the second movement looks back in principle to the C major quartet, but with greater tonal experimentation. Here again, thematic recapitulation refuses to coincide with the return of the tonic in that Theme 1 is initially restated in D major before a transition back to the tonic, F major. With the recapitulation of the tonic, a further (but truncated) form of Theme 1 recurs, yielding rapidly to a more substantial restatement of Theme 2. The effect of this method greatly diminishes the impact of the restatement proper. In the case of the early C major quartet where the subdominant was used for the recapitulation of Theme 1, the effect was one of relaxation—but the route back to the tonic was after all a simple one of modulating to the fifth above. Parry's choice of a third relationship (F/D) not only heightens the relaxation of the restatement, but necessitates a more involved return to the tonic. Both factors contribute to the ambiguity of thematic material and tonal recapitulation, and consequently, there is some uncertainty between what is strictly developmental and recapitulatory.

This experimentation was almost certainly due to Dannreuther's influence. From the study of Mozart and Beethoven piano works, Dannreuther soon weaned Parry on to those of Brahms. By July Parry was hard at work on the Op. 5 Piano Sonata and he was also acquainting himself thoroughly with the two-piano version of the Piano Quintet, Op. 34b. But although within the province of instrumental composition Brahms remained the focus of attention, he also began to feel profoundly the magnetism of Wagner generated by a renewal of interest in *Lohengrin*. Hitherto he had only been introduced to this in the form of a concert performance at the Crystal Palace, but on 28 May he was able to hear his first live performance of the work at the Royal Italian Opera. His comments confirm the deep impression left by Wagner's concept of music-drama together with a somewhat impetuous dismissal of earlier stylized operatic forms:

I think Wagner is right in his idea of what an opera should be. Nothing can be more ridiculous than stereotyping human nature as it must be portrayed on the stage into a system of arias, recitatives, trios, etc. in fixed plan. No dramatic effect can come of it. And the best music can only serve as an excuse and save you from being insufferably bored with such trivial and unmeaning scenes. A great deal of the music is perfectly wonderful . . . the story and the situations are very dramatic and interesting, and leave a profound impression . . .[47]

Later in June, he made use of Dannreuther's box at Drury Lane to hear *Lohengrin* again, this time being rehearsed under Costa. But perhaps more significant than *Lohengrin* was his growing preoccupation with *The Ring*. Already Parry and others like him had been tantalized with snippets of the vast tetralogy primarily through the Wagner Society, but again the experience had been limited to concert performances, and in some cases extracts had been represented purely by vocal lines and piano reduction. 'When', the newspapers and journals complained, 'was this giant of all operatic works to be performed?' With his teacher being the foremost champion of Wagner's music in England, Parry had the rare chance to learn of the *The Ring*'s progress which by now formed as important a part of his lessons as did the improvement of his piano technique. In April, after a perfunctory day at Lloyd's, he made for 12 Orme Square to find Dannreuther 'deep in the Götterdämmerung, the last of the Nibelungen set of Wagner operas which had just arrived'.[48] At last there was the prospect of a complete staging of the work, and there was the thrilling possibility that Dannreuther might obtain tickets for the future performances at Bayreuth.

Although Parry was to be most frequently found at Orme Square, he was also a regular visitor at the house of the von Glehns, a rich and leisured family, who settled in Sydenham at Peak Hill Lodge. In particular Parry was the guest of Mary Emilie (Mini) von Glehn, a fine amateur pianist who took lessons with von Bülow, and she, being struck with the quality of Parry's Shakespeare Sonnets, used her influence with her sister-in-law, Sophie Löwe, the singer. After rehearsing 'When in disgrace' at Sydenham, Sophie Löwe proceeded to include the song in her programme for the Stuttgart Tonkünstler-Verein[49] where it was received with some enthusiasm. A close neighbour of the von Glehns was George Grove who was very much the central figure in the lively gatherings at Peak Hill. It consequently provided Parry with a rare opportunity to acquaint himself more intimately with one of the most influential musical personages in London. Parry of course had known Grove intermittently since 1868 and they had met numerous times both at the Crystal Palace and at Dannreuther's home, but since the beginning of 1875 their friendship had deepened significantly. As editor of *Macmillan's Magazine* Grove included in the May edition Parry's six poems under the title *A Sequence of Analogies*, a series of mild lyrical poems modelled on Meredith. But the magazine was by now not Grove's

---

[47] Diary, 28 May 1875.
[48] Ibid. 29 Apr. 1875.   [49] Stuttgart Tonkünstler-Verein, 7 June 1875.

prime concern; rather he was absorbed with the idea of *A Dictionary of Music and Musicians,* the prospectus of which had been announced in January 1874. In July Grove wrote to Parry (using his affectionate Homerian nickname 'Paris') with an invitation to contribute an article on 'Arrangement':

My dear Paris,

I have been intending to favour you with a letter for a long time past, but have never succeeded in screwing up my courage sufficiently . . . as now I want you to do an article for my Dictionary of Music: I am quite determined that you shall have something to do with it, and now that I have got a lovely subject for you, you *must* consent—you must be 'beautiful Paris' and not 'evil hearted Paris'. The subject that you are to write about is 'Arrangement' . . . Oh very dear Paris, it's a jolly subject . . . I took Miss M. E. von Glehn into my counsel about it lately and she agreed that it was the very thing for you. I should be so *very much* pleased if you would do it. Don't go and burst out laughing and reject the whole idea at once but set to work on it and just write me a nice little note to say so.[50]

Parry accepted at once and shortly left for a holiday in the Channel Islands with his friend, Robert Oldham. He returned with agonizing earache and, after seeking medical advice, was ordered to rest. This provided a welcome pretext to stay away from Lloyd's as he was not only engaged in the collection of material for Grove's article, but, more significantly, he was busy sketching ideas for a Duo for two pianos. This work was to represent a crucial departure in his creative development.

[50] Letter from George Grove, 14 July 1875, ShP.

6

Stylistic Experimentation

MOST of September 1875 was devoted to the completion of the *Dictionary of Music* entry 'Arrangement' with which Grove appears to have been delighted. Amongst those who were asked to write articles in these early stages were Davison, Prout, Hullah, Stanford, Pauer, Sullivan, and Dannreuther. Ouseley also contributed an article on 'Augmentation' but soon became too ill to complete its counterpart on 'Diminution' so Grove turned to Parry who quickly obliged, finding that this work provided a valuable supplement to the meagre income from Lloyd's. By November Grove had become so overwhelmed with editorial responsibilities that he decided to employ Parry as sub-editor. It was an undertaking that Parry accepted with open arms:

When we came up to town in November, Grove asked me to take a larger share in the work of the Musical Dictionary and to help him to edit it. A grand opportunity for me both to work and to learn. It was very kind of him. I soon had lots to do. Reading all the articles through and correcting and cutting down those that are too long, and adding to those that were incomplete etc. and best of all going to the British Museum to get up my own work which there will be plenty of.[1]

The rest of his time was divided between two engrossing activities. The first was the newly formed Bach Choir which he joined and sang in as a bass for many years. In the back row of the second basses he sat next to Charles Stuart Wortley, the politician, whom he quickly and lastingly befriended. The second, and more intellectually absorbing exercise was a detailed study of Brahms's Piano Quintet and the earlier version for two pianos whose discrepancies were the source of correspondence with Macfarren. By 28 September, the first movement of a grandiose *Großes Duo* in E minor was completed and Eddie Hamilton came down to Ottershaw at the beginning of October to play through it along with the Brahms Duo. After returning to Cranley Place in November, work continued at a feverish pace until, before the end of the year, he had finished two further movements: a pastoral slow movement in 6/8 and an imposing Romantic fugue based on a subject sketched originally for the organ in 1872 and one on which he had extemporized in May 1873.[2] The

---

[1] Diary, [Nov.] 1875.   [2] Ibid. 26 May 1873.

complete work was then played through at Erards with his old friend, Susan Stephenson, in January 1876.

A popular impression of the *Großes Duo*, related by commentators ranging from Ernest Walker to Gerald Finzi, is the 'somewhat anachronistic effect' produced by the 'frank adoption of eighteenth-century formulas'[3] in which Parry 'looks back to Bach in nineteenth-century terms, in the same way that certain neo-classical works of recent years look back to Bach in twentieth-century terms'.[4] This is true certainly of the quasi-Baroque 'pastorale' and the severity of the fugue (almost redolent of a Busoni arrangement) with its extraordinarily angular subject, and one cannot ignore Parry's deference to Bach's organ music in the opening material of the first movement (Ex. 8*a*). Yet the Duo has never been examined in terms of structure to see how this might reflect on Parry's developing concept of instrumental form. In fact, for all their eighteenth-century allusions, neither the slow movement nor the studious finale succeeds in achieving a convincing sense of cohesion; indeed Parry's worst enemy here seems to be relentlessness. On the other hand, the critics' preoccupation with Bach caused them to overlook Parry's chief aim in the first movement, which was to consolidate that mastery of Brahmsian sonata technique which had been essayed only tentatively in the violin sonata.

This is especially apparent in the greater complexity of the exposition's thematic and tonal organization. The first group (see Ex. 8*a*), constructed on an ABCA basis, is much more extensive than anything Parry had yet composed, and with the return of the opening material in the tonic (bar 21), it falls back on the Schubertian practice of 'closed forms'. In this regard Parry was fully aware of such structural devices as one finds in, for example, Schubert's A minor Quartet (D. 804) and the piano sonatas in A (D. 664), G (D. 894), and B flat (D. 960) which all show a preference for ABA forms in their first groups. Parry would also have seen the same methods at work in Brahms's Sextet, Op. 18, the Piano Quartets, Opp. 25 and 26, and, perhaps most significantly, in Brahms's greatest tribute to Schubert, the Piano Quintet, Op. 34. All these works Parry would have known intimately.

His indebtedness is perhaps most conspicuous in the second group which exploits the possibilities expounded by Brahms in his G minor Piano Quartet. Here the first movement contains one of the largest, most prodigiously integrated second groups in sonata literature, infused by a strong contrast between the minor and major modes of the dominant key—a method Brahms no doubt borrowed from the first movement of

---

[3] E. Walker *A History of Music in England* (Oxford, 1907; 3rd edn. revised and enlarged by J. A. Westrup, Oxford, 1952), 330.

[4] G. Finzi, 'Hubert Parry: A Revaluation', *Music Maker* (Summer 1949), 5.

Schubert's G major quartet (D. 887). Brahms begins his second group
with a new theme in the dominant minor which soon gives way to a
longer (and thematically richer) section in the dominant major. Parry
reverses the procedure and introduces his second group in the dominant
major (Ex. 8*b*) and concludes with the minor (Ex. 8*d*) which reiterates

Ex. 8. *Großes Duo* in E minor (1876), first movement. *a* first-group idea;
b second group, first part; *c* second group, middle part; *d* second group, final
part.

cont. over/

Ex. 8. cont.

the opening material, now recomposed. Between the two statements occurs a new theme in G major (Ex. 8*c*) which is more analogous with the type of transitional third relationships heard in Schubert (cf. the second group of the G major quartet). The transition to G major is prefaced by a passage through the Neapolitan of B (achieved by a reinterpretation of the German sixth in bar 43 as the dominant seventh of C), of which G is naturally the dominant. G major, although much more prolonged, acts

cont. over/

as the Neapolitan to the dominant of B to which it drops in bar 62. Such an extensive use of the Neapolitan again suggests the strong influence of Brahms's Piano Quintet whose first movement is finely balanced between established keys and their Neapolitans.

Parry's exposition has no repeat (a tendency he was to adopt regularly in his later instrumental works) which is perhaps more reminiscent of some Beethoven contexts than of Schubert or such Brahms as Parry had

Ex. 8. cont.

heard at that time. His comments on this very subject, made much later in his *Art of Music* of 1896, are revealing in the schemes of his own sonata movements:

In the early sonatas both halves of the movement were played twice. As artistic feeling developed, the repetition of the second half was frequently dispensed with, but the repetition of the first half was maintained, mainly to help the mind to grasp firmly the principle of contrast between the two keys. In modern times the repetition of the first half is also commonly dispensed with, because the musical instinct has become so quick to grasp any indication of design that it no longer requires to have such things insisted on; and also because the progress of music towards a more passionately emotional phase makes it noticeably anomalous to go through the same exciting crises twice over. Beethoven's practice illustrates this point very happily; for in the less directly emotional sonatas in which design is particularly emphasized, he gives the usual direction for the repetition of the first half; as in the early sonatas, when the possibility of dispensing with such conventions had not dawned upon him, and in the first movements of such later sonatas as the Waldstein (Op. 53) and the one in F sharp (Op. 78). In movements which are so decisively emotional and expressive as the first movements of the Appassionata (F minor, Op. 57), of the E minor (Op. 90), of the A major (Op. 101) and the E major (Op. 109), the repetition is dispensed with, and the movements are made as continuous as possible from end to end, so as to hide the formal element and guard against the mind's being distracted by it.

The Duo's recapitulation provides further confirmation of the Brahmsian model. The first group is almost totally recomposed with the original 'closed form' being abandoned in favour of new tonal exploration. This eventually culminates on F sharp minor which forms the supertonic in a cadence to E major for the second group. The tripartite plan of the second group is also subject to a number of modifications. It exemplifies Parry's solution to the problem of having material originally in foreign keys restated in the tonic, while at the same time allowing the most striking key relationships to be experienced again. Parry's restatement of the second group's opening theme (see Ex. 8*b*) in the tonic major is more reminiscent of Schubert (cf. Schubert's A minor sonata (D. 784)). In preserving the pattern of tonal events, the central idea, originally in G (Ex. 8*c*), appears transposed down a fifth on C which, as the submediant of E minor, facilitates a quick transition back to the tonic. At this juncture first-group material, originally heard in B minor (Ex. 8*d*), returns to complete the final part of the second group as well as supplying the coda.

In the *Großes Duo* Parry expresses for the first time a much greater degree of not only musical but personal self-confidence. Much of this was due to the injection of intellectual activity demanded by Grove's Dictionary. But Parry must also have felt that his position as sub-editor at last accorded him some form of professional status. A much larger portion of his income was now derived from musical work, be it editing, writing, or teaching private pupils, and this undoubtedly brought with it a greater degree of financial security. Grove made it quite plain that work on the Dictionary would increase dramatically and with this in mind, Parry at last had the vital pretext to abandon his life at Lloyd's.

Even though it was only a matter of time before Parry could turn his back on the world of insurance for good, domestic circumstances prevented a quick decision as Maude was about to give birth to their first child. On 13 January 1876, a daughter, Dorothea, was born after some skilful operating by the doctor. Parry wrote to his mother-in-law with the happy news which, instead of gratifying her, only served to open up old feelings of animosity and reproach:

I wrote to her Ladyship the same day. And never was her singular character more clearly displayed. Instead of being pleased at Maudie's being safe, she was miserable on receiving the news. Mary said she turned quite pale and then burst into tears. She wrote to me and said she was horribly *mortified* at not having been present. Not because she loves Maudie or to sympathize with her, but because she loves the excitement of it, and delights in retailing the horrors with unlimited exaggeration to everyone she meets . . . Mary said that when my letter arrived she read it out (ostensibly) to them at breakfast . . . She was furious with me and with Dr Black for not sending for her immediately, though Maudie had told her long ago that it would kill her to have her in the room during her confinement . . . The many other exasperating things which she did would fill volumes if they were set down. And through them all alike runs a vein of blind egotism. I never saw so clearly before how every action she does, even her great charities and her profuse generosity, is prompted by the lowest vanity and egotism. She seems to me utterly without heart or sympathy, or truthfulness and honesty. A creature whom only the customs of society, which she worships as her real God, keeps from any conceivable enormity.[5]

The strain of childbirth took its toll on Maude and she remained confined to bed for weeks as the narrative of Parry's 1876 diary confirms. Furthermore the stress of her predicament was not helped by the constant interference of Lady Herbert:

We had the greatest difficulty in keeping Lady Herbert away . . . Lady H[erbert] loves to produce strong emotions in the minds of her hearers . . . and so things went wearily on. Maudie wavered about between a little better and a little worse for weeks and weeks . . . The baby grew strong and healthy and was christened Dorothea after our favourite character in Middlemarch.[6]

The seemingly endless fluctuation in Maude's condition consequently precluded time for composition and what spare moments Parry enjoyed were spent in editing articles for Grove or lessons with either Macfarren or Dannreuther. Both teachers were encouraging in their verdict of the *Großes Duo* and he was particularly heartened by Sullivan who, writing to thank him for kind words expressed about his work, declared: 'Not only do I appreciate this thoroughly, but I value the praise of an accomplished musician like yourself. Why do you not do more? Have I not a fine band at my disposal whenever you want a thing tried?'[7]

[5] Diary, 13 Jan. 1876.   [6] Ibid. [? Jan.–Mar.] 1876.
[7] Letter from Arthur Sullivan, 19 Feb. 1876, ShP.

But life at Cranley Place was constantly overshadowed by Maude's fragility and, perhaps inevitably, Parry began to form close friendships with other women, even though these remained strictly platonic. One such female companion was Tora Gordon to whom he always remained deeply attracted:

I also had a very sweet little Idyll which cheered my somewhat dreary and sorrowful life a great deal; and this was the friendship which grew up between Tora Gordon and me. I got to frequent the Gordons' house a good deal and went to see Irving with them, as we sympathize strongly in our admiration for him. Then Tora got engaged to Victor Marshall and my excitement on this occasion being considerable I said partly in fun that I would write a Sonata in honour of it; but fun soon became earnest and as I began the sonata I began to idealize the object of it and to make a Romance out of it; and love grew till in my heart she was only second to Maudie. The result was a rapidly produced work. I wrote my four movements and an introduction in less than 3 weeks and with the doctoring it afterwards received partly from my own criticisms and partly from Macfarren's valuable suggestions I think it is the best work I have written yet.[8]

Evidently the passion felt for Tora was deep but necessarily restrained and the composition of the Piano Sonata in A major was a perfect outlet for his sense of loneliness. Macfarren praised the slow movement which no doubt appealed through its extensive Schubertian lyricism and piano texture. However, both the Scherzo and the gentle Rondo finale suffer from somewhat banal thematic material where the style of piano writing seems to fluctuate between Schumannesque delicacy (Parry perhaps harking back to his *Charakterbilder*) and the thicker timbre of Brahms. The most successful movement, in which his real yearning finds utterance, is the first. Even though there is a degree of stylistic inconsistency between the strongly Schumannesque Maestoso introduction and the Brahmsian Allegro grazioso, this is to some extent transcended by Parry's inventive structure. Thematically the movement is not especially distinguished, and tonally it is less ambitious than the Duo's first movement. Nevertheless it does demonstrate three individual features which were to be realized more fully in instrumental works of 1877 and beyond. Perhaps the most simple of these is the absence of expositional repeat which, as already stated, owes more to Beethoven at this stage than Brahms. Indeed one is more conscious of Beethoven in this movement than in either the Violin Sonata or the Duo. It is highly likely that Parry's inclusion of the introduction and its recurrence as a transition to the recapitulation in the main sonata movement was gleaned from the punctuative role of Beethoven's Grave in his Sonata in C minor, Op. 13 *Pathétique*—though Beethoven's material recurs before the

---

[8] Diary, [? Jan.–Mar.] 1876.

development and not after it. The internal treatment of the two introductions is, however, quite different. Beethoven's introduction makes use of just one theme, with the whole paragraph rooted in the same key as the subsequent Allegro. Parry opts for an opening in the tonic minor (a device he had already used in the first movement of his 'Oxford' C major quartet) together with two distinct thematic ideas in closed form (A B A), which is ostensibly more reminiscent of the type of introduction found in the first movement of Schubert's 'Great' C major Symphony. Furthermore, the restated theme before the recapitulation is not, as one might expect, the first theme but the second, with a very brief reference to the quasi-recitative in its final phrase. Yet despite these divergences the structural role of Parry's introduction is thoroughly Beethovenian.

The main Allegro grazioso also displays some interesting procedures. The 'closed form' of the first group is highly unconventional in the way the central material deviates as far afield as the dominant of C sharp before abruptly returning to the opening idea in the tonic. But no sooner has this repetition occurred when C sharp major rears its head again together with a new thematic strand as part of the second group. C sharp is, however, short-lived, being superseded by a repetition of the same thematic material in the dominant, E major, in which the rest of the second group is based. The modifications of the restatement further establish the principles applied in the Duo. To begin with, the 'closed form' of the first group is abandoned, but this is not justified simply for reasons of brevity. The unresolved dominant of C sharp in the exposition (unresolved because it was expunged by a return of A major and a repeat of the first theme) is this time permitted its rightful conclusion without interruption. The abruptness of the transition from first to second group, brought about by the juxtaposition of A major and C sharp major is effectively dissipated. Yet Parry also allows the striking key relationships of the exposition to be heard once more, by transposing the third-related tonality down a fifth into F sharp major—it is then succeeded by a return to A major, consistent with events of the exposition.

Soon after the completion of the Sonata in A major, Maude was strong enough to withstand journeys, first to the Majendies at Hedingham and then to Wilton for Easter. Her family, overbearing as ever, insisted that she stay at the house for a long period. Ironically once there she sickened for diphtheria and scarlatina which necessitated complete isolation. During Maude's quarantine Parry wrote a second sonata for piano, this time in F major. Evidently his intention was far less ambitious, and stylistically much of it appears regressive in its deployment of an unabashed Mendelssohnian language. Only the last movement, which attempts to combine the virtuoso element of Chopin's finales with the 'hunting motifs' of Schumann's *Papillons*, comes near to expressing anything more contemporary and even here the material barely rises above the commonplace. In a letter to Eddie Hamilton, to whom he sent the sonata, he mentioned the sympathy that Lady Pembroke had shown for the work, but since personal relations with her were nearly always strained, he withdrew the idea of dedicating it to her in favour of Grove, 'the most excellent of kind friends':

Wilton House,
Salisbury.

My dear Eddie,

You are a great brick to be so prompt in looking over and sending back my movement, and altogether for being so ready to help me. What you say of it is very nice, but I fear your kind old friendly heart makes you think too well of it. I sent it to old Lamborn Cock and that excellent old party *thinks* he will bring it out in the Autumn. I hope he will. That'll be fine; because Stanley Lucas is going to bring out the other, and I shall quite feel as if I was getting on, and begin to get quite bumptious. Isn't it odd now? I fixed my attention on things rustic when I wrote the F Sonata, and intended to call it Arcadia; and Lady P having shown much apparent sympathy with music I had intended to dedicate it to her, and to make a little joke about a second Arcadia dedicated to a second Countess of P—— (Philip Sidney you know). But it's all busted. Such is life![9]

In fact Lady Pembroke (or George's 'cruel wife' as he once referred to her) exasperated him almost as much as Lady Herbert, so that by the beginning of May he was longing to return to London. Besides the excesses of 'aristocraticisms' which he by now abhorred, he felt starved of musical company and pressures were mounting in his responsibilites for Grove:

I am going to leave her [Maude] in charge of Pre [Maude's former governess] tomorrow in order to hear the B minor Mass, which I have been abominably done out of. And I am then going to stop and try and get on with my Dictionary work and other things; as you see Maude has a most pertinacious hatred to being in London any time except in the winter . . . She wants to go to Highnam straight after the sea and straight away to Hugh Montgomery's from Highnam. It doesn't give a chap much chance. It's that diseased aristocratic education which emasculates both moral and physical . . .[10]

Evidently Maude's demands on his time together with the constant recriminations of her family were causing frustration and resentment. Having returned to London he found little respite there for he felt obliged to look for more spacious accommodation as well as a retreat for Maude somewhere on the coast. Relief came with the Garretts who

---

[9] Letter to Edward W. Hamilton, 7 May 1876, BL Add. MS 48621.
[10] Ibid.

invited him to spend a fortnight at their home at 2 Gower Street. In their company his morale was transformed:

I was never so spoilt in my life. They seem to divine all one's wants before one has thought of them oneself. They are the best company I ever knew, and to live in their house is a very great element of happiness in itself. The quiet and soothing colour of the walls and decorations and the admirable taste of all things acts upon the mind in the most comforting manner.[11]

This change of mood immediately turned his mind to the thought of leaving Cranley Place and finding somewhere more ample, less central, and, at the Garretts' suggestion, in close proximity to Gower Street. This is clear in a letter to Maude of 19 May:

I am quite out of love with Cranley Place since I have been in this part of the world. It seems so fresh and healthy up here, I feel quite different from what I ever do there. R[hoda] and A[gnes] think it is quite natural—That S. Kensington is not healthy for itself and the bad water and drainage there make it quite poisonous. The houses here are so fine and airy and they have such jolly gardens. If we lived in Russell Square for instance we should get a grand big house with lots of room for Dorothea to play about in, a garden to itself and the biggest and I should think best kept square in London for *less* than we pay for Cranley Place; and we should be in the middle of everything except Society and that's just what we want to avoid.[12]

From Gower Street he was able to visit the British Museum regularly, dine at the 'Women's Club' with the Garretts and Mrs Fawcett, and edit articles for Grove without interruption. But once the fortnight was over he was obliged to stay at Chesham Place with Lady Herbert. The contrast with Gower Street was disturbing. 'Here instead of comfortable happiness and quiet good sense in everything,' he wrote, '—perpetual racket, and bustle, and gossip and aristocraticisms; no time to do anything reasonable, no practising possible, or work of any kind. Everlasting bustle, chatter, dressing and self admiration.'[13] In the second week of June Maude returned to London pale and thin, whereupon the Garretts intervened to recommend some accommodation close to their own seaside home in Littlehampton, Sussex, where she could recuperate. Rooms were subsequently ordered at a quaint, rather old-fashioned hotel called 'Beach Hotel' where they moved on 12 June. Maude's health improved with 'rather unsound-seeming rapidity' which restored sanity to Parry's domestic life and at last he was able to focus his attentions on musical study again.

During the first half of 1876 London had continued to show a healthy interest in new music. As part of his Lisztian crusade, Walter Bache

[11] Diary, [May] 1876.
[12] Letter to Lady Maude Parry, 19 May 1876, ShP.
[13] Diary, [June] 1876.

produced *The Legend of St Elizabeth* in February, and in March Dannreuther gave the first English performance of Tchaikovsky's Piano Concerto in B flat minor at the Crystal Palace. This formed part of an enterprising programme including Joachim's arrangement of Schubert's Duo in C Op. 140 and Rubinstein's ballet music from his opera *Feramors*. Parry was able to take advantage of these concerts until the end of March when contact was completely severed until May. On returning to London he heard *Tannhaüser* at the Royal Italian Opera and was able to attend some of Anton Rubinstein's recitals at St James's Hall. With Grove he was able to interview the pianist-composer in connection with the Dictionary.

Although Rubinstein's new Fifth Piano Concerto and 'Dramatic' Symphony (both recently performed at the Philharmonic Society) interested him, as did Tchaikovsky's concerto with which he became acquainted through Dannreuther, Parry's unwavering preoccupation was with Wagner and the prospect of attending Bayreuth to hear the complete *Ring* cycle. Before leaving London Dannreuther had been successful in obtaining free tickets for him to attend the festival's second cycle of performances between 20 and 23 August. Anxious therefore to acquaint himself fully with the entire trilogy he took the published vocal scores to Littlehampton:

I worked at the great Trilogy. Playing it all through more than once (which was no inconsiderable labour and which I did not finish until after I had left Littlehampton) also working all through the German with a Dictionary and reading the music to myself, so that when I came to hear it I may miss nothing. I shortly began to understand Dannreuther's enthusiasm about it. The man has grown so enormously since the earlier works I have heard of his and I miss now the occasional vulgarity and weakness which appeared to me in them. He seems entirely master of himself and his resources and capable of carrying out his great intentions without a flaw in the result.[14]

After a few weeks in Littlehampton they returned to London resolved to move from Cranley Place, but Bedford Square, which seemed so congenial to Parry, did not appeal to Maude who felt that such a large premises would entail more servants and consequently greater expense. Their search for a new house was suspended by a month at Highnam, after which Parry left in haste for Bayreuth.

It seems that anyone who wished to be associated with the progressive in music was drawn to this small Bavarian town. Composers, critics, writers, artists, and philosophers were full of anticipation for the three promised cycles of the *Ring* which had been in a state of planning so long, and for many months afterwards the subject would dominate every

[14] Ibid. 1876.

journal from Moscow to London. The musical contingent who gradually congregated there formed perhaps the greatest tribute that any composer has ever experienced. For Parry such company seemed overwhelming. Besides Liszt, who was almost as much an attraction as Wagner himself, there was Tchaikovsky, Cui, Nikolay Rubinstein, and Klindworth from Russia; from France came D'Indy and Saint-Saëns; from Norway Grieg, and from Vienna Bruckner. Last but not least, there was Dannreuther and Stanford from England. The critics (also well represented by Hanslick (Vienna), Filippi (Milan), Wolff (Paris), and Davison (London)) were quick to note those, such as Verdi, Gounod, Brahms, Anton Rubinstein, Raff, Thomas, Joachim, von Bülow, and Hiller who had made it their business to stay away. Indeed it was a credit to Parry's single-mindedness and his faith in the ideals of Dannreuther that he rebutted the severe castigations of Macfarren (who had, incidentally, inflicted the same opinions on Stanford[15]). Shortly before he left for Germany, he had received a letter in which Macfarren made plain his absolute disgust for the entire affair:

I am sorry you are going to Bayreuth, for every presence there gives countenance to the monstrous self-inflation. The principle of the thing is bad, the means for its realization preposterous. An earthquake would be good that would swallow the spot and everybody on it, so I wish you away.

Yours with kindest regards,
G. A. Macfarren

Is it possible you are the same you whom I met at the Bach?[16]

But Macfarren's prejudices were left far behind as Parry was drawn into Wagner's mythical world. His diary account, written after it was all over, provides sure evidence that, for the moment at least, he had become a fervent Wagnerite:

I give up all attempts to describe my own feelings. I never was so perfectly satisfied in my life. Rheingold was first of all perfect to my mind. The Walküre came up to my anticipations which were of the very highest. Then Siegfried I found certainly hard to understand; and I did not enjoy it so much as the others at the time—but on looking back upon it I got to enjoy it more, and the impression afterwards became very strong. As for Götterdämmerung it utterly surpassed my anticipations. I was in a whirl of excitement; and quite drunk with delight. The 1st Act satisfied me most, with its three great climaxes piled on one another like Andes on Himalayas.[17]

On returning to England, the euphoria of Bayreuth was soon dissipated by the time-consuming task of finding a new house. After much searching, and little work, a decision was made to purchase

[15] Sir C. V. Stanford, *Pages from an Unwritten Diary* (London, 1914), 167-8.
[16] Letter from Sir George W. Macfarren, 12 Aug. 1876, ShP.   [17] Diary, [Aug.] 1876.

Lincoln House in Upper Phillimore Place, Kensington. But all this energy was expended needlessly as the verdict on Maude's health was blacker than ever. An infected lung would not improve in the smoke-filled air of London so they were advised to return to Littlehampton where they remained for just over a month. It was an anxious time for Parry. An antagonistic landlady frequently prevented him from playing the piano and, as he said in a letter to Eddie Hamilton, most of the day was absorbed in attending to his wife: '. . . Maudie takes up a good deal of my time, exercising her and doing various things that she cannot do for herself . . .'[18] Matters were not improved when they came into possession of Lincoln House. Intense consultations with several doctors ensued and their advice was to go abroad as soon as possible. It was recommended that they go up the Nile, or as Montgomery suggested, to Algiers; but as Maude was a bad sailor, it was decided, with not a little interference from Lady Herbert, to go to Cannes.

The prospect of spending at least three months in the south of France immediately filled Parry with gloom and despondency. To have contact with London and his colleagues severed for such a period made him anxious. In Cannes there would be precious little opportunity to hear new music in the concert-hall, the opera, or in anything approaching the intimate atmosphere of Orme Square. Moreover he was anxious of the effect his absence would have on his commitment to Grove, and, perhaps more importantly, how it might disrupt the steady improvement in technique he was enjoying under Dannreuther and Macfarren. Mont-gomery attempted to quell his friend's anxieties. He, with his own delicate health, was already familiar with the Mediterranean and its potential benefits, and felt sure that this interlude would not harm his future:

As far as your art goes, now I am going to be a Job's comforter—you will not lose so very much ground, after all—at any rate now, that you cannot gain again. You are not so very old yet that you need despair at having to hibernate or artistically go to sleep for one winter or even two—I know that ars longa vita brevis est—but then, you see, we must entsagen some portion of this brief life— 'That's the humour of it'. Fortunately you are not only a musician—no offence to the art—and there are many books to be read etc. etc. which may make the hibernation not unprofitable. Even in the science of your art there must be things you have not gone to the bottom of, which may be worked at in winter quarters with books and paper and pen . . . If books and thoughts and a little microscoping will not carry you through your time with comfort to your soul, you should try a little drawing. You gave me a very good reason once for not dabbling in the fine arts, but if you must be temporarily divorced from music, you could not fail to be the better for developing the talents you must have in this direction.[19]

    [18] Letter to Edward W. Hamilton, 29 Oct. 1876, BL Add. MS 48621.
    [19] Letter from Hugh Montgomery, 10 Nov. 1876, Blessingbourne, County Tyrone.

But Parry was not to be comforted. On the day before they were due to leave Upper Phillimore Place his frustrations further intensified when he learned that there was likely to be considerable delay over Breitkopf und Härtel's decision to publish the *Großes Duo* which Dannreuther had recommended to them. Much to his annoyance it was news for which he would have to wait several months.

On 24 November they arrived in Cannes and made for the Hôtel Paradis where rooms had been arranged for them. Yet, notwithstanding the obvious comfort of his surroundings, Parry chafed at the dearth of stimuli. 'For all the beauty we saw,' he wrote, 'I spent part of the day and all the evening swearing at my exile, to which I am by no means reconciled.'[20] Maude's condition was a source of constant apprehension which was compounded by Dorothea who also fell ill with an attack of croup. There seemed little sign of escape from this domestic monotony until he was introduced to a young, energetic Italian violinist, Edward Guerini. Guerini in turn introduced him to his wife who was herself a composer and fine pianist and to the cellist, Feri-Kletzer. This did much to restore Parry's sagging morale. He advertised harmony classes which he began to hold at the Hôtel de Provence at the end of December, and he also began to work with Guerini whose reputation was already well established for his chamber concerts. Guerini insisted that Parry should be involved in his series of 'six séances de musique classique et moderne', the first of which took place at the Hôtel Dupart on 11 January 1877 and featured a performance of Rubinstein's Sonata No. 2 in A minor, Op. 19 and Beethoven's Piano Sonata in E minor, Op. 90. The concert proved so popular that the remaining five were moved to a more spacious venue at the Hôtel de Provence. The two main works of the second concert on 18 January were Schumann's Violin Sonata in A minor, Op. 105 given by Parry and Guerini, and Mendelssohn's Piano Trio in D minor, Op. 49 performed by Guerini, his wife, and Feri-Kletzer. After the third concert on 25 January Guerini agreed to include Parry's Suite for Violin and Piano (a reworking of his earlier *Suite de Pièces* of 1873) in the fourth concert. The Suite was encored and, by public demand, was repeated at the sixth concert on 24 February.

In retrospect, Guerini's concerts were extremely beneficial to Parry in several ways. First and foremost they brought him into close contact with a variety of chamber works by Bach, Beethoven, Schumann, Mendelssohn, Rubinstein, and Brahms. Secondly, in having the opportunity to participate in performances (and taking advantage of Dannreuther's technical instruction), he learned valuable practical lessons in ensemble. Last, the experience of public performance helped

---

[20] Diary, 24 Nov. 1876.

him to some extent to conquer a natural shyness and acute nervousness that would overwhelm him in such situations. After Guerini's six concerts were over, Feri-Kletzer organized a 'Grande Matinée Musicale' at the Hôtel Beau-Site on 28 February in which the other three artists participated, and then it was the turn of Parry himself to be the centre of attention. On 8 March, at the Hôtel de Provence, he was the pianist in Beethoven's Piano Trio in B minor (with Guerini and Feri-Kletzer) and soloist in works by Bach, Couperin, Schumann, and in the first performance of his own *Variations on an Air by Bach*.

Though these concerts provided a valuable distraction from domestic worries and some useful income, there is no doubt that at Cannes he continually fretted at being away from England and felt compelled to extract as much news as he could about London's musical events from those who visited him. This he explained in a letter to Eddie Hamilton:

I was uncommonly glad to get your letter, for I have not been overwell supplied with information by my friends since I have been away. I suppose it's my own fault in some respect as I am such a bad correspondent myself. I got a good deal out of old Spencer and enjoyed his visit really immensely. . . . he told me a great deal about how things were going on in England in musical and other ways and freshened me up all round. But most of your news was fresh all the same . . . and your criticism of Cowen's opera about which I had endeavoured to extract some information from Grove, but failed as I haven't heard from him for about six weeks.

. . . There are a lot of nice people here, some old friends and one or two nice new ones. The ones we liked best have gone away, viz. the brother and sister of the headmaster of Harrow; they were about the only people of any lively qualities we have had in our hotel, which though a good one and small, is frequented greatly by old maids and parsons. At one time we had 8 old maids at table d'hote out of about 16 or 18 people—and as for parsons I have mostly been the only man without a white tie.[21]

But Parry's most intense frustration was with his environment. In December he had begun to sketch an *Aurora* overture but, through incessant interruption, periods of work became more and more disconnected until composition became virtually impossible. He did succeed in finishing one song, 'Love and Laughter' to words by the Revd Arthur G. Butler, which was eventually published in 1902 as part of the fifth set of *English Lyrics*, but anything large-scale had to be abandoned. The stress of this predicament was again confided to Eddie Hamilton:

As to the envy you express of the quiet time I get in banishment, nothing could be more inappropriate. Sometimes I feel as if I should go mad with worry and irritation; our life is the most dismally unquiet thing a human being with anything to do could have to live through. In the first place hotel life is

[21] Letter to Edward W. Hamilton, 20 Feb. 1877. BL Add. MS 48621.

notoriously liable to constant interruptions. Then my only place to work in is also Maude's sitting room and she is nearly always moving about after something or other, besides that it is Dolly's day nursery and our dining room and breakfast room, and is only separated from Dolly's sleeping apartment by a wooden partition through which her frequent yells come as easily and fully as if she was in the same room. I have been desirous enough to write, but haven't managed to get a chance to put 50 bars on paper in as many days. I can get no quiet by any means. Many a time I have thought to get a quiet half hour and sat myself down opposite my paper and then Dolly has . . . howled for half an hour and after that was over if my patience lasted so long, judge for yourself the fitness of mind one would be likely to be in to settle down to write anything. Sometimes I have been so wild that I have wondered if anything could be worse. The opportunity for doing anything in composition is slipping further and further away from me; and all you musicians at home are slipping by me; and I shall have to end up with being the musical scrub and bottle washer, and teaching young ladies their common chords, or how to play a Mozart variation or two; and after one has devoted oneself to one's art as I have done it's a bit of a sickness to face.[22]

In fact not long after this gloomy letter was written, Parry received an ecstatic letter from the long-silent and apologetic Grove with enthusiastic reports of the new symphony by Brahms which he had heard in rehearsal at the Royal Academy of Music. This was in preparation for the auspicious Joachim–Brahms concert in Cambridge on 8 March when Joachim was to be awarded an honorary Mus.D. by the university. Brahms had also been invited, but despite impassioned pleading from Joachim and Clara Schumann, he refused to leave Germany. Nevertheless, Joachim agreed to conduct the symphony and his own *Elegiac Overture in Commemoration of Kleist*, with the rest of the concert, which included Brahms's *Schicksalslied*, taken by Stanford. After the Cambridge performance Grove was determined to have the work performed at the Crystal Palace and it was given under the baton of Manns on 31 March. Grove very much hoped that Parry would be able to travel over for it but this was impractical as Maude had still not fully recovered.

It was in fact to be another whole month before they left Cannes on 19 April. After breaking the journey in Paris to hear Meyerbeer's *Robert le diable*, they arrived at Upper Phillimore Place on 24 April. The suspense of waiting to hear whether Breitkopf had agreed to publish the *Großes Duo* was dispelled by a note from Dannreuther, the work's dedicatee. The state of business in the city was, by contrast, quite hopeless. In his absence McDonnell had been forced to borrow money contrary to their partnership agreement. This, for Parry, made the situation financially intolerable. Without any further hesitation it was decided to pay all

---

[22] Letter to Edward W. Hamilton, 20 Feb. 1877. BL Add. MS 48621.

outstanding debts and wind up the business. Though initially he regretted the end of his personal connection with McDonnell, Parry was happily aware that the decision had brought him the long desired freedom that would enable him to concentrate entirely on music.

The disappointment at not being in England for Brahms's First Symphony was mitigated by the excitement of Wagner's imminent visit to London. Dannreuther, as the leading light of the Wagner Society, was responsible for suggesting the idea of a Wagner Festival as a means of making good the deficit created by the pecuniary failure of Bayreuth. As it turned out, his valiant attempt to assist Wagner failed utterly, for the losses incurred by the six scheduled concerts were colossal, and even the arrangement of two further concerts did nothing to rectify the financial disaster. Yet, at the outset, the risks were submerged by the exhilaration of Wagner's presence in the capital. Moreover, with Wagner the guest of Dannreuther, 12 Orme Square became a hive of social activity for all devoted Wagnerites.

The chance for Parry (who was himself a member of the Wagner Society Committee) to meet Wagner at Orme Square came on 2 May but, tantalizingly, he did not record his immediate impressions. At his second meeting on 5 May he did comment on the extraordinary conversational magnetism of the master: 'there was a goodly company of artist folk to see Wagner who was in great fettle and talked to an open-mouthed group in brilliant fashion. He talks so fast that I could catch but very little of what he said.'[23] But it was Wagner's flamboyance as a conductor that delighted him most:

Wagner's conducting is quite marvellous; he seems to transform all he touches; he knows precisely what he wants and does it to a certainty. The 'Kaisermarsch' became quite new under his influence, and supremely magnificent. I was so wild with excitement after it that I did not recover all the afternoon. The concert in the evening was very successful and the Meister was received with prolonged applause, but many people found the Rheingold selection too hard for them.[24]

In fact the festival as a whole proved too exacting for the general musical public. The long first act of *Die Walküre* without scenery and action was a severe test on the audience and many walked out. Nevertheless a rapturous reception was always provided by the loyal nucleus of Wagner supporters. On 16 May extracts from *Götterdämmerung* were met with applause that went on for nearly a quarter of an hour. 'Siegfried's Tod', Parry wrote, '. . . seems to me the greatest thing in the world and made me quite cold with ecstasy.'[25] The following day he was at Orme Square again to hear Wagner 'read the newly finished text of Percival [*sic*] . . .'[26]

[23] Diary, 5 May, 1877.   [24] Ibid. 7 May 1877.   [25] Ibid. 16 May 1877.
[26] Ibid. 17 May 1877.

which he found somewhat baffling though he was once again enormously impressed at Wagner's capacity to dramatize. On 18 May he attended the rehearsal for the final concert which was to include three substantial extracts from *Tristan* (the *Vorspiel*, the duet from Act 1, and the *Liebestod* from Act 3), a work, though familiar in reduction, he had not yet heard in its full realization:

I enjoyed them fully and so did Maudie, who is keener about Wagner's music than I ever saw her about anything except the Rights of Women. We sat with George Eliot and Madame Wagner. . . . Wagner got into a charmingly unsophisticated rage at some of the band for beginning badly; and threw down his baton and seized his coat and comforter and put them on (for no ostensible reason except the need of doing something) and walked up and down the platform in front of the orchestra till time and the appeals of those of the orchestra more in favour had cooled him down a bit.[27]

The Festival brought its fair share of social responsibilities for Parry who was frequently charged with the duty of entertaining Wagner's wife. On 9 May he was forced somewhat reluctantly to leave the rehearsal of *Die Walküre* to find somebody willing to escort Madame Wagner to the Grosvenor Gallery for a soirée:

I tried Mrs Rot and her friends and failed, and then went to Mama [Lady Herbert] who to my surprise was quite willing, and I thought rather pleased to have a lioness in tow, notwithstanding the inclination of Society to taboo a person who puts 'Wagner-Liszt' on her cards and was as long as the humour lasted the wife of Bülow. But I put it to Mama that she would be escorting the daughter of 'her old friend Liszt' and that bait took . . .[28]

Much of the escorting was done by himself which included the despondent journey back to Bayswater after Unger's 'painful collapse' in *Götterdämmerung*. He was, however, spared the task of taking the Wagners to a reception at the Millais' on 20 May after the sixth and final concert. Wagner, in a bad temper, had a sore throat and refused to go despite his promises. From Parry's comments the decision was a wise one for he judged the occasion to be purely one designed to enhance the Millais' social kudos:

So in the evening the Millais's had to have their Hamlet with an extra ghost, for Wagner certainly went not, and there was a great company to meet him who were thoroughly sold. And as many of them were of those whose understanding or constitutions, not being of the right calibre, prompted them to much hypothesis-making in contempt of him and his works, I was rather pleased. Their snobbishness is obvious. They love not his works, but they would be glad

---

[27] Diary, 18 May 1877.
[28] Ibid. 9 May 1877. Also cf. Charles L. Graves, *Hubert Parry* (London, 1926), i. 178 where Graves substitutes 'Mama' [Lady Herbert] for 'a lady of high rank' and 'my friend'!

to get near him because he is big, and they could tell their friends lightly that they had met him, and then cast some more dirt no doubt.[29]

Wagner was, however, obliged to attend several receptions at Orme Square given in his honour by Dannreuther, whose mood by this time was subdued owing to the meagre profits earned by the concert series. The two further hastily planned concerts on 28 and 29 May included music from *The Ring* and *Tristan* but these did little to improve the financial situation, and when Parry saw Wagner and his wife off at Victoria Station on 4 June the profits of one of London's most historic musical events amounted to no more than £700.

During the festival Parry had begun to sketch a new work, but it was Brahms not Wagner who provided the inspiration. The new work, a Piano Trio in E minor, was the first indication of a conscious decision on Parry's part to pursue Brahms's method of 'intellectualism' in the composition of abstract instrumental music and to avoid the endemic Wagner fever that was sweeping Europe. However, it is clear from the numerous chamber and orchestral works which followed the Trio in quick succession, that Parry needed the freedom to experiment before he could be convinced that this road was the most appropriate one. None the less, this period of experimentation ensured that Parry's attitudes to structure and tonality would not simply result in enslaved emulation of Brahms but show a distinctive and personal approach in which influences of other composers, such as Schumann and Liszt, would play an important role.

The first movement of the Piano Trio was completed in sketch on 13 May and by 30 May he was already at work on the Finale. Dannreuther seemed 'tolerably pleased'[30] with it and agreed to oversee the work's completion, for his pupil had by this time ceased taking lessons with Macfarren. By 23 June the work was finished. 'He [Dannreuther] said mighty compliments over my slow movement,' Parry recorded excitedly, 'and that the Scherzo is also good, but the first movement fails here and there because I haven't rightly expressed my intentions.'[31] His excitement at Dannreuther's satisfaction was well justified, for all four movements showed a yet more confident handling of the Brahmsian principles of tight motivic and tonal integration. The basic contour of the opening thematic idea of the first movement, B-C-B (see Ex. 9*a*), and in particular the central pitch C, play a vital role in determining the tonal scheme of the entire work. Within the first movement this can be seen in several different contexts. The first group, for example, includes a deviation to C major for 13 bars (bars 34–46) before reverting to the

---

[29] Diary, 20 May 1877. Also cf. Graves, *Hubert Parry*, i. 180 where Graves substitutes 'Millais' for '——'.

[30] Diary, 17 June 1877.   [31] Ibid. 23 June 1877.

Ex. 9. Piano Trio in E minor (1876). *a* opening theme, first movement; *b* transition to second group, first movement; *c* beginning of the Trio.

(c) vn. **Meno mosso**

dominant of E minor (bar 47). The move to the submediant occurs again at the end of the first group (bar 65) but this time C helps to establish the new second-group key of A flat (Ex. 9*b*). Other important instances include the integral unison shift from C to B (bar 170) at the end of the development in preparation for the return of E minor, and, perhaps most arresting of all, the sudden change of direction to C minor (bar 275) at the outset of the dramatic coda. C major continues to assert itself in the Scherzo in A major in that it forms the key of the Trio (Ex. 9*c*), and the Schumannesque slow movement, the emotional centre of the work, is set in C major. Finally, the virtuoso sonata-rondo of the last movement also deploys C major prominently as its second-group key.

When he was not occupied with the Trio in E minor, Parry devoted the rest of his time to Grove who was especially anxious to press ahead with the next instalment of articles. Macmillan were already showing signs of impatience after Grove had projected that the Dictionary would not be completed until December 1880. Consequently once Wagner had departed for Bayreuth, work began again in earnest. In addition to the editing of numerous articles by other authors such as Helmore, who irritated him with his extravagant 'polemics and digressions',[32] Parry was required to make analyses of Haydn's quartets, Mozart's symphonies, concertos by Corelli, oratorios by Handel, and keyboard music by Couperin. Much of this useful work on repertoire was done at Littlehampton during the summer months and at Highnam where he and Maude stayed for the Gloucester Three Choirs Festival. However, it was not until Parry returned to London in September that he felt disposed to begin 'Form', the first of his more substantial articles for the Dictionary. These articles, which later were to include penetrating appraisals of 'Sonata', 'Symphony', and 'Variations', provide us with a fascinating insight into the composers and works which Parry himself considered seminal to an understanding of the subject, and, furthermore, they often shed light on his own compositional processes.

September and half of October proved to be a time of intense loneliness for Parry. Maude, who was pregnant with their second child, went first to Roehampton and then to the Majendies at Hedingham. 'Tried to work after but was very depressed and didn't succeed much,' he wrote dejectedly; 'it is horrid this loneliness, not a soul to speak to, or to look into their eyes and catch a gleam of sympathy.'[33] Yet despite the misery of his solitude he was able to drive himself to finish a *Concertstück* in G minor for orchestra on 22 September which may well have been a reworking of the abortive *Aurora* overture begun in Cannes in December 1876.

It seems likely that the *Concertstück* was written purely as an orchestral exercise in order to gauge his ability to use the apparatus developed in the *Großes Duo* and Piano Trio. Furthermore it appears that once Parry had completed the score, the work was shelved. It remained unperformed until 1982. Its construction shows distinct similarities with the first movement of Schubert's 'Unfinished' Symphony which Parry greatly admired. Initially this can be felt in the way the expositional key scheme of the *Concertstück* (g/E flat) mirrors that of Schubert's movement (b/G); but the parallel is more telling in the restatement where Parry not only follows an identical tonal procedure (g - B flat - G - g; cf. Schubert's b - D - B - b) but also emulates Schubert's technique of thematic displacement. The internal proportions of Parry's work are appreciably larger, with an especially elaborate development of over 200 bars. No less elaborate is his organization of thematic material and here the *Concertstück* differs markedly from Schubert's plan. One major divergence lies in the huge oblique opening paragraph which lasts over 60 bars while the other occurs at the point of recapitulation which commences

[32] Diary, 25 May 1877.   [33] Ibid. 24 Sept. 1877.

dramatically outside the tonic in the key of A flat minor (though curiously Parry may well have gleaned this technique from the Finale of Schubert's Ninth Symphony). Besides these interesting structural comparisons with Schubert, the *Concertstück* betrays a number of diverse influences. The oblique opening, for example, is strongly reminiscent of a similar process at the beginning of the Scherzo of Brahms's Piano Quintet, while the monothematic element of the piece perhaps owes more to Schumann. Yet the most striking passages in the *Concertstück* are those which reveal Parry's fascination for Wagner and Liszt. The rising muscular arpeggiation that occurs at the end of the second group momentarily reminds one of the 'sword' motive in *The Ring*, while the influence of Liszt is apparent in the dissonant osinati and the harmonically experimental fugato at the end of the development (Ex. 10).

Ex. 10. Fugato at the end of the development of the *Concertstück* in G minor (1877).

The latter part of 1877 was absorbed mainly in work for the Dictionary. Visits to the British Museum intensified though these were occasionally interspersed with trips to Buckingham Palace to view manuscripts of *Messiah* and *Israel in Egypt* together with a number of Purcell autographs. The atmosphere of the Crystal Palace was enlivened by the playing of the new virtuoso violinist, Sarasate, as well as the presence of Max Bruch who had come to London to conduct the prelude to his opera *Lorelei* and his Violin Concerto in G minor. Parry was much impressed with the music: 'The works both gave me great pleasure, being richly coloured and warm with the healthy glow of a true musician's heart.'[34] Sarasate appeared on 20 October in Mendelssohn's Violin Concerto, but this time the main attractions for Parry were the youthful and previously unperformed Symphony No. 2 by Schubert and a new symphonic poem, *La Jeunesse d'Hercule*, by Saint-Saëns, which did little to raise his opinion of French music: '[it] displays many touches of the French taste for peculiar noises, but it is not without a few touches of good material. I thought it altogether a failure however'.[35] The most rewarding musical experience was Dannreuther's preparation for his performance of Scharwenka's Concerto in B flat minor at the Crystal Palace on 27 October. The concerto's Lisztian cyclic design in one consecutive movement (consisting of elements of several traditional movements) captivated Parry, particularly in the way the Finale functioned as a free recapitulation of the opening 'allegro'. Indeed, his impression of Scharwenka's concerto was so strong that he soon began to contemplate the composition of a cyclic work of his own.

On 21 October he wrote in his diary: 'To Dannreuther directly after luncheon and had a famous grind with him over . . . a new Wind Nonetto I am writing as an experiment.' By 4 November he had finished the first movement and Dannreuther seemed pleased with the result. 'We had a delightful couple of hours together which refreshed me wonderfully,' he recorded, 'for I have been getting terribly dazed and sick under the pressure of C[hesham] P[lace] aristocraticisms; . . . The constant strains of trying to take an interest in the lists of aristocrats who were present at this and that gathering and the many personal facts of upper ten life is more than one can bear for more than a very limited period.'[36] But he and Maude soon freed themselves of the stultifying, overprotective atmosphere of the Herberts and work progressed quickly, the Scherzo and slow movement being completed by 25 November. The Finale, begun on December 6, gave him more trouble and much time was spent poring over the manuscript with Dannreuther, who was, none the less, highly taken with it and impressed by his pupil's rapid

[34] Diary, 13 Oct. 1877.   [35] Ibid. 20 Oct. 1877.   [36] Ibid. 4 Nov. 1877.

development. 'Dannreuther alarmed me a good deal by expressing a very high opinion of what I ought to do as a composer. I am afraid he will be disappointed,'[37] he wrote nervously, but two days before Christmas, shortly before the completion of the Nonet, Parry was left in no doubt about his teacher's belief in his abilities:

At the end of my lesson he [Dannreuther] made a declaration which moved me so much that I could not make answer. He said he had been so lonely for so long, and I might be a brother to him and help him on in life and he would not let me consider myself as having lessons from him any longer, and so on. I can't write all the sweet things he said. They almost hurt me because I felt I was unworthy, and it might so wound him in the future if, after having put his trust in my abilities, he found me wanting.

The Nonet's intense cyclic organization attests Parry's description of the work's 'experimental' nature. Though he did not yet feel ready to confront the problems posed by a one-movement structure similar to that of Scharwenka's Concerto, he did nevertheless attempt to create a four-movement work unified by a minimum of thematic ideas and their transformations. The exposition of the first movement introduces three distinct thematic strands which subsequently pervade the material used in all the later movements. The first of these, a three-note 'motto', is heard at the very opening (figure 'x'; Ex. 11*a*) out of which ensues the first main thematic idea (figure 'a'; Ex. 11*b*). A secondary fragment, characterized by its fluctuating harmonic progressions, occurs fourteen bars later (figure 'y'; Ex. 11*c*) which is followed by a return of figure 'x'. The motto is then repeated, but this time on the flat submediant level which signals a temporary diversion to G flat and the introduction of a third, subsidiary idea (figure 'z'; Ex. 11*d*). The motto also dominates both the opening and closing ideas of the second group (Ex. 11*e* and 11*f*) which are interspersed with a reference to figure 'y' (Ex. 11*g*). Besides its obvious thematic interest and concentration, the first movement also displays a similar propensity to that of the *Concertstück* to recapitulate material outside the tonic. The drama of this event (Ex. 11*h*) is heightened by the arresting juxtaposition of the spacious Bb octaves (bars 165) played by the entire ensemble at *ff* (reminding us of the movement's opening) and the sudden contradiction of an A flat minor triad (bar 166) at *pp*. These spacious octaves prove to be an anticipation of the motto which returns persistently on a B flat triad (bar 167). Yet even this reassertion fails to swing the balance back to the tonic, for a further contradiction to the A flat minor triad continues to undermine any sense of stability. After a further statement of the motto on the dominant of C,

---

[37] Ibid. 11 Dec. 1877.

Ex. 11. Wind Nonet in B flat (1877). *a* motto figure (figure 'x'), first movement; *b* opening theme (figure 'a'), first movement; *c* secondary fragment (figure 'y'), first movement; *d* third subsidiary idea (figure 'z'), first movement; *e* opening idea of second group, first movement; *f* closing idea of second group, first movement; *g* reference to figure 'y' in second group, first movement; *h* point of recapitulation, first movement; *i* opening idea, Scherzo; *j* figure 'y', Scherzo; *k* opening theme of slow movement; *l* climax of cyclic scheme at the end of the Finale.

(g)

(h)

(i)   **Allegro molto**

(j)

cont. over/

Ex. 11. cont.

figure 'a' returns in the 'wrong' key (cf. Ex. 11*b*) which is only rectified rather crudely by the precipitate interjection of the oboe (bar 176).

The material of the Scherzo is clearly derived from the motto and figure 'y' (Ex. 11*i* and 11*j*) but the Trio, replete with drones and shepherd's pipe tune, attempts to create a pastoral evocation in total contrast. The motto also permeates the lyrical idea of the slow movement though it is more elusively positioned (Ex. 11*k*), and Parry also incorporates the contour of figure 'x' into the basic outline of the second-group material. The final movement of the Nonet represents the climax of the work's cyclic construction, in that its sonata structure is built on all the principal themes from previous movements. The main climax of the cyclic scheme, however, occurs at the end of the movement where most of the main themes appear simultaneously above a protracted dominant pedal (Ex. 11*l*).

The fact that Parry was preparing a set of parts for the Nonet in February 1878 is confirmation of his intention to have the work performed. A pencilled note in another hand at the end of the score ('Fine copying 22/1/78. S. West. Crystal Palace Orchestra') suggests that the work was looked over by a member of the Crystal Palace Orchestra, and markings in the parts also suggest that it was rehearsed. What is clear, however, is that the Nonet received no public performance during Parry's lifetime and had to wait until 1937 before it was heard. The Nonet is a fine example of pioneer wind writing and is all the more remarkable in that it pre-dates nearly all the major works for wind written in the second half of the nineteenth century such as Dvořák's Serenade, Op. 44 (1878), Strauss's Serenade Op. 7 (1881), and Gounod's *Petite Symphonie* (1885). Brahms's Serenade in A, Op. 16 which is predominantly for wind instruments, was particularly well known to Parry and he would have learnt much from copying out the score. Yet the unusual instrumentation (for flute, oboe, cor anglais, two clarinets, two horns, and two bassoons), the intense cyclic organization, and a lyricism frequently combined with excursions into Wagnerian harmony reveal an inclination to experiment beyond the parameters of Brahmsian severity.

1878 was to be an auspicious year for Parry in terms of both creative productivity and the opportunities to hear his works performed. Early in January Stanford paid him a visit: 'We played my Duo in E,' he recorded, 'and he played me his brilliant Toccata and some bits out of his opera from Lalla Rookh. He reads wonderfully and has great facility generally and power also, and enthusiasm.'[38] Then on 22 January Dannreuther agreed to perform the Piano Trio with Holmes and Lasserre at the next of his fifth series of chamber concerts at Orme Square. This was his first chance to have a work performed publicly in London. His diary entry for 31 January conveys a mixture of suppressed excitement, apprehension, and finally, disappointment:

At 10.30 to rehearsal of my Trio with Maudie. The first movement was dreadfully troublesome and kept them at work for about an hour and a half. Scherzo soon went with a little trouble with the passage in the Trio. Slow movement also not very troublesome and the last not nearly so troublesome as we expected, though Mr Lasserre the Frenchman was very much bothered by the syncopations.

Lots of friends came to hear my Trio. Eddie, Spencer, Benson, etc. . . . The first movement went fairly well, but the Scherzo which I expected to be best of all to the public [came] to grief. The loose MS fell down on Dannreuther's hands in turning over and put him out. Then Mr Holmes who otherwise played very steady and well missed a point. Then at a place where Mr Lasserre had to come in by himself he missed altogether and for several bars there was a complete blank; a further confusion occurred in other important points and the movement was quite spoilt. I felt very disappointed and an encore of the slow movement failed to bring back my spirits, though they played it very well the second time. Most of the last movement went well. People seemed very pleased at it . . .

[38] Diary, 11 Jan. 1878.

Aware that the performance had been defective, Dannreuther included it in his next concert on 28 February which 'went splendidly and the musicians present seemed very pleased.'[39]

On 6 February there was a new addition to the Parry family with the birth of a second daughter, Gwendolen—a choice of name which continued to reflect a passion for George Eliot's novels, in this case the last and most remarkable, *Daniel Deronda*. The question of Gwendolen's christening soon led to a considerable dispute amongst both families, for memories were still fresh in their minds of his deliberate absence at Dorothea's baptism. Yet, ultimately, his concern for the feelings of his rapidly ageing father (though probably appreciably less for his over-bearing mother-in-law) led him to give up his stand, though it was evidently done wholly reluctantly: 'It really is an absurd pitch of constraint that I should not only yield to the baby's being jabbered over and splashed by a parson in the interests of "the Church" for the sake of other people's feelings, but also have to endorse his nonsense by my presence—and yet I was absolutely driven to it by the unforeseen force of circumstances.'[40] His acquiescence was largely due to Maude's delicate state of health which he did not wish to exacerbate; nor did he wish to compound the offence to his father who was by now more distraught than ever over the deterioration of Clinton's condition. There can be no doubt that Parry was himself profoundly upset by his brother's progressive illness. In his more lucid moments Clinton still showed sparks of his real intellectual potential. These he committed to paper. His mistake, however, was to send his articles to his father. In October 1877 Parry received one such article entitled 'Cosmic Emotion' from an irate Thomas Gambier Parry:

He does not make a word of comment in sending it to me but Clin writes to me that he had received a furious letter from Possie about it, which Clin describes metaphysically as a 'foaming at the mouth'. The article is very poetical, philosophical, full of Clin's old warm-hearted breadth of feeling, but containing many allusions to advanced views of Unitarianism and Biology and reference to modern philosophers quoting them with approval; which of course raised Possie's High Church ire to a terrible degree.[41]

But glimpses of Clinton's sobriety were now extremely rare and, during a meeting in London, Parry found himself uncomfortably confronted with the pathetic reality of his drunken brother's condition:

His humours alternated between violence and swearing and crying, extravagant demonstrations of affection for me, and collapse. When I got him to Phillimore Place I found I could not manage him. He was perfectly wild for more drink and my only chance seemed to get him down to Swindon [to the asylum]. I had to

[39] Diary, 28 Feb. 1878.   [40] Ibid. 5 Mar. 1878.   [41] Ibid. 22 Oct. 1877.

hold him always as he seized every opportunity to try and get after more drink. Altogether he was a most piteous and sickening spectacle.[42]

He was also faced with the difficult predicament of Clinton's separated wife and children whom the rest of the family now preferred to ignore. 'You are the *only one* of all your family', wrote Florence Parry, 'who ever writes to me in a really affectionate way, and you have always been the same to me.'[43] For Parry it was a typically humane response both out of pity for the harsh social ostracization she and her children had suffered, and out of loyalty to his brother who now had no real future.

This inter-familial bitterness, though it was always distressing, would earlier have deflated him, but such was the momentum of his creativity and new-found confidence that he was able to surmount any feelings of encroaching depression. Already he had begun to give composition lessons and spent much time in correspondence with Charles Stuart Wortley who frequently sought his advice on musical matters. More significant was his intoxication with the sound of his Trio whose first performance spurred him on to commence a string quartet. Without the familiar pianistic idiom, however, he soon began to encounter problems: 'I've stuck fast in a bit in my Quartett in G and remain puzzled, and neither walking or sitting can I grapple with it.'[44] Nevertheless, work continued at a furious rate. By 11 March he had written a large portion of the 'death's head Scherzo with gleams of hope in it'.[45]. A diary entry of 17 March mentions Dannreuther's approval of the first movement and a similar reaction was noted a week later on 24 March to the 'new slow movement'. By May 13 he had finished the last movement and was copying out parts for an impending performance. Unfortunately Dannreuther's concert series was fully booked and other potential performers, such as Franke, were too busy to consider rehearsing it, so it was temporarily shelved.

During this period of boundless energy Parry and Dannreuther were also preoccupied in rehearsing the *Großes Duo* in preparation for a concert in Orme Square in April. As a trial run a performance was given to a select audience on 31 March, and then on 11 April he made his 'first appearance in public in London' receiving warm accolades from his friends and musical colleagues. Two days later he had the satisfaction of hearing Brahms's Symphony No. 1 for the first time. His expectations of the piece were naturally high and these had been reinforced ever since he had received Grove's glowing report in Cannes the previous year. His reaction, surprisingly, was one of disappointment: 'He does not seem quite at his ease in the orchestration and there are many bits which don't

---

[42] Ibid. 1 May 1878.
[43] Letter from Florence Parry, 25 August 1878, ShP.
[44] Diary, 25 Feb. 1878.
[45] Ibid. 11 Mar. 1878.

come out at all, and the work doesn't seem to me to hang well together, and what is most curious of all there are some decided reminiscences in it, especially in the last movement.'[46] After the serious challenge and assessment of Brahms's new work, Parry simply could not countenance the lightweight musical language of Sullivan's new operetta *The Sorcerer*. Artistically Sullivan's score seemed bereft of ideas and was consequently the victim of some scathing criticism. '[I] thought it the poorest flippant fooling I ever sat through;' he wrote heatedly, 'Gilbert has made some good bits in the dialogue, but it is cheap and second rate altogether.'[47] Rarely thereafter did Sullivan's music ever strike a note of sympathy with him.

Two months after the birth of Gwendolen, Maude was still unwell and her doctors were once again recommending her to go abroad for the winter. The thought of another enforced six months' exile at such a crucial time in his career was intolerable. To stem any worsening of the situation the family left London for Wilton on 18 April. With an interlude of a few days in London at the end of April they remained there until 6 May. For Parry the affluent surroundings of Wilton were utterly enervating, added to which the differences in political views between the Herberts' arch conservatism and his allegiance to Gladstone's Liberalism were irreconcilably entrenched:

The violence with which the family—i.e. George, Gety and Sidney—talk about Gladstone is perfectly astounding. As Eddie said, it is quite indecent. According to their views, everything he does is for the sake of popularity. . . . Their way of talking is so extraordinary that I can only listen with gaping mouth and answer not a word, for I simply don't know what to say to such a torrent of invective. If one attempts to say a word in his defence one is gaped at as if one was a lunatic.[48]

It was therefore a great relief to find himself back in Phillimore Place even though he was once again alone, for Maude was away staying with friends. As a member of the organizing committee (along with his friends Robin Benson, Arthur Balfour, and Stanford) of Franke's series of Tuesday-evening chamber concerts, he took advantage of having his Trio performed again on 14 May with Dannreuther, Franke, and the cellist, Hausmann, though it was, unfortunately, 'abominably done'.[49]

During the subsequent revisions of the Trio Parry began to consider the notion of a Lisztian one-movement work which had so captured his imagination in Scharwenka's concerto. So powerful did the idea become that he took to sketching a *Fantasie-Sonate in einem Satz für Violine und Clavier* on 22 May. For ten days, spending up to nine hours a day composing, he was possessed by the piece until it was finished on 2 June:

---

[46] Diary, 13 Apr. 1878.   [47] Ibid. 17 Apr. 1878.
[48] Ibid. 18 Apr. 1878.   [49] Ibid. 14 May 1878.

'Got to the end of my Fantasie Sonata for piano and violin in B major in the morning and took it to Dannreuther,' he wrote triumphantly, 'He was pleased with it, especially the Lento part.'[50]

The scheme of the Sonata is a particularly interesting attempt at a solution of the one-movement design with internal structural features that are far more experimental than the Nonet. The work commences with an expansive first group in B major which introduces four distinct ideas (Ex. 12*a*, *b*, *c*, and *d*) of which three (Themes 1, 2, and 4) share similar rhythmical or melodic features. The lyrical penchant of this section is continued in the second group which redeploys Theme 1 (with new consequent material) in the third-related key of A flat. However, Parry did not intend this to be a stable tonal area for the music soon passes to the dominant of F minor which is drawn out emphatically over the closing 12 bars of this paragraph. The open-ended preparatory nature of the second group is the first of numerous unconventional tonal procedures that ensure the continuity of this piece. The next section is especially remarkable for the way in which Parry seeks to create the illusion of a Scherzo but which is at the same time both tonally and thematically developmental. It begins by stepping up the tempo ('più moto') and reworking Theme 2. A further change in tempo ('poco più moto') accompanies a sudden radical alteration in texture to an imitative one using two new fragments. After a passage of rather austere 'Beethovenian' contrapuntal treatment the music begins to gather momentum, eventually climaxing on a prolonged dominant of F. Resolution of this dominant is tantalizingly denied as the rhythmical dynamism subsides, first to the dominant of D, and then finally to the dominant of B in preparation for the return of the tonic. With the recapitulation of expositional material it would appear that the form of the work is destined to follow the conventional sonata plan. Themes 1 and 2 are restated identically but Theme 3 is extended, and after a sudden climactic switch to the Neapolitan the violin embarks on an impassioned, angular, and distinctly chromatic passage. This change of direction heralds the preparation of another new section—a slow movement (marked 'lento') in E minor. It was this part of the Sonata that earned the greatest praise from Dannreuther, and from its structural originality it is clear why he thought so highly of it. Perhaps the most remarkable aspect of the movement is its total independence of formal models by European composers. Although precedents have been cited in connection with Parry's unusual recapitulatory procedures in the Violin Sonata in D minor, the *Concertstück* and the Nonet (which were undoubtedly partially responsible for the slow movement's integral

[50] Ibid. 2 June 1878.

Ex. 12. Fantasie Sonata in B major (1878). *a* theme 1; *b* theme 2; *c* theme 3; *d* theme 4; *e* theme 5; *f* theme 6.

(*a*) *Allegro quasi maestoso*

Theme 1

(*b*)

Theme 2

(*c*)

Theme 3

(*d*)

Theme 4

(*e*)

Theme 5

Theme 6

complexity), there is little evidence to suppose that the sophisticated through-composed design, coupled with the 'transformed' recapitulation would suddenly emerge in this section of the Fantasie Sonata.

The slow movement presents two further thematic ideas (Exx. 12*e* and *f*) both of which are derived from earlier material. After the rather dark, brooding tones of Theme 5 in E minor, the mood becomes more emotionally charged with the introduction of Theme 6 in the relative. This is an inspired, sweeping melody covering over two octaves and vividly coloured by inflections of the minor subdominant and the Neapolitan. In moving away from G major, however, Theme 6 attempts to behave developmentally both in its move to a third tonal area of B minor and in its further treatment of established motivic ideas. In rising to a passionate climax, still within B minor, Parry's stirring sequential phrases seem uncannily to foreshadow those of Elgar, particularly in the broad piano texture which seems more orchestral than pianistic. A radically modified form of restatement follows in which an abridged Theme 5 returns on the dominant of E and the establishment of the tonic is given to a radiant Theme 6 in E major. At this stage, conscious of this movement's function as an interpolation, the tonality is steered back towards the dominant of B in preparation for a second recapitulation.

Parry naturally felt the need to avoid further simple repetition of material at this stage, having already restated much of it literally in the first 'abortive' recapitulation. Yet though his attempts to rework his ideas are brave and resourceful such as the restatement of Theme 4 in D major and the truly Lisztian memory of the slow movement just before the coda, there is an overall sense of anticlimax, for something much bigger is required here as a peroration of the entire Sonata. It is a feeling that is particularly emphasized by the weak coda which fails to give the work a real sense of finality.

The energy expended in the furious bout of work on the Fantasie Sonata left Parry in a state of nervous elation bordering on hyperactivity. Though his duties for the Dictionary absorbed most of his daytime hours (he completed articles on 'Harmony', 'Kirchen Cantaten', and many shorter ones such as 'Imperfect Cadence', 'Interval', 'Italian Sixth' and 'Key'), the compulsion to explore other new avenues continued unabated. Even the potential distraction of finding new accommodation for Maude in Littlehampton failed to upset his concentration. Through-out June and July he worked at a Fantasia and Fugue in G major for organ, using sketches made in 1877. Then, in mid-July he found and rented Cudlow House in Rustington not far from Littlehampton which was ideal, for here, with no restrictions from cantankerous landladies, he could compose and practise unhindered. Invigorated by his new surroundings and by the company of the Dannreuthers who were holidaying in Littlehampton during July and August, he embarked on a detailed study of *Tristan und Isolde* and renewed his acquaintance with Bach's keyboard music. His revival of interest in Bach was later reflected in the original subject that formed the basis of his Theme and Nineteen Variations in D minor for piano which were composed rapidly between 25 and 28 August (though the work itself was not performed in its final version until February 1885). The first version contained seventeen variations, but Parry added two more in October 1882 when he was considering the work for publication.

This set of variations shows a considerable advance on the modest Variations on an Air by Bach. The model for the latter, no doubt recommended by Macfarren, was primarily Mendelssohn's *Variations sérieuses*, but it is clear from the opening variations of the later work that the procedures exhibited in Brahms's sets Opp. 21, 23, and 24 had become the dominant precedents—a fact that is later confirmed by Parry's 'Variations' article for Grove, written in October 1884:

His [Brahms's] principles are in the main those of Beethoven, while he applies such devices as condensation of groups of chords, anticipations, inversions, analogues, sophistication by means of chromatic passing notes etc., with an elaborate but fluent ingenuity which sometimes makes the tracing of the theme in a variation quite a difficult intellectual exercise.

Parry's set shows the well-established method of commencing with variations that adhere strictly to the bar structure and harmonic pacing of the theme. Having laid this foundation, the variations are allowed to expand (e.g. Variation 8) and contract (e.g. Variation 16) to become melodically and harmonically more abstract. This technique reaches a point where the enumeration of variations becomes intriguingly ambiguous as the clear delineation of them is obscured by skilful elision. Indeed, when challenged to disclose the nineteen variations, Parry abandoned the attempt after coming to two different totals. One organizational feature, the tonal plan, is unequivocally clear, however, for the variations are grouped and given fixed key areas (Ex. 13) which enhances the already strong sense of homogeneity; Tovey also maintained that the scheme provided the foundations for the much later Symphonic Variations of 1897 (in which, significantly, the variations are all numbered).

Ex. 13. *Theme and Nineteen Variations in D minor* (1878); tonal and thematic scheme.

Variations:	1-3	4-5	6	(trans.)	7-8	9-11	12-14	(trans.)	15 - 16	17	18-19
Key:	d	D			A	a	F		d -----		----D
									(♭II)	(V)	

The tranquil atmosphere at Rustington during the summer months of 1878 gave him ample time to satisfy his voracious literary appetite. He buried himself in Darwin's *Descent of Man*, Arnold's *Essays in Criticism*, Tennyson's *Harold*, and Swinburne's *Songs before Sunrise*. More significantly he became infatuated with Shelley's epic poem *Prometheus Unbound* (which was to have more momentous consequences two years later) and *The Troubadours* by the avid Wagnerian and new critic of *The Times*, Franz Hueffer. What particularly caught his imagination in Hueffer's book was the story of Guillem de Cabestanh, the late twelfth-century troubadour, quoted from a Provençal manuscript in the Laurentian Library in Florence. It began by telling of Guillem's attachment to the court of Sir Raimon de Rossilho and his favours towards Sir Raimon's wife, Lady Margarida, which resulted in a secret, 'Tristanesque' declaration of love and the composition of many of Guillem's most passionate love songs. By contrast, the tragic dénouement is violent and gory. Raimon, moved by jealousy and revenge eventually meets Guillem in a lonely place, slays him, cuts off his head, and tears out his heart. He then returns to the castle and has the heart roasted for his wife's dinner. After she has consumed the heart, Raimon divulges his secret, presents the head of her lover, and asks whether she enjoyed the flavour of the meat. Her noble answer, 'that never other meat or drink shall take from my mouth the sweetness which the heart of Guillem has left there', causes her enraged husband to fly at her with sword in hand, whereupon she runs to the balcony, throws herself off, and dies. Here was admirable potential for a symphonic study and it was not long before Parry had sketched the design of a 'concert overture'. It is clear from Grove's programme notes for the first performance that Parry was not tempted to treat the work programmatically. Instead, he preferred to restrict himself to a representation of Guillem's emotional responses and his relation to Margarida and Raimon by use of distinctive thematic ideas treated in sonata form—an approach Grove paralleled with the famous Beethovenian canon at the head of the 'Pastoral' Symphony—'Mehr Ausdruck der Empfindung als Malerei'.

On 10 September Parry completed an arrangement for four hands and by 24 September a draft score was delivered to Dannreuther. 'There's plenty in it that might be a deal better,' he wrote to his master, 'and I'll hope to improve upon it in the scoring. Meanwhile I hope you will use that blue pencil of yours to score things that look particularly unsatisfactory to you.'[51] After a lesson on 25 October Dannreuther gave his approval and, using his influence, approached Manns with a view to the overture's inclusion in a concert at the Crystal Palace early the following year. No sooner had Parry put the finishing touches to the score than he conceived the idea of a Piano Concerto in F sharp major, composing the outline of the first movement by 7 November. Yet, with another burst of creative energy, these sketches were set aside as he became preoccupied with plans for another chamber work, a Piano Quartet in A flat.

For most of January 1879 Parry was engrossed in the composition of the Piano Quartet and the revision of the Fantasie Sonata. Already, during the previous December, he had written a first movement and had sketched ideas for the Scherzo and slow movement. Completion of the Scherzo did not occur, however, until 3 January, while the extensively reworked slow movement was finished on 5 January. The last movement took longer to shape but when finished Dannreuther declared it 'better than any of the others except the slow movement'.[52] The rest of the month was spent revising the score in preparation for its performance in February. The Fantasie Sonata was also due for its first performance with Holmes and Dannreuther on 30 January which seemed to go well, but its reception was somewhat pallid compared with that of the Piano Quartet on 13 February. Parry's diary account gives a vivid picture of the final rehearsal two days earlier:

In the morning last rehearsal of my Quartett for Thursday. Of course it gave them a good deal of trouble, but they seemed much pleased with most of it. And with their expression of approval I was utterly happy. I was strangely intoxicated with much of it myself and astonished at the tone and richness which appeared. One thing pleased me especially. The effect of the Scherzo had been doubtful before. But this time it went and D[annreuther] at the end turned quickly to the others [Gompertz, Gibson, and Lasserre] and said loudly 'Superbe Satz'. The slow movement they expressed emphatically 'magnifique', 'ganz himmlisch' and so I was wild with delight. The end of the last movement went like mad.[53]

His singular satisfaction with the Piano Quartet was justified for it was by far his most assured instrumental work to date. In the majestic slow

[51] Letter to Edward Dannreuther, 24 Sept. 1878, Bod. MS Eng. Letters e.117.
[52] Diary, 12 Jan. 1879.   [53] Ibid. 11 Feb. 1879.

introduction of the first movement one already senses a work of much greater ambition, and the subsequent large-scale sonata movement shows a higher degree of tonal and thematic involution. The first movement, for all its impressive workmanship, does not rise to the level of inspiration conveyed by the Scherzo and slow movement. Indeed the Scherzo, set in the relative F minor, must surely stand as one of Parry's most outstanding contributions to the form. Structurally it moves on from the modified ternary design used in the Scherzo of the earlier Piano Trio, for here Parry combines elements of recomposition with rhythmic dynamism in the outer two sections and a melodious Trio in a radiant C major. The slow movement is yet more masterly in the way Parry succeeds in fashioning protracted, self-developing thematic paragraphs together with a series of broad, cumulative climaxes, and these are further enhanced by the sense of continuity created by the avoidance of full closes. The latter technique in particular caused his critics to associate him more readily with Wagner, even though similar procedures had already been widely essayed in earlier chamber works. The movement, an abridged sonata, commences with a wonderfully spacious theme (Ex. 14*a*) which subsequently forms the basis of a sumptuous contrapuntal texture projected over 40 bars. After a splendid *ff* climax, the return to D flat is replaced by a striking interrupted cadence taking us on to a chord of A major. This initiates a second paragraph and a further accumulation of tension generated in particular by the prolonged central pedal over which the strings weave their wide-ranging contrapuntal lines (Ex. 14*b*). This second, more dissonant climax is spread over at least 20 bars which, after subsiding, leads to a restatement of the opening theme though without reaching a full close. These two main sections are both recapitulated, but being grounded in the tonic they are subject to extensive reworking. Similarly neither section enjoys a resolution of its climax and this is reserved until the end of the coda. To provide a finale after such a movement was indeed a considerable challenge, but Parry's last movement continues to explore the idiom thoroughly, and there is much effective writing for the strings particularly in their solo trio in the second group. Furthermore, the references to material from the first movement and Scherzo within the development and coda provide an interesting cyclic dimension to the piece as a whole.

The Piano Quartet was performed again, albeit rather roughly, on 1 April in front of a larger audience in Carlton Gardens at the home of Arthur Balfour. The programme consisted entirely of Parry's works: songs sung by Sophie Löwe and Mrs Godfrey Pearse, the *Großes Duo* (played by Dannreuther and Parry), the Piano Trio, and of course the Piano Quartet (Dannreuther, Straus, Jung, and Lasserre). The critic of the *Pall Mall Gazette* was quick to point out the 'modernisms' of the

Ex. 14. Piano Quartet in A flat (1879), third movement. *a* opening theme; *b* passage leading to climax of second group.

instrumental works which he felt were a significant departure from standard English practices:

In Mr Parry's works we have the inspiration of a composer supported by the learning of an earnest and eclectic student who is no less at home in Bach than in Wagner. 'In polyphonous treatment', says a writer who has made a careful study of Mr Parry's compositions, 'and continuousness in his thematic work, avoiding formal cadences, he ranges himself with the most recent school of composition; breaking away entirely from English ideas, which, submitted to the influence of Mendelssohn, have not dared or cared to look beyond the limits that master may be said to have defined . . . This performance has taken him out of the category of mere amateurs, and future public opportunities will no doubt enable us to recur to his works and criticize them from the only possible standpoint, as we would those of Messrs. Stanford, Gadsby, Wingham, Davenport, and other young aspirants to fame—on the real merits they display as music appertaining to the English school, in which Mr Parry promises to take a leading place.[54]

This was heartening criticism but the suggestion that Parry had allied himself with Wagner was to trigger opposition from several of his friends and colleagues. Ludwig Straus, the violinist, voiced his objections at a rehearsal which Parry recorded with amazement: 'Straus does not like the Violin Fantasie and the [Piano] Quartett because *there are not enough cadences* in them, and too many keys!!'[55] Joachim, who played through the Fantasie Sonata with the composer on 25 March offered little comment, but his sympathies with Parry's music were gradually declining as he detected the influence of Wagner. Davison, writing the programme notes for the first performance of the Piano Quartet at a Monday Popular Concert four years later (3 December, 1883), was grudgingly magnanimous, though he too was suspicious of Parry's Wagnerian tendencies:

Of what especial school Mr Parry is a steadfast disciple needs not to be told. He is no timid believer, but a proselyte through intimate persuasion, as is proved in the works he has hitherto given to the world, and would scorn to repudiate the convictions that have guided and are still guiding his artistic career . . . it would answer no purpose to follow the *péripétie* of this movement, with its several themes rolling, more or less unexpectedly, into and out of each other, with an utter (though, be it added, thoroughly honest) disregard for what has been inculcated as 'form' by the example of the recognised great masters of art, from the first quartet of Mozart to the last of Beethoven, which show imagination as well as abstract musical beauty.

Scepticism also continued to dog Parry during the rehearsal of *Guillem de Cabestanh* on 14 March when Manns became awkward about the changing tempo and dynamic markings. Though the rehearsal the following day seemed more promising, the performance came to grief:

---

[54] *Pall Mall Gazette*, (12 Apr. 1879).   [55] Diary, 23 Mar. 1879.

'at the concert it began badly,' Parry wrote furiously, 'and the horn played the tune jauntily instead of in wafted softness and it all went to pot. In my estimation it was a complete fiasco.'[56] The conductor of the New Philharmonic Concerts, Wilhelm Ganz, after asking to see the overture, abruptly refused it on account of its technical difficulties. 'I readily helped him out,' Parry recorded sarcastically, 'as he is a kind of animal that doesn't suit me—then I got out of the house as quick as I could with the rejected work under my arm.'[57] At about the same time he received a letter from Montgomery who was holidaying in San Remo. Through the newspapers and reports from a mutual friend, Robin Benson, Montgomery had received encouraging news of Balfour's concert and the performance of *Guillem*, but he too could not refrain from making disapproving remarks about the insidious infiltration of Wagnerian traits in Parry's musical language. His letter was couched in the frank language of the 'Essay and Discussion Club':

The overture, I gathered from 'The Times', was badly played in parts and, partly for this reason, partly for others, not enthusiastically received, but I suppose you could hardly expect to take the world by storm with the first performance of [an] orchestral work—especially when written—as I gather—on very heretical lines . . . From a purely personal and selfish point of view, I'm not much pleased with the account of your recent and more important compositions. All I hear promises well for your success and tells well for your power and originality, but the remarks point to that quality in your work which makes Wagner so unsatisfactory to me and *immoral* in the effect he produces on my emotional condition. A tendency to promiscuous intercourse with all sorts of loose keys instead of that faithful cleaving to one only—in an enlarged sense—to which one is accustomed in the respectable masters. I speak with insufficient information and with insufficient knowledge and have considerable hopes that I shall find my misgivings removed when I come to hear you; but the observations I have seen certainly point to a sort of independent Wagnerism as your present style and in Wagner I undoubtedly find too much excitement of a disorderly kind and too little—or rather *no* repose . . . I said that all I heard promised well for your success—but here too I have a few doubts as to whether your present style of work does not appeal to too small a section of mankind . . .[58]

This lack of empathy began to rankle until, in early September, Parry's patience ran out after Dannreuther passed on a trenchant note from Manns who did not mince his words in writing: 'Friend Parry's Overture is a downright bad piece of music from sheer want of proper self-criticism on his part.'[59] Parry was sorely hurt by this accusation. 'A fair example of the "insolence of office",' wrote the composer angrily; 'and,

[56] Ibid. 15 Mar. 1879.   [57] Ibid. 22 Apr. 1879.
[58] Letter from Hugh Montgomery, 20 Apr. 1879, ShP.
[59] Graves, *Hubert Parry*, i. 204.

even though it may be true and I not he am the fool, it is an evil and bullying way of expressing his opinion.'[60]

Though Mann's antipathy towards *Guillem de Cabestanh* stemmed largely from his dislike of Parry's 'modern' Wagnerian rhetoric which was, on the whole, uncongenial to him, he was discerning enough to sense the structural flaws in the work. It is clear from the design of the overture, with its peculiar adaptation of sonata principles and particularly its multi-sectional development, that the Lisztian genre of the symphonic poem was in Parry's mind. This is further substantiated by the 'psychological' dimension of the work (i.e. the study of Guillem's character and the love of Lady Margarida) which is a predominant feature of Liszt's own works such as one finds in *Prometheus*, *Orpheus*, or the *Faust* Symphony. Surprisingly, however, there is no attempt to integrate the incongruities of the diverse thematic material by means of a series of Lisztian transformations, and the sonata organization comes to grief in a tortuous and unbalanced recapitulation. Moreover, there is not enough conviction in the dramatic potential of the story and several of the crucial dramatic gestures, in particular that of Lady Margarida's noble retort to Raimon immediately prior to the coda, seem rather tame in comparison with similar contemporary contexts in Liszt, Smetana, or Tchaikovsky.

Notwithstanding its faults, however, *Guillem* is an important work in this experimental period of Parry's output. Many of the gestures are unashamedly Wagnerian, and perhaps express more than any other of his instrumental works his reverence for that composer's art. This is clear in the secondary idea of the first group (Ex. 15*a*—what Grove labelled as 'the first dawn of the unlawful passion in [Guillem's] heart') and the main second-group theme (Ex. 15*b*—Guillem's 'disloyal, traiterous love') which recall the rich lyricism of *Die Meistersinger*, while the closing material of the exposition seems almost self-consciously reminiscent of *Tristan* (Ex. 15*c*). These references are, however, not simply an interesting indication of Wagnerian deference, for they are significant in the later crystallization of Parry's melodic style, particularly in the assimilation of accented passing notes (both diatonic and chromatic), appoggiaturas, enhanced dominant chords of the ninth, eleventh, and thirteenth, and various methods of delayed melodic resolution, not to mention one of the most distinctive features of all—sequence.

One might assume from *Guillem* that Parry had totally succumbed to 'Wagner fever', but instead it appears that this work represented a watershed in his stylistic development. The belated reply to Hugh

[60] Diary, 7 Sept. 1879.

Ex. 15. *Guillem de Cabestanh* (1878). *a* first group, secondary idea; *b* second group, opening idea; *c* second group, closing idea.

Montgomery's letter, fuelled by the continuing anger over Manns's allegations, makes his position clear:

Your criticisms of my attempts at composition are founded upon not over trustworthy hearsay, so I need not answer them. I like my compositions as little as possible. I feel that they are far from what they ought to be; but I take a good deal of pains and do not write ill considered reflections of Wagner, and though I feel the impress of his warmth and genius strongly, I am not tempted to tread in the same path in the matter of construction, because what is applicable to the province of 'dramatic' music is entirely alien to instrumental music. I have my own views on the latter subject, and if they differ from the expositions of the pedagogues, that is chiefly because I have endeavoured to see with my own eyes instead of following blind leaders of the blind. No doubt my attempts at music are destined to failure. I am not keen about success. It is not my business; and though I cannot say that it does not often cost me a great effort to keep at work, on the whole I have such a strong sense that earnest work is the greatest and surest source of happiness in life, that I am able to grind on without considering anything but that what I do shall be the best I can, and leave reward of any sort out of the question as superfluous.[61]

It was a single-minded declaration. He was determined to work on regardless, even though he did not carry the sympathies of his friends or his colleagues, save Dannreuther and Stanford. Montgomery replied with even greater frankness complaining that his attempts were of 'a perverse kind':

If you have worked out your vein of what I may—with rather a stretch of language—call *altruistic* music, God forbid that I should say a word to discourage you from lightening the troubles of your life by such an innocent pursuit as the production of purely egoistic music. But neither I, nor any of your friends believe that if you go the right way to work, you cannot write more music by which the world may be benefitted and as, compared with the production of music which we can all enjoy, and which makes us all feel better for listening to it, the production of such stuff as your own language, coupled with what others have told me, seems to point to, [it] appears to me, an unworthy employment for you—a sort of intellectual or aesthetic onanism; I venture—at the risk of not hearing from you again for six months and then getting snubbed—to raise my feeble protest.[62]

It was a protest that Parry, fully convinced of the direction of his stylistic development, chose wholly to ignore. He felt buoyed up by Dannreuther's unshakable faith, which counted for so much at this time. Dannreuther still vociferously encouraged Parry to hear all the newest works that were appearing in London be they Brahms's Violin Concerto (6 March), Tchaikovsky's Third Symphony (24 April), Wagner's *Siegfried Idyll* (3

---

[61] Letter to Hugh Montgomery, 15 Sept. 1879, ShP.
[62] Letter from Hugh Montgomery, 1 Dec. [1879], Blessingbourne, County Tyrone.

May), or Raff's 'Frühling' Symphony (15 November), and he paid Parry a rare compliment by including his *Großes Duo* together with illustrations from Brahms, Volkmann, Rubinstein, Saint-Saëns, Grieg, Tchaikovsky, and Liszt as part of a lecture entitled *Living Composers for the Pianoforte* which he delivered at the London Institution on 20 March. This level of activity and contact ensured that there was no check in Parry's creative momentum. Work on the Piano Concerto resumed in March and by 1 June he had completed a slow movement and had reached as far as the cadenza of the finale. 'He [Dannreuther] seemed well pleased and made exclamations of much satisfaction as he went through it,'[63] Parry wrote elatedly. At Rustington, where he found absolute tranquillity and no danger of interruption, the draft of the work was soon finished, and after suffering some 'excrutiating trouble'[64] with the highly original structure of the slow movement, the concerto was scored by 3 August. Dannreuther, who professed the concerto to be Parry's best work so far, then set plans in motion to perform it at the Crystal Palace in April 1880, with Manns, even though the latter believed that the experience would simply teach Parry another sobering lesson in composition.

Since the beginning of June Parry and Maude had resided at Cudlow House in Rustington where, with brief interludes at Highnam and Wilton, they based themselves until well into the new year, often in the company of the Garretts. Maude's health continued to give him cause for concern, so they decided to remain by the sea rather than risk a relapse by returning to London. As a result, Parry passed much of his time travelling between Victoria and Littlehampton. The attraction of the Crystal Palace concerts plus the new 'Orchestral Festival Concerts' under Richter at the St James's Hall was as potent as ever, and his work with Grove was now beginning to come to fruition with the first volume, containing parts i–vi, now available in print. Having reached the letter 'S' Grove delegated to him the responsibility of two large articles 'Sonata' and 'Symphony' as he felt that 'the author of Form should treat the two great vehicles of it'.[65] These articles occupied him during the lonely evenings at Phillimore Place, but back at Rustington the compulsion to compose soon returned as he conceived ideas for a Cello Sonata. This was begun in early November with the first movement complete by the end of the month. The slow movement took longer to form in his mind. 'I took a brisk walk beyond Preston along the sands,' he wrote, 'intending to work out a movement in my head, but when I got home I found the result extravagant and gave it up.'[66] The last movement also left him dissatisfied but work was spurred on by the offer of a

---

[63] Diary, 1 June 1879.   [64] Ibid. 18 July 1879.
[65] Letter from George Grove, 13 Oct. [1879], ShP.   [66] Diary, 29 Nov. 1879.

performance at Orme Square with Lasserre the following February. His motivation was, however, given a greater boost by an invitation from his old friend Charles Harford Lloyd and the Gloucester Three Choirs Committee to write a new choral work for the Festival in September. Such a commission at last beckoned the prospect of wider recognition.

7

Prometheus Unbound
Depression and Resolve

BEFORE Parry could begin work on his first choral commission, there were other priorities. In early January he negotiated the purchase of a field in Rustington where he planned to build the seaside home he had long dreamed of. Dannreuther was also anxious to perform both the Cello Sonata and the String Quartet in G in his new series of chamber concerts. The Sonata still had many deficiences of which he was rudely aware after a rehearsal at Orme Square in mid-January. 'First two movements were satisfactory,' he recorded, 'the last would not go at all, and was as rough as a hedgehog. Consequently I came away feeling miserable.'[1] More worrying, however, was the recurrence of the debilitating heart trouble of his teens. As Parry described it, the problem was an 'extraordinarily irregular action of the heart which hardly gave me an hour's peace. During the fits work was impossible, as it was almost unendurable except by walking rapidly about the room.'[2] His physician maintained that there was no permanent functional disorder, but strongly advised his patient to refrain from work for six weeks. This advice was heeded for no more than two days before his usual routine of vigorous exercise and long periods of 'brain work' was resumed. It was a pattern of behaviour that was to be repeated over and over again, much to the annoyance of his doctors and his closest family. Physiologically it was a familiar situation: an excitable, nervous temperament exacerbating a weak heart condition. Yet without the capacity to relax mentally there was little prospect of the condition ever improving. Moreover, in Parry's case there remained a dogged, almost lunatic defiance of any medical prognosis. The danger of a total breakdown in health was considerable and indeed soon became a reality; but having recovered to a certain degree, he could never then be dissuaded from continuing his punishing schedule.

[1] Diary, 18 Jan. 1880.
[2] Ibid. 19 Jan. 1880. Parry's heart condition was most probably a combination of angina and rheumatic heart fever, the former most likely to have been congenitally inherited from his father. It was common usage in the Victorian age to refer to an attack of angina as a 'heart attack', though the latter should not be confused with modern usage of the term which refers to a much more serious and often fatal coronary condition (such as, for example, a coronary thrombosis).

The performance of the Cello Sonata on 12 February pleased him greatly. 'The last movement took most apparently which surprised me,' he wrote, 'as I had thought it to be far inferior to the others . . . Lasserre sang the slow movement divinely.'[3] Contrary to his expectations, however, the audience found it difficult to understand in spite of the work's predominantly lyrical content. Subsequently this reaction seems to have accentuated his dissatisfaction with it and his discomfort with the idiom. After further extensive revisions Novello agreed to publish it in 1883, but, with the possible exception of the magnificent slow movement, he continued to feel dissatisfied with it. This is evident from the comments in his diary after a performance of the work at Orme Square on 3 December 1885 when he remarked: 'it went down pretty well, specially the slow movement. But it all sprawls about and is too long and indefinite.'

On 26 February Holmes, Gibson, Jung, and Lasserre performed his String Quartet in G which also delighted him, though the reception was similarly lukewarm. 'I had very few words of sympathy said to me after', he noted. The work was never heard again and was not submitted for publication. Perhaps the most tantalizing aspect of the piece, however, has been its mysterious disappearance, for although it is clear that it was in the possession of Gerald Finzi in 1948, the manuscript did not find its way into the collection of Parry autographs which Finzi later deposited in the Bodleian Library, Oxford in the 1950s. Dr Emily Daymond's catalogue of Parry's work gives brief details of the four movements (1. Allegro, G major 4/4; 2. Andante, C major 4/4; 3. Allegro molto, C minor 6/8; 4. Allegro moderato, G major 3/4) but the only commentary of the music occurs in an article provided by H. C. Colles for Cobbett's *Cyclopaedic Survey of Chamber Music* published in 1930. Colles's remarks suggest that the Quartet continued to reflect an experimental approach to structure consistent with other chamber works written at the time (e.g. the Nonet and Fantasie Sonata) as well as exhibiting an interesting attitude towards string sonorities:

The first movement of the quartet dashes straight into a fervent first subject which is never repeated in its entirety, though its figures pervade the greater part of the movement, even appearing in contact with the more expressive second subject. A critic has recently pointed out that 'there is no surer touchstone' of a classical composer's treatment of form than the precise way in which his recapitulation differs from his exposition [Tovey on Schubert, *The Heritage of Music* (Oxford, 1927), 102]. In this quartet the way in which Parry eludes a full-dress recapitulation of his first subject, which would necessitate a break in the texture, and, sweeping over the point of the return, recalls its features, presently extending a subsidiary idea of the second subject into a

[3] Diary, 12 Feb. 1880.

culminating coda, is a piece of masterly manipulation exactly suited to the special case.

. . . In the quartet the four movements are quite independent of one another as far as their thematic material is concerned. The scherzo (which here follows the slow movement; . . .) is the most strongly emotional of the four. Parry described it as a 'death's-head scherzo with gleams of hope in it'; and the expression is justified in a grim touch given to the rattling theme announced on the viola by the prominence of an augmented fourth interval. The recurrence of this theme on the fourth string of each instrument exemplifies in the string quartet, what is more obviously apparent throughout the wind nonet, the desire of the composer at this period to associate his musical ideas with distinctive qualities of tone colour.[4]

His disappointment with the reception of the String Quartet soon evaporated as he became absorbed with the more pressing matter of the Piano Concerto which was to be performed at the Crystal Palace on 3 April. Parry approached this second appearance at the Crystal Palace with greater reserve and not a little dread, for at the back of his mind was the memory of Manns's unpleasant admonishment after the performance of *Guillem de Cabestanh* and he was naturally anxious to avoid any further difficulties with the conductor. Manns's abrasive personality flared up again at the final rehearsal which ended in their having a 'loud wrangle before the whole orchestra'.[5] Yet, in spite of this clash of personalities, the performance turned out well, though the critic of the *Monthly Musical Record*, himself enthusiastic about the work, maintained that it 'was coldly, almost frigidly received' by the audience. Parry appears to have been largely satisfied with the performance though he felt that the orchestra was at times too heavy for the piano. This view was echoed in a letter of congratulation from Grove:

I think that there are one or two places where the piano did not come out as it ought, but whether that was D's fault or arose from a little overscoring or (as Taylor thought) from the pf. passage being too quiet to be heard I can't judge. I thought the sound of the orchestra very good, very pleasant to hear and also very individual and like no one else . . .

As to Manns I think if I were you I should write a note and thank him for having afforded you the opportunity of bringing forward the Concerto; and you might say some civil thing about his being hard worked. He told Taylor that he thought it *very good*, but that it might have been more easily written for the orchestra as to keys.[6]

Other complimentary letters were received from Davison (who thought it 'very clever indeed'[7]), from Franklin Taylor, and from his old friend

---

[4] H. C. Colles, s.v. 'Parry', in W. W. Cobbett (ed.), *Cyclopaedic Survey of Chamber Music* (Oxford, 1930; repr. 1964), 208–9.

[5] Diary, 3 Apr. 1880.

[6] Letter from George Grove, [Apr.], 1880, ShP.   [7] Ibid.

Mini von Glehn. But perhaps the most gratifying letter came from Frederick Corder after a second and more satisfactory performance under Richter on 10 May:

I hoped to have had a talk with you last night, but was disappointed, so I must write and thank you, first for your note and praises of my Suite, and secondly for demonstrating in your Concerto (I must consider last night as its *first* performance) that there are English composers who can write. I was impressed by the slow movement even at the Palace, and a proper rendering makes it perfectly charming. The last movement has great 'go', but if I may venture to find fault, the cadenza is a little long, though you have so much to bring into it that I'm sure I don't see how you could shorten it.[8]

Of the performance conducted by Richter, Parry made no comment except for a brief remark at a rehearsal on 8 May regarding the orchestra's considerable difficulty in negotiating 'the 6 sharps business'[9] and that attention to detail was prevented by Richter's giving too much time to the rehearsal of other works. Some small alterations for the concerto's second performance were made, but the work was given a major revision in 1895 when it was revised for a concert on 19 October as part of a series celebrating the fortieth anniversary of the institution of the Crystal Palace Saturday concerts. The pianist this time was Frederick Dawson.

Although the three-movement design of the concerto seems conventional enough, the internal structural organization of the movements, particularly the first and second, show thinking of a cogent, complex, and most unconventional nature. The scheme for the revised first movement is a curious and intriguing one. The model of the classical Brahmsian orchestral introduction (ritornello) has no part to play here, for after a short statement of the main thematic idea (Ex. 16*a*) shared by piano and orchestra, the piano breaks loose with a cadenza-like flourish which recalls the similar procedure of Liszt's Concerto in E flat with which Parry was extremely familiar. This cadenza does not act purely as an interruption, for it functions as a transition and tonal preparation to a startlingly remote key area. The piano eventually concludes its cadenza on the dominant of G after which the orchestra alone takes up the opening material in G major. This remarkable change of direction was one that Parry subsequently chose to integrate into the fabric of the entire concerto. Over the next 18 bars G major is gradually eroded as the tonality finds its way back to the dominant of F sharp. A further repeat of the principal material in the tonic follows played by the orchestra with accompanying elaborations from the piano. A similarly arresting tonal contrast occurs with the lyrical second group, which, recalling the first-

[8] Letter from Frederick Corder, 11 May, 1880, ShP.   [9] Diary, 8 May 1880.

Ex. 16. Piano Concerto in F sharp (1878–80). *a* main thematic idea, first movement; *b* opening of second group, first movement; *c* opening of Finale.

group material in its opening strain (Ex. 16*b*), is set in D major.[10] The significance of this tonality is felt most strongly at the point of recapitulation, for here the return of the tonic is briefly but radically interrupted by a restatement of first-group material in D major. This sudden shift vividly parallels the move to G major experienced at the beginning of the exposition, though this time it is intensified by a further extraordinary shift back into F sharp from which point the recapitulation unfolds more conventionally.

The second movement of the concerto is yet more fascinating for it is one of Parry's most imaginative through-composed structures as well as one of his most thematically economic. Certain features, such as the extensive developmental second-group (itself a reworking of first-group material), are reminiscent of the 'lento' section of the Fantasie Sonata. This may also be said of the 'transformed' recapitulation, though in the concerto this is far more extensive and intricate. Parry's article on 'Symphony' for Grove suggests that Brahms's Second Symphony may have provided the initial ideas for such a process:

In the laying out of the principal sections as much freedom is used as is consistent with the possibility of being readily followed and understood. Thus in the recapitulatory portion of a movement the subjects which characterise the sections are not only subjected to considerable and interesting variation, but are often much condensed and transformed. In the first movement of the second symphony, for instance, the recapitulation of the first part of the movement is so welded onto the working-out portion that the hearer is only happily conscious that this point has been arrived at without the usual insistence to call his attention to it. Again, the subjects are so ingeniously varied and transformed in restatement that they seem almost new, though the broad melodic outlines give sufficient assurance of their representing the recapitulation.

It was almost certainly this aspect of the movement that profoundly impressed Corder. Evidently Parry was also highly encouraged by the success of the movement as a musical unity, for his later instrumental works show a similar mode of thought.

The last movement, though thematically less inspired, is significant from a cyclic point of view. Of particular interest is the long cadenza (again extensively revised for Dawson in 1895) in which the two main

[10] It is clear from the manuscript that the decision to set the second group exclusively in D major raises some interesting questions. For the two performances under Manns and Richter in 1880 the orchestra initially introduced the second-group material in the dominant, C sharp major, before moving to D. This scheme is described in Grove's programme notes for the Crystal Palace performance, and the same analysis appears in the programme for the performance under Richter. However, the autograph manuscript and parts show that Parry dispensed with the orchestral passage in the dominant for the 1895 performance. It is also clear from the manuscripts that the transitional cadenza and the arresting move to G major early in the movement were also results of the extensive revisions in 1895, and were included undoubtedly to enhance both the significance of the shift to D major at the point of recapitulation and to the frequent shifts of similar character in the finale.

thematic ideas of the first movement reappear. But perhaps more important still is the way in which Parry re-incorporates the precipitate harmonic changes of direction so characteristic of the first movement. This is immediately apparent in the highly unusual nature of the opening theme of the finale (Ex. 16*c*) which always begins obliquely in D major before reverting to F sharp. The full potential of this tangential beginning is more fully realized in the numerous recurrences of this theme, for each time it is heard, it is preceded by dominant preparation for F sharp, and so consequently the brusque semitonal shift upwards to D major vividly reminds us of previous contexts in the first movement. This progression occurs on two occasions within the first group, but the full impact is reserved for the recapitulation and, most notably for the transition from cadenza to coda where the effect is momentous.

The overall success of Richter's performance of the concerto did much to cement Parry's relationship with the great German conductor, and it kindled an enthusiasm for Richter's concert series of which Parry became an ardent follower. During the 1880 season he attended all of Richter's concerts though he was sometimes perplexed by the un-conventional planning of the programmes. Nevertheless he remained deeply impressed by the quality of interpretation and the seed was planted in his mind to write a work for Richter to conduct.

At Rustington there was little time for relaxation during the summer. A price was agreed with the architect, Norman Shaw, to design and build a house on the recently acquired plot of land, and after negotiating with the builders in Littlehampton, the first brick was laid by Dorothea on 16 August. Of greater concern, however, was the distress caused by Clinton's restive condition at Highnam. Disturbing letters had arrived from his father with news that asylums and personal nurses had failed to subdue him, and that now the only alternative was to send him to the colonies again to keep him away from his wife and children. Having decided on New Zealand, Clinton left England on 29 June. Parry was there to see him off; it was the last time he would see his brother alive.

Before the première of the Piano Concerto he had begun to consider a suitable text as the subject of his commission for the Gloucester Festival. Since the summer of 1879 he had been attracted by the radical ideology of Shelley's *Prometheus Unbound* which, as part 'psychodrama' and part political allegory, expounded a combination of the Aeschylian myth of Prometheus, the champion of mankind, with the poet's own thesis of a heroic Satan and an oppressive God. Such epic ideas suggested a canvas on which his experience of dramatic vocal music could be mounted. The Wagnerian possibilities were also highly persuasive, as Shaw noted:

Wagner was anticipated in the year 1819 by a young country gentleman from Sussex named Shelley, in a work of extraordinary artistic power and splendour.

Prometheus Unbound is an English attempt at a Ring . . . Both works set forth the same conflict between humanity and its gods and governments, issuing in the redemption of man from their tyranny and by the growth of his will into perfect strength and self-confidence; and both finish by a lapse into panacea-mongering didacticism by the holding up of Love as the remedy for all evils and the solvent of all social difficulties.[11]

The major problem in setting Shelley's drama was the reduction of four Acts into a workable model. On 29 February he had discussed the possibilities with Dannreuther and went back to his teacher on 2 March with a proposed scheme of a 'Dramatic Cantata' in five scenes. Having obtained Dannreuther's approval, he instantly set to work and completed the first two scenes by 21 March. The response to his efforts augured well: 'went to Dann for a bit in the afternoon with the first scene of Prometheus, over which he seemed so much pleased that I went away intoxicated with delight at his commendations . . . Frank Pownall came after to Phillimore Place and sang it and the 2nd Scene and seemed also much pleased.'[12] With the distraction of the Piano Concerto the sketching of further scenes became irksome as he was 'stuck fast in the Jupiter and Demogorgon scene'[13] and his constant concern with the new house put paid to any resumption until after the Richter performance was over. By the middle of May he was at work again on the Chorus of Furies which gave him immense trouble. Nevertheless, progress was rapid. Dannreuther was shown each new scene as it was finished and towards the end of June he was nearing the end of Part 2 Scene 3. But no sooner was the last chorus completed when serious doubts began to loom over its construction which eventually led to despair:

I worked at Prometheus for about three and a half hours and discovered suddenly to my horror that the last chorus is an utter hodgepodge of jumpy and unassimilable sections. I had not realised the general effect in totality before and it came upon me suddenly. There is nothing to be done now as there is no time to rewrite it, but to face it and despair. It appears to be the fault of having taken such a helterskelter of disconnected choice songs which nothing can even make into a continuous musical whole—as far as I can see at present. It is heartbreaking after such a persistent and heavy grind as I have had.[14]

A letter to Dannreuther of 13 July expressed the same misgivings:

I have run my head into a trap in the last chorus. I had to grind so furiously hard at the scoring of it that all my attention got centralized in the details, and it was not till I got near the end that I found these short isolated verses by the Spirits of the Hour and Spirits of the Air and what not get most abominably choppy. It's impossible for me to do it over again now, and it will probably have to go for

---

[11] G. B. Shaw, *The Perfect Wagnerite* (London, 1898), 230–1.
[12] Diary, 21 March 1880.   [13] Ibid. 10 Apr. 1880.   [14] Ibid. 7 July 1880.

first performance as it is, but I think it's very bad . . . I shall get you to have a look at it, and save me from any very atrocious exhibition.[15]

But the problems over *Prometheus* were destined to worsen. Word arrived at the beginning of August that the copyists had mislaid the score and parts and the situation was exacerbated by the delay in correcting choral and orchestral parts. Worse still the first rehearsal in Gloucester on 6 September, the day before the performance, proved disastrous. The orchestral parts were found to be ridden with more errors. Moreover the 250-strong chorus, drawn not only from the three cathedral cities, but also from London, Bristol, Oxford, and Huddersfield, were bewildered by the work. The rehearsal went on from ten in the morning until five in the afternoon; and then after a rest for two-and-a-half hours, it resumed at half-past seven and went on until past midnight. Matters were improved the following day when a large company of chorus members from Huddersfield arranged a private rehearsal and, as Parry explained in a letter to Dannreuther written four days after the performance, lifted the general morale of the choir: 'the result was astounding. The first Chorus went admirably, and the constant crescendo up to the *ff* sounded all I could wish. But still more astonishing was the Fury Chorus. Almost directly they started I felt we were quite safe and went ahead without hesitation; and though it was pretty rough, it had lots of go and sounded furious, and there was no question for a moment of coming to grief.'[16] Some sections were, however, not so successful. The *Chorus of Spirits* in Part 1 degenerated into confusion, and in Part 2 Jupiter's scene broke down completely. Fortunately Parry's morale was restored with the superb singing of the 'Spirit of the Hour' by Anna Williams.

The reaction to *Prometheus Unbound* in the press seems to have been mixed. Some critics immediately took a dislike to the work, first because they detected the strong presence of Wagner and secondly because they objected to Shelley's atheistic philosophy. Others such as Shaw, Prout (in the *Athenaeum*), and Hueffer (in *The Times*) were more constructively critical in their comparisons with Brahms and Wagner. With regard to Parry's assimilation of Wagnerian declamation, Hueffer was particularly adroit in his criticisms though these have been obscured to some extent by later commentators. As A. E. F. Dickinson considered: 'The free declamatory melody of "Prometheus Unbound", with which critical reporting has been somewhat obsessed, is an integral feature and a striking one'.[17] And Colles, writing for the *Oxford History of Music*, stated even more categorically:

[15] Letter to Edward Dannreuther, 13 July 1880, Bod. MS Eng. Letters e.117.
[16] Letter to Edward Dannreuther, 11 Sept. 1880, Bod. MS Eng. Letters e.117.
[17] A. E. F. Dickinson, 'The Neglected Parry', *Musical Times* (Apr. 1949), 109.

The choice of subject, 'Scenes from Shelley's *Prometheus Unbound*', itself proclaims a new freedom, and the opening prelude declares the composer absorbed in the imaginative spirit of the quasi-dramatic poem, while the first monologue of the enchained and rebellious Prometheus shows a sense of forceful declamation which English music had not known since Purcell. Contrast it with the opening words of Lucifer in the prologue of Sullivan's *Golden Legend*, so much admired for its dramatic quality when it first appeared at Leeds six years later. Beside Parry's Prometheus the declamation of Sullivan's Lucifer is flaccid and nerveless.[18]

Certainly when viewed in an 'English' context, Colles is justified in making his substantial claim. Critics were unanimous in deciding that Parry had allied himself with 'the music of the future', many expressing doubts about such a choice. Yet in applauding Parry's attempt to embrace Wagnerian declamation, commentators have tended to overstate the extent of his technique. It is evident from Prometheus's first phrase 'Monarch of Gods and Demons' that he was unable to prise himself away from regular four-square phrase patterns and the regularizing of Shelley's irregular metres. This declamation is still symptomatic of the aftermath of Mendelssohnian recitative or arioso, as Hueffer took pains to indicate:

Mr Parry is unmistakably a disciple of Wagner's school, and the declamatory style adopted, for example, in Prometheus's first monologue is therefore sufficiently familiar to him. He indeed treats the words with laudable attention to their poetic as well as their metrical significance. But that is not all that is necessary. The declamatory type of music, paradoxical though the statement may sound, requires an infinitely greater fount of melody than the ordinary hum-drum style of Italian opera. This melody, though it only at intervals develops into a distinct rhythmical phrase, is always potentially present, being heard now in the orchestra, now in the voice parts. Without it the declamation is dry and void of interest. It is in this 'endless melody', as it has not inappropriately been called, that Mr Parry seems somewhat deficient.[19]

What Parry failed to absorb into his musical style (even if he fully recognized it) was Wagner's crucial break with traditional periodic structure. The metrical irregularity of Wagner's verse (*Stabreim*) caused by the irregular number of strong accents, and the indeterminate number of unaccented syllables between these accents, gave rise to a rhythmic irregularity, which in consequence caused the musical periodic structure to break down into prose. Such a prose structure effected a change in musical syntax where two-bar and four-bar phrases existed on an equal level with three-bar and five-bar phrases. In *Rheingold* and particularly *Die Walküre* it is this technique that is predominant, where

[18] H. C. Colles, 'England 1850–1900' (Chap. 13), *Oxford History of Music*, 468–9.
[19] F. Hueffer, *The Times* (8 Sept. 1880).

Wagner no longer relies on primarily syntactic musical structures of antecedent and consequent phraseological patterns (i.e. 2 + 2, 4 + 4, 8 + 8). His declamation is allowed to develop freely, and to compensate for the absence of conventional periodic form, the music is woven together with leitmotiv.

It is evident from the regular two-bar phrases of Parry's opening monologue (Ex. 17*a*) that Wagner's declamatory technique has not been adopted. Parry's melody is still that of the arioso line, with more obvious antecedent and consequent phraseological divisions (i.e. traditional periodic structures), and also Parry is perhaps overfastidious in his need to respond to every important word of the text (e.g. *Monarch* of *Gods* and *Demons*, And *all spirits* but *one*) either with registral emphasis or longer note-values; this tends to restrict rhythmical freedom that is such a striking part of Wagner's declamatory technique. One major redeeming feature of the monologue, however, is Parry's bold use of the orchestra, particularly in the way he attempts to lift it from its traditional accompanying role. This is apparent, not only in the use of the orchestra as a vehicle for melodic and harmonic continuity, but also in the numerous purely instrumental pasages which intersperse the vocal phrases. It is perhaps this factor (together with some imaginative scoring) that raises Parry's declamation above that of his English contemporaries.

Throughout *Prometheus* Parry's orchestral technique is inventive and assured. Nowhere is this clearer than in the short but dramatic prelude to Part 1 whose opening chords announced by the wind contrast vividly with the solemn agonized fugato played by muted strings. Equally dramatic, though much more animated, is the accompanying music to the Chorus of Furies which shows a flair for instrumental colour redolent of some of Liszt's most vibrant scores. Wagnerian timbres are conspicuous in Jupiter's scene, notably the mysterious passage beginning 'And though my curses through the pendulous air' which is strongly reminiscent of *Siegfried*—an influence confirmed at Jupiter's terrible realization of his imminent demise ('No refuge! no appeal!') with the appearance of low solo bassoons and low horns (Ex. 17*b*). But without doubt the most voluptuous Wagnerian scoring occurs in the *Spirit of the Hour* which recalls the lush sonorities of harp and divided strings found in *Lohengrin*. The sound of the Brahmsian orchestra is also present in various guises. The song of *The Earth* for contralto solo ('I felt thy torture, son'), with its use of divisi cellos, recalls the first movement of the *Deutsches Requiem*, while the arrival of the Demogorgon attempts to draw on the grandeur of Brahms's First Symphony (it even shares the same key!).

Of the solo vocal movements by far the most satisfactory is *The Spirit*

Ex. 17. *a Prometheus Unbound* (1880), beginning of opening monologue; *b Prometheus Unbound*, Jupiter's realization of his demise; *c Prometheus Unbound*, orchestral opening of the *Spirit of the Hour*; *d Die Walküre*, the 'love' motive of Siegmund and Sieglinde; *e Prometheus Unbound*, opening phrase for Soprano in the *Spirit of the Hour*; *f Die Walküre*, 'Volsung' motive; *g Prometheus Unbound*, thematic connection between the chorus 'Thrice three hundred thousand years' and the opening idea of the orchestral introduction; *h* main leitmotiv of *Prometheus Unbound*: 'the prediction of Jupiter's downfall'.

"Die Walküre" C.V.S.

(d)

(e)

SPIRIT OF THE HOUR

Soon   as   the   sun   had   ceased

(f)

cont. over/

Ex. 17. cont.

of the Hour for soprano. Here one is aware of a more successful application of Wagnerian declamation and the essential role of the orchestra. Moreover, the through-composed structure with its constant development, interaction, and extension of its two main thematic strands comes much closer to a Wagnerian continuity. Parry's deployment of chromaticism and diatonicism is dramatically more emphatic in the way it reflects the changing sentiment of the text, and this also recalls similar Wagnerian contrasting passages in the *Ring* and *Parsifal*. Scene 4 is flanked by an instrumental introduction and postlude which makes use of a melodic idea 'a' (Ex. 17*c*) that is extended sequentially. To Stanford this treatment was so Wagnerian that he was provoked to write in the autograph manuscript 'Die Walküre C. V. S.' (see bars 8–9)—no doubt he had the context of the 'Love' motive of Siegmund and Sieglinde in mind (Ex. 17*d*). A new idea 'b' is introduced in the first phrase of the opening vocal paragraph (Ex. 17*e*) which, besides being loosely related to 'a', closely resembles the 'Volsung' motive (Ex. 17*f*) which also figures prominently in *Die Walküre*. The orchestral introduction and this first vocal section, with their deployment of a luscious chromaticism, portray the subsidence of chaos and transformation of the world. But when the text transfers its attention from the ecstasy of these events to 'the dwellings of mankind', the past chromaticism is eroded by the emergence of diatonicism to accentuate the moral affirmation: 'and men walked one with another'. Such contrast between the sensual and the moral (often a euphemism for godly or religious) is not unlike Wagner's use of the same harmonic device where he sets 'Valhalla' apart in the purity of a diatonic D flat. But perhaps most significant is not so much the contrast of harmonic languages as Parry's manipulation of diatonicism.

Here for the first time we have a passing taste of a more intense, higher diatonic style which he was to adopt with greater assurance in the next few years, added to which it was a language, once consolidated, which would bring about the establishment of a distinctive 'English' musical dialect synonymous with Parry's style.

The choral sections of *Prometheus*, like the solo movements, show a diverse set of approaches ranging from the inventive to the banal. On the imaginative side the chorus's first appearance as the *Voice from the Mountains* ('Thrice three hundred thousand years') is highly effective in its gradual accumulation of volume against an almost static harmonic background, with the result that Parry's change of tonal direction from C major to E minor ('We trembled in our multitude') is particularly stirring. In the final section of Part 1 (beginning 'Life of life'), soloists and chorus share a magnificent modified strophic design. The final strophe, set over a protracted dominant pedal, is taken by the chorus and has the effect of a majestic apotheosis in the manner of a quasi-operatic finale. The impact of other choruses by comparison is disappointing. After the evocative thunder and lightning of the orchestral prelude to the *Furies*, the chorus itself is utterly tame and rhythmically poor. The same may be said of Parry's inadequate representation of the Demogorgon by male chorus which retreats into conventional Victorian part-song textures, as does the *Chorus of Spirits* in Part 1 which is reminiscent of similar movements in the operettas of Sullivan. But the most sorry lapse into commonplace choral procedures is that of Part 2 Scene 3. This can be felt essentially in the disjointed plan of short sections in which Parry relies on simple repetition or on fugal technique. These techniques one traditionally finds in the finales of nineteenth-century English oratorios and cantatas, but they are antipathetical to the whole concept of forward motion in dramatic music, to which (judging from the title of *Prometheus*) Parry had aspired. He was perhaps too conscious of writing a traditional finale, and consequently slipped too easily into conventional procedures, forgetting that the essence of his cantata was its active theatrical effect.

An additional Wagnerian dimension of *Prometheus* is Parry's limited use of leitmotiv technique. His article for Grove on the subject, completed in March 1879, provides a valuable insight into his loathing for the musical expectations of contemporary audiences with regard to the simplistic 'cutting up [of] large musical works into short incongruous sections of tunes, songs, rondos, and so forth'. The article reveals a considerable enthusiasm for the technique and a comprehensive knowledge of its dramatic purpose, and hence it would seem to predict a wide and varied application of Wagner's principles, but surprisingly Parry restricted himself to only one distinctive idea which is first heard in the accompaniment to the *Voice from the Mountains* in Scene 1. This new orchestral motive is itself a conflation of the vocal shape 'Thrice three hundred thousand years' which is in turn derived from the fugal idea of the opening prelude (Ex. 17*g*). This short idea appears to represent the essential philosophy running through Shelley's drama, that omnipotence or absolute power possessed by Gods and Governments will one day be overthrown by the greater power of humanity. The leitmotiv recurs in various other transformations throughout the cantata, notably during the dialogue between Mercury and Prometheus in Part 1 where Prometheus predicts the inevitable fall of Jupiter (Ex. 17*h*), and it is ubiquitous during Jupiter's scene in Part 2 especially where it signals his downfall (see Ex. 17*b*).

In spite of some resultant stylistic inconsistencies, there can be little doubt that Parry was thoroughly capable of handling the technique of transformation essential to leitmotiv. What is surely lacking in *Prometheus*, however, is the confidence and sheer experience of sustaining and manipulating leitmotivs for each and every new dramatic situation. Moreover, it is disappointing that he limited himself to the one abstract idea and ignored the possibilities of character portrayal. References to the leitmotiv are comparatively few in number, and consequently, its rather sporadic occurrences hardly contribute seriously to the overall unity of the work. In fact, *Prometheus* relies little on the interplay of thematic material across its five scenes, and what little is used seems either arbitrary, underdeveloped, or isolated.

These criticisms may seem harsh in view of the important historical position bestowed on this work by many scholars of British music; and even if some commentators have not concurred in their appraisals, *Prometheus* has still proved to be the most convenient point of embarkation when discussing the so-called 'English Renaissance'. It was probably Ernest Walker who was responsible for establishing the now popular belief: 'If we seek for a definite birthday for modern English music, September 7, 1880, when *Prometheus* saw the light at Gloucester and met with a distinctly mixed reception, has undoubtedly the best claim.'[20] It has also been tempting to interpret Elgar's 'practical starting-point' of 1880 in his inaugural lecture at Birmingham University in 1905 as being an indirect reference to *Prometheus* though he made clear that this was purely a date of convenience. Since then the emphasis on *Prometheus* as the vital breakthrough as stated by Howes, Colles, and Howells has continued to gather weight.

There can be little doubt that *Prometheus Unbound* excited scholars and performers alike. For example, Prosper Sainton, violinist and leader

[20] E. Walker, *A History of Music in England* (Oxford, 1907; 3rd edn. rev. and enlarged by J. A. Westrup, Oxford, 1952), 331.

of the festival orchestra, was one who was greatly impressed by it. Writing from France he declared to C. Harford Lloyd: 'Let me add one line more to tell you the deep, very deep impression "Prometheus" has made upon me. There is the *étincelle électrique* so seldom found nowadays. With a fine refined performance, Mr Parry's work must create a great sensation'.[21] Certainly, in embracing, at least in part, Wagnerian techniques of declamation and leitmotiv, the cantata automatically set itself apart from other contemporary English works in the same idiom (such as Sullivan's *Golden Legend* or Barnett's *Paradise and the Peri*); this Sainton evidently recognized. Yet it has to be said that the association of the revolutionary vision and intellect of Shelley and Parry's apparent literary temerity has tended to blind commentators to the cantata's purely musical quality. In other words, although *Prometheus* is full of potentially striking ideas that display an awareness of dramatic music of the European mainstream, one soon becomes uncomfortably conscious that the Handelian and Mendelssohnian conditioning of Parry's early musical training and experience of English choral festivals lurks just beneath the surface in all the scenes (except perhaps Part 2 Scene 2). Scene 5 is a particularly telling example of this lapse into the security of established pedagogical procedures; and the declamation, perhaps the feature most responsible for the work's historical veneration, is ultimately marred by the same precepts. Seen in this light, the substantial claims for *Prometheus* as a revolutionary work seem excessive, not only in the context of the English Renaissance but also within Parry's own compositional development. The work's stylistic instability suggests more readily a composer with an admirable technical proficiency, but with as yet little personal conviction. In fact *Prometheus* bears all the symptoms of immaturity, experiment, and the uncertainty of a composer who had not yet found himself; and its most 'modern' traits are precisely those which later Parry chose to jettison.

Numerous commendations and congratulations arrived after the performance in Gloucester from friends and fellow professionals, but the general consensus especially among the publishing fraternity was one of indifference. In November he was thoroughly demoralized by Lucas's outright rejection of *Prometheus*: 'Found a letter from Lucas refusing to have anything to do with the publication of Prometheus, whereat perhaps being out of sorts and tired I was cast down; I think I can bear the want of publicity far better than the irritation of having to *ask* a publisher to undertake a work and to be somewhat abruptly refused, as is now my constant luck'.[22] To his rescue during this time of disillusionment came Stanford whose pioneering ventures with the

---

[21] 'Charles Harford Lloyd', *Musical Times*, (1 June 1899), 373.
[22] Diary, 21 Nov. 1880.

Cambridge University Musical Society were already both nationally and internationally renowned. Having read some of the unsympathetic accounts of *Prometheus* in the press, Stanford's interest in the work immediately increased. At first Parry was somewhat disenchanted by Stanford's demeanour when they met at Broadwood's to go over the work: 'His criticisms were confined to objections to passages which smell too strong[ly] of Wagner [see Ex. 17c]; and on the whole not particularly useful or remarkably wise; and whenever he played a bit to me it was cold and unmeaning in his hand.'[23] Nevertheless Parry found Stanford's energy and vitality reassuring and a performance was fixed for May 1881 in Cambridge. This had the effect of turning his mood of depression into one of resolve. As his letters to Dannreuther indicate, he was spurred into several revisions of the opening monologue, the dialogue between Prometheus and Mercury, the Furies chorus, and 'Life of life'. He was also greatly relieved when Novello agreed to publish, though the pressures on him to meet their deadlines prevented him from making a more thorough revision of the cantata.

Although Parry had already achieved much by the end of 1880, the one idiom he had fought shy of was the Symphony. A few sketches were made in Rustington in 1876 but these were abandoned when other opportunities presented themselves. That he was still considering the possibility of a symphony for the Crystal Palace is confirmed in a letter from his father[24] at the end of 1879, though in a letter to Charles Stuart Wortley in May 1880 it is clear that he had still not made up his mind. 'As to Symphonies I shall wait awhile yet,' he wrote, 'but I hope to have a try someday.'[25] That day was not long in coming, for on 23 December 1880 he commenced work on the first movement of a Symphony in G with a view to having it performed at the next series of Richter concerts. The symphony became the major focus of his attention for the whole of 1881 though its progress was constantly subjected to interruptions. In January he had to break off, first to dispatch the proofs of *Prometheus* to Novello, and then to complete an Evening Service in D promised to Stanford for the choir of Trinity College, Cambridge. By mid-February, however, he had sketched the complete outline of the first movement but remained dissatisfied with it. Composition then proceeded in fits and starts for he was regularly needed at Cambridge for choral rehearsals, and travelling back through London there were always the distractions of Dannreuther's concerts (in which new works by Grieg and Dvořák featured), while at the Crystal Palace Manns had embarked on a

[23] Diary, 26 Nov. 1880.
[24] Letter from Thomas Gambier Parry, 25 Dec. 1879, ShP.
[25] Letter to Charles Stuart Wortley, 16 May 1880, RCM Add. MS 4764.

complete cycle of Schubert's symphonies. Joachim and Madame Schumann were also in London, but after visiting Joachim 'behind the scenes' after a 'Pops' concert on 21 February Parry's diary reports signs of a souring in relations between the two men. 'He looks as hearty and strong as ever,' he recounted, 'but eyes me askance.'[26] Early in March both Dannreuther and Parry were abused by the 'Joachim clique' for reasons neither could understand, but it is likely that Joachim, with his Wagnerian antipathies, viewed both men with suspicion for he simply could not comprehend how they could show sympathy for the so-called opposite poles of Wagner and Brahms. For Parry it caused great sadness, but from then on his relationship with Joachim never truly healed, and on Joachim's part his response to Parry's music was always tempered by bad feeling.

During March work on the symphony gathered pace as Parry laboured feverishly at the slow movement and Scherzo. Richter's new concert season was looming ominously and there was little hope of having it ready; hence it was with some relief when Franke, as Richter's emissary, relayed the message through Dannreuther that there would after all be no room for the symphony that year. With the pressure off, Parry was able to concentrate on other pressing matters such as the entire recasting of the slow movement of the Cello Sonata, and then in May rehearsals began in earnest for *Prometheus* in Cambridge. After initial difficulties with Stanford over tempi (which for Parry always remained a sensitive musical issue), the performance on 17 May was a great success and just recompense for the confusions of Gloucester. That Parry was overjoyed is evident from a letter to Eddie Hamilton: 'It was a performance indeed! I never hope to hear anything finer than Anna Williams or King in their respective parts. And how the band did play! and the Chorus sing! And everybody was so overwhelmingly kind, and you most especially; Maude was so wild with delight over your telegram that she told me that bad as she was, she got up and jumped about the room'.[27] The triumph at Cambridge also did much to boost Parry's reputation in London for in September he received a memorandum from Arthur Prendergast, the Secretary of the Bach Choir, saying that their conductor, Otto Goldschmidt, had expressed the wish to introduce *Prometheus* to a London audience as an extra concert in 1882.

Parry's only musical recreation during the summer months was the regular attendance at Richter's concerts during which time he came to know the conductor very well. His main duties, however, were domestic and concerned with the move into 'Knight's Croft', his new house. Maude's health was still delicate and he took most of the responsibilities

---

[26] Diary, 21 Feb. 1881.
[27] Letter to Edward W. Hamilton, 18 May 1881, BL Add. MS 48621.

on himself. One important issue was the interior decoration of the house for which he sought advice from the Garretts. The Garretts were expert interior decorators and Parry had had the opportunity while staying at their Gower Street home in 1876 to savour the artistic taste of their designs. Consequently he wished to decorate Knight's Croft in the same manner with furniture from their warehouse together with wallpapers by Morris and tiles by De Morgan.

On 22 July Parry and his family moved in, though, with so many practical distractions, it was some time before he felt comfortable enough to resume any writing or composition. His 'Sonata' article for Grove occupied him throughout August and entailed endless analyses of Baroque, Classical, and nineteenth-century works, many of which bored him. Alleviation from this came with the regular visits of Ethel Smyth who was a guest of the Garretts: '[She] introduced herself to me in a singularly bold and offhand manner which quite alarmed me.'[28] In fact Parry found her manner and forceful personality somewhat over-powering, though her company was stimulating in that she was 'open and unsophisticated',[29] commanded a wide knowledge of music, and had no pretensions. Her music he found less impressive, though he appreciated the assimilation of 'Brahms's characteristic modulations and the use of subsidiary key centres' in her Quartet in C minor. But the one side of her musical personality with which he could find no sympathy was her violent antipathy to Wagner, which seemed even more polarized than Joachim's:

She is the most extreme anti-Wagnerite I have yet come across. Every touch of him she feels with equal aversion; she is contemptuous both of his poetry, charm and music. We played the Brahms variations on the Schumann theme in E flat and when we got to the last one she said 'I can't bear this; it's like Wagner'. 'There, that ninth, it's Lohengrin. I have got to detest the very sound of a ninth from him.' After she said 'It is impossible for anyone to like Brahms and Wagner.' I demurred. She answered 'Well Amateurs of course are different, but no professed musician can possibly accept the two. No man can serve two masters. They are so utterly opposed in harmonic principles, it's not possible.'[30]

For the rest of 1881 there were few interludes in which Parry was able to settle long enough to compose. Concentrated work on the symphony seemed to be receding further into the distance. With the constant disturbances of workmen, friendly neighbours, and visits to the British Museum for more material to supplement the 'Sonata' article, small-scale works seemed his only recourse. As he wrote in a letter to Dannreuther: 'I have also set myself seriously to consider the matter of songs, and have tried my hand at about half a dozen of the old lyrics.

[28] Diary, 28 Aug. 1881.   [29] Ibid. 29 Aug. 1881.   [30] Ibid. 6 Sept. 1881.

You will have to decide someday on what they are fit for.'[31] After abandoning a setting of 'Absence hear my protestation' which he felt to be too plagiaristic, he attempted a setting of Shakespeare's Sonnet 'How like a winter hath my absence been' but gave up, having become uncomfortable with the words. Fortunately he did manage to complete several songs including settings of 'And wilt thou leave me thus', Sidney's 'My true love hath my heart', and Shakespeare's 'Take, O take those lips away' which he took to London for Dannreuther's perusal at the beginning of November. But the compositional difficulties he experienced were put down to the long periods of isolation in Rustington. 'I get so musically depressed in the complete loneliness here with not a single soul to speak to on a musical subject that I get almost desperate',[32] were his anguished words to Dannreuther. 'I begin fifty things and doubt in a short while whether they aren't poor stuff after all and give them up.' His faith was, however, restored by Anna Williams's fine performances of the songs at Orme Square on 1 December, and the thought of organizing them into a set of vernacular lyrics (or *English Lyrics* as he termed them) began to loom large in his mind. The interest in songs continued with settings of Shelley's 'Goodnight' and Bodenstedt's translation of Shakespeare's Sonnet XLVI 'Leb' wohl du bist in Preis zu hoch' ('Farewell thou art too dear'), but these in turn became compositional interludes as he turned once again to the serious matter of his unfinished symphony.

In late December and early January the whole of the first movement was orchestrated. Appreciable alterations were then made to the slow movement, and the two Trios of the Scherzo were totally recomposed. At the beginning of February he was occupied with the last movement which took him another four weeks to complete. Finally, after revisions which largely centred on the slow movement, and having gained Dannreuther's endorsement, Parry once again decided to approach Richter for his 1882 season of concerts. Richter's schedule during May and June promised to be more exhausting than ever, for besides his usual series of novel programmes (which this time included Brahms's Piano Concerto No. 2 and Dvořák's Symphony No. 5), he and Franke had planned an enormous 'Wagner Cyclus' to be held at the Theatre Royal, Drury Lane consisting of two series of performances during which *Lohengrin* would be given four times, *Der Fliegende Holländer* three, *Tannhäuser* three, *Tristan und Isolde* three, and *Die Meistersinger* four (not to mention several performances of *Così fan tutte*, *Fidelio*, and *Euryanthe*). These would interleave Richter's nine orchestral concerts. Perhaps still more astonishing, however, was the sheer saturation of

---

[31] Letter to Edward Dannreuther, 19 Oct. 1881, Bod. MS Eng. Letters e.117.
[32] Letter to Edward Dannreuther, 7 Nov. 1881, ibid.

London's concert world at this time, for competing with Richter's operatic exploits during the whole of May was Angelo Neumann's staging of four cycles of *The Ring* at Her Majesty's Theatre conducted by Anton Seidl.

Parry was only too well aware that Richter's punishing itinerary might well once again lead to an exclusion of the symphony, but he decided not to forgo the opportunity. On 1 May he went to Franke's home in Vere Street to meet Richter. Eight days later, by appointment, they went through the work: '[He] seemed to like the slow movement and Scherzo and promised to do it,' he wrote, 'Rehearsal to be early in June.'[33] Richter's intentions at last seemed positive and Parry was consequently buoyed up with enthusiasm for the conductor's interpretations of Wagner which he attended throughout the rest of May. But having been summoned to Vere Street on 2 June for news of the impending rehearsal, his morale slumped as Richter, not surprisingly weary, was vague and somewhat unconcerned:

Had to go to Vere St in the morning and was kept waiting for an hour and a half as Franke was so busy. All that came of it was that Franke couldn't tell me anything, though the rehearsal was fixed for tomorrow; only I had better bring the parts to Richter. Did so in the afternoon and saw Richter who said he was very tired and had too much to do—couldn't have rehearsal tomorrow; but would try to find an opportunity before long; any spare hour in the theatre. Don't much expect it will come off and shall not believe in any performance at all till the rehearsals are over and it is definitely announced. They always seem to want to back gracefully out of it.[34]

Eventually the rehearsal was fixed for 13 June, but, as Parry's exasperated diary account conveys, it was a fiasco:

Unfortunately great part of the band did not come. No first clarinet, no 3rd Horn and great part of the strings absent. We struggled on roughly for a long while, against heaps of mistakes in the parts and finally it became evident that with the one rehearsal which only is possible, Richter could not make it go and so it was given up. A good deal of it sounded well; but even the men who were there were tired and not up to the mark and shirked their work. Dann came and supported me nobly in the trying ordeal.

His disappointment was naturally immense and his faith in Richter's attitude to his music was shaken to its foundations. News of the symphony soon reached his old Etonian friend Robert Lyttelton now working in Birmingham, who at once suggested to the Festival Committee there to include it in their forthcoming Festival. The Committee proved amenable, terms were agreed, and with that Parry was at long last assured of a performance, albeit outside London.

[33] Diary, 9 May 1882.   [34] Ibid. 2 June 1882.

When the extraordinary run of Wagner operas came to a conclusion at the end of June, Parry's appetite for the composer had increased rather than waned, for into Dannreuther's possession had come *Parsifal* which was due to be premièred in Bayreuth in late July. After spending many hours together at Orme Square acquainting themselves with the score, they departed for Bayreuth. The first performance of *Parsifal* took place on the evening of 26 July:

and a marvellously perfect one it was. All the singers did better than I ever heard them do before. Scaria was superb as Gurnemanz; Materna even better as Kundry; Winkelmann excellent as Parsifal and Hill's Klingsor as good as possible. The scenic management and tableaux were supremely effective, and all the difficult points I had dreaded—the swan, the Blumenmädchen, were all just perfect. As a work of art it is at the very highest point of mastery. The religious element makes it seem to me a little hollow, and I was not satisfied with the climaxes of first and last acts being chiefly scenic and not humanly emotional. But the impression is very great.[35]

The following day they were both invited to a reception at Wagner's house 'crowded with all the notablities and nullities . . .'[36] which precluded any conversation with the great man or with Liszt who was also present. As he explained in a letter to Maude:

Wagner doesn't like those sorts of gatherings, and only presented himself for a little while. I kept at a good distance and watched him, which was sufficiently amusing. He looks old and white but wonderfully boyish. There is a curious gleam of fire and geniality and freshness about him. A sort of elasticity and irrepressible informality. It was great fun to see him . . . I couldn't get a word with Liszt. He was incessantly sidling about caressing everybody like an old bogey at a witches' sabbath who had got hold of all the pretty rascals he liked best.[37]

Parry attended two further performances of *Parsifal* on 28 and 30 July, but he was anxious to return to England for Costa was already worrying over the parts for Birmingham.

The first rehearsal at St George's Hall on 9 August went better than he expected and the orchestra responded well except in the slow movement. But, largely through lack of time and poor organization, there was little improvement at later rehearsals which did not augur well, and at the first Birmingham rehearsal on 26 August things seemed to go from bad to worse. 'Sainton who leads was very sulky and impatient and altogether I had a bad time', Parry wrote. 'It was listened to with absolute coldness and the band showed no signs of anything but indifference throughout.'[38] How the nightmare of Richter's abortive rehearsal must have flooded

[35] Ibid. 26 July 1882.
[37] Letter to Lady Maude Parry, 28 July 1882, ShP.
[36] Ibid. 27 July 1882.
[38] Diary, 26 Aug. 1882.

back, added to which the apparent failure seemed all the more emphatic in the light of the favourable reception accorded to Stanford's *Serenade* also included in the festival. Yet this familiar gloom was dispelled absolutely by the fine performance that took place on 31 August. According to the *Musical Times* 'Every movement of the Symphony was warmly received, and the composer was loudly applauded on his retirement from the orchestra.'[39] Parry preferred to be more cynical about the applause which he felt to have been whipped up by friends and affable stewards. He could not, however, ignore the genuine commendation of his professional colleagues, such as Stainer, Benedict, Hueffer, and Prout who had, prior to the symphony, vacillated in their opinion of his abilities. Stanford offered to take it to show Bronsart in Hanover who had the previous winter produced the Irishman's opera *The Veiled Prophet*. Manns was also persuaded to perform it at the Crystal Palace the following April, though once again he found the score difficult to penetrate. Nevertheless he was most impressed by its assurance as he made clear in a letter to Grove after the performance:

H. Parry's Symphony is a very remarkable work. A little less 'polyphony' and a little more 'placido' in the midst of the ceaseless *Sturm und Drang* would be improvements at least to my enjoyment of such genuinely enthusiastical flow of high-souled aspirations. Such music is awfully difficult to master and my ears will ring with it for some time to come, in consequence of the close study which I had to make of the score. However I am myself pleased with the result.[40]

Grove presented the letter to Parry who preserved it carefully. But perhaps the most treasured letter of congratulation came from his father:

Dearest Hubert,

It was but a tantalising sight of you yesterday! We caught a glimpse of Maude in the gallery—and saw that some of the Lyttelton party were about perpendicularly above us. We were not well placed being partly under the side gallery. The sound did not reach us *fully*. It was what a picture is, not in a perfectly good light but with just a shimmer of glaze, which *takes the bloom off*. Linda got a little better into the open, in a seat temporarily vacant just when your music was being performed. As all I can do to express myself as to music is by feeling and not by knowledge, I do not pretend to any criticism,—but I must not let a day pass without just a word to say how deeply Linda and I were impressed with your work. It is a great work —and can only be properly appreciated by being perfectly known. It will surely be given again—and I do hope indeed to be within reach, to hear it.[41]

---

[39] 'The Birmingham Musical Festival', *Musical Times*, (1 Oct. 1882), 537.
[40] Letter from August Manns to George Grove, Apr. 1883. See Charles L. Graves, *Hubert Parry* (London, 1926), ii. 42.
[41] Letter from Thomas Gambier Parry, 1 Sept. 1882, ShP.

Thomas Gambier Parry's claims for the symphony as a 'great work', though somewhat excessive, were the words of a now proud father, for in his eyes such a work represented the very pinnacle of Victorian secular composition and his son had acquitted himself with honour.

The fact that Parry had already gained considerable experience in the handling of large-scale instrumental music through his chamber works, and that familiarity with orchestral technique had been enhanced through the *Concertstück*, *Guillem de Cabestanh*, and the Piano Concerto, meant that his First Symphony showed fewer signs of tentativeness. Certainly there is nothing indecisive about the first movement which combines a bold Schumannesque lyricism (in which the 'Rhenish' never seems far away) with moments of true Wagnerian passion, framed by a strong Brahmsian sense of working out. Indeed, so vigorous is Parry's intention to compose 'symphonically' that exposition, development, and recapitulation seem almost too protracted; nevertheless the rhapsodic development in particular reveals a bold inventiveness in its contrast of poetry and dynamism. The slow movement is the most individual movement of the symphony for, besides the unusual rhythmical features of the opening idea (Ex. 18*a*), Parry achieves a compelling momentum through the more animated sections. Here he makes extensive use of dotted rhythms and the anticipatory semiquaver—a stylistic thumbprint which he was to use repeatedly in later works (Ex. 18*b*). The Scherzo, like the first movement, is perhaps unduly long largely owing to its two Trios (another similarity it shares with the 'Rhenish' Symphony). Yet the blend of rhythmic drive, imitative counterpoint, and pastoral melody (notably engendered by the splendid quartet of horns in the first Trio) is imaginative, as is the experimental central return of the Scherzo material in a developmental role. Of all the movements the last is the most unashamedly eclectic especially with regard to Schumann whose Fourth Symphony appears to have been a powerful subconscious influence on several of the thematic ideas. Nevertheless, the splendid lyrical second group introduced in the sonorously contrasting key of E flat is especially characteristic (Ex. 18*c*), its yearning diatonicism prophetic of some of Parry's most muscular themes in later works. The cyclic dimension of the symphony is also brought to a stirring conclusion in the coda, where the main theme of the first movement, referred to in both the slow movement and Scherzo, is restated with noble grandiloquence.

The impact of the First Symphony did much to consolidate Parry's reputation both publicly and professionally but he remained cynical about the intentions of conductors and performers. At the end of October, Barth, the concert pianist, expressed a desire to perform the Concerto in Germany. Parry had also been immersed in the revision of the D minor Variations for piano in which he added two new variations.

Ex. 18. First Symphony (1882). *a* opening theme, second movement; *b* main second-group material, second movement; *c* second-group melody, Finale.

He then sent the work on to Oscar Beringer in the hope that the eminent pianist would include it in his next recital programme. But neither Barth nor Beringer took up their respective challenges which fuelled Parry's scepticism even further. However, a genuine cause for optimism came with a commission from Cambridge (no doubt on the strength of Stanford's recommendations) to write another symphony for May 1883. 'The Cambridge people have asked me to let them have a Symphony for their May Concert', he wrote to Dannreuther, 'I must have a try, but I daresay it won't come off.'[42]

The other major issue of 1882 that gave Parry cause for concern was the imminent foundation of a new college of music that was to replace the National Training School for Music that had been in existence since 1876. The function of the National Training School was to provide a form of free musical education to those who could not afford the course offered by the Royal Academy of Music. In the hands of Sullivan, Stainer who succeeded him in 1881, and the staff (which included Pauer, Visetti, Prout, and Carrodus), the School had certainly raised public consciousness to a modest degree by fostering such talents as those of Eugène d'Albert and Walter Alcock, but its national impact had been extremely limited. The Prince of Wales and various other members of

---

[42] Letter to Edward Dannreuther, 18 Oct. 1882, Bod. MS Eng. Letters e.117.

the royal family were anxious that the status of this institution should be raised. Ideas for a scheme to amalgamate the School with the Royal Academy had been voiced in 1878 under the presidency of the Prince of Wales, but Macfarren and his colleagues eventually declined the proposal in 1879, a decision that was often vehemently criticized in the press. But the idea for a newer, larger, and more prestigious music college did not die. Under the chairmanship of Prince Christian, a charter was drawn up in 1880 and presented to the Privy Council by the Prince of Wales.

The main problem for the new college was, needless to say, a financial one. The generation of public support was of paramount importance as was the patronage of the Royal Princes, the Duke of Edinburgh, Prince Christian, and the Duke of Albany who spoke at the first great meeting publicizing the college on 11 December, 1881. This meeting, at the Free Trade Hall in Manchester, was but a prelude to the meeting presided over by the Prince of Wales in the Banqueting Hall of St James's Palace on 28 February, 1882. It was attended by a vast and impressive array of politicians, the prime minister, the Archbishop of Canterbury, the Lord Mayor of London, composers, publishers, patrons, journalists, and many influential amateurs. Immediately after the meeting Grove was appointed to organize meetings throughout the country to explain the aims of the new college, as well as to raise funds to the sum of £300,000 deemed necessary to establish the college on a secure financial footing *ab initio*. Grove's efforts to solicit money from every echelon of society were ceaseless, a fact recognized by the Executive Committee who subsequently asked if he would accept the position of Director-designate. *The Times* announced the news on 20 October which immediately triggered a bombardment of enquiries from those who believed the opportunity was ripe to secure one of the many new professional posts on offer.

Parry had watched the developments of the new college plans with interest. After all, there was every opportunity of obtaining inside information from Grove through his close connections with the Dictionary and at almost every musical gathering it was the sole topic of conversation. He had attended the great meeting at St James's Palace in February and, at the Café Royale afterwards, had been subjected to the sour words of Bennett and Sainton who felt that the Academy and Macfarren in particular had been shamefully treated. His enthusiasm for the project was as great as Grove's and there can be no doubting that Parry was one of the young aspirants for a position. We might naturally think that his appointment was inevitable and that the whole affair was a *fait accompli*; but, with his characteristic shyness, cynicism, and self-doubt, he seriously believed that no invitation would come from Grove.

This is evident from a letter written by Maude to Eddie Hamilton in which her personal dislike for Grove, provoked by the latter's aversion to strong-minded women such as Mrs Fawcett or Agnes Garrett, is unambiguously expressed:

He [Hubert] is working now at a new Symphony for Stanford which is to be done at Cambridge in the spring . . . I am cross with Mr Grove only I try and realise to myself that after all he is a baby and can't help it. He seems to me to be totally devoid of moral courage. Hubert says he is almost positive he will throw him over about the Musical College, for he has implied as much to Hubert. Such a shame.[43]

Rumours began to fly. Interpretations hung on every word Grove uttered. Maude believed that Stanford would be asked to join the staff to the exclusion of her husband but suggested in an angry letter to Eddie Hamilton that 'eventually public opinion would force Mr Grove to have him',[44] and that Stanford, despite his kind words, had been inconsistent in his support. But all the bitter words, false accusations, and wayward assessments proved futile when a letter of appointment arrived on New Year's Day, 1883.

[43] Letter from Lady Maude Parry to Edward Hamilton, n.d. [? end of 1882]. BL Add. MS 48621.
[44] Ibid.

8

Grove and the Royal College of Music

> Temporary Offices,
> Duchy of Cornwall Office,
> 1, Buckingham Gate,
> London, S. W.
> Royal College of Music
> December 30, 1882

MY dear Parry,

I write by desire of the Prince of Wales to ask if you will assist him in his great experiment by taking the Department of Musical History with a seat on the Board of Professors. It is our wish to make lectures an important part of the College course, and into no hands could those on the history and development of music be put with more propriety than into yours. As the College grows I hope that there may be some other opportunity of turning your great abilities to account—as in Composition etc. but the lectures will be your cardinal occupation.

I ought to tell you that we must begin the College on the same low rate of remuneration to the Professors that the National Training School proceeded upon during its whole existence:- namely for the Professors who form the Board 15/- an hour. When we come to our full strength, I am not without hope that that rate may be increased; but at first it must rule; and I trust that it may not deter you from accepting His Royal Highness's invitation. He hopes to open the College in April or May.

> yours ever sincerely,
> G. Grove
> Director[1]

Grove's letter heralded a year of much greater optimism, accomplishment, and pecuniary stability for Parry. Moreover, in inviting him to join the College staff as Professor of Musical History, Grove acknowledged Parry's scholarly achievements for the Dictionary which bolstered his public status as an academician of note. The result was an invitation from Macfarren to act as the external examiner for the Cambridge Mus.B. and Mus.D. examinations in February. Consequently, in the latter part of January his work on the new symphony was temporarily

---

[1] Letter from George Grove, 30 Dec. 1882, ShP.

interrupted in order to go through the exercises. It was then necessary to join the board of examiners in mid-February to reach a decision on the candidates. It was an experience that proved exasperating for it confirmed in Parry's mind the shocking disparity between the pedagogy of the ancient universities and contemporary European developments. Perhaps inevitably, his ideals clashed with those of his former teacher:

Over the exercises we disagreed plentifully. Mac wanted to pass the worst of all of them—a wretched, commonplace, empty piece of stuff in which I and Steggall were thoroughly agreed to reject. I wanted to pass two others; one of which had a good deal of musical sentiment, and attractive musical qualities though mild. This they would have none of. The other I think they were most unjust to. In many respects it was quite masterly, specially as counterpoint. The 8-part writing most remarkable; and well and thoroughly worked; but they rejected it on the grounds of overelaboration, which was very hard. It is the cry of second rateism, as raised against Wagner and everything good that is done. The fogeys won't have it because it is not done as they would have it after the manner of their younger days. I don't see what they are to pass. As we were constituted nothing could well have done so. For I certainly would not pass such dull triviality as Mac favoured and Mac would not pass anything that I thought up to the mark. He was pretty avid however on the whole. He had one hit at Wagner. 'If work made a man great, Wagner ought to be one of the greatest, but unfortunately everything he has put down is wrong.'[2]

While undergoing these trials and tribulations, news came that he was to be admitted to Trinity College, Cambridge and proposed for an Honorary Doctor of Music. For Parry this was a gesture of professional recognition which compounded that of his College appointment. His father was one of the first to congratulate him and with his letter came an informal commission to write a work for the Gloucester Festival:

I heartily congratulate you on your honours which you thoroughly deserve. I am delighted at the whole affair. You say that you are already admitted to my old College—Trinity—fancy that! *but how?* I have no recollection of any means of transfer from an Oxford Coll. to one at Cambridge but by taking the ad eundem degree—your old university owes you something—mine alas! owes me nothing—I only took an inglorious 'Poll'!

Williams, organist at Gloucester, and I suppose future conductor of the Festival next September (some day in the first week) asked me whether you had anything *within our scope* that you particularly wished to be done here—something already written—sacred for the morning or secular for evening. The system adopted by the Stewards is to invite 2 modern composers to write specially. They invited Stanford and Stainer. The former offered to finish specially a Mass Service—which, to be written specially for our Cathedral, was seriously objected to—an old mass, as a *study* of music of established high class for sacred purposes was placed in a totally different category. We cannot regard

[2] Diary, 13 Feb. 1883.

such matters merely and nakedly from the musical side alone. We much regret Stanford not caring to produce anything else—unless it be a Symphony which would be somewhat beyond our ability for want of time and means of rehearsal—so another composer has promised something.[3]

Parry and Maude were guests of the Stanfords at their home in Hervey Street in Cambridge during the conferring of the degree on 1 March. In the Senate House he was 'presented' by Sir John Sandys, the Public Orator, who read a felicitous Latin eulogy which drew attention not only to Parry's musical achievements (with particular reference to *Prometheus*) but also to the artistic contribution of his father at Ely cathedral and to his deceased father-in-law, Sidney Herbert. Thereafter Parry was referred to in the press as 'Dr Parry'. This title soon began to irritate him as he preferred the more natural 'C. Hubert H. Parry' with which he used to sign himself. He was also undoubtedly aware of Shaw's tongue-in-cheek, anti-academic use of the title in his outspoken criticisms of the late 1880s and early 1890s.

Parry's links with Cambridge at this time were as close as ever. In addition to the symphony for CUMS he had agreed at the suggestion of Stanford and F. J. H. Jenkinson (the classics scholar also of Trinity College) to compose the incidental music for the university production of Aristophanes' *The Birds* in November. This had arisen after Parry and Stanford had attended a performance of *The Ajax of Sophocles* in Cambridge the previous December with music by Macfarren, in which the university had taken up the idea of presenting Greek plays with musical scores by contemporary composers from Oxford's production of the *Agamemnon of Aeschylus* (music by Parratt). However, work on *The Birds* necessarily had to wait until his two other commissions, the symphony and the choral work for Gloucester, were completed.

The composition of his Second Symphony, which had occupied him since October 1882, absorbed the best part of the first six months of 1883. It appears that the first movement was finished before the turn of the year, and the Scherzo was rapidly composed in early January. But the slow movement's progress was particularly sluggish and took much longer to complete owing to the interruptions of examining for Cambridge. 'Got to the end of slow movement at last,' he wrote despairingly on 20 February, 'and quite sick of it. So many and so long interruptions—one after another have just ruined it—if the idea was ever workable at all! Perhaps not. Now it goes sprawling; and some of it just commonplace; but it must stop; for waiting longer won't mend it.'[4] Fortunately his characteristic self-doubt was met by encouragement

[3] Letter from Thomas Gambier Parry, 20 Feb. 1883, ShP.
[4] Diary, 20 Feb. 1883.

from Grove who had heard Stanford play the first movement through to him:

Dearest P.

I saw Charlie yesterday morning and he played me the first movement of your Symphony and I can't help telling you of the *very great impression* it made on me. It is splendid —so clear and tuneful and fresh, and so like your own dear old self. I particularly admired the absence of that *priggish musicianship* that is such a bore in so many new German works.

The Introduction is lovely and the connexion between it and the Allegro struck me as being most happy—close and yet quite unforced.

I long to hear it again for it has left the impression on my mind of a really original, great, and most interesting work. Except a Brahmsy★ bit once or twice nothing *reminded* me of anything else—but, as in the finale of the other Symphony, I felt its kinship to the greatest; and again No.7 seemed to stand by as if to *welcome it into the family*.

It really has made me quite proud—and did a good deal to support me through a very trying day yesterday when I was bothered and worried very unnecessarily . . .

. . . Tomorrow of course you'll be at Cambridge taking your new honour. There will be nothing left to give you after people have heard the new Symphony!

yours
G.

★ and they were reminiscences of the composer and not of passages.[5]

Completion of the last movement of his Second Symphony dragged on through February and March as he remained unconvinced of its structure. '[It] seems more and more hopeless', he wrote in frustration, 'The plan I projected may be possible but it's beyond my powers at present.'[6] By 27 April he finished it 'at a struggle', but Stanford found the last movement too short and persuaded Parry to rewrite it which he did in May after the official opening of the Royal College.

The Second Symphony in F was, appropriately enough, nicknamed 'The Cambridge'; it was also known as the 'University Symphony' though not published as such. With regard to the latter this subtitle had relevance for a 'programme' which Parry imparted to the author of the programme notes. Still more significant, however, are the conjectures of the author, who suggested that such a programme might be auto-biographical. Indeed, from the description given, it is certain that something of the composer's immensely happy, yet romantically turbulent life at Oxford, with all the uncertainties of what lay beyond, are contained therein:

[5] Letter from George Grove, [28 Feb. 1883], ShP.
[6] Diary, 4 Apr. 1883.

It may be that (like Berlioz, who, in his 'Harold' Symphony, has given us a picture of his feelings and adventures while resident in Italy) it is his *own* reminiscences of life at the sister University that he has here put upon record. Be that as it may, the life of an undergraduate is the theme upon which he has worked; and it is one which is easily traceable throughout the Symphony. In the introduction we are brought face to face with the novel sensations and high aspirations which an undergraduate feels on reflecting that from lately being a mere school *boy* he has suddenly become a University *man*, and are further furnished with some premonitions of his character. The Allegro, which immediately follows, might be regarded as descriptive of the jollity of University life: health, high spirits, happiness in making new friends, with some prefigurement of that which *must* come—the dawn of love. In the Scherzo we realise all the jollification of a home scene: rustic merrymaking at a harvest festival during the long vacation; with (in the 'Trio') not a little serious flirtation in a corner. The Slow Movement reveals to us our hero's first real passion and ardent lovemaking; its anxieties as well [as] its happier phases. In the Finale we are alive to his delight at having taken his degree, his grand resolves for the future, and determination to make his way in the world.[7]

The work was first performed at the Cambridge Guildhall on 12 June 1883. It was extremely well received by an enthusiastic audience, though as Parry explained in his diary, Maude's 'poor' health inhibited his full enjoyment of the occasion:

The Symphony got fair consideration, and in the afternoon went most admirably and sounded to me well. It was wonderfully well received, and the friends I like to please seemed well delighted with it. On account of Maude's weakness we had to hurry away before the end of the concert, and the worry incident to getting away and leaving so many people I wanted to see and so many things I wanted to do at Cambridge spoilt a very great deal of my pleasure. We got back in time for dinner and Maude did not seem much the worse.[8]

Whereas the First Symphony, with its sense of effusive enthusiasm, left the impression of symphonic earnestness, a quality underlined by its considerable length, the 'Cambridge' at once exudes a new, maturer confidence in the medium. Parry, who retained a deep affection for the work, evidently intended that the symphony should convey a sense of grandeur and optimism in which the cyclic design, explored on a smaller scale in the First Symphony, is, with its added programmatic significance, given room to expand more spontaneously. Grove's comments in his letter to Parry, quoted above, are especially apposite in this context. The slow introduction in F minor presents thematic material that is not only vital to the overall plan of the first movement but also to the entire work. The opening idea 'x' (Ex. 19*a*) is especially seminal, though (as Grove

[7] See Richter Concert programmes, summer season, Monday evening, 27 June 1887, 203–4.
[8] Diary, 12 June 1883.

Ex. 19. 'Cambridge' Symphony (1883). *a* opening idea (figure 'x') of introduction, first movement; *b* secondary idea (figure 'y') of introduction, first movement; *c* second-group melody (showing figure 'y'), first movement; *d* second-group material (showing figure 'x'), slow movement; *e* opening theme, Finale.

(*b*)

(*a*)

(*c*)

(*d*)

(*e*)

noted) the secondary idea 'y' heard on a solo clarinet (Ex. 19b) prefigures the main second-group idea (Ex. 19c) which, moving on from the similar context in the last movement of the First Symphony, is a quite outstanding lyrical paragraph replete with soaring counterthemes. Still more significant is Parry's use of essentially three-part counterpoint combined with his own personal development of diatonic dissonance and wide registral tessitura that seems to foreshadow the expressive language associated with Elgar's musical style. This surely is a taste of the mature Parry! The development is also an impressive display of Parry's symphonic ability in the way he 'composes out' the falling seventh that characterizes and initiates the second group. Moreover, in contracting the seventh interval to a third, Parry also increases the rhythmic momentum which gives this section of the movement a powerful sense of forward motion. The Scherzo in D minor is perhaps the most Brahmsian-sounding movement notably in the opening material, though the secondary idea with its quasi-modal accompaniment seems momentarily to step outside the prevailing Teutonic idiom. The Trio in the tonic major, particularly with the prominent horn solos, is also strongly reminiscent of Brahms, yet the central, sudden, and passionate deviation to B flat major threatens to remove us to a quite different stylistic sphere. Indeed, the language and rhetoric of the slow movement has more in common with Dvořák than Brahms particularly in the simple manner in which Parry prepares the way for the long lyrical span of the main theme (a comparison with the opening bars of the slow movement of Dvořák's Sixth Symphony provides a telling parallel), and the reorchestrated recapitulation of the main subject on the cellos also seems to recall similar contexts in Dvořák's orchestral works. Less redolent of Dvořák, however, is the polyphony of the inner parts which derive their figurations from 'x' referred to in the movement's opening bars. Figure 'x' also becomes more melodically preponderant in the second group (Ex. 19d). By comparison with the invention of the previous three movements, the finale (which was later performed on its own in Antwerp on 18 October 1885) is somewhat dry and uninteresting, a feeling immediately invoked by the rather tired opening thematic material and its subsequent rondo treatment. Conscious of this inadequacy, a completely new finale was composed in 1895 and performed by the Philharmonic Society under the composer on 30 May. In this revision Parry obviously hoped to create a feeling of diatonic grandiloquence using the rich 'sul G' effect of the upper strings for the long opening theme (Ex. 19e), and this trend is continued in the sonorous secondary material of the second group in which the well-known sounds of the finale of Brahms's First Symphony spring immediately to mind. The cyclic dimension is also further strengthened by the reintroduction of the first movement's principal theme which makes a dramatic Wagnerian entry at the outset of the development. This material subsequently dominates the development and later, after the recapitulation, it is further elaborated and developed in the coda which functions both as a grand conclusion to the last movement and an apotheosis to the entire symphony.

In the month before the first performance of the Second Symphony, the Royal College of Music was officially opened by the Prince of Wales on 7 May. Out of 1,581 applicants from all parts of the British Isles 480 students were chosen to audition in front of the Director and Board of Professors in London during April. From these the 50 original scholars were selected to which another 44 pupils were added. These 94 students constituted the first year's intake amongst whom were Emily Daymond (who was later to figure prominently in Parry's life), Charles Wood, Hamish MacCunn, and A. Herbert Brewer.

As a 'political' gesture Macfarren, as Principal of the Royal Academy of Music, and Arthur Sullivan, former Principal of the National Training School, were honoured with knighthoods as was Grove on his entry as the first Director of the Royal College. The teaching staff numbered 31 in all. Parry's main task was to teach musical history, though he was also expected to assist Stanford in the teaching of composition. Many of those appointed Parry already knew well such as Pauer, Franklin Taylor, and Arabella Goddard (pianoforte); Gibson (viola); Jenny Lind-Goldschmidt and Visetti (singing); Walter Parratt and Frederick Bridge (organ). Many would remain his colleagues during his long association with the College.

Before setting to work on the Gloucester commission Parry completed a setting of Shelley's 'I arise from dreams of thee' which he had sketched way back in January 1876. His new attempt still left him ill at ease and eventually he shelved it after Hugh Montgomery had sung it through at Phillimore Place. He then turned his mind to the task of finding a suitable text for a simple choral work in accordance with his father's directives. James Shirley's dramatic debate, the 'Contention of Ajax and Ulysses' (also known as 'The Glories of our Blood and State'), had lain at the back of his mind for many years as is confirmed by a few skeletal jottings in a manuscript book of 1872. The short text seemed eminently suitable and he began to sketch ideas on 27 May. Even though the first performance of the 'Cambridge' Symphony interrupted its progress, he evidently finished the work quickly for the piano score is signed June 1883.

Only days before travelling to Highnam, where he was to stay for the Gloucester Festival, a letter arrived from his father with devastating news:

Our dear Clinton is no more. He died on the 7th. of July. He appears to have been long ill—the last letter received by anyone of us was to B.[eatrice] dated as long ago as about the middle of last December. She didn't keep this letter. The precious letter had mentioned his being ill . . . It is too long a story to write now. I write to Australia today. About your coming here, all this must make no difference—especially as it is most necessary for you to go through your Cantata with the Conductor . . . The Conductor spoke of the originality of your work making it very difficult to deal with without your help or explanation . . .[9]

Parry was immediately plunged into depression. The last pathetic letter from his brother, full of familiar sentiments of remorse and good intentions, had been dated 21 January 1881, when Clinton had been sheep-farming in the Wanganuï valley on the north island of New Zealand. Life there had been hard, spartan, and desperately lonely. News of *Prometheus* had reached him and he at once hoped to return to England in August if Thomas Gambier Parry would agree to send him money. But rather than allow him to come home, Thomas Gambier Parry agreed to fund Clinton's passage to Australia, where, largely as a result of alcoholism, his health eventually failed. 'Tragically lonely,' was Parry's diary response; 'What an end to such abilities and such a genial widely sympathetic nature.'[10] A bad London rehearsal of his *Shirley Ode* hardly helped to revive him, and the atmosphere at Highnam was sad beyond measure as Thomas Gambier Parry mourned inconsolably.

'The Glories of Our Blood and State' was performed in Gloucester on the evening of 4 September. 'Performance of my ode very good—Public not much taken with it apparently,' Parry recorded in his diary. Several members of the press were keen to draw a parallel between it and Brahms's *Schicksalslied* as this extract from the *Musical Times* demonstrates:

The music of this piece is so decisively founded on the modern German models as almost to seem like an imitation of Brahms's 'Schicksalslied'; but we cannot say that there is the slightest suspicion of plagiarism. In the concluding portion, however, we have some relief from the absolute gloom which pervades the composition, and the instrumentation throughout shows the hand of a master.[11]

It is true that Parry's ode reveals the influence of Brahms in general design and style, though in detail there are numerous divergencies. The main similarity is the ternary plan where slow outer sections flank a central animated paragraph. Parry's opening section is divided between the dark orchestral prelude in D minor and the first chorus in D major. The central paragraph marked 'allegro molto' is set in the relative, B

[9] Letter from Thomas Gambier Parry, [29 Aug.], 1883, ShP.
[10] Diary, 30 Aug. 1883.
[11] 'The Gloucester Musical Festival', *Musical Times*, (1 Oct. 1883), 541.

minor, which then subsides into a recapitulation of the opening
orchestral prelude, accompanied this time by a unison counterpoint in
the chorus. After eight bars of literal repetition the music temporarily
modulates to the Neapolitan to emphasize a moment of hushed
solemnity ('To the cold tomb'). But E flat major soon yields to the
dominant of D, at which stage the chorus embark on a final fugal episode
in a tranquil mood of didacticism ('Only the actions of the just smell
sweet'). Superficially the organization of the *Schicksalslied* appears very
similar with its opening orchestral prelude, followed by the chorus and
then the animated central section in the relative minor. Its influence on
Parry therefore seems highly plausible. But beyond this simple
comparison the parallels end. Brahms's opening chorus is considerably
more unified in its use of sonata elements, and the longer central
paragraph, also a sophisticated sonata, shows a greater degree of tonal
dissolution and thematic development. Brahms's restatement is also
more striking for its magical return in C major (not E flat) and for its
being entirely without chorus. Though the contrast of minor and major
modes shows some degree of invention in the outer sections of 'The
Glories of our Blood and State', this level of comparison shows Parry's
work to be much less imaginative. Indeed, the lack of such an approach
(i.e. that of the sonata) in Parry's vocal music is a significant indication of
his attitude towards the composition of music and words. Unlike
Brahms, who evidently viewed the adaptation of sonata form to vocal
music as a structural problem that could be intellectually solved (as is
boldly demonstrated in the *Schicksalslied*), Parry regarded the sonata as a
form to be used exclusively for instrumental music:

The sonata, therefore, is of all things the most perfect representative type of
abstract principles of organization. It can only exist under conditions in which
nothing hinders or distracts the attention of the composer from manipulation of
design. Directly words are used, the sonata type becomes not only an anomaly
but an irrelevancy. The value of the sonata as a type lies in its being absolutely
and unqualifiedly an exposition of certain ideal principles of design or
organization. To adapt it to words would imply the necessity that the writer of
the words should also write them in sonata form. The absurdity is at once
apparent. The sonata form is essentially a form devised for music; it is no more
adapted to literature (except as an occasional sport) than it is to crockery ware.
Parenthetically also it may be said that the style of sonatas is equally
inappropriate for other departments of music. For it must be obvious that the
more perfectly anything is carried out to suit special conditions the more
impossible is it that it should serve equally well for totally different conditions.
And this is indeed what practical experience has proved to be the case where
predetermined forms of the sonata order and the reserved style of the sonata
kind have been employed for operas. It is true such works may have great
beauties and a special charm of their own, but they cannot be regarded as

adequate or final solutions of the problems of either opera or song or any music wedded to words, either in form or style.[12]

One may naturally infer from Parry's remarks that he believed that words should always be allowed to dictate their own form and not be restricted by 'predetermined' ones. This statement dates from 1911, but the view was almost certainly forged much earlier. In forming such an attitude, Parry believed that his duty to the words was paramount, a perception which seems consistent with his over-fastidious response to *Prometheus Unbound*. It was an approach to which he unerringly adhered, often at the expense of structural considerations. It may also explain the reason for the 'patchwork' structure of 'The Glories of our Blood and State', which, with the one exception of the chorus's reiteration of the opening orchestral prelude, is a series of episodes thematically unrelated to one another.

Nevertheless, there are some fine ideas within these episodes. The sombre orchestral introduction is particularly striking, as is the first expressive choral entry, and the poignant sequences of the passage that concludes the first section ('With the poor crooked scythe and spade') again seems to foreshadow Elgar. The prevailing atmosphere of the work is pensive and mournful and therefore appropriate to Parry's subtitle of 'Funeral Ode'. It was later dedicated to the memory of Rhoda Garrett who had died in November 1882 and to Henry Fawcett who died almost exactly a year later. The loss of these two close friends was a severe shock to Parry but neither death moved him so much as that of his brother, alone in ignominy on the other side of the world. Therefore it seems reasonable to suggest that the memory of Charles Clinton Parry is also enshrined within the pages of this tenebrous work.

After the Gloucester Festival, Parry retreated to Rustington in order to make headway with the incidental music for *The Birds*. Jenkinson, whom Parry consulted regularly on details of stress, rhythm, and interpretation of the Greek text, came to stay for a week in mid-September. After Jenkinson had returned to Cambridge, the correspondence between them was brisk and, on Parry's part, contained many humorous grumbles at Jenkinson's meticulous attention to detail. Having attempted to rewrite several choruses, Parry felt that he still had not come to terms fully with the Greek text:

I have stuck determinedly to mending the Choruses. Some of them have given me very great trouble; but I have done all but three. Some of them are the better for it, but some again are no better than poor compromises. I think I shall send you a couple of those which I am most doubtful about to see if you think they can pass . . . While I was in the stress, and sorely worried over it, I growled at

---

[12] C. Hubert H. Parry, 'Form and Style', *Style in Musical Art* (London, 1911), 96.

you a little; but when the bother isn't going on I am very grateful to you for pointing out the better way to manage it all; and I shall continue to be so. . . . It will take me a long time to better my confusticated style. I suppose it has grown up with its heels in the air, and it's no joke getting it round into a proper posture . . .[13]

On one point Jenkinson was forthright. He wanted melodrama for the Parabasis, the effect in Greek drama where the Chorus come forward to address the audience on behalf of the poet. Parry felt that he had precious little time to compose one or for the Choragus to learn it. 'Of course I am still open to discuss the matter with you,' he wrote, 'if the difficulty of reciting it proves insuperable . . . But at present I can see no way of doing it which seems to me even tolerable.'[14] By the end of October he finished the various revisions and scoring, though after rehearsals in Cambridge, Jenkinson requested another Entr'acte which caused a 'fierce grind'.[15] The dress rehearsal proved to be chaotic as the chorus were bewildered by the orchestral accompaniment, but the first night and the subsequent four nights at the Theatre Royal were a great success with all the reserved seats sold out. The performances were conducted by Stanford with costumes by J. W. Clark (Registrar of the University) and Charles Newton (Professor of Zoology), and scenery by John O'Connor. Many of the cast, amongst them M. R. James (later Provost of King's College and Eton) as Peithetairos, Arthur Benson (later Master of Magdalene College) as the Priest, and Harry Cust (later a Unionist Member of Parliament and a talented poet) as Prometheus were destined to have distinguished careers. An edition of the music with songs, choruses, and the orchestral music in arrangement for four hands was published by Stanley Lucas in 1885 (with a translation by Arthur Verrall, Fellow of Trinity College and later Professor of English Literature) but the full score was not published.

Aristophanes' satirical comedy afforded Parry the opportunity to combine light-heartedness with pathos. Since he was catering for modest vocal abilities, the technical range and syllabic delivery of the solo numbers and the numerous choruses had to be relatively undemanding. Consequently, the vocal sections are, on the whole musically less ambitious, relying largely on simple unison lines of two- and four-bar phrases which were enhanced to a large extent by the more elaborate orchestral support. Nevertheless, Parry was able to inject moments of subtle artistry into such pieces as 'The Song of the Hoopoe' and the rumbustious Finale (Bridal March and Chorus); and some of the choral interjections ('Tho' a man, as from infinite proof we needs must fear'

[13] Letter to F. J. H. Jenkinson, 28 Sept. 1883, CUL Add. MS 6463.
[14] Letter to F. J. H. Jenkinson, 21 Oct. 1883, ibid.
[15] Diary, 17 Nov. 1883.

(line 451), and 'What a terrible tale is the tale of our downfall' (line 539))
have a distinct charm. But the originality of the score lies in the purely
instrumental portions which proved so popular that, with the further
addition of horns, trumpets, and trombones, a number of them were
performed as a suite of pieces at the Crystal Palace under Stanford's
direction on 8 December.

Parry scored the incidental music for a reduced orchestra of 2 flutes, 2
clarinets, 2 bassoons, 2 horns, harp, timpani, and strings (a simple oboe
part also appears at the bottom of the score, though this seems to have
been a last minute addition). This, however, did not restrict his
expressive range. The Introduction to Act I is a beautifully through-
composed piece, particularly in the way he restates the opening material
in augmentation as a means of winding down the energetic mood. 'The
gathering of the birds', with its careful wind writing and incessant yet
gentle quaver motion, is even more delightful. But perhaps most
delicious are the more restrained, slower sections which bring out
Parry's lyrical gifts. This is certainly true of the long melodic lines of the
Introduction to Act III which are skilfully developed in canon, and the
delicately scored Entr'acte (Ex. 20*a*), occurring prior to the Finale, is a
gem. The Wedding March (to Sovereignty), which was subject to later
revisions, is undoubtedly the best known of all the orchestral pieces and
largely gained its popularity through its concert version (and by Alcock's
arrangement for organ). For the main march tune (Ex. 20*b*) Parry drew
on the rich sonority of violins in their lowest register (a sound later
explored in the revised finale of the Second Symphony) giving us a
surprisingly early introduction to the 'nobilmente' strains associated
with the broad melodies of Elgar's *Pomp and Circumstance* marches
seventeen years later. This tune, featuring a bold use of appoggiaturas,
sequence, and diatonic harmony, is an indication of new stylistic
confidence which is later ecstatically exemplified in the ebullient coda
(Ex. 20*c*).

As recognition of Parry's music increased significantly during 1883, he
seems to have chosen to orientate his social life around non-musical
people. To a large extent this was undoubtedly a reaction to his life at the
Royal College where he was daily surrounded by musicians, while his
continued attendance of concerts given by Richter and Manns brought
him into contact with Joachim, Sullivan, Cowen, Ethel Smyth, and
Mackenzie. But with the exception of Dannreuther (his 'most excellent
best soul'), he found that he could only completely relax in the company
of truly close friends such as Spencer Lyttelton, Robin Benson, and of
late, Jenkinson (or 'Jinks' as he became affectionately known). Parry also
enjoyed the companionship of the painting fraternity, in particular that
of William Richmond and Edward Burne-Jones. Richmond often visited

Rustington with his children and Parry, who always delighted in the company of children, warmed to Richmond's daughter, Helen. Her lively interest in music, which prompted Parry to send away for a volume of Bach's '48', and her love of the sea forged an intimate relationship which gave rise to a gentle and sometimes amusing series of correspondences. 'Most dearest belovedest and best of Podgelfats'[16] Parry would often write, lamenting her absence during his expeditions out in the new canoe he had bought in Littlehampton. '[Y]ou must come back next year and have lots. And I have ordered the sailing boat, and expect it will be all ready for you,'[17] he wrote excitedly, for these modest expeditions had

Ex. 20. *The Birds* (1883). *a* opening of Entr'acte at line 1693; *b* theme from the Wedding March; *c* opening of coda from the Wedding March.

[16] Letter to Helen Richmond, 8 Sept. 1883, RAA RI/3/4/1.
[17] Letter to Helen Richmond, 20 Oct. 1883, RAA RI/3/4/2.

ignited an interest in the sea which was to become his chief source of
recreation, and later of escape, away from the exacting demands of his
musical career. The new sailing boat referred to in his letter to Helen
Richmond, the *Ornis*, a small open cutter built by Harvey of
Littlehampton, was sailed for the first time on 15 April. It gave him
immeasurable pleasure, even when he encountered potentially dangerous
weather conditions. This activity, an extension of his natural affinity for
strenuous exercise, was unquestionably a form of catharsis.

On 5 March 1883, Parry heard Brahms's new String Quintet, Op. 88
(completed in 1882) at a Popular Concert under the leadership of
Joachim. '[It] is of course masterly but not it seems to me musically
effective throughout',[18] was his critical appraisal. Yet the work evidently
left a deep impression, for on 10 December he began work on his own
Quintet in E flat which Dannreuther offered to include in his next series
of concerts in the spring of 1884. During the Quintet's composition there
were the usual distractions—Cambridge Doctoral exercises, examination
papers for Trinity College of Music, and journeys to Wilton House
where, over Christmas, illness had first beset his eldest daughter and
later his brother-in-law. 'I am all behind hand,' he wrote to Dannreuther
from Wilton, 'I've not given up the Quintett, but I'm sure it's dreadfully
spoilt by all this delay, and there's no chance of its being ready in time
for rehearsal except for the last concert.'[19] In spite of his initial fears, it
was completed by mid-February and performed at Orme Square on 18
March. In his quintet Parry attempted to mirror many of the features of

[18] Diary, 5 Mar. 1883.
[19] Letter to Edward Dannreuther, 4 Jan. 1884. Bod. MS Eng. Letters e.117.

Brahms's work. The first movement has a similar fresh lyricism, though it lacks the vibrancy of Brahms's thematic and tonal contrast. The Scherzo, on the other hand, is a vigorous, inventive movement imbued with Brahmsian seriousness and characterized by the explosive chords heard at the opening which are then dramatically extended in the coda. The slow movement is perhaps the finest in idiomatic terms. Parry makes felicitous use of the two violas in a luxuriant, rhapsodic context of extended melodic lines. The finale, a sonata rondo, appears to have given him more trouble. Originally, for the second-group tonality, he settled on C major, but in later revisions (in 1896 and 1902) he altered this to B major. He also complained of an unhappiness with the idiom in general, and felt that it was often too heavily scored—a problem he sought to alleviate in the later revisions which inevitably delayed its publication until 1909. Stanford, who admired the work, persuaded Parry to approach Joachim hoping that the latter would perform it at a 'Pops' concert in 1886. The suggestion proved to be a further blow to Parry's already fragile relationship with the violinist: 'he criticised my string quintett which he evidently dislikes thoroughly. He said "the slow movement is much too long and very wearisome". Thought the Scherzo best. He is certainly utterly out of sympathy with me in music and has long felt; I have no hope of any help from him ever. I should never have sent the Quintett to him but for Stanford'.[20]

Joachim's polarized Brahmsian view soon reared its head when he and Ouseley were invited by Grove to examine the student composers at the College. 'Joachim none too agreeable', Parry wrote irritably in his diary, 'Got it into his head that MacCunn was influenced by Wagner and said "he has been subjected to pernicious influence"'.[21] There was no doubt in Parry's mind to whom the accusation was directed, since MacCunn was his pupil. Ouseley, on the other hand seemed even more comical, for he complained of MacCunn's 'putting a 2nd subject of a minor movement in the Dominant major and said, as if it settled the question, "That is not in my book, you know."'[22] But the contentious reputation often arising from his examining exploits did not, it seems, cause any disadvantage to Parry. On the last day of January he received a telegram from the Vice-Chancellor of Oxford informing that he had been elected Choragus for the university and would also receive an Honorary Doctorate. As an acknowledgement of this appointment and honour, *Prometheus Unbound* (which Parry revised in April) was performed in Oxford on 21 May. The main consequence of his new position was the obligation to act as a regular examiner for the degrees and help with the university's lecture programme.

[20] Diary, 6 Apr. 1886.   [21] Ibid. 4 Apr. 1884.   [22] Ibid.

Parry's general misgivings about the Quintet did not, however, deter him from composing further chamber works. After the composition of the Quintet was finished in February, his academic commitments afforded little time for large-scale composition in the following months, but in early March a brief interval allowed him to write two simple *Intermezzi* for string trio (published in 1950). These were dedicated to Kitty, Margaret, and Susan Lushington, daughters of Vernon Lushington QC whose home in Kensington Square was a popular meeting-place for artistic, musical, and literary people. It was not until the late summer that ideas began to crystallize for another Piano Trio, on a more ambitious scale than the first. After a number of rehearsals, in which Holmes and the cellist Ould were somewhat diffident, the new Trio was given at Orme Square on 25 November and later published by Novello.

The Piano Trio No. 2 in B minor combines severity and intensity with great tenderness in a wealth of melodic invention. The work was, however, not without its critics, the most vociferous of whom seems to have been Stanford who, after hearing a performance at Cambridge in February 1886, 'thought the first movement quite unintelligible and the last much too restless and foggy in sound.'[23] Brahmsian intellectualism is the dominant force behind the prevailing turbulence of the first movement, which is only temporarily relieved by the Schumannesque 'reverie' of its second-group material. The Scherzo, by comparison, is thematically less interesting, though it is redeemed to some extent by its lyrical Trio. The finale suffers from undue length, and the coda in the tonic major is a disappointing anticlimax. Nevertheless, the movement is distinguished by a magnificent broad Rondo theme of which Brahms would surely have been proud. The emotional centre of the Piano Trio is, however, the sublime slow movement which is one of the finest in all of Parry's chamber works. One senses that he felt happiest when exploiting the lyrical potential of the strings—a fact borne out by the extended opening melody for cello. Moreover, with the lessons he had learned from similar lyrically dominated movements in the Fantasie Sonata and Piano Concerto, he was able to use this propensity for extended melody to construct a through-composed movement of great structural originality and assurance.

Furthermore, within the domain of four-movement schemes, it is one of his most sophisticated cyclic designs—a design that compares favourably with that of the 'Cambridge' Symphony. The Trio has a close affinity with Schumann's D minor Violin Sonata, notably in the way material from the introduction is subsequently incorporated into the first theme of the 'Allegro con fuoco'. The opening theme of the introduction

[23] Ibid. 20 Feb. 1886.

(which is characterized by a three-note figure similar to that of the Wind Nonet) also recurs as material for a fresh thematic episode in the Scherzo. The finale commences with what appears to be the same slow introduction, but it proceeds differently with a combination of material from the slow movement (the main theme), the Scherzo (the Trio theme), and the main theme of the first movement. A last reference to the cyclic idea is used to form the cadential progression before the final statement of the Rondo theme. But perhaps more significant than the motivic interplay is the harmonic foundation of the first four bars of the introduction to the first movement which asserts the progression: $Ib-II^7b-V-I$. This harmonic cell also plays a cyclic role, existing independently of the thematic ideas it initally accompanies. We hear this partially as the opening progression of the 'Allegro con fuoco' and in a more protracted state in bars 4–13 of the slow movement. As a constituent of this progression, II^7b provides an added dimension, recurring as a sort of *idée fixe*. For example it is the penultimate chord of the entire work, and in the opening of the slow movement it receives particular dynamic and registral emphasis.

The Quintet and Piano Trio in B minor were the two major creative offerings of 1884. In between times Parry occupied himself with small assignments. In April, for example, he made certain minor revisions to the cadenza of his Piano Concerto in the hope that Dannreuther would take up the work again.[24] He completed his 'Variations' article for Grove, and read a paper for the Musical Association. He also agreed to contribute a series of articles to Miss Leith's *Every Girl's Magazine*, the first of which was on Mozart. Eventually these informative short studies were published by Routledge in 1887 in a collection entitled *Studies of the Great Composers* and were accompanied by a preface explaining their purpose was to help 'people of average general intelligence to get some idea of the positions which the most important composers occupy in the historical development of the art'. As biographical thumbnail sketches they were not intended as probing, philosophical, or analytical discourses; none the less, they provide an interesting general historical perspective of the 'great masters' seen through the eyes of a scholar of the 1880s, particularly with regard to Wagner (which is indebted to Dannreuther), Haydn (to the work of C. F. Pohl), and Schubert (which benefited enormously from the recent pioneering work carried out by Grove); added to which they act as a useful point of reference in our understanding of Parry's more penetrating scholarly articles and books.

---

[24] A performance of the Piano Concerto was subsequently given in Richter's season of concerts on 9 June with Dannreuther as soloist.

Yet, above all these varied undertakings, there lay one project which was to preoccupy him for the next four years. With two symphonies, two choral works, a large corpus of chamber works, and numerous songs behind him, the time seemed ripe to contemplate the one genre that had remained as yet unexplored—opera. For Parry it was cause for great excitement which increased after discussions with Dannreuther in late May. But in years to come it would prove to be the one artistic decision he would bitterly regret.

9

Guenever
Despair and Bitterness

THE idea of writing an opera had been in Parry's mind since the latter part of 1882 when he looked at a libretto by his friend, the Revd Arthur Butler, whose acquaintance he had renewed on a visit to Oxford in November. Parry subsequently rejected Butler's project, but the search for a suitable text went on. Another incentive was undoubtedly the operatic activities of his contemporaries. Goring Thomas's *Esmerelda*, commissioned by Carl Rosa, had enjoyed tremendous success at Drury Lane in March 1883, and further recognition in Cologne and Hamburg. Mackenzie's 'Lyrical Drama' *Columba* written in collaboration with Hueffer and also produced by Carl Rosa at Drury Lane in April 1883, scored an equally resounding triumph. Stanford had enjoyed the attentions of Bronsart in Hannover with his *Veiled Prophet of Khorassan* (libretto by Barclay Squire) in the spring of 1881. More recently his second opera, *Savonarola*, had been performed with acclaim in Hamburg in April 1884, under the baton of Josef Sucher. Acutely aware of the importance of international recognition, Stanford had also worked feverishly to have yet another opera, *The Canterbury Pilgrims*, ready for Carl Rosa to produce at Drury Lane in April 1884 which he no doubt hoped would lead to further performances abroad.

On 28 April 1884, Parry went to the first performance of *The Canterbury Pilgrims*. It impressed him in parts, but he was rather bored and disappointed with it as a whole. 'The pilgrims song is the most attractive thing in it to me. The fugal entry of pilgrims taking too. I didn't think anything else particularly noticeable. It was very well received of course . . .'.[1] The last somewhat acid comment alluded to the clique of followers whom Stanford contrived to be at first performances of his works in order to be sure of vociferous applause. This, Parry maintained, helped to heighten the farce of the first and only performance of *Savonarola* at Covent Garden under Richter in July. The lessons of *Savonarola* were fundamental: a poor libretto, an inconsistent dramatic scheme which situated much of the drama in the Prologue instead of the Third Act, and musical ideas poorly conceived for the

---

[1] Diary, 28 Apr. 1884.

stage. On all these counts Parry hoped to improve where Stanford's efforts had, as yet, fallen short. Unfortunately, the first of these, the libretto, proved to be a major stumbling-block from which the musical composition of his own opera never recovered.

It was Sir George Grove who suggested that Una Taylor, daughter of the author Sir Henry Taylor, would be a suitable librettist. Although as a novelist her success had so far been modest, Grove believed that her enthusiasm for opera, and more particularly Wagnerian music-drama, would be appropriate to Parry's own operatic conceptions. Unfortunately she had no experience of the theatre. In her correspondence with Charles Graves, Parry's first biographer, she maintained that Parry also professed an ignorance of theatrical practicalities which caused him to rely entirely on the judgement of Dannreuther. As to the subject, Parry settled on the epic story of Lancelot and Guenever—a bold decision viewed in the light of the Arthurian precedents of *Tristan* and *Parsifal*. A diary entry of 28 May reveals that Lancelot was to be the main protagonist of the opera. But after discussion, Una Taylor asserted, their perception of the story changed:

His conception of the story and mine differed. As you know, the Morte is a medley of various versions of the stories it tells, and it seemed to me one could legitimately base our plot on a less commonplace one than the generally received tradition, and make Gareth's death, not Guenever's faithlessness, the main motive in the tragedy. After Hubert Parry had read up the chapters in the Morte [a book which naturally appeared in his 1884 reading list] which I thought justified this rendering, I think he agreed willingly to work on those lines.[2]

There being a modicum of agreement between them, Parry recorded on 20 June that he finished a sketch on Act I. Work was then interrupted until the beginning of August when Una Taylor visited Rustington for a week in order to discuss the development of the story in the later acts as well as a complete recasting of Act I. Though ideas for *Guenever* were undoubtedly forming at the back of his mind after sketching some ideas in June 1884, Parry did not resume work until January 1885. By this time, however, his health had started to deteriorate seriously and he was obliged to give up the attempt. He was unable to return to the sketches of Act I until November 1885.

After the Christmas vacation, Parry's return to the College was marked by unpleasant wranglings. It is evident from numerous diary entries, that Parry's opinion of Stanford was by no means a high one. Maude's correspondence reveals that Parry, besides having doubts about the real quality of Stanford's compositional talent, also fostered a deep suspicion of the Irishman's motives. On the one hand he was deeply

---

[2] Charles L. Graves, *Hubert Parry* (London, 1926), ii. 210.

grateful for Stanford's support in the performances of *Prometheus* and the 'Cambridge' Symphony, but he also recognized a side of Stanford's personality that was charged with virulent ambition and self-aggrandisement. This mistrust surfaced at a Board meeting early in January:

Stanford has been playing some curious tricks. We sent him only one small batch of paper work to look over at the exams; and now I hear he refused even to do that, and sent it onto Parratt, who was too good natured and did it for him. His way seems to be to shirk his work, and to get himself conspicuous with outsiders by writing memoranda to the Council behind the backs of the Professors and the board. He will probably end by being the prominent man of the College, and having a testimonial for his devotion, when in reality he is the only man in the place who shirks his work.[3]

In March Parry went to Cambridge to hear a performance of Stanford's new Elegiac Ode, written for the Norwich Festival in 1884. His remarks, particularly with regard to the setting of Walt Whitman (whom Parry greatly admired but never set himself), were more biting than ever: 'There are good points in it. Or rather attempts at good points, most of which are not very profound in conception, not musicianly and not at all up to the mark of the poem in character. Had to come back by special train and did not get to Phillimore till near 2 in the morning. Such sacrifices has one to make to accommodate people's sensitiveness'.[4] Except to close friends such as Jenkinson, Parry's criticisms of Stanford's music remained wholly private. During the fiasco over *Savonarola* when Stanford fell into disfavour with the critics, Parry, who detested the press, felt disposed to support the work after encountering adverse criticism from Hueffer. 'To him I stuck up for the work all I could,' he wrote to Jenkinson, 'To Charley I shall be as nice as I can you may be sure. But I am afraid nothing short of enthusiastic praise will comfort him.'[5] And later to Jenkinson he expressed in a nutshell the main obstacle to his appreciation of Stanford's work: 'It wouldn't be fair to say I don't praise C.V.S.'s music; only I rarely get to that pitch of boiling enthusiasm which is necessary to produce complete satisfaction in others.'[6]

At the end of 1884, with the exertions of the Piano Trio over, Parry felt an inclination to return to song writing, a genre he had for some time neglected. In the last days of December he began revising a number of the songs which Anna Williams had performed at Orme Square. This soon induced him to compose a number of new ones. One of Keats's poems, 'Bright Star! would I were steadfast as thou art' which particularly gripped him, was set early in the new year, and the

---

[3] Diary, 2 Jan. 1885.   [4] Ibid. 13 Mar. 1885.
[5] Letter to F. J. H. Jenkinson, 21 Sept. 1884, CUL Add. MS 6463.
[6] Letter to F. J. H. Jenkinson, 2 Dec. 1885, ibid.

Shakespeare Sonnet *Wenn ich, von Gott*, originally composed in 1874, was presented to Dannreuther in a revised version. Publication of two sets of *English Lyrics* and a separate collection of Shakespeare Sonnets lay at the heart of this renewed energy for song composition. On 16 January two further settings of Shakespeare, 'Willow, willow, willow' and 'Blow, blow thou winter wind', were written rapidly, the latter after experiencing (as Parry himself put it) 'the howling and soaring and booming of the wind outside'.[7] The first volume of *English Lyrics* Parry envisaged as a soprano set. Initially a setting of Shakespeare's 'Crabbed age and youth' had been sketched in November 1882 but he had been at a loss how to treat 'the rapid dramatic changes of sentiment in the latter part'.[8] This sense of dissatisfaction still prevailed so 'Willow, willow, willow' was written as a replacement. Once Dannreuther's approval had been obtained, Parry approached Stanley Lucas who agreed to publish them.

With the exception of the setting of Scott's 'Where shall the lover rest', the quality of this first volume of *English Lyrics* is consistently high. Schumann is particularly prominent in the setting of Shelley's 'Goodnight' (Ex. 21) which shares a distinct textural affinity with the tranquil 'innig' style of songs such as 'Am leuchtenden Sommermorgen' and 'Im wunderschönen Monat Mai' ('Dichterliebe', Op. 48). In addition to the gentle arpeggiation and appoggiaturas that both songs have in common, Parry's initial tonal obliquity is especially reminiscent of that composer. But what is more intrinsically Brahmsian is the meticulous motivic integration of the vocal line which exemplifies Parry's attention to detail. The seminal motive of Parry's vocal line, a rising fifth (figure 'a'), underpins the central word 'Goodnight' (itself a recurring textual motive) in Shelley's poem. This musical interval is anticipated in a veiled fashion by the accompaniment's initial arpeggiation, and embellished by one of the many poignant appoggiaturas. In answer to this phrase, the textual contradiction of the first statement 'Ah no!' is conveyed by a rising fourth (the intervallic inversion of the fifth), which ascends to high F. In relaxing the tension created by both the rise in register and the prolongation of the dominant, Parry moves, not to the tonic as we expect, but to the dominant of E flat (bar 3) and answers with a falling phrase incorporating the preceding fourth interval in inversion. The second line of text ('That severs those it should unite') proceeds to develop these motivic precedents by first outlining the fifth ('severs those') and then the fourth ('it should unite'). Line 3 ('Let us remain together still') opens with a virtual inversion of 'the hour is ill' (cf. bars 3 and 6) concluded by two falling fourths (bars 6–7); and the final line of the stanza not only mirrors its previous phrase by incorporating two

[7] Diary, 16 Jan. 1885.   [8] Ibid. 1 Nov. 1882.

Ex. 21. 'Good night' (1881–5), bars 1–12.

rising fourths, but it also recalls the first line's more anxious ascent to top F which is here mollified by the first statement of the tonic in the piece. Moreover, in playing on the word 'goodnight', Parry takes the opportunity of echoing the first word and motive of line 1, but reversing the pitches. To add to the contrast of rhythmical figuration and tonal divergence, Parry introduces a new melodic motive for his central section (figure 'b') which, with its upper neighbour-note motion, is related to the opening piano figuration (namely the appoggiatura figure at the end of each pattern). The motive is then combined with the main 'fifth' motive of the first section and can be observed in the first phrase (bars 11–12) which is constructed on a sequence of two rising fifths of which the first is decorated by the new motive (it is also significant to note that the second of these rising fifths accompanies the textual motive, though with the two words in reverse order (i.e. 'night good' (bar 12)). This idea is developed sequentially in line 7 ('Be it not said, thought, understood'), before line 8 recalls the now established textual and motivic association of 'goodnight' at its conclusion in another rising fourth.

Having concluded the central section in C major (the dominant of the dominant), Parry quits the key in a chromatic modification of the bass motive (see the beginning of bar 18) which is then mirrored at the end of bar 19. This not only maintains harmonic continuity but also facilitates a return to the oblique progression at the opening of the first section. The final vocal section is a fine example of melodic variation. Line 9 mimics the beginning of line 1 with its ascent to C, though intervallically it is modified to a fourth, recalling the recent cadence of bars 17–18. But having avoided the literal quotation of the fifth interval, Parry proceeds to incorporate it into the rhythmically displaced ascent to high F (bars 20–1), and, with this added rhythmical momentum, produces some appropriate textual imagery ('which near each other move'). Line 10 continues to work the fourth interval in its initial stages ('From evening's close') before ascending to the climactic high G, registrally the highest point of the vocal line ('to morning's light'). This climax is also coupled with the only variation in the harmonic scheme which moves on to the dominant of F. Line 11 commences with a literal repetition of line 3 ('The night is good'), though Parry indulges in an augmentation of the original rhythm in the second part not only for textual emphasis ('because my love'), but so as to link the phrase with line 12 ('They never say goodnight'). Here also Parry rhythmically displaces the ascent to C to the third beat, throwing emphasis on to the word 'say'; the final reference to 'goodnight' is then sung more poignantly over the greatly enlarged interval of an octave. Even at this cadential point, Parry continues the sense of variation by developing and extending the original feminine cadence of the first section (bar 9) delaying for two bars what is only the second pure tonic root of the song.

'My true love hath my heart' and 'Willow, willow, willow' also show a similar propensity for vocal integration though with relatively less complexity. In 'Willow, willow, willow', Parry captures Desdemona's grief with a profound simplicity, and most telling of all is his introduction of a 'new' pitch at a crucial stage of the text ('and *soften'd* the stones'—i.e. the F natural) an effect reminiscent of those in Purcell.

The second set of *English Lyrics* was published by Stanley Lucas in 1886 and consisted of five settings of Shakespeare. The first, 'O mistress mine' from *Twelfth Night*, has been one of Parry's most enduring songs. This is largely owing to an original piano accompaniment which sets the mood with its coquettish chromaticisms and irregular phrase lengths in the introductory bars. It is also an interesting song from the tonal point of view for it underlines Parry's increasing reliance on diatonicism and its modal potential. In this regard it is fascinating to observe how Parry avoids the platitude of modulating to the dominant and instead gives greater status to the mediant (A minor) and the supertonic (D minor) which have more modal implications. 'Take, O take those lips away' from *Measure for Measure* curiously looks forward to the brevity of Wolf's late songs. The song displays a mature handling of tonality, notably in the sensuous move to D flat ('And my kisses bring again'), but most impressive is the interdependence between voice and piano, a feature emphasized in the final bars where the piano is left to resolve the open-ended vocal line. Third in the set is 'No longer mourn for me' which was composed ten years earlier and which Parry evidently decided to discard from his projected volume of Shakespeare Sonnets in Bodenstedt's German translation. 'Blow, blow thou winter wind' from *As You Like it* and 'When icicles hang by the wall' from *Love's Labour's Lost* were more recent compositions and evoke a contrasting rustic mood. 'Blow, blow' is equally balanced between the minor mode of each verse and its refrain ('Heigh ho! sing heigh ho! unto the green holly'), a disputation distilled in the epigrammatic final bar in the minor. 'When icicles hang by the wall', the final song of the set, is more humorous with its hooting owls and amusing quotation of 'For he's a jolly good fellow' (see bars 40–2) as part of an effective evocation of a winter landscape.

The words 'Felt desperately tired', written in his diary on 3 January 1885, were indicative of the state of Parry's health. The constant travelling to and from Rustington to be with his ailing wife, together with ceaseless writing, composing, examining, research at the British Museum, proof-reading, and part-correcting, not to mention his teaching duties at the Royal College were rapidly taking their toll on his physical endurance. But faced with the prospect of relinquishing his work-load, his reaction was always to double his efforts. He therefore could not refuse the invitation from Stanford to give a series of weekly lectures at Cambridge between 4 and 25 February, and there was no let-up in his attendance of concerts in London. Eva James gave the first performance of his *Theme and Nineteen Variations* at Orme Square on 10 February and the Bach Choir gave a performance of *Prometheus* on 19 February which was well received save for a savage attack made by the critic of the *Pall Mall*. Though for several years Parry had been a regular contributor to both the *Pall Mall* and the *Saturday Review*, he had come to detest the press and to ignore their futile jibes and remarks; yet such was his innate sensitivity that he was always intimidated by them. 'I know it is stupid!', he wrote tormentedly, 'But it is cruel to struggle wearily on, and have to endure the vile sneers of these curs.'[9] His anger subsequently exploded when, on attending a concert at Orme Square on 24 February, he found that Dannreuther had relented to pressure by Hueffer to perform some of the latter's songs. 'The most outrageous rubbish', was Parry's fuming response; 'Hueffer is beginning to put pressure on singers and others to perform his wretched productions, under pain of being suppressed by the Times.'[10]

A combination of these irritations and an excessive number of commitments undoubtedly helped to accelerate the decline in his health, and more particularly his uncertain heart condition. Already in January the strain of correcting orchestral parts for a performance of *The Birds* in Manchester caused severe palpitations and headaches which frequently left him drained and unfit for work. His close friends, William Richmond, Jenkinson, and Hugh Montgomery soon began to sense that his intrepid constitution showed signs of collapsing. Yet still he went on. Having become accustomed to the absence of Maude at Phillimore Place, he felt more inclined to cultivate the Victorian habit of dining out regularly with friends. He was a constant visitor at the Richmonds' home in Hammersmith and he was invited to dinner parties at the Balfours. At Rustington there were visits from Una Taylor about the opera libretto and from Jenkinson who sailed with him on the *Ornis*. Moreover, he did a little work on a *Suite Moderne* for violin and piano intended for Kitty Lushington (this eventually became the Suite in D for Violin and Piano published in 1907). But his condition did not improve, and it was perhaps inevitable that, at the end of April, he should suffer a severe attack of angina.

Unfortunately the domestic climate at Highnam was not conducive to his making a full recovery. A visit to his father in May confirmed his fears that the house and estate were in decline. Already in early March,

<hr>

[9] Diary, 22 Feb. 1885.   [10] Ibid. 24 Feb. 1885.

Parry had made a brief visit to Highnam and had been subjected to the violent diatribes of Thomas Gambier Parry who vehemently blamed the Liberals for 'ruining the country gentlemen who are the mainstay of the nation'.[11] Yet it is also clear from Thomas Gambier Parry's letters that he harboured many regrets about purchasing the estate in the late 1830s. An appreciable slice of income to the estate came from the cultivation of the land by tenant farmers, but with the decay of agricultural prices, his farmers had given up paying rent altogether, and with the increasing tax burden (for which he held the Liberals entirely responsible) he began shutting up vineries, hot houses, and even rooms in the house. In May the situation seemed more acute than ever:

Poor old Highnam is depressingly changed. Reductions have had to be made so universally that the house can hardly be kept up. Nearly half the gardeners have been dismissed (6 out of 13), one groom, one lady's maid, one footman cut off. [Barely] enough horses left to take people into Gloucester for shopping and station and things sadly out of repair.[12]

Of course in accusing the Liberals Thomas Gambier Parry was also indirectly accusing his son whom he knew to have Gladstonian sympathies. Parry was also aware that one day he would inherit the estate with all its problems. Yet it was not so much the financial difficulties that daunted him; rather it was the prospect of running the estate from London where his professional life kept him. It was this very question that surfaced years later and which was to be the source of intense bitterness, jealousy, and animosity between Parry and his eldest half-brother, Ernest, who, sick and emotionally unbalanced, had recently returned to England an invalid. For the moment, however, it was a dilemma that remained at the back of Parry's mind, but undoubtedly added to the weight of mounting responsibilities.

With the resumption of lectures at the College, his heart trouble worsened to the point where he was forced to consult a doctor. 'He examined away for a long while', Parry wrote ominously, 'and looked so awfully grave at first that I began to think he was going to condemn me.'[13] So serious was the state of his heart that his physician immediately recommended a complete cessation of work of any kind, including composition. In order that he might divorce himself entirely from work, Hugh Montgomery suggested that he go on a voyage to South America with Sedley Taylor as his companion.

On 17 June they left Liverpool on the Pacific Mail Company's liner, the *Aconcagua*, bound for Valparaiso, Chile. 'I watched the land fading away in the distance thinking of Maude', he recorded sombrely, 'but not

[11] Diary, 5 Mar. 1885.   [12] Ibid. 22 May 1885.   [13] Ibid. 3 June 1885.

daring to think of how long it will be before I see the land again.'[14] Despite Sedley Taylor's positive reports home telling of the good effect of sea air and absence of worry, Parry was soon bored, homesick, and fretful. There were few passengers on board who made interesting conversation, and Sedley Taylor's 'fidgety' personality irritated him, a fact intimated in a letter to his wife written off the coast of Portugal: 'I'm writing this under difficulties, as Sedley Taylor is playing within a few yards to an admiring group of passengers and officers, on a cracked old pianoforte which stands at the end of the saloon; and accompanying wild attempts at ballads.'[15] From Lisbon, a city that enraptured him, the liner made out into the Atlantic packed with hordes of Portuguese emigrants. After stopping at Pernambuco, the ship sailed south for Rio and Montevideo, panoramic views of which he carefully sketched. From Montevideo they continued south to the Straits of Magellan. This was for him potentially the most exciting portion of the voyage, but his mind remained fixed on home and he longed for his wife in an almost adolescent fashion:

Here we go still, always due south; and 500 miles further from my own dear. We are near the Straits now; and are running slow as it is night and we don't want to run on this wild and lighthouseless coast. We shall most likely be in the Straits tomorrow morning, and at a little station called Sandy Point, half way through I shall have to post this letter. It's over 300 miles from the Atlantic to the Pacific, and part of the way it is said to be the wildest thing imaginable. The cliffs of solid rock almost hang over head as the steamer goes through, and the tide whirls between them, black with tremendous depth of water; and round about will be glaciers, and snow covered peaks;—and even possibly a few cannibals. I must bring this to an end I'm afraid. And this is the last letter I shall be able to write. Perhaps you will only get it a week or so before I come back. Oh! that coming back, how dreadfully far off it seems. Dear love how I do long to be with you again. You dear, dear sweet, good, owniest of owns; your boy knew he loved you a great lot before; but he didn't know how much till now.

                    Goodie bye my own dearest.[16]

After Montevideo the atmosphere on board deteriorated. The vulgar tones of the ship's doctor singing a mixture of Sullivan, music hall and patter songs brought him to boiling-point: 'One can endure in silence for some time, but a whole hour is maddening.'[17] Moreover, Sedley Taylor's company was unsettling and seriously upset his heart. On their arrival at Valparaiso things were no better and he cursed 'the uselessness' of this voyage.[18] In the three weeks they were ashore they took a train about sixty miles inland to Los Andes and, with a guide, took mules into the

[14] Ibid. 18 June 1885.   [15] Letter to Lady Maude Parry, 22 June 1885, ShP.
[16] Letter to Lady Maude Parry, 20 July 1885, ShP.
[17] Diary, 17 July 1885.   [18] Ibid. 28 July 1885.

lower mountains along the Uspallata Pass where they spent several nights eating and sleeping in the spartan conditions furnished by the local farmers. For Parry the experience was fascinating and unforgettable, but Sedley Taylor's health could no longer tolerate the life-style and they were forced to return—much to Parry's disappointment as he hoped to get nearer the high peaks of the Andes. After hearing *Aida* 'very fairly performed'[19] in Santiago they made their way back to Valparaiso, spent some time with the numerous English residents there, before boarding the ship again on 14 August. The return journey, which took over four weeks, had much the same effect as the outward-bound voyage. He frequently shied away from the motley assortment of continental passengers and chaffed at the delays in Montevideo, St Vincent, and Lisbon. Among the passengers who came on board at Lisbon was the Portuguese Military Attaché at Berlin who confirmed in Parry's eyes the frivolous Latin attitude to music, and, furthermore, galvinized his own antipathy to that aesthetic:

Among other things we talked of Germany where he has been a good deal. He said Germans were quite inartistic. I said at all events they were great musicians. 'Well, yes, in a fashion they are. But it is their own fashion. Quite different from other people. They take it so seriously. It is strange. When you go to the opera in Germany they do not talk or laugh—never—It is just as if they were at Mass!' It is much the same view of the Art that a refined and cultured old Brazilian expressed to S.[edley]T.[aylor] on the way out—'Music', in his view, 'was not a matter for men of sense to consider. Rather a frivolous art—Better be left to Italians.' S.T. has been rather lucky catching things of the kind. Some commonplace plutocrat once said to him. 'Ah you like music do you. Well it's a nice *amusement for people who can't afford to hunt.*'[20]

On 18 September he was back at Rustington with great relief though there was little real improvement in his health. Shortly after his return he underwent a minor operation for an inflamed cyst on the neck, which interrupted his teaching routine at the College, and his heart seemed no better. His specialist, Sir Andrew Clark, whom he consulted in November, maintained that the very absence from work had if anything served to provoke his complaint by causing additional anxiety. Such a diagnosis was to Parry a pleasant surprise, since he was half-expecting another period of enforced rest. With the consultation over, he lost no time in preparing a revision of the Shakespeare Sonnets for publication. He also began a set of *Characteristic Popular Tunes of the British Isles* for his daughters to play as piano duets. These technically undemanding arrangements were finished in January 1886 and later published by Stanley Lucas in 1887 in two volumes; the first, dedicated to Dorothea,

---

[19] Diary, 4 Aug. 1885.   [20] Ibid. 13 Sept. 1885.

contains English and Welsh tunes, and the second, dedicated to Gwen, Scotch and Irish.

It was *Guenever*, however, that totally preoccupied Parry in the last months of 1885 and was to dominate the first half of 1886. Even before his consultation with Clark, he had yielded to the temptation of resuming work on Act I, which he began afresh so that a complete sketch of the new First Act was finished by 2 December 1885. Early in 1886 Una Taylor's visits to Phillimore Place were frequent as the libretto for Acts II, III, and IV was digested and revised. Evidently Parry found her personality uncongenial. He described her as 'one of the most singular miniatures of cleverness and silliness'[21] he had ever met and found her affectation thoroughly annoying. 'When she first came, she cackled and giggled incessantly', he wrote irritably, 'and by degrees under our silent habits she toned down.'[22] After she had gone (which was a relief to the entire Parry household), progress on Act I and Act II was swift. In March Parry showed the First Act of the opera to Stanford who approved of it. Dannreuther similarly professed himself pleased with Act II, especially the Pendragon song and 'tender bits of Guenever'.[23] The real problems seem to have begun with Act III which was drafted at the end of March. The chief obstacle was the language of the libretto which he wrestled with for several days, sketching one unsatisfactory idea after another, and when he presented the portion of Act III to Dannreuther, the latter expressed unequivocal disgust with the words and thought it inevitable that much of it would have to be rewritten. His advice was always heeded. It was not until the end of April that Acts III and IV approached their final forms, after which Parry began to consider the best way of confronting Carl Rosa. Stanford, who had worked with Rosa, and moreover approved of *Guenever*, seemed his most favourable advocate, so the complete piano arrangement was sent to him in mid-May. Stanford subsequently suggested various emendations to the score but was full of praise:

I have just finished playing it through, and I think it's quite superbo, *really* superbo. Dramatically and every way I bet my hat on its success. The words are fine, and the book is quite admirable in my humble judgment. I would like you to alter one or two small things which I will show you (stage waits) and one or two *Parsifal* effects . . . No time to lose. I want to strike while the iron is hot.[24]

Stanford and Dannreuther took the opera to Rosa in late June, yet in spite of their fervent recommendations, he refused to undertake it for

---

[21] Ibid. 16 Jan. 1886.   [22] Ibid.   [23] Ibid. 21 Mar. 1886.
[24] Letter from C. V. Stanford, 21 May 1886. Graves, *Hubert Parry*, ii. 211.

various reasons, the prime one being the poor libretto. From a letter to
his wife we may gauge the extent of Parry's disappointment:

Dearest owniest,

the news is as bad as it well can be. I saw Stanford last night and he told me all
about it. Rosa doesn't like the libretto at all. The 2nd act he thinks hopeless—
quite impossible! And even the music drags, as well it may with Una's
successive processions of 'mailed' knights, who all must come in to slow march
time. He liked the last act best, and the tail end of the 3rd act—when the barge
comes in. But he will have nothing to do with performing it so as I said it will go
into a drawer for good, and all that work is done with. I suppose it was good
practice for me. Don't worry yourself about it. I must go on as before and try
and be as useful at the College as long as they will let me.[25]

He also had the duty of writing to Una Taylor with the bad tidings,
though he was careful to hide his own misgivings about the libretto:

My dear Una,

I have been expecting you in town for a long while. You said you should
probably come up in May. I finished the pianoforte arrangement of the opera
about 6 weeks or 2 months ago. I went through it with Dannreuther and he
expressed himself much pleased with it. Then Stanford took it and also was
pleased and offered to take it to Rosa. He and Dannreuther went together
yesterday and I am sorry to say he as good as declined to have anything to do
with it. He says in the first place anything to do with Arthur 'means ruin' in this
country. 2ndly the third act drags and will have to be entirely rewritten
librettoly and musically—the whole conception of it changed in fact! What he
likes best is the tail end of the 3rd and the 4th act entire. I am so accustomed to
disappointment that I shall probably soon shake it off after a bad night or two,
when as last night bits of it will keep ringing in my head whether I will or no.
But I am very sorry for you. I think it will disappoint you. There is no help for
it. The best that could be done was done for it and there it ends.[26]

With Rosa's rejection, Stanford and Dannreuther immediately suggested
that a German opera company might be interested. Parry, who was
somewhat reticent about such a move (particularly after Stanford's
unfruitful attempts with the First Symphony), consented simply because
he saw no other alternative. Consequently, in July he handed over the
score and libretto to his former German tutor, Friedrich Althaus, who
promptly obliged with a German translation. In August the opera was
shown to Emil Neckel of the Mannheim Theatre, but he expressed
doubts. On Stanford's instigation, Carl Armbruster, the conductor,
talked about it to Häckel of the Münchenoper. He declined it. There was
an additional problem in that Goldmark's opera *Merlin* was due to be

[25] Letter to Lady Maude Parry, 29 June 1886, ShP.
[26] Letter to Una Taylor, 29 June 1886, Bod. MS Eng. Letters c.2.

staged at the Vienna Hofoper in November—subject matter that was precariously close to that of *Guenever*. When Dannreuther returned the score early in January Parry's cynicism was complete: 'He [Dannreuther] gave me back the MS of my opera which has been returned from Germany and is not to be tried. I knew that before it went. [The] excuses are polite; Goldmark's "Merlin" is too near the same subject—and Stanford's [work] is better backed with money guarantees.'[27] But perhaps the final nail in the coffin for Parry in terms of morale was Rosa's acceptance of Mackenzie's second opera, *The Troubadour*, on a libretto of Hueffer's. His scathing assessment of the opera suggests that nepotism was as useful to the composer as his talent:

Hueffer's libretto is unsurpassably bad. Structures all obviously borrowed from Tannhäuser, Tristan or Flying Dutchman and invariably spoilt. The development of the plot depends on grimaces and unintelligible actions and drags fearfully and comes to no climaxes anywhere. There is no action in the first and 2nd acts, the latter of which simply comes to a stop when the curtain comes down . . . By the end of the performance, half the stalls were empty. There is some fine and effective scoring and some fine music here and there, but the general impression to me was hollow and rather meretricious . . . It seemed a complete failure, but as the book is Hueffer's, the press will doubtless push it through and make the public think they ought to like it.[28]

The essential problem with *Guenever* undoubtedly lay, not only with the language of the libretto, but the plot itself which was subject to innumerable changes and recastings. The manuscript which exists in the Royal College of Music in its piano arrangement, is largely inconclusive as to the definitive order of events. Even though there are potentially helpful markings such as 'Dritter Act, Szene 1' (in Althaus's hand) these frequently bear no relation to the order of events so as to make sense of the story. It is also not clear whether Parry made attempts to condense the plot and the four acts after receiving Rosa's criticisms.

What is apparent, however, is that in early August 1884, Parry and Una Taylor came together to recast large sections of the libretto including the whole of Act I. This is explained in a letter to Dannreuther:

I've got my librettist here, and we have been discussing the alterations in Guenever; and it strikes us that it will simplify matters altogether if we take up the story further back. We shan't have to go in for so many retrospective allusions. What we have got to is this. Act I—opens outside the walls of Chester. People moving about, and anticipating good sport at the burning of Guenever; and making up the pile of faggots. Enter Mordred and Gareth; Mordred is trying to persuade the latter to join in enforcing the sentence on

---

[27] Diary, 9 Jan. 1887.   [28] Ibid. 8 June 1886.

Guenever, and tells him that Lancelot is expected to try and rescue her. Guenever is brought in and protests her innocence bravely, and tells Mordred he has slandered her to the King. Mordred answers more or less mockingly and persuades the people that the sentence of burning is quite just. Guenever is tied to the stake and the fire lighted. Lancelot charges in with a small party of knights, knocks over a few knights and people and kicks the faggots out of the way—breaks the chain that binds Guenever to the stake and exits with her. Gareth, unarmed, is seen lying wounded close by as Lancelot goes out, and the curtain comes down. The old first act as you have seen it then follows. The main alteration being that Arthur is obviously at war with Lancelot, and Lancelot tries to make it up with him but fails. There is no need to explain why Arthur is going out to battle, and Mordred merely makes use of his opportunity to fall traitorously upon Arthur at the beginning of Act 3 and so on as before . . .[29]

From this account it is clear that the original conception of the First Act became absorbed in a reconstituted Second Act. In the manuscript the First Act is musically complete in this new version which was completed finally at some time in early 1886. The question of plot in the Second Act is less certain (unfortunately Una Taylor destroyed the manuscript libretto when she learned that the opera would not be performed), but would appear to be as follows: the Act is set at the castle and opens with a female chorus recounting the story of Tristan and Isolde and the mistrust of King Mark. A horn sounds outside and Mordred and his knights approach bearing the body of Gareth. Lyones, Gareth's wife, laments the death of her husband. Encouraged by Mordred she curses her husband's killer and plans revenge. Mordred also succeeds in encouraging Arthur to believe in Lancelot's treachery. Consequently, when Lancelot enters in the next scene, his pleadings for his own honour and that of Guenever fall on deaf ears. Lancelot withdraws knowing that he and Arthur are at war. Guenever likewise pleads with Arthur not to go to battle. He refuses, but forgives her. At this stage the manuscript breaks off, for the conclusion to Act II has been incorrectly bound between the end of Act I and the beginning of Act II. With Arthur's exit, Guenever is alone. Mordred enters to seek her pardon. She naturally condemns him, which excites his feelings of hatred and treachery. Mordred then reveals his plan to slay both Arthur and Lancelot and to rule in Arthur's stead. Guenever in despair pleads with him, but it is too late. The death oath has been sworn. The curtain falls.

It is evident from Parry's letter to Dannreuther that he intended that Act III should begin with Mordred's attack on King Arthur and his wearied army, but this part of the manuscript is missing. The section that commences this part of the opera is a lament sung by Lyones on the death of Gareth. She is subsequently joined in scene 2 by Mordred

---

[29] Letter to Edward Dannreuther, 1 Aug. 1884, Bod. MS Eng. Letters e.117.

bearing the news that he believes Arthur to have died from a fatal spear thrust administered by Mordred during the battle. And yet he has searched in vain to find Arthur's body amongst the dead. In scene 3 Arthur suddenly enters. During an extensive orchestral interlude he and Mordred fight until Mordred falls and dies. Arthur drops, weak from his wounds, and is confronted by Lyones. Knowing that to seek revenge on Lancelot would be in vain, she swears to wreak vengeance on Guenever. Arthur's appeals are rebutted, but he begs her to take his ring to Guenever with a message of eternal faithfulness. The fourth and fifth scenes recount the hurling of the sword into the lake and the placing of Arthur in the barge which bears him to Avalon.

The final act is set in a courtyard in front of a large abbey. In the first scene Guenever, who has retreated to a convent to seek God's pardon and refuge from the curses and hatred of her people, sings farewell to her past life. As the doors of the abbey open to take Guenever in, Lancelot enters and implores her to go with him. She relents, but as they prepare to depart they are confronted by Lyones, who, bearing Arthur's ring, seeks Guenever's life. A large body of knights and women sworn to avenge Gareth's death approach, but Lancelot bolts the door to the courtyard. The doors soon give way. Guenever retreats up the steps to the great door of the church as Lancelot attempts to fend off the hordes of knights. But with Lancelot fully occupied, Lyones slips past him up the steps and stabs Guenever. The fighting stops, Guenever dies and the nuns carry her body into the abbey.

Although the new libretto purged the opera of 'retrospective allusions' many dramatic problems remained unsolved. For example, Act III was still in danger of detracting from the main thrust of the story by focusing too heavily on Arthur's death. The end of Act IV is dramatically inconclusive so far as Lancelot is concerned. There were also intrinsic musical flaws, such as the poor dramatic contribution of the chorus. As Parry himself recognized, the incessant march time of the various groups of knights soon became rhythmically stereotyped giving little scope for contrasting gestures. This is also reflected in the banal choral writing throughout the opera whose incessant, unimaginative homophony rarely rises to a level commensurate with the epic dramatic strokes he wished to convey. The light-hearted opening chorus ('Winter love lies cold'), for example, has more in common with a Sullivan operetta and seems to parody the gravity of their work as they gather wood for Guenever's pyre. Worst of all, the choruses of knights, who spend most of their time swearing loyalty to their lords, have no rhythmical flexibility or dramatic impact, and seem to bear all the weakest attributes of an English nineteenth-century part-song texture. The strongest music is to be found in the larger solo paragraphs (such as Guenever's soliloquy in Act I (Ex.

22) and Arthur's first appearance in Act II), though even here there are few occasions when Parry achieves a truly high level of dramatic and musical continuity. That he contemplated a canvas of Wagnerian proportions, using leitmotiv, declamation, and seamless melody fully integrated within the orchestral canvas, there can be little doubt. The use and variety of leitmotivs in particular confirm this approach and they show a far greater degree of thematic contrast than Parry's first major Wagnerian essay, *Prometheus Unbound*.

It is of course impossible to obtain a comprehensive view of *Guenever* since we only have the piano arrangement and a few sketches to study, and within these there are precious few allusions to instrumental timbres. Occasionally there are references to strings or the odd abbreviation (Ob. or Cl.), but a comparison of Parry's vocal-score reductions with full scores show that he was in the habit of omitting important elements such as florid inner parts or essential suspensions. In orchestral garb the skeletal ideas outlined in short score would therefore undoubtedly have sounded more idiomatic, particularly the purely orchestral entr'actes such as the extensive sword fights in Acts III and IV. One may also surmise that Parry was sensitive to the possibilities of increasing the impact of his leitmotivs through the use of distinctive instrumental timbres. In this regard one suspects, for example, that for Arthur's motiv, the sound of brass would be prominent, for Lancelot the full orchestra, and for Guenever the rich sonority of divided strings.

However, one of the prime weaknesses evident from the vocal score of *Guenever* is the poor vocal rhythm. It was already apparent from *Prometheus Unbound* that Parry's understanding of vocal declamation was open to question in that he lacked the Wagnerian sophistication of phrase structure and sustained melodic interest. There are, from time to time, glimpses of inspiration. Arthur's entrance in Act II shows much greater rhythmic resourcefulness and its 'orchestral' support is far more integral in the development of his leitmotiv. Likewise, Guenever's soliloquy in Act I, already mentioned (see Ex. 22) is more imaginative as is her duet with Lancelot at the end of Act IV Scene 2. Nevertheless, in general the flexibility of solo vocal writing is wooden and enslaved to a regular periodic structure that is sadly detrimental to the forward momentum of the drama. This is evident in Lancelot's entreaty to Guenever ('Canst thou forget the days long gone'), but nowhere more so than in Mordred's confrontation with Guenever at the end of Act II where his murderous ambition and her guilt are emasculated by inadequate melodic and rhythmic invention which in turn undermines the sense of dramatic climax.

As Parry's letters convey, the failure of *Guenever* was more than a temporary disappointment. Its composition had cost him two years of

Ex. 22. *Guenever* (1885–6), the opening of Guenever's soliloquy, Act I.

earth - ly sin · · · slay the one hope · · that I · have · had therein

arduous labour. His librettist had proved to be artistically wanting and theatrically inept. The outcome appears to have been a somewhat ambiguous attitude towards opera. His admiration for the operatic achievements of Beethoven and Wagner never waned, and he held Humperdinck's *Hänsel und Gretel* and Mussorgsky's *Boris Godunov* in high regard. But he remained dubious of opera's capacity to be sincere. Before going to South America his reaction to Massenet's *Manon* had raised such a question: 'An utterly unsound piece. Bits of pretty and effective music; but full of falsities of character, cynical, inconsistent. Points that might be effective and interesting spoilt through the fact that the writer is thinking of stage effects instead of human nature.'[30] His perception of Verdi, Berlioz, Bizet, and later Debussy was much the same, and he found the brashness of Strauss's *Elektra* and *Salome* alarming not to say indecent. But these views he largely expressed privately, either in his diaries or to his close friends, for rarely does a prejudicial sentence appear in any of his lectures or writings. However, the question of sincerity in opera is a point that Parry returned to on several occasions in his notebooks. From the following caustic remarks it seems logical to interpret that the despair and bitterness left in the wake of his only operatic attempt had left their mark: 'Opera is the shallowest fraud man ever achieved in the name of art. Its invariable associates are dirt and tinsel. Its history is falseness, intrigue, shallowness, levity and pretension. It is the appanage of the wastrels, the home of the humbugs. No composer who is worthy of any reverence at all ever wrote an Opera.'[31] Also inherent in these dismissive comments is the sense of regret that he had chosen to explore this artistic avenue in the first place. The result, none the less, was decisive in that Parry firmly disregarded opera for the rest of his life and his involvement in the theatre was thereafter restricted to the composition of incidental music.

[30] Diary, 28 May 1885.   [31] Notebook, [? 1918], ShP.

While efforts to stage *Guenever* were going on abroad, Parry was forced to concentrate on an orchestral commission from the Gloucester Festival. As time was short he decided to write a Suite which traditionally demanded uncomplicated structural designs, an emphasis on thematic material, and orchestral flair. The *Suite Moderne* or *Suite Symphonique* not only reflects his predilection for movements with a more contemporary flavour (a tendency shown a year earlier in the *Suite Moderne* for Violin and Piano), but was also intended to be analogous to the four movements of a symphony (hence the title *Suite Symphonique*). This can be seen in the arrangement of movements—the Ballade and Rhapsody as the quicker outer movements and the Romanza as the slow movement. The choice of Idyll in place of the Scherzo is more unconventional. Evidently Parry regarded this as the 'Dance' movement, a term he used consistently in his diary,[32] and that he clearly intended it to correspond to a Scherzo is confirmed by the Festival programme, even though this confused the critics: 'many were wondering why a quiet and melodious piece should have been termed a "Scherzo"'.[33] The internal structure of each movement also tends to confirm the sense of symphonic allusion. The Ballade, full of strong, characteristic diatonic melody, is a sonata of reduced proportions with a short development. The broad second-group melody (Ex. 23a), introduced by the full complement of cellos (and first bassoon), is particularly fine and harks back to those broad melodic strains of the 'Cambridge' Symphony and the March from *The Birds*. More typical still is its recurrence in the upper strings under which the cellos provide a magnificent countertheme. Such stylistic

Ex. 23. *Suite Moderne* (1886). *a Ballade*, second-group melody; *b Romanza*, opening melody.

[32] Diary, 3, 8, and 9 Aug. 1886.
[33] 'The Gloucester Musical Festival', *Musical Times*, (1 Oct. 1886), 592.

fingerprints in the Ballade, set in A minor, prefigure the more mature and expansive *Overture to an Unwritten Tragedy* composed in the same key nine years later. Still within the vein of tragedy, there is much in this movement rhythmically reminiscent of Brahms's *Tragic* Overture. The Idyll and Romanza, with their simple ternary 'song' designs, continue the strong melodic orientation of the suite. While in the Romanza Parry's exceptional ability is clearly exemplified in the handling of strings that dominate the movement (Ex. 23*b*). In keeping with the finale of a symphony, the Rhapsody is a delicately scored, highly attractive sonata-rondo and makes a brief cyclic reference to the *Ballade* in its initial bars.

Though the *Suite Moderne* was a success, it very nearly did not figure in the Gloucester Festival at all. At rehearsal in London on 1 September, things got so behindhand that the suite was not even played through once. So enraged was Parry that he threatened to withdraw the work but was persuaded otherwise by Lloyd and Williams. At the Gloucester rehearsal the organization was little better: 'The band tried their best, but there was not even time to get them to play the notes. Affairs were so disorganized that Williams had forgotten to prepare for my rehearsal and the Chorus had to wait impatiently all through it. There was no "bâton" ready and I had to begin with an umbrella and go on with a walking stick.'[34] For the evening performance at the Shire Hall on 9 September, the work had been whipped into some semblance of order though it was nevertheless extremely rough. The overall impression was, however, highly favourable and requests for further performances came from Riseley of Bristol (where it was given on 11 October) and Henschel (at the St James's Hall on 6 December). It was revised in 1892 but, despite its initial popularity, was never published.

Amongst Parry's small-scale musical accomplishments in 1886 was the submission of the final version of the *Four Shakespeare Sonnets* to Stanley Lucas. These songs form an intriguing contribution to the small catalogue of songs with German texts by English composers, and bear worthy comparison with Stanford's two sets of *Heine* songs, Opp. 4 and 7, and with Stainer's highly assured settings of the *Seven Songs* composed in 1892. For his set, dedicated to Hugh Montgomery, Parry finally decided on Sonnets XXIX ('When in disgrace'), LXXXVII ('Farewell! thou art too dear'), XVIII ('Shall I compare thee to a summer's day'), and XXX ('When to the sessions of sweet silent thought') having rejected 'If thou survive my well-contented day', which remained unpublished, and 'No longer mourn for me', which was later included in the second set of *English Lyrics*. With the problem of the

[34] Diary, 6 Sept. 1886.

content resolved he still faced bothersome decisions over the volume's presentation, particularly in justifying the inclusion of Bodenstedt's German text. 'I am so bothered over the title page for those Sonnets', he wrote to Dannreuther, 'that I want you to help me out with your wisdom. Do you think it would do to put this note on the first page? "The German version is given because owing to certain peculiarities in the diction of these Sonnets it produces a better musical effect, without much loss to the sense"'.[35]

Dannreuther's advice was to hold out for both texts but to dispense with any explanation, and judging from the published edition, it was advice Parry heeded. His Partita for Violin and Piano, a work also composed many years before, was also published, this time by Czerny (and later by Chanot in 1890) much to the joy of its dedicatee, Edward Guerini, who had known the work since his performance of it in Cannes in 1877. 'I am quite *proud* of the dedication my dear Parry', wrote Guerini from his new London home, 'and I only wish I were more talented in order to do full justice to your admirable inspiration.'[36]

   Guerini's praise was not echoed in other quarters, however. Difficulties had begun to arise with his last few articles for Grove's Dictionary in which he had felt disposed to take a firm stand against some of Grove's misconceptions. Fortunately no rift occurred, but life at the College, which was already trying his patience to the limit owing to the lack of space, threatened to become intolerable when his own competence as a teacher and lecturer was called into question. Barnby, who had been appointed as one of the Board of Examiners for the annual examinations in May, had launched a fierce attack on him in an address to the other examiners. Drawing attention to the 'bad influence' Parry had on pupils of the College he evidently hoped that a dismissal would follow. Dannreuther, who, as an appointee to the Board, vociferously opposed Barnby's onslaught, reported the news as the situation progressed. Parry's reaction was a combination of rage, despair, disenchantment, and stoicism. At the root of Barnby's objections were Parry's methods of teaching composition which he regarded as unconventional and ill-disciplined. And yet the fruits of his tutelage were already emerging in the work of Charles Wood and, most notably, Hamish MacCunn, who, having enjoyed a performance of his Concert Overture *Cior Mhor* at the Crystal Palace in November 1885, was due to have a second overture, *The Land of the Mountain and Flood*, rehearsed at the Crystal Palace in July. Such results, Parry believed, rendered Barnby's criticisms

---

[35] Letter to Edward Dannreuther, 4 June 1886, Bod. MS Eng. Letters e.117.
[36] Letter from Edward Guerini, 26 Nov. 1886, ShP.

incomprehensible. The effect of Dannreuther's news was, none the less, dispiriting:

You are a good friend! and it is kind of you to take so much trouble for me. But I'm afraid it's no good. With a noodle like Barnby in charge of course the report will be unfavourable. And then I shall simply clear out. But I shall demand an enquiry and the name of the Chairman of the board and if I don't make Barnby dance it will not be for want of tearing him to pieces. But it makes me very sick of the whole job. I really have got my heart in the College, and I feel I am some use there, and if it comes to what I expect, I shall feel inclined to make my final bow to the race of professional musicians, all except you and Stanford, for good and all. And it will be a little compensation not to have to keep company any more with men who know nothing about any subject but their own, and are generally stupid about that.[37]

Barnby's report, which was unfavourable as Parry had predicted, was rejected. The relief stemmed the threat of his departure, but it caused his heart trouble to return and upset his nerves to the point where he could barely face his colleagues.

It was at harrowing times such as these that Rustington proved to be a haven of peace and escape. At times, even for Parry, London seemed all too claustrophobic and the need to divorce himself entirely from music was paramount. A reflection of this was the upgrading of his yachting pursuits in which the *Ornis* was superseded in October by the larger seven-ton yawl *Hoopoe* purchased at Woolston docks in Southampton. As a more robust boat, the *Hoopoe* enabled him to sail further afield along the south coast of England and provided him with enough experience and enthusiasm to contemplate the idea of more protracted voyages in the future. His friendships and association with non-musicians also intensified. In March he was proposed by his American friend and novelist, Edward Bellamy (famous for his Utopian romance *Looking Backward: 2000–1887*) for the Savile Club, an institution with a strong literary tradition. Among those who signed their names in the Candidates' Book were Robert Bridges, Sidney Colvin (famous for his criticism of history, literature, and art), his old friend Donkin from Oxford, Henry James, and James Bryce (the Regius Professor of Civil Law at Oxford). His social circle was further enhanced when he and his family left Phillimore Place for their new home at 17 Kensington Square, which Parry had purchased from the banker and book collector, Alfred Huth. The drawing-room was 'christened with a Brahms song and my Shakespeare sonnets',[38] and later he gave a house-warming party that included Arthur Balfour, Eddie Hamilton, Lady Elcho, and the Burne-Joneses. As Arthur Ponsonby's pamphlet *Records of Kensington Square*

[37] Letter to Edward Dannreuther, 7 May 1886, Bod. MS Eng. Letters e.117.
[38] Diary, 10 Dec. 1886.

(published by the Kensington Society in 1936) has shown, the Square boasted a list of distinguished inhabitants including celebrated church-men, authors, critics, politicians, scientists, lawyers, scholars, and artists. Edward Burne-Jones, who lived at No. 41 and with whom Parry was already well acquainted, became a neighbour and close friend as did Vernon Lushington at No. 36. These two were well known for their artistic gatherings through which Parry came to know William Morris, William de Morgan, Rossetti, Swinburne, and Madox Brown. His great friend Robin Benson, a renowned art connoisseur, lived next door at No. 18, where his family stayed until the move was completed at the end of November, while others such as Sir John Simon, General Sir Thomas Gore Browne, Mrs J. R. Green, widow of the eminent historian (famed for his voluminous study *History of the English People*), the diplomat H. F. Wilson, and R. B. Litchfield (founder of the Working Men's College and a music critic) also resided in the Square.

The atmosphere of Kensington Square was, on the whole, a happier one than he had known at Phillimore Place. It was also more conducive to composition and witnessed the creation of all his finest works until his death thirty-two years later. The change of environment coincided with a hardening of Parry's stylistic parameters and ideals. Because of the rejection of *Guenever*, he seriously started to reassess his artistic capabilities and those genres in which he had been creatively most successful. In many ways his decisions were assisted by Richter. In November 1885 Richter had asked Parry for a new work, though, owing to his health and preoccupation with *Guenever*, the idea was dismissed. However, Richter's performance of Brahms's Fourth Symphony in the following May had impressed him so much that the idea of a new, large-scale orchestral work once more became an exciting proposition. On that occasion unfortunately Richter had not been at all cordial with him after the performance, but Parry was still determined to woo the great German conductor. Late in June Richter asked him to bring *The Glories of our Blood and State* and the 'Cambridge' Symphony for his perusal:

I played him the Ode and he said he liked it. Then we went at the Symphony together. He read it amazingly; always seeing where the instruments were that were prominent, and never making a mistake in transposition but reading it right off, horns, clarinets, and all—and all I had to do was to fill in and play the bass, which I did abominably. He offered to try it in the autumn and thinks he will play it next season. Of course I know it won't come off. But he was pleasant.[39]

The pessimism of those final remarks was of course the inevitable result of so many past disappointments at Richter's hands. This time, however,

[39] Ibid. 24 June 1886.

there was to be no such disappointment, for Richter agreed to include the 'Cambridge' Symphony in his 1887 season of concerts. It was to signal the beginnings of an important collaboration over the next few years which led to the commissioning of *Judith* for Birmingham and a symphony for Richter's concert season in 1889.

Though Richter was undoubtedly a key element in Parry's compositional revitalization at this time, he was not the only one responsible. Some credit must also be accorded to Stanford who had recently succeeded Otto Goldschmidt as conductor of the London Bach Choir and was determined to improve the choir's flagging standards. As part of this process, and in connection with the Bach Choir's celebration of Queen Victoria's Jubilee, Stanford was keen to perform Parry's *The Glories of Our Blood and State*. But objections were raised by the committee at the words 'Sceptre and crown must tumble down' which were felt to be unsuitable for such a celebration, so they commissioned the composer to write a new choral work on a similar scale for the choir's concert the following May. Grove, who was consulted by Stanford on the subject of an appropriate text, suggested Milton's *Ode at a Solemn Music*, a poem which had also been lying dormant at the back of Parry's mind for many years. Grove's idea seemed eminently attractive. Stanford was satisfied, as was the Committee, while Parry was eager to begin sketching the work as soon as the College term was over. As he read through Milton's ode at Wilton over Christmas, Parry could not have known that this new piece would almost at once prove to be one of the most popular English vocal works of the age, bringing with it unrivalled national recognition together with a new sense of stylistic assurance, maturity, and optimism.

PART III

1887–1897
Years of Renown

'O may we soon again renew that song': *Blest Pair of Sirens* (1887)
(By permission of the Master and Fellows of Trinity College, Cambridge)

10

Blest Pair of Sirens
National Prominence

JUST as *The Glories of Our Blood and State* was the result of much earlier meditations on Shirley's poem, thoughts of setting Milton's *Ode at a Solemn Music* had occurred to Parry as far back as 1867 when he had sketched a few ideas in an early manuscript book; but these had come to nothing. Stanford's commission for a short choral work, and Grove's suggestion, consequently reawakened his natural affinity for the text and work proceeded swiftly. This rapid progress was only checked by a lack of satisfaction with the last line of text; even so, it was complete enough for Dannreuther's perusal on 13 January, after which it was dispatched to Stanford. A stringent programme of rehearsals was put under way by 1 March reaching a climax on 29 March when Grove, Bridge, and Joachim attended. Perhaps understandably there is no mention in his diary of Joachim's response, but Grove's reaction he did record: 'At the end old G. jumped up with tears in his eyes and shook me over and over again by the hand and the whole choir took up the cue . . . and applauded vociferously. It was encouraging.'[1] The full score was completed soon afterwards on 2 April, but it was another six weeks before the work was performed under Stanford's direction on 17 May at the St James's Hall. To use Parry's words, it was 'quite uproariously received'.[2] On coming on to the platform he was greeted with shouts from the choir, and his many friends and acquaintances in the packed hall were equally enthusiastic.

Apart from the magnificent eight-part choral writing (the quality of which evidently impressed the Bach Choir at its first performance) and the apt orchestral scoring, the success of *Blest Pair of Sirens* may be attributed to two main factors. The first is undoubtedly its taut musical structure and simple tonal scheme which complement the Pindaric form of the ode. Furthermore, the integration of the superb orchestral introduction displays a degree of unity far in advance of the 'patchwork' design of *The Glories of Our Blood and State*. The second and perhaps most significant aspect of the piece is its musical language in which a higher diatonic dissonance is used with absolute mastery.

[1] Diary, 29 Mar. 1887.　　　[2] Ibid. 17 May 1887.

Within the first section of the Pindaric design (i.e. the strophe or 'Turne') Milton's words depict the heavenly unity of 'Voice and Verse'. Tovey, who was particularly intrigued by the problems of the poetical structure, drew attention to the first eleven lines which, although ending with a comma, provide 'the first possible stopping-place after telling what Voice and Verse are to do'.[3] This section outlines the main musical event of the shift from E flat to the bright foreign tonality of G major. The process is not a simple one. E flat is firmly established in the muscular diatonicism of the orchestral prelude (Ex. 24*a*), after which the chorus, in a paraphrase of the orchestra's opening bars (which, incidentally, paraphrase the opening bars of *Die Meistersinger*), reiterate E flat before moving away to the dominant of G with a fitting blaze of sound ('able to pierce'). This preparatory modulation marks the beginning of a fugal passage, 'And to our high-rais'd phantasy present'— the only clause which Parry repeats. As Tovey explains:

this is no vain repetition, nor is it a rhetorical point to emphasise those words. It does not emphasise them; it does not even suggest that anybody is saying them twice over. The eight-part chorus is broken up into its main divisions, and we hear these words in one group of voices after another till they gather together again in 'That undisturbed Song of pure concent,' thus throwing into relief the meaning of the word 'concent'.[4]

The next line ('Aye sung before the sapphire-colour'd throne') not only fulfils Milton's 'concent' but also marks a brief return to E flat. We expect this return to be affirmed with a forceful perfect cadence ('To him that sits thereon') but it is instead deflected to the flat submediant (C flat). After a prolongation of this flat submediant harmony (now reinterpreted as the dominant of E), Parry then repeats the same harmonic move again on to C which subsequently functions as the subdominant of G major in which the music cadences in line 11 ('Their loud uplifted angel-trumpets blow'). Although G major has already been anticipated to some extent by its dominant touched on in line 4, the impact of this third-related key is considerably enhanced by its oblique preparation. Lines 12–16 of the strophe are taken up with a consolidation of G major. Here Parry returns to the antiphonal texture heard in line 3 ('Wed your divine sounds') and he extends this over the next 30 bars with mounting harmonic intensity and exemplary motivic economy to the first emphatic cadence of the work which is made all the more momentous by the restatement of the introductory orchestral theme.

At this point in the text we move from strophe to antistrophe (or 'Counter-Turne') where the harmony of heaven is contrasted with the

[3] D. F. Tovey, 'Parry: CCXVIII. "At a Solemn Music", for Chorus and Orchestra', *Essays in Musical Analysis*, v. (Oxford, 1937), 232.

[4] Ibid. 233.

Ex. 24. *Blest Pair of Sirens* (1887). *a* bars 1–5 of the orchestral introduction; *b* beginning of epode, 'O may we soon again renew that song'.

sinful discords of earth. This is made all the more vivid by Parry's sudden change of tempo, metre, and mode that is executed mid-phrase ('Till disproportioned sin Jarr'd against nature's chime'). The 'harsh din' is evoked with a solitary but pronounced reference to the *Tristan* chord, a harmony thrown into relief by the context of its diatonic environment. The penitential mood of G minor is not maintained for long since the text returns to the subject of concord ('perfect diapason') and this is paralleled by a gradual transition back to the dominant of E flat (at letter E). Tovey has stated: 'Here is Milton's first full stop! And here, too, in spite of (or rather because of) his beautifully clear form, is Parry's first real full stop; for the orchestra now enters with a new theme and thus carries the mind definitely away from any longer retrospect over what has been so firmly welded together.'[5] There can be no doubt that the orchestral interlude succeeds in articulating both the poetical and musical structure with its fresh material, but it is also perhaps the only moment in the work where, through the sequential extension of the one phrase, Parry comes precariously close to being mechanical. The passage is, however, redeemed by the oblique transition into the final choral section where the violins rise to join the sopranos on E flat as part of a poignant supertonic seventh chord (Ex. 24*b*).

Reconciliation of the strophe and antistrophe occurs in the four-line epode (or 'Stand') which expresses a yearning for the ultimate reunification 'To live with Him, and sing in endless morn of light'. As a final musical paragraph Parry divided this into two distinct sections. The first, mirroring the aspiratory nature of Milton's words ('O may we soon again renew that song'), is built on a splendid lyrical theme (Ex. 24*b*) whose opening phrase was derived from the introductory material of the orchestral prelude (cf. bars 4–5, Ex. 24*a*). In being loosely imitative it shows a similarity with the lyrical coda of *The Glories of Our Blood and State*, but here it functions differently as preparation for the final ebullient fugato ('To live with Him'). This fugato is constructed within the confines of a hugely protracted dominant pedal over which harmonic and thematic tension are paced to perfection. Parry times his departure of the first pedal point (from letter G) from the moment when he begins adding to the four-part choral texture, initially established in the previous lyrical section. This accumulation of parts towards the original eight-part texture is then directed towards a second, more emphatic pedal (letter H) which extends over 16 bars. With the resolution of line 16 ('singing everlastingly') relatively fresh in our minds, we half expect this pedal point to resolve in a similar manner with a restatement of the orchestra's introductory theme. However, Parry does not fulfil these expectations, for he delays these events with an arresting modulation to C minor as the beginning of a final peroration in double time. This grandiose peroration eventually concludes with the long-awaited cadence and recapitulation of the orchestral theme which is subsequently given more climactic weight with the addition of the chorus (particularly the first soprano doubling the main inner contrapuntal voice five bars from the end) and is surely one of Parry's most epigrammatic choral statements.

Few of Parry's choral works display such an acute sense of preparation

[5] D. F. Tovey, 'Parry: CCXVIII. "At a Solemn Music", for Chorus and Orchestra', *Essays in Musical Analysis*, v. (Oxford, 1937), 234.

and climax as *Blest Pair*. Much of this is generated by the consummate understanding of Milton's poetic structure which in turn produced a cohesive musical form of powerful simplicity. But the momentum of the work is also carried through by a mature and consistent language that relies exclusively on diatonicism and a sophisticated vocabulary of higher dissonance. Already Parry's predilection for sturdy diatonic melody has been witnessed in the lyrical second-group themes of the First and Second Symphonies and the *Suite Moderne*, but the concept of a more highly developed harmonic dimension had been less prominent, appearing in isolated situations such as *The Spirit of the Hour* from *Prometheus Unbound* and with limited success in the Evening Service in D and *The Glories of Our Blood and State*. In *Blest Pair* Parry's use of double and triple appoggiaturas, multiple suspensions, sequences, falling sevenths, and extended pedal-points are exploited with great resource—all of which can be observed in the prelude alone. These stylistic features betray his indebtedness to the tradition in which he had been raised, namely one in which diatonicism had predominated as a 'moral' alternative. Such techniques Parry experienced at first hand in the music of composers close to him such as S. S. Wesley (in his anthems 'Cast me not away from thy presence' or 'Ascribe unto the Lord') and Stainer ('Drop down ye heavens from above') and their pedagogical attitudes he was conversant with from his days at Eton. Though he had attempted, in the main successfully, to emancipate himself from the moral prejudices of his forebears by consciously removing himself from the trappings of sacred music, it is clear that the influence of his formative years had not been swept aside. That he continued, for example, to be moved by the sounds and sensibilities of S. S. Wesley's *The Wilderness*, is borne out by the following diary entry made on 5 September 1880 after hearing it in Gloucester Cathedral:

[The Wilderness] affected me a good deal probably through old associations. There are very fine and also tender and well realised passages in it, though it is essentially an English work and such as I can well understand a German being doubtful about. Its home is an English Cathedral and it speaks the best language and the best thoughts people who frequent such places of worship are in a state to comprehend.

It is positively significant that Parry should have attached the label of 'English' to such a work and to such an environment, and moreover, that he drew attention to the cultural differences between the English Cathedral idiom and German music. This is particularly intrinsic to the development of Parry's musical language for *Blest Pair* not only formed an important stylistic precedent for his later choral and instrumental works but also contributed to the composer's strong desire to create something that was itself distinctively national in character.

In one sense, therefore, in fully assimilating diatonicism, Parry acknowledged his country's indigenous tendencies, but his development of such a language had the effect of establishing and consolidating diatonicism as a quintessential element of a future national style. That so much of his music from *Blest Pair* onwards sounds characteristically 'English' is largely due to this stylistic dimension, but we can also see how, as a result of Parry's influence, it also became an essential ingredient in the formation of Elgar's style. A detailed study of Elgar's earlier cantatas and the *Enigma Variations* (particularly *Nimrod* and the Finale) shows that, besides the various continental influences of Wagner, Brahms, Massenet, and Delibes, diatonicism and its techniques are central to his language. It is also surely significant that Elgar, who had played in numerous performances of *Blest Pair* as a violinist (sometimes under Parry's baton), drew attention to the work and Parry's artistic leadership in his inaugural lecture (16 March 1905) as Peyton Professor of Music at Birmingham University. These stylistic influences did not, however, stop with Elgar, for they resound strongly through later generations of British composers such as Vaughan Williams (whose choral song 'Toward the Unknown Region' and *Sea Symphony* firmly betray their roots), Bliss, Howells, Walton, and in particular Finzi, whose admiration of Parry's music is so vividly portrayed in the yearning appoggiaturas and falling sevenths of *Dies Natalis*.

The excitement generated by *Blest Pair of Sirens* was very much in keeping with the general level of public enthusiasm for the Queen's Golden Jubilee. In the usual way, the music profession made its contribution to the occasion with the composition of new anthems, part-songs, and patriotic hymns epitomized by Mackenzie's *Empire Flag*. Amongst the numerous odes commissioned were Mackenzie's *Jubilee Ode* (with words by Bennett) and Stanford's *Carmen Saeculare* (Tennyson). A similar fervour was reflected in the concert seasons and festivals up and down the country. Richter, who was equally keen to infuse his own concert series with the same public spirit, ventured to commission a Jubilee Overture from Parry. But Parry's response was one of outright rejection as is evident from a letter to his wife: 'I had a letter from Richter this morning inviting me to write a Jubilee Overture!!!! I really can't. The idea is disgusting. I am so stupid! It's just as if all my wits were clean gone.'[6] And in his reply to Richter we are left in no doubt as to why his rejection of the idea was so vehement:

It is kind of you to propose my writing something of the Jubilee order; and if I had not the most invincible repugnance to it I should gladly do it rather than not meet your kindness halfway. But what with Jubilee buttons, and Jubilee cards,

[6] Letter to Lady Maude Parry, 18 Apr. 1887, ShP.

and Jubilee Anthems, and Jubilee hymn tunes, and Jubilee bunkum of all sorts, I cannot bring myself to join the company. Too much use has been made of the occasion in ways that are not pleasant to meet with, and even if I could put my own dislike of it in my pocket my friends would not like it I'm sure. Forgive me![7]

Fortunately Richter was not deterred by Parry's refusal and suggested instead that he would do the 'Cambridge' Symphony. It was a contrite gesture on the part of the German conductor who, after the abortive attempt to perform the First Symphony in 1882, was keen to reassure the composer of his admiration. 'Any misunderstanding between us is impossible,' he had written in May 1883; 'I hope very soon to find the opportunity to show you how sincerely I esteem you, and to perform another of your works.'[8]

With an assurance from Richter that the Symphony had gone into the concert programme, Parry immediately set about revising and re-orchestrating large portions of it. Then, on 22 May, a pressing letter arrived from Richter:

My dear Mr Parry,

Could you come tomorrow in the rehearsal, or in the concert? I must leave Tuesday morning, but at 9½ o'clock we could look through your score of the Symphonie. I want this, as I cannot return sooner than on the 2nd of June and the first rehearsal will take place on the 3rd. I must be prepared; one looking through with you on Tuesday at 9½ in the morning, and another study in the evening of the 2nd of June would do. If you could spare an hour on Monday afternoon—3 till 4—or 4–5—you would oblige very much.

yours truly,

Hans Richter.[9]

It was a tight schedule, but during their private sessions together, Parry's confidence in Richter's interpretative powers was reinforced by the German's extraordinary ability to score read:

We went through my F Symphony and he professed to be delighted with it. His reading was perfectly miraculous. He played the upper part and I the lower, and even at Presto pace in the Scherzo he was hardly ever at a loss, always picking out the particular part of the score that would be prominent at the moment, and playing fiddles, clarinets, and horns with equal success. It is a very astonishing gift. Even when he couldn't play the notes he could give some idea of the general effect.[10]

His extensive revisions, however, had meant that all the parts needed to be rewritten, and this led to major anxieties during the first rehearsal

[7] Letter to Hans Richter, 29 Apr. 1887. In the possession of Sylvia Loeb.
[8] Charles L. Graves, *Hubert Parry* (London, 1926), ii. 179.
[9] Letter from Hans Richter, 22 May 1887, ShP.   [10] Diary, [May] 1887.

when Richter became increasingly angry over their inaccuracy. Things reached a point where Parry feared that Richter would withdraw the work, but tempers cooled and the parts were taken away for a major overhaul. Dannreuther, selfless as ever, stepped in to assist in the short time Parry had to check through everything before the next rehearsal on 6 June. As it transpired, Richter was in better humour despite threats beforehand that he would withdraw the work over the least mistake. Moreover, Parry's anxiety evaporated at the concert when he received an ovation from the audience and the orchestra who rattled their bows loudly in approval. Even the press were less grudging in their praise.

The triumph of the revised version of the 'Cambridge' Symphony provided a welcome distraction from his otherwise fraught professional duties. Besides his history lectures and lessons at the College, Mackenzie had invited him to assist in examining for the Lucas scholarship at the Academy, and there was also his course of lectures at Oxford, not to mention his duties as Choragus. His College obligations in particular proved stressful for, in many ways, the institution had been a victim of its own success. In four years the numbers of students had increased to such an extent that the premises were no longer adequate. Some classes had to be held in the Albert Hall Mansions, while the concerts took place in the West Theatre of the Royal Albert Hall. As a temporary alleviation to the latter problem, the Alexandra House with its Concert Room was opened on 14 March 1887. However, for many members of staff the cramped conditions remained intolerable. It was a situation of which Grove was only too well aware. Along with the College Council he made an urgent appeal for the granting of a new site on which a building of considerably larger dimensions could be erected.

Undoubtedly a factor that continually restored Parry's morale during this period of difficulties at the College was his relationship with the students. They held him in the highest regard, not only for his musical achievements but also for his approachable manner and sincerity. Nevertheless, there were occasions when his patience and sympathies were tried by those who chose to be more aberrant in their behaviour. This was certainly the case with Hamish MacCunn who had studied composition with him until 1886 when he resigned his College scholarship. In appreciation of MacCunn's considerable talent in producing the overtures *Cior Mhor* and *The Land of the Mountain and Flood* and the cantata *The Moss Rose*, Parry had remained tolerant of his pupil's refractory personality. But there came a time when MacCunn, with his bull-headed views and resentment of the College staff, decided to make a point by declining his Associateship of the College, which in turn gave rise to some strongly worded correspondence with his master:

My dear Dr Parry,

After leaving you today I could not help thinking a good deal about our conversation and the nature of its subject. I allude to the attitude which I assume, with your deprecation towards the question of the A.R.C.M. degree, and my action at the time of the examination. It is my desire to lessen the extent of that deprecation on your part by endeavouring to further explain the feelings and reflections which caused me to act as I did. In the first place, none is more alive than I am to the practical view of an examination as a scholastic trial, with all its necessary and attendant discipline and minute exaction. It was not with the examination I found fault. But I have always felt, while at the College, what was to me an entirely foreign sensation, namely, that, while meeting the various men there in their several capacities, I had not met one man, bar yourself, who had acted to me, during the most ordinary intercourse common to society, with the remotest vestige of a supposition that *possibly* I might *be* a gentleman!

Their opinion was, of course, not my criterion of myself, but, in this associateship business the 'last straw' seemed to me to be arrived at when they offered me *their* associateship, *their* patronage, *their* God-forsaken passport to society under conditions which appeared to me only consistent with their former demeanour and uncouth behaviour. Hence my reasons for declining the degree were simply that musically I did not esteem it, and socially I thought of it and those who conferred it with infinite and undiluted disgust. Remember I am always particularly speaking of the College *without your* personality.[11]

It is clear, particularly from the last remark, that MacCunn wished to dissociate Parry from the prejudices and condescension he felt were part and parcel of the College's internal social structure. But this was only a prelude to another, perhaps even deeper source of bitterness which MacCunn expressed with characteristic abrasiveness:

My acquaintance with you has been the one instance in which I have met a musician and gentleman combined, but you (owing as I have always tried to think, to your scarcity of leisure time) have not yet received me in your house as a guest, nor have you shown much desire to know more of me than my music. I am speaking as plainly as I can and because I think and know you to be of a generous and noble nature and it is my earnest wish to retain and increase upon your friendship.

What do *you* know of *my* nature? How do you know that socially and in my secluded life in rooms, I am not going to the devil? What reason have I to suppose that, apart from the loss of me as a man of an imagination sympathetic with your own, you *care* whither my body and soul are going?

Deep, true and lasting friendship is not begotten over sympathy in art, any more than it is over sympathy in the business of trade, and your many expressions and acts of kindness and friendship to me long ago gave me hopes that I should some day know you better socially and artistically. I have spoken plainly to you, and I now ask you to speak plainly to me. Why have you not even

11 Letter from Hamish MacCunn, 11 July 1887, ShP.

once asked me to come to your house?—you know well enough in what sense I mean— . . . much as I would deplore it I must insist that, if you do not recognize me as being on the same social footing as yourself, and if you do imply, as you have (possibly unconcernedly) done, that for me to meet your family, your friends and yourself, in the ordinary sense understood by society in general, would be to their and your disadvantage, then, I say, if such be the case, I insist that you look into your heart, and there you will see that in answering this letter you would be writing to an utter stranger.

Don't misinterpret this, nor fail to understand me. I would gladly have your true artistic and social friendship and it is because I desire both of these not one without the other that I write this.

The furious tone of MacCunn's letter would undoubtedly have wound many of Parry's colleagues up into a state of apoplectic rage. Indeed, after a furious row with Stanford in November 1888, a letter from MacCunn demanding an apology actually brought Stanford up to London to see his lawyer.[12] Parry's response was disarmingly calm. He recognized in MacCunn's emotionally tangled resentment and disappointment a deep sense of loneliness with which he himself could identify. Coolly refuting his pupil's insinuations of class superiority, he alluded to his own unpleasant experiences at the hands of the Herberts. Certainly the word 'gentleman' was not part of his vocabulary:

I should be glad if the English language could do without the word, for it is so misused. A man in the same sentence will use it to denote all the better and most refined qualities in man, and also to denote a member of a particular class—and then he will go on to attribute all these nice qualities to every member of the class he is talking about because he calls them by the same name. Many are the protests I have made against it with my own family and even my wife—and I naturally detest the word because I feel its uncertainty of meaning leads it to [the] very impudent assumption of empty superiority of so-called rank and moneyed position.[13]

Even more significantly MacCunn's somewhat gauche question as to why he had not been invited to Kensington Square forced Parry to speak of intensely personal matters:

You say I have not recognized you 'as being on the same social footing as myself.' This is of itself sufficient to show how morbidly your mind must work, and what tricks your imagination plays you. I do not recognize distinctions of rank and society in any way more than I am absolutely forced to. My life is an excessively secluded and domestic one; partly owing to having more to do than I can get through, and partly to my wife's excessive delicacy. For years we were cut off from almost any kind of society altogether. And as she has to spend the greater part of her life on her back, she is excessively sensitive on the score of many people coming in; as she is shy of being found in that position by anyone;

[12] Diary, 23 Nov. 1888.   [13] Letter to Hamish MacCunn, 13 July 1887, ShP.

and if she sits up she soon breaks down. In fact no small part of my care in life is to see that she is not tired and worried with people coming in. If she was strong and well it would be delightful to have our house as a sort of open meeting ground for all the pupils who were in earnest about their art. But such a condition of things is impossible.

This is one of the few letters in which the circumstances and constraints of Parry's private life are admitted so openly. Though in his diaries we are aware of his wife's continuing fragility, rarely is there any word of complaint, impatience, or irritation brought about by his enforced seclusion. It is quite likely that, after fifteen years of domestic life spent chasing after her every whim, frustrated mentally (and no doubt sexually) by her mixture of hypochondria and valetudinarianism, he began to doubt their compatability; but owing to his profound sense of moral duty, his devotion to her remained unstinting. The success of *Blest Pair* and the revised Second Symphony, however, was set to intensify the contrast between his public and private existences for it was certain that new commissions would increase to the detriment of what little time he already could afford his wife. Maude in turn preferred more and more to spend her life at Rustington and showed a decreasing interest in her husband and his musical achievements. In this sense, therefore, 1887 marked a watershed in Parry's emotional relationship with his wife, for thereafter he was destined to love her as the memory of what she once was. This seems implicit in so many later diary accounts of their domestic rapport, for often he would talk of her irritability, lack of understanding, and at times of her unrelenting bullying. And yet, out of an almost naïve devotion, he would always find a reason for her lack of humour. In a combination of regret, desperation, frustration, and despair he would confine himself to his room the better to come to terms with his own depression. One such diary entry was made on his birthday in 1892:

I have had some wretched birthdays, but none to come near to this one for thorough misery . . . When I got home I found Maude very unwell with cold, and in a most irritable humour—which worked upon my weariness so desperately that, though I was fit for nothing in the way of work, I had to go and sit in my room by myself. For it was no use even by silence to stop her bullying me. She couldn't stop herself, being out of health; so the only thing to do was to remain apart, and the result of course was that I was most thoroughly wretched for all the rest of the day.[14]

In consequence, as he became increasingly emotionally estranged from his wife, his love and affection began to centre on his eldest daughter,

[14] Diary, 27 Feb. 1892.

Dorothea, in whom he would later confide his most intimate thoughts and reflections.

The excitement generated by *Blest Pair* soon spread to the provinces and it was not long before commissions from festival committees began to arrive. In August an invitation for a choral work came from Leeds for the 1889 festival, and Richter, presumably still enthusing over the success of the 'Cambridge' Symphony, was instrumental in persuading those at Birmingham to commission a large-scale work for their 1888 festival.[15] Parry also began to sketch a small symphony though with no performers as yet in mind, and as if that was not by any reasonable standards enough, the publishers Kegan Paul asked if he might reconsider the preparation of an 'outline of the Evolution of Musical Art'[16] which they had requested in 1884.

The Birmingham commission, while welcome, posed a real dilemma. Parry knew that the committee hoped he would furnish them with a traditional 'Old Testament' oratorio—a stereotype he wished to avoid; added to which, the problems of finding a text that would placate the Festival Committee would be extremely time-consuming and might prevent him completing the work in time. Hence before accepting the invitation he wrote to Dannreuther:

Most best of men,

here's more advice I want from you. A few weeks ago I got an application from the Leeds' Committee for a Choral and Orchestral work, about an hour and a half long, for their festival in '89. I thought that gave me nice pleasant lots of time to find a good subject, and think well about how to deal with it. So of course I accepted. Now today comes another application from Birmingham for a work of the Oratorio Order two hours long for *next* year's festival. I think I ought not to let such a chance slip if I can do it. But it's very short time to find a subject, and get it into shape and write the stuff. Moreover, I don't like the Oratorio notion—though of course one can make a work on Oratorio lines which shall be perfectly independent of ecclesiastical or so-called religious conventions. Do you think there is anything to be made of the poetical material in the same neighbourhood as Parsifal? Do you think there are any stories of the Albigensians or some such types? It must be something with lots of chance for chorus—and just at this moment—when I haven't thought much about it, it seems to me it might be worked by having a 'Narrator' as in the early Oratorios and in the Passions and Resurrections; introducing the characters in propriâ personâ as well.[17]

---

[15] According to Stanford, however, it was he who had originally urged the Festival Committee to request such a work from Parry during a conversation with Richter in the garden of George Mathews at Birmingham in 1885. See 'A Tribute from Sir Charles Villiers Stanford', *RCM Magazine*, 15/1, 7, and Graves, *Hubert Parry*, ii. 196.

[16] C. Hubert H. Parry, *The Art of Music*, 2nd edn. (London, 1896), v., Preface.

[17] Letter to Edward Dannreuther, 2 Sept. 1887, Bod. MS Eng. Letters e.117.

Dannreuther sympathized with Parry's dislike of the traditional oratorio genre, and suggested various themes including German versions of Sanskrit poetry, Simrock's *Mythologie*, and the *Edda*; but it was the story of Columbus that appealed to him most: 'I have often thought something might be made of that subject. There is plenty of life and colour and no need of God or Devil to set matters going.'[18] Barclay Squire, who had provided the libretto for Stanford's opera *The Veiled Prophet of Khorassan* was also consulted but little progress was made. Finding a text that provided enough purely choral opportunities was beset with difficulties as was the task of contriving appropriate material for both male and female soloists. Eventually, pressed for time, Parry came to a decision and approached the Birmingham committee with his ideas. They were not impressed and dug their heels in, as the following disconsolate letter to Dannreuther relates: 'The Birmingham people stood out for a regular Oratorio. I hope you won't swear! After some correspondence in which they declined my alternative proposals, I caved in. But with a mental reservation that there shouldn't be much of religion or biblical oratorio beyond the name.'[19]

In his disappointment, Parry opted for a compromise and turned to Dean Prideaux's speculative work *The Connection of the Old and New Testaments* where he hoped he might find a subject that concentrated on human passions and emotions rather than religious ones:

When endeavouring to get materials together for an Oratorio in September, 1887, I consulted the learned work of Dean Prideaux, known as 'The Connection of the Old and New Testaments,' for details of one of the Jewish captivities. I here came across his speculation, which he worked out with some show of historical probability, that the exploit of Judith occurred in the reign of Manasseh. I had already been attracted to the story of Manasseh, as its salient features, though merely suggested in the Biblical summary, have a breadth of significance and a force of character that seemed likely to lend themselves to treatment in an Oratorio form. The excuse for introducing Judith afforded me by Dean Prideaux decided my choice, but it was not my original intention to call the work by her name; for though her heroism is most admirable, the sanguinary catastrophe of the story is neither artistically attractive nor suitable for introduction into a work in the Oratorio form. Nevertheless, in working out the subject, I was partly carried away by the superior interest of her personality, and partly by the advice of friends in whose sagacity I had confidence, and her share in the action became at least equal to Manasseh's. But I did not at any time wish to centralize the interest entirely upon individuals, but rather upon popular movements and passions, and such results of them as recur a hundred times in history; of which the Israelitish story is one vivid type out of many.

---

[18] Letter from Edward Dannreuther, 4 Sept. 1887, ShP.
[19] Letter to Edward Dannreuther, 20 Oct. 1887, Bod. MS Eng. Letters e.117.

Parry's initial inclination was to name the oratorio *The Regeneration of Manasseh*—a deliberate attempt to focus less on Judith and more on Manasseh as the representative of the fallen Israelites, their Assyrian captivity, and the eventual restoration of their liberty. Later, however, he was persuaded by Dannreuther and Squire to reconsider in favour of *Judith*.

The first sketches of the oratorio's plan contained in a notebook reveal that he originally conceived the 'argument' in four acts. The first act was concerned primarily with the worship of Moloch, the demands of Moloch's high priest to sacrifice Manasseh's children to the god, Judith's and Isaiah's vain protests, the sacrifice of the children, and Isaiah's execution. Act Two dealt with the news and coming of the Assyrians, the vain cries of help to Moloch, the fall of Jerusalem, and Manasseh's captivity. Act Three (which Parry subtitled 'Captivity') was one of lament on the part of Judith, the Israelites, and Manasseh, finishing with their penitential calls to Yahweh and the promise of relief. Finally Act Four (subtitled 'Deliverance') recounted the subjugation of Manasseh in Jerusalem under the power of the Assyrians, Judith's exhortation of Manasseh to free Israel, the coming of Holofernes, Judith's appeal to God and her departure for the Assyrian camp, the death of Holofernes together with the destruction of the Assyrian army, ending with Judith's song of triumph. This scheme soon proved to be too long and Parry subsequently condensed it into two acts (consisting of three scenes each) with a central Intermezzo. In achieving this, the new Act One became a conflation of the original first two acts though omitting the speculative material about Isaiah and introducing the more prominent role of Meshullemeth, Manasseh's wife; Manasseh's repentance was enacted in the Intermezzo; and lastly, Act Two was largely devoted to those events of the former Act Four, though commencing with a compression of the laments in the original Act Three into a single scene. Whether Parry chose to omit the gruesome event of Holofernes' beheading at the initial stages of planning is not clear, but the revised libretto of Act Two recounts it in the form of a narrative delivered by Manasseh.

The composition of *Judith* proved to be a most unsettling affair from the outset, and the one major interruption to his routine—a trip to Oxford to examine—did little to improve his humour. A letter to Maude tells all: 'Tonight I have got to dine with Lloyd to meet Ouseley again. It will be a real bore; and I look forward to it with despair. They will talk what they call music, which is dull scholastic shop; and probably after dinner they will play Mozart symphonies on the pianoforte as duets.'[20] Work on the oratorio progressed in fits and starts, and there were seldom

[20] Letter to Lady Maude Parry, 19 Oct. 1887, ShP.

times when he felt satisfied with it. In accordance with the Festival Committee's desires, there was a great deal of music for the chorus. He also attempted to comply with his original conception of a Passion design using the chorus as the 'Turbae', though he dispensed with the idea of an 'independent' Narrator (this was eventually deployed in *Job*). The form and style of the text, however, continued to irritate him as his diary entry for New Year's Day 1888 reveals: 'Stuck fast in the middle of a stupid chorus in the 2nd half "The God of our Fathers". Wrote it over and over again—working morning, afternoon, after tea and night and always find it beastly. The words aren't sufficiently telling.' Nevertheless, he was spurred on to finish it by Dannreuther who was particularly impressed with the Intermezzo and Watchmen's chorus in Act Two. By the beginning of February the second act was complete. This left only the second and third scenes of Act One and an orchestral introduction all of which were composed by 5 March. Extensive revisions absorbed him for the rest of the month. Still his dissatisfaction remained and was in no way relieved by Stanford's initial reaction to Act Two which he saw at the College in mid-February:

He [Stanford] didn't take to it, and played much of it as if he didn't see the sense of it; and made some very severe criticisms. There seems to him too much praying—too much sameness in the style; too little rhythmic and vigorous stuff—and he wants to take out Judith's prayer . . . and also (probably) Manasseh's last song. He read the things very quickly, but played them abominably; with not the very least sense of their meaning. It was pernicious!![21]

Later, however, Stanford professed a change of mind and became one of the work's keenest advocates.[22] The Birmingham Committee, on the other hand, were seriously worried about the oratorio's length, notably with regard to Act Two, and after a meeting on 6 July at Kensington Square with Charles Beale, the chairman of the committee, it was made clear that Parry would have to make substantial cuts. This was followed on 9 July by a serious wrangle in Richter's lodgings in Bentinck Street when Beale suggested that the whole oratorio could be represented by the Second Act. He also told Parry that Novello would have to publish the work in that form so that the public would not be conscious of what had happened. This proposal met with Parry's total disapproval: 'When I pointed out that the work would look rather queer in that form he said: "Well we shouldn't mind publishing an announcement that Dr Parry meant to elaborate his work more fully afterwards". "But," said I, "here is the work complete, and it's impossible people should not find it out; besides such an arrangement would not be at all fair to me, and would be

[21] Diary, 14 Feb. 1888.
[22] This is revealed in Stanford's article 'Hubert Parry's *Judith*' originally published in the *Fortnightly* and later reprinted in *Studies and Memories* (London, 1908), 139–55.

untrue into the bargain." [23] But Beale dug his heels in and the meeting ended with the prospect of a severely truncated oratorio. After Beale had departed, Parry played through the whole work for Richter, 'and he called it a "splendid work;" but', wrote Parry somewhat sceptically, 'I think he did so more out of kindness than sincerity.'

Richter, however, was true to his word and subsequently persuaded the committee not only to abandon the notion of cuts but to devote the whole morning performance to the work. Nevertheless, that was not the end of the problems. Much to Parry's annoyance Hueffer had been engaged to provide an analysis for the programme: 'I found him totally stupid as far as music is concerned, but sharp enough though very "doctrinaire" in matters of drama and plot. He was pleasant enough though, on the whole; but as I was leaving his door after 3 hours of it he amused me by saying "I wish you all success, but it's a pity you haven't a better book." An eminently appropriate remark from the author of the "Troubadours".'[24] Furthermore, it became obvious during the full rehearsals that Richter was experiencing difficulties with tempi and Parry began to regret that he had not undertaken to conduct himself. However, at the performance on 29 August, a grand affair involving an orchestra double the ordinary size, Richter's conception improved and the general reception was excellent:

The chorus was, of course, splendid. Band ditto. Anna [Williams] threw herself into the part in a way that threatened to extinguish her before she got to the end. Lloyd was perfect, and the boys extremely good. People seemed to take to it very soon, and all the friends I saw after the first half were evidently much pleased. The scene of the children seems to have affected people most, and the last chorus of the 1st Act came off splendidly. The rule that no applause is allowed after separate numbers is rather trying, as it is hard to tell whether people are liking it or not. But there was a good row after each half, and my dear chorus shouted and waved their pocket-handkerchiefs like mad.[25]

Many parts of the performance pleased him greatly, especially the Intermezzo, but there was much that disappointed him. In consequence he decided to cut down the last chorus and add brass to the processional music in the first scene of Act One. He also introduced several optional cuts including the Intermezzo, and, in Act Two, half the opening chorus and the Trio in scene one, and a substantial portion of Judith's solo 'Let us give thanks' in scene two. This was done so that smaller provincial choruses might find the work more accessible.

The success of *Judith* at Birmingham consolidated Parry's national reputation and the work was taken up by choral societies up and down the land, the most notable being perhaps those given by the Edinburgh

[23] Diary, 9 July 1888.   [24] Ibid. 22 July 1888.   [25] Ibid. 29 Aug. 1888.

Choral Union in November and Mackenzie's two performances in London at the St James's Hall on 6 December and the Crystal Palace on 15 December with the Novello Choir. It was Parry who suggested that the London performances were entrusted to Mackenzie, though as Mackenzie duly admitted, he was never able to satisfy Parry's wish to take the tempi fast enough.[26] Indeed, privately, Parry felt that his colleague was somewhat 'deficient in spiritual and intellectual energy' as he failed to capture the spirit of the work.[27] But the response from the London audiences was clamorous, something borne out by the rapturous letters from Barclay Squire, Edward Burne-Jones, and Arthur Somervell. Two other admirers who sang in the Novello choir during both performances were to become lifelong friends and colleagues: one was Charles Larcom Graves (who would write the first biography of Parry); the other was August Johannes Jaeger who would develop a close working relationship with the composer in the years to come.

The criticisms of Parry's first oratorio could not be more conflicting and confusing in their polarities. Stanford's article 'Hubert Parry's *Judith*', written in 1888 for the *Fortnightly*, was undoubtedly the most eulogistic in which he defended Parry's 'judicious reticence' and obedience to the best principles of Greek tragedy particularly with regard to the omission of Holofernes' death. This he also tried to justify by drawing an unlikely parallel with the last act of *Carmen*. We might nowadays see this as no more than an excuse for the traditional reserve of the English Oratorio style which generally avoided such dramatizations. But it is also likely that such a scene demanded a dramatic skill which Parry lacked—a failing he himself recognized from his experiences with *Guenever*. Only with Elgar's dramatic cantatas such as *King Olaf* and, *par excellence*, in *The Dream of Gerontius* do we see a genuinely operatic approach in the context of English Oratorio. Nevertheless, Stanford offered a number of useful criticisms in his defence of Parry's stylistic imitation. Here he was not only referring to the deliberate archaicisms of the Bachian *Intermezzo* and Manasseh's Handelian aria 'God breaketh the battle' at the end of Act Two, but also (and much more significantly) to the elements within the work that are more distinctly English and which point to the influence above all of S. S. Wesley.

Shaw's attack in the *Star*[28] gives us a very different picture. To him the composition of Oratorio was 'perhaps the most gratuitous exploit open to a XIX century Englishman'. Associated with it was the legacy of Handelian and Mendelssohnian works mechanically thrown together

---

[26] Sir A. C. Mackenzie, *A Musician's Narrative* (London, 1927), 159.

[27] Diary, 13 Nov. 1888.

[28] G. B. Shaw, 'Parry's Judith' (signed 'By The Star's Own Captious Critic', the *Star* (18 Dec. 1888).

using stereotyped structural procedures of chorus and aria, not to mention 'the worn-out novelties of modern scoring'. On a deeper social level, Shaw the active socialist also regarded the Oratorio as a symbol of the establishment in all its cosy respectability which he believed Parry, 'who had proved the constant elevation of his musical ideal', might well have avoided. With all his characteristic eloquent humour (a chief reason why his musical criticisms have survived), Shaw could find very little in the work to applaud, yet ironically he sensed an improvement towards the end; whereas Stanford, with his operatic instincts, considered the work to sag and recommended instead the advantages of a short theatrical ending. Shaw also felt inclined to parody mercilessly the one number of the work, Meshullemeth's ballad ('Long since in Egypt's plenteous land'), which has endured in the form of the hymn 'Dear Lord and Father of Mankind'. But owing to his delight in sarcasm largely engendered by dramatic and musical incongruities, this obscured the fact that the ballad contains one of Parry's finest, some might say 'classic', tunes.

Sarcasm and parody aside, Shaw undoubtedly hit on the work's major defects—namely its moribund choral techniques which significantly contribute to the oratorio's unsuccessful structure. In this regard A. E. F. Dickinson's penetrating remarks seem particularly pertinent:

Oratorio is a grand opportunity for creative expanse, but has its problems of structure and content. Pieces of solo-work, buttressed by massive and severely contrapuntal choruses, do not necessarily make a water-tight structure. Dramatic narrative and pious choral reflection do not easily blend; a lecturer may point to a screen and comment, but can a chorus? 'Judith', a document in 'popular movements' (the phrase comes in the composer's own preface), is a naif stylised epic tale which it is difficult to take seriously except as religious satire . . . and despite fine passages the oratorio is far too long for its reflective, non-operatic treatment.[29]

Though there was public jubilation after Birmingham, Parry was relieved that the affair was over and relished his retreat to the Sussex coast. There was to be little respite from the public gaze, however, for Hereford had included *Blest Pair of Sirens* in its festival programme and had asked him to conduct. Once again its reception was rapturous but Parry had some strong words for the works by Ouseley and Cowen that also formed part of the programme: 'Much of Cowen's "Thanksgiving Ode" utterly vulgar and vile. Ouseley's Polycarp really worse than I expected; purely asinine. Antidramatic and ineffective. The Sirens went well and everybody expressed themselves delighted with it.'[30] The rest of his time at Rustington he spent sailing, with intermittent bouts of work

[29] A. E. F. Dickinson, 'The Neglected Parry', *Musical Times* (Apr. 1949), 109.
[30] Diary, 13 Sept. 1888.

on the new symphony that Richter had requested for his 1889 concert season. Moreover, as a creative diversion from the production of large-scale pieces, he turned once again to writing songs in which he felt increasingly disposed to express his more private thoughts; indeed, it was often the case in later life that he found solace in this most intimate of genres as a means of escape from the vicissitudes of festival commissions. One exquisite miniature to come from his pen during the latter part of September was a setting of Beaumont and Fletcher's 'Lay a garland on my hearse' (which later appeared in Set V of the *English Lyrics* published in 1902.

More portentously 'Lay a garland' seemed to presage the news of his father's death which arrived by telegram on 29 September. 'Utterly bewildered'[31] he and his youngest half-sister, Hilda, took the train to Highnam where the rest of the family were assembled. Several painful days followed. The Sunday service at church disgusted him even more than usual with its 'totally senseless forms of modern continental religion . . .'[32] but the actual funeral he found deeply moving.

In spite of the religious and political differences that had separated them since 1873, father and son had grown closer in the last months of Thomas Gambier Parry's life. Parry's visits to Highnam in 1888 had been a little more frequent than before and they had been able to spend pleasant and affectionate hours together discussing the progress of *Judith* and other commissions. But even though his father had not looked well, there seemed no hint that his death was imminent. Fortunately when it came, it did so quietly and without the harrowing circumstances of any lingering illness:

The death of that dear old father of mine hit me rather hard. I scarcely realised how fond I was of him till he departed, and it seems to me now as if the attraction he had for me was different from that of any other person in the world. Though we disagreed, as you know, about many things, the last year drew us together more than ever before. I never was more drawn to him, nor was he ever more loving to me than in the last few months; and his going made me feel strangely lonely. However, we were better off than many people, for his death was singularly painless and quiet. I wasn't at home, unluckily, but they tell me he just passed quietly away in his chair, where he always sat reading of an evening, and there was nothing to aggravate the sadness of it, either for him or the rest of the family—and they seem to have been better prepared for the parting than I was.[33]

But facing up to grief and regret proved to be the least of Parry's familial problems. For the moment, Highnam remained in the possession of his stepmother. Sooner or later, after the death of Ethelinda Gambier

[31] Ibid. 29 Sept. 1888.   [32] Ibid. 30 Sept. 1888.
[33] Letter to Edward Dannreuther, 26 Oct. 1888, Bod. MS Eng. Letters e.117.

Parry, the house and estate would fall to him as the eldest male heir. An acknowledged fact this may have been, but already seeds of contention and jealousy had begun to take root in the mind of Ernest Gambier Parry. Since his return to Highnam in 1885 Ernest's continuing poor health had given rise to a delicate mental condition, a major consequence of which was a tendency to exaggerate feelings and responses. Love for his father, his estate, his religious convictions, and his achievements turned into a worship of the worst, sanctimonious kind, which, though they recognized it, other members of the family felt powerless to stem. After Thomas Gambier Parry's funeral Hubert for the first time took cognizance of his half-brother's predicament and was alarmed at the absurdity of many of his judgements and remarks which he perceived to lack real sincerity. Of more immediate concern, however, was the future financial management of the estate on behalf of Ethelinda Gambier Parry. This the family agreed should for the moment fall to Ernest. Though in many ways it seemed the natural and most reasonable decision to make, the responsibilities would only serve to amplify Ernest's sense of adoration for Highnam to a point where his perception became utterly distorted. This sentiment largely contributed to his personally held conviction that he cared far more for the estate than did Hubert, who was, he imagined, too busy in London to care. This in turn led Ernest to believe that Highnam was therefore his spiritual and, consequently, his rightful inheritance. When these feelings at last became known after Ethelinda's death in 1896, it was inevitable that a violent quarrel would break out between Hubert and Ernest. But when Hubert was forced into a position where he had to exercise his right of primogeniture, he did so not out of spite, but because he feared that the future of Highnam would be seriously threatened if Ernest continued to manage it.

1. Thomas Gambier Parry

2. Isabella (Hubert's Mother)

3. Hubert at Eton

4. Hubert at Oxford

5. Family Photo

(standing from left to right) Hubert, Clinton with Owen, Linda, Thomas Gambier Parry; (seated from left to right)
Beatrice with Noel, Florence Hinde (Clinton's wife) with Bluebell, Ethelinda with Hilda: (seated on grass from left to
right) Ernest, Sidney, Geralidine

6. Lucy Parry

7. Lady Maude Herbert as a teenager

8. Hubert and Maude at Wilton
(with Lady Adine Murray)

9. Highnam Court

10. Wilton House

11. Knight's Croft, Rustington

12. Parry's Music Room at Knight's Croft

13. Sketch from the Cruise to South America: 'A little bit of Bahia from the bay'

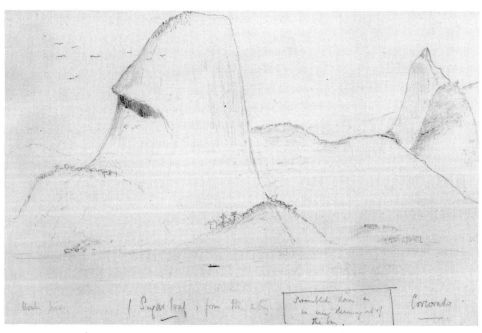

14. Sketch from the Cruise to South America: '*Sugar loaf* . . . scrambled down as we were steaming out of the bay'

15. 17 Kensington Square

16. Parry and Family with Emily Daymond (arms folded) at Rustington

17. Dolly (right) and Gwen (left)

18. Parry with Grieg at Oxford (1907)

19. Bournemouth (1910)
(standing from left to right) Parry,
German; (seated from left to right) Elgar,
Godfrey, Mackenzie, Stanford

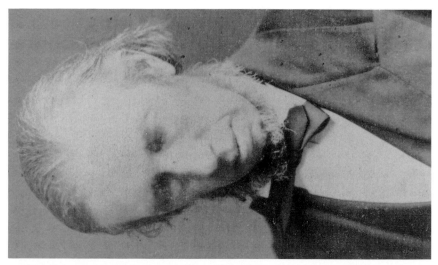

21. Sir George Macfarren

20. Edward Dannreuther

22. Staff of the Royal College of Music (1883)
Parry (second row, five from right); Stanford (third row, fourth from right); Grove (seated top centre)

23. Parry and Crew of the *Humber* (later the *Wanderer*)
including (seated far left) Sidney Gambier Parry; (seated centre) George Robertson
Sinclair

24. The *Wanderer*

25. 'Off to sea!'

26. Family Group at Shulbrede

(from left to right) Parry, Dolly (with Elizabeth), Arthur (standing), Maude, and Matthew

27. Gwen and Harry Plunket Greene on their Wedding Day (1899)

28. The Choir and Orchestra of the Three Choirs at Highnam (September 1910)

29. Delegates of the International Musical Congress at London University (1911) Parry can be seen seated in the centre with Mackenzie (Chairman of the Congress) to his right. Stanford can also be seen seated six to his left.

30. Parry (*c.*1898)

31. Parry and Maude at
Rustington (*c.*1910)

32. Parry and Maude at
Shulbrede (*c*, 1910)

33. Parry (1917)

Dilemma
The Response to Public Demand

A SURE sign that Parry had become something of a national celebrity
was signalled by his election to the Athenaeum Club in April 1888. He
had originally been proposed by Lord Lyttelton, Spencer Lyttelton's
father. But on Lord Lyttelton's unexpected death, Lord Leighton, the
Nazarene painter and great friend of Parry's father, had stepped in with
Grove who was the second sponsor. On 1 May Parry made his first visit
to the club to have tea with Grove and Alfred Ainger, the popular
lecturer, preacher, and biographer of such famous literary names as
Charles Lamb and George Crabbe. In the ensuing years the Athenaeum
proved to be a significant refuge for him in times of increasing loneliness
for at the club he was sure to meet and dine with 'sundry sage and
worthy men'.[1] After a day choked with teaching, concerts, and other
public functions, the dread of returning to Kensington Square without
wife or children often became overwhelming. Hence he looked to this
pre-eminent institution to satisfy the gregarious nature (albeit a selective
one) within him—a nature which needed to share time with other
kindred spirits. When he was not at the Athenaeum he would
occasionally visit the Savile Club, though his presence there became
increasingly rare as he told Adrian Boult many years later when the
young conductor was a candidate for membership: 'I shall be very glad if
I can be of any use in connection with your candidature for the Savile. I
am not much good as a member as I never use it, and have not been
inside it half a dozen times in the last 10 years.'[2]

Wilton also provided him with a growing source of friends and
acquaintances. George and 'Gety' Pembroke invited him, Maude, and
the family to the house for Easter and they were there again at
Christmas. At these gatherings he met Matthew Arnold whose writings
had so influenced him during his late teens, and there were others such
as Edmund Gurney and Auberon Herbert. One aristocrat he particularly
warmed to was Lord (Charles) Beresford whose affinity with the sea gave
them a common bond. Through the Pembrokes he also gained an

[1] Diary, 1 May 1888.
[2] Letter to Adrian Boult, 27 Apr. 1915, BL Add. MS 60499.

introduction to many other aristocratic personages such as the Tennants, the Cowpers, and the Duchess of Rutland who shared a love for literature and art, and there were of course Lady Pembroke's two sisters, Lady Brownlow and Lady Lothian. This circle of friends, which also included Lord and Lady Elcho, Arthur Balfour, the Wyndhams, and Spencer Lyttelton, soon earned the nickname 'The Souls' which was reputedly given them by Charles Beresford at a dinner-party given by the Brownlows in the early summer of 1888. From the time of his first visit to 'Clouds' (the Wyndhams' enormous and architecturally superb country house in Wiltshire) at Christmas 1888 until well into the 1890s, Parry was often involved on the fringe of this élite coterie. There were Easter houseparties at 'Clouds' which 'began the season'. In the summer Saturday-to-Monday parties took place at Panshanger and Wrest Place (the homes of the Cowpers), Ashridge (the home of the Brownlows), Wilton, Stanway (the home of the Elchos), and Taplow (the home of the Grenfells). In London there were dinners with the Tennants in Grosvenor Square, with the Cowpers at 4 St James's Square; the Wyndhams entertained in Belgrave Square and the Duchess of Rutland organized various gatherings at her studio in Arlington Street. Many of the circle's members he had known for a considerable time such as Balfour and Spencer Lyttelton, and their interest in art also attracted the company of Edward Burne-Jones, Edward Poynter, and Alma Tadema. 'The Souls' enjoyed the company of writers such as Henry James, Oscar Wilde, and Pearl Craigie who later (in 1900) asked Parry to provide incidental music for her play *A Repentance*. Many of these eminent people Parry knew well as part of London's artistic life, and from his own habits of regularly dining out. He had, for example, become better acquainted with Poynter, Alma Tadema, Browning, and George Du Maurier at a dinner given by the explorer and traveller, Douglas W. Freshfield, at his home in Airlie Gardens. However, a large proportion of the central characters of 'The Souls' he did not know and during many of their parties he frequently felt emotionally excluded. This was not to say that he did not find their artistic amusements harmless, light-hearted, and fun, but too often the atmosphere conveyed a sense of complacency, *laissez faire*, and sometimes condescension which he abhorred. There were times too when he questioned their genuine love of the arts, particularly after the terrible howler of the 17-year-old Ettie Desborough (then Ethel Fane) who sat next to him at dinner and opened the conversation with 'I do hate music, don't you?'[3] But what perhaps more than anything else confirmed his alienation and distrust of the

---

[3] J. Abdy and C. Gere, *The Souls* (London, 1984), 63.

aristocratic way of life were comments such as those made by Lady Ailesbury:

Maude went to see Lady Ailesbury [her aunt] and gave me a vivid picture of the state of existence of the household. The first thing her ladyship said was (in a most concerned way) 'My dear, I hear you have not gained anything'. Maude could not for the life of her think what she meant, but at length it came out she was afflicted because we had no increase in fortune to speak of. So utterly mundane is the aristocratic view of life.[4]

Had it not been for such as Lord Beresford, Lord de Vesci, and later Lady Radnor, his withdrawal from aristocratic society might have been swift. But fame had its price and as he was loath to offend his brother-in-law whom Maude adored, he seldom refused. This inability to say 'no' was also reflected in his professional life as he took on more examining duties, more lecturing (for such bodies as the Royal Institution), and more commissions, many of which were promised to friends whom he did not wish to let down. One such promise was for another Violin Sonata for Dannreuther's chamber-music concerts at Orme Square which he wrote at a furious pace partly in London and partly at Wilton during the Christmas break. By 3 February 1889, the Sonata was being rehearsed in Bayswater by Dannreuther and George A. Gibson and the performance on 14 February went well though Parry's personal impression was 'mild'. This reaction may have stemmed from his recollection of the earlier Fantasie Sonata which was much more overtly hot-blooded and virtuoso. The D major Sonata, though less impassioned, exudes a much greater confidence in terms of structural balance, harmonic and thematic consistency, and instrumental interplay. At once we are aware of the striking rhythmical flexibility of the first movement's opening theme played by the violin, particularly the falling seventh at the end of its first phrase (Ex. 25*a*). Moreover, Parry's mature diatonic language is evident both in the closing material of the exposition and in the wonderfully reflective coda. The slow movement in B flat major is yet more lyrical and shares the same pathos as the great slow movements of the Piano Quartet, Cello Sonata, and Piano Trio in B minor; indeed, the beautifully constructed second-group melody (Ex. 25*b*) is one of Parry's most inspired thematic inventions. The brilliant Finale, revealing Parry in delicate mood, appears from the diaries to have been written first. In February 1894, when the Sonata was subject to revision, this movement remained virtually untouched. However, the first movement, which is accorded the most intellectual treatment, was evidently the cause of some uneasiness since he devoted nearly all his revision time to its perfection.

[4] Diary, 24 Nov. 1888.

Ex. 25. Violin Sonata in D (1888–9). *a* first movement, opening theme; *b* slow movement, second-group melody.

(*a*)   [*Allegro*]

vn. *p*

(*b*)   [*Andante sostenuto*]

pf. *mf*   *3*   *3*   *cresc.*   *3*

   In addition to honouring his promise to Dannreuther, Parry also had his sights on the Leeds Festival commission for the following October, but before he could fully immerse himself in the task, a request came from the Philharmonic Society for an orchestral work of symphonic proportions, though smaller than a full-blown symphony. In answer Parry mentioned that he had 'a short and very slight symphony all but finished'[5] which might be suitable. This he had sketched out during 1887, but had not designed it for an orchestra of the Philharmonic's size. As a result of these misgivings he suggested that the Society might consider a performance of the 'Cambridge' Symphony which he believed was worth playing again. But the Philharmonic opted for the smaller symphony which they felt was more appropriate for their programme schedule. In reply Parry voiced his disappointment at their decision and was even faintly disparaging about his new symphonic creation:

I apologize for being so slow in answering your note. I can't help being sorry you should choose the small symphony I spoke of, but as you prefer it, I must of course accede. It is quite a small and unimposing kind of symphony, in the plain key of C major and consists of an opening Allegro, a slow movement in A minor, Scherzo in F, and a set of variations. I suppose it must be announced as a Symphony—Sinfonietta looks too affected. The announcement might perhaps give it as a 'Short Symphony'. As to naming me, I really don't care. Somehow people have got to call me Dr H. P., but C. Hubert H. Parry seems more natural to me personally.[6]

Extensive revision of the so-called 'small symphony' (or 'Symphony for Small Orchestra' as appears on the original autograph) took up most of January, though further small amendments were subsequently made as the score was not dispatched to the copyist until the beginning of April.

   [5] Letter to Philharmonic Society (Mr Berger), 25 Nov. 1888, BL Loan 48: 13/26.
   [6] Letter to Philharmonic Society, 14 Dec. 1888, ibid.

The first performance took place on 23 May under the composer's direction.

The impression left by Parry's Third Symphony proved to be more profound than either of his two previous efforts. Indeed, the work soon became his most popular orchestral essay and received regular performances. Henry Hadow made it the subject of his first Oxford lecture in 1892. However, acclaim for what in the opinion of the composer was no more than a lightweight composition tended to irritate Parry, who believed that more serious and worthwhile music could be found in the other symphonies.

Much of the Third Symphony's popularity was owing to its accessibility. Conceived for forces barely larger than a Mozartian orchestra, it soon found a place in the repertoires of many amateur orchestral societies. Furthermore, its appeal also lay in the national distinctiveness of the work. The writer of the programme notes (one presumes Joseph Bennett) suggested that the nickname of 'English' be attached to the symphony owing to the prevailing character of the thematic material. It was with this subtitle that the work was published in 1907 after numerous revisions. The first of these revisions took place in 1895 for the Leeds Subscription Concerts on 30 January when the composer conducted Henschel's Scottish Orchestra. For this performance the first movement was rescored and three optional trombone parts were added; moreover, in the last movement two new variations were substituted for variations two and three. Then, in November 1902, the first movement was painstakingly rescored again before its performance at Bournemouth on 18 December.

Without doubt the 'English' Symphony exudes the fresh, sturdy diatonicism (such as the main theme of the first movement, six bars after letter A) with which we have become so familiar in Parry's mature language. Certain other stylistic features, such as his propensity for three-part contrapuntal textures (e.g. in the first movement four bars after letter B, and in the slow movement at letter B), a texture one more readily associates with Elgar, are even more prominent than before. In being deliberately 'classical' in his formal approach the nature and treatment of the material is much more simple and direct than in either of Parry's earlier symphonies, having instead more in common with the lighter vein of the *Suite Moderne*. Both thematic groups in the first-movement sonata are clearly defined and the ideas themselves are concise and infectiously melodious. The first group in particular demonstrates the Classical orientation in the way it is presented in two parts, one a lively passage in semiquavers, the other noble and 'largamente'. The second of these ideas begins the recapitulation, a procedure thoroughly reminiscent of the Mannheim school. Consistent with the immediacy of the expositional ideas, the development is less discursive, though interest is maintained through variations in tempo. If the first movement has a flaw, it lies in the excessively regular periodicity of the phrase structure which occasionally borders on the mechanical. However, notwithstanding these reservations, it is a lively characteristic movement thoroughly consistent with the aspirations of its title. The Scherzo is perhaps the least interesting movement for not only does it share similar phraseological weaknesses, but, despite its 'busy' rhythmical activity, it is thematically dull. The theme of the last movement, on which Parry bases his twelve variations, is by comparison much better and full of potential. Yet Parry's response to the classical constraints imposed by the small scale of the symphony is disappointingly conservative. In preserving both the phrase and harmonic structure of the theme throughout without once resorting even to a change of mode, the series of variations (with repeats) courts a sense of monotony—a feeling that is thrown into relief by the sudden excursion into new tonal areas in the extended coda. As a complete contrast, the 'andante sostenuto' stands out as a real gem. Of all the movements this is the most lyrically expansive and shows a greater degree of structural invention in its use of thematic displacement; it is also here that Parry's orchestral textures are at their most sumptuous. Of particular note is the wonderfully soaring second-group theme in the violins and its radiant return in A major in the recapitulation.

Only five weeks after the first hearing of the 'English' Symphony, Parry's Fourth Symphony in E minor (unofficially named by the composer the 'Richter' Symphony) was given at a Richter concert on 1 July. Although greeted with enthusiasm, the public and critics were less vociferous than they had been in May. One commentator described the first movement as 'too restless'[7] and too difficult to follow. It is evident from numerous diary entries and various correspondences that the gestation of the work had been tortuous and problematic. Much of it was composed in March in periods between sittings for the painter, Herman Herkomer, who insisted upon Parry wearing his doctoral gown.[8] Having finished the greater part of it by the end of the month, Parry was alarmed to discover that it had not been announced in Richter's new concert season. When the news reached Richter he wrote immediately reassuring the composer that it had been omitted as a cautionary measure only because he had heard no news of it during the winter. With Richter's confirmation scoring commenced in earnest, but with each page he began to feel a powerful sense of dissatisfaction. By the end of April the initial heavier orchestration had been replaced by a lighter one and the

---

[7] 'Richter Concerts', *Musical Times*, (1 Aug. 1889), 473.

[8] Herkomer's portrait appeared in the New Gallery catalogue of 1889, p. 16 no. 55. A sketch of Parry by Herman Herkomer also appeared in the *Daily Graphic* on 17 June 1891.

development of the first movement had been entirely rewritten. Richter approved much of the first movement when he played through it in May but there was doubt over the last movement. Indeed at the rehearsal of the symphony on 29 June Parry's misgivings over the whole work, with the exception of the Scherzo, were verified: 'My Symphony didn't get along well—and I felt very dissatisfied with it. Slow movement doesn't come off as I had hoped. Scherzo the only effective movement. Last one quite ragged.'[9] At the concert two days later his reservations became more specific: 'Parts of it came off pretty well. First part of 1st movement—Ditto of Scherzo. Middle of 1st movement and Ditto of slow [movement] didn't please me, nor last movement either. It was much better received than I expected, and after Scherzo I had to go up and make a bow or two.'[10]

The serious mood of the Fourth Symphony, with its severe Doric architecture, moves beyond the intellectualism of either the First or Second Symphonies. Clearly Parry had attempted to inject a new level of pathos into this score, and certainly this is the case with both the first movement and the affecting Lento. The latter is particularly rich in original melodic ideas, striking a much deeper note than its counterpart in the 'Cambridge'; the fine closing idea of the first group, with its sequence of falling figures is prophetic of Elgar (who, incidentally, was at the first performance) and bears interesting comparison with some of that composer's most mature thematic utterances (Ex. 26*a*). Though the symphony as a whole lacks the cyclic thread that runs through its predecessor, there is one fascinating structural innovation in the second movement, entitled *Intermezzo* (Ex. 26*b*) which functions as a link between the first and third movements not only in atmosphere but also in a tonal sense, since the initial tonic major (E major) yields to the dominant of C major, the key of the impending slow movement. The Scherzo in A minor (also available in an unpublished version for four hands), was the only movement with which Parry felt satisfied. It is certainly an intriguing piece. Described as 'an *al fresco fête* in the olden time—a coquettish dance of lords and ladies, interrupted by a song'[11] it has more in common with the lighter vein of the *Suite Moderne* with which it shares the same key. Thematically, however, it is less distinguished, though this is made up for by greater rhythmical interest, notably in the fluctuations of metre between triple and duple.

Disenchantment with the first and last movements led Parry to shelve the Fourth Symphony for many years. Eventually he was persuaded to exhume it by Dan Godfrey for a single performance on 29 December 1904, at Bournemouth; but this only increased his resolve to recast the

⁹ Diary, 29 June 1889   ¹⁰ Ibid. 1 July 1889.
¹¹ 'Richter Concerts', *Musical Times* (1 Aug. 1889), 473.

work entirely. With an ever-increasing work-load, however, the task was postponed for several more years, until an opportunity at last presented itself in 1910.

While working on the Fourth Symphony Parry was also obliged to tackle his Leeds commission which had to be ready well in advance of the Festival in October. Originally Leeds had envisaged that, along with Corder, Cowen, and Goring Thomas, Parry should provide a short cantata, but the Committee, having suffered a refusal from Brahms for a new symphony, no reply from Rubinstein, and an unacceptable suggestion from Saint-Saëns to write an oratorio on the death of Moses, finally turned to Parry who agreed to compose a secular work for the occasion. Possible themes for the text included the Albigensian Crusade, a setting of the *Te Deum*, and Pope's *Ode on St Cecilia's Day*. He settled on Pope's ode and began to sketch his ideas at the beginning of November 1888.

On completing the Ode in June 1889, Parry found he had reached the familiar stage of complete exhaustion. Gloucester were once again demanding his presence for *Judith* which was due to be given at the Three Choirs Festival at the end of August, and rehearsals for Leeds had been fixed for September. In order to avoid the possibility of a nervous collapse, Barclay Squire enticed him to go to Italy for three weeks' rest. Taking in Trent on the way Parry was able to see the famous codices. 'They are in excellent condition,' he wrote excitedly, 'written clearly on rough paper and in *score*. We found things by Dunstable, Dufay,

Ex. 26. Fourth Symphony (1889). *a* slow movement, closing thematic idea of first group; *b Intermezzo*, opening.

(a) [*Lento espressivo*]

vn. 1

(b) *Allegretto semplice*

str.   *pp*

pp

Binchois, etc. . .'.[12] Then, leaving Squire at Trent, he went on via Verona to Venice where he stayed for three days. On August 15 he went to St Mark's for the Feast of the Assumption only to have his illusions shattered by the lamentable level of the music which was 'plain, empty, and in every attempt at effect or expression purely meretricious'.[13] The latter part of the holiday was spent first with his Oxford friend, Heathcote Long, at his villa at Cadenabbia and then with the Blumenthals at their chalet in Bern before returning via Paris.

The performance of the Ode at Leeds on 11 October was undoubtedly for Parry the high point of 1889. 'It was a wonderful performance and a most unexpected success,' he wrote to Helen Richmond; 'I expect it was greatly owing to the way the chorus and Miss Macintyre sang. It will never sound like that again.'[14] In gratitude he dedicated the work 'to my friends of the Leeds Chorus and their zealous chorus-master Alfred Broughton 1889'. The Ode's success, underlined by a similar triumph at the Albert Hall in November, immediately brought it into close competition with *Judith* and placed Parry's name at the top of every festival committee's list of 'modern' composers.

For the *Ode on St Cecilia's Day* Parry opted for a much more conventional 'episodic' structure—that is, a series of individual movements for soloists and chorus culminating in a grand Finale. Though overtly more simple in style than *Judith*, it is at once more confident—a mood established by the spacious diatonic gesture of the opening of the prelude and chorus in which Parry was also able to show off his abilities as an orchestrator. In general the technical demands made on the chorus are far less exacting, relying largely on four-part textures, much of it homophonic. Some of the choral writing comes near to being sentimental such as one finds in the part-song-orientated 'By the streams that ever flow', and yet its effect is strangely touching with its use of grace notes and unexpected tonal divergencies. However, the forced patriotism of 'But when our country's cause' is amongst Parry's more unimaginative choral utterances, and one feels (as he himself later expressed) that the text conveyed a sentiment with which he felt uncomfortable. The most directly emotional music can be found in the solo passages, notably 'But when through all the infernal bounds' for soprano. Parry's yearning voice comes to the fore in the latter part, beginning 'But hark he strikes his golden lyre'.

Having achieved a second major coup with *St Cecilia*, Parry was naturally aware of the dilemma which confronted him. He knew that the public would now demand new choral works on an annual basis and that this would largely preclude the composition of instrumental music, an

---

[12] Diary, 12 Aug. 1889.   [13] Ibid. 15 Aug. 1889.
[14] Letter to Helen Richmond, 20 Oct. 1889, RAA RI/3/4/13.

idiom he was loath to ignore. The Third and Fourth Symphonies had clearly demonstrated his continuing interest in orchestral composition, but the indications were that such music would not form a welcome part of his response to public demand. Indeed, it would be eight years before he would attempt another major orchestral piece (the Symphonic Variations) and another twenty-one years before he would again turn his attention to a symphony. As for chamber music, he composed only one further major work: a piano trio which Dannreuther commissioned from him for his 1890 season of concerts at Orme Square. Though being a less challenging work than the earlier Trio in B minor, the Piano Trio in G shares many of the same lyrical preoccupations as the Violin Sonata in D major. This is certainly true of the first movement which is beautifully scored. Parry, however, found it 'too sugary'[15] and the main first group theme 'too feminine and characterless'.[16] The third movement entitled 'Lament' he was particularly pleased with and along with the somewhat Brahmsian 'Capriccio' (second movement) it sounded especially well at its first performance on 13 February 1890.

In terms of sheer compositional activity 1890 was considerably less phrenetic than 1889. Nevertheless, the pressure of history lectures continued unabated at the College including a particularly interesting and pioneering one on viol and lute music in which Dolmetsch, Fuller Maitland and Hipkins participated. This schedule was intensified by a further series of lectures at Oxford (on early Opera, Oratorio, Monteverdi, and Carissimi), a lecture at Birmingham on madrigals, one for the Leeds Philosophical Institute, and several for the Royal Institution on the evolution of music. The substance of the last was already taking shape in a new book, 'The Art of Music', though this undertaking was largely put to one side while he concentrated on the completion of a 'History Summary' (the full title of which was 'Summary of the History and Development of Medieval and Modern European Music') for Novello who were pressing for a new and more authoritative reader for young musicians. This was finally dispatched in July, but was not published until 1893. Its subsequent popularity, however, warranted a second edition in 1904.

There had also been the possibility that his academic responsibilities would be augmented in 1889 by the Professorship at Oxford, which had been vacated by the death in April of Ouseley. His old Exeter College friend, the historian Henry Pelham, persistently encouraged him to apply. But there was uncertainty over Stainer's intentions. Parry enjoyed the support of many people at the university including C. H. Lloyd and there seemed to be a strong possibility that, if Stainer declined the post

---

[15] Diary, 2 Feb. 1890.   [16] Ibid. 13 Feb. 1890.

on the grounds of failing sight, he would succeed to the chair. Parry wrote to Stainer in April generously exhorting him to accept, as he would be more than willing to fill the role of Choragus. In time the matter was resolved, for Stainer's eye problems improved and he felt more disposed to accept. Parry accordingly withdrew, not wishing to stand against him.

In many ways it was providential that he did not secure the Oxford chair for there were more than enough difficulties at the College to occupy him. The crisis of working space had continued to grow, and at last a decision was made to erect a new building to accommodate the burgeoning number of students. The foundation stone was laid by the Prince of Wales on 8 July 1890 at which ceremony Parry conducted the College Choir and Orchestra in a performance of *Blest Pair of Sirens*. The projected time of opening was 1893, but for various official reasons this was delayed a year.

In addition to his College-teaching schedule for 1890, he accepted a number of new private pupils. One significant name on his list was Donald Francis Tovey, an individual he had heard much about through Jenkinson and Parratt. Parry saw and heard Tovey for the first time on 17 May, but the boy did not make a good impression. 'He played to me very mildly;' Parry wrote dismissively, 'and with a [pretentious] manner and conscious phrasing. I was not prepossessed.'[17] However, it was agreed that Tovey would have a course of lessons in analysis and composition. The first encounter took place six days later and did little to improve the initial impression. The second lesson, a week later, was no better as Parry's diary reveals: 'Donald Tovey for another lesson with sheets and sheets of dull and respectably correct twaddle which he seems to pour out with as much ease as water out of a jug.'[18] Finally a lesson in June seems to have angered him so much that he was moved to chastise the youth vehemently: 'I got so riled with his self-satisfied complacency over his idiotic compositions that I gave him a regular lecture. He played me a Fantasia 950 bars long, which took over 20 minutes to play which hadn't more than 3 bars in the whole thing that were not utterly vapid rubbish.'[19] His response to Tovey did not improve and in January 1891 he felt obliged to inform Sophie Weisse that Donald was 'very scatterbrained and unconcentrated, and needs firm discipline to correct flightiness from growing into a confirmed habit.'[20] She was much dejected by Parry's assessment, but was heartened by his readiness to carry on teaching her protégé. Tovey's attitude to composition changed noticeably during 1892; lessons continued, though more sporadically than before, until he went up to Balliol College, Oxford in the autumn of 1894.

[17] Ibid. 17 May 1890.   [18] Ibid. 30 May 1890   [19] Ibid. 6 June 1890.
[20] M. Grierson, *Donald Francis Tovey* (Oxford, 1952), 22.

More important than Tovey, however, the other auspicious name to appear amongst the names of Parry's pupils was Vaughan Williams who entered the Royal College of Music as a student in September 1890. In his essay, 'A Musical Autobiography', Vaughan Williams recorded not only his own admiration for Parry's stylistic distinctiveness, but also, and perhaps more importantly, his teacher's ideology concerning composition. His famous moral dictum to Vaughan Williams, that he should 'write choral music as befits an Englishman and a democrat',[21] says much about Parry's belief that music and life, humanity and creativity, were indivisible. Leading on from this ideal, perhaps the most essential directive that he taught was that 'a composer must write music as his musical conscience demands'.[22] In other words, composition presented choices that were not only artistic but also moral, and this morality was, in Parry's eyes at least, synonymous with complete sincerity. In this regard Parry was at one with G. F. Watts who also asserted that Art was indivisible from morality. Parry's criticism of Wagner's Prelude to *Parsifal* as 'mere scene painting' epitomized his dislike of what he understood to be mere colour. Dvořák's *Requiem* (as 'Roman Catholic scene painting'[23]) was later dismissed for the same reason. For Parry, form and organic growth, based solidly on Teutonic precepts, were the predominant issues which, if lacking, could not be compensated for by the addition of colouristic effect. This belief in musical architecture was as much a question of 'morality' on Parry's part as it was of technique, for he saw musical structure as substance which in turn corresponded with the artistic sincerity of the human personality. Likewise, pure colour and affect without substance were superficial which subsequently reflected on artistic and intellectual honesty. As Vaughan Williams wrote in his obituary to Parry in 1918: 'Is a nation given over to frivolity and insincere vulgarity? We shall surely see it reflected in the music of that nation. There was no distinction for him between a moral and an artistic problem.'[24]

Parry's social life-style in 1890 continued much as it had done in 1889. To combat the solitary evenings in Kensington Square he dined out even more regularly than before. Maude was, as usual, at Rustington for most of the spring, autumn, and the whole of the winter, and so the routine of weekend journeys to the Sussex coast soon established itself and became a pattern for the rest of his life. Weekly visits to 'Rusty', as he affectionately called it, enabled him to oversee the gradual realization of

---

[21] R. Vaughan Williams, 'A Musical Autobiography', *National Music and Other Essays*, 2nd edn. (Oxford, 1987), 183.

[22] Ibid. 180.   [23] Diary, 9 Oct. 1890.

[24] Vaughan Williams, 'Parry' (an obituary), *Music Student* (Nov. 1918), 79. See also Charles L. Graves, *Hubert Parry*, i. (London, 1926), 363.

his sailing aspirations as Harvey's boatyard at Littlehampton began the construction of a new ketch (the *Dolgwandle*—an elision of 'Dolly' and 'Gwandle') which was to be used for commercial ventures up and down the south coast of England.

The dissemination of his works continued to increase nationally. *St Cecilia* was given in Dublin, at the Three Choirs in Worcester, and by the Bach Choir in London. He also attended two performances of *Judith*, the first at York and the second at Bristol where he was a guest of the Roothams. His other main concert venue was Norwich who had commissioned him to write a choral work for their October festival. For this new work he envisaged a cantata which might more successfully integrate the somewhat inchoate procedures of *Prometheus Unbound*, though much would depend on the choice and handling of the text. In December 1889, after he had spent many days in a vain search for suitable poetry, he came across Milton's 'L'Allegro ed Il Penseroso', a work he had known for over twenty years. Although he struggled with the manipulation of the text from beginning to end, it is evident that Parry enjoyed Miltonic lyricism and symbolism—a fact already apparent from *Blest Pair of Sirens*. This empathy seems to have existed particularly with the poet's early verse in which the clarity, urbanity, and classical symmetry of Jonson had been the prime influence. Dannreuther recognized this innate response and pronounced the work to be far superior to *St Cecilia*. Parry, who had been generally despondent about the work since its conception was much encouraged. After the Norwich performance he wrote to his wife:

[Dannreuther] volunteered the remark that he liked it better than Cecilia, which is very comforting. He thinks it better all round, and new. I was rather down about it, because it seemed to me that my friends didn't really take to it as they took to Cecilia, and though people were very nice, it seemed to my innermost self that it rather hung fire. But if Dann[reuther] thinks so well of it, I think it must be all right.[25]

Similarly Shaw, who had condemned *Judith* so categorically, found much to praise after attending the first London performance in December; 'now that his genius, released from an unnatural and venal alliance, has flown back to the noble poetry that was its first love,' he wrote, 'let the hatchet be buried—and Judith with it as soon as possible. This new cantata of his is happy, ingenious, as full of contrapuntal liveliness as Judith was full of contrapuntal deadliness, and genuine in feeling throughout.'[26]

The parallels and contrasts of Milton's two poems constantly outlined impressions of an ideal day and night interspersed by images of darkness

[25] Letter to Lady Maude Parry, 26 Oct. 1890, ShP.
[26] G. B. Shaw, *World* (10 Dec. 1890).

and light. The two universal abstractions of Milton's age, Mirth and Melancholy (or Contemplation) were the subjects of an academic disputation in which ultimately the quiet, meditative solitude of Melancholy prevailed. Nevertheless, Mirth was not simplistically portrayed as a frivolous pursuit that could not be reconciled with the heavenly ideals of Contemplation. Milton's poetical flexibility had the power to express the virtues of both emotional states with the result that both have an affinity with heaven. It was this essential interaction between the two abstractions that Parry was able to exploit more effectively in terms of tonal organization. Furthermore, the recurrence of thematic material was handled with greater textual significance, and the orchestral prelude, which introduces much of the material, plays a more integral role in the cantata than that of *Prometheus*. It was not the first time Milton's text had been set. Handel had used it in 1740 together with a rather inept Georgian appendage entitled *Il Moderato* by Charles Jennens, intended to resolve the apparent dichotomy. In organizing his text, Handel chose constantly to alternate between 'L'Allegro' and 'Il Penseroso' for the first two parts, and then conclude with 'Il Moderato' as the epilogue. Parry was almost certainly acquainted with Handel's setting, but was not tempted to treat the poems in the same way. Selected parts of 'L'Allegro' were set first and appear in three scenes beginning with an orchestral prelude. The key of G minor, approached by a series of powerful diatonic, almost modal progressions, dominates the orchestral introduction, which, with its quasi-Baroque counterpoint conveys a mood of severity (Ex. 27*a*). This is taken up by the soprano's initial declamation 'Hence, loathed Melancholy', but G minor is appropriately dispelled as Mirth is invoked ('But come thou goddess fair and free') in the relative B flat. The rejection of G minor is significant, as this tonality is never heard again. Instead, B flat major becomes the key around which the cantata is orientated, and in which Mirth and Melancholy become reconciled. This move is also further emphasized by the presentation of a new theme (Ex. 27*b*) by the soprano and chorus which forms the basis of Scene 1. Having established B flat major, Parry sets his second scene in the dominant for solo soprano, which, replete with drone, is a pastoral evocation in a modified ternary form using essentially trochaic and iambic vocal rhythms to stress the simple classical metre of Milton's verse. Scene 3 commences resolutely in D major with the chorus ('Towered cities pleased us then') though this is soon expunged as the tranquillity of F major is recalled ('There let Hymen oft appear'). However, F major itself is short-lived as it functions as dominant preparation for B flat which again symbolizes the pleasures of Mirth as the soprano embarks on her most voluptuous solo 'And ever, against eating cares'. The chorus, in concluding the scene, take up the soprano's material before launching into a more contrapuntal episode that is gradually superseded by homophony. This change of texture symbolically alludes to the text's 'Untwisting all the chains that tie the hidden soul of harmony' which in turn prepares for the final affirmation 'Mirth with thee I mean to live' and the return of the main theme of Scene 1.

From the concluding statement in B flat emerges a more extended orchestral transition that leads directly into 'Il Penseroso' (Scene 4) which also provokes a change of key. Furthermore, with the challenge 'Hence vain deluding joy', the bass soloist is introduced for the first time in E flat major (significantly the key used for the contrasting 'dolce'

Ex. 27. *L'Allegro ed Il Penseroso* (1890). *a* opening of orchestral introduction; *b* main theme representing 'Mirth'; *c* the 'dolce' theme, orchestral introduction; *d* theme representing 'Melancholy'.

cont. over/

Ex. 27. cont.

theme before letter D in the orchestral prelude (Ex. 27*c*)). E flat major is soon quitted for B major (another tonality introduced in the prelude) to portray the textual references to Morpheus, the god of dreams. These key changes, however, are only a preparation for the invocation of Melancholy ('But hail thou goddess sage and holy, Hail divinest Melancholy') which is marked by a further shift to D major and the recurrence of the 'dolce theme' (Ex. 27*d*; also cf. Ex. 27*c*). The use of D major to highlight this new emotional state also recalls and integrates two earlier references to the tonality: first, the abortive opening to Scene 3 of 'L'Allegro'; second, in the same scene, the final sensual passage for soprano in her shared structure with the chorus ('The hidden soul of harmony').This new theme is also the subject of another shared structure. Initially it appears as a bass solo, but after it comes to a half close in the relative minor, the hushed chorus take up a repeat which resembles the version of the orchestral prelude more closely (modulating to the dominant). The consequent material of this extended melody with its gradual shift to the dominant of B flat, exactly parallels the tonal movements of the prelude. Equally significant in this passage is the union of soloist and chorus which more closely interact as if to represent symbolically Melancholy's richer powers of fulfilment. Moreover, symbolism is also present in the tonal movements in which for the first time there is a hint of reconciliation between Mirth and Melancholy. It is at this stage that the disputation between the two humours begins to gather momentum, and this is consistently realized in the fluctuation between B flat and D major during the rest of Scene 4. Perhaps the most magnificent movement in the work is Scene 5 ('And when the sun begins to fling His flaring beams'). Dannreuther regarded this as the finest section of the piece. Certainly the exploitation of the sumptuous texture together with a wonderfully controlled sense of harmonic pacing and tonal variation is masterly, and without doubt this enhances the rapturous 'dream' of Milton's text. With the conclusion of the six-part chorus, the bass's last passage of declamation supplies the necessary transition to B flat, where the key once associated with Mirth is at last symbolically reconciled with Melancholy in a grand ecstatic Finale (Scene 6) for chorus. It is interesting to note that Parry's final text is not in fact the end of Milton's poem. 'Il Penseroso' concludes with a similar affirmation to parallel 'L'Allegro' ('These pleasures, Melancholy, give, And I with thee will choose to live'); but evidently Parry sensed that such an affirmation might seem too unaccommodating in its preference for Melancholy rather than Mirth, destroying or at least confusing the conciliatory balance and unity created by the musical structure.

L'Allegro ed Il Penseroso was designed as a series of scenes in the same way as *Prometheus Unbound*. But whereas *Prometheus* was divided into two halves, *L'Allegro* is treated as an homogenous whole, a fact clearly apparent in the tonal plan, the characterization of the two humours by soprano and bass, and the greater conciseness of the internal structures. One is aware of the symmetry created by the first two scenes and the last two, for the simple structure provides a framework within which the main textual and tonal argument takes place. This is especially well calculated by the manner in which Scene 3 functions not simply as a textual and tonal peroration of the first poem, but also as a point of departure for the more exploratory Scene 4, to which it is linked. Scene 4, in which the main musical argument is centred, provides the necessary transition to the final two scenes whose cogency is further assisted by the system of tonal associations. Undoubtedly the success of *L'Allegro* is largely due to its more thorough integration of the underdeveloped procedures of *Prometheus*. Another feature that may have unconsciously aided Parry was Milton's intrinsically meditative poetry as opposed to Shelley's radically dramatic, though often inflexible prose. *L'Allegro* is not cluttered with bombastic gestures or self-conscious Wagnerian rhetoric, nor does it fall victim to the stylistic unevenness that is so rife in *Prometheus*. This is perhaps most evident in the declamatory passages which are treated with a refreshing elasticity. Though *L'Allegro* drew praise from Dannreuther, Shaw, and William Hannam who arranged to have it performed in Leeds in March 1891, the public did not take to it, and there have been very few performances of what is in fact a fine work.

The negative reaction to *L'Allegro* left Parry feeling disillusioned, not a little angry, and entirely out of sympathy with the public's seemingly insatiable appetite for specific types of choral work. This sense of demoralization he expressed in a letter to his wife:

Frank [Pownall] came after tea and we had one of our old-fashioned times, he sang [and] I played a lot to him, and enjoyed having someone to sympathize. It seems to me as if no-one cared really for what is first rate in music, such as the greatest Beethoven things and Bach things—and at times I do feel that lonely and disheartened I am almost desperate. But when Frank comes I feel there's somebody worth playing to. I think it's the total lack of sympathy that's made me give up my playing.[27]

Judith, which he had viewed as a grudging concession to oratorio was enjoying nationwide acclaim, and already there were signs that a new oratorio would be demanded by the Gloucester Committee for their 1892 festival. Hence the dilemma presented itself—should he accede to contemporary taste and convention, stoically accepting the penalty of his environment, or should he follow the road towards iconoclasm and artistic integrity, and risk a decline in public attention?

For the moment, it seems, he decided to compromise. He accepted Gloucester's commission for an oratorio, in the knowledge that there were also openings for experiment. One such opportunity came with Dr G. R. Sinclair's request from Hereford for a choral work for the 1891 Three Choirs Festival. For this he looked to the Latin text of Psalm 130 'De profundis clamavi' and conceived a most ambitious canvas for twelve-part chorus, soprano solo, and orchestra. Though less musically consistent than *L'Allegro*, *De Profundis* contains some fine music, and is particularly impressive in the dexterous manipulation of the twelve parts which vary from three choirs (*a*4) in the first section, double choir (*a*6) in the second, and full choir (*a*12) together with the soloist in the third. Of the three movements, the first is perhaps the most substantial and inventive, notably in the way in which the chorus's first entry is thrown into relief by the radical tonal shift to F sharp major, away from the dark brooding orchestral prelude in G minor. Moreover, Parry's sense of harmonic rhythm is masterly in the way he judges the gradual transition from F sharp to the dominant. The sheer sound and texture of the

[27] Letter to Lady Maude Parry, 26 Oct. 1890, ShP.

choir's opening passage (which builds on the polyphony of *Blest Pair*) is Parry at his most awesome and visionary and was only to be surpassed by the inspired sonorities of Elgar's *Dream of Gerontius*. The two sections for solo soprano—'Fiant aures tuae intendentes' which concludes the first section, and 'A custodia matutina usque ad noctem' which commences the last—continue the trend of rhythmically flexible lyricism essayed so convincingly in *L'Allegro*. The main flaw occurs in the third movement where Parry regrettably resorts to a worthy but somewhat laboured fugue to restate G major. The twelve-part writing is undoubtedly a *tour de force*, but the 'learned' counterpoint is a feeble and rather tired recourse which hardly matches up to the original substance of the previous two movements.

Before *De Profundis* was performed in September 1891, Parry was asked to provide a short musical setting of Swinburne's ode, *Eton*, for the 450th Anniversary of the foundation of the College on 28 June. A slight work, composed to suit the modest abilities of its performers and to appeal to a select audience, it strikes a note which nowadays seems altogether dated in its nostalgic, patriotic triumphalism. The restrained central interlude, 'Still the reaches of the river', is strangely moving, largely because of Parry's subtle progressions. Later in 1892 Warre Cornish and others attempted to entice Parry to accept the post of precentor and music instructor at Eton in succession to Barnby, but the offer was quietly refused. After Parry had dissuaded Parratt from accepting,[28] the post was eventually taken up by C. H. Lloyd.

In many ways Parry's links with 'high society' reached a watershed during 1891. He continued to dine out regularly, was a frequent visitor to summer garden parties such as those given by Sir Henry Thoby Prinsep in Hyde Park Gardens. But his abhorrence of small-talk, blasé attitudes, and political apathy frequently led to more furious outbursts in his diaries and notebooks:

The upper classes for the most part regard music with much the same feelings as a savage regards paintings. From the most obvious short simple tunes they do get some sense of [definition] as the savage would analogously from simple paintings, but from anything the least approaching to high art they get at most but a hazy feeling and vague impression as the savage would get from the combination of colours without the smallest notion of what it is about.[29]

His impatience and discomfort also extended to meetings with the 'Souls'. In 1891, one week-long gathering brought him into contact with Oscar Wilde. As Parry's lengthy diary account reveals, Wilde helped form a symposium in the smoking-room at which he would be the centre

---

[78] see D. Tovey, and G. Parratt, *Walter Parratt* (London, 1941), 86–8.
[29] Notebook, ShP.

of attention. The 'incessant blather' that he talked, plus the affected 'tête-à-têtes' he took with all the female members of the party, soon galvanized Parry's utter dislike:

As long as Oscar [Wilde] was at Wilton he was the centre of attraction—always talking either to a solitary lady or a group of entranced listeners. Sometimes I thought him amusing, once or twice brilliant, often fatuous. His great gift is personal assurance—truly brazen when he is talking nonsense. For when he is quite tired out he trusts to his deliberate manner of slow enunciation to carry off perfectly commonplace remarks. One evening, when he was quite tired out with successive *tête-à-têtes*, the symposium in the smoking room formed itself as usual with George Wyndham for leader. G.W. really did all the talking, and all O.W. could do was to reiterate very slowly when reference was made to somebody or another: 'How old is he?' at which the assembly looked immensely interested.[30]

A comment in one of Parry's notebooks—'Aphorisms are the vapid platitudes of ordinary conversation disguised in the bombastical language of egotistical complacency'[31]—might easily have been inspired by this ordeal. Such pretentiousness combined with the façade of personal confidence and dilettantism left Parry detesting him by the end of the visit and his encounter with Mrs Wilde left an equally bewildering impression:

I made friends with Mrs Wilde, who is a very strange person who has abnegated all balance of mind and all self-control, but is at the same time kind, natural, and willing to serve her friends at any moment. Maude took a walk with her and thought her almost crazy with eagerness about spiritualism, suicide, and her singular views of the relations of the sexes. She says she never would think any worse of a married woman having children with strange men. For said she 'love comes and what can one do?'[32]

This sentiment Parry felt to be part and parcel of the moral decadence of the 'naughty nineties'. The events of the early 1890s only served to confirm his doubts. There was Parnell's love affair with Kitty O'Shea, which irreparably damaged the Irish leader's political career; this was soon followed by the Tranby Croft case, which opened the eyes of the middle-class public to the reckless habits of the Prince of Wales. Last but not least, there was the Queensberry affair in 1895—the scandal of the decade—in which Wilde was vilified and during which Parry afforded Wilde little sympathy.

During the summer months while these smart parties were in full swing, Parry gave much of his time to the preparation of the choral numbers for a production of *The Frogs* of Aristophanes commissioned by the Oxford University Dramatic Society and during August at Knight's Croft, while awaiting the completion of the *Dolgwandle* in Harvey's

[30] Diary, 27 July 1891.   [31] Notebook, ShP.   [32] Diary, 27 July 1891.

boatyard, he composed most of the instrumental music. By 19 October he was putting the final touches to the score, though he was forced to make a fair number of minor changes (mostly on the question of accents) after discussions with Lord Warkworth. C. H. Lloyd undertook most of the rehearsals until February 1892, when Parry stepped in to direct the orchestra. After a promising start, it seemed that the production was doomed to failure. Initially this feeling appears to have been caused by a misunderstanding disseminated by the *Pall Mall Gazette* who maintained that those with critical authority were disappointed with the music. 'It's silly to be affected by such things,' Parry wrote woundedly, 'but it did upset me sorely and I had a bad night of it.'[33] Furthermore, the two main dress rehearsals were a near fiasco with the chorus 'hopelessly at sixes and sevens all the while'.[34] Two new entr'actes were hastily written before the final dress rehearsal but even then Parry had to request a further run-through. The first performance in the evening of 24 February however, was an overwhelming success:

I pulled myself together with a fierce effort, and all the music, with but rare slips, went to perfection. The chorus really attended to me and the band played their very best. Even the Overture was vigorously applauded . . . Ponsonby as the Dead Man [was] unsurpassable, and very good as Euripides. Furse's Heracles was a little overdrawn but very funny. So, too, with Helbert's Dionysus. Charon was supremely good also—specially his lesson to Dionysus in the boat crossing the Styx, and of course that was received with shouts of joyful laughter. Talbot was excellent as Aeschylus and Lyon as Xanthius. The chorus was as pat and vigorous as conceivable and their tone splendid. There was grand enthusiasm at the end, and everybody had to go before the curtain.[35]

The final performance on 1 March was met with 'wild uproar' as everything was encored (even the Overture). So the happy memories of *The Birds* were recaptured and new friendships with younger faces were cemented. Undoubtedly the most significant of these was with the young Arthur Ponsonby, the third son of General Sir Henry Ponsonby, principal private secretary to Queen Victoria. After *The Frogs*, Ponsonby summoned enough courage to visit Kensington Square—'and that was the beginning of it all' wrote Ponsonby in his diary referring to his protracted courtship and marriage to Dorothea Parry whom he had met at Eton in June 1891 during the first performance of the college ode.

From an orchestral standpoint, *The Frogs* is not such a consistently striking and memorable score as *The Birds*. For instance, there is nothing to equal the final march or the radiance of the Entr'acte in Act III. The Overture to *The Frogs* is nevertheless extremely attractive, light-hearted, and delicately scored, as is the *Barcarole* (Entr'acte for Act I Scene 2).

---

[33] Ibid. 15 Feb. 1892.   [34] Ibid. 22 Feb. 1892.   [35] Ibid. 24 Feb. 1892.

The Introduction to Act III (subtitled 'Poet's tempers'), replete with quotations (including one appropriate 'tragic' reference to Beethoven's Fifth Symphony) is also very funny. The music for chorus, on the other hand, is more assured and is certainly amongst the best that Parry produced in his catalogue of incidental scores for Greek plays. As much can be said of the extended medley of the 'Chorus of the initiated', particularly with its recurrent tripping syncopated figure and the charming final section in A major ('Iacchus honoured of all men'). A number of the choral items are also highly amusing, notably the first chorus of croaking Frogs ('Brekekex koax koax'), a canon 4 in 1 at the unison as they cry out against Dionysus, and Chorus No. 13 which compounds the hilarity of the 'Poet's tempers' by including quotations not only from Beethoven's Fifth but also the 'Ode to Joy' from the Ninth.

Parry's links with Cambridge University were reinforced when, after attending a celebration in honour of Dvořák at the Cambridge Guildhall in June, he was invited to write a new choral work for CUMS to be done the following year. For this he decided to tackle Tennyson's Choric Song from 'The Lotos-Eaters', a poem derived from Book IX of Homer's *Odyssey* in which Odysseus' mariners, drugged by the honeyed fruit of the Lotos flower, resolve never to return to their homeland. Work on *The Lotos-Eaters* could not, and did not, actually begin until after completion of *The Frogs* at the very end of October 1891; it was, however, written extremely quickly—in Parry's opinion 'too fast to be good'.[36] By 15 November he had reached the end of the first complete sketch, after which the usual extensive revisions followed. Scoring took place during early December, some of it in the billiard-room at Highnam during a visit to see the havoc caused by a severe gale. On 10 December he took the entire score to Dannreuther: 'He approved very highly and said much of it was quite wonderful. I only hope it may "come off"— sometimes I'm much out of heart about it and at others that there are very good points in it for me.'[37] A week later, Stanford had his first scrutiny of the score. '[He] pronounced it "lovely"' Parry recorded in his diary, adding with a certain diffidence: 'May he keep in that mind!'[38]

Parry had informed Tennyson of his plans in November 1891. A reply came from his son, Hallam:

My dear old friend,

My father is delighted that Hubert Parry should set the 'Choric Song' in the Lotos Eaters. No-one could do it better. He also says 'Will you ask him to come and hear me read it if he can before he goes to work.'[39]

[36] Ibid. 31 Oct. 1891.   [37] Ibid. 10 Dec. 1891.   [38] Ibid. 18 Dec. 1891.
[39] Letter from Hallam Tennyson, 19 Nov. 1891, ShP.

A visit to Tennyson's home, Farringford, near Freshwater on the Isle of Wight was accordingly arranged in January as a welcome interlude to his Christmas holiday at Wilton. This was a rare chance to meet one of the most pre-eminent of poets and to learn his views on this latest setting of his verse. Indeed, the opportunity was made all the more poignant by Tennyson's death later that year (6 October). Parry's lengthy account of his stay at Farringford is full of curious and intriguing impressions:

He and his wife are very decrepit. Was introduced to her first; as she lay well muffled in furs and rugs on the sofa in the drawing room. The rest of the party were merely Hallam and his wife and their child. Tennyson turned up at tea time, and immediately fell foul of me for using the slang word 'awfully'—we had a little passage of arms and I confessed that I did not put much guard on my tongue, but used the words in familiar use and familiarly understood. He growled out: 'I'd sooner you said "bloody"', but was good-humoured in the end, though he often attacked me laughingly again on the same score. I sat with Hallam in his little snuggery at the top of the house for some time, and when Tennyson took his regulation half-hour's walk up and down the 'ball-room' before dinner, I walked with him. He brightened up considerably and seemed less deaf and decrepit than before. But he had an apparent penchant for coarse stories and harped much upon Brantôme and the French novelists; and told me at least one fearfully loathly item. At the same time he was savagely severe upon sins of sexual indulgence, especially on seduction. Talked about Hell and said he had been telling the new Bishop of Manchester he did not believe in it, and the Bishop retorted in a whisper that he didn't either. He also talked a lot about his critics, and the unfavourable way they had treated him, which seems always in his mind.[40]

This last observation substantiates Tennyson's sensitivity to hostile criticism from which he had been largely protected by his son. However, Tennyson had the reputation of being amiably sociable, and he much enjoyed declaiming his work for Parry in the library after a sumptuous dinner:

He soon set to work reading, and began with the 'Lotos-Eaters'. It soon struck me it was not at all a prepared or careful performance as he frequently ignored stops and ran phrases in[to] one another with little apparent sense; but he evidently greatly enjoyed it himself. The manner of reading is most strange—I should think something after the manner of the ancient professional reciter of epics and songs among barbarous people. He poised his voice rather high for average intoning, and raised and dropped it for special words. Moreover he was much given to a rather commonplace lilt; a sing-song method of enforcing the accents which rather jarred with my sense of the rhythmic variety of the written verse. If I had heard him read before I read his works I never should have thought him capable of such exquisite effects of subtle variety or the treatment of his metres. But it was a most interesting experience. After 'Lotos Eaters' he

[40] Diary, 2 Jan. 1892.

began talking about 'Maud' and then read a great deal of that too. Then he got discussing critics again, and the [worst] of sense of measure and rhythm in poets generally. Of Browning he said: 'It's strange; Browning was a musical man, and understood music, but there's no music in his verse; now I am unmusical and don't understand it, but I know there's music in my verse.' I asked him if he ever deliberately adopted alliteration as an effect. He said he often found that some passage sounded particularly pleasant and attractive, and when he came to examine, found it was some accidental alliteration—'but then I often take it out.' He kept talking till quite late, and then went off to say good-night to his wife. It's the most old-fashioned house I ever saw. With dim candle lamps in the passages, and four-posters, and hundreds of Mrs Cameron photographs, ugly paper and early Victorian furniture. But I slept well all the same!

The recitation continued the following day with the 'Wellington Ode' which Tennyson hoped his guest would also set, but Parry was less enthusiastic. With the poetry readings over, Parry played him his setting of 'The Lotos-Eaters', though he was uncomfortably aware that it meant little to him. Tennyson's response was, however, perfectly cordial though it appears that, from his declared lack of musical knowledge, he refrained from any significant criticism. Nevertheless, he did go on hoping that Parry would keep the 'Wellington Ode' in mind since he admired the composer's ability for the kind of grandiose and solemn effects he considered germane to the poem.

Tennyson's fondness for recitation almost certainly had an influence on the construction of Parry's work, for in printing the entire poem at the front of the vocal score, he insisted that the introductory stanzas prior to the Choric Song should be recited. This he made clear in a letter to Elgar in April 1902 weeks before a performance by the Worcestershire Philharmonic:

I hope you have got a good reciter to recite the preliminary stanzas [Elgar marked this with blue pencil]. That is a very important part of the business— and I always begin the soft clarinet bit directly the reciter finishes 'we will no longer roam'—That is if people will let me. For they generally applaud the reciter very warmly. I think they like that part of it best.[41]

The eight stanzas of the Choric Song are cast within a one-movement structure held together predominantly by material presented in a sylph-like introduction scored for clarinet, muted horns, and pizzicato lower strings. Functioning at intervals as a form of ritornello, this sets a mood of extraordinary lightness and delicacy of touch that prevails throughout. This is complemented not only by the transparent scoring and imaginative harmonic colouring (that finds its sources chiefly in Liszt and Wagner) but also by the often sparing use of the chorus (which is

---

[41] Letter to Edward Elgar, 19 Apr. 1902, HWRO 705.445:5247/8:2797.

frequently restricted to either purely male or female choirs) and the textural contrast with the soprano soloist. Moreover, the tonal design of the work is agreeably sensuous in its subtle employment of third-related keys, notably in the first of the soprano's three stanzas (3, 5, and 7) set in the sonorous region of G flat major/F sharp minor. In a letter to Sedley Taylor written in connection with programme notes for the first performance, Parry attempted to give an explanation of the work's design:

I tried to make the music a comment on the poem and to follow the alternation of the human longing for ease and repose and languorous self-indulgence, and the irrepressible impulse that reminds men that they were not meant to take their ease and do nothing in 'Lotosland'. The soprano solo is as it were the 'inner spirit' referred to in verse 2, and the chorus the human creatures with their protests against their haunting memories and their restless feelings of destiny driving them whither they would not. The moods are alternated and so are Solo and Chorus. But for the life of me I cannot put it decently. Perhaps the best way will be just to print the words of the poem, and have done with comment.
Forgive me for being so stupid.[42]

Certainly the seductive, morphetic atmosphere, particularly apparent in the stanzas for soprano, underlines Parry's interpretation of the human craving for 'ease, repose, and languorous self-indulgence', but perhaps more engaging is the way this reflects on the composer's own personality. None of the latter dispositions realistically formed part of Parry's philosophy, nor indeed lay within the remit of his musical language. His children frequently commented that he increasingly cultivated a spartan life-style. Yet in one sense *The Lotos-Eaters* gives us a rare glimpse of Parry the aesthete and hedonist who loved fine architecture, the countryside, travel, wine, cigars, good food, yachts, and (later) cars. Furthermore, it appears to suggest that, in spite of his self-imposed puritanism and profound humanitarian morality, he at times needed (and, moreover, could not deny himself) the artistic outlet of 'Lotosland' with all its sensuality and escapism. This is surely nowhere more apparent than in the final stanza 'The Lotos blooms' with its magical languid return to D major and the deliciously luxuriant final pages ('O rest ye brother mariners, we will not wander more') which bear witness to the breadth of Parry's harmonic vocabulary.

After several frustrating rehearsals which had presented numerous problems of choral declamation and orchestral balance, the first performance took place in Cambridge on 13 June under Parry's direction. 'The audience seemed to like it well enough,' he wrote

---

[42] Letter to Sedley Taylor, 4 June 1892, CUL Add. MS 6259.

somewhat reservedly in his diary, 'but strangely enough it evidently did not please F[uller] Maitland and Graves. I suppose they have made up their minds what sort of music I ought to write and object to my trying to widen my field.'[43] The number of performances over the next twenty years, which amounted to no more than half a dozen, also seemed to emphasize the public's lack of enthusiasm. Stanford performed it with the Bach Choir in 1896 and an American performance also took place in Milwaukee the same year. Elgar, who thought highly of the piece, performed it in Worcester in May 1902, and Vaughan Wlliams conducted a performance many years later (April 1912) in Petersfield. Since then it has been neglected until the Bach Choir under Sir David Willcocks gave what was probably the first performance in living memory in June 1985.

The other commission which occupied Parry during a large part of 1892 was very much the sort of music the public expected from him. While the finishing touches were being made to *The Lotos-Eaters* he was already busy with the drafts for his second oratorio *Job*. The original suggestion for this subject (with Robert Browning as the librettist) had been made by William Richmond (one of the work's most steadfast advocates) in October 1887 when Parry was still searching for literary material for his first oratorio. At that time the appeal of Dean Prideaux's work prevailed. However, at the end of August 1891 he gave more serious attention to it, devised (with considerable aggravation) a libretto, and sketched out a possible first scene. But owing to the more pressing duties of examining at Oxford and for the newly instituted music degree at London University, and of course the composition of *The Lotos-Eaters*, he was not able to resume work until January 1892. By 24 January he had completed the third and focal scene 'The Lamentations of Job' which he showed to Dannreuther. Dannreuther's enthusiasm gave him the energy to finish the oratorio despite increasing pressure of academic work, including the time he had to devote to the earlier chapters of his projected book 'The Art of Music' which Kegan Paul were anxious to publish the following year. It was therefore not until March that he was able to return to *Job* once again. Encouragement from Dannreuther persisted but his own view of the work deteriorated. 'It's flabby,' he wrote half-heartedly, '. . . and wanting in real vitality'[44], and this general dissatisfaction with the oratorio's construction continued to haunt him despite its instant acclaim by the public. In July 1894 Sedley Taylor wrote to him with the criticism that the allusion to Job's 'friends' (or 'comforters') had been omitted to the detriment of the work. Parry defended his original scheme, but conceded that there were defects:

[43] Diary, 13 June 1892.   [44] Ibid. 18 Apr. 1892.

I'm sure you will believe that I gave the scheme quite the uttermost consideration I was capable of, and searched out my materials with very great pains and concentration of attendance. I altogether failed to see how to make the friends musical. No doubt there is much beautiful literature, grand phrases which would adapt themselves splendidly to musical declamation which occur in connection with them; but in such matters the grand scheme has to be considered; and it is a most familiar experience of everyone who has to deal with making a work on a large scale that moments which in themselves seem most interesting and attractive have often to be abandoned because they cannot be brought into the scope of the whole; and won't fit with the pressing necessities of development and balance. To introduce the friends into the scheme would necessitate an absolutely different plan and a different principle of treatment. My whole plan would have to go overboard. The first part gave me great difficulty and I was quite aware of its deficiencies. The materials available at my disposal were not so full or so attractive. I did what I could with them. As it is, I always recast and rewrite to such an extent that it pretty nearly wears me out— and I don't think now I could do much with the first half.

I have considered the matter of breaking up the last chorus; but I am quite convinced what it might gain in some directions it could lose in continuity and development. I derived it with great care so as to get contrast, balance, continuity, and make it as much of the complete thing as I could. One always has to console oneself . . . that human efforts must always be imperfect in some respects, and all we can do is the best we can. I often 'squirm' over my own deficiencies—But I have to brave them as best as I can. In such a case as Job the scheme is too complicated to revise without complete rewriting and recasting.[45]

Though the omission of 'the friends' was not lost on some critics, it did not mar one of the most rapturous of receptions Parry ever enjoyed—one no doubt enhanced by the sensitive interpretation of Plunket Greene. This response was further reflected by performances at successive Three Choirs Festivals in Worcester (1893) and Hereford (1894)—a rare honour for any English composer. Yet conversely it was subject to some of the most acerbic words to flow from the pen of Bernard Shaw, who, after hearing *Job* sung by the Middlesex Choral Union in 1893, pronounced it 'the most utter failure ever achieved by a thoroughly respectworthy musician'.[46] Notwithstanding his prejudices and caustic remarks, Shaw genuinely believed Parry to have made an artistic error which he construed to be symptomatic of academia—'an attempt to bedizen a dramatic poem with scraps of sonata music'. Hence his suggestion that Parry would do better to 'confine himself to the composition of "absolute music"' and 'burn the score [of *Job*], and throw *Judith* in when the blaze begins to flag'. It seems, however, that few people recognized the essential drift of Shaw's criticism and ultimate

---

[45] Letter to Sedley Taylor, 20 July 1894, CUL Add. MS 6259.
[46] B. Shaw, *World*, (3 May 1893).

objective which was to eradicate the stultifying effects of oratorio—an effect he genuinely considered to have distorted Parry's own natural gifts for instrumental music.

In spite of Shaw's blistering attack, *Job* remained immensely popular, possibly even more so than *Judith*. In comparison with the earlier oratorio *Job* was altogether more concise in construction. The choice of literary material, though still faithfully (or perhaps one should say compliantly) biblical, indicates a conscious shift away from Old Testament histories towards philosophical allegory and may well have been influenced by the deep impression left by the text Bridges provided for Stanford's abstractly sacred oratorio *Eden* which Parry (as the dedicatee) had heard at the Birmingham Festival in October 1891. The structural design in *Job* of four individual but interdependent scenes, unified by common themes or leitmotivs, demonstrates a return to the well-tested ground of *Prometheus* and particularly *L'Allegro*. Because of its more concentrated organization, *Job* is much shorter (lasting no more than an hour) and immediately proved itself to be more practical for future festival programmes. Yet, even though there is merit in the design, the content of the oratorio is but another example of Parry's incapacity to create vivid musical images commensurate with the dramatic events and contrasts of a text, and consequently the same deficiencies that stultified *Prometheus* are also evident here. The representation of God (a taxing musical image by any standards!) is declaimed by a male chorus, replete with part-song homophony and regular rhythms (cf. the Demogorgon in *Prometheus*). As Dickinson has pointed out, 'the divine voice [is] too literary to be coherent'.[47] Satan unfortunately gives the impression of a flamboyant, mischievous rogue in a melodrama with whom it is almost impossible to equate the scale of cruelty and tragedy inflicted (Jupiter in *Prometheus* suffers from the same lapse of characterization). Such dramatic polarities and their successful depiction appear to have been beyond the musical imagination of Parry. Another of the work's lamentable failures lies in a sterile declamatory style that is rhythmically restricted in its delivery. The arioso passages are punctuated by frequent cadences that undermine the composer's attempts to sustain longer musical paragraphs. This is particularly apparent in the *Lamentation* whose only respite is the fine lyrically reflective section in D flat ('Man that is born of woman' Ex. 28*a*)). Indeed Parry's extraordinary inability to get the scale right can be seen by reading the text which is wildly unrealistic in its length. It is perhaps significant that the more meditative parts of the text elicited a more interesting response from Parry. The opening orchestral theme as a

[47] A. E. F. Dickinson, *Vaughan Williams* (London, 1963), 83.

representation of Job's holiness is a fine idea; the affecting pentatonicism of the Sheperd-Boy's music is pastorally evocative and harmonically inventive in its brief excursion to the flat mediant (Ex. 28*b*); and rather reminiscent of Brahms, is Job's calm affirmation of faith (Ex. 28*c*) sung against a yearning theme for muted strings. These may be inspired utterances displaying an affinity with the contemplative sentiments of *L'Allegro*, but they are isolated by much longer paragraphs of Mendelssohnian sanctimoniousness that seem merely perfunctory by comparison. Parry tried hard to unify his four scenes with recurring thematic material. A simple instance is the use of the oratorio's opening idea which not only concludes Scene 1 but also more symbolically Scene 4 (Ex. 28*d*)—an attempt by Parry to represent Job's sanctification and the restoration of his former blessed state. This material is subject to transformation. Towards the end of the first choral episode in Scene 2 ('The song of the shepherd has ceased') a version appears in the form of a lament (Ex. 28*e*). This transformation then forms the basis of Job's affirmation of faith (see Ex. 28*c*) and further references in Scene 3 ('I will say unto God') and Scene 4 ('Who shut up the sea with doors') which are interrelated by their similar harmonizations. The somewhat lukewarm material that is associated with God (Ex. 28*f*) becomes a broader lyrical statement enriched with diatonic dissonance and greater rhythmical freedom (Ex. 28*g*), and when it recurs at the end of Scene 2, Job's theme is also skilfully incorporated (Ex. 28*h*). Finally, throughout all four scenes, a second theme associated with Job undergoes numerous rhythmical and melodic modification (Ex. 28*i*), most discursively in the *Lamentation* (Ex. 28*j*).

Some writers on Parry have tended to over-emphasize *Job*'s indebtedness to Wagner, simply because leitmotiv technique is applied more comprehensively in the work than in, for example, *Prometheus*, and because few other English oratorio composers had yet embraced the method at that time. Its greater imagination and structural conciseness have been the subject of considerable eulogy by composers such as Elgar, Vaughan Williams, and Finzi. Sir Adrian Boult even described it as 'a work of the future'. Doubtless they all saw the work as a useful and significant prototype, and as the progenitor of genuinely new explorations in oratorio. However, the inescapable impression left by *Job* is one of stylistic limitation; a period-piece that pales in comparison with Elgar's more dramatic cantatas and oratorios such as *King Olaf* (1896), *The Light of Life* (1896), and *Caractacus* (1898) written only a few years later.

Twice during the summer of 1892 Parry found himself in Ireland, first to receive an honorary Mus.D. from Trinity College, Dublin as part of its Tercentenary celebrations. As the guest of Sir Robert Stewart he stayed in Dublin for a few days and drove up to Mount Merrion in order,

Ex. 28. *Job* (1892). *a* 'Man that is born of woman', Scene III ('The Lamentation of Job'); *b* the Shepherd-Boy's music, opening of Scene II; *c* Job's affirmation of faith, Scene II; *d* opening idea, Scene I ('Job's holiness'); *e* transformation of Ex. 28*d* at the end of the first choral episode, Scene II; *f* theme representing God, Scene I; *g* lyrical interpretation of theme representing God, Scene I; *h* combination of themes representing God and Job, conclusion of Scene II; *i* main secondary theme associated with Job, Scene I; *j* opening of 'The Lamentation of Job', Scene III.

(c) **Andante sostenuto**

JOB

str. (muted)

poco cresc.

The Lord gave,

(pizz.)

and the Lord hath ta - ken a - way;

(d) **Maestoso sostenuto**

Tutti

(e) **Meno mosso**

ob.

ch. (S.)

(The song of the

shep- herd has ceased in the land)

cont. over/

Ex. 28. cont.

as he recorded nostalgically in his diary, 'to revive my loving memories of the place'.[48] Within five weeks he was back at Mount Merrion again, this time as an interlude to a more protracted sailing expedition around Ireland with George Pembroke on the *Black Pearl*. Having put into Kingstown on the morning of 13 August, he visited the house in the

---

[48] Diary, 6 July 1892.

afternoon. There, in the gardens, he recalled the passionate romance of his early life:

I went all over it again and revived the memories of that delightful time when Maude and I were there alone, many years ago. A time I like to look back to almost more than any in my life. It was so peaceful and happily contented. It's funny though how I had forgotten the house and the lie of some of the rooms. But the garden—every inch of it—was perfectly familiar.[49]

The Irish coast, particularly the bays of County Mayo, thrilled him and he developed a love of the Irish landscape that remained with him for the rest of his life, a fact borne out by his constant return to the coasts of Counties Cork, Kerry, Clare, and Galway in his yacht.

During the voyage, when he was not distracted by the unpredictable behaviour of Lady Pembroke, he was preoccupied with ideas for an incidental score to Stuart Ogilvie's romantic tragedy *Hypatia* based on Kingsley's novel. The request had come from the actor-manager Sir Herbert Beerbohm Tree who wanted an overture, preludes and several entr'actes for his elaborate production at the Haymarket Theatre in January 1893. This was the first serious London theatre commission Parry had undertaken, and, perhaps aware of his own shortcomings when it came to stage music, it was one to which he gave a painstaking amount of attention and care. As one critic remarked—'In point of mere bulk—setting aside the questions of merit altogether—it has about as much matter in it as would make two symphonies.'[50] At first Parry was full of enthusiasm for the project since he much sympathized with the story of the beautiful fourth-century pagan philosopher, who, amid the strife between Christian fundamentalism, anti-Semitism, and those who hoped for the restoration of paganism, died for her beliefs. There was also much dramatic potential in the characters and situations. The scheming Jew, Issachar, produced a striking Wagnerian idea (Ex. 29*a*) which opened the overture. Orestes, the ambitious Prefect of Alexandria, inspired a fine processional march (Ex. 29*b*). The hopeless love for Orestes of Ruth, Issachar's daughter, is encapsulated by some impassioned music in Act 2 (Ex. 29*c*), and the Nitrian Monks are given some modal chant which pervades much of the incidental fragments. At one stage the chant material was designed as an important number with orchestral accompaniment, but much of this had to be scrapped after Tree made numerous major alterations. Consequently a substantial portion was condensed and sung in unison without any orchestral support.

Unfortunately Tree proved to be an infuriating collaborator and caused Parry's initial excitement to wane rapidly. In a letter to his wife,

---

[49] Ibid. 13 Aug. 1892.
[50] 'Dr Hubert Parry's "Hypatia" Music', *Musical Times* (1 Feb. 1893), 91.

Ex. 29. *Hypatia* (1892–3). *a* Issachar's theme; *b* main theme from Orestes' march; *c* Ruth's love for Orestes.

written on New Year's Day, 1893, he was quite frank about Tree's incompetence:

We had more rows yesterday. My temper is getting so bad I'm fit to do nothing but shout blasphemies at Tree's head before all the assembled public. But it's obvious it's only his hopeless impractical ignorance of all that concerns music. I daresay he means well enough. The worst of it is his stage management is so bad that you can never depend upon things going the same way twice; and so the music has to fit a shifting quantity. And then when through his own fault the music doesn't chime exactly, he literally shrieks and tears his hair on the stage. I was perfectly worn out yesterday afternoon, but I got a nap and so got through the evening's rehearsal fairly well. But I didn't get back here till nearly 2, and I expect the theatrical people must have been at it till 3 this morning.[51]

[51] Letter to Lady Maude Parry, 1 Jan. 1893, ShP.

Tree continued to demand changes during the final rehearsal, and at the eleventh hour even suggested the provision of new music to underpin an extensive scene. Utterly maddened by this display of ineptitude, Parry was heard to exclaim apoplectically: 'Look here, Tree, what you ought to do is to go out into the street and hire a damned barrel organ.'[52] Though Armbruster, the Haymarket's resident conductor, did his best to realize the composer's intentions, Parry was, not surprisingly, totally dissatisfied with the outcome. Fortunately the opportunity to recast some of the music came with a request from the Philharmonic Society for an orchestral work for their 1893 season of concerts. Parry had been forced to turn down similar commissions in both 1891 and 1892 under the pressure of *The Lotos-Eaters* and *Job*, but it was suggested that some of the music of *Hypatia* could be arranged as a Suite. Eventually five movements were cobbled together from the lengthy score, but, pressed for time, Parry was forced to adopt a completely haphazard tonal plan in order to preserve a sense of programmatic chronology. The scheme devised was: (i) Overture—Allegro con fuoco—E minor; (ii) Entr'acte—Hypatia and Philammon (from the Prelude to Act 3)—Andante—B flat; (iii) a market scene (which was intended to correspond to a Scherzo)—Allegro—G major; (iv) Entr'acte—Orestes and Ruth (from Act 2)—Allegretto—D major; (v) Orestes' processional march—A major. A sixth movement, taken from music preceding the final scene of Act 4 was also devised to function as a form of finale, but this was later rejected. The ordeal of Tree's production left Parry's nerves in tatters and when it was proposed that Mackenzie, the newly elected conductor of the Philharmonic Society's orchestra, should take the score in hand, Parry was appalled and threatened to withdraw it unless he could conduct himself. After a reassuring letter from the Society, Parry dispatched a reply explaining why he wished to direct the performance:

I am sorry such misunderstanding arose. Perhaps I was too easily harassed about it. But the truth is I have been so tortured time after time by having to attend performances of my own works when conducted by other people that I have been almost driven to vow I would never go to such performances again. It sometimes almost makes me quite ill. And I think if I was to sit and look on while this set of movements was being conducted for me at the Philharmonic, it would make a very convenient precedent for insufficient conductors to quote on other occasions as an excuse for keeping the stick to themselves at the expense of unfortunate composers. It's all very well when the works have been before the public for some time, and the composer's traditions are known; as would be the case with Sullivan's work or Stanford's Irish Symphony; but if a composer is not

---

[52] Graves, *Hubert Parry*, i. 351.

to conduct his own work when it is new, how is he ever to show how he wishes it to be rendered . . .?[53]

The first performance of the *Hypatia* Suite was given on 9 March, under, as the critic of the *Musical Times* noted, 'the proper conditions' and with notable success. The strain of the last few months, which included an arduous series of four lectures at the Royal Institution (entitled 'Expression and Design in Music'), had left Parry in a state of nervous exhaustion. Grove, writing from Sullivan's villa on the Riviera, congratulated him on the success of *Hypatia* but knew only too well that the whole escapade had been a 'fiery . . . trial'.[54] Grove also instinctively sensed that his most valued colleague was once again on the point of complete breakdown. 'I feel considerably guilty about it,' he wrote somewhat anxiously, 'because I can't help feeling that the constant College work must be a dreadful weight round your neck. Such pupils as Davies and Phillips are worth all your attention—but don't you think that such girls as Molly Carpenter (bless her)—with all their *niceness* . . . might be taken from you, and given to someone else?' Grove's exhortation at once went to the heart of the problem. Parry's belief in the College's 'mission' meant that he would hardly ever refuse a new pupil, or turn down any other necessary teaching. With deserving 'outsiders' such as Tovey, this was also the case. Indeed, aware of Parry's heart condition, Grove chafed at this inability to decline work, fearing that a serious relapse might prove fatal. After returning from Italy he wasted no time in recommending a trip to the continent. After receiving a gloomy prognosis from his doctors Parry reluctantly agreed. At the end of April he made his way to Naples where he found George Pembroke and the Brownlows, and for six weeks he convalesced aboard the *Black Pearl* visiting Rome, Pompeii, Sardinia, Minorca, and Corsica. Grove was then moved to explain his absence in an address to Parry's students that contained a grave warning:

You all of you know that he was very ill before Easter. But you are perhaps not aware how very serious his illness was. His doctors warned me then that unless his work were lightened, the worst consequences would probably follow. Now Dr Parry's lessons and lectures at College are only a part of his work. He is one of the greatest English musicians of to-day, and as such is constantly being applied to for oratorios or overtures, or other such little compositions: *and he never refuses*. It is a characteristic of his beautiful nature. For instance, he will never say *no* to any one of you who asks him for an extra ten minutes: never scold you or refuse to take you if you bring your work badly done. But I entreat you, don't do it. Those ten minutes—those little extra worries are death to him: they are the things that send hard-worked men to their graves. You must

    [53] Letter to the Philharmonic Society, 28 Feb. 1893, BL Loan 48:13/26.
    [54] Letter from Sir George Grove, 14 Jan. 1893, ShP.

carefully avoid them, or you may be responsible for something *very* serious indeed.[55]

But this was not simply an expression of profound concern on the part of a friend. Grove himself was also experiencing failing health and for some years he had been aware that the Directorship of the Royal College of Music must soon fall to someone younger. On 1 February 1891 a memorandum in his notebook read: 'N.B. to write to the Prince and tell him about the qualifications of C.H.H.P to succeed me.'[56] Three years before he would eventually retire, Grove had no doubts about his successor.

---

[55] Graves, *Hubert Parry*, i. 354.
[56] Id., *Life of Sir George Grove* (London, 1903), 364.

12

Climax

Directorship of the Royal College of Music

DURING the late spring and early summer of 1893 Parry was able to let the demands of the Royal College of Music recede into the background. The break was undoubtedly beneficial for it also gave him time for the gestation of a new orchestral commission for Worcester. By mid-June he was back in London, but apart from the exigencies of the Associated Board, and the need to see Ibsen's 'brilliant' *Enemy of the People*, he felt the need to withdraw to the quietness of Rustington where he spent much of the time sailing with his half-brother Sidney Gambier Parry. The initial ideas for his Worcester work had now crystallized into an overture which he dispatched to Goodwin's for copying on 14 August. The work, listed in the programme only as an 'Orchestral Piece' with no public allusion to its form or 'tragic significance', was subsequently given at the Worcester Festival on 13 September under the composer's direction. After a moderate reception, all save one of the critics were perplexed at the work's 'meaning'. The exception was Herbert Thompson, critic of the *Yorkshire Post*. Thompson, who had seen the superscription 'For an unwritten tragedy' added by the composer at the top of the manuscript score, believed that:

it would be suited admirably as a prelude to Shakespeare's *Othello*. A somewhat lengthy introduction, in which the wailing tones of the oboe give a feeling of sadness to the music, leads by a strong and vigorous crescendo to the allegro, the two chief subjects of which might be taken as representative of the hero and heroine of the tragedy. The first, with its passionate accents, would stand well for the jealous yet noble nature of the Moor; while the second, melodious and clinging, is equally fitted for Desdemona, whose purity and innocence are the more manifest by contrast with the atmosphere of jealousy and passion by which she is surrounded.[1]

Parry was amazed:

Thank you so much for sending me the cutting from the Yorkshire Post; and thanks also for writing it! It's wonderful how you manage to spy out so much of the construction and material of a new work at one hearing. And it's flattering to

[1] H. Thompson, *Yorkshire Post* (14 Sept. 1893); see also the papers of Herbert Thompson, BLUL MS 164/3.

my vanity that you hit so exactly on my intentions in the chief subjects. It's not only 'near the mark' but right on it. It really is very pleasant when one's ideas are so truly grasped; but it's very rare that the intention can be so exactly seized. I haven't looked at the Overture again. It's not even extracted yet from the parcel in which the Librarian of the Festival packed it. But I have my doubts whether I shall change the name by which it was first made known. I have such a strong feeling of the immensity of the tragedy of Othello that I hardly like to venture to associate any work of mine with it. It's a sort of presumption. It was the feeling that my attempt was not comprehensive or complete enough that made my choose another name.[2]

The first London performance of the *Overture to an Unwritten Tragedy* (but with no hint of its connections with Othello in the programme notes) was given in a revised version by the Philharmonic Society on 19 April 1894 under Mackenzie. It was well played, but, as Parry noted, 'not very well received'.[3]

In spite of its unenthusiastic reception, the *Overture to an Unwritten Tragedy* was the first of Parry's orchestral works to be published, though not until 1906. Why it should have elicited such a response is unclear, but its serious, discursive Brahmsian method may have jarred with a public more accustomed to the Parry of *Judith*, *Job*, and the *Hypatia* Suite. The design of the overture merits detailed analysis, particularly the manner in which the introductory lento plays an integral motivic role by first building to the allegro, and then, transformed, returning nostalgically in the coda. Moreover, motivically the introduction is also vital in presenting a seminal motivic cell (A—G $\sharp$—A) which is worked with an intellectual ingenuity and thoroughness similar to the first movement of Brahms's Second Symphony. Particularly discursive is the development or 'free fantasia' which, as Tovey aptly described, aims 'to assimilate the material of the introduction to the tempo and style of the Allegro'. This tendency is continued in the developmental treatment of the coda which subtly brings together elements of the introduction while alluding suggestively to the lyrical second-group material. Much of the potency of Parry's developmental process is due to a vibrant and varied rhythmical inventiveness. This is also prevalent in the frequent use of three-part contrapuntal textures which Parry had already explored to some extent in the 'Cambridge' and 'English' Symphonies but is here deployed with much greater confidence and aplomb. Once again this characteristic sonority seems to foreshadow the technique that Elgar was to take up so readily in his own orchestral works. Since the younger composer was to be found among the first violins of the Worcester Three Choirs orchestra during the overture's first performance, it seems highly

---

[2] Letter to Herbert Thompson, 22 Oct. 1893, BLUL MS 361/185.
[3] Diary, 19 Apr. 1894.

plausible that this work, with its swirling sequential passages, dramatic orchestration, and expansive lines, exerted a profound influence.

Before the end of 1893 Kegan Paul, Trench, Trubner & Co. Ltd at last managed to launch Parry's second book, *The Art of Music*, which had occupied him for several years and absorbed many of the lecture-series given at Oxford and the Royal Institution. As he had once stated in a draft intended for Grove's Dictionary in the 1880s, he had been much preoccupied with a theory of the evolution of modern music analogous with Darwinian concepts, and this book was largely the outcome of those explorations; indeed, when it was republished in 1896 it was renamed *The Evolution of the Art of Music*. Moreover, as volume lxxx of Kegan Paul's voluminous *International Scientific Series* this additional slant proved more consistent with the philosophical, political, and scientific contributions of Herbert Spencer's *The Study of Sociology*, Walter Bagehot's *Physics and Politics*, William Graham's *Socialism: New and Old*, and T. H. Huxley's *The Crayfish: An Introduction to the Study of Zoology*. The book was an instant success, and even Shaw, who once more felt obliged to vent his spleen on the academic establishment, admitted that it should not be left unread by any aspiring student of music. Although there are weaknesses, particularly in the earlier chapters where research was still in its infancy, one of its strengths is the way Parry was able to communicate abstract ideas in approachable language. This is done most successfully in the later chapters when he is dealing with contemporary repertoires. The discussions relating to the evolution of sonata form, for example, are extremely penetrating, not to say pioneering, and tell us much about the composer's own attitudes to the form in compositional terms. His essays on 'Modern Tendencies' (Chap. 13) and 'Modern Phases of Opera' (Chap. 14) are equally lucid, especially the discussion of Wagner's harmonic language and operatic procedures.

1893 closed on a solemn note with the death of his former teacher, Sir George Elvey, whose funeral took place at Windsor on 14 December. It was a sad, moving ceremony in which memories of his Eton days were inevitably recalled. Christmas was spent at Wilton, though miserably by all accounts. George Pembroke was unwell, and the company of Lady Pembroke was insufferable. 'One has to put up with a good deal from her ladyship and his aunt,' he wrote to Barclay Squire, 'but its gone almost beyond endurance. She is perfectly infernal when she gets started the wrong way—like a mad mule . . .'.[4] To add to his discomfort, Dorothea was confirmed in Salisbury Cathedral. This he deemed to have been the result of 'pressure of the world overcoming her somewhat slender

---

[4] Letter to Barclay Squire, 1 Jan. 1894, FzMC.

scepticism—and Maude being all for it from the practical point of view—and I having nothing to say one way or another.'[5] He was, however, revived by a visit to Longford Castle where he spent some happy hours in the company of Lady Radnor. As an energetic and ebullient amateur conductor, she persuaded Parry to compose a work for her ladies' string orchestra who intended to give a London charity concert at the St James's Hall in the summer. By 9 February the 'Lady Radnor' Suite was finished and was later included as planned in a programme on 29 June that also contained Boyce's Sonata No. 10 in E minor to which Parry had added a viola part. Lady Radnor conducted the work from memory and the 72 strings of her orchestra acquitted themselves superbly. The Suite, as the critic of the *Musical Times* remarked, 'proved a delightful work, in which the composer . . . caught the spirit of the eighteenth-century music with rare success.'[6] Undoubtedly the work reflects Parry's considerable interest in the Baroque period and his knowledge of dance-movement design. Yet it is by no means a pastiche, for there is much in the attractive and rich idiomatic string writing that is individual and distinctive. The lyrical Prelude (particularly the second idea) and the spacious Sarabande are fine instances of the composer's natural ear for string sonority. But the most tender and characteristic movement is surely the exquisite Slow Minuet where the muted timbres of divided strings seem to encapsulate (as did the central movement of Elgar's Serenade of 1892) the real affinity for string music that was to emerge with such a wealth of creativity in succeeding generations of British composers.

Though Parry's health had only marginally improved by the spring of 1894—he only just avoided peritonitis—the pressures of public life continued unabated. One disagreeable episode which did little to calm his nerves was a highly unpleasant row with the *Pall Mall Gazette* in March that was whipped up by Stanford in one of his worst quarrelsome tempers. The root of the problem lay in a strongly worded criticism of the Bach Choir's performance of Bach's *St Matthew Passion* written by Vernon Blackburn, which Stanford hoped would be rebutted by a reply from Parry. 'I insisted that it was always a great mistake to meddle with the press,' Parry wrote in his diary, 'and the private person always got the worst of it.'[7] A letter was eventually written, much to Stanford's delight, by Fuller Maitland, and Parry was persuaded (or as he put it— 'driven') to add his signature together with Grove, Mackenzie, Goldschmidt, and Parratt. This action he privately regretted for, as he ruefully recorded later: 'the letter simply "gives us away" at Stanford's

[5] Diary, 5 Jan. 1894.
[6] 'The Countess of Radnor's Concert', *Musical Times* (1 Aug. 1894), 536.
[7] Diary, 16 Mar. 1894.

bidding.'[8] From this last remark it is obvious that Parry was only too well aware of the accusations that would fly from the pens of those less charitable towards the 'academic' establishments—in particular Bernard Shaw. Indeed, Shaw, who considered the clique of London's musical institutions to be a mutual admiration society, produced his own letter for the *Pall Mall* in which, to his credit, he suspected that both Grove and Parry had been signatories under duress. His own murderous review of the concert was not published and was in fact suppressed by the *World* who took fright over its possible legal consequences. This contributed to Shaw's decision to resign from the *World* at the end of the season.

Nationally Parry's reputation as a composer was at an all time high—a fact acknowledged both by the conferral of an honorary DCL by the University of Durham and his election to the Philharmonic Society on 7 July 1894. However, there can be little doubt that his fame was largely due to the enormous success of his oratorios. In 1894 alone he attended performances of *Job* in Cardiff, Hereford, Leeds, and Liverpool, and *Judith* in Warwick and Chester. Conscious of this widespread appeal, Birmingham had once again made a request for an oratorio for their festival in October. Swept along, it seems, by public fervour, Parry agreed, though with his usual misgivings about the form. Before the project could get under way, he had to fulfil the obligation of providing a short anthem for the Festival of the Salisbury Diocesan Choral Association. For 'Hear my words, ye people' he put together a text drawn from Job, Isaiah, and the Psalms, finishing with Sir H. W. Baker's free adaptation of Psalm 150 'O praise ye the Lord' which later became well known as a hymn ('Laudate Dominum'). For the main choral sections of the anthem (sung by a body of 2,000 singers), Parry kept the technical demands to a minimum, and reserved the more modestly complex material for Semi-Chorus (of 400) and soprano and bass soloists. For instrumental support the organ was joined by a brass ensemble (provided by the band of the Royal Marines from Portsmouth) comprising cornets, trumpets, horns, trombones, euphonium, and tuba. Since the first performance on 10 May 1894, 'Hear my words' has formed a regular part of the repertoires of cathedral and good parish church choirs, using Novello's edition with organ reduction. However, it should be acknowledged that the effects Parry envisaged for the piece were the contrasts of massed voices, semi-chorus, and soloists which are today generally lost in performances with a small number of singers. Likewise, Parry's original scoring has rarely, if ever, been taken up.

When Parry embarked on his third oratorio, he had almost certainly decided that it would be his last contribution to the genre. In the press a

---

[8] Diary, 18 Mar. 1894.

counter-attack had been mounted against Shaw (though without naming him) whom, the critics feared, would discourage Parry from producing further oratorios:

In a review of Dr Parry's new book, 'The Art of Music,' which appeared in the *World*, the critic [meaning Shaw] was good enough to go out of his way to give that distinguished Englishman [Parry] advice as to his proper sphere in art. Leave oratorio writing, he said, and turn to instrumental music, of which you have given us such splendid examples. 'Job' and 'Judith' are not to be compared with the 'Overture on an Unwritten Tragedy' and the 'English Symphony'. Now these are the sort of thoughtless remarks which have lately become common in certain circles. It is the fashion to point the critical finger of scorn at our Cantatas and Oratorios; to call them 'Festival manufacture' . . . and in general to discourage the only national school of music we possess . . . We must have something new to sing. Our provincial Festivals, which multiply yearly, are the direct cause of a great deal of music being written, and, on the whole, adequately performed. It must be, therefore, in this direction that any greatness that is to fall to our lot will come upon us. We have no instrumental traditions, and but little adequate performance of instrumental music. The best of it is under foreign direction, and comes from foreign sources. Who, then, in their senses, could advise Dr Parry, or any other English composer, to turn away from all the national traditions and devote himself to those which we have derived from Germany?[9]

But, in spite of such pleadings, Parry had already conceded privately that, consistent with Shaw's advice, his excursion into 'dramatic' oratorio had been a mistake, for he had realized that no amount of theological unconventionality or philosophical allegory could of themselves bring about a transformation of the genre. Furthermore, he must also have been conscious of his shortcomings in the sphere of dramatic music and of his failure to make the epic gestures commensurate with either the violence of *Judith* or the sheer scale of *Job*. This failure, therefore, must have loomed large in his mind when confronted with the psychological tragedy of Saul—a drama for which he could ultimately provide only a reflective response. Hence, with no conviction in the work, the completion of *King Saul* for Birmingham became principally a matter of honouring his agreement to the Festival Committee.

If anything, the most impressive feature of *King Saul* is the well-contrived libretto which draws freely not only on the First Book of Samuel but also on other Old Testament texts including the Psalms and the Song of Songs. Indeed, in Act III the contemplative setting of Psalm 121 ('Let us lift up our eyes unto the mountains') sung by David and the chorus, the lyrical duet for Michal and David ('I am my beloved's and my beloved is mine' and 'Set me as a seal upon thine heart') from the

---

[9] 'English Music', *Musical Times* (1 Sept. 1894), 592.

Song of Songs, and their subsequent farewell accompanied by female chorus produced the most convincing utterances in the work. The merits of these seemingly more spontaneous passages are thrown into striking relief by the weaker characterization of Saul and the dramatically vapid portrayal of The Evil Spirit. Much of this weakness lay in the stiff declamatory style; but Parry's attempt to create a greater cohesion through more extensive use of representative themes also gave rise to a work which, with its more conventional choral approach, seemed unable to commit itself to either an older or a more contemporary style. In addition, the representative ideas and their ensuing transformations were of themselves simply not immediate enough for their dramatic contexts, and it was only in the more 'symphonic' environment of the Introduction to Act I that they were rendered musically satisfying. As the critic of the *Musical Times* wrote:

Dr Parry would have done just as well had he avoided representative themes altogether. I say just as well, because the rather elaborate use made of them in the present case is productive of neither good nor harm. The device should be so used as that it cannot be ignored—as that the purpose for which it is employed stands out clear, distinct, and unmistakable. But the *Leitmotiven* in 'King Saul' are, for the most part, obscured by other features more strenuous, direct, and powerful. I find the old plain oratorio fashion here mixed with a modern ingredient, and the two will not blend in required proportion. The old overpowers the new and practically annihilates it. Dr Parry may rightly conclude, I think, that his style and method do not assimilate with the dovetailing and inlaying process which seems to have such a charm for contemporary writers.[10]

The first performance of *King Saul* took place on 3 October under the composer's direction with Henschel in the main role of Saul. The first London performance, in a revised cut form, was given by the Royal Choral Society at the Albert Hall on 7 February 1895. Like *Judith* and *Job* before it, the oratorio was hailed as a triumph for English choral music. But the absence of any comment about the performance in Parry's diary clearly suggests his relief that the event was over.

He was almost certainly exhausted by the exertions of his last and longest oratorio, and, on returning to London, would have benefited from another period of rest. Yet there was a nervous atmosphere of expectancy at the College, for the Prince of Wales had accepted Grove's resignation in mid-October, and the College Council were eager to settle the matter of his successor. At a special meeting on 5 November, Grove delivered his formal resignation to the Council, after which, the names of five contenders were debated, one of which would go forward to the

---

[10] 'The Birmingham Festival', *Musical Times* (1 Nov. 1894), 743.

Prince. The five were Parry, Parratt, Stanford, Taylor, and Bridge. For some time many had considered Parratt as the most likely successor, but more recently his unpredictable personality had somewhat diminished his standing. As for Stanford, Grove found him 'tiresome'[11] (no doubt still smarting from the *Pall Mall* fracas), and, anyway, the Irishman was also in the running for the vacancy left by the death of Sir Robert Stewart at Trinity College, Dublin. As it transpired, Grove was not disposed to Stanford's appointment there either, favouring instead George Robertson Sinclair, though the job eventually went to Prout. Frederick Bridge also seemed a bright prospect, but perhaps did not carry quite so much public recognition as Parratt. As for Parry, it is clear that Grove wanted him to be appointed, but a question mark lay over his health.

Nevertheless, good health or bad health, the Council, chaired by Prince Christian, unanimously recommended Parry. Delighted at the result Grove wrote: 'He is the best, but O my dear—in many things he will be very poor—no backbone, no power of saying no, or of resisting those whom he likes.'[12] Parry accepted but it was decided not to publicize the appointment until six weeks before he was due to take office. But once publicized, there was unstinting congratulation from all sides. Grove, saddened by his own retirement, was heartened by Parry's support and friendship—a feeling he intimated to Louie Heath: 'Parry is to succeed me and as I talked to him yesterday, the sight of his dear young face and his cheery way comforted me in a way I cannot "exclaim" to you. I have been sadly under a cloud for three months past, and now it seems to be lifting. It is far the best appointment that could be made . . .'.[13] And to Florence Coleridge he wrote warmly: 'I am most encouraged by Parry's appointment. He has all my virtues and others which I never could aspire to. It depends upon the pupils to make him an excellent Director. If they put the same confidence in him that they have put in me, he will rise to the occasion; so please remember *that* and act upon it . . .'.[14] In accepting the post, Parry must have sensed that he had arrived at the peak of his vocation. Yet he was also full of foreboding at the responsibilities the post would bring. When questioned by the editor of the *Scottish Musical Monthly* he replied: 'I cannot say the appointment makes me in any degree jubilant, for the loss of such a friend as Sir George Grove, and the irreparable gap his retirement will make at the College, makes everyone connected with the place feel depressed'.[15] This

[11] Percy M. Young, *George Grove* (London, 1980), 241.
[12] Ibid.
[13] Charles L. Graves, *Life of Sir George Grove* (London, 1903), 416.
[14] Ibid.
[15] 'Dr Hubert Parry', *Scottish Musical Monthly*, 2/16 (Jan. 1895), 75.

he also expressed in a sympathetic letter to Grove written from Wilton during the Christmas vacation:

I can't express myself about the situation . . . I realize too vividly and painfully what it must be to you, with all your energies and sympathies fully alive, to be giving up a thing so engrossing and valuable as the College work. It's too painful to speak of. It may be a comfort to you to feel how intensely everyone from the topmost Professor to the smallest boy feels your going. I hope it is. I feel very strongly that my first efforts will be enveloped in gloom! It will be a long while before the place regains any of its cheerfulness . . .[16]

The offer of the position of Directorship to Parry not only affirmed his achievements as a composer, scholar, and teacher, but also, and more importantly, was testimony to his extraordinary charisma. He was an eminently likeable man, generous and open. All those who came into contact with him found it impossible not to be touched and changed. This could be felt in a composition lesson, a history lecture, or rehearsal. He was able to engender aspiration, vision, sympathy, and self-belief. His manner was unfrightening, paternal yet youthful, and without a hint of condescension and quickly put the young at ease. Publicly he radiated a feeling of immense warmth, of happiness, geniality, and an infectious love of life. Choruses and orchestras, amateur or professional, throughout the country responded to his urbanity and abounding interest in their well-being and purpose. Indeed he would stop at nothing to promote the cause of music as an essential facet of the nation's strength, and was fiercely protective of musicians who were struggling to make their way. His conscientiousness and selflessness were unshakable. Failing to attend a concert, a lesson, or a lecture rankled, for he hated to disappoint those who depended on him. Motivated by this sense of duty he fought continuously against his ill health and did everything possible to prevent it from impeding his work. Only his family and his closest colleagues knew anything of his heart condition. That was how he wished it to be. Some of his pupils, notably Vaughan Williams, perceived that behind the face that Parry presented to the world there lay a nervousness and depressive temperament, but the deepest impression that remained with him was the aura his teacher exuded. In the obituary for Parry written for the *Music Student* in November 1918, he remarked:

Walt Whitman says: 'Why are there men and women that, while they are nigh me, sunlight expands my blood?' Parry was one of these. You could not hear the sound of his voice or feel the touch of his hand without knowing that 'virtue had gone out of him'. It would not have mattered what we went to learn from him— it might have been mathematics or chemistry—his magic touch would have made it glow with life. Half-a-dozen of his enthusiastic eloquent words were worth a hundred learned expositions.

[16] Graves, *Life of Sir George Grove* 416–17.

Arthur Ponsonby was similarly awestruck in his company and recalled an occasion in which Parry had conducted one of his own works in St Paul's Cathedral: 'I see most vividly now that fine shaped head and that look of solemn inspiration as he lifted his baton—an unforgettable figure of power and dignity, a perfectly appropriate physical frame for the whole mental and moral attitude of his life, a real conductor of human aspirations leading men to the highest they could reach.'[17] It was such personal attributes as these—a magnetic personality, an encyclopaedic knowledge, the ability to stir the imagination, and the capacity to lead— that set him apart from other contenders. In order to revitalize the visionary fervour that had been, twelve years earlier, the driving-force behind the foundation of the College, the institution needed a man of charismatic stature; Parry was all this and more.

If there were any misgivings about Parry's appointment to the Directorship of the Royal College, they were founded on a fear that, with the time-consuming duties demanded by the post, he would have less and less time to devote to creative work. The *Musical Times*, for one, expressed such an apprehension, as did Stanford in a letter written shortly after the news of Parry's appointment had been publicized:

It is not in my heart to 'congratulate' you, because I think your music much more important than any office in the world, and I only hope you really won't let it interfere with your private work and that you will make them give you lots of devils to do the grind. You know you may rely on me to help you in any way I can, in and out of season . . . Dear old man, it is the greatest pleasure I could have to be under your thumb.[18]

These doubts were well justified, for within a matter of weeks the College found itself in a pressing financial situation. With the move to the new building and the necessity of employing extra domestic staff, the savings of some £7,000 accumulated by Watson and Grove had evaporated. Immediately Parry had to instigate major economic changes, the most draconian of which was the dispensing with terminal examinations in favour of a single annual one. Bridge and Taylor were enraged by this decision, but had to accede reluctantly. One other, more delicate area for Parry was Stanford's opera expenditure; 'that', wrote Grove, 'will want all Parry's resolution and tact, God help him!'[19]

On 7 January 1895 Parry delivered his first address to the students in his new position. It was inevitably devoted to the contribution of Grove, and to personal reminiscences of their first professional collaboration, the *Dictionary of Music*. In honour of Grove the scholar, as well as the administrator, Parry organized a special concert of Schubert's music;

[17] A. Ponsonby, 'Brief Glimpses', unpub., ShP.
[18] Graves, *Hubert Parry* (London, 1926), i. 355.   [19] Young, *George Grove*, 247.

'the concert depends on your presence,' Parry wrote, 'I want to have the String Quartet in D minor; the String Quintet; some pianoforte pieces and some songs. I do hope you will be able to come.'[20] It was an appropriate farewell gesture to the former Director who was about to begin his next scholarly task of writing a book on Beethoven's nine symphonies.

It seems nothing short of the miraculous that, with the substantial increase of more onerous public responsibilities (not to mention those of the Associated Board and the degrees at Oxford and London Universities), Parry was able to find time not only to compose, but also continue to hear music new to the London concert scene. Humperdinck's *Hänsel und Gretel*, staged at Daly's Theatre, was playing to packed houses. Parry attended two performances and was entranced. 'I enjoyed it immensely', he wrote, 'A most lovable affair and beautifully done. Music almost all inspired by Meistersingers etc.'[21] Later in the year he heard the first English performance of Smetana's *Bartered Bride* at Drury Lane, met Richard Strauss at the Imperial Institute, and looked on with admiration not only at Richter, whose concerts were still attracting large crowds, but also Nikisch who was making a name for himself, and Henry Wood who scored a success with the first of his Promenade Concerts at Queen's Hall.

Compositionally the last few months of 1894 had been given over to the completion of two smaller assignments that Novello agreed to publish in 1895. The first was a series of delicious miniatures which were published as *Twelve Short Pieces for Violin and Piano* (and, for commercially expedient reasons, were divided into three sets). These pieces had been written over a number of years for purely domestic enjoyment and had been designed to suit the technical proficiency of Gwendolen and the Lushington sisters who were learning the violin; the dedication to Maude, Gwen, and Dolly (with the exception of the very first piece, *Idyll*, to 'K.M.', who may well have been Kitty Maxse, née Kitty Lushington) emphasizes their intimate nature. Moreover, the mixture of tenderness, nostalgia, melancholy, light-heartedness and simple melodiousness makes for attractive variety which is rare in pieces at this level of technical assurance. In terms of structure they are likewise uncomplicated, forming neat ternary designs resembling earlier small-scale movements found in, for example, the 'Lady Radnor' Suite. Some pieces are decidedly reminiscent of other composers. The 'Romance' (Set I No. 2) and 'Capriccio' (Set II No. 3) are successful pastiches of Dvořák, while the 'Romance' (Set II No. 2) shows an indebtedness to Schumann, and the central section of 'Capriccio' (Set III No. 3) almost

---

[20] Letter to Sir George Grove, 27 Feb. 1895, ShP.
[21] Diary, 11 Jan. 1895.

paraphrases the opening of Franck's Violin Sonata. Most nostalgic are the gentle 'Idyll' (Set I No. 1) and the soaring phrases of the 'Romance' (Set III No. 2) which seem to encapsulate everything that is 'English' about Parry's melodic phraseology (Ex. 30). There is also the wonderfully introspective, almost tearful 'Lullaby' (Set I No. 4), which contains material in its central section that was used later in the corresponding section of the 'Sarabande' of the posthumously published *English Suite*.

The other obligation to Novello concerned a genre which Parry had largely neglected for almost ten years. Apart from 'The Maid of Elsinore', composed for Harold Boulton's *Album of New Songs* in 1891, and 'Rock-a-bye', a children's ditty written for the Columbian Exposition in Chicago in 1893, he had not had occasion to bring together a new collection of songs in the same vein as the two sets of *English Lyrics* published between 1885 and 1886. However, by the end of 1894, there were enough songs to warrant a new set which were then dedicated, in admiration, to Harry Plunket Greene who performed several of them at a recital on 14 December at St James's Hall with Leonard Borwick. By comparison with the first two sets, this new collection of lyrics is less consistently good, though there are a number of fine songs amongst them. The first of the two settings of the Jacobean poet, Lovelace—'To Lucasta, on going to the Wars'—is a delicate, through-composed interpretation of the three four-line strophes; the other, 'To Althea, from Prison' is less strong, except for the robust opening material. The setting of 'If thou would'st ease thine heart', by Beddoes, an early Victorian poet much influenced by Elizabethan and Jacobean writings, is a fine example of the modified strophic design that Parry often favoured, and one enhanced by the constant change of tempi and piano texture. 'Why so pale and wan', by another Jacobean, Sir John Suckling, is less distinguished, though it might well have benefited from the orchestration for strings, double woodwind, and horns which was sketched but never

Ex. 30. Theme from *Romance* (Set III No. 2); Twelve Short Pieces for Violin and Piano (1894).

completed. Perhaps the finest and by far the most original song in the collection is 'Through the Ivory Gate', a setting of a text by his old Eton friend, Julian Sturgis. It is perhaps odd that this song was not scored, for its texture and delivery readily suggest a dialogue between voice and orchestra (and indeed one that foreshadows the whole manner of Elgar's vocal and orchestral technique in his later choral works). The vocal line is predominantly declamatory rather than lyrical and relies largely on the thematic support of the piano for continuity. Much of the material is reminiscent of the inspired outpourings of *L'Allegro*, particularly the rapturous interaction of the central passage beginning 'Then answer had I made' with its poignant appoggiaturas in the piano. This, together with a beautifully modified restatement of the opening music, makes for one of Parry's most interesting contributions to the art of song-writing. Perhaps most telling about this song, however, is its sense of personal intimacy. As Parry grew older he became more and more attracted to the poetry of his British contemporaries, and though, in many cases, their verse inclined dangerously towards insipid Victorian sentimentality, he frequently experienced a personal empathy with it. As regards Parry's partiality to Sturgis's work, Colles stated that it 'often gave him [Parry] the things he wanted to talk about, and that became more essential . . . than the pure beauty of rhythmic language which had first attracted him to the Elizabethans.'[22] In 'Through the Ivory Gate' Sturgis attempted to capture something of 'immortal friendship', albeit as a dream. For Parry this sentiment undoubtedly had a private significance. An ideal, platonic, male friendship, permanent, unfickle, and always close at hand, was something for which he yearned to replace the growing indifference of his marriage. It was to this theme of 'lost love'—a recurrent idea in Sturgis's poetry—that Parry was to return again and again as a private means of imparting his intense inner loneliness as well as the wish to withdraw from the public gaze.

Parry had every intention of devoting the best part of 1895 to the composition of the work he had been commissioned to write for the Leeds Festival in October. Since the year also marked the Bicentenary of Purcell's death, many cathedrals, choral festivals, and concert series were taking the opportunity to revive Purcell's little-known output. Parry considered that the occasion would be a rare chance to pay homage to the great Baroque genius in an ode. As regards the libretto, he had been impressed by Bridges' contribution to Stanford's *Eden* in 1891, and since then he had been privately entertaining the idea of a collaboration. Bridges was sympathetic:

[22] H. C. Colles, 'Parry as Song Writer', *Essays and Lectures* (Oxford, 1945), 60.

My dear Parry,

Squire has written to me to say that you might be writing a Cantata or short choral piece for the Leeds Festival next year and that you would do an 'Ode to Music' which might also serve for the Purcell Festival, and that you [would] like to hear my ideas on the subject.

I have yesterday sent in a piece of work to the publishers which has engaged me all the summer, so that I am quite at leisure to think this over.

I write at once to you to say how glad I should be to do it with you, lest you might think I was indifferent. Also to prevent there being any misunderstanding. I should wish you to understand that whatever passes between us I shall never consider you in the least bound but free to give up the notion at any time.

On my side I can't promise to have the requisite inspiration to order, but I see a splendid opportunity for something new, and popular. My idea is to show music in its various relations to the passions and desires of man: as something supernatural mysterious and consolatory: which it always is to me. Also it seems to me that something quite new might be done in the music by the *blending* of the different attitudes of mind or spirit, instead of their merely *isolated* contrast as in Handel's Alexander's Feast.

If you have any idea on the subject send me a line. I shall think it over and if I get any lights will write again in about a fortnight.

I could not get to hear Saul and the papers don't give one much information. I hope it satisfied you, and that you are not overdone.

yours ever,
R Bridges

P.S. If a definite musical scheme presents itself to your imagination I could work my stuff to fit it, and this recommends itself to me as a satisfactory procedure.[23]

Bridges was evidently much excited by the idea of the ode for within a week of his first letter, a second was written setting out a scheme for the work describing not only its literary content but also its basic musical shape as well. In it he proposed a celebration of the beauties of nature, a contemplation of the mysteries of death, including a lament (in this context on the premature death of Purcell himself) and a choral dirge for the dead artist, thereafter passing into triumph, joy, and dance with, as Bridges described, 'the theme being the identification of music with the religious (or whatever you call it) spirit, which corresponds with the aspirations at the bottom of the social movements of our time'.[24] Bridges envisaged only one soloist, a soprano, who would be the personification of sorrow; this he also believed would make the work more accessible for smaller choral societies. Parry, though agreeing with many of the essential aspects of Bridges' proposals, had in mind a rather different overall scheme which explored the theme of 'Man, Woman, and Music'

[23] Letter from Robert Bridges, 10 Oct. 1894, RUL MS 1399/2/2.
[24] Letter from Robert Bridges, 16 Oct. 1894, ibid.

involving several soloists. Bridges soon submitted two further plans, the second of which attempted to incorporate both conceptions. Eventually a compromise was reached in which the essence of Bridges' original plan was preserved though room was made for a passionate duet (soprano and tenor) on the theme of Universal Love, while the personification of sorrow would instead be taken by a bass solo. The scheme of the ode was later included by Bridges in the publication of the poem in 1896 by Elkin Matthews (pp. 19–20):

I. An invitation to Music to return to England: that is, in the sense that England should be again pre-eminent for music above other European nations, as she was in the 16th century. The three English Graces are Liberty, Poetry and Music.
II. Music invited in the name of Liberty: the idea associated with the forest.
III. Music invited in the name of Poetry: the idea of Poetry associated with pastoral scenes and husbandry.
IV. The Sea introduced as the type of Love; isolating our Patriotism, and making our bond with the rest of the world.
V. The national intention gives way to wider human sympathies. Music here considered as the voice of Universal Love, calling and responding throughout the world. A national meaning also underlies, in respect of our world-wide colonisation.
VI. Sorrow now invites Music; asserting her need to be the chiefest. The occasion being the celebration of Purcell's genius, her complaint implies a call for some musical lament for his untimely death.
VII. Music replies with a dirge for the dead artist; offering no consolation beyond the expression of woe.
VIII. The chorus consoled praise dead artists, and pronounce them happy and immortal.
IX. A picture of the ideal world of delight created by Art.
X. The invocation repeated, with the idea of responsibility of our colonisation.

Bridges began work on the text in November and proceeded cautiously, constantly referring back to Parry for instructions on the type of verse required. 'If you want me to go on,' he wrote insistently, 'write soon and tell me if you prefer smoother and less individual rhythm. I shall not do any more till I know from you what sort of rhythm you want . . .'.[25] Unfortunately Parry's response to Bridges' enquiries became more and more delayed as the yoke of his administrative responsibilities at the College began to mount. For Bridges the situation became increasingly frustrating. On Christmas Eve he wrote again, this time in the hope of enticing Parry to his home at Yattendon where they could 'tackle the matter in detail'. But familial duties at Wilton and Highnam took priority, especially since both George Pembroke and Ernest Gambier Parry were unwell. Parry was, however, able to supply

[25] Letter from Robert Bridges, 19 Nov. 1894, ibid.

Bridges with basic directives over the Dirge, and most specifically for the soprano solo. With this Bridges attempted to sketch out suitable verses. By the end of the year he had completed the magnificent words of the Dirge ('Man born of desire | Cometh out of the night') and in full flow was inspired to produce perhaps the most memorable part of the poem which he jotted down in a letter to Parry of 2 January 1895:

> Rejoice ye dead, where'er your spirits dwell,
> Rejoice that yet on earth your fame is bright,
> And that your names, remember'd day and night,
> Live on the lips of those who love you well.
>
> Tis ye that conquered have the powers of hell,
> Each with the special grace of your delight.
>
> Now ye have starry names,
> Behind the day ye climb
> To light the glooms of Time
> With deathless flames.[26]

After this emotional climax, Bridges' intention was to sum up the work in two stanzas with 'a description of ideal art'[27] and a triumphal conclusion. 'I think you [would] be sympathetic with this,' he stressed to Parry, 'I don't know that it has ever been done: and I think I can do it in objective terms.' But though Parry admired 'Rejoice ye dead', the finale was to prove a sticking-point in spite of Bridges' numerous suggestions.

Decisions were once again put back by other pressing business—a delay which undoubtedly caused Bridges considerable vexation. But it was not simply pressure of work at the College which prevented Parry from progressing with the ode's text, for both the Leeds Subscription Concerts and the Philharmonic Society had made requests for orchestral works. Parry was, of course, in no position to furnish either institution with a new work, but instead offered Leeds a revised version of the 'English' Symphony and the Philharmonic (who had erroneously heard rumours of a new symphony) a revised version of the 'Cambridge'. Revision of the 'English' Symphony entailed an extensive overhaul of the first movement together with the addition of trombones, and a replacement pair of variations in the finale. This work he managed to complete during December 1894 and January 1895, but gathering the performing material together proved to be an irksome experience. With the symphony still unpublished, and yet remaining very popular, the manuscript score and parts had been lent out on numerous occasions only to be lost. As Parry explained to William Hannam, the secretary of the Leeds concerts:

[26] Letter from Robert Bridges, 2 Jan. 1895, ibid.
[27] Ibid.

That 'English' Symphony is one of the most unfortunate pieces of MS I ever had to deal with. The first score was lost, and a fresh copy made in a hurry (for a performance) from the parts, and now the parts are lost! I lent them to a friend and he without giving me any notice has disappeared up the Nile, and his relations can't find any trace of the parts. I am having fresh ones made as fast as I can . . .[28]

Fortunately the old parts were eventually found, and the performance, played by Henschel's Scottish Orchestra and conducted by the composer, was well executed. As for the 'Cambridge' Symphony, Parry decided to use the opportunity to compose a completely new finale. Much of the work was done during February, though the final touches dragged on into May. Writing to Berger at the Philharmonic he declared: 'My revision [of the symphony] has been done under almost insuperable difficulties, for it's almost impossible for me to get more than a casual half hour in any part of the day for my own work. The score of the last movement has consequently only just gone to the copyist . . .'.[29] The new version of the 'Cambridge' Symphony was performed at the penultimate Philharmonic concert of the season on 30 May under Parry's baton. Curiously it was announced as Symphony in F (No. 3) in accordance with a letter Parry had sent to the Philharmonic in January, though in a list of Parry's orchestral works published later, the numbering reverted to its original chronological position.[30]

With these interruptions it was not until the end of February that Parry was able to resume work on the ode. By this time Bridges was anxious: 'If you wish to give the Ode up,' he wrote in the postscript of his letter of 25 February, 'do not hesitate to say so—just now I should profit of the freedom'.[31] Parry, rather contritely, made clear his determination to finish the work, but admitted that, though he admired much of the text, he had found some parts less congenial from a musical point of view, and had consequently been struggling with them for the best part of two months. Bridges immediately attributed this to the lack of communication:

Did it not strike you that the two numbers which you like best *are those which I wrote* after *consultation with you*, and the one which you like the best of those is the one *concerning which you gave me a pretty good notion of what form you would like?*

Surely if you have now been wrestling with its awkwardness for 2 months you could write and tell me *where the chief hitches are*—so that I may get rid of

---

[28] Letter to William Hannam, 4 Jan. 1895, McUL.
[29] Letter to the Philharmonic Society, 17 May 1895, BL Loan 48:13/26.
[30] see 'Hubert Parry', *Musical Times*, (1 July 1898), 446.
[31] Letter from Robert Bridges, 25 Feb. 1895, RUL MS 1399/2/2.

them. And *which lines and passages you would like altered* and what rhythm *you wish for in their place.*

There!

Now don't *write* anything till we have gone over details together.[32]

But a meeting was not to be. Instead there was a three-week lull in their correspondence before the exchange of ideas began to intensify once more.

Musical ideas for the ode, sketched at the beginning of 1895, began to take more definite shape at the end of March, and with this clearer vision of the work, Parry's correspondence with Bridges began to include numerous instructions for changes—mainly structural requirements for the sake of musical unity. Indeed a comparison with the published poem reveals the considerable number of alterations that were made. For instance Parry demanded that the fourth section ('The sea with melancholy war') needed to be more obviously tripartite in design with a recapitulation of the turbulent opening section; this necessitated the omission of many of Bridges' original lines. A similar demand was made with regard to the end of the second section ('Turn, O return!') where, as a spacious affirmation of the ode's key (F major) he required the return of the opening choral material from the first section ('Myriad voiced Queen'). For the bass solo (section six) a decision was made to use the last four lines of the second verse as a refrain to both stanzas: this proved to be a masterstroke in terms of the musical effect. The Dirge, like section four, was also subject to considerable surgery, and much to Bridges' dissatisfaction, a large portion of stanza two was excised. As for the finale, matters still remained undecided, for Parry was not wholly convinced of the necessity for two further sections after the consolatory mood of section eight. Bridges did all he could to provide a satisfactory conclusion, but Parry found the end textually flat, so at the last, sections nine and ten were heavily adapted. With such extensive omissions, particularly in the Dirge, Bridges felt that the essence of the poem—the allusions to Purcell—had become too obscure and remote. Hence for musical purposes he agreed to Parry's more general title of *Invocation to Music*, but when the original poem was published the following year he restored the title he had first envisaged—*Ode to Music written for the Bicentenary Commemoration of Henry Purcell.*

During June and July Dannreuther was shown the *Invocation to Music* as it slowly but surely progressed and he expressed himself particularly pleased with the Dirge and following chorus. In August Parry made a frantic effort to finish the work and to score it before going off to the Gloucester Festival to conduct *King Saul*. Thereafter he hoped to clear

[32] Letter from Robert Bridges, 5 Mar. 1895, RUL MS 1399/2/2.

his mind with a sailing trip to the Devon coast accompanied by his friend C. H. Lloyd.

The first performance of the *Invocation* took place in Leeds on 2 October with Parry conducting. It was a great success and the chorus acquitted themselves splendidly. Then attention moved to London where the ode formed part of a series of celebrations in honour of Purcell during the latter part of November. At the Lyceum Theatre Stanford conducted a performance of *Dido and Aeneas* with students from the Royal College. On the following day (21 November) a grand service of commemoration took place in Westminster Abbey which Parry attended, joining Stainer, Stanford, Grove, Mackenzie, Bridge, Cummings, and Squire in procession to Purcell's grave where wreaths were laid. In the evening, to complete the celebrations, the *Invocation* was given by the Royal Choral Society in the Albert Hall. Parry received an ovation.

A letter written to Hannam a few weeks before the Leeds Festival reveals that Parry's feelings about the Ode were mixed: 'Some of the words are indeed extremely fine. Parts do not satisfy the poet himself. He [Bridges] got bored with it, and the result in those cases was not at all sympathetic to my mind. But I am most thankful for the parts in which he turned out such noble lines and thoughts as the Dirge.'[33] Yet, despite the difficulties, Bridges' verse appears to have truly inspired Parry. The chorus material has a breadth and grandeur which seems to anticipate his later ceremonial vein. This is revealed in the broad opening chorus ('Myriad voiced Queen') which returns even more majestically in the coda after section two of the poem. The tempestuous fourth section is also rich and effective, especially in the more tranquil central passage where Parry gives special attention to word-painting. The Dirge had a particular significance for the composer in that it was unofficially dedicated to the memory of George Pembroke who had died in the late spring. Bridges' text, largely derived from the cynical questioning of Ecclesiastes, therefore had a particular poignancy and solemnity. Its meditative tone is expressed primarily with a dignified homophony that seems hauntingly to recall the mood of Purcell's own 'Man that is born of Woman' from the Funeral Music to Queen Mary. The impact is enhanced by a tonal instability, fluctuating between A flat and F minor, which interacts powerfully with the C major of the preceding bass solo (section six) and the stable A flat at the end of the section ('Rejoice ye dead').

Commentators who attended the Leeds and London performances were quick to note the consistently high quality of the solo material which is among the finest Parry ever wrote. The brazenly Miltonic flavour of the third section of the poem for tenor ('Thee fair Poetry oft

[33] Letter to William Hannam, 5 Sept. 1895, McUL.

hath sought') rekindled that power of invention which had produced the luscious pastoral solos of *L'Allegro*. To contrast with this gentle atmosphere, the duet for soprano and tenor ('Love to Love calleth') is an unabashedly emotional affair which, evoking the passion, desire, and sensuousness of Bridges' words, provides an interesting not to say significant precedent to Elgar's impassioned duet for Eigen and Orbin in *Caractacus*. Bridges' text seems to have released Parry from the trammels of poor vocal rhythm, for here the declamation has a genuinely operatic flexibility. Much of the yearning nature of this movement is created by the frequency of intense appoggiaturas, the most powerful of which is unleashed, appropriately in true Wagnerian fashion, at the words 'But out of his heart there welleth ever' (Ex. 31*a*). Nowhere had the sound of *Tristan* been so overt since the days of *Prometheus Unbound*. In many ways the bass solo that follows acts as the emotional watershed of the work. Here Parry once again deploys declamation, but of a much more reflective kind than was evident in the duet. To this, in the guise of a refrain which he himself contrived from Bridges' original text, Parry introduced a passage of arioso which looks forward to the lyrical conclusion after the Dirge. The melody, with its hymn-like resoluteness, is a fine one, but the tender closing phrase ('And drinketh up our tears'), projecting the gentle spirit of *Through the Ivory Gate*, is sublime (Ex. 31*b*). During their correspondence about section eight of the poem ('Rejoice ye dead') Bridges explained how he envisaged its approach and ambience: '[The] orchestra make an effect of rhythmic silence, gradually asserting itself as music—like a dead march heard in the distance and approaching—but mere rhythm. Then on the top of this suddenly steals a romantic melody, "weird" in character, of uncertain interpretation, like as modern "dead marches" are. The phrase when once stated is then interpreted by voices . . .'.[34] To some extent this conception influenced Parry. At the conclusion of the Dirge, a slow, distant, repetitive, funereal rhythm asserts itself which steadily grows in forcefulness. From this point, however, Parry's interpretation differed. As a culmination of the march rhythm he allowed the music to reach a full climax which at the same time marked the departure for A flat. The climax having subsided, the 'romantic melody' was introduced by the soprano, but was not in any 'weird' or 'uncertain' vein as Bridges had imagined. On the contrary, Parry's remarkable melody was very definite in its expression of consolation (Ex. 31*c*). With its luxuriant diatonic harmony and the English yearning of its many falling phrases, not to mention the sumptuous modified repetition for chorus, this melody is on a par with 'O may we soon again renew that song' from *Blest Pair*. It must soon

[34] Letter from Robert Bridges, 6 Mar. 1895, RUL MS 1399/2/2.

Ex. 31. *Invocation to Music* (1895). *a* 'But out of his heart there welleth ever', duet for tenor and soprano; *b* 'And drinketh up our tears', bass solo; *c* 'Rejoice ye dead', soprano solo.

have occurred to Parry that the pathos of this statement marked the emotional climax of the work, with the broad choral statement of Bridges' last four lines ('Now ye are starry names') affirming the immortality of the artist. After such stirring ideas, the last two sections are textually less impressive; nevertheless, Parry provided a fine trio for the soloists, and a spacious final chorus which brings to a fitting end this imposing *pièce d'occasion*.

In the course of 1895, Exeter College, Oxford conferred an Honorary Fellowship on Parry in recognition of his achievements. But a shadow was cast over the thrill of this accolade by George Pembroke's untimely death. Maude, the Earl's favourite sister, was acutely distressed, as were Dorothea and Gwen who had acted very much as substitute 'children' to the Pembrokes' otherwise childless marriage. The household at Wilton was too traumatized to host any gathering at Christmas, so instead this task was taken in hand by the Pembrokes' close relations, the De Vescis, who entertained them along with a number of 'Souls' at their beautiful home at Abbeyleix, County Leix in Ireland.

Pembroke's death seemed to act as a sombre prelude to a year beset with tragedy and, worst of all, lasting bitterness. Early in February Parry attended the funeral of Lord Leighton, shortly after which George Watson, secretary at the College, suddenly died. Then, in May, word came from Highnam that his stepmother had not long to live. More worrying than Ethelinda's death, however, was the future of the estate and the question of Ernest Gambier Parry's role in it. Since the death of Thomas Gambier Parry in 1888 he had managed the estate, but his highly nervous disposition was exacerbated by the strains of audits, maintenance, investments, and agricultural prices, particularly since the financial state of Highnam was under enormous pressure. But more sinister was Ernest's hidden desire to inherit the estate. This emanated not only from an almost irrational adoration for his father and his achievements, but also from a secret hope that Parry, who was due to inherit Highnam after Ethelinda's death, might relinquish it owing to the responsibilities of his musical work in London. On the day of the funeral the matter was 'tactfully' raised by a relation:

In morning before the funeral 'Uncle Frank' asked if he could have an interview with me. We went into the billiard room and sat down opposite one another. He had a paper in his hand to which he constantly referred. He gave me the impression that he had been carefully primed by Ernest, and that the paper was either written or arranged by Ernest. Uncle F. said—'There are 3 courses open to you. The first is to come to live here yourself, and take the full responsibilities of the position. This I suppose you do not wish to do. The 2nd alternative is to put an agent in to manage for you. This would be very unkind and painful to your brothers and sisters, so I suppose you would not do that. The third alternative, which I happen to know is *what your father wished, is that you should hand the place over to Ernest*, and that he should hand over to you any margin of income which might be left over, though of course under the present circumstances there could not be much.' I went into Ernest after and he showed by his manner, and by the passionate eagerness, when I expressed doubts as to whether it really could be any great advantage to hand the place over to him, that he was fully conversant with all that had been going on in the billiard room. My expression of doubt made him leap from his invalid chair onto his feet with the exclamation 'You're wrong Hubert, I can prove to you you're wrong!' He carries his sentiment about Highnam to a point of positive extravagance. And of course he has his own interest in his own possible succession, and the succession of one of his boys after me. Eva [Ernest's wife] makes arrangements difficult because she refuses to live at Highnam unless the whole establishment is kept going at its full extent.[35]

It was an issue which deserved very careful consideration. Parry himself loved Highnam, but without any of the obsession shown by his half-brother. He was undoubtedly aware of the time-consuming obligations of managing the estate, which, when looked upon objectively, were unwelcome additions to an already overcrowded itinerary. In one sense

[35] Diary, *Memoranda*, 27 May 1896.

to 'hand over' the estate to Ernest seemed practical—a thought he evidently entertained since he was subjected to a fierce attack by Lady Herbert who accused him of 'defrauding Maude and her children.'[36] Eventually, however, the decision hinged on financial savings that needed to be made on the estate and, more important still, on Ernest's suitability. In order for Highnam to survive the possibility of increasing debt, cuts had to be made in staff and household expenses. Ernest's reaction was predictably hysterical and self-righteous:

For the first time in my life I feel as if I could run for escape anywhere, not to get free of the worry, but because of the horror of the past months, and the horror of what you speak of, but which I, at present, can neither bring tongue nor pen to mention. There are to me—to us all, I think—traditions here so sacred, that to touch them seems almost sacrilege. I have been round and round, month by month, year by year, doing this, doing that; and it seemed to me always that I was pointing father's walls, guarding father's trees: they were his, *his*—he did it all, and I was only the family's servant who was set to guard them—nothing else. And while I acted thus, and I swear its truth, I added always—'his work shall not go back, no stranger shall ever touch it, Hubert shall find it nice— clean, undamaged, free from debt, as father left it.' I worked for you, I tell you, and I never thought of self or son. One aim alone I had in my mind—to keep father's handiwork safe and secure, that these walls and these walks should know only the voices he knew and the tread of the feet that had tried hard to follow in the course he set. Will you then give me time. There is only one thing that I could not see, it may be weak to say so—I could not see a strange foot here and live. *Somehow* the family must go on, and I will sacrifice all I have in the world to keep the stranger out. This may be madness; it may be wrong, God help me! but it is a madness that springs from a passionate determination to guard this very sacred home of ours.[37]

Soon word came from Ernest that reductions had been made by giving notice to a housekeeper, several maids, a groom and a footman; horses had been sold and much in the way of stable accessories was also up for sale. It was a small beginning, but it became clear towards the end of the year that, with accumulating debts of over £1,500, further changes would have to be made. At this stage, Henry Nicholl, Parry's own solicitor, advised him that Ernest was not fit to do the agencing. It was then decided to relieve Ernest of his duties and to find another agent. Ernest continued to express his readiness to take up the succession at Highnam, but because the estate finances were in such a poor state, there would be little or no income. This Parry could not entertain, so at last he resolved to assume residence at Highnam himself. This sparked a terrible row between him and Ernest which was to create a rift that refused to heal. Bitter and angry, Ernest and his wife took themselves off

---

[36] Diary, 24 Sept. 1896.   [37] Letter from Ernest Gambier Parry, 3 June 1896, ShP.

to Goring-upon-Thames. There Ernest's animosity smouldered, and in spite of entreaties by Parry to return to Highnam, he would not come. As time passed, the misunderstandings between them grew, until Ernest declared openly that he believed Parry incapable of comprehending his feelings and motives. Correspondence between them grew increasingly acrimonious. Then, most unfortunate of all, irregularities in the accounts uncovered by the estate solicitor, cast such doubts over Ernest's conduct and competence:

You have often been told during the past year and more of my willingness to see you; but the time has gone by, and I have come to feel that [it] is far better that we should not meet. In my broken condition the ordeal would be more than I could bear; and it is quite possible that one or other of us might utter words to be afterwards regretted. I have suffered in a way that I thought it impossible I could ever be called upon to suffer, least of all by one who claimed the same father; and this does not make meeting easier. There are some wounds that can never heal, and it is not the least pitiful part of this business that it is totally irremediable: the damage inflicted has been too great and has gone too deep: the effects have been too widespread and lasting: the mental suffering too fearfully acute. What has been done cannot here be undone, and I must perforce carry this with me through such margin of existence as may be left to me.

It seems to me therefore best, having said what I have above, that, though we may never meet, we should yet both of us make endeavour to deal charitably with each others faults; . . .We may then, it seems to me, go our separate courses in silence . . .[38]

It was a devastating letter which caused Parry appreciable distress. Much time was spent in anger and sadness trying to compose a suitable reply, but having written it, he could not bring himself to send it.

Perhaps the greatest tragedy of this appalling quarrel was that no reconciliation ever came about; if anything, the resentment and rancour on Ernest's part worsened to the extent that the rift became permanent. For Ernest Highnam was tantamount to a sacred shrine which not only embraced the artistic ideals of Thomas Gambier Parry, but also embodied his father's hopes of establishing a dynasty. This had already been 'tested' with Clinton's disinheritance and premature death, and the constant financial pressures on the estate (which Thomas Gambier Parry himself predicted) also seemed to threaten the family future. But while Ernest was obsessed with the 'spiritual' consequences, Parry was preoccupied only with the practical realities of preserving their father's achievements. With Ernest in charge (who seemed to show a similar strain of mental instability as had Clinton) he feared for Highnam and its precious contents. He himself adored the estate in every way, but with a sanity and pragmatism his half-brother lacked. He loved the paintings;

[38] Letter from Ernest Gambier Parry, 28 Nov. 1898, ShP.

he enjoyed billiards (with a lunging cue-action that proved detrimental to the glass cases that bordered the room!); he took every opportunity to revisit the favourite haunts of his youth, such as May Hill and Elmore, and he drew enormous pleasure from walks in the Pinetum—as one of his bailiffs, Alfred Eels, recalled:

Whatever the time of the year or the weather he was very fond of walking in the woods—especially the plantation of Spanish chestnuts near the Pinetum known as Sandy Hill, about the highest point in Highnam, and so called from the red sandy soil. The plantation contains about 600 clean, well-grown trees, and here he liked to stand and listen to the wind whispering through the leaves. From the Pinetum itself there are fine views looking over the woods to Gloucester and the Cathedral; and another from the seat under the Deodara-cedar, looking west over Churcham and right away to the Forest of Dean beyond.[39]

Clearly then, Highnam was close to his heart, and full of memories; yet he also had to face the ultimate reality that, on his death, Ernest and his sons would after all inherit a bitter legacy. This was confirmed in 1904 when Parry had occasion to read Ernest's *Highnam Memoranda*. Here it was clear that Ernest was attempting to boost his own branch of the family to the exclusion of his half-brother's. It was 'as if the first family had never existed', wrote Parry angrily in his diary, 'and Highnam was only for the Lear Parrys.'[40]

A saving grace which did much to lift the gloom of family friction was the acquisition of the *Latois*, a 21-ton yawl, purchased at Southampton. For the *Latois* Parry enlisted a crew from Littlehampton and immediately planned the first of a number of extensive summer voyages well beyond the modest excursions along the south coast of England. During August he sailed with his half-brother Sidney and Aveling (from the College) to the Scilly Islands. From there they made for the Irish coast—Waterford harbour, Queenstown, Crookhaven, and Valentia harbour. The conditions were often dangerous—sometimes treacherous—but a mountainous rough sea inspired him, danger seized him, and the flow of adrenalin invigorated him just as it had done on the football field of Eton thirty years ago. For a while at least, the College, the staff, the pupils and all the pressures of commissions, revisions, and publishers could fade away. He was away from Maude too, from her whims, her bullying and her capriciousness—and yet, ironically, he as her 'loving Boy' suffered an almost pathetic, agonizing loneliness parted from her and his two daughters. His letters were often lengthy and re-echoed the same passion for life as he had shown in the Oxford years, before their marriage. The Skelligs, two impressive, jagged island outposts off the coast of County Kerry held a special fascination for him and he longed to set foot on

[39] Graves, *Hubert Parry* (London, 1926), ii. 6. [40] Diary, 3 Jan. 1904.

them, despite persistent remonstrations from Pengelly, his skipper. This he related to his wife in a colourful, breathless letter of 23 August:

The sea outside was monstrous big—perfect mountains after nearly a week's hard blowing. But I made up my mind I would have one more try at the big Skellig. I didn't say anything about it till we were well out in the open, and then when Pengelly [the skipper] said something about running down fast southward with the NW breeze, I told him I hadn't done with the Skellig yet. His face was quite a study. Suppressed disgust, amazement, incredulity! 'I know it's impossible to land there in that little boat today' said he. Said I 'Well we'll just look at it at all events'. He bore it rather well on the whole, though he clearly thought the little boat would be dashed to pieces. I more or less argued with him, and very nearly gave up when I saw the wind getting momentarily worse and the sea more turbulent. But when we got a little under the lee of the big rock it was a little quieter, and we slipped the boat into the water very quickly and Jack and I were into her before a wave could catch her and we cast off successfully. It really was extremely exciting, for it was risky for the yacht as well as for us. We saw a man gesticulating wildly from a crag on the rock to warn us from the place we were going to attempt; and he pointed out a narrow gully where we might possibly get the boat near. It was a sort of lofty cave with rough steps cast in the side, and I jumped from the stern and the man on the rock caught my hand [and] there I was after all on the big Skellig. I really bounded for joy.[41]

In the eyes of most human beings, this sort of adventure bordered on lunacy. Even today the risks of landing on Skellig Michael are immense; indeed in retrospect it seems quite extraordinary that Parry did not perish as a victim of his own intrepidity and impetuosity. Yet those who accompanied him on his long sailing excursions confirmed that he thrived in dangerous situations. This was to be his annual cure, as therapy, recuperation, and, most important of all, removal from the high public profile of his country's revitalized musical life.

A further cathartic aspect of Parry's maritime escapism was the marked difference in the company he kept. Life on board with Pengelly and the crew was uncomplicated and down to earth. They had little knowledge of his life as a musician or of his professional standing; hence, his relationship with them was devoid of the worship that his personality engendered amongst staff and students at the College. This 'worship' was understandable enough. MacCunn, Daymond, Vaughan Williams, and Holst all talked of the spell he cast over them both privately and publicly; even Bernard Shaw feared meeting him in case he should succumb to the same effect. But the corporate nature of running the yacht, a responsibility in which he took a full and active part, dispelled any sense of hierarchy or rank. Parry's close friends—C. H. Lloyd,

[41] Letter to Lady Maude Parry, 23 Aug. 1896, ShP.

Frank Pownall, George Robertson Sinclair, and later (from his Professorial days at Oxford) Sir Walter Raleigh and Logan Pearsall Smith—who
had first-hand experience of Parry the sailor, saw how he came alive at
sea, taking long, vigorous swims off the side of the yacht, perusing the
charts, or superintending the purchase of victuals when they could get
ashore. One amusing account of a somewhat gruesome experience off the
Kerry coast took place on his first trip to Ireland. He had just left
Derreen House, the Irish seat of Lord Lansdowne, when they were
forced to take shelter in Ballinskelligs:

it came on so bad we had to take shelter in the very dirtiest, ugliest, dullest,
gloomiest and most out of the way place I have been in; and here we are stuck.
The rain comes down ceaselessly and the wind howls. You can't see anything a
mile off, but you can hear the thunder of the sea; and we know if we tried to face
it we should most probably lose our boat . . . The people here seem a fearfully
low lot of creatures. I went to the post office last night and found it was also the
local pot house and the general store. The inside was so dark when I got in that I
could only distinguish a lot of gloomy savages lolling about and drinking. One,
utterly drunk, was lying across the counter, which was flooded with dregs of
porter and spirits, and several others were well on the way to be equally drunk.
But the girls who came in for little shoppings and the other soberer people
seemed to take it as a matter of course; and I suppose it goes on every day. I was
short of meat, and was directed to the local butcher about a mile away. I found it
was just an ordinary cottage with the dissected portions of the recently killed ox
hung up in the living room, and the head nailed onto the front door. The house
was surrounded with a sea of liquid manure, which some ducks were sinking in
with much appearance of satisfaction, and which the children walked through
straight into the house. I suppose the dismal rain and mud and dirt makes it
look extra repulsive—but so far I don't think I ever saw a more hopeless corner
except in city slums.[42]

The comparatively hardy existence of cabin life contrasted vividly
with the type of society he moved in during the rest of the year. The
greater kudos of his public position brought more and more dinner
invitations from the 'Souls', though he found their conversation
increasingly artificial. More significantly, his position as head of an
institution enjoying royal patronage meant that his contacts with the
Royal Family became a regular part of his professional duties. There
were garden parties at Buckingham Palace and Sandringham, dinners at
Kensington Palace with Princess Louise, official parties with Prince
Christian, the Dukes of Edinburgh and Cambridge, and, of course, the
Prince of Wales. Though many of these occasions were purely protocol,
there were difficult situations to negotiate especially in the sphere of
nepotism, an aspect of elevated society he abhorred. One instance was

---

[42] Letter to Lady Maude Parry, 21 Aug. 1896, ShP.

the Princess of Wales's insistence that Olga Neruda be appointed to the College staff. 'She is very pertinacious about such matters,' was Parry's recollection, 'but I told her it was impossible . . .'.[43] It turned into a long-running saga, dragging on until 1908; letters were exchanged; Olga Neruda even visited Parry with a letter from the Princess addressed to 'Sir Hubert Parry' (before he was knighted!); but he risked royal disfavour and remained firm.

The style of numerous entries in Parry's diary of 1896 initiated a trend that was common to his diaries for the rest of his life. There we find a catalogue of short, sharp factual statements ranging from meetings with parents of aspiring young musicians, administration, examinations, illustrations for lectures (though by this time he had stopped teaching composition and had delegated all pupils to Stanford), student problems, and concerts. Hence, composition and writing were pushed to the further extremes of the day, to the early morning and late evening. Perhaps fortuitously there were no large-scale works to complete during 1896 which gave him time to meditate on two major commissions from the Philharmonic Society and the Hereford Festival for 1897. Apart from a series of three lectures on 'Realism and Idealism in Musical Art' for the Royal Institution, the chairing of the Musical Association, and the revision of *The Art of Music*, he gave his time entirely to miniature forms, the most substantial of which was a fourth set of *English Lyrics*. With the exception of 'Weep you no more, sad fountains', a beautiful setting of an early anonymous Jacobean poem, this collection drew exclusively on words by nineteenth-century poets. The success of 'Weep you no more' is due mainly to two factors: a well constructed vocal line, and deft simplicity of form. With regard to the latter, Parry skilfully enhanced the two-strophe design by recasting the G minor material of the first strophe into G major for the second. This change of mode in turn mirrors the change of mood in the second strophe. Of the two settings of poems by Byron, certainly the finest is 'There be none of beauty's daughters', dedicated to Evelyn de Vesci. The expansive interpretation of this text is strongly reminiscent of Brahms, particularly in the significance given to the flat submediant deviation in the second stanza, and the splendid recovery from it. 'When we two parted', though equally well composed in terms of accompanimental interplay, motivic thoroughness, and tonal cogency (G minor is well integrated as a subsidiary tonal level to E flat), is rather less distinctive from the standpoint of vocal rhythm. Parry seems to have been unable to resist the tendency for one-bar or two-bar units to close off, prompted, no doubt, by the intentionally cheerless regularity of Byron's short lines. Nevertheless, when the poem's

[43] Diary, 26 July 1897.

dolorous message of 'silence and tears', lost love, and memories of passionate youth is considered in the context of the composer's own emotional predicament, it is deeply moving. The setting of Keats's 'Bright Star', dedicated to his friend Robert Benson, was first composed in January 1885 but very thoroughly revised for publication. It is one of Parry's most impressive responses to the sonnet form, producing a well-proportioned through-composed structure. The tonal scheme is also well planned, especially with regard to the climax of the first part of the poem ('The moving waters at their priestlike task of pure ablution round earth's human shores') which emerges in B major. The move back to the tonic (A flat) is then executed with great skill, notably in the subtle manner in which Keats's resolute ninth line of text ('No—yet still steadfast') coincides with the switch from the dominant of G to the dominant of A flat. The two settings of poems by American poets are much less distinguished. 'Thine eyes still shined for me', words by Ralph Waldo Emerson, was first composed in a quite different version in A minor for the October edition of the *Atalanta* magazine in 1893. Evidently Parry was not satisfied with it and completely reinterpreted the text in a new version in D major. Yet, although there are some nice touches, particularly the tonal obliquity of the prelude and postlude, this song's through-composed design tends to adhere to a stereotyped procedure common to many of Parry's small-scale harmonic structures. A comparison of 'Thine eyes' with 'To Lucasta' (*English Lyrics* Set III) reveals a similar method of working-out. Both are settings of three stanzas in which a modulation to the dominant is incorporated at the end of the second stanza. The succeeding interlude is then suspended over the dominant in preparation for a return to the tonic. The move to the tonic is, however, delayed as the music moves towards the subdominant; this invariably underpins the main climax of the song in the third stanza. The second of the two American settings is 'When lovers meet again' with words taken from a recent publication (*Poems* (1894)) by Langdon Elwyn Mitchell (John Philip Varley). Set very much in the style of a Victorian parlour song, this is the least attractive of the set; however, the appearance of Mitchell is significant, for his words, like those of Sturgis, proved to be a recurrent source of inspiration in later songs, one of which ('From a city window') stands out as one of Parry's most striking contributions to the repertoire.

Much new music came to Parry's notice during 1896. He was pleased to hear the first London performance of MacCunn's opera *Jeanie Deans* given by the Carl Rosa Opera Company, and he was exceedingly impressed by the directness of Stanford's *opéra comique*, *Shamus O'Brien*. In contrast, Boito's *Mefistofele* which was being revived at Covent Garden in July, he thoroughly disliked, finding it 'raw and crude . . .

extremely second rate and insufficient';[44] it was to be his common reaction to the Italian musical sensibility. One interesting occasion appears to have been a most enjoyable function at Visetti's in honour of Gabriel Fauré who was over in London to hear his duet *Larmes* (*Pleurs d'or*) sung by Camille Landi and David Bispham at the St James's Hall. Visetti had organized a concert of Fauré's music which gave Parry the opportunity of hearing the Frenchman's work for the first time. 'Some of it [was] delicately and artistically good. Very sensitive stuff',[45] were his diary comments. These run contrary to his usual cynical reaction to the French musical temperament demonstrated by his verdict on Saint-Saëns' *Samson et Dalila* heard in January 1897 which he described unmercifully as being 'such miserable, empty, common, trashy stuff that I came away'.[46] The Richter Concerts, however, remained the chief attraction for there he heard the first London performances of Dvořák's Ninth Symphony, his overture *Otello*, and Strauss's *Till Eulenspiegel*. In the next few years Strauss's symphonic poems, notably *Don Juan*, *Till Eulenspiegel*, and *Tod und Verklärung* would conquer the concert-halls of London. This new progressivist 33-year-old German fascinated Parry enormously though he admitted to finding his work 'problematical'.[47] One other composer who was at last making headway was a name with which Parry was as yet relatively unfamiliar, largely because London had heard so few of his works; his name was Elgar. Jaeger, the publishing office manager at Novello, who had known Parry professionally since joining the publishing company in 1890, was the first to draw Parry's attention to the man he saw as a potential force in British music:

Look out for Elgar's 'King Olaf'. Though unequal and in places open to criticism I think there is some *fine* stuff in this. The young man has imagination, beauty, strength, 'go'. He is exceptionally gifted and will 'take the shine out of' some of the gentlemen at the top of the profession (excuse the slang!). I believe in him; and oh! he has *melody*!! melody that touches one. He is not yet very *deep*, but he will grow, I feel sure. 'The light of life' I do *not* care for, *nor does he*! He spoke of it as a 'written to order' effort. 'Olaf' is very different stuff. Whether he will ever do anything *great*, the future will prove.[48]

In a few years Elgar would eclipse Parry himself in terms of national popularity.

For several years Parry had been impressed by Lionel Benson's Magpie Madrigal Society (founded in London in 1885) and had enjoyed their concerts. Since the early 1890s he had begun to sketch out various ideas for a group of songs specially for them. Eventually these sketches, when polished up, divided themselves into two distinct collections: one

[44] Diary, 1 July 1896.   [45] Ibid. 30 Apr. 1896.   [46] Ibid. 16 Jan. 1897.
[47] Ibid. 7 Dec. 1897.   [48] Letter from Augustus J. Jaeger, 25 Sept. 1896, ShP.

of Elizabethan texts (which paralleled Stanford's sets of *Elizabethan Pastorals*), the other of modern lyrics. Both were dispatched to Novello in early 1897. The *Six Modern Lyrics*, dedicated to the 'Magpies', had already gained some prior publicity with the publication of Tennyson's 'There rolls the deep' which appeared in the March edition of the *Musical Times* in 1896. This part-song had been written quickly in early February for one of the College concerts in response to the deaths of Prince Henry, Sir Joseph Barnby, and especially Lord Leighton. Parry drew his text from Tennyson's *In Memoriam* (CXXIII), setting three of the verses. It proved very successful and Jaeger pressed him to publish it, hence its rapid appearance in the *Musical Times*. Somewhat less attractive, though not uninteresting texturally, is a setting of Moore's 'How sweet the answer' which was first performed by the 'Magpies' on 17 May 1892. Two of the settings are of words by Robert Bridges. During 1896 Parry had read several of Bridges' volumes of *Shorter Poems* from which he set 'Since thou O fondest and truest' (Book III) in a simple strophic form. More ambitious, however, is 'What voice of gladness' (known as *Larks*; Book V). Bridges had urged Parry to look at this text in November 1894, while they were corresponding over the initial schemes for the *Invocation to Music*. In this strongly Elizabethan lyric, Bridges hoped that the poetic sentiment might produce a setting 'corresponding in musical significance . . . with the old madrigal'.[49] Parry's interpretation partially suggests a certain madrigalian polyphony as does the strong vein of word-painting, yet much of the song is homophonically conceived and is dominated by some attractive melodic writing in the top voice. The most effective gesture, however, is reserved for the final climactic passage ('with joy as bright as heaven's best azure') in which Parry attempted to evoke the ecstasy of the lark's song by halving the rate of harmonic change. This technique he had used once before, over thirty years ago in his madrigalian setting of Herrick's 'Fair Daffodils'. 'If I had but two little wings' (Coleridge) appeared in the April edition of the *Musical Times* as an advertisement for the whole set. Perhaps a little over-sentimental in parts, especially the central section in third-related E flat, the gentle conclusion ('and still dreams on') is beautifully handled. The last of the six, 'Music when soft voices die' (Shelley), is in many ways the most affecting, and for the composer, the most personal. Simple in phrase structure and uncomplicated tonally, the song relies for its richness on wilting appoggiaturas and poignant cadential suspensions to convey something of the poet's tender melancholy.

The *Six Lyrics from an Elizabethan Song-Book*, dedicated to his old friend Spencer Lyttelton, concentrated more readily on humorous and

---

[49] Letter from Robert Bridges, 19 Nov. 1894, RUL MS 1399/2/2.

naïve elements, such as in the mock modality of Samuel Daniel's 'Love is a sickness' or the sardonic 'Whether men do laugh or weep'. The most memorable setting is without doubt the six-part 'Tell me, O love'. The opening portion is cast in the form of a dialogue between the male and female voices, the one wooing, the other denying, and which moves tonally from F major to the dominant of A. This prepares for the ultimate reconciliation in a radiant A major in six parts ('yet stay sweet love'). Through a series of smooth sequential modulations this brief episode cadences in C major, making way for the final section back in F ('Time brings to pass') whose concluding bars once again exhibit the expressive capacity of Parry's diatonic language.

Most of the part-songs from the two sets were performed by the 'Magpies' during May and June of 1897 at the time of their issue by Novello. Unfortunately they did not receive the interpretation Parry had hoped for; 'Lionel B[enson] quite lost his head,' Parry wrote despairingly afterwards, 'and ruined nearly all my partsongs by utterly impossible tempi. It was most depressing.'[50] One or two other songs which were also performed, but not included in either collection, later found their way into a third publication which Novello issued in 1898. The *Eight Four-part Songs* were first given at the Albert Institute by the Windsor and Eton Amateur Madrigal Society conducted, more sympathetically, by Walter Parratt, who received their dedication. The texts for this set are a mixture of Elizabethan and contemporary poetry ranging from the *Elizabethan Song-Book*, that had figured so prominently in the earlier 1897 set, to Arthur Benson and Robert Bridges. Perhaps the finest and most characteristic song is the nostalgically Romantic 'O love, they wrong thee much', which, though rhythmically simple and often texturally uniform, has a powerful harmonic intensity that so aptly expresses the fervent entreaties of the lover to his beloved. The melancholy, falling phrases of the opening, replete with diatonic suspensions, are particularly characteristic of the composer, while the restrained, solemn coda ('and fall before thee') is deeply touching. In a similar mood is a setting of Arthur Benson's 'Home of my heart'. Benson's words are largely on a level with those of Sturgis, but the message behind them, of estranged love, had an autobiographical significance for the composer; a sentiment which makes the returning strains of 'Home of my heart, why stand so cold and silent?' especially heartrending.

As a contrast with the intimate, almost private world of the part-song, Parry found creative satisfaction in being able to return to the abstract

[50] Diary, 3 June 1897.

composition of orchestral music, an opportunity brought about by the commission from the Philharmonic Society. Variation form, together with its structural problems and challenges, was a province of instrumental music that held a fascination for him, a fact confirmed by the early Bach variations, the finale of the 'English' Symphony, and most significantly of all, the *Theme and Nineteen Variations* for piano. The plan of this latter work, no doubt prompted by and imbued with the Romantic models of Brahms's *Haydn Variations* and more so of Dvořák's Symphonic Variations (which Parry first heard under Richter in 1889), led him to conceive a set of orchestral variations with a 'symphonic' dimension. This 'symphonic' dimension was not, however, to be simply a description of a developmental process consistent with Beethovenian or Brahmsian techniques; it was also to refer concisely to the matter of overall design—namely, that the variations would be grouped in such a way as to correspond in terms of key relationships, tempi, and mood with the four movements of a symphony. This Parry confirmed in a letter to Richter seven years later in 1904, shortly before the conductor was to perform the Variations in Manchester:

I.   Theme and Variations 1–11
    Maestoso energico
    E minor and major
II. Variations 13–18
    Allegro scherzando.
    C major
III. Variations 19–22
    Largo appassionato.
    A minor
IV. Variations 24–7
    Vivace.
    E minor [*sic*][51]

Tovey suggested that the basis of such a scheme was derived from the earlier D minor piano variations (see Ex. 13), though he also argued that the analogy of four symphonic movements raised certain problematic questions and could 'not be pressed too far'.[52] One objection was that the work as a whole would require a more substantial finale to balance the much larger first movement, which Tovey suggested might easily be seen as two movements rather than one. This point carries some weight when one considers that the opening twelve variations are divided into two

[51] Letter to Richter, 29 Feb. 1904. In the possession of Sylvia Loeb. The key of the fourth group of variations, stated as E minor, must be an oversight by the composer, since the key is clearly E major.

[52] D. F. Tovey, Parry: LXIII Symphonic Variations for Orchestra, *Essays in Musical Analysis*, ii. (Oxford, 1937), 144.

groups of six, contrasted not only by minor and major modes, but also by tempo (maestoso energico followed by allegretto grazioso); and as Tovey indicates later in his analysis, they are also divided by a short transitional cadenza on the flute. The only feature to suggest that these two groups of variations form a single movement is the return of the minor mode in variation 12 with an augmentation of the theme in the brass (the so-called 'Pause' variation).

Parry maintains the basic harmonic and melodic structure of the theme throughout the first 18 variations; interest is sustained through the irregular six-bar thematic structure and continuity is facilitated by each variation's closing on the dominant. Curiously, Tovey ignored these two important differences in his otherwise fascinating comparison of Parry's theme with that of the slow movement of Beethoven's last quartet (Op. 135). The slow movement breaks more radically with these classical restraints in its four variations. For example, variation 19 extends to twice the length of the theme but avoids the familiar phraseology by combining an accompaniment of triple metre with constantly irregular melodic phrases that are forever changing their emphasis. Variations 20, 21, and 22 continue this trend (14 bars, 10 bars, and 18 bars respectively), with the last variation (22) culminating on II⁷b of E minor before subsiding on to the dominant. Not only does this climax on II⁷b facilitate a transition back to E, but it also ties in neatly with the same chord at the end of the first movement (cf. Variation 12), which in its earlier context dissolved on to a first inversion of C major at the beginning of Variation 13. As Tovey states, the Finale acts mainly as a restatement of the opening theme in the tonic major with further variations reverting to the norm of six-bar phrases. The only exception to this is Variation 26*B* which occurs immediately before the final amplification of the theme, where Parry briefly develops a rhythmically modified version of the theme by imitation together with tonal instability. The technique of tonal expansion at the end of the variations had been tried in the last movement of Parry's 'English' Symphony and was a method almost certainly gleaned from Brahms's tonal adventures in the coda of the Passacaglia in his Fourth Symphony.

Dannreuther was particularly impressed with the Variations when he saw them for the first time in piano-duet form on 21 March 1897, shortly after they were completed. At the first performance on 3 June they were warmly received; 'band played up like bricks—went capitally,' Parry wrote in his diary, evidently delighted with the orchestra's response. The work proved to be immensely popular both at home and abroad. On 4 December the Liverpool Orchestral Society directed by Richter's only conducting pupil, Alfred Rodewald, gave a lively performance of the work, even though, according to Parry, the audience seemed rather indifferent. Wood conducted the work at a Queen's Hall Saturday Symphony Concert on 5 March 1898, albeit rather roughly; by request it was also repeated at a Philharmonic concert on 31 March, and in October of that year Parry was invited by Halford in Birmingham to conduct the Variations as the central work in the programme. On the continent the Italian composer and conductor, Guiseppe Martucci, included the work in his broadly eclectic programmes in Bologna in 1898 and again in Naples in 1906; later still, the Variations were performed at a Gürzenich concert in Cologne in February 1912. Indeed the Symphonic Variations (as they became known) was Parry's only orchestral work to achieve a modicum of international renown. Clearly its design captured the imagination of several foreign commentators (such as Friedrich Blume) for it was seen as an important contribution to the canon of late nineteenth-century cyclical variation forms along with Dvořák's Symphonic Variations, Franck's *Variations symphoniques*, and Strauss's *Don Quixote*. Last but not least, Parry's Variations also provide a fascinating and significant prelude, and, more than likely, an important stimulus, to Elgar's *Enigma* Variations produced two years later in 1899.

One of the more rewarding aspects of his role, first as a full-time teacher, and later as Director of the College, was to see the blossoming of compositional talent in younger generations. For them his position as artistic mentor was unrivalled. Parry, as we have seen, also took a keen interest in contemporary continental developments; he made a special point of hearing new works, and frequently encouraged foreign conductors and composers to visit the College both formally and informally. But of those generations of composers and performers who had been his mentors in the 1870s and early 1880s, many were now dead, and the artistic world he had known was fast being superseded by new, modernist ideas. The passing of the old order was for him most emphatically symbolized by the death of Brahms on 3 April 1897. As a tribute to 'the greatest and most noble members of the brotherhood of artists of our time', the whole of his May College address was devoted to 'the last of the great German heroes of musical art'.[53] Brahms was, however, more than a great German musician, for he epitomized Parry's ideal of all that was artistically sincere, single-minded, and intellectually honest. Perhaps most important of all, his music was full of individual character and personal conviction. This Parry stressed to his students, laying open his own creative affinities:

A man may utter artistic things with the technique of a superhuman conjuror, and if he have not temperament and character of his own he is become but a spinner of superfluities and a tinkling cackler.

[53] Sir C. Hubert H. Parry, 'Johannes Brahms', in *College Addresses*, ed. H. C. Colles (London, 1920), 46.

And it is worth remembering that it is in that respect that the English race is so peculiarly deficient. In the intensity and fervour which gives the full nature without stint to the expression of artistic ideals, foreign natures have much better aptitudes. We are too cautious and reticent to abandon ourselves to the full absorption in a musical thought or expression. We have too much respect for grand and wide principles of organization to give our individuality full scope.

But here, too, the example of Johannes Brahms is full of encouragement for us. His was no nature always laid open to receive any chance external impression. He was no expansive, neurotic, ecstatic, hysterico-sensitive bundle of sensibilities, but even as full of dignified artistic reserve and deliberate artistic judgement as the most serious of our own people. But he joined with it the great nature, the cultivated comprehensive taste, the imagination fostered and fed by dwelling on noble subjects and keeping far from triviality and conventions.[54]

Parry noted in his diary that during the delivery of the address he was 'too much overcome in talking about Brahms'. At the end of May he gave vent to his grief in the composition of an orchestral elegy which he hoped he might finish in time for the College's planned commemoration concert in early June. But time was against him, and what with the pending Hereford commission, he was unable to finish it. Subsequently, the work seems to have escaped Parry's mind, for work on it was not resumed and it was confined to the shelves until after his death when Stanford exhumed it, revised it, and performed it at the Parry Memorial Concert in November 1918 at the College. Ultimately, therefore, the *Elegy for Brahms* became a poignant elegy for its author.

The *Elegy for Brahms* in A minor, a key Parry seemed to favour in expressing the darker, more brooding side of his temperament (cf. the *Overture to an Unwritten Tragedy*), displays a striking consistency with the structural methods of his first mature instrumental works, notably with the slow movement of the Piano Concerto. The loose sonata structure of the *Elegy* is delineated more sectionally than the Concerto movement, but it does share the same 'recomposed' approach to the recapitulation with the second group establishing the tonic outright. Other unusual events occur in the development. One is the incorporation of a new theme (initially in F sharp minor—bars 104–8—Ex. 32c) at the outset which, after a brief extension, is never recalled. Another is the almost literal repeat of second-group material between bars 141–51 (cf. bars 84–100) transposed into the subdominant. This material, which had appeared at the end of the exposition, had a preparatory function in paving the way for the new theme at the beginning of the development. Its inclusion later in the development has a similar preparatory effect, this time for the main theme. It is at this juncture that, once again, we

[54] Sir C. Hubert H. Parry, 'Johannes Brahms', in *College Addresses*, ed. H. C. Colles (London, 1920), 46–7.

experience the ambiguity of development and recapitulation. The main theme returns, not in the tonic, but still in the subdominant, augmented (three times its original note-values), reorchestrated, removed to a register three octaves lower, and in a new harmonic context (Ex. 32*d*; cf. Ex. 32*a*). A repetition of the same phrase follows, a third higher as if to mirror the sequential descent of the theme in the exposition (bars 3–7). But this attempt at some kind of expositional imitation is curtailed by fragmentation which rises to an impassioned Wagnerian climax on the dominant of F (bars 168–76). Over the dominant pedal another rhythmical variation of the main theme is introduced, at something approaching its original register. Through a diminished seventh in bar 184 the tonality slips gently on to the dominant of A where at last the music becomes stabilized (bar 185 onwards), though during the bars of totally fresh melodic expansion (bars 189–96) we never once hear a root position of A minor. The final, slightly protracted bars of this transformed 'first group' are taken with the same solo violins heard in the exposition (cf. bars 43–6 with 200–4) which acted as a transition to the second group. It is only with these bars of the first group that we can find some form of recognizable and corresponding counterpart in the exposition.

The *Elegy* shows a high degree of involution. Certainly it is one of the most original sonata movements Parry produced; moreover, the techniques of recomposition, reconstitution, and transformation reveal a new, mature assurance that would reach a climax fifteen years later in the *Symphonic Fantasia*. Besides the structural sophistication of the *Elegy*, one other point of great interest lies in the integration of style. In one sense the work reveals Parry's obvious deference to Brahms, a fact evinced by such instances as the second-group material (which even resembles Brahms's style of orchestration—Ex. 32*b*), and the strong vein of metrical opposition that runs through the development and coda. Yet, beyond these deliberate reverential gestures, the full-blooded passion of the piece is couched, perhaps ironically, in Wagnerian terms. This is clear from the expressive use of melodic appoggiaturas and the dramatic climax of the first group, but Wagner's influence is nowhere more concisely demonstrated than in bars 168–76 of the recapitulation, particularly the ejaculatory dominant eleventh (bar 176) and the ecstatic relief thereafter; such moments as these belong to the sensuous world of *Tristan*. Yet the Wagnerian agitation does not dominate the *Elegy*, for much of the lyrical material is Parry's own. For example, the plaintive first-group material, constructed solely on a sequence of one-bar phrases, is typical of the composer, as is the unusual and distinctive oblique opening progression (VI—II^{7}b) that yields unconventionally to the tonic in bar 3. Surely most characteristic of all, however, is the expansive,

Ex. 32. *Elegy for Brahms* (1897). *a* opening idea; *b* main second-group idea; *c* new thematic idea, beginning of development; *d* recapitulation of opening theme in new context.

panegyric mood of the coda which dispels all sense of mourning and sorrow.

To a large extent the shock and sadness of Brahms's death was eclipsed in Britain by the overwhelming spirit of national celebration; 1897 was the year of the Queen's Diamond Jubilee. For Victorians it was time to express feelings of national pride, confidence, and above all patriotism. This patriotism—conservative and right-wing (and profoundly influenced by notions of racial superiority)—was one which, for many

Britons, was synonymous with the longevity and fortitude of the Queen's sixty-year reign. Parry, however, felt uncomfortable expressing his patriotism in these terms; he was not like Elgar, who, as an aspiring squire, ardent monarchist and Conservative, had no problems about his own overt participation. Parry, unlike his colleagues, had no desire to write a march or a Jubilee ode, so instead he opted to use Robertson Sinclair's commission from the Hereford Festival to compose something more esoteric. The result was a setting of the Latin text of the Magnificat, which, interestingly enough, paralleled Elgar's setting of the Te Deum and Benedictus commissioned for the same festival. The Magnificat was first performed in Hereford on 15 September with Anna Williams as the solo soprano. The chorus, evidently delighted with their own music, sang splendidly, but Parry felt that Anna Williams was not equal to the emotional intention of her part, a fact which had become apparent in the earlier rehearsals. The general response to the Magnificat was extremely positive. The *Daily Telegraph* hailed it to be 'one of his finest, as well as his ripest productions' while the *Athenaeum* stated categorically that 'no finer setting of the canticle has ever been penned'. Henry Wood, who performed it in Queen's Hall on 19 February 1898, and then later revived the work in one of his Promenade seasons, was one of its greatest advocates. In sharp contrast, Jaeger, writing anonymously for the *Musical Times* was more critical, and, in fact, he resented having to temper some of his more adverse criticisms on the instructions of the journal's editor. To Elgar he stated that he considered it 'Poor Parry' and among the weakest things that the composer had ever written.[55] It was a sweeping denunciation, which, one suspects, stemmed from his dislike of the weaker solo numbers and the somewhat perfunctory closing fugue. This, however, seems to have distracted him from the strength of the two central choral movements which are exceptionally fine and well composed.

Most of the critics were struck by the composer's deference to the 'Baroque masters', a feature particularly apparent in the melismatic style of the solo material; Jaeger, with perhaps a certain tongue-in-cheek, drew attention to the Purcellian characteristics of the melodic writing,[56] while others were quick to forge a link between the second aria, 'Fecit potentiam', and the Handelian manner of 'God breaketh the battle', from *Judith*. An archaic vein is given to the work as a whole by the extensive use of the original plainsong hymn (tone 8). This is introduced in the opening orchestral prelude (Ex. 33*a*) but is given greater breadth in the polyphony of the almost Bachian opening chorus. It also figures prominently in the soprano's 'Fecit potentiam' and returns with

[55] J. Northrop Moore, *Elgar and his Publishers* (Oxford, 1987), 66.
[56] A. J. Jaeger, 'Festival of the Three Choirs', *Musical Times* (1 Oct. 1897), 678.

Ex. 33. *Magnificat* (1897). *a* opening of orchestral prelude and opening
statement of solo soprano in the first choral section; *b* orchestral opening of
'Suscepit Israel' and comparison with first choral statement; *c* orchestral
opening of 'Et misericordia'.

augmented grandeur in the closing bars of the final chorus. Its most
subtle appearance, however, is reserved for the sonorous six-part chorus
('Suscepit Israel') in which two distinct transformations are heard (Ex.
33*b*). Especially effective is the oblique opening progression in the
orchestra which is used later with great skill to deflect the final cadence
of the chorus away from C major to F. 'Suscepit Israel' is undoubtedly
one of the high points of the work, but most commentators were

unanimous in judging the pastoral 'Et misericordia' to be the emotional centre. This tender pastorale is characterized by the transparent scoring of two clarinets, two horns, a single bassoon, pizzicato lower strings and a lyrical obbligato solo violin (Ex. 33*c*), which, after a lengthy emotional prelude, proceeds to embellish the gently rising phrases of the chorus. Introspective, rueful—and perhaps giving us a taste of a violin concerto that, sadly, he wanted to write but never did—it is a unique movement in Parry's choral output, and demonstrates once again how sensitive he could be towards the question of orchestral colour. Perhaps more significantly, the sonority of the extended violin solo prefigures and gives context to the most passionate and imaginative of all English Romantic violin obbligati in 'The sun goeth down' from Elgar's *The Kingdom*.

Having moved into Highnam in late December 1896, Parry found himself in the role of squire, sitting on the Parish Council, responsible for the school, the church, the vicar, the well-being of his tenants, the upkeep of their cottages, and, of course, the maintenance of Highnam Court itself. In Gloucester he was also sworn in as a Justice of the Peace and made his first appearance on the bench in September 1897. One of the duties he felt obliged to perform in this new role, as an example to his servants and those working on the estate (though one which he carried out at times with considerable torture and frustration), was the attendance of church on Sundays. 'To church in the morning, which was just hateful', began one indignant entry in his diary, 'To hear all these people calling themselves "miserable sinners" in such a complacent way makes me squirm.'[57] In one sense it does seem curious that a man with a natural revulsion for dogma and organized religion should take such a course of action. Some might, understandably, view it as an inconsistency, not to say a shortcoming, in his strongly articulated radicalism, and that had he had the courage of his convictions he would have stayed away. Yet this reaction would have also flown in the face of Parry's acute sense of public responsibility. As a patriarchal figure in high public office, his perception of morality and the law was profound, and he held the view that any institution that instilled a keen sense of ethical awareness had an important part to play in promoting the ideals of humanitarianism. In the one department of his professional life this strong moral stance was expressed to his students through the vehicle of his College addresses, and in his music it was soon to gain utterance in a series of 'ethical' choral works; at Highnam, however, there was no such mechanism, and so the church, in spite of her unpalatable dogmas and interminable sermons, seemed the best and most readily available replacement.

[57] Diary, 24 Jan. 1897.

His obligations to his tenants at Highnam was matched by his generosity towards them. For the Jubilee he organized, with the co-operation of the Parish Council, a celebration in the grounds of the estate. There were races, fireworks, feasts, and cigars for all. This was combined with a celebration of his own silver wedding anniversary. Festivities also took place aboard the *Latois* which he and Pengelly sailed down to the Solent for the Jubilee naval review on 26 June. This was the first of four sailing excursions he made during the year. With Sidney Gambier Parry he spent the first half of August exploring the lowland waterways of Flanders, visiting Ostend, Flushing, Ghent, and Bruges. After a brief interlude back at Rustington to check the orchestral parts of the Magnificat and the proofs of the full score of *Job*, he was off again with Aveling to Calais and Amiens. Then, with only a few days remaining after the Hereford Festival before College duties called, he met Pengelly and the yacht at Guernsey from where they sailed home to Littlehampton.

Another significant and happy family event was Dorothea's 21st birthday party which took place early in the year at Highnam. Her life was about to take a new turn. Arthur Ponsonby, who had been known to the family since 1891, had fallen deeply in love with her. In 1894 he had joined the diplomatic service and, having been assigned to the Eastern Department of the Foreign Office, he was posted to Constantinople as the junior of eight diplomats. Being so far away, this understandably put a strain on the progress of his relationship with Dolly and two emotionally turbulent years followed in which Maude imposed severe restrictions on their correspondence. Then, after more than two years in Turkey, he left Constantinople in November 1897 with the prospect of a new posting in Copenhagen. Back in London he wasted no time. After several previous 'refusals' on Dolly's part, she finally accepted him. The news was broken to Parry at Highnam. He was delighted, and yet feared that his closest and most intimate female companion might now be taken far from him. His apprehension was, however, unfounded, for Ponsonby proved in the coming years to be as close an ally as his daughter—a fact later attested by his objective and penetrating psychological reminiscences of the father-in-law he adored.

PART IV

1898–1918
Decline

13

Knighthood
Philosophical Introspection—the 'Ethical' Oratorio

DOROTHEA and Arthur Ponsonby were married on 12 April 1898, in St Mary Abbots Church, Kensington. 'No hysteria', wrote Parry in his diary, 'and Doll as quiet and cool as ordinary.' Dolly and Arthur then departed for Copenhagen where Arthur was to join the diplomatic Legation. But Arthur was not content with the 'gentleman's' diplomatic lifestyle and all the while looked for something more energetic, vocational, and creative. His activities in amateur theatre, which dated back to his days at Oxford, led him to ponder for a time a career in acting, but he was quickly dissuaded by Parry and others from resigning his position. Instead, he applied for a transfer to the Foreign Office and in February 1900 brought Dolly back to London, much to the delight of her father.

In May 1898, Parry received what he described as a 'rather harassing' letter from the Prime Minister, Lord Salisbury:

Private.   18 May, 1898
My dear Mr Parry,

I have ventured to submit to the Queen that the honour of knighthood should be conferred upon you on the occasion of Her Majesty's Birthday: and, the Queen having been pleased to signify her entire approval of my submission, the agreeable duty falls to me of communicating her gracious intention to you. I trust that you may be disposed to accept this mark of Her Majesty's favour as a recognition of the great services you have rendered to the advancement of the teaching of music in this country and especially of the eminent position which you hold in the musical world.

Believe me,
Yours very truly,
Salisbury.[1]

In a carefully worded letter to Lord Salisbury, voicing some reservations, he accepted. It was just as well he did, for on 21 May he received a telegram from Arthur Johnstone of the *Manchester Guardian* congratulating him. 'Couldn't make it out', he wrote in his diary, 'till I looked in the

---

[1] Letter from Lord Salisbury, 18 May 1898, ShP.

paper and saw the "Honours" list. So my name must have been sent in before my acceptance was received.'[2] On 25 May he wrote to his daughter: 'There was no way out of this business. The Queen had passed it before they sent me notice; and when I went down to find out if the Prince wished me to accept, I was made to see he would be the reverse of pleased if I didn't. And after all it does savour of bumptiousness to decline what is meant for a compliment.'[3] Congratulations from friends and family poured in, and though these were accepted in good heart, he made clear his qualms about the matter:

It was no doubt considered advisable that the *status* of the head of the R.C.M. should be of the same sort as the head of the R.A.M. I made such investigations as I could to find out how my declining would be taken, and they were not encouraging. But I didn't do it out of any idea that it wasn't fully up to my deserts, but rather because titles of this sort are apt to distract certain kinds of minds from judging a man as he is, and hinder them from estimating him at what he is really worth. However I suppose I shall have to make the best of it.[4]

Parry was knighted at Windsor on 13 July. It was an occasion that was not without its light-hearted side. Parry recorded in his diary that the Queen 'laughed all the while she was dubbing me in the most genial manner!'[5] Frederick Ponsonby, elder brother of Arthur and the Queen's assistant private secretary, also remembered the occasion, and of the fear which the Queen had a habit of instilling into those who were about to be invested: 'What a ripper he is. He [Parry] told me he had had a private rehearsal and had split his breeches in trying to kneel down in his velvet pants. Some of the others who came to be decorated were chattering with fear and one of them kept on repeating his name to me, he was so frightened.'[6]

The same month Parry was profiled in the *Musical Times* as part of the journal's series of 'Portraits'. For the first time the public at large knew something of his background, his formative years, his teachers, his rise to fame, and his creative achievements, as well as a taste of his most absorbing outside interest, yachting. It was a fitting if rather cursory tribute.

At the same time as these public accolades came two deaths that deeply saddened him. One was the passing of his friend, the artist Edward Burne-Jones, for whom he organized a Memorial Service in Westminster Abbey. The other was the death of his political mentor, William Ewart Gladstone, whose funeral he also attended in Westminster Abbey.

[2] Diary, 21 May 1898.   [3] Letter to Dorothea Ponsonby, 25 May 1898, ShP.
[4] Charles L. Graves, *Hubert Parry* (London, 1926), ii. 9.
[5] Diary, 13 July 1898.
[6] R. Mullen and J. Munson, *Victoria: Portrait of a Queen* (London, 1987), 136.

The spirit of Gladstonian reform, change, and progress always remained an integral part of Parry's *persona*. On becoming a Vice-President of the Incorporated Society of Musicians' Orphanage he was proud to represent the institution, but was fiercely insistent that it should not be closed to those who had not been connected with the Society. He was also keen to support Stanford's new opera scheme, though he was extremely perturbed by the suggestion that he and Cummings might be asked to take over the management as joint impresarios. Unfortunately for British opera the scheme failed to materialize beyond the planning stage. Much more to his liking was his attempt to reform the degree system at Oxford. In 1891 he had successfully pressed for the abolition of the public performance of the Doctorate exercise (that of the lower degree having long since been excused) and he had done the same for the Doctoral degree at London University in 1897. But the reforms up for discussion in 1898 were far more momentous for it was proposed that, in order to ameliorate the standard of the Bachelor of Music degree, a compulsory three-year period of study should be enforced before its conferment. Parry, Hadow, Parratt, and Stanford ardently supported this line believing that it would immediately raise the status of music graduates to that enjoyed by other faculties in the university. Moreover, they held the firm opinion that music degrees were granted too easily and would inevitably be improved if candidates were resident and were obliged to attend courses of lectures. Already a Special Board of Music had recommended compulsory residence for music students at Cambridge, which the University wisely adopted in 1893. Parry wrote to C. H. Lloyd about the urgent need for such reforms at Oxford:

About the reforms in the method of granting degrees I am very keen, and I think it a deadly mistake on the part of the profession to oppose it. It's all for their good. Why should a place like Oxford grant degrees wholesale to the rank and file of the profession, for just a fee and an examination? Their being in no real sense University men only maintains the old prejudice that musical men are an inferior caste. There are plenty of places for them to go to and get degrees and diplomas—Dublin, London, Durham. Oxford ought to show something that more definitely belongs to the place. The degree is granted too easily now, and lets in much too much of very second-rate rank and file. I don't pretend that the actual details of the scheme may not be advantageously reconsidered, but the principles seem to me essentially good. I don't think an exercise is sufficient by itself to pass for the Mus.Doc. There ought to be several works submitted, to cover more ground, as at Cambridge.[7]

Regrettably Stainer, Prout, and especially Bridge opposed the proposal on the ground that there was still no established system of teaching

---

[7] Graves, *Hubert Parry*, ii. 11.

music at Oxford. Moreover, it was suggested that musicians earning a living could neither spare time away from their professional duties nor afford the necessary fees. Hadow, however, suggested that those students with pecuniary difficulties could obtain degrees through the Royal College; this met with Parry's approval. Nevertheless, Bridge, with whom Parry had frequently crossed swords during the examining of degrees, took the extra step of obtaining signatures from seventy Oxford graduates who were against the proposal. This evidence proved crucial at the Hebdomadal Council who rejected the scheme much to Parry's indignation. In a letter to Hadow he could not but help pour out his abhorrence at the consequences of the decision: 'I am always trying to bring the tests and questions up to date as much as possible, and we will go on doing that. But you will never prevent "scugs" and mechanic and plodding duffers getting degrees as long as exams and technique are the only tests required.'[8] Music at Oxford did not acquire full faculty status, with a salaried staff and appropriate premises, until 1944.

Things were quite different at the College, and it was with some pride that he could point to several generations of composers who were either now well established or well on the way to being so. Hurlstone and Holst were beginning to show real promise; Samuel Coleridge-Taylor had scored a success with *Scenes from the Song of Hiawatha* and his orchestral Ballade in A minor, while D'Albert enjoyed the honour of an entire Philharmonic concert devoted to his music.

In July Parry met Norman O'Neill for the first time and in September was at last introduced to Elgar during the London rehearsals of *Caractacus* for the Leeds Festival. Parry was deeply impressed by the new cantata and, after its London première on 20 April 1899, he wrote to Elgar: 'I was very glad to be able to be at the performance of Caractacus. I thought it went remarkably well and it certainly is brim full of life and colour and artistic detail.'[9] It was to be the beginning of a relationship, which, although it was never especially intimate, was nevertheless infused with mutual admiration, respect, and encouragement. Moreover it was a friendship which was to remain stable and unbuffeted in later years when other members of the 'establishment'—one thinks especially of Stanford—fell out with Elgar.

Only weeks before the Leeds Festival Parry himself had enjoyed a certain success with a new cantata, *A Song of Darkness and Light*, which had, once again, been composed in collaboration with Robert Bridges and written as an apotheosis to Gladstone. During 1897 Parry had been in touch with his friend on several occasions, first over the production of Bridges' *Yattendon Hymnal*, and secondly over Bridges' recommendation

[8] Graves, *Hubert Parry*, ii. 12.
[9] Letter to Edward Elgar, 23 Apr. 1899, HWRO 705:445, 5247/8:2790.

to the artist William Rothenstein to include Parry (and Stanford) in a series of 'English Portraits' to be published by Grant Richards. Writing to the poet, Parry happily consented to Rothenstein's request,[10] and at the same time put to Bridges the suggestion that they might once more work together for the Gloucester Festival commission in 1898. Brewer, the director of the Gloucester Festival, was hankering after another oratorio-style work of the kind Parry was eager to avoid. Bridges, who was equally out of sympathy with the idea, reinforced Parry's resolve to stand firm in the event of Gloucester's objections; 'Don't you think,' Bridges wrote to his friend, 'that we might hit off a new sort of thing?'[11] Indeed, during the past few years, Parry had been contemplating the means whereby he might express more concisely his own philosophical beliefs and spiritual unorthodoxy through the choral idiom, and this new commission seemed to provide an opportunity.

It is clear from the extensive reading lists at the back of his diaries that Parry's literary tastes were also beginning to reflect such a development. Much of his non-fictional reading, which had shown a predilection for philosophical texts by Spencer and G. H. Lewes, began to encompass the 'agnostic' writings of Huxley and Sidgwick as well as political theses by Lecky, such as *Democracy and Liberty* and *The Map of Life*. As for fiction, the delight he had felt for the works of Samuel Butler, George Eliot, and Meredith, while by no means spent, had been superseded by a fascination for newer writers such as Kipling, Henry James, Thomas Hardy, and Émile Zola. Zola's nineteenth-century panorama of the French middle and working classes, replete with a detailed picture of misery, vice, and poverty coloured by powerful human instincts and appetites, undoubtedly served to raise Parry's moral consciousness. This is confirmed in an outspoken memorandum at the end of his 1898 diary where he attempted to expound the meaning and purpose of art as a moral ideal (consistent, as he saw it, with Zola's paradigms) while also finding time to criticize the artistic discrimination of the privileged classes who set themselves up as arbiters:

Zola and his fellows are right after all. Those who describe and make us realize what is hideous and repulsive and painful and irritating are right. We must look trouble straight in the face. What business have those who have time and opportunity to go in for culture to select just those particular things only which are pleasant to contemplate, and which flatter their selfish indolence—Their meanly lying indolence—and to ignore the facts of human degradation, vice, and suffering. Art is not solely for consolation—though that be one of its

[10] The drawing was made at the end of October 1897; the original [?] is now housed in Reading University Library. Another (presumably) rejected sketch made by Rothenstein is housed in the National Portrait Gallery, ref. 3877.

[11] Letter from Robert Bridges, 30 Sept. 1897, RUL MS 1399/2/3.

functions. It is not merely for refinement though that is one of its many benefits. It is not merely for interest though that may save many from folly and misspent lives. But to make men realize their fellowmen's conditions—and to know and feel the many sided aspects of their sufferings, and joys, and to enlarge their sympathies and their understandings.

The compelling nature of Zola's approach with its mixture of pessimism, optimism, and faith in social meliorism led Parry to other writers of a similar 'naturalistic' persuasion such as George Moore, whose novel *Esther Waters* he devoured immediately it was published in 1894; likewise he showed a consuming passion for Gissing's work, in particular the disheartening *New Grub Street* where self-advertisement triumphs over artistic conscience. In the province of theatre, Parry immediately appreciated the worth and relevance of Ibsen's social comment in *Hedda Gabler*, *An Enemy of the People*, and *The Doll's House* at a time when the Norwegian playwright was reviled by the public; moreover, he soon came to admire Shaw, one of Ibsen's most ardent champions, through such pieces as *Major Barbara* and *The Devil's Disciple* in spite of the fact that the Irishman had made Parry the brunt of so much merciless criticsm in the past.

Bridges' personal philosophy—one of man's longing to identify himself with an ideal spiritual reality, which the poet saw in the beauty of the natural world—also seemed admirably suited to Parry's desire to express the unconventional. In addition, Parry admired Bridges' capacity for discipline, clear language, and cogent form which was very much akin to his own modes of thinking. However, in order to avoid any inconsistency and misunderstanding, such as had existed during their collaboration on the *Invocation to Music*, Bridges insisted on regular meetings. In early November 1897 they met for the first time, after which Bridges drew up a plan:

The idea was that the orchestra was always to show the way, and give the picture (as it were) and the voices to join in with the words as if elicited by the music rather than conditioning it.

I can't imagine how long these orchestral pictures are to be. Suppose we call the thing a 'Hymn of Nature' and have sections of this sort:

1. Power and infinity and awe
2. Evil and Terror
3. Beauty and calm of mind
4. Pleasure of labour and mirth
5. Art
6. Tears
7. Faith [*not* Churchy]

Taking this as a rough sketch to amend. *Is it too long*? Would six lines of 10 syllable verse be enough for each section? Is the transition (contrast) between 2 and 3 too abrupt?

NB. I think a great effect might be got by No. 6. The suggestion of weeping by the orchestra and the totally unexplained intrusion of the tears should be very pathetic.

I should be glad if you would tell me what you think of this. I don't know whether I can do it.[12]

In fact Bridges' doubts were unnecessary for Parry was much encouraged by the design and barring some minor alterations, this first sketch remained intact. By 7 December Bridges had drafted the entire poem which he showed to Parry at a meeting in London a few days later. The composer was once again delighted, as was Dannreuther who saw the text and some early musical ideas in late January. The only stanza to cause a modicum of debate was the final one which Parry wished to use as a means of thematic recapitulation. This, they agreed, should be constructed after the music of the first six stanzas had been sketched. Much of the music was composed in March, but examinations and a 'Parry Concert' in Newbury (which, as a special feature, included the *Invocation*) prevented Parry from commencing the finale until the beginning of May. By 5 August after a violent struggle, the score was finished and sent off to Jaeger. The chorus coped well with the new ode at rehearsal and were rewarded the day before the performance by a party at Highnam: 'The Chorus went to the Pinetum and all the band came over to the garden where I had a marquee for them and whiskys and sodas and fruit and cigars . . .'.[13] Such occasions were to become frequent occurrences at Gloucester Festivals.

For Parry the overall title of the work was an important issue to be settled. Bridges put forward two simple suggestions: *Festival Ode 1898* and *Power Eternal* (derived from the first line of text). But Parry wanted something that alluded more to the philosophical vein of the work. He was attracted by Bridges' original title for the poem *Hymn of Nature* (which the poet assigned to it when it was published in the September edition of the *Cornhill* magazine) and in the July edition of the *Musical Times* advertised the work as *A Hymn of Nature and Man*. This title was evidently given to Jaeger sometime in May or June for the urgent purposes of Novello's publicity; yet it is clear in various letters from Bridges in June that Parry was still unhappy with it:

I quite see the sort of thing that you want—and really I have no objection to your calling the cantata by any name that you like. I expect Novello & Co. would know best what would 'take on' . . .

---

[12] Letter from Robert Bridges, 8 Nov. 1897, ibid.   [13] Diary, 14 Sept. 1898.

Honestly I think that the public will be expectant enough at the sight of your name—and if the music satisfies their expectations no name would identify it better than such a title as 'Festival Cantata 1898' which would recall when and where it was first heard . . .

There is a difficulty in giving a name which would cover the intention of the piece (as far as I am concerned) because it is an attempt to picture or sketch various irreconcilable moods—and it would require either a long prosy title or something which (as your suggestion does) would imply a solution or at least a onesided view. '*Power Eternal Festival Cantata for 1898*' seems to me a rather good title.

My original title was '*Hymn of Nature*'.[14]

In an addenda to the letter Bridges put forward four further titles: *Darkness and Light*, *A Song of Darkness and Light*, *A Song of the Earth*, and *A Song of the World*. Parry opted for the second title which he began to use by the end of July. This introduced to the work a more polemic viewpoint by which the 'eternal power' of Nature could be contemplated. Each of the seven stanzas—'Mystery', 'Terror', 'Peace', 'Toil', 'Art', 'Tears', 'Faith'—was given subtitles at Parry's insistence (though they do not appear in Bridges' published text) in an attempt to articulate the meaning of Nature as seen and experienced by man. Regarding the theistic dimension, however, Bridges was a little concerned that the clergy at Gloucester might protest at the somewhat vague definition of God in the strictly Christian sense. Hence, in the finale, he introduced the notion of a doxology in which 'Beauty, Truth, and Love are one'. This he hoped would satisfy the 'parsons' to some extent, though he was aware of one other potential criticism:

There is a general objection to the whole ode which may very well be raised viz. that it is not consistent. It may be asked what is this '*Power*' in stanza one? and what is its relation to the '*God*' in [the] last stanza?

I do not mind this conflict of ideas—you will remember that we agreed that you were to have the words as explanatory of the music—and if they appear in that way there is no reason why they should be consistent. There are the ideas, there is no doubt about their existence. The audience must reconcile them as best they can.

The absence of this desirable reconciliation appears to me to be better, truer, and more poetic than a onesided solution. I can't imagine what the parsons will say, but I expect that the doxology will satisfy them.[15]

The musical structure of *A Song of Darkness and Light* is quite simple in that it mirrors the clear-cut episodic design of the poem, and each new stanza is accompanied and clarified by the introduction of new musical ideas. However, though the form is in one sense sectional, the cantata

[14] Letter from Robert Bridges, 10 June 1898, ShP.
[15] Letter from Robert Bridges, 25 Apr. 1898, RUL MS 1399/2/3.

runs without a break as a single movement. This is consistent with the composer's desire to create an overall symphonic unity which he planned to achieve through the more prominent use of the orchestra. The instrumental dimension of the work is emphasized by the lengthy orchestral prelude which introduces several well-contrasted clue-themes (Ex. 34*a*, 34*b* and 34*c*); these subsequently recur throughout the work in a series of transformations in both the individual episodes and intervening transitions that culminate in the finale, 'Faith', whose plangent latter stages function as a form of recapitulation. Moreover, the role of the chorus is frequently musically subordinate to the orchestra which carries the main thematic momentum; only in 'Toil' and 'Faith' do the chorus assume something of their more traditional role, and this tends to occur where Parry deploys more conventional techniques of fugue and imitation. The two most striking and musically successful sections using the new approach are 'Mystery' and, above all, 'Tears'. Both are dominated by the orchestra. The darkness of 'Mystery' is extensively foreshadowed in the discursive orchestral prelude which forms an important organic part in the emergence of the first episode. The clue-theme of 'questioning' (Ex. 34*a*) continues to figure conspicuously after the entry of the chorus, but more predominant is the thematic material symbolizing 'dread' (Ex. 34*b*) which appropriately asserts itself during the chorus's opening declamatory statement ('Power eternal, power unknown, uncreate'). This material, heard first in the orchestral prelude, frames the entire episode, and its recurrence at the end (four bars before figure 14) provides a dramatic intrusion to the evocative tranquillity of the last lines of the stanza ('All things pass as a dream Of thine unbroken slumber'). These concluding bars are especially fine. Not only is the orchestra given space to blossom lyrically above the unison strains of the chorus, but there is a also a masterly manipulation of harmony. This can be felt most notably first in the sonorous tonal divergence to the Neapolitan (D flat), but more moving still is the richness of the recovery back to the dominant of C. Such inventive and experimental progressions as these, while remaining firmly bridled within Parry's diatonic language, mark a definite step forward in the composer's harmonic vocabulary. Similar tonally fluid progressions are present in the most memorable of all the episodes, 'Tears', whose immediacy depends largely on the uncomplicated through-composed structure and tonal scheme, and on the touching simplicity of the 'weeping' figure on the oboe that permeates the entire orchestral accompaniment (Ex. 34*d*). Nostalgic and melancholy, yet capturing something of the 'sweet compassion' of Bridges' words, this is Parry at his best and most apposite. With the exception of these two episodes and the dark, brooding orchestral introduction, the cantata is, nevertheless,

Ex. 34. *A Song of Darkness and Light* (1898). *a* theme representing 'Questioning'; *b* theme representing 'Dread'; *c* theme representing 'Questioning of Dread'; *d* theme representing 'Tears'.

(a) **Andante**

cl./ b. cl./ bn.

(b)

hns.

vc./ d.b.

(c) **Animando**

str./ w.w.

cresc.

(d) **Lento espressivo**

ob.

hns.

str.

vc./ d.b.

pizz.

disappointingly inconsistent in the quality of its ideas. 'Terror' and 'Toil' are, by comparison, rhythmically and harmonically bland and the two solo episodes, 'Peace' and 'Art', while containing some effective orchestral writing, are melodically undistinguished. Only 'Faith', where Parry's shows his uncommon ability to create intensity by a radical deceleration of harmonic pace, is more meritorious, though it is spoilt by the empty rhetoric of the hymn tune ('Thy work with beauty crown thy life') before the close.

During the last quarter of 1898, Parry was occupied primarily by a commission from Hadow and Oxford University Press to write Volume III ('The Music of the Seventeenth Century') of the *Oxford History of Music*, a task that was to last the best part of four years. In December he also set to work on some incidental music for Pearl Craigie's one-act play *A Repentance*. The acquaintance of Mrs Craigie ('John Oliver Hobbes') had been made many years ago through his connections with the 'Souls', and he had watched her career with interest during the 1890s as she established her reputation first with novels such as *An Emotion and a Moral* (which he read in 1893) and later with plays such as *The Ambassadors*, which had scored a great success in London during 1898. Their paths crossed again in June 1898 when Parry and an orchestra of College pupils were asked to participate in a charity concert organized by the Polish pianist and one-time pupil of Madame Schumann, Natalie Janotha. The main attraction of the concert at the St James's Hall was a performance of Bach's Triple Concerto which Parry had conducted, the soloists being Miss Janotha, Lady Randolph Churchill, and Mrs Craigie. It was after this concert that Mrs Craigie asked Parry if he would provide an overture and incidental music for her new play which was due to be staged at the St James's Theatre in late February 1899.

Set in Spain in 1835, *A Repentance* attempts to be a psychological diagram of the abnormal political crisis created by the Carlist question. As Mrs Craigie explained to E. Fordham Spence:

The Carlist question seemed to make men—and women—absolutely unstable, inconsequent, desperate, and inexplicable. Great deeds of heroism were done: and also extraordinary acts of treachery, followed by repentances as sudden as the one I have described. I was ill with nervousness about the play (before the first night) because I felt I was presenting something violently 'impressionist'. I crowded—as you say in so many words—the history of an epoch into a short act.[16]

This 'crowding' proved to be the resounding criticism from all quarters of the press who felt that such a theatrical denouement would have been best achieved in four acts. Much of this was justified. In one act alone the

[16] John Morgan Richards, *The Life of John Oliver Hobbes* (London, 1911), 155.

drama is hurried; it is difficult to absorb and comprehend the import of the main protagonists' psychological predicaments; many of the events seem melodramatically sensational, and consequently implausible. Nevertheless, the play ran for 35 nights between 28 February and 15 April as a *lever de rideau* to the main attraction of the evening, *The Ambassadors*, and was much admired by Edmund Gosse, Benjamin Swift, Thomas Hardy, and George Wyndham.

During the composition of the incidental music Parry was very ill, but obstinately refused to stay away from the College. Although the short play did not demand such an extensive quantity of music as *Hypatia* had done, it still gave him a considerable amount of trouble and worry. The rehearsals were also plagued with difficulties, particularly with the co-ordination of the off-stage band, though this was overcome by a primitive Tannoy system installed specially by the telephone company. Mrs Craigie, on the other hand, was more patient and, fortunately, lacked the histrionic temperament that had so aggravated Parry in his relations with Beerbohm Tree. She genuinely liked Parry's music which made the task more agreeable and efficient, and Robins (director of music at the St James's Theatre), who took over the baton after the first night, was equally congenial. The overture to *A Repentance*, by far the most substantial musical piece in the play, is interesting and imaginative, and deserves to be exhumed. The tonal obliquity of the main leitmotiv, that of the Carlists' cause, also assists the fitting portrayal of the politically cynical, treacherous nature of the aristocratic Des Escas in the opening bars. This idea is effectively transformed into various forms as the play progresses.

Apart from *A Repentance*, Parry wrote very little music during 1899. Only two miniatures came from his pen: one was an orchestral song, *The North Wind*, written for Ivor Foster who sang it at New Brighton on 9 July; the other was a fine five-part 'choral song', 'Who can dwell with greatness' (Henry Austin Dobson), composed in response to a request from Walter Parratt who was compiling a volume for Macmillan entitled *Choral Songs by various writers and composers in honour of Her Majesty Queen Victoria*. Parratt's aim, as he explained in the preface to the edition, was to create a modern-day *Triumphs of Oriana* in which the thirteen composers and poets would attempt to emulate, in Victorian terms, the spirit of the Elizabethan madrigal.[17] Two of the songs, by Elgar and Parratt, had been sung at Windsor at the Serenade given on Queen Victoria's 80th birthday in 1899. Several more were performed by

[17] The other contributors to the edition were Mackenzie (Austin), Stanford (A. Benson), Walford Davies (Bridges), Bridge (Earl of Crewe), Martin (Davidson), Goodhart (Gosse), Wood (A. C. James), Somervell (Marquess of Lorne), Elgar (Myers), Lloyd (Newbolt), Stainer (J. F. R. Stainer), and Parratt (Warren). The volume was published in 1900 as a limited edition.

the Windsor and Eton Madrigal Society on 10 February 1900 and Parry's own song was sung at a concert by the same society on 29 May.

Nearly all Parry's creative time was taken up with the 'Oxford' book. Just as he had done in the days of Grove's dictionary, he made regular and intensive visits to the British Museum to look at Lully operas, Scarlatti keyboard sonatas, part books of viol compositions by Lawes, Christopher Gibbons, and Rogers, and numerous vocal pieces by Purcell and Schütz. He also availed himself of the extensive collections in the Bodleian during his visits to Oxford as examiner. But other things besides examinations brought Parry to Oxford during 1899. On 20 June the university conferred upon him an honorary DCL after which there was a lively party with Stainer and Hadow at the Christ Church Deanery where he met the Duke of York, Lord Kitchener, and Cecil Rhodes. One topic of conversation must almost certainly have been Stainer's resignation of the Heather Professorship in May, and the likelihood of his successor. Parry's honorary degree seemed to be a sign that he was the most favoured candidate, and when applications were invited later in the year, Stainer stood over him 'like a gaoler'[18] until he had submitted his. It was therefore no surprise when the telegram arrived on 30 November announcing his election to the Professorship.

During 1899 Parry's participation on music committees and in new societies seemed to reach saturation point. On 2 February he gave the inaugural address at the first meeting of the Folk-Song Society and subsequently became a member of the standing committee.[19] He found time to attend meetings of the Brahms Memorial Committee (headed by Joachim), the Society of Antiquarian Musicians with Squire, with whom he also helped (along with Lionel Benson) to edit a *A Collection of Madrigals by Ancient Composers* (published by Laudy & Co. of London and Leipzig), and he took an active role in the Church Congress in October where he delivered a paper on 'The Essentials of Church Music'.[20] Committees of the Associated Board and Hymns Ancient and Modern continued to claim his time, as did the Board of the Mendelssohn Scholarship which seems to have been a particularly acrimonious business as one diary account relates: 'Mendelssohn Scholarship Meeting most amusing—everyone at daggers drawn. Bridge in fury with Stanford; Mac[kenzie] with Sullivan; Stanford with Mac; Cummings with representative of both RCM and RAM and Otto Goldschmidt stirring up strife whenever he could.'[21] Some of this ill feeling almost certainly stemmed from recent developments in the Philharmonic Society. Parry had been asked if he would take the Conductorship, but he refused; this left the way open for Cowen who

[18] Diary, 9 Nov. 1899.
[20] See ibid. (1 Dec. 1899), 815–17.
[19] See *Musical Times* (1 Mar. 1899), 168–9.
[21] Diary, 6 Nov. 1899.

took up the post again, much to the annoyance of Sullivan, Cummings, and Stanford.

Performances of his choral works took him all round the British Isles. In early March he conducted *De Profundis* in Cambridge, and shortly after he travelled to Ireland for performances of *King Saul* in Dublin and Belfast where Agnes Nicholls and Muriel Foster acquitted themselves superbly. A revised *Prometheus Unbound* was given by the Bach Choir on 24 March while in October *A Song of Darkness and Light* was one of the focal points (along with Elgar's new *Sea Pictures*) at the Norwich Festival. There were also two concerts devoted entirely to his music during the year. On 27 April the Richmond Philharmonic Society honoured him with a festival concert at the Star and Garter Hotel in a programme consisting of the 'English' Symphony, the *Hypatia* Suite, *The Lotos-Eaters*, *Best Pair*, and one of the part-songs, 'There rolls the deep'. An interesting novelty was also an orchestrated version of 'Where shall the lover rest' (from *English Lyrics* Set I) specially arranged for Agnes Nicholls. In New Brighton on 9 July, as part of a series of concerts organized by Granville Bantock featuring Stanford, Parry, and Elgar, Parry conducted a programme primarily of orchestral music, though the 'Dream of King Saul' and a new orchestral song *The North Wind* were included.

As usual in London his curiosity for new names drew him to the Philharmonic, to Richter's concerts and to the opera house. Rachmaninov's first appearance in London on 19 April was marked by the performance of his Fantasia in E *The Rock*, Op. 7, which, as Parry noted, delighted the public. He greatly admired Stanford's *Dead Men* Variations which he heard for the first time in early May. At the same Philharmonic concert the Symphony in D minor by Martucci was also performed, and the following day Parry attended a dinner in the composer's honour. At the opera his experiences were well contrasted by, on the one hand, De Lara's *Messaline*, which made him feel physically sick, and on the other by the first staging in London of Puccini's *La Bohème* which he liked wholeheartedly. With regard to English music it appears from his diary that he missed the concert on 30 May at the St James's Hall devoted exclusively to the music of another newcomer, 'Fritz' Delius, but he continued to follow the rapid progress of Elgar. He was impressed by *Caractacus*, less so by *The Light of Life* which he heard in Worcester in September, but he reserved his most eulogistic comments for the *Enigma* Variations which he heard Richter conduct on 19 June. 'Elgar's Variations first rate', he wrote excitedly in his diary; 'Quite brilliantly clever; and genuine orchestral music.'[22] Parry's involvement with Elgar's

---

[22] Diary, 19 June, 1899.

Variations gave rise to a mythology which lasted for many years. It was suggested in Plunket Greene's biography of Stanford that Jaeger showed the score of the work to Parry, who, being highly taken with it, left his after-dinner armchair and went immediately to Richter on an inclement night with the manuscript score under his arm in order to show it to the conductor.[23] Jerrold Northrop Moore has demonstrated that matters could not have happened in this way. Since Elgar had not yet finished the score of the Variations, Parry could not therefore have seen the completed manuscript as Plunket Greene suggested. Nevertheless, a corrected version of the story (by Dora Penny) confirmed that Jaeger, full of unbridled enthusiasm, did call on Parry at Kensington Square on a rainy night soon after seeing Elgar's unfinished score. Parry heard all that Jaeger had to say, and was then persuaded to go to Richter's house in order to exert some influence on the German to conduct the work. Unfortunately when they arrived at Richter's house they found that he had already gone abroad. The next best course of action left to them was to apply to Richter's London agent, N. Vert, who agreed to forward the score to Richter in Vienna after it was completed.[24] After the June performance Parry wrote an exuberant letter to Elgar in praise of his masterpiece and was delighted when Elgar offered him a copy of the published score early the following year:

I am afraid my slowness in answering may seem rather unappreciative, but it is really owing to my being completely overworked. I should indeed very much like to have the copy of your Variations which you so kindly offer me. I have not the luck to possess a copy yet, but it will be extra pleasant to have one from the composer himself. You know how much I admire them, and I shall be delighted to revive my impressions of the brilliant orchestration by reading them to myself.[25]

Yet away from this energetic display of interest and selfless generosity, Parry was inwardly depressed. He was disturbed by the developments in South Africa, the sieges inflicted by the Boers at Ladysmith, Kimberley, and Mafeking, and by the black week in December when the British Army suffered three consecutive defeats and the loss of nearly 3,000 lives. This combined with certain events at the College had, as he explained in a letter to Dolly, 'nearly broken [him] up' and he was 'all to pieces'.[26] One student had been killed in a street accident, another had run off, and one professor had been caught flirting with a student which

[23] H. Plunket Greene, *Charles Villiers Stanford* (London, 1935), 157–8. This charming anecdote was later quoted in Vaughan Williams's essay 'What have we learnt from Elgar?'. (See *National Music and Other Essays*, ed. Kennedy, 2nd edn. (Oxford, 1897), 254.)

[24] J. Northrop Moore, *Edward Elgar: A Creative Life* (Oxford, 1984), 259 n. See also id., *Edward Elgar: Letters of a Lifetime* (Oxford, 1990), 74 and n.

[25] Letter to Edward Elgar, 1 Feb. 1900, HWRO 705:445 5247/8:2791.

[26] Letter to Dorothea Ponsonby, 2 Mar. 1899, ShP.

had necessitated a severe reprimand. A final devastating blow was Dannreuther's resignation on the grounds of deteriorating health. Though in Parry's mind he was unreplaceable, there was still the strain of finding someone suitable to take his pupils. Dannreuther's poor condition was worrying. Pneumonia had been diagnosed and there was concern that he might live only a few more months. Fortunately he pulled through, but he was thereafter only a shadow of his former self. Even more upsetting was a valedictory note from Grove. It was to be the last he would receive from the great man:

Dear Hubert,

Just a line to say good-bye, for I am afraid it has come to that. I intended to come and see you this morning, but when I tried, my wife would not let me and I have no alternative to give to her many arguments.

I hope you may fill my place for many a long year to come, as well as you are doing it now.

Please say good-bye to all my old friends on the staff—to Parratt and Taylor and the rest. I am terribly sorry to say good-bye and wish I could do it more effectually.

G. Grove.[27]

Parry had been concerned with Grove's failing health for some time, particularly the loss of the power of speech and the greater part of his memory. Grove had not appeared at the Brahms Memorial Committee— a clear sign to those attending that he was not well. During October there were reports that he was close to death but he rallied through the spring of 1900 before dying on 28 May. The day after, Parry noted in his diary: 'Richter to luncheon. And after Charlie and his new Violin Concerto, with Arbos playing the solo . . . At end I made a little speech about Grove, the announcement of whose departure from the world came this morning and the band played the Funeral March from "Eroica".'[28] On the day before the funeral at St Bartholomew's Church, Sydenham, he reflected briefly on his friendship with Grove in a letter to Eddie Hamilton: 'Morley and Pownall and I am going down tomorrow; and I have ordered a big wreath from the College. Now he is gone, the tragic recent condition seems to pass out of my mind and I only think of the wonderfully genial and brilliant friend he was years ago.'[29]

On a happier note, the marriage of his younger daughter, Gwen, had been announced to Harry Plunket Greene, the well-known baritone. In a letter to his old Cambridge friend Jenkinson Parry wrote:

It's nice to hear from you and to receive such sympathetic references to Gwen's engagement. She's radiantly happy, and he seems no less so. He's a fine tower of

---

[27] Letter from George Grove, 3 June 1899, ShP.   [28] Diary, 29 May 1900.
[29] Letter to Edward Hamilton, 30 May 1900, BL Add. MS 48621.

strength to bring into the family and I should be hopeful about their making a good thing of their lives together. I hope it won't take her quite so far away from us as Dolly is. At least they won't have to be away for such long stretches of time. Doll's very happy too, and we hope to have her back for a time soon.[30]

In June Plunket Greene came to live at Kensington Square for the few weeks before the wedding. The marriage, a quiet one, took place at Highnam on 20 July, Gwen and the rest of her party walking across to the church from the Court. The best man was Herman Herkomer and among the congregation were Maude Valérie White and Plunket Greene's accompanist, Leonard Borwick. Then Parry was off sailing again in the *Latois*, to Dartmouth, the Isle of Wight (where he briefly met the Queen at Osborne), and to the Channel Islands.

During the relative calm of 1899, Parry was contemplating three new and very different commissions that would come to fruition in 1900. One was a request from Robertson Sinclair at Hereford for a new choral work. For this Festival Parry composed a *Thanksgiving Te Deum* 'to commemorate the noble achievements of the British Forces in South Africa'; it was first performed at Hereford on 11 September—as it turned out, an apt moment, for the Boer War had at last begun to turn in Britain's favour. The Te Deum is, as Jaeger aptly described in his analysis for the *Musical Times*, 'hewn in granite, noble structures erected in the architectural style of Bach, a wealth of new thought expressed in the beautiful classical language bequeathed to us by the immortal Leipzig cantor'.[31] Indeed Jaeger had no hesitation in dubbing Parry the 'English Bach' on the strength of the resourceful and imaginative 'quasi-baroque' fugal style that prevails in much of the choral writing. Such consistency of treatment and technical skill have the effect of enhancing the deliberately archaic orientation of the piece and create a congruity that avoids the impression of mechanical academicism (which occasionally let Parry down in other contexts, such as the finales of *De Profundis* and the *Magnificat*). To contrast with the contrapuntal earnestness, several of the more devotional sections are homophonic. The setting of the Sanctus (which, Jaeger maintained, was 'one of the serenest things Sir Hubert has ever given us')[32] is one such example, while the emotional supplication 'Miserere nostri' combines homophony and imitation with an affecting language of modal harmonic progressions. Nor should one overlook the diatonic breadth of the two bass solos—'Tu Rex gloriae' and 'Salvum fac populum tuum'—which combine pathos with simplicity.

---

[30] Letter to F. J. H. Jenkinson, 1 June 1899, CUL Add. MS 6463, fol 1229.
[31] A. J. Jaeger, 'Sir Hubert Parry's Te Deum', *Musical Times* (1 Sept. 1900), 600.
[32] Ibid.

The Te Deum is also structurally inventive. The monothematic orchestral introduction is important for several reasons. The first is the central theme (Ex. 35*a*) which is sounded three times in keys a major third apart (F, A, and D flat) before returning to the tonic (F major) by way of the dominant. This scheme functions as a useful anticipation of the significant tonal areas and relationships in the work as a whole. An overview of the piece shows a liberal division of the text into a series of seven substantial paragraphs. The first, constructed of four smaller sections, acts both to establish a firm foundation for the tonic key and as a choral exposition of the 'Te Deum' theme which is treated fugally at the outset and in grandiose augmentation at its close. At this juncture the connections with the third-relationships of the orchestral prelude become clear, for the second paragraph ('Te gloriosus Apostolorum') moves to D major, and the third ('Tu Rex gloriae Christe') to B flat ('Tu Rex gloriae'). The fourth part ('Aeternam fac cum sanctis tuis'), centred around E flat major, performs a pivotal role to the next series of third-related sections. 'Salvum fac', a more lyrical episode for bass and male chorus, passes on to the albeit less distinctive 'Per singulos' in E major for female chorus, and the sequence of major-thirds is completed by a move to C major ('Miserere nostri'). Having arrived at the dominant, the duet for soprano and bass ('Fiat misericordia') serves as a brief preparation for the finale which is, as Jaeger rightly stated, an imposing example of contrapuntal architecture. Within this spacious movement, Parry attempts to draw together elements of the entire work. On a tonal level, third-related keys (such as D and B flat) are touched on once again, while the eventual return to the dominant of F is executed through D flat—a shift which mimics that of the orchestral introduction. Thematically, the fugal point 'In te Domine speravi', and its persistent consequent phrase 'non confundar in aeternum' (Ex. 35*b*), reiterate the seminal shape of the work's main theme to such an extent that the

Ex. 35. *Te Deum* (1900). *a* central theme; *b* concluding fugal theme.

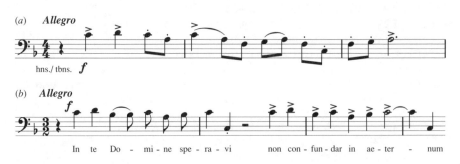

(*a*) *Allegro*

hns./ tbns. *f*

(*b*) *Allegro*

f

In te Do - mi - ne spe - ra - vi   non con - fun - dar in ae - ter - num

epigrammatic restatement of the 'Te Deum' idea (letter OO) seems inevitable.

Shortly after the performance of the Te Deum, Parry was in Birmingham to conduct *De Profundis* and the first hearing of his new scena, *The Soldier's Tent*, written specially for the festival and sung by its dedicatee, Harry Plunket Greene. The scena was performed on 2 October, the day before the first and ill-fated performance of Elgar's *Dream of Gerontius* in which Plunket Greene also sang. That Elgar's work was causing considerable difficulty in rehearsal is clear from Parry's diary entries in the days approaching the festival week. At one Queen's Hall rehearsal Richter took more than a fair share of time over *Gerontius* and parts of *Götterdämmerung*. Plunket Greene was exhausted and *The Soldier's Tent* therefore suffered an 'appalling rehearsal' which had to be abandoned. Fortunately, the following day, things fared better for the scena and *De Profundis*, but the rehearsals in Birmingham did not augur at all well for the psalm. On 29 September Parry wrote in his diary with some irritation: 'To rehearsal in afternoon in Town Hall. Elgar's Dream of Gerontius gave a vast amount of trouble and kept chorus and orchestra at work till past 5.30. No use trying to get anything out of "De Profundis" with them all tired out.'[33] With so little rehearsal and a choir sapped of enthusiasm, the performance of *De Profundis* inevitably came to grief. Parry was furious: 'Terrible performance of "De Profundis". 1st sopranos came in a bar too soon in the opening passage and ruined it. And it all went as flabbily as possible. Nothing to be got out of the chorus by any means.'[34] By comparison, *The Soldier's Tent*, 'went fairly' but was undoubtedly overshadowed by the previous misfortunes of the concert.

For his one experiment in the genre, Parry selected his text—a Romanian folk poem—from Alma Strettell's collection *The Bard of Dimbovitza*. The poem, with its repetitive pattern, was an imaginative choice. There was much potential in the dichotomy between the beguiling spirits and the courage of the sleeping soldier who, resisting them, is doomed to die. Certainly the opening lines ('Across the mountains the mist hath drawn a cov'ring of bridal white') inspired Parry to produce an evocative orchestral prelude and postlude that seem strongly reminiscent of Wagner's idyllic 'forest murmurs' in *Siegfried*. It is an impressive romantic picture of nature—a phenomenon rare in Parry's music—enhanced by rich harmony and deft orchestration. Hence it is disappointing that Parry failed to imbue the vocal section with the same enchanting vision. The two main ideas—one in a tranquil 6/8, the other a martial fanfare—are not strong enough ideas in themselves, and there is a surprising lack of variation in the treatment of

---

[33] Diary, 29 Sept. 1900.   [34] Ibid. 2 Oct. 1900.

repeated sections which require modification to mirror the subtle changes of textual nuance. Sadly, these deficiences detract from the fine music that frames them.

The main work that occupied Parry during 1900 and which overlapped both the composition of the *Te Deum* and *The Soldier's Tent* was the music commissioned by Cambridge University for Aeschylus' *Agamemnon*. It was the only occasion on which Parry turned to tragedy. Evidently he was deeply impressed with the play's imagery of impending doom and foreboding, its dire seriousness subsequently prompting him to compose his most ambitious score. This was also due to the fact that the 'choral' dimension of the play was extensive and the Cambridge Committee wanted as many as possible of the 840 lines allocated to the chorus set to music. Eventually they agreed on 660, but this still added up to a mammoth task along with other purely instrumental numbers such as an Introduction to Act I, a triumphal March at the beginning of Act II, a brief Intermezzo at the end of Act II, and a tragic Coda. In the daunting job of word-setting Parry had the best classics scholars of his day to rely on: there were his old friends Jenkinson and Verrall from the days of *The Birds*, as well as Henry Jackson, the Regius Professor Sir Richard Jebb, and Sir John Sandys who many years ago had 'addressed' him at the conferral of his honorary doctorate at the university. Great pains were taken over rhythm and stress. There were long meetings in the College with Jebb and the stage manager, J. W. Clark, to go through the Greek and the dramatic exigencies of the production, and there were also numerous discussions with Charles Wood who undertook the training of the chorus as well as the responsibility of conducting all but the first and last performances.

One of the major problems with which Parry was confronted was the enormous lengths of the choruses. There was so much to learn, and so little time to learn it. A solution was found by assigning the Strophes to one voice (e.g. the tenors) and the Antistrophes to the other (basses). This division immediately suggested a natural means of musical variety for, in order to create the necessary contrast between Strophe and Antistrophe, Parry set one against the other by means of more remote key relationships. This can be seen clearly in Strophe B (tenors) and Antistrophe B (basses) of the first chorus which juxtapose C major and A flat (Ex. 36*a*), while the succeeding Strophe and Antistrophe Y contrast C minor with D flat major. As Parry explained in a letter to F. G. Edwards of the *Musical Times*, there were also other possibilities:

then there was the artistic opportunity of making the Antistrophe a variation of the Strophe in almost every case. Sometimes turning the accompaniment upside down, as in the latter parts of Strophe Y and Antistrophe Y in No. 4 (pp. 65 and 67 [of the vocal score]) (the third Chorus) and sometimes when the words of the

Ex. 36. *Agamemnon* (1900). *a* the openings of Strophe B (Tenors) and Antistrophe B (Basses); *b* Clytemnestra's theme; *c* Helen's theme; *d* Agamemnon's theme.

cont. over/

Ex. 36. cont.

Strophes and Antistrophes conveyed a different sentiment, the same tune or something like it was accompanied by quite different figures. And in one or two instances by a quite totally different orchestral colour e.g. Strophe B in the first chorus [p. 23] is accompanied by strings and Antistrophe B altogether by low wind.[35]

Since much of the vocal delivery is traditionally syllabic and in unison, the variety created by antiphony, arresting tonal shifts, and orchestral accompaniment does much to avert textural monotony. This is also avoided, as Graves noted in his review for the *Spectator*, by confining vocal utterance to the chorus, which is then pitted against the spoken delivery of the main dramatis personae. However, music and spoken (or 'intoned') word are combined with great effect, notably towards the end of Act III with Clytemnestra's furious Antistrophe ('At last you see the future and the truth') which is dispatched with a Wagnerian fury reminiscent of Hagen's vengeance in *Götterdämmerung*.

In writing to Edwards Parry declared that he believed that leitmotiv could not be the 'allsufficing means of artistic organisation', but there were nevertheless plenty of opportunities where they could function as 'subordinate elements of coherence'.[36] The main antagonist, Clytemnestra, is portrayed by a figure introduced by the chorus when they first address her in Act I Scene 2 (Ex. 36*b*). Whenever there is allusion to anything ominous her motif recurs, just as the 'ring' motif does in Wagner's tetralogy with which Parry's material shares a distinct harmonic similarity. Furthermore the rhythmic character of Clytem-

[35] Letter to F. G. Edwards, 20 Nov. 1900, BL Egerton MS 3090.   [36] Ibid.

nestra's motif is subsequently extended to infuse the lament over Agamemnon in Act II ('Tell me why, at ev'ry hour, haunting, ever haunting fear round my soul foreboding evil hovers'), and later becomes the tragic funeral cortège of the Coda, attempting to conjure up heroic visions of Siegfried's awesome *Trauermarsch*. Other ideas are equally all-pervasive. The phrase 'Sing me a burden of sorrow but good shall triumph!' recurs with increasing irony, especially in Act III, while Helen, purportedly the main cause of the ensuing tragedy, is represented by a more lyrical 'undercurrent' (Ex. 36*c*) which is beautifully worked in the orchestral Introduction. By comparison, the motif representing Agamemnon, the eponymous hero, is somewhat less interesting (Ex. 36*d*), and though his material is subject to appreciable transformation and amplification (e.g. in the Coda), it lacks the colour and distinctiveness of its counterparts.

Agamemnon was performed by the Cambridge ADC during the week of 16–21 November; 'Chorus first rate', Parry recounted in his diary, 'everything went pat—no hitch whatever.' But its reception undoubtedly lacked the enthusiasm excited by either *The Birds* or *The Frogs*. Commentators were confused by the mixture of antiquity and modernity. The play was performed by an all-male cast singing in Greek and clothed in classical garb, but critics from the *Saturday Review*, the *Westminster Gazette*, and the local *Granta* could not reconcile this deference to antiquarian accuracy with Parry's 'modern'-sounding score. In this respect, the *Saturday Review* was particularly dismissive, though others such as the *Granta* and the *Athenaeum* were prepared to admit that the musical quality often rose above that of the dramatic adaptation. The theatre too, Parry recalled, was very bad for sound, and this probably affected the audience's perception considerably. One cannot escape the suspicion, however, that Parry was not entirely happy with the score. After the first performance he felt the music 'fell quite flat' and in no way truly measured up to the inspiration of Aeschylus' masterpiece. Other tragedies, namely Macfarren's *Ajax of Sophocles* (1880), Stanford's *Eumenides* (which Parry had heard in Cambridge in 1885), and even parts of Wood's slighter *Iphigenia in Tauris* (1894), showed a greater flair and dramatic spontaneity which, while present and virile in his interpretations of Aristophanic Comedy, seemed to elude him here.

Parry's social and academic ties in 1900 were augmented by a number of new obligations. He accepted the Presidency of the British branch of the newly inaugurated International Musical Society and he was asked to chair meetings of the People's Concert Society, an organization close to his heart for its efforts to banish élitism by the dissemination of serious music among the poorer strata of society. There were also dinners for the Wagner Society, the Magpie Madrigal Society, the Literary Society, the

Musicians' Company and the London County Council, not to mention the public protocol of royal functions at the Imperial Institute, Windsor Castle, Buckingham Palace, and Kensington Palace.

The previous year he had agreed to give a series of three lectures for the Royal Institution in January and February which he entitled 'Neglected By-ways in Music'. Exploring areas which he considered 'survivals of an intermediate stage of human development' (such as 'Fancies', 'Divertissements', 'Masques', 'Ayres', 'Monologues and Dialogues', the 'Cantata a voce sola', and 'German by-ways'), these lectures continued to reflect Parry's allegiance to the Darwinian precepts set out in *The Evolution of the Art of Music*. Much of the subject-matter under examination had also been thrown up by his study of seventeenth- and eighteenth-century music, and many of the arguments appear again in his Oxford book.

Having been admitted to Convocation in late January, Parry's Inaugural Lecture at Oxford, the first in his new professorial capacity, took place on 7 March. In order to accommodate more people, the venue was moved from the Sheldonian Theatre to the Town Hall; even so, the hall was packed and the reception tumultuous. The lecture, published in pamphlet form by the Clarendon Press, was entitled prophetically 'Style in Musical Art'. It was a theme on which Parry was to base his future lectures at the university, and from which he was eventually to compile a new book. In addition to his Oxford commitments, he found much of his time consumed by the demands of the London University Commission who were keen to associate the London Music Colleges with the newly reconstituted university. The delicate negotiations involved a heavy and lengthy correspondence. Many of Parry's College colleagues were vehemently in favour of maintaining independence from London University, from whom they feared interference. While understanding this view, and to an appreciable extent sympathizing with it, Parry was also aware of the public interest in the association and the advantages it would bring with the opening up of facilities, the widening of the syllabus, and the evaluation of degrees using a broad reservoir of expertise from all the institutions. Consequently, through Parry's patient negotiating skills and his overall willingness to listen, the various Music Schools were persuaded to enter the scheme. He oversaw the beginnings of this co-operation until his retirement from the University Senate in April 1901.

1900 brought with it a mixed bag of domestic blessings. The arduous schedule of weekend travelling to Highnam, Rustington (where Maude was almost permanently settled), and back to London, began to convince Parry of a hopeless, inescapable loneliness. Solitary train journeys and hermetic evenings in Kensington Square were the cause of long periods of depression that were only partially mitigated by intense 'scrambles' of work cutting down his book for the Oxford History series or attending novelties such as Isadora Duncan's 'entertainments' at the New Gallery or Puccini's *Tosca* at Covent Garden. Some solace came with Gwen and Harry's move to Kensington Square, and positive delight when Dolly and Arthur arrived home from Denmark. With his family once again around him, and the addition of a grandchild, Elizabeth, born to Dolly and Arthur in December, some of the depression lifted.

Although there was little time for sailing during the year—there being only room for ten days in the English Channel with Pownall—Parry was not prevented from looking out for a larger yacht. He had already intended to visit the Irish coast again the following year but considered that the smaller ketch had suffered too severely in the Atlantic seas. Having charged Harvey's boatyard in Littlehampton with the responsibility of finding a new boat, he was pleased to hear from John Harvey in mid-December that a spacious 63-foot ketch called *Humber* had come to his notice that might suit. With characteristic alacrity, Parry scuttled down to Littlehampton to view her, and perceiving the yacht's potential quickly purchased her. Having been built in Hull specifically as a pilot for the river Humber (hence her name), she needed extensive refitting which Parry himself designed. Harvey's undertook the work and she was seaworthy in time for the summer of 1901.

Just as George Pembroke's death in 1895 seemed to signal a spate of deaths during that year, Grove's death in May 1900 similarly prefaced another series of mortalities. Sullivan died in November and Parry was requested by the Prince of Wales to attend the funeral as his representative. Ranald McDonnell, Parry's former business partner at Lloyd's, died in early January 1901, and Stainer, who had died suddenly after a heart attack in Italy at the end of March, was buried in Oxford. Overshadowing this grim chain of events was the death of Queen Victoria at Osborne on 22 January. The whole country mourned. The Queen, who had asked to be buried at Windsor, was brought to London from Portsmouth. As the train passed through stations on the way to London, people were seen solemnly kneeling on the ground. Then, as the body was taken from Victoria to Paddington Station for the journey to Windsor, Londoners were able to participate in the funeral of their sovereign. The streets were bedecked in purple and white precisely as the Queen had wanted; her coffin was placed on a simple gun carriage and was accompanied by the new King, members of the Royal Family, and the Kaiser. Parry watched the events from the balcony of his friends the Horners at Buckingham Gate. 'The new King on a tall horse looked imposing. The Emperor extremely pale,' he wrote afterwards. 'Too much dazed by the feeling of the Queen being inside the little coffin to take much notice of other people or what was going on—It seemed to come upon us all of a sudden.'[37]

The loss of friends and colleagues, plus the fact that Dannreuther was still extremely ill and unable to work effectively, was a salutary reminder of his own age and frailty. At 53 Parry was by now beginning to feel the strain of ceaseless activity. At the end of his diary entries, phrases such as 'ached with weariness' or 'too tired to work' become increasingly common as do references to a lack of appetite and his heart disorder. In February 1901 he once again became rudely aware that his physical condition was rapidly declining. For several days he lay incarcerated at Highnam, 'stupified' and 'disgustingly ill'. His doctors delivered a gloomy diagnosis and an even more grave prognosis unless he refrained from work for at least a month. A holiday abroad was once again prescribed so Parry, with Sidney Gambier Parry, boarded the *Norham Castle* bound for Madeira where they spent the next three weeks in Funchal, Tarovante, Santa Cruz, and Tenerife, enjoying the mild climate, subtropical vegetation, and picturesque scenery. Nevertheless, the noise at the hotels and the bustle of people made him anxious and militated against any physical improvement. Ill and depressed he wrote home to Maude: 'In my present condition hardly anything could be worse than the life I have to lead. As you know well, society always tries me very much and this is a perfect pandemonium.'[38] On his return it was therefore no surprise to find his doctors disappointed in his progress. Further rest was recommended, but, typically, Parry refused for there were important matters to oversee at the College.

In June the New Concert Room was due to be opened and for the occasion he had composed a short *Ode to Music* to include the new organ that he had bought for the College as a gift. The words of the ode were by Arthur C. Benson, a housemaster at Eton. Benson's poem, constructed in four uncomplicated stanzas, was full of subtle metaphor and simile to which Parry immediately responded. Surviving correspondence also shows that Benson, an able amateur musician himself, was a most congenial and amenable collaborator who quickly and willingly carried out any desired changes to the text. The *Ode to Music* was performed at the College on 13 June and again on 23 July being received with enthusiasm. Benson was delighted:

I could not find words truly to express to you my admiration of the music of the Ode or my gratitude to you for the subtle and glorifying interpretation of the words. I thought too that the performance was wonderfully perceptive and beautiful. It was the purest pleasure to me, and I thought it a *great* work. I can only say that I am proud to have been so honoured.[39]

[37] Diary, 2 Feb. 1901.   [38] Letter to Maude Parry, 7 Mar. 1901, ShP.
[39] Letter from A. C. Benson, 13 June 1901, ShP.

Benson's assessment may have been somewhat exaggerated, but the ode, though slight in structure and scope, is certainly an attractive piece of choral and orchestral writing. The 'nobilmente' orchestral introduction, with its swirling appoggiaturas, muscular harmony, and rich tessitura, is comparable in mood and breadth with that of *Blest Pair of Sirens*, and the opening chorus is effective in its simplicity. Only the central march-like paragraph ('O march of years') is wanting in inspiration, but this is offset by the broad, harmonically slow-moving gestures of the fervent last chorus ('Music, be this thy temple hourly blest') where Parry shows himself to be a consummate master of choral texture.

During the summer of 1901 Parry set other projects in motion. Without the pressure of any big commissions, he sketched several songs and outlined the first chapter of a book he had always wanted to write on J. S. Bach.[40] He took his first extended voyage in the *Humber* to the south coast of Ireland where he enjoyed the traditional regatta and fireworks in Cork harbour and visited Baltimore Bay and his 'beloved' Crookhaven.

Ireland was badly needed therapy and he came back restored to something of his former vigorous constitution. The Gloucester Festival included *The Soldier's Tent* sung by Plunket Greene and *Job*, both of which were performed well. But only days after the festival was over he was thrown back into a state of debilitation. The first illness was due to a bicycle accident in which he seriously injured his shoulder and imbedded some thorns deep in his head. The thorns had to be removed under anaesthetic and his shoulder remained so painful that he was obliged to conduct the Leeds rehearsals of *A Song of Darkness and Light* with his left arm. At the end of September he was operated on again, this time to remove a sebacious cyst in his back. The eucaine anaesthetic left him 'utterly feeble' for several days, but fortunately he was strong enough to conduct at Leeds on 10 October, this time with his right arm.

The year ended much as it had begun, on an unhappy note. There were some signs that although Gwen had given birth to a son her relationship with Harry was not living up to their hopes and expectations. Consequently her marriage and well-being continued to be a major cause for concern for Parry. At the College personal relations with Stanford were also at a worrying stage. Stanford had asked the College to provide him with a fixed salary, but the Executive had refused and Stanford held Parry partly responsible. There followed many months of unpleasant confrontations and correspondence as the matter was thrashed out. So enraged was Stanford that his anger spilled over into other business as Parry's account of an Exhibition meeting relates: 'Unfortunately I came

[40] The impetus to begin the book seems to have been provided by an article commissioned by an American Encyclopaedia and written in February.

into conflict with Stanford who disputed a suggestion of mine in a most offensive manner, and caused me tired and irritated to break out into a furious wrath. He also turned green with rage . . . Very unfortunate, and upset me frightfully.'[41] Parry also learnt of others who were experiencing grave problems with the Irishman's fractiousness. Hannam at Leeds foresaw difficulties over the next festival (a situation exacerbated by Cowen's involvement) while Arthur Coleridge, an old and close friend, spoke bitterly of Stanford's obnoxious manner stating that 'Charlie *will* have his quarrel.'[42] Eventually matters came to a head in March when Parry decided to confront Stanford and resolve the deteriorating situation. Voices were raised, frank opinions were exchanged, tempers cooled, and a compromise was reached; but the dispute was only the first of many that would exhaust Parry's patience with his colleague and ultimately result in an irreparable rift between them.

Whereas Parry's rapport with Stanford was becoming ever more brittle, a more positive and blooming relationship was materializing with Elgar. In 1899 the younger man had already invited Parry to become an honorary member of the Worcestershire Philharmonic. Parry, extremely reluctantly, was forced to refuse on the grounds of College rubric:

It is contrary to the rule of the Royal College that the Director shall accept honorary positions in connection with Musical Societies and institutions which are not connected with the R.C.M. And I have been trying to see what excuse I could make. Your Worcestershire Philharmonic is in charge of a very exceptional musician it is true, and one whom I should like to support. But, suppose that distinguished musician went off somewhere else and the philharmonic went into the charge of someone of more *in*artistic ideals! Where would the Director of [the] R.C.M. be then poor thing? I should be proud to have my name associated with yours; or to be of any help I could. You honour me too by your invitation. How can one find an implied connection with the R.C.M.? If I could only puzzle that out![43]

Elgar accepted Parry's dilemma, and as if to make up for it, he produced *The Lotos-Eaters* in Worcester on 10 May 1902. Parry on his part contributed to the purchase of Elgar's Cambridge Doctoral robes and was delighted when they arrived on Elgar's doorstep: 'I am very glad the festive raiment has safely arrived, and I hope it fits. I should like to see you in it. I think it would suit you very well!! I am very proud to have been allowed to take part in providing it.'[44] Parry tried hard to secure Elgar both to conduct the *Enigma* Variations with the College orchestra in November 1901, and in March the following year as an external

[41] Diary, 27 Mar. 1902.   [42] Ibid. 24 Jan. 1902.
[43] Letter to Edward Elgar, 11 Mar. 1899, HWRO 705:445 5247/8.
[44] Letter to Edward Elgar, 11 Dec. 1901, ibid. Others to contribute to Elgar's robes were Plunket Greene, Jaeger, Percy Pitt, Alfred Kalisch, Nicholas Kilburn, and Henry Wood.

examiner in composition. Elgar was not able to fulfil either invitation, the second of which he countenanced with his characteristic diffidence and mistrust of academia. Parry continued to praise and admire Elgar's music. The *Enigma* Variations, as we know, he held in high esteem, but he was also generous in his appreciation of *Cockaigne* which he heard both at the Philharmonic and the Gloucester Festival in 1901. 'Brilliant piece of work and quite up to date,' he noted in his diary. 'Even Circus music at times. But vivid.'[45] Parry's admiration for Elgar was reciprocated by the younger man. The Director of the Royal College of Music was not only, in Elgar's eyes, the most important instigator of all that was flourishing in modern musical England, but he was also an eminently likeable and approachable man. Indeed Elgar respected and trusted Parry to such an extent that, during the last stages of the *Apostles* in 1903, he felt able to write for advice on word-setting:

Will you tell me how *you* would accent in music the word 'toward'. I have searched Saul, Job etc. in vain. At school I was taught to say '*to*-wards' and my dictionary (Webster) gives a lot of others who say the same thing. But some well educated persons still say 'to*ward*'—this is naturally easier to sing—but is there any authority? Now *do not, please*, answer this except on the enclosed *p.c.*—you are too busy to be bothered; just write the word for me, and your petitioner will ever play b.[46]

It was a letter that reflected not only Elgar's high regard for Parry's choral music but also a reverence for the older man's knowledge and experience. In the near future, when he was surrounded by controversy, accusations, and bitterness from other well-established British composers, his recollections of Parry's ungrudging kindness, combined with a genuine esteem for the man and his music, never faltered.

One of the main focal points of 1902 was of course the Coronation of King Edward VII, and every British composer hoped to gain public kudos from a commission for the service itself, or for auspicious occasions connected with the celebration. Parry's first assignment arrived at the end of 1901 when Arthur Benson (who was already actively collaborating with Elgar on a Coronation Ode) asked for a tune for his words 'God of all Created Things' which Novello subsequently published. The main assignment, however, came from Sir Frederick Bridge, the Director of Music for the Coronation, who wanted a new style of processional anthem using the opening words of the service 'I was glad when they said unto me' (from Psalm 122) to accompany the King and Queen's entrance into Westminster Abbey. Work on 'I was

---

[45] Diary, 20 June 1901.
[46] Letter from Edward Elgar, 27 May 1903, ShP. See also Parry's reply in J. Northrop Moore, *Elgar: Letters of a Lifetime*, 130.

glad' was begun in mid-May, and after consultation with Bridge over choreography and the incorporation of the *Vivat*s, the anthem was completed by 25 May. During June Parry spent time scoring the anthem for the huge orchestral forces, and after rehearsals in the Abbey he wrote a cadenza for the organ which could be inserted in case of delays. The public and press meantime awaited the novel manner of the composition with considerable excitement.

Parry's Coronation Anthem is universally recognized as a masterpiece of ceremonial music—perhaps the finest of its genre in modern times. It exhibits the same natural affinity for massive choral effect and regal majesty as *Zadok the Priest*. Evidently it made such an impression that it was included in George V's Coronation in 1911 and afterwards became a regular fixture at later Coronations and many other royal occasions. For King Edward's Coronation 'I was glad' was performed with a choir of 430, a large orchestra, organ, and ten fanfare trumpeters from the Royal Military School, Kneller Hall. The skill and stylish aplomb which Parry demonstrated in successfully deploying these lavish forces with imaginative variety and, moreover, musical ingenuity—as well as accomplishing the desired functional effect—was a remarkable achievement and the key to its abiding success.

The first part of the anthem (SSATTB) was sung by the Abbey choir at the West End of the building. Their opening phrase, greeting the monarchs, is surely one of the most famous choral exclamations in the English repertoire, particularly in the way Parry highlights the word 'glad' with a sudden deviation from B flat to the dominant of C minor. The diatonic dissonance of the next strain ('Our feet shall stand in thy gate') harkens back to the intense language of *Blest Pair of Sirens*, a connection which becomes more obvious during the antiphonal exchanges with the 'General Choir' ('Jerusalem is builded as a city'). Cadencing in the tonic (B flat) this first section gives way to fanfares and the *Vivat*s, shouted vociferously by the King's Scholars of Westminster School aloft in the Triforium and answered by the full choir below. Then comes one of the most affecting moments in the anthem when Parry quits G major by the smoothest of modulations to G flat, the key of the Semi-chorus ('O pray for the peace of Jerusalem'). The Semi-chorus (or Quartet) acts as a calm interlude before the final section, sung by the full choir, re-establishes the march rhythms and brings the anthem to a strenuous conclusion.

The version sung at the 1902 Coronation was not quite the one we know today. Apart from minor disparities in the fanfares (and the *Vivat*s which naturally change from monarch to monarch), the major difference lay in the orchestral introduction (Ex. 37*a*) whose rising phrases were derived from the vocal imitation 'We will go' (see bars 4–7 after letter

A). In 1911 Parry revised the orchestral prelude into a much grander affair, making more overt use of additional brass. Moreover, since the work as whole was unified by the opening choral motive and its diminution in the orchestral ritornelli (Ex. 37*b* and 37*c*), he decided to give prominence to it in the introduction where it is announced by the massed trumpets (Ex. 37*d*).

The full rehearsal to co-ordinate music and liturgy in the Abbey took place on 24 June, two days before the Coronation. Little did the public know that the King had suddenly been taken ill at Buckingham Palace. There the King had had an emergency operation for appendicitis in a hastily constructed operation room. The medical bulletins assured the public that he was recovering satisfactorily, but it was announced that the service at the Abbey was to be postponed indefinitely. Parry, who had recently heard from Lord Salisbury that the King wished to make him a Baronet, had gone straight from the College to the Abbey unaware of the news. His diary account gives a vivid picture of events:

Went through the Cloisters and into the S[outh] Transept and came into the Chancel just as the Bishop of London stepped onto the dais where the carved thrones are, and, addressing mainly the performers on the organ screen and the choir, for the rest of the Abbey was almost empty, announced the necessity of the King's undergoing an operation and the Coronation being postponed—and he ended with an appeal to all to join him [directly] in a Litany. He then went up to the altar and began. The choir joined in with a most superb tone, and produced an effect I have never experienced before. So solemn and pathetic. A few kneeling figures on the floor of the Chancel. The sun light streaming in on the ancient recumbent figures on the tombs, the thousands of empty seats! I came away soon after 2 back to College—passing through merry crowds who did not know the news![47]

The whole country was naturally anxious as all the festivities were cancelled. Multitudes of visitors in London hotels invited from the far-away colonies and dominions of the Empire started to pack their bags for the long sea journey home.

The Coronation was deferred until 9 August, but Parry was determined not to cancel his sailing trip to the west of Ireland. At the end of July, he, C. H. Lloyd, Pownall, and Sidney Gambier Parry made their way to Valencia Island where Pengelly was waiting with the *Humber*. For a week he made lightning visits to the Aran Islands, the cliffs of Moher, Galway, Skellig Michael, and the rarely frequented Little Skellig before it was necessary to leave for London on 7 August. At the Abbey on 8 August, Bridge 'scrambled' through 'I was glad' in such a perfunctory way that Parry was worried as to how it might turn out the following day. His uneasiness was justified. In his diary he noted: 'Bridge made a sad

[47] Diary, 24 June 1902.

Ex. 37. *I was glad* (1902). *a* original orchestral introduction; *b* first choral entry; *c* main ritornello; *d* opening of the revised orchestral introduction (1911).

mistake in the processional music and seemed to lose his head. Finished the whole anthem before the King came in at all, and had to repeat all the latter part when he did.'[48] The reason for this hiatus was the result of confusion in the King's procession which had got behindhand, and Bridge, unaware that the King had not entered the building, plunged into his *Vivat*s and the last part of the anthem. When the King finally entered the Abbey he had to be accompanied up the Nave by further organ improvisation. It was necessary therefore, when he reached the organ screen, for the King's Scholars to sing the *Vivat*s once again, before choir and orchestra repeated the end of the anthem. It was an unfortunate mishap, but catastrophe was avoided.

With the Coronation over Parry quickly made his way back to Ireland to resume his holiday. With Lloyd, Pownall, and his half-brother he had a delightful fortnight exploring the Blasket islands, the peninsulas of Dingle and Bere, and the south coast of Ireland. After crossing the channel to Milford Haven, he took the train to Gloucester to attend the wedding of his half-sister, Hilda, to Egerton Tymewell Cripps. Then it was back to Milford and home by yacht to Rustington. The day after his arrival on 1 September, word came from Dolly and Arthur who were most eager for him to travel down to north-west Sussex to see an 'ancient' house between Midhurst and Haslemere they wanted to lease. For Arthur, who had resigned from the Foreign Office and given his services to the Liberal Party, the house—Shulbrede Priory—was an ideal retreat, nestling amongst wooded hills to the south of Hindhead (in Surrey). The basis of Shulbrede was the remains of a substantial twelfth-century Augustinian settlement that had almost fallen into ruin after the Dissolution of the Monastaries in the sixteenth century. But the old part was preserved and lived in by generations of farmers who developed and expanded it. Like his son-in-law, Parry was captivated by the lofty rooms, the stone hall, the vaulting, the ancient water source, the splendid fireplaces, and the overall remote location. After Dolly and Arthur moved in at the end of September he quickly grew to love the place and Shulbrede, which was purchased outright in 1905, became a regular and convenient stopping-off point during journeys between London and Rustington.

The latter part of 1902 saw Parry back to something of his old active self. With regard to revisions, he once again turned his attention to the String Quintet which he had tinkered with in 1896, but to no avail; it was still not as he wanted it so that, even after its performance at Leighton House in March 1903, it was put away. The first movement of the 'English' Symphony was also revised and rescored for a concert in the

---

[48] Diary, 9 Aug. 1902.

Winter Gardens in Bournemouth. There was much proof-reading to do
for the publishers. Jaeger was anxious to publish the 'Lady Radnor'
Suite and reprint the Trio in B minor. Augener had also reprinted the
Characteristic Popular Tunes of the British Isles in 1901, and wanted to do
the same for the A major Piano Sonata and later the *Shakespeare Sonnets*.
The major publications of the year were, however, his volume for the
Oxford History of Music, and two further volumes of *English Lyrics*.

Set V of the *English Lyrics* contained several songs of a much earlier
date: 'Love and laughter' was written in Cannes in December 1876, was
revised in 1882, and appeared first in *Girl's Own Paper* in January 1892;
'Crabbed age and youth', almost certainly a discarded contribution to the
second set of *English Lyrics* (consisting exclusively of Shakespeare
settings), was composed in 1882; while Beaumont and Fletcher's 'Lay a
garland on my hearse', dates from 1888. The miniature scale of 'Lay a
garland' has Wolfian affinities, notably its postlude in the tonic major.
However, the idea of the lament in which the fullest pathos comes in the
postlude goes back to Purcell's 'When I am laid in earth' (the actual
sound of which is concealed in bars 2–4), though the use here of the
tonic major is pure Romanticism. In 'Proud Maisie', also an early song,
the clear-cut dialogue of Scott's poem is symbolized by the fluctuation of
F major ('proud') and D minor ('mortal'). The song also provides an
example of an unusually good use of an opening ritornello as the epitome
of the entire song which complements the 'olde' Baroque sense of
pastiche, a style prevalent in 'Crabbed age and youth' and 'A stray
nymph of Dian'. The outstanding song of the fifth set, which eclipses
even the tonal and structural economy of 'Proud Maisie' is 'A Welsh
lullaby', a setting of a translation from the Welsh by Edmund Jones. The
'lullaby' charm is evoked by a gentle ostinato and the harmonic structure
attains a great sense of repose through its use of a static tonic/dominant
drone. This feeling is further reflected in the contours of the vocal line,
particularly the refrains which are mainly orientated around an inverted
dominant pedal. The fundamental harmonic vocabulary also rarely
strays from tonic or dominant triads which reinforces the aura of
innocence. As a result of this diatonic purity, the textual catastrophe of
the second verse ('torn') is successfully thrown into relief by the tonal
divergence to the flat mediant (A flat).

By comparison, the sixth set of *Lyrics* is less distinguished, though still
preserving the composer's characteristic freshness and unsentimental
manner. 'When comes my Gwen', another of Edmund Jones's translations,
belongs to the ballad style of 'When lovers meet again' (Set IV); it was
dedicated to Harry and Gwen as a 'Christmas box' in 1901. The slightly
sardonic 'Love is a bable', a setting of Elizabethan lyrics, is an attractive,
scherzo-like ditty. Plunket Greene was a regular exponent of 'A lover's

garland', one of two settings 'from the Greek' by Alfred Perceval Graves composed in February 1902. Most affecting, however, are the sighing phrases and melancholy cadences of 'And yet I love her till I die', which anticipates the many settings by later English lyricists.

One major feature of Parry's musical life which differed widely from those of Stanford and Elgar was his lack of international recognition. Stanford, as we know, enjoyed considerable success in Germany with his operas, and his *Irish* Symphony was performed widely by such eminent conductors as Martucci and Mahler. Elgar achieved an even greater reputation abroad: Mahler and Julius Buths took on the *Enigma* Variations which were also given at Cologne, Mainz, and Wiesbaden; *Gerontius* was performed in Düsseldorf, Darmstadt, Brussels, Vienna, Paris, and New York; the First Symphony was played in Berlin, Bonn, Leipzig, Vienna, St Petersburg, and in several American cities. With the exception of a few disparate performances of the Symphonic Variations and the odd chamber work, Parry's music was barely known to the European public. Hence it was with some interest that Jaeger learnt of an invitation from Dr Emil Streithof, the Director of the Duisburger Gesangverein, for Parry to attend the 50th anniversary celebrations of the society at the Duisburg Festival in May. For the occasion Dr Walter Josephson, conductor of the festival, had prepared a German translation of *Blest Pair of Sirens* and very much wanted Parry to hear it. Strauss's promised choral ballad *Taillefer* could not be made ready so Parry's work was the only choral novelty in the programme. Jaeger was delighted:

You really *must* go over and be present . . . I shall *most* likely be there and you can *order me about* if I can help you at all (I am not sure whether you speak German). Oh yes! you *really must* go. Why, you are always travelling about England conducting your works; why then not please those good Germans? They will make you feel at home; Rhinelanders *can* do that. Ask Elgar!

Sincerely yours,
A. J. Jaeger.

Even my dear wife who sends her kind remembrances says 'You *really MUST* go'.[49]

But Parry vacillated for a while. There was, as usual, much work at the College, and there were degree papers to look over at Oxford. Jaeger was vociferous in his persistence as Novello had now asked him to go as a representative of the firm:

And now we all hope devoutly that you *will* go. It would be a terrible disappointment to the Committee and especially to Dr Josephson and the Chorus if you stayed away, while your going would, I feel sure, give English

[49] Letter from A. J. Jaeger, 25 Apr. 1903, ShP.

music a tremendous push uphill *abroad* (—which it wants badly, don't it?). If Oxford Examination papers keep you, why—take 'em with you and do them in the train; there's plenty of time going and returning. It is an exceptional occasion and surely for once you may be allowed to take exceptional liberties with your work. The Committee are inviting *all* the conductors of big societies in Rhineland and Westphalia (Steinbach, Buths, Schwickerath, Heubner, Haym, Reuter, Müller etc etc etc). They can do much for your music and English music generally. So once more—*DO* go![50]

To Jaeger's relief, Parry, realizing the rare chance put in his way, relented and travelled to Duisburg with Plunket Greene who was also engaged to sing in the festival. *Blest Pair* took its place in a vast four-hour concert on the second day which included the first German performance of Bruckner's Ninth Symphony. The programme also contained Bruckner's Te Deum, piano music played by Busoni, and Strauss's *Tod und Verklärung* which immediately preceded Parry's work. This juxtaposition evidently worried the composer, but the audience were unperturbed by it and gave Parry a clamorous reception. He received a large bay wreath and was the centre of attention at the banquet afterwards. The German press were equally full of praise. The *Rhein- und Ruhr Zeitung* remarked on the powerful impression made by the work and called it a 'pearl amongst English compositions'.[51] Elgar, who was better known to German audiences, was curious to know how *Blest Pair* fared. 'I regret very much that I could not get away,' he wrote on Parry's return to England; 'I would have added a good English yell to the Deutsche's plaudits had I been free: I hope the chorus was good in your "Sirens" which is amongst the noblest works of man!'[52] News came from an ecstatic Jaeger: 'Parry had a really great success. In fact his "Sirens" had more success than Strauss "Tod & Verkl". They nearly killed Parry with Kindness, especially the ladies! I was very glad the venture turned out so well.'[53] And the following day the man from Novello confessed to Elgar that, in spite of all the Brucknerian and Straussian modernities, Parry's music was an 'oasis'. 'It was the only work which really *thrilled* & *elevated* me. And I have Known it for nearly 20 years! Not a bad test!'[54]

The music of Strauss and Elgar featured prominently in the months after Parry's return from Duisburg. Between 3 and 9 June at the St James's Hall, Strauss was honoured with a festival of his music in which eight of his symphonic poems were heard. Parry, who owned several of the scores—*Tod und Verklärung* he particularly admired—went to several of the concerts and 'was fairly stunned' by the brilliance of the

[50] Letter from A. J. Jaeger, 13 May 1903, ShP.
[51] *Musical Times*, (1 July 1903), 452.
[52] Letter from Edward Elgar, 27 May 1903, ShP.
[53] J. Northrop Moore, *Elgar and his Publishers*, i (Oxford, 1987), 440.   [54] Ibid. i. 442.

music.[55] He also entertained Strauss to lunch at the College and, taking the orchestra through *Tod und Verklärung* afterwards, the German *enfant terrible* was greatly impressed by their playing.

Strauss had paid Elgar many compliments in a speech after the Düsseldorf performance of *Gerontius* which, as C. W. Orr remarked later, 'caused some fluttering in the academic dovecots' in England.[56] Parry, however, felt no animosity (even though Stanford, always volatile, may have had his feathers ruffled). He was keen as ever to follow the progress of his great contemporary. On 9 October he heard *The Apostles* in rehearsal which he found 'remarkable for the richness of its colour and the directness of its appeal'.[57] He also heard *Gerontius* at its first London performance in the newly opened Westminster Cathedral, though this time Elgar's now famous work elicited a quite different gut reaction:

In afternoon to the new R. C. Cathedral at Westminster to hear Elgar's Gerontius. The place very imposing indeed—and good for sound too. The work gave me a better impression than when I heard it at Birmingham, the surroundings lent it additional effect. But it reeks too much of the morbid and unnatural terrors and hysterics engendered by priestcraft to be congenial—vivid though it certainly is.[58]

It was no better at Hereford in September. The subject of *Gerontius* was 'revolting. Debased and craven religion, hysteric and morbid'.[59] Newman's blatant exposition of Roman theology ran in violent contradiction to the sentiments to which Parry himself was aspiring both in life and in art. For him *Gerontius* excited a revulsion against dogma, superstition, guilt, and power which prevented liberation of the intellect. The ferocious outbursts of his notebooks clearly show his rabid antipathy:

The chief object of Roman Catholic education is to prevent people being educated.

Those who are responsible for it are aware that the smallest freeplay of the intelligence must make the whole edifice of the creed and the power of the priest likely to collapse.

Roman Catholicism is the most gigantic imposture ever devised by the mind of man—and it is an imposture which has been maintained by all the most horrible means which man could use. By fraud, treachery, falsehood, violence, murder, assassination, the slaughter of helpless innocent women and children, the laying waste of fertile countries, by torture, by burning people alive (there is no history of anything that has ever happened in this world that is so utterly cruel, horrible, and unscrupulous) and yet it has inspired some of the purest and

[55] Diary, 9 June 1903.
[56] C. W. Orr, 'Elgar and the Public', *Musical Times*, (1 Jan. 1931), 17.
[57] Diary, 9 Oct. 1903. [58] Ibid. 6 June 1903. [59] Ibid. 10 Sept. 1903.

finest and most gifted human beings that ever lived—Dante, Palestrina, Bellini, Michelangelo, Raphael.

To infer from these outspoken comments that Parry was, in the best traditions of Victorians, inherently anti-Catholic would be too simple an analysis. Romanism represented the pinnacle of organized religion which he vehemently disliked and which he saw all too readily paraded in his mother-in-law, sister-in-law, and her husband, Friedrich von Hügel. Yet there was almost as much in Anglicanism and biblical Protestantism to rouse his ire. The Athanasian Creed, for example, he detested, refusing to say it at church; and the sacraments of Baptism and Confirmation were similarly berated. Likewise he could give no credence to the literal interpretation of scripture which, while acknowledging its power of moral and philosophical allegory, he took to be myth. It would be quite wrong, however, to suggest that Parry was irreligious purely because he was hypercritical of the Church and its doctrine. He never abandoned the assertions made in the letter to his father in 1873 that he believed in a god that was good, but beyond that nothing more could be known of him. 'God's goodness', to Parry, was manifested in *A Song of Darkness and Light*, in the mystery of nature, beauty, art, and the 'divinity' of human nature and aspiration. Darwinist to the end, Parry also intrinsically believed in man as a developing species which necessarily embraced numerous modern scientific notions of anthropological development and, perhaps most important of all, social behaviour. Responsible social behaviour implied moral choice, and it was this precept, perhaps more than any other, that infused Parry's being. To this end, as Arthur Ponsonby observed, he was instinctively and observantly religious.

Filled with the compulsion of his own idealism, Parry spent the next six years of his creative life attempting to express this in the form of ethical cantatas and oratorios. It might seem paradoxical that many of the texts he constructed for these works were drawn from the Bible, but he saw no inconsistency between core elements of Christian morality and his own principles. It was perhaps inevitable, however, that his strongly personal orientation would prompt the partial contribution or complete provision of his own words as well. These were written in a style somewhat akin to the manner of Walt Whitman, a poet very much in vogue and one Parry had for many years admired for his 'lack of elaborate speechmaking and elegance of literature' as well as his own powers of ethical affirmation and belief in the justice of democracy.[60] Unfortunately Parry did not share Whitman's power of language, imagery, or conciseness, nor did he have the poetical strength or imagination to sustain major emotional or moral issues. Consequently

[60] Notebook, ShP.

this failing gave rise to long stretches of prosaic dullness where, in spite of their worthy sentiment, the words are often trite and, as Alexander Brent Smith pointed out, the meanings are quite often obscure. It was, none the less, a failing which resulted purely from a lack of poetical flair rather than, as Smith suggested, from 'emotions common to humanity . . . which were out of range of Parry's understanding and sympathy.'[61] This was a common enough misapprehension of those who could not see beyond the numerous photographs of Parry in old age as the landowning country squire, apparently godfearing, socially conventional, extolling the virtues of his privileged class through the conceit of wealth and high public office. Such a posture automatically precluded compassion, political radicalism, and an awareness of suffering, poverty, and deprivation—the very qualities which gave Parry his innate sense of social duty, responsibility, and artistic motivation.

The first work to reflect this ethical stance was *War and Peace*, written expressly for Sir Frederick Bridge and the Royal Choral Society, and dedicated to those who died in the Boer War. It was not, however, designed to bolster the sense of jingoism that had emerged during the struggle in such poetry as W. E. Henley's 'For England's Sake' or 'Last Post' set by Stanford. Parry was seeking something eminently more objective and universal not unlike the sentiments of later twentieth-century works on the same theme such as Vaughan Williams's *Dona Nobis Pacem*, Ireland's *These Things Shall Be*, and Bliss's *Morning Heroes*. He had hoped initially that Benson would write a text for him, but the now famous author of 'Land of hope and glory' was acutely reticent about such a task. 'It seems impossible for a struggling poetaster to say anything new,' Benson wrote. 'Moreover my capacity, such as it is, lies in observation of the minute and precise order. But I'll have a try, and if in a fortnight or so I can't get on, I will confess it and you shall absolve me—I fear the thing is too *big* for me; I am a poet of the poky order!'[62] Benson provided some of the words and ideas but generally retreated from the project so that the lion's share of the libretto fell to Parry. For the structure of the ode the composer looked to expand the episodic design of *A Song of Darkness and Light*, similarly linking the sections with an all-pervasive clue-theme. It was also intended that the initial dissonant musical fragment should gradually evolve from the tumult of 'War' to the consonant serenity of 'Peace', a process which no doubt led Parry to add the descripton of 'symphonic' to the title. The plan was safe enough, but the quality of ideas and their subsequent transformation are disappointingly poor. There is a weariness and banality in the diminished-seventh harmony of the opening bars and its

---

[61] A. Brent-Smith, 'Charles Hubert Hastings Parry', *Music and Letters*, 7/3 (July 1926), 223.
[62] Letter from A. C. Benson, 27 Sept. 1902, ShP.

various strained reappearances in other forms of seventh harmony throughout the work. This is epitomized at the pivotal climax ('Far, far off is the beacon that guides the soul of man') in the eighth episode, 'Home', which is feebly underpinned by a dominant-seventh outline in the orchestra. Only in 'Aspiration' is there a real glimmer of inspiration. Here Parry was able to draw on his ability to capture the redemptive sentiment of 'Oh, for that day when all men's hearts shall beat' in which the falling seventh figure of the vocal line recalls the epode of *Blest Pair of Sirens*. Nevertheless the finale lapses into bland triumphal rhetoric and the final supplication 'Grant us thy peace', so effective in Vaughan Williams's *Dona Nobis Pacem*, is accompanied only by colourless diatonic progressions. A. E. F. Dickinson, perhaps more than any other commentator of his day, was able to articulate the essential creative shortcomings of the ode, though his comments could easily be extended to Parry's later ethical works as well:

The Ode carries a burden of strained and conflicting sentiment which in the long run it proves unable to bear or to be moved by. The listener, tired of truthful declamation and humane observations waits vainly for two or three vital themes, such as attend the dignitaries and demons of *The Dream of Gerontius*, or even the muddled tale of *King Olaf*, with penetrating or far-reaching results. He waits vainly, because such themes are moulded by craftsmanship but called into existence by a central musical inspiration that makes itself felt at once or cumulatively. Such illumination is not perceptible here, to my observation.[63]

War and Peace was first given on 30 April 1903 at the Albert Hall and conducted by the composer. It scored a moderate success owing largely to the fact that it struck a contemporary note in the national consciousness. The effect, however, proved ephemeral for, after performances in Bermondsey and Leeds the following year, the work quickly fell out of the repertoire. On the other hand, the Motet *Voces Clamantium*, composed for the Hereford Festival in September the same year, received more attention, mainly through the efforts of Walford Davies who performed it regularly with organ accompaniment at the Temple Church. Davies was himself keenly sympathetic to the ethical dimension, as is evident from the spirit and literary content of his own music (such as *Everyman* which he was presently composing for Leeds), but Parry was rudely aware that an appreciable proportion of his performers and audience were not responsive to his visionary interpretation of Isaiah's prophetic cries. At the Hereford rehearsals in London he had considerable difficulty in communicating to the orchestra and soloists the work's meaning, and at the performance on 10 September he felt 'as if everybody was bewildered and bored'.[64] The main problem once again

---

[63] A. E. F. Dickinson, 'The Neglected Parry', *Musical Times*, (Apr. 1949), 110.
[64] Diary, 10 Sept. 1903.

lay in a lack of really striking material epitomized by the undistinguished 'trumpet' ritornello accentuating the central symbolical theme (the 'voices of them that cry' (Ex. 38)). No amount of seventeenth-century Baroque allusion, esoteric form, antiquated choruses (reminiscent of S. S. Wesley), or faithful speech-rhythm in the solo arioso can help to raise the general level of inspiration above the commonplace. Moreover, Parry's rather superficial Latin titles ('Vox clamantis in deserto', 'Adventus populi', 'Vox prophetae', 'Vox consolatoris', and 'Vox Dei') appear somewhat incongruous with the vernacular text, as do the composer's culminating words.

Ex. 38. *Voces Clamantium* (1903), main ritornello 'the voices of them that cry'.

Among other works to come from his pen during 1903 was a setting of Tennyson's 'Crossing the bar' written for Novello's *Parish Choir Book* and later incorporated into the newly revised *Hymns Ancient and Modern*. He also produced, at the behest of Herbert Brewer, an amusing madrigal *Orpheus* (words and music) for the Gloucester Orpheus Society of which he was President and which the society performed under his direction in January 1904. But most fun and frivolity was derived from a revival of *The Birds* at Cambridge in November for which he revised and appended the score, writing a new Parabasis and a new trio (in A flat) for the Wedding March. The production was a great success, but the record of it was accompanied by sadness: 'I felt sad,' he wrote ruefully after the final performance, 'at feeling it was the last I should see and hear of it'.[65]

This doleful frame of mind was provoked by continued trouble with his heart which was causing him debilitating pain and even moments of brief unconsciousness. Furthermore, the pessimism of his doctors must undoubtedly have caused him to dwell on the possibility of his living only a few more years. Deaths of those connected to him professionally or personally also served to remind him of the possibility. In August the death of his niece, Lilian Parry, in tragic circumstances in Munich, seemed to underline the curse on his elder brother's family. Of the four children, Isabel had only lived to 19, Owen to 21, and now Clinton's younger daughter at 31 (this left only Noel who lived into his 70s but showed the same depressive tendencies as his father, committing suicide by taking poison). 'Mungo' Herbert, his brother-in-law, died suddenly

[65] Ibid. 28 Nov. 1903.

in September. Brind, Parry's first piano teacher, died in December and was buried at Highnam. Sowray, his trusted estate manager, who had been suffering from cancer, died in February 1904. Then, in May, there came the death of Dvořák—a composer he considered to be one of the nineteenth century's finest symphonists. As a tribute, the College held an 'In Memoriam' concert which included the Ninth Symphony, the overture *Carnival*, and the Cello Concerto.

There seemed little prospect, however, of Parry cutting down his workload. With the inception of the Patron's Fund,[66] its administration and the selection of works, it was in fact increasing. There was pressure too from Novello who wanted to publish the 'Cambridge' and 'English' Symphonies, marches from *The Birds* and *The Frogs*, and a revision of the History Primer. The Berks., Bucks., and Oxon. Competitive Music Festival commissioned a part-song ('In Praise of Song'). Finally, when the Gloucester Committee wrote commissioning a new work for the 1904 Three Choirs Festival, Jaeger, deeply concerned, tried to be protective:

I feel almost inclined to commiserate with you, because those kind Gloucester people want another *new* work. Let them do the splendid Te Deum and allow you to devote your time to clear up arrears . . . a little! Why not? Why *won't* they leave you alone for once and give you rest?[67]

But Jaeger knew Parry's temperament only too well: the perennial inability to say 'no', to delegate, to accept help, or to refuse his services or advice to those who needed it. Such was the case in early 1904 when his old Twyford friend Sir Cavendish Boyle, Governor of Newfoundland, asked him to provide a tune for the Newfoundland National Song. Jaeger pleaded with him to farm out some of his orchestration. 'You are *too* conscientious over your scoring,' Jaeger insisted. 'Why, Sullivan's "Golden Legend" was largely scored by Hamilton Clarke, as *we* know very well *here*! No-one thinks the worse of S. for that! And he wasn't as busy as you are!'[68] The following year Elgar offered his services in just this way; 'anything in fact that an ordinary copyist could or could not quite do, I would take the greatest pride and pleasure in doing it for you.'[69] But the replies, when Parry could find time to write them, always came back with excuses and worthy reasons for refusing assistance. 'You are *too* kind,' chided Jaeger, 'and goodnatured and complacent—you

---

[66] The Patron's Fund was founded in 1903 by Sir Ernest Palmer. Its purpose was to provide an opportunity for young composers to hear their works in concert. Though administered from the Royal College of Music, the Fund was open to any student, and the adjudication of submitted works was undertaken by a panel drawn partly from the colleges and partly from outside the institutions. Composers such as Holst, Bax, and Hurlstone all benefited from the generosity of the Patron's Fund.

[67] Letter from A. J. Jaeger, 20 Nov. 1903, ShP.

[68] Letter from A. J. Jaeger, 11 June 1904, ShP.   [69] Graves, *Hubert Parry*, ii. 35.

won't let anybody help you! I wish you could display some wrathful temper and drive out these people with a whip and a few strong words. It's too bad!'[70] Jaeger's friendly counsel was to no avail. Not wishing to disappoint Brewer, the Gloucester commission had been accepted, and Parry had to search for another ethical theme.

In the spring of 1904 Parry began work on *Misericordia Domini*, a moral oratorio which, illustrated by the examples of Moses, David, and Peter, has as its central theme the inherent frailty of man, perfected by the power of Divine Love. As the composition neared completion Parry changed his mind about the title, opting first for *The one thing that availeth* and finally settling for *The love that casteth out fear*. The work was divided into two parts, the first dealing with the Old Testament, the second with the New. A further novel dimension for the composer (and one that clearly shows the influence of *The Apostles*) was the spacial contrast of a hidden Semichorus (the 'mystic' chorus'), who were positioned in the Choir at the back of the orchestra and the Full Chorus. The differing sonority and volume of these two bodies are constantly juxtaposed, the Full Chorus embodying man's search for the meaning of life, the Semichorus providing Divine 'suggestions'.

Just as *Voces Clamantium* had attempted to capture something of the spirit of seventeenth-century vocal forms with its subtitle of 'motet', *The love that casteth out fear* is similarly styled 'Sinfonia Sacra'. This description clearly relates to the vocal and instrumental forms—the *Symphoniae Sacrae*—of earlier Baroque composers such as Giovanni Gabrieli, and more significantly his German pupil, Heinrich Schütz. Aware of the links between Schütz's spontaneous vocal structures and the symphonic choral works of later centuries (most notably those of Brahms such as the *Requiem* and *Gesang der Parzen*), Parry felt the desire to assimilate the devotional solemnity of this style of vocal music into his own choral meditations. Solemnity is immediately apparent in the orchestral prologue of *The love that casteth out fear* which presents two seminal ideas: one more chromatically orientated and sequentially treated (Ex. 39*a*) representing man's pessimism; the other purely diatonic (Ex. 39*b*) as the analogue of 'The love that casteth out fear'. These clue-themes, together with the Semichorus's opening bars ('O my people, what have I done to thee?'), itself derived from the initial orchestral utterance, recur throughout the work as punctuative ritornelli. It is distinctive material with potential, yet Parry's treatment of it rarely rises above the innocuous, particularly in the second part where invention hopelessly flags. As Dickinson remarked: 'The crucial "There is no fear in love" is introduced by two bars not easily distinguished from

[70] Letter from A. J. Jaeger, 6 July 1904, ShP.

Ex. 39. *The Love that casteth out fear* (1904). *a* theme representing 'Man's pessimism'; *b* theme representing 'The love that casteth out fear'.

the sound of the village organist eking out the Collection hymn.'[71] Furthermore one wearies of the uneventful arioso and the incessant homophonic textures of the choral writing whose mannerisms are flagrantly exposed in the final bars.

The love that casteth out fear was given at Gloucester on 7 September. It was well performed by the choirs and by Muriel Foster and Harry Plunket Greene. Parry was pleased, but he was unsure of the public's reaction. Friends and relatives who knew him were sympathetic; the press was kind; yet he was conscious that his music and philosophical sentiment was not making its mark. For the Leeds Festival in the autumn he revised the scoring of *Voces Clamantium*; it was cordially

[71] A. E. F. Dickinson, 'The Neglected Parry', *Musical Times* (Apr. 1949), 111.

received, but was hardly noticed in the company of Elgar's *In the South*, Stanford's new and attractive *Five Songs of the Sea*, or even works by Walford Davies (*Everyman*) and Holbrooke (*Queen Mab*). This had the effect of intensifying his introspection and caused him to dwell on the future of his creative ideals.

14

Breakdown in Health
Resignation

To combat his inner loneliness and an inbuilt lack of confidence in his own abilities, Parry continued to find contentment and consolation in his maritime pursuits. Ireland's remote western coastline became a habitual retreat—a place far removed from the bustle of the Metropolis where he could read, smoke, and contemplate the rugged beauties of nature. His 'most darlingest' Maude, who had now become accustomed to her husband's long summer absences, learned to picture the panoramic grandeur of Kenmare River and Bantry Bay in his frequent letters home:

When I got up at 8 we had got to one of the finest bits of coast scenery in the whole of Ireland, just off Bantry Bay; where the sea is studded with rocks varying from little points with white foam roaring over them to monsters of 200 feet, and one of over 700. I really think as I saw it this morning it was one of the most splendid sights I ever saw. The sea was all the deep Atlantic blue, and raging; great rollers and peaks with white foam or their crests tearing along and sweeping over the low lying rocks and dashing up the sides of the big ones, and the islands at the mouth of the Kenmare river all shining in the blazing sun with a background of countless rugged peaks and crags and black precipices, split up into gullies and ravines, and here and there a sward of green down with sheep feeding on it, and a white cottage nestling in some more sheltered corner. I felt inclined to shout with delight.[1]

To add to the excitement afforded by his long nautical escapades, he had his yacht renamed the *Wanderer* (since 1903) and lengthened by ten feet in Harvey's boatyard, which enabled the accommodation to be more sumptuous and capacious for those who accompanied him on his voyages.

As exciting as the transformation of his yacht, was the purchase of his first car, a 'Gladiator'. The employment of a chauffeur, however, did not prevent him from taking the wheel himself which he did with the same sense of adventure and gay abandon that he steered the *Wanderer*. Soon he was driving everywhere, to Highnam, Shulbrede, Hurstbourne (the home of Harry and Gwen), and Rustington. Journeys were, for those

---

[1] Letter to Lady Maude Parry, 17 Aug. 1904.

times, executed with frightening speed—his chauffeur was sometimes literally sick with fright. Cars—a Panhard, a Charron, a Rolls Royce— were driven recklessly, were often in consequence breaking down, and were sometimes written off; violent accidents were frequent yet somehow he survived. He was also, perhaps inevitably, one of the first drivers in the country to have his licence endorsed for speeding!

Two important events made 1905 a significant year for Parry. The first, of deeply personal consequence, was the death of his lifelong friend and mentor, Dannreuther. The 'most excellent and best of men' had been ill for several years and it had been heartbreaking for Parry to see him at the College slowly wasting away to a shadow of his former self. By the end of 1904 he was very weak; there were visits from a despairing Mrs Dannreuther and Parry did what he could to help financially. Then, on 13 February, news came of his death at his seaside home in Hastings; he was 60. Parry was devastated. The following day he attended the cremation in Golder's Green with Dannreuther's three sons, Sigmund, Tristan, and Hubert (his namesake) and felt desperately alone. As a tribute the College concert that same evening concluded with a performance of Brahms's Chorale Prelude 'O Welt, ich muss dich lassen'. Later, as he witnessed the dismantling of Dannreuther's studio in Gerald Road, Pimlico, Parry remembered the happy pioneering days in Orme Square, Wagner, Bayreuth, and the gentle guiding hand of man who had brought the wider world of music to him. Now there was no one to whom he could confide his doubts, or with whom he could discuss the progress of each new work as he had done assiduously with his 'beloved master'. It was the end of a thirty-two-year relationship and the end of an era.

The passing of Dannreuther more or less coincided with the second major event of the year: Elgar's series of lectures as Peyton Professor of Music at Birmingham University. In 1904, after two fruitless attempts, Parry and Stanford saw Elgar successfully elected to the Athenaeum. Later, on 7 February 1905, Elgar received an honorary doctorate from Oxford largely upon the recommendations of its Professor of Music. Moreover, at Parry's instigation, the London Symphony Orchestra was brought to the city for a concert to honour its new D.Mus. which included *Blest Pair* and the *Enigma* Variations, each conducted by its composer. Then, on 16 March, came Elgar's inaugural lecture—'A Future for English Music'. Without naming names, tactfully worded attacks were launched at the lecturing profession and at academic musicians, but he saved much of his ammunition for British composition, quoting Richard Strauss's speech in Düsseldorf, and taking indirect snipes at one or two well-known British composers. 'Stanford in a great rage about Elgar's inaugural address at Birmingham', Parry noted in his diary.[2] A fiery letter from Stanford appeared in *The Times* (3 November 1905) vehemently challenging Elgar's statement that English music was held in no respect abroad. In the years that followed, Parry looked on helplessly as Stanford's hostility to almost everything Elgar wrote, said, or did grew more and more rabid. He tried to bring the two men together, but their conflicting personalities—Stanford's quarrelsome temperament, tainted, one feels, by a certain jealousy, and Elgar's suspicion of academia's condescension—lay even beyond Parry's generous powers of reconciliation. In July 1910, during a concert of British music in Bournemouth, the thought crossed his mind when he observed the two men being organized for a photograph with German, Mackenzie, and Godfrey. He was, however, shocked to see Stanford refuse to speak to Elgar, and when the Irishman stubbornly sat at the opposite end of the row, it became clear that the situation was irrevocable. It was perhaps symbolic that the two men were finally made to shake hands by Brewer at the unveiling of the Parry Memorial Tablet at the Gloucester Festival in September 1922, though by then the gesture could have meant little to either.

Of course from Parry's point of view the Birmingham lectures were a source of gratification as well as, in his professional circles, something of an embarrassment. He was the only composer Elgar chose to single out:

> The one exception is a name which shall be always spoken in this University with the deepest respect, and I will add, the deepest affection—I mean Sir *Hubert Parry*, the head of our art in this country, who produced a serious work at the Gloucester Festival [*The love that casteth out fear*]: with him no cloud of formality can dim the healthy sympathy and broad influence he exerts and we hope may long continue to exert upon us.[3]

In the course of 1905 Parry's admiration of Elgar continued with the *Introduction and Allegro*; 'very ecstatic', he described, 'with the usual rits and accelerandos and spasms . . .'.[4] And with this ringing in his ears he strongly recommended the Philharmonic Society, as one of the Directors, to include one of Elgar's works in the next season's programme. As if to complement the gesture, Elgar wrote to Parry requesting copies of all his available books and full scores for the Birmingham University Library.

Parry heard the *Introduction and Allegro* at the Worcester Festival at which his own newly revised version of *De Profundis* was revived by Atkins. It was a fine performance, but the most memorable performance of the year was in Huddersfield on 3 March. 'Performance of Judith the best it has ever had', he noted; 'Chorus magnificent. Agnes [Nicholls] better than ever—and all most sympathetically received.'[5] In recent

[2] Diary, 20 Mar. 1905.
[3] Percy M. Young, *A Future for English Music and Other Lectures* (London, 1968), 49.
[4] Diary, 13 Sept. 1905.   [5] Ibid. 3 Mar. 1905.

years the Huddersfield Choral Society had benefited from the training and pioneering ideas of Dr Henry Coward who had moulded the chorus into a virtuoso instrument of national renown. In appreciation of the detailed attention given to the work, Parry expressed his feelings in a letter to the secretary of the Society: 'As for the chorus, of course they quite beat my resources of expression to convey even approximately my sense of their truly superb performance. Their vigour and certainty, and dramatic intelligence are quite amazing, and as for the volume of tone, I can positively feel it inside still. It is a perfect delight to hear such singing.'[6] It was a warm and heartfelt accolade to a chorus who, having played such a valiant part in rescuing *Prometheus Unbound* in Gloucester twenty-five years before, always remained deep in his affections.

Apart from a setting of Shakespeare's 'Fear no more the heat of the sun' (written for an album of Shakespeare songs edited by Charles Vincent for the Ditson Publishing Company, Boston, Mass.), and the revival of the 'Cambridge' Symphony at one of the Charles Williams Concerts at Queen's Hall on 21 March, the year provided the opportunity for an amusing diversion from the otherwise earnest nature of Parry's creative energies. During the latter half of 1904 the OUDS asked if he would write an incidental score for their new production of Aristophanes' *The Clouds*. Without much hesitation, Parry, or 'Paristophanes' (as Bailey later affectionately dubbed him) agreed.

At the heart of the play lay the disputation between 'Right', the old education and morality (of which Aristophanes himself was an advocate), and 'Wrong', the new-fangled ideas of the sophists preaching atheism, speculation, rhetoric, and scientific enquiry which the playwright quite unjustly ascribed to Socrates. The argument is exposed with biting satire, but there is also an element of real tragedy in the way the Clouds (just like the gods in tragedy) manipulate the main character, Strepsiades, to confound himself by yielding willingly to evil. Strepsiades takes revenge on Socrates by burning down the 'Thinkery', but not before he himself has been aptly chastened. *The Clouds* (or *The School for Sophists*), an unusually serious comedy which proved too serious for its original audience, gave Parry a splendid opportunity for purely musical parody. Distorted quotations of other composers, already a feature of *The Frogs*, were used without inhibition or respect. In a letter to Cyril Bailey in January 1905, Parry explained some of the ideas behind the music:

The Overture is, as I told you, called a 'Notturno', and as a hit at the modern programme-music people, I want to call it 'Insomnia Strepsiadis'—will that be right? It represents the nightmare he has been suffering from just at the beginning of the play. Then he is also the subject of the movement before the scene where Socrates talks of him as such a fearful idiot, and I want to call that movement 'Passacaglia' and either 'Rusticus expectans' or by the hideously burlesque title of 'Rusticus aratur in Parvis', which I leave you to translate. Perhaps the first is more respectable. Also do you think 'Fuga pessimistica' is too atrocious for the name of another movement? I think you will guess what I mean, and perhaps can suggest a better and less canine name. About the movement in which I told you I had introduced a solo bit from Beethoven's Violin Concerto: how would it be to bring in some one made up like Joachim to pass on the stage as if playing it in the street and seeking admission to the school?—which is denied him, and he passes sorrowfully out before Strepsiades comes to knock at the door. The Orchestra practically snuffs him out and extinguishes him as I have it. The point would be the exclusion of Music in accordance with the statement of Adikos, and it would be a hit at the modern scoffs at 'old-fashioned music'. It fits on very deftly to the movement suggesting the knocking at the door.[7]

The opening of Beethoven's Violin Concerto is only one of many hilarious citations used in the choruses and the series of five substantial incidental orchestral movements. As he explained to Bailey, the introduction to Act I 'Notturno: Strepsiadis Insomnia' depicts the restless tossing and turning of Strepsiades and his final abandoning of sleep. Besides his own leitmotivic fragment—a chain of rapid diminished sevenths—the poor man's insomnia is portrayed with satirical reference to Tchaikovsky's *Pathétique* Symphony and several motives from *The Ring* (including the 'curse' and the 'Ride of the Valkyries'). The *Sinfonia Academica*, which directly preceded Act I Scene 2, mercilessly fragments the opening of Beethoven's Violin Concerto, the meaning of which is clear from Parry's letter, combined with passing allusion to Wagner's 'curse' motive, Mendelssohn's Wedding March, and the topical popular song 'Wait till the clouds roll by'. The first of the three Entr'actes, the *Passacaglia: Rusticus Aratur*, which refers unflatteringly to Socrates' impatience with Strepsiades' idiocy, is based on a subject not unlike W. H. Monk's hymn tune to 'All things bright and beautiful' (Ex. 40a). Initially this movement attempts to begin solemnly, reflecting Socrates' efforts to teach Strepsiades the subtleties of verse measures; this is musically characterized by the learned, Bachian contrapuntal treatment and even the suggestion of Bach's own Passacaglia in C minor for organ. But the serious tone degenerates into farce as the passacaglia theme accompanies strains of the 'sailor's hornpipe', becomes a march, and then proceeds to coexist with 'For he's a jolly good fellow'. After an animated climax, the music subsides; 'For he's a jolly good fellow' becomes a rhythmic echo, and the hornpipe is heard as a memory in the

[7] Letter to Cyril Bailey, 19 Jan. 1905 (see Charles L. Graves, *Hubert Parry* (London, 1926), ii. 264–5).

flat submediant. Finally the passacaglia theme returns in a restrained compound duple metre which Parry could not resist 'souping up' before the precipitous coda with a quotation from Strauss's *Till Eulenspiegel*. The second Entr'acte, the *Fuga Pessimistica* (or *Fog-fugue*) is, as the title would imply, a structurally 'liberal' affair and, ushering in the third scene of Act I, it anticipates the lengthy central discourse between 'Right' and 'Wrong'. Musically this is symbolized by the respect for counterpoint—a revered tool of the 'old school'—and the post-Wagnerian chromatic tendencies of the modernists which the angular, skulking subject amply exaggerates (Ex. 40*b*). Parry had observed such fugal practices in Strauss (notably *Ein Heldenleben* and, recently heard in London, the *Sinfonia Domestica*) and Reger who are undoubtedly parodied here. Finally there is the rumbustious *Quodlibet* which begins Act II, in which Parry tries to portray a duped Strepsiades, educated in the ways of the new morality, meditating on how he is going to cheat his creditors. The musical result is an almost chaotic volley of quotations, many already familiar, but introducing 'Waltzing Matilda', 'John Peel', 'We won't go home till morning', and several new quotations from *Die Walküre* which are all combined in an uproarious climax.

Shortly after *The Clouds* Parry suffered another severe 'heart attack' and was strongly advised to banish all activity from his life for several months. In response the Easter vacation was spent more quietly at Rustington interspersed only with visits to London to hear Rimsky-Korsakov's 'Antar' Symphony and the London début of Pablo Casals in Saint-Saëns's A minor Concerto. In mid-April he spent a weekend at Highnam with Dolly and Arthur and organized a meeting in the parish to debate the Free Trade issue. Parry chaired the meeting with speeches from Arthur, Sir Harry Johnston, and George Fox Pitt (all Liberal candidates) after which a party was held at the Court which included Lady Queensbury, the Johnstons, Lady Edith Fox Pitt, Louis Mallet, Jack Gordon, and Logan Pearsall Smith, the man of letters. Arthur Ponsonby, who was by now becoming increasingly active politically, invited Parry to Shulbrede for a few days before the beginning of the new term. There he was able to enjoy the company of Elizabeth and the new addition to the family of Matthew who had been born the previous year. It also gave him the opportunity to minister to Dolly who, like her mother, seemed to have an inclination for 'poor' health. Shulbrede lifted his spirits but he was still far from well. After delivering his address at the College he had another medical examination which prescribed a holiday. In consequence May was passed motoring around Normandy and Brittany with Maude who for once braved the sea crossing.

After three weeks in France Parry returned to London preoccupied by the subject of a commission for the Norwich Festival in October. Jaeger,

Ex. 40. *The Clouds* (1905). *a* opening of *Passacaglia: Rusticus Aratur*; *b* opening
of the *Fuga Pessimistica*.

who had been extremely ill himself with progressive consumption and
had spent the winter convalescing in Davos, Switzerland, had been
suggesting for some time that Parry could at last bring forward his long
withheld setting of Browning's ballad 'The Pied Piper of Hamelin'. This
had reached an advanced stage in 1893, but was quickly withdrawn when
his pupil, Richard Walthew, produced a setting of the same text for the

Highbury Philharmonic Society. 'It would be *extremely* interesting to hear you in a humorous mood!!' wrote Jaeger to Parry in September 1896,[8] evidently trying to coax the composer into exhuming his own version, but because Walthew's setting was still enjoying a modicum of popularity at that time, it was postponed yet again with no definite prospect of its ever seeing the light of day. Then, having experienced the 'truly fearful libretto . . . [and] drivelling feebleness' of Mackenzie's 'narrator' cantata *The Witch's Daughter* at Leeds in 1904 (so grim it justly deserved the invective spoonerism *The Ditch's Water*), and Novello publishing Cowen's mildly amusing *John Gilpin*, Parry at last sensed that the time was right to unearth his cantata.

The fact that *The Pied Piper* was in an advanced state of composition proved an advantage in Parry's present physical condition. With only a moderate amount of revision and the orchestration to do, the task was a relatively easy one. The short score was completed and dispatched to Novello on 19 June and the scoring (much of it highly colourful) occupied him for the following six weeks barring the addition of parts for cor anglais and bass clarinet in late September. Besides recommending that Novello should publish a full score, Jaeger, in his enthusiasm for *The Pied Piper*, produced an analysis for the *Musical Times* summarizing its simple raiment as 'beautiful and original'.[9] Jaeger also predicted that the cantata would become immensely popular, and so it did, remaining firmly in the repertoire until the 1930s when, with so many Victorian and Edwardian choral works, it became unfashionable.

In response to Browning's simple, clear-cut poetical structure, Parry created a musical design that was equally concise. Stanzas (such as 1–3, 5, and 6) that introduce characters or set the scene have their own self-contained tonal structures, most notable of which is the introduction of C major at the entry of the Piper (stanzas 5–6). To contrast with the relative stability of these opening episodes, the later stanzas employ a much greater degree of tonal dissolution and fluidity to portray the main action of the poem. Stanza 7 marks this departure as it depicts the ever-increasing procession of rats whose demise is signalled by a temporary move back on to the dominant of G ('Wherein all plunged'). The first attempt at a cadence into G is denied by a satirical and 'reharmonized' quotation of Chopin's Funeral March. Once over, the original vivace tempo is resumed, the funereal mood sardonically dismissed, and a return on to the dominant of G is effected. The re-establishment of G major initially symbolizes the apparent stability of the dramatic situation, but as we know, at this central stage of the poem Hamelin's victory is a hollow one. The swift departure from G major and the

[8] Letter from A. J. Jaeger, 25 Sept. 1896, ShP.
[9] Jaeger, 'Sir Hubert Parry's *The Pied Piper of Hamelin*', *Musical Times*, (1 Nov. 1905), 726–8.

chorus's jubilant carillon marks the beginning of a much longer paragraph of tonal development through stanzas 7 to 13 as joy is transformed into tragedy. As a climax of this tonal development stanza 13 enhances the unity of the work by significant references to previous tonalities such as G major ('The Mayor was dumb'), B flat major (the mesmerized children's procession of stanza 12), D minor (related to stanza 2), and B minor (cf. stanza 3). These events are curtailed by an augmented triad on G which has the dual function of being a distortion of the tonic triad as well as behaving as a dominant substitute of E minor, the key of the lament at the head of stanza 14 ('Alas for Hamelin'). Finally, with Hamelin's memorial to the children, G major is restored ('And opposite the place of the cavern') and affirmed by the elevating tone of the closing chorale ('And on the great church window').

To complement the simplicity of the tonal construction, Parry created what was to be one of his most subtle and complex motivic infrastructures. It was also a feature which evidently impressed Jaeger since it was the dexterity of Parry's motivic metamorphosis of the Piper's thematic material that formed the basis of his analysis. The Piper's main leitmotiv is anticipated embryonically by the four-note figure 'a' in the opening bars of the orchestral introduction (Ex. 41a), but it is not until stanza 5 that the main character's idea crystallizes fully (Ex. 41b—Theme 1) along with a second, more lyrical theme incorporating figure 'a' more elusively (Ex. 41c—Theme 2). After punctuating the Piper's charming soliloquy in stanza 6, both ideas are subjected to development in stanza 7. Perhaps the most noteworthy transformation at this juncture is the combination of Theme 2 with a counterpoint in the sopranos largely derived from Theme 1 (Ex. 41d). There is also considerable skill in the way Parry introduces to this new counterpoint another brief idea (figure 'b'—itself related to figure 'a') characterizing the Piper's 'little smile', foreshadowing the strident accompaniment to the Corporation's renegation of their agreement in stanza 9. Last but not least, the soprano line also contains a third thematic germ (figure 'c') symbolizing the Piper's magic intention which is destined to take on a more ironic flavour in the accompaniment to the lament in the final stanza. As a counterpart to this motivic concentration and its assocation with the Piper's first act of hypnosis, Parry introduces a yet more enchanting series of thematic metamorphoses for the procession of mesmerized children in stanza 12. This is initiated by a choral statement deploying a conflation of figures 'a' and 'b' ('Once more he stept into the street') from which a solo oboe emerges with the Piper's call of two notes derived from 'a' (Ex. 41e). Repeated ten times, the Piper's hypnotic ostinato eventually settles into a rhythmically transformed and melodically extended version of the new counterpoint in stanza 7 (Ex. 41f—cf. Ex. 41d). Other transformations of this idea occur in the latter stages of the work, as accompanimental figures in the last stanza. But perhaps the most impressive example of the composer's motivic inventiveness is the chorale theme clearly derived from figure 'b' which precedes it, and which also has much in common with the Piper's original motive (Ex. 41*g*—cf. Ex. 41*b*).

The Pied Piper of Hamelin is by far the best example of dramatic continuity, stylistic consistency, and motivic homogeneity in any of Parry's dramatic works. Leitmotivs in particular recur with a tangible significance and are happily distinct from one another by means of characteristic melodic twists or neat individual harmonic progressions.

Ex. 41. *The Pied Piper of Hamelin* (1905). *a* opening of orchestral introduction (showing the embryonic shape of the Piper's theme); *b* crystallization of Piper's theme (Theme 1), stanza 5; *c* secondary theme representing the Piper (Theme 2), stanza 5; *d* combination of figures 'a' and 'b' and Theme 2, stanza 7; *e* conflation of figures 'a' and 'b' and the emergence of the Piper's call, stanza 12; *f* transformation of Ex. 41*d*; *g* the concluding chorale and its derivation from figure 'b'.

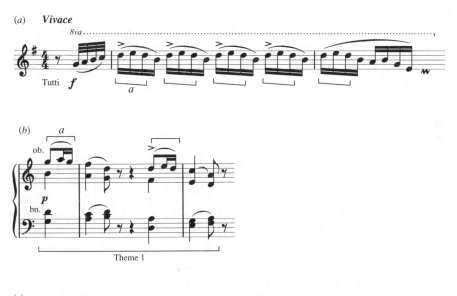

cont. over/

Ex. 41. cont.

(*d*)

(f)   *Poco più mosso*

(g)

An additional unifying factor is the effective and evocative manipulation of diatonicism. The scalic phraseology of the chorus's music in many of the stanzas (notably 2, 5, and 13) is reminiscent of simple nursery rhymes (an environment in which Parry's regular phrases are not detrimental) and the pastiche hymnody at the end of stanza 14 is another well-integrated application. Yet perhaps the most striking harmonic feature is the use of modal harmony which recurs at intervals throughout the cantata, becoming prominent in the choral lament ('The Mayor sent East, West, North and South'). It is the Piper's own music, however, which is most imaginative where Parry succeeds in creating a romantic image of minstrelsy.

During the latter part of the year bad health continued to dog him. After returning from another sailing holiday around Ireland, he again underwent an extremely unpleasant operation for a suppurated cyst in his neck, after which he was weak for several days from the effects of ether. But London beckoned and he became restless. One of the most astounding features of Parry's later diaries is the unstinting generosity and loyalty shown to members of the younger generation of composers who were striving to find a platform for their works; for this he could always spare his time. The Patron's Fund has already been mentioned which gave assistance to Bax, Bowen, Holst, Frank Bridge, and Hurlstone, the latter three for whom Parry had an extremely high regard. Other names also began to appear such as Balfour Gardiner,

Benjamin Dale, John Ireland, and Ernest Farrar. He was a regular visitor to the Broadwood concerts that frequently featured new music, where he became acquainted with works by Percy Grainger, Cyril Scott, Roger Quilter, and the music of his most illustrious pupil, Vaughan Williams. He was often at the Royal Academy of Music to follow the activities of the new Society of Young British Composers but had to be helped home on the verge of another major attack of angina after their second concert on 21 November.

In further recognition of his services to the nation's musical life, the King made him a Commander of the Royal Victorian Order on 18 December 1905. No one was more pleased than Dolly and Arthur. Parry was characteristically reticent about the honour, but was touched by the King's kind thought. The composer's mind was in fact concentrated on the more important business of the General Election at the end of January 1906. Arthur, who had become a staunch supporter of Campbell-Bannerman, was now taking the opportunity to participate in practical politics, standing as the Liberal candidate for Taunton. During the campaign Parry assisted his cause by picking up voters in the 'Gladiator' and running them to the polling stations. In Gloucester he was equally active attending Liberal meetings, and undertaking a little gentle canvassing. When the news came that the Liberals had won a landslide victory he was elated, though this was tempered by Arthur's narrow failure to win Taunton from the Tories. Arthur's hour would, however, come with a by-election in the Stirling Burghs two years later.

Parry's generosity to his son-in-law was also reflected in other sympathetic gestures he performed for his family, friends, and colleagues. One was the provision of two songs for Harry Plunket Greene: a sacred song, 'Praise God in his holiness', written for the inauguration of the new organ at Hurstbourne Church; and 'The Laird of Cockpen', composed specially for one of his many recitals. Another was the publication of Dannreuther's songs by Stainer & Bell, the editing of which Parry undertook personally. He was greatly supportive to Hurlstone's family after the young composer's tragically premature death on 30 May 1906 from bronchial pneumonia. That same evening Parry had attended a concert by the Magpie Singers in which Hurlstone's part-song 'Litany' had been encored. On going into College the following morning he was greeted with the calamitous news and wrote disconsolately of the 'great loss to English music and to his friends. A most admirable and lovable disposition.'[10] A similarly disturbing shadow seemed to hang over the welfare of Jaeger. During his incarceration at Davos in 1905 they had corresponded. Parry was eager to know if his friend was recovering, and

---

[10] Diary, 31 May, 1906.

Jaeger, restive as ever, was keen to offer his comments about musical events in England. He congratulated Parry on his success with *The Clouds*, but was particularly enthusiastic about the success of *Judith* in Huddersfield: 'I have *just* received a letter from my sister-in-law with cuttings from a Huddersfield paper describing your *great Triumph* there with "Judith". I am *delighted*, for I *love* "Judith" and remember with pleasure "our" performance ("Novello" Choir ages ago . . .)'.[11] In the same letter Jaeger turned his attentions to his wife who was left alone to worry in their home in Muswell Hill. Through her Jaeger wanted to hear how the revival of Parry's 'Cambridge' Symphony fared:

I have told my wife to go and tell me all about it, for she wrote that she would like to hear the work. She is *very* partial to your music; loves its strength, directness, and loveable Humanity. So I hope she will go and enjoy herself to her heart's content. She told me that Elgar sent her a ticket for his concert the other day and that she had a quiet cry when it came to No. IX ('Nimrod', of the Variations, which is 'me') which the orchestra played most beautifully. Elgar wrote to me about his Oxford degree day and how 'dear Parry was in great form'.

Parry was much moved by Jaeger's pitiable predicament. He was still very ill and another serious operation brought his wife and children to Switzerland, a journey they made with financial help from Parry. Later in the year Jaeger returned to England but he was far from cured. In the dirty London air he quickly suffered a relapse and left for Davos again in November. Parry sent more money and once again helped to pay for the passage of Jaeger's wife. Rested but weakened, Jaeger came home from Switzerland in June 1906 in the hope that he could get back to work to repay the kindness of his friends and his firm who had kept on his salary despite months of absence.

In September 1905 Parry began an extensive revision of the *Overture to an Unwritten Tragedy*, but work was broken off for the *Pied Piper*. It was resumed in the first few weeks of 1906 and the overture was performed in its new version by the London Symphony Orchestra on 25 February at Queen's Hall. So that the revised version would become better known, the overture also featured at the Lincoln Festival in June and later at the annual concert of the Royal Society of Musicians where it took its place in a programme made up entirely of British works. The overture was the first of Parry's full orchestral works to see print. Novello also printed a full score of the *Pied Piper* which was being widely performed. During 1906 alone Parry attended and conducted three performances in Gloucester, Leeds, and Southport, the last of which was especially fine thanks to the training of Henry Coward.

[11] Letter from A. J. Jaeger, 20 Mar. 1905.

Encouraged by the popularity of the *Pied Piper*, Parry began the composition of his latest commission for the Hereford Festival with renewed zest. It was to be another 'moral oratorio' called *The Soul's Ransom—A Psalm of the Poor* styled once again as a 'Sinfonia Sacra' like its Gloucester predecessor, *The love that casteth out fear*.[12] The subject was one close to the composer's heart—the poor in body and in spirit. Most of the text was taken from the prophetical words of Ezekiel with Parry providing the final moral of the last chorus, just as he had done in *Voces Clamantium*.

Structurally *The Soul's Ransom* is the most concise of all Parry's ethical choral works in its four-movement design, and there is at times a more convincing adaptation of Baroque 'style-form'. This is true of the affecting recurrences of the clue-theme symbolizing comfort and compassion (Ex. 42)—a fine, characteristic idea; and even more so in the second movement where the three beatitudes of the solo soprano ('Blessed are ye poor, for yours is the kingdom of heaven') are answered in turn by the contrapuntal ritornello of the chorus ('It is the spirit that quickeneth'). In this section Parry was able for once to ally a reflective text to the lyrical style in which he excelled. It is therefore to be regretted

Ex. 42. Theme representing 'comfort and compassion'; *The Soul's Ransom* (1906).

[12] Originally Parry had a mind to call the work *Sursum Corda*, but this title was changed owing to the coincidence that Walford Davies's commission for the same festival was to be entitled 'Lift up Your Hearts', and clearly with Parry's Gloucester model in mind, was subtitled 'A Sacred Symphony'.

that this untrammelled and unforced utterance is marred by the stilted didactic choral statement ('God is a spirit') at its conclusion. This form of declamatory mannerism is also death to the end of the first movement ('If thou desire wisdom keep the commandments') and a greater part of the third movement ('Prophesy unto these bones, and say'). Most disappointing of all, however, is the anaemic finale which, as the ethical culmination of the work, fails to make an impression. Significantly perhaps, it was also a shortcoming sensed by the composer at the last rehearsal, but by then it was too late for remedies. At its first and only performance in Parry's lifetime (12 September), the chorus, who had lacked verve in the hurried rehearsal, pulled themselves together, and barring one or two accidents on the part of the soloists, Plunket Greene and Emma Albani, it seemed to go well. 'People seemed pleased',[13] wrote Parry afterwards, but the press were lukewarm.

After the somewhat tepid experience of Hereford, Parry returned to Rustington tired and exhausted and frail. In August he had limited his sailing to the south coast and the south-west peninsula on the advice of his doctors. The vigorous exercise still interfered with his heart, and during a choral rehearsal at Hereford at the end of August, he had suffered a spell of unconsciousness and could not stand. For this reason Robertson Sinclair had kept a close eye on him during the performance of *The Soul's Ransom*. As it happened, nothing untoward occurred, but there were to be many more occasions in the future when anxious friends armed with full scores and seated in the front row of the audience were ready to take up the baton should the composer collapse under the physical strain.

At Rustington he had much proof-reading to do. Novello were about to publish two new sets of *English Lyrics*, two suites for violin and piano, and the *Overture to an Unwritten Tragedy*, besides which there was also progress to be made on his Bach book after which Putnam's were enquiring.

Set VII of the *English Lyrics* is much like Set III in that, with the exception of one song to words by Sturgis, all are settings of Elizabethan or Jacobean poetry. Of the three light-hearted songs, 'Ye little birds that sit and sing' (Heywood), 'Julia' (Herrick), and the anonymous 'On a time the amorous Silvy', the last is the most memorable in its coy dialogue between shepherd and shepherdess sweetened by deft key changes and a charming final cadence through the flat mediant. 'Follow a shadow' (Jonson) is a fine example of terse harmonic organization, though it lacks sufficient motivic consistency in the vocal line, particularly in the second stanza. Perhaps the finest of the set is the

[12] Diary, 12 Sept. 1906.

turbulent setting of Shakespeare's Sonnet CIX 'O never say that I was false of heart' where the composer makes skilful use of tangential harmonic progressions at the outset. This is observable not only in the preludial material, but also in the extraordinary delay of the tonic (E flat) which appears only in the final bars.

By contrast Set VIII is made up entirely of settings of nineteenth-century poems: three by Sturgis, two by Meredith, and one by Langdon Elwyn Mitchell. 'Marian' (Meredith) and 'Grapes' (Sturgis) are lively, buoyant songs executed with craftsmanly panache. 'Nightfall in winter' (Mitchell), composed several years earlier, is a bleak song chilled by the vision of a winter landscape—a picture enhanced by the remote tonal contrasts of E minor and E flat minor. Similarly the Brahmsian 'Dirge in woods' (Meredith) is dark and sullen in its stoicism. Most personal to Parry, however, is 'Looking backward'. Although Sturgis's words are at times wincingly banal, they nevertheless capture a sentiment that is virtually autobiographical. Again the theme of lost love is central, but here the relevance of childhood love, loss of faith in God, and the desire to rediscover the passion of youth have an added poignance. Musically it may not be one of Parry's best songs, but seen in the context of his private life it is one of the most moving.

The two suites for violin and piano, consisting of five movements each, had been composed over many years. The Suite in D was largely the product of a *Suite Moderne* sketched in 1885 for Kitty Lushington, its movements reflecting a more 'modern' character, notably No. IV 'Dialogue'. The Suite in F is more satisfying in its level of inspiration. So thought Jaeger after Parry sent him a gift of both copies:

On the whole I prefer the second Suite . . . The two slow movements are splendid, especially the second ('Retrospective'); and the middle section in 3/2 time is not only one of the most beautiful things you have ever uttered, but in mood,—deeply felt resignation or longing, most affecting. When I first played it, my heart opened out like a clenched fist under the impulse of a warm friendship or love welling up in the heart (I know that Goethe uses a simile like this in a letter to Zelter, after he (Goethe) had listened to some good music at Carlsbad or Teplitz). I thought of Dante's famous lines:

> Nessun maggior dolore
> Che ricordarsi del tempo felice
> Nella miseria

True, the prevailing note in this short and beautiful section is not sorrow; but then I have always held that in a musical reproduction of the mood of these lines there should be a perfect blending of the 'tempo felice' with the 'misericordia', thus producing the exquisite tenderness tinged with longing which I seem to recognize and which holds me enthralled in these lovely bars.[14]

[14] Letter from A. J. Jaeger, [?] Nov. 1907, ShP.

Jaeger also conjectured a programme in the 'Scherzo' of the Suite in D. 'What is it about?', he wrote quizzically. 'An exciting motor-ride with "hoot" obbligato (and a fine for "furious driving" at the end??).'

Poor Jaeger was simply not well enough to get to Hereford to hear *The Soul's Ransom*, nor to Birmingham to hear the première of Elgar's *The Kingdom* which broke his heart. Though only 46, there had been mention of his retiring permanently from Novello, since his health had failed to improve. His doctors had ordered him to take a holiday by the sea in preparation for another journey to Switzerland. At the end of September he called at the College to make his farewells, but Parry was at Highnam:

I'm off for another 6 months 'Holiday' (how I *loathe* these 'Holidays'!) early next week. My lungs are bad again—worse are they than before—and I shall have to make another desperate attempt at getting 'cured' . . . My expectoration has been *much* worse than ever before. Oh dear, what a dreary business it is and how despairing . . .
Goodbye, dear Sir Hubert and good health to you. Keep well! English music can't afford to see you ill as you were a short time ago, at Hereford. I leave England with a very heavy heart. Heaven knows how I may feel six months hence.
I'll let you know occasionally *if* I make any progress towards recovery.[15]

Parry sent further cheques to pay for accommodation and the expenses of treatment in Davos. Jaeger, whose financial situation was perilously low, poured out his heart:

How I have worked (in my own spare time at home) to help people in every way I could, making myself ill with writing and working till past the midnight hour, night after night—and how few have ever moved a finger to do me a kind turn, or my wife. You, for whom I have done *nothing*, have been kindest to me, and the thought of it moves me to tears . . .[16]

Jaeger's homesick letters were not encouraging. Tuberculosis was gradually sapping away his strength and will to live.

But Parry himself was far from fit. During a performance of *King Saul* in Halifax on 22 November he had staved off another heart attack purely by force of will. A car journey to Highnam had to be abandoned, and after his last Oxford lecture of the year he had to be helped back to his rooms in Grove Street. Beauchamp, his doctor, recommended a month's holiday, and so, after Christmas, he and Maude made for the Italian Riviera where they passed the whole of January in Mortola, Genoa, Florence, and Pisa.

Having marginally recuperated, he was back in time to hear the Bach

[15] Letter from A. J. Jaeger, 27 Sept. 1906, ShP.
[16] Letter from A. J. Jaeger, 11 Mar. 1907, ShP.

Choir perform *The love that casteth out fear* on 8 February. This performance took place only two weeks before the founder of the Choir, Otto Goldschmidt, died at his home in Malvern. Then, at the beginning of March, news came of the death of August Manns. To both men Parry owed a debt of gratitude for the performances of his earliest major works. He was also distressed later in the year by the deaths of Joachim, who in spite of their differences had remained a cordial friend, and Grieg, whom he had only recently 'presented' to Oxford University for the conferral of an honorary D.Mus. in May 1906. The most shattering bombshell, however, was the sudden death of one of his most intimate of friends, Eddie Hamilton, which left him numb for several weeks.

Parry's duties at Oxford brought him into contact with a number of eminent personages during the year. On 18 June 1907 he 'presented' Glazunov to the University for an honorary D.Mus. and just over a week later, in the auspicious company of Kipling, Mark Twain, and Campbell Bannerman, he did the same for Saint-Saëns. One of the most important dates in the University calendar was the reception of Kaiser Wilhelm II who visited Oxford to receive an honorary degree in November. After the conferment, the Kaiser was driven to Windsor Castle where he was introduced to a deputation of professors from the University. Parry was amongst them:

To Windsor. Paid the Parratts a visit. Joined the Deputation from Oxford at the White Hart, and when we were all robed drove up to the Castle where we were ushered into a long drawing-room. We formed ourselves into a horse-shoe, and the Kaiser came in in uniform with D.C.L. robes over it and stood facing us. Curzon made an admirable speech and the Kaiser responded. Then he shook hands with all of us in very frank and pleasant fashion, saying a few words when he found opportunity. He completely fascinated me, and I quite fell in love with him.[17]

Though the Kaiser's charm won Parry over in the artificial atmosphere of a formal gathering, his imperialist actions and the growing military postures of his nation began to worry the composer. He was concerned that a dangerous arms race was now in progress as he watched the serious augmentation of Germany's naval strength which was being matched by the British construction of Dreadnought battleships. Arthur's close relationship with the Prime Minister and the Liberal Cabinet also gave Parry a stimulating insight into decision-making at the highest level ranging from the latest legislation to the Honours Lists. With regard to the latter, he was eager to voice his opinions as to whom he considered deserving of national honour. Occasionally, when he saw that credit was being given where it most definitely was *not* due, he was vociferous in his

[17] Diary, 15 Nov. 1907.

opposition. Such was his reaction in June 1907 when Arthur informed him that Wilhelm Ganz, the singer, conductor (with whom Parry had had a brief and unsavoury encounter over *Guillem de Cabestanh* almost 40 years earlier), and now professor at the Guildhall School of Music, had been proposed for an honour:

The news you gave me last night is so serious that I feel I must say a word about it. Wilhelm Ganz is not regarded as a musician at all, but merely a sort of unclean bird of prey which loiters on the outskirts of music and picks up its living in not over reputable fashion. His business is to purvey parties of musicians for the parties of smart folk who are too indolent or too ignorant to get their performers for themselves. It's a very ancient means of obtaining a livelihood, and it is regarded by people intimate with such matters as a shady one. And Ganz's reputation in the connection is the reverse of good. The things I have myself heard of his cheating young performers of the fees which the careless rich folk paid to him for them make one mad with rage. To give such a man an 'honour' would seem to anyone who knows anything about music of the present day as incredible, portentous, utterly ridiculous. Little better than an insult to hundreds of loyal hardworking Englishmen who have, like William Cummings head of the Guildhall School, deserved well of their country and are left in the lurch while a notorious little foreign jobber is singled out for distinction.[18]

Recognizing his father-in-law's strength of feeling, Arthur was quick to recommend the erasure of Ganz's name—a recommendation that was subsequently heeded by those in authority.

The most radical political issue to affect Parry domestically, however, was women's suffrage. Since May 1905, when the Commons had 'talked out' a bill to give women the vote, the Women's Political and Social Union had been gathering momentum; and when Christabel Pankhurst (daughter of Emmeline Pankhurst, founder of the Union) was imprisoned for assaulting the police, the indignation of the suffrage movement began to spill over. Noisy protests halted parliament, and large crowds gathered in Trafalgar Square to demonstrate their anger over the government's equivocation. Imprisonment of many 'suffragettes' brought similar action outside the Houses of Parliament. Both Parry and his wife expressed sympathy for the suffrage cause, but it was Maude's energies that were rekindled by the debate. She began to attend meetings regularly with Edith Fox Pitt, Gladys Holman Hunt, Agnes Garrett, and Mrs Fawcett. On occasions too, Parry was able to go along. After one suffrage meeting in Queen's Hall he noted: 'G[eorge] B[ernard] S[haw] made a marvellously good speech with lots of real humorous points and excellent sense underlying it all. Dickinson good. The lady speakers mostly tiresome—except a plucky little woman who proposed an

[18] Letter to Arthur Ponsonby, 14 June 1907, ShP.

amendment advocating universal suffrage. Her seconder was offensive and spoilt her case. Maude enjoyed it hugely.'[19] Soon there was to be no holding Maude's enthusiasm as her allegiance to the Women's Movement reached fever pitch, falling short only of chaining herself to railings and imprisonment. Parry was delighted that his wife had at last found her *raison d'être*, but there reached a point where the constant bustle of meetings (some of which were at Kensington Square and Rustington), processions, petitions, and representations began to play on his nerves.

The year 1907 witnessed a brief vogue for *The love that casteth out fear* which was heard at Gloucester and Leeds. Parry's main sights, however, were set on the Cardiff Festival at the end of September where his newest choral offering, *The Vision of Life*, was to be performed. This was intended to be his ethical *apologia*: a work in which he could fully expound, through his own poem, a 'vision' of evolving humanity through the ages, fired by optimism, aspiration, spiritual fellowship, and the thirst for knowledge. These abstract philosophizings are personified by 'The Dreamer' (Bass), who is more inclined to pessimism in his search for meaning, and 'The Spirit of the Vision' (Soprano), who steadily leads him and *The Dream Voices* (played by the chorus) on to higher ideals and into a spiritual state 'purged of earthly stain'. Such high spiritual attainment is achieved, so Parry believed unshakably, through man's capacity to help his fellow man and contribute to a common good. Having played his part, he dies and is of no account, yet the 'vision' is passed on to successive generations. W. A. Morgan, the secretary of the Cardiff Festival Committee, was decidedly reticent about the non-Christian slant of the work, but it was too late for the Committee to demur, particularly since the Festival programme was also to include the unorthodox convictions of Bantock's *Omar Khayyam* Part II.

Parry had great hopes that, with this summit of his ethical explorations, he would score a success with the public. But at the final rehearsal in Cardiff on 24 September he was extremely disappointed. 'Thought it rather tedious', he concluded dejectedly.[20] The performance, however, seemed to go more satisfactorily in spite of the fact that Agnes Nicholls had to step in at the eleventh hour after Miss Gleeson-White's voice had given out. The press were also charitable about the work. There were kind words from the *Musical Times* as there were from the *Tribune*. Yet the overwhelming impression seems to have been that the audience was most attracted by the directness of the *The Kingdom* which was drawing large crowds wherever it was performed. Elgar, Parry concluded magnanimously, had captured the hearts of the people. Nevertheless, Elgar was genuinely enthusiastic about *The Vision*

---

[19] Diary, 26 Mar. 1907. [20] Diary, 24 Sept. 1907.

and certainly responded to 'The Dreamer'—one of the 'old men who dream dreams'—a theme which he himself explored through Arthur O'Shaughnessy's poem *The Music Makers* in 1912. During the final rehearsal Elgar sat with Parry and talked through the work with him, and afterwards marked his vocal score with the correction of misprints and some suggestions for improvements sending it on with an appreciative letter. Parry was greatly touched by this act of kindness and never forgot it. In May 1909 he returned Elgar's vocal score and with it expressed his gratitude for the empathy Elgar had shown towards the work:

At last I am returning your copy of 'The Vision of Life' with the heartiest thanks for your kindness in marking such a lot of things that need correcting, and the very warmest appreciation of your generous and sympathetic attitude towards it. If I ever have the chance of conducting it again your suggestions will be very helpful; and if I do not the kindly feeling you have expressed for it will be the most permanent of consolations.[21]

It was, like *The Soul's Ransom*, to be the only performance in Parry's lifetime. Elgar, who concluded that the work was 'too strong for the Church',[22] tried in vain to have it included in the Leeds Festival in 1913, but it was turned down. Elgar and Jaeger both hinted that he might revise the last chorus, a suggestion he acknowledged. In 1914 he rewrote the final chorus for the proposed Norwich Festival, but the War intervened and the Festival was cancelled.

The symphonic concept of *The Vision of Life* is, as its subtitle would suggest, far more amplified than any of his other ethical works. A smaller number of clue-themes are subjected to a more thorough reworking, and the purely instrumental dimension is considerably extended, there being many protracted passages for orchestra alone. The structure, however, is less satisfactory for, after three clear-cut paragraphs in E minor, C major, and E flat (which roughly constitute the first half of the poem), it becomes evident that Parry's inspiration seriously began to flag. Indeed, the second half of the work rambles and lacks grip, a feeling reinforced by the effete finale which remains bafflingly unmoved by the impassioned Wagnerian orchestral climax that precedes it. In 1914 he sought to remedy this deficiency, and the revision was certainly a considerable improvement, but he still failed to create a musical paragraph ample enough as a peroration, an impression confirmed by the lack of real symphonic inevitability in the last stages of musical transformation. The most successful parts of *The Vision* are, like *The Soul's Ransom*, those expressed through a purely lyrical idiom associated with 'The Spirit of

---

[21] Letter to Edward Elgar, 7 May 1909, HWRO 705:445 5247/8.
[22] M. Kennedy, *Portrait of Elgar* (Oxford; rev. and enlarged edn., 1986), 157.

the Vision'. The second of the soprano's four sections ('Yet while the roar of power triumphant rings') shows Parry at his most eloquent. The transformation of the original yearning motive first exposed in the orchestral introduction (Ex. 43*a*), sounds a note not unlike the aspiratory tone of Shelley's 'Spirit of the Hour' in *Prometheus Unbound*, and the material has a distinct similarity in melodic contour to Elgar's 'New Faith' motive in *The Kingdom*, a work with which Parry was quite familiar (Ex. 43*b*). The tranquil orchestral conclusion (figure 29) also provides an expressive commentary, but the most compelling orchestral statement occurs in the thirteen bars prior to the entrance of the 'The Spirit of the Vision' ('lento teneramente') where the composer looks forward prophetically to the ecstatic melodic invention of the Symphonic Fantasia five years later (Ex. 43*c*).

From Parry's letters of 1907 it is increasingly clear that his illness was gradually undermining his apparently unassailable *joie de vivre* with which his friends and family were familiar. His voyage to Ireland in the summer had been ruined by atrocious weather and sea-sickness, and the condition of his heart had been so bad that he even expressed an indifference to the sea. 'I can't look forward to my cruise this time as anything but a sort of penance,' he wrote jadedly to Maude; 'I'm actually longing to be home again. I'm possessed by a sudden revulsion against sailing. I wonder if I shall get over it.'[23] Fortunately for him, and for the Royal Yacht Squadron who elected him in May, his fervour returned in time, but for the moment he could not escape the insidious reality that he would have to take more time off from the College. On the recommendation of his London doctors, Beauchamp and Dawson, he resigned the Presidency of the Mendelssohn Scholarship and, though elected as a Philharmonic Director against his own advice, he warned the Committee that his contribution to the new season would be extremely slim. He also intimated to Hadow that he would resign the Oxford Professorship in June 1908. Nevertheless, the stress of work continued. His old String Quintet, now extensively revised, went off to Novello for publication, and he struggled to finish the last chapter of his book on Bach. He also insisted on keeping up his concert attendance. He wanted to hear Vaughan Williams's setting of Whitman's 'Toward the Unknown Region' at the last College orchestral concert of the year, and early in 1908 he forced himself to attend the Joachim Memorial Concert, the whole of *The Ring* under Richter in English, and gain his first impressions of Sibelius through *Finlandia* and the Third Symphony.

It was perhaps no surprise therefore that the frequency and severity of his 'heart attacks' grew, until in mid-February he endured three fierce

---

[23] Letter to Lady Maude Parry, 3 Aug. 1907, ShP.

Ex. 43. *A Vision of Life* (1907). *a* theme representing 'yearning'; *b* transformation of 'yearning' (Fig. 27), 'The Spirit of the Vision'; *c* theme of orchestral interlude prior to the entry of 'The Spirit of the Vision' (nine bars before Fig. 26).

(*a*)

(*b*)

(*c*)

attacks which swiftly brought the attendance of Beauchamp. The diagnosis was bleak. His liver was seriously enlarged, there was dropsy in both legs, and, needless to say, acute heart strain. Beauchamp was of the opinion that both the College and Oxford should be given up immediately. Parry would not entertain abandoning the former, but he agreed to resign his Professorship and wrote at once to Sir Herbert Warren:

My doctors are so severe in their verdict that I evidently shall not be allowed to superintend the examination in May. They talk airily of my applying for excuse from my duties for 6 months. But that does not seem to me the right view at all. If a man cannot do the work which belongs to my responsible office, he must make way for someone who can. So, though it is painful to me beyond expression, I feel the only right course is to tender my resignation of the Professorship. I had hoped I might hold on at least till the end of the year of tenure—June 30th—but I think as I cannot do the work even now it will be only right that I should resign at once.[24]

'The severance and end of my work there simply stupifies me with distress',[25] wrote Parry desolately in his diary after Warren's acceptance of his resignation reached him. On this sombre note he boarded the *Japan* bound for the Mediterranean. There he visited Malta, met Arthur and Dolly at Taormina, and toured the Italian coast from Palermo as far as Genoa with them. Music, however, was not banished from his existence. He read through the score of Strauss's *Sinfonia Domestica* and sketched a number of songs to texts by Mary Coleridge, but the majority of hours were wiled away reading or in lively discourse with his son-in-law.

After arriving back in England on 1 April, Parry was determined to return to his duties at the College. This he did in May, but placated his doctors by considerably reducing his teaching hours. With more time than he had had for many years, Parry set to work on two choral works: one for Atkins and the Worcester Festival, and another for the opening of the Memorial Buildings at Eton in November for which Robert Bridges had also been commissioned to provide the words. Much time was spent at Highnam and he was able to see more of his wife at Rustington. For once there was the opportunity to enjoy a modicum of tranquillity but there were moments of excitement. News of Arthur's successful election to the House of Commons came in May, and in June he joined Maude and Mrs Fawcett in a suffrage demonstration from the Embankment to the Albert Hall. Towards the end of June he began to resume his normal duties at the College whose affairs had largely been overseen by Claude Aveling; there was, moreover, the official courtesy of entertaining Saint-Saëns who was due to visit the College to conduct his Third Symphony. Parry's health, however, was still far from being restored. Jaeger, himself recuperating in Exeter, was alarmed:

I am sure all your multitudinous friends and admirers do wish you would let the College *go to the D*—— and that you would look after yourself and the

[24] Graves, *Hubert Parry*, ii. 45.   [25] Diary, 24 Feb. 1908.

prolongation of your life, a life splendidly spent and filled with sufficient first-rate and unequalled work to 'adorn' half a dozen ordinary men's existences. You have done *enough* work, dear Sir Hubert,—enough of the College Drudgery, the 'presiding' at innumerable Dinners and meetings, the speechmaking and advice and encouragement-giving, the bracing up and cheering of *other* people. Do rest on your laurels, and devote yourself to composition only, within such bounds as your Doctors prescribe . . . It is the everlasting 'rush', the working against time, the sweat and anxiety of getting your compositions ready 'in time' for this or that fixed date, that plays such havoc with your health . . . Why *risk* another relapse? Do not give your heart a *chance* of playing pranks again.[26]

Jaeger's words were wise and were to some extent acknowledged. With his heart attacks persisting, further resignations took place including the Presidency of the Musical Association and his Directorship of the Philharmonic Society. Yet such action had its emotional price. 'I am going through a spell of the most outrageous despair I have ever lived through', he confided to Harry Plunket Greene. Both Dawson and Beauchamp's assessments of his physical condition were extremely gloomy and there was some uncertainty as to whether he would be able to conduct at Worcester in September.

In the event, two gentle sailing excursions along the south coast and to France helped him recover sufficiently to superintend rehearsals and the performance of *Beyond these voices there is peace* for the Three Choirs Festival. With words extracted from Ecclesiastes and Isaiah, *Beyond these voices* continued the thread of the earlier 'moral oratorios' with the theme of 'all encompassing peace' made possible through the emanciption from discontent, bitterness, vanity, and wordly pleasures. It was a subject close to the composer's heart, and for the rest of his life he continued to be most attached to it above all the other ethical works for chorus and orchestra. But with the exception of the one chorus 'To everything there is a season', with its simple ritornello structure and quasi-baroque counterpoint, the work failed to make any lasting impression on the public, and despite attempts to revive it by isolated advocates such as W. G. Whittaker, it quickly dropped out of the repertoire along with his other ethical choral works. In his article 'Hubert Parry', R. O. Morris did much to articulate the reasons for such a catalogue of 'noble failures'; it was due, Morris maintained, 'to a refusal to bow to his own limitations' brought about primarily through musical conservatism and the inability to 'weld his style into such an instrument of such infinite subtlety, flexibility and expressiveness as would be needed for the translation of this philosophic survey of human affairs into terms of music.'[27] Frank Howes's criticisms are also

---

[26] Letter from A. J. Jaeger, 20 May 1908, ShP.
[27] Graves, *Hubert Parry*, ii, 207.

enlightening with regard to the composer's faltering capacity to frame his religious unorthodoxy and broad philosophical insight within effective or memorable prose:

Parry was too busy, too quick, too inexperienced in rigorous philosophical thinking, to have got life's major issues either focused into philosophical sharpness or made incandescent in poetry. He was so keen on the ideas and had so much of the evangelist in him that he was content to throw the ideas into pedestrian verse which could inspire no-one to musical utterance, not even the poet himself.[28]

But it was Dickinson who was most apposite in his appraisal of the crucial problem:

It is apparent that Parry grew weary of the 'family' atmosphere of Old Testament oratorio and sought to strike a rarer, more intellectual, more pertinent note. The aim seems to have deafened his ear to the limitations of the lectern style (in an ethical church). Or he did not give himself time to let the central impulse of his conception sink beneath consciousness, there to join with other archetypes and then issue in appropriate musical symbols?[29]

After the Three Choirs at Worcester was over, Parry set about finishing and orchestrating the *Eton Memorial Ode* which was performed in the presence of the King and Queen on 18 November. 'No hitches,' he noted in his diary, 'Ode vigorously sung. Boys delightful—I loved them . . .'.[30] What with the rough yet exuberant tones of the Eton College Musical Society, and the incorporation of both the 'Eton Volunteer Call' and 'Assembly Call', the occasion was a nostalgic reminder of his own schooldays. Music for young people seemed to feature prominently during the last part of the year. For some time he had been promising Arthur Peppin at Clifton to write a school song. The result was a setting of Henry Newbolt's 'The best school of all' which Harry Plunket Greene sang at Clifton on 21 December. At the end of November he also sketched four unison songs for children—'The Owl' (Tennyson), 'A contented mind' (Sylvester), 'Sorrow and Song' (Hedderwick), and 'The Mistletoe' (Father Prout)—which the Year Book Press published the following year. His main task, however (at Allen's request), was the revision and re-orchestration of *The Glories of our Blood and State* which formed part of a concert consisting of the 'English' Symphony, *Job*, and Bach's G major Brandenburg Concerto, given at Oxford on 2 December—a concert given in his honour at the instigation of the new Heather Professor, Sir Walter Parratt.

---

[28] F. Howes, *The English Musical Renaissance* (London, 1966), 142.
[29] A. E. F. Dickinson, 'The Neglected Parry', *Musical Times* (Apr. 1949), 110.
[30] Diary, 18 Nov. 1908.

The happy memories aroused by Eton and Oxford at the end of 1908 did much to brighten a year that had otherwise been physically painful, demoralizing, and unpredictable. The tepid response to his 'ethical oratorios', of deep significance to his creative *persona*, gave him cause for greater soul-searching. The reality was unpalatable, but he knew that he would have to abandon his ethical evangelism as defined through the medium of works for chorus and orchestra. But though his spirits were at a low ebb, events were soon to revive his creative drive.

15

Indian Summer
Symphonic Renewal

SINCE the composition of the Symphonic Variations and the shelved *Elegy for Brahms* of 1897, Parry had not contemplated the possibility of writing a symphonic work for orchestra alone. In spite of the fact that orchestral music afforded him the greatest satisfaction, the pressure of choral commissions had simply been too great and he had been forced to turn down requests for large symphonic works from the Philharmonic Society on more occasions than he cared to remember. Such was, to use Elgar's phrase, 'the penalty of his environment'. But others were aware of the fallow side of Parry's creative powers. On many occasions in the 1890s Richter had begged him to write another symphony, but when Elgar appeared on the scene at the end of the decade these requests evaporated. Napier Miles, one of his long-standing private pupils, suggested a violin concerto in 1904. This came to nothing, but Miles continued to make enquiries about all four symphonies and some of the chamber music. Jaeger too dropped hints:

I have often thought, dear Sir Hubert, and I think so again . . . that you really reserve your most beautiful, *innermost*, deepest and tenderest thoughts for your instrumental compositions. I think of the 4 Symphonies—especially their slow movements—and the classic breadth of the long-drawn melodies there to be found. *There* your muse has time or opportunity to 'expand' into long, spacious melodies and no restriction is placed on your imagination by 'words', which—since you never repeat a syllable—seem to me to put a bar in the way of your melos growing into the long melodies I love in your Symphonies.[1]

Jaeger's letter arrived providentially at the same time as a major incentive from the Philharmonic Society. Since Parry had recently severed his executive connection with the Society, the Committee decided that a fitting gesture would be the commission of a large-scale orchestral work for the new season which would form part of concert consisting entirely of the composer's music. Parry meditated on the proposal for the rest of 1908 and the first few months of 1909, during which time he heard the first London performance of Elgar's First

---

[1] Letter from A. J. Jaeger, [?] Nov. 1907, ShP.

Symphony under Richter at Queen's Hall. 'Place packed,' he noted, 'Work received with enthusiasm. Very interesting, personal, new, magnetic. A lofty standard . . .'.[2] Perhaps more than anything else, the success of Elgar's new work encouraged him to contemplate the provision of a symphony. On 29 December 1904 his Fourth Symphony had been included in one of Dan Godfrey's enterprising programmes in Bournemouth, but during the rehearsals and performance he had been rudely reminded of its structural defects. However, he had also been struck by the potential of the material and considered that the symphony might be recast and expanded in the future. The Philharmonic invitation provided such an opportunity. With this resolution in mind he wrote to Berger but at the same time pointed out that an entire concert of his music was not desirable. From the letter it is clear that he was now keenly conscious of his own total eclipse and that London's public had all but forgotten him:

I am ashamed to have kept you waiting for an answer to such an extremely attractive invitation. The truth is one needs to think such a matter over quietly and coolly. At first blush an opportunity to conduct the Philharmonic Orchestra seems such a delightful prospect that one would rush impetuously into accepting it. But indeed I must consider the interests of the Society as well as my own personal enjoyments. And I feel only too painfully confident that it would be impolite in the Society's interests for me to accept. Nowadays, as we all recognize, the Conductor is taking the place of the Singer as the centre of attraction, and I am quite aware that I should be no attraction at all, if not indeed the reverse. Partly for reasons of health I have had almost to give up conducting entirely for some years, and the London public at least does not regard me as a conductor at all—and the result might be absolutely the emptiest house that ever fell to the lot of the Society. The venture is too serious to be risked—and so with hearty appreciation of the honour which your invitation implies, I think it wiser in the Society's interests not to accept. But if you will still allow the Symphony to stand, of course I shall be delighted to conduct that . . .[3]

Parry's wishes were respected, and the proposal of an expanded Fourth Symphony accepted with a view to its performance in February 1910. It was to be the beginning of an Indian summer of creativity.

Besides work on the Symphony, which did not begin in earnest until the end of October 1909, various other enterprises were brought to a successful conclusion. He revised *L'Allegro* for the Southport Festival. OUDS revived *The Frogs* in February replete with additions. Singing in the chorus of the Initiated was one of his most dedicated future advocates, Adrian Boult. In March Richter conducted the Symphonic

[2] Diary, 7 Dec. 1908.
[3] Letter to the Philharmonic Society, 16 Apr. 1909. BL Loan 48:13/26.

Variations with the London Symphony Orchestra; it was to be the last time Parry heard the great German maestro conduct one of his works. Putnams published his book on Bach which joined the ranks of several recent studies by Abdy Williams, Rutland Boughton, and most notably Albert Schweitzer (in Newman's translation). 'I owe him [Bach] a debt', Parry explained to William Hannam, 'which I wanted to repay for many years past . . . I'm afraid it will be too stiff reading for the uninitiated public. But I had to do it from the highest point of view I could attain to, and I live in hope that it may be useful to some few people who take their music wholeheartedly.'[4] His fears proved unfounded. The book enjoyed a wide readership and was reprinted in 1910. His devotion to Bach meanwhile was gestating in the form of the chorale preludes for organ which would eventually take shape three years later.

In the meantime Novello published two further sets of vocal miniatures: the ninth set of *English Lyrics* and *Six Part-songs*. Most of the *Six Part-songs* date from the period 1905–6. Dedicated to Lionel Benson, they were written with the Magpie Madrigal Society in mind who most commonly performed them. Five of the songs are in the standard four parts of which the wittily canzonetta-like 'Prithee, why?' (Suckling) and the soothing pastoral 'Sweet day so cool' (Herbert), with its gently variegated refrain, are the most distinguished. Of greater textural and personal interest, however, is the tortured 'Sorrow and Pain: A Meditation' (Lady Charlotte Elliot), which essays a more intense harmonic language foreshadowing the rich, autumnal sensibilities and sonorities of the *Songs of Farewell*. This is particularly evident in the striking harmonic progression of the opening phrase ('O sweet are sorrow and her sister'), but it is the refined control of harmonic progressions in the final didactic affirmation that is most prophetic of the late motets' profundity.

Set IX of the *English Lyrics*, composed in 1908 (several on board the *Japan*), were written in response to the death of the poetess, Mary Coleridge, who died in 1907 at the age of 45 from appendicitis. It was the nearest thing Parry ever came to a song cycle. Her style, if lacking somewhat in sensuousness, was an unostentatious one which the composer found himself in sympathy with and his choice of seven poems attempted to explore the delicate imagery, ingratiating allegory, and spiritual searching expressed within the limitations of her unobtrusive artistic personality. These features are touched upon in the Brahmsian 'Witches' Wood', 'Armida's Garden' (a favourite song of the fleetingly famous Elsie Swinton), and the more broadly eschatological 'There'. By contrast, 'Three Aspects', a song suggesting an orchestral orientation,

---

[4] Letter to William Hannam, 22 Nov. 1909, McUL.

carries us through the conflicting emotions of Parry's own life—'a royal game', 'a terrible fight', culminating in 'a vision of . . . deep happiness' in which, as Stephen Banfield has pointed out, 'it is tempting to see the dramatised first-person form as a telling self-revelation'.[5] The most overtly emotional statement, however, is reserved for 'Whether I live' which, in its marrying of the minds of two souls, probes an intimacy which was denied the author, and one which was gradually slipping away from the composer.

Hard on the heels of Set IX of the *English Lyrics* was a tenth set written expressly for and dedicated to Agnes Hamilton Harty (née Nicholls) who sang the set in a recital at the Bechstein Hall on 16 November 1909. They were not published until 1918, by which time Parry had subjected a number of the songs to considerable revision, especially 'My heart is like a singing bird' (Rossetti). The latter was not included in the set as sung by Agnes Nicholls who chose instead to sing an extensive recasting of Shelley's 'O World, O Life, O Time', set initially during the composer's days at Oxford. However, when Novello expressed a wish to publish in 1917, Parry asked her which song she would prefer to head the set and 'My heart is like a singing bird' prevailed. It is a fine, dramatic piece with a touch of the Edwardian drawing-room, especially the panache of the final stanza's top A. The rest of the set is rather mixed in quality. 'One silent night of late' (Herrick) and 'The child and the twilight' (Mitchell) belong to the world of 'On a time the amorous Silvy' and 'Love is a bable' with their bluster, unexpected tonal divergences, and light-hearted delivery, though both lack the sustained melodic interest of the earlier songs. Allan Cunningham's 'Gone were but the winter cold', with its allying of winter and the solitude of death, has a certain Brahmsian melancholy, but is vocally less imaginative, and the coda ('Let none tell my father') courts over-sentimentality. There is a certain refinement in 'A moment of farewell' (Sturgis), but this, along with the worthiness of the other songs pales alongside 'From a city window' (Mitchell) which is undoubtedly one of Parry's finest contributions to the genre. Here again there seems to be a personal significance in the nocturnal solitudes of the onlooker hearing the shuffling of feet below 'in the dark street'. One imagines that, in later life, this was the daily experience of the composer, unable to combat the overwhelming sense of loneliness in Kensington Square. The restless sentiment of much of the song is complemented by the animated accompaniment, and the tranquillity of the central episode conjures up a curious conflation of Wolf and Debussy (Ex. 44), a more sensuous evocation which also haunts the final bars. But most striking of all is the

[5] S. Banfield, *Sensibility and English Song* (Cambridge, 1985), i. 21.

Ex. 44. English Lyrics Set X (1910), bars 12–15 of 'From a city window'.

precipitate return of the 'hurrying, restless feet below', a fascination for which becomes larger than life in the spacious swell of the climax ('Like a great tide ebb and flow') accentuated by the unexpected shift to the Neapolitan directly before the cadence.

In spite of two minor operations in November 1908, and another the following January to remove a cyst, Parry's health began to improve. That Christmas his heart had still been capricious in its behaviour, but a short trip to Mortola proved highly theraputic. Life at Kensington Square was lively. Maude's enthusiastic support for the suffrage movement brought the Pankhursts to the house on several occasions and there was much discussion excited by the arrests and force-feeding of suffragettes in prison. During visits to Shulbrede he was also given detailed accounts of Arthur's activities in the House of Commons and found great solace in his company. They frequently went to the theatre together—one of Arthur's eternal passions—and enjoyed such pieces as Galsworthy's social realist play *The Silver Box*. By contrast, Parry's relationship with his other son-in-law was not so agreeable. Like Stanford, Plunket Greene was a staunch Irish Tory, supporter of Balfour, member of the Anti-Women's Suffrage Committee (which did not endear him to Maude), and a dominant personality. In April 1909 he entered into a fiery correspondence with his father-in-law which grew more and more animated as it progressed. At its heart was the German scare, but other political issues found their way into the argument including Home Rule and Toryism. Gwen begged Harry to curtail the correspondence so as not to hamper her father's improving health. He did so immediately and wrote an apologetic letter half wishing the altercation had never begun. The cordiality of their relationship resumed, but thereafter it never existed at the more intimate level enjoyed by his other son-in-law.

The death of Jaeger in May did much to override the sores of disagreement with Plunket Greene. During 1908 Parry had interceded at Novello to obtain work for the ailing German as his tuberculosis steadily worsened, and to supplement what the firm could pay him for the 'Foreign Notes' in the *Musical Times* Parry sent along numerous cheques. The tone of his last letter to Parry in October 1908 was distressing: 'I am made of *very* ordinary clay and kick with all my futile strength against the kind fate that chains me to the procrustean bed of an aimless, useless life. Cui bono? you may say. I know it's useless, yet a D——! does occasionally relieve one's feelings.'[6] Jaeger was too weak to reach the College in 1909 and so was not able to see Parry again. On 18 May a letter from Jaeger's wife arrived at the College:

My dear Sir Hubert,

My dear husband wished me to write to you, and give you his love, and bid you goodbye. He had the greatest love and admiration for you, and he would have loved to see you again. He died very peacefully early this morning.

Yours very sincerely,
Isabella Jaeger.[7]

Another cheque was dispatched immediately to assist Mrs Jaeger and her children together with a letter praising her husband's invaluable service to British music. 'How I wish he could have read the letters I have,' replied Mrs Jaeger, 'telling me of the warm appreciation, and admiration everyone has for him. But maybe he knows now.'[8] To benefit the Jaeger family, a Memorial Concert took place on 24 January 1910. Muriel Foster sang Elgar's *Three Songs*, Op. 59 and Richter conducted the *Enigma* Variations. Coleridge-Taylor and Walford Davies were also there to conduct their own works. As his contribution, Parry took the baton for his *Overture to an Unwritten Tragedy*.

During the summer of 1909 Parry made another sailing expedition to the west coast of Ireland including his usual 'pilgrimage' to the Skelligs. With Pearsall Smith, his companion, he discussed Nietzsche's *Also sprach Zarathustra*, a text he probably had been prompted to read by the first performance in England of Delius's *Mass of Life* on 7 June under Beecham. Delius's pugnacity over the Musical League at the end of 1907 had not endeared him to Parry, and Delius for his part dismissed the Director of the Royal College of Music as a man 'rolling in wealth, the

---

[6] Letter from A. J. Jaeger, 12 Oct. 1908, ShP.
[7] Letter from Mrs Jaeger, 18 May 1909, ShP.
[8] Letter from Mrs Jaeger, 19 May 1909, ShP.

lord of many acres and living off the fat of the land';[9] as an outdated academic, a stultifying influence on British music, and a standard-bearer of the status quo. And Delius's opinion of Parry's music was never expressed without biting sarcasm as witnessed by Elgar (*teste* Fenby) when he visited Grez-sur-Loing in 1933. At the Three Choirs Festival at Hereford in September 1909 the two men might have met again as rooms were reserved for both of them at the Bishop's Palace by Robertson Sinclair. But Delius, the ardent Socialist, had no wish to mix with the privileged classes, and instead stayed at the Queen's Arms in Broad Street. Parry, typically, was more magnanimous. He may have been disparaging about Delius's 'stiff, amateurish' conducting of his *Dance Rhapsody* (a view later reinforced by Beecham), and suspicious of his pretentious behaviour afterwards,[10] but he took a genuine if critical interest in the younger composer's progress.

This open-mindedness was borne out by the extraordinary catalogue of new works and first performances Parry heard during 1909 and 1910. Besides the vogue for Delius's music, London had also succumbed to Debussy fever, principally through *Pelléas et Mélisande* which Parry attended twice. He exhibited a similar inquisitiveness over Charpentier's *Louise* in 1910, but was thoroughly hostile to the eroticism of Strauss's *Salome* which he found 'a very foul affair altogether. Pitiful to see crowds of people engrossed in the degradation of human nature.'[11] In the province of instrumental music he was intrigued by the 'curious plethoric ruminations' of Reger's chamber works featured in two concerts at the Bechstein Hall in May 1909 in the presence of the composer.[12] The first performance of Vaughan Williams's *Fantasia on a Theme of Thomas Tallis* at Gloucester on 6 September he described as 'queer', but he was deeply impressed by Elgar's Violin Concerto. 'It's of the very finest quality', he wrote to the composer, 'and the spirit of it and the intention and the wonderful lot of sincere and skilful work in it are all after my own heart.'[13] He was similarly generous in his praise of Rachmaninov who visited the College in October to play his Piano Concerto No. 2 and conduct his Second Symphony.

It was against this diverse musical backdrop that Parry's Fourth Symphony was extensively rewritten. Under the composer's direction it was first performed at Queen's Hall on 10 February 1910 in the presence of Queen Alexandra. The performance by all accounts was good, but the

    [9] L. Carley, *Delius: A Life in Letters* (Aldershot, 1988), ii. 24.
    [10] 'They told me at the Palace', Parry noted in the Memoranda of his 1909 diary, 'that Delius was so excited about the performance of his work that he had to remain in his room all day and live upon gruel. He conducts very badly—stiff, amateurish.'
    [11] Diary, 8 Dec. 1910.   [12] Ibid. 14 May 1909.
    [13] Letter to Edward Elgar, 21 Nov. 1910, HWRO 705:445, 5247/8:2815.

audience, who were by now more accustomed to the richness of Rachmaninov, the flamboyance of Elgar, and the challenging sonorities of Reger and Scriabin, were in no mood to comprehend the forbidding severity of Parry's symphonic style. They had, moreover, been tired out by a long programme in which the Symphony featured at the end; 'people didn't understand the first movement,' he noted, 'and I didn't think they understood much of any of it.'[14] Walford Davies and Napier Miles both wrote letters admiring the work, but harboured similar reservations. In replying to Miles, Parry wrote:

I'm very glad you thought well of the Symphony. They certainly played it splendidly. I suppose it is a bit stern as you say. On the whole I'm glad you thought so. Just at this time of day it seems to me inevitable; though it militates against its acceptance. It seemed to me it said what I wanted it to say—but it's not likely to be taken in at a first hearing, and as generally happens in such a case it may be a good while before it gets another.[15]

Though Parry's fears for the Symphony's future lack of popularity were largely justified, the work did receive two further performances on 27 May 1910, at the Birmingham Promenade Concerts (at the invitation of the organizers, Landon Ronald and Hamilton Harty) and on 13 April 1911 at Bournemouth.

One of the chief motives for the extensive recasting of the Symphony was that the composer wished to attach an autobiographical programme to the four movements which had been in his mind during its original composition in 1889. In this Parry wished to portray a series of universal emotions and instincts in which man seeks not only to find himself but also something of the meaning of life. Each substantial movement is given a title, 'Looking for it', 'Thinking about it', 'Playing on it', and 'Girt for it', with the whole work summarized as 'Finding the way'. Clearly, therefore, it was an attempt to imbue instrumental music with the spirit of his ethical choral works. In describing the programme or 'meaning' of the work, there was none the less an inner conflict in Parry's mind. In the past he had been called upon on several occasions to 'analyse' his instrumental and choral works in the form of programme notes, but felt distinctly uneasy about trying to describe them in detail by means of purely musical terms. Nevertheless, he was equally concerned that audiences and commentators might misconstrue the basic essence of the scheme, and that to give a clue was a more desirable alternative than to leave it to the intuition of another writer, or even worse, to the press. In consequence, when hustled by custom to explain the significance of form and design in his music, he somewhat reluctantly

[14] Diary, 10 Feb. 1910.
[15] Letter to Napier Miles, 4 Mar. 1910, BUL DM47/62.

resorted to loose symbolical or metaphorical descriptions of events. The inadequacy of these, however, left him discontented and restless, as is evident from a letter written to Herbert Thompson:

the older I get the more intolerable it is to me to try to explain what I mean in any musical work I attempt. I thought of trying to account for my own distaste and trying to account for it to you; . . . I suppose my feeling is what everyone must feel who goes to work seriously, that one means so much more by what one puts down than can be explained short of a big treatise that the few obvious points that can be given just make one shudder. Every moment in Art ought to look several ways at once. Mere symbolical references are but one aspect of it. They also have their places in the design—psychological as well as objective. But it's no use. I can't set to to appraise my doings like a commercial traveller to a customer. I know one can't expect people to find out what one means. They mostly suppose one doesn't mean anything. But to say 'I mean this or I mean that' has become beyond me. Whenever I have tried it it has made me feel sick afterwards. . . . be as lenient to my insufficiency as you can![16]

But despite his recalcitrance, he still felt obliged to give some indication of the Fourth Symphony's ethical course in the Philharmonic programme, and he was moved to do so again for his last two orchestral works, the Symphonic Fantasia '1912' and *From Death to Life*.

The first movement of the Fourth Symphony, 'Looking for it', is an imposing sonata structure, on an epic Brahmsian scale. The main forceful Doric idea, intended to show man rejoicing 'in the consciousness of effectual forces working within him' (and no doubt articulating Parry's own belief in the morality of work), is essentially unchanged from that of the first version as is its dark stirring consequent material (Ex. 45*a*) in the low tessitura of massed violins. The subsidiary subject for horns, symbolizing the ideas of man's questioning and destiny (Ex. 45*b*) shows some rhythmical and melodic similarities with the original idea, but were, nevertheless, radically recomposed and expanded tonally. This leads, as did the original, to G major for the second group, though here both ideas are quite new. The wistful melody heard on the solo clarinet (Ex. 45*c*), accompanied by other mellifluous strands in the bassoons, violas, and cellos, is an attractive idea (though very different from the more lyrically voluptuous strains of the 1889 version). It was inspired by lines from Milton's 'Lycidas':

> Were it not better done as others use,
> To sport with Amaryllis in the shade,
> Or with the tangles of Neaera's hair?
> Fame is the spur that the clear spirit doth raise
> (That last infirmity of noble mind)
> To scorn delights, and live laborious days;

[16] Letter to Herbert Thompson, 10 Sept. 1911, BLUL MS 361/189.

Ex. 45. Fourth Symphony 'Finding the Way' (1910). *a* main first-group theme, first movement ('Looking for it'); *b* secondary material of first group, first movement; *c* main second-group theme, first movement; *d* secondary material of second group, first movement; *e* opening theme, slow movement ('Thinking on it'); *f* closing material of first group, slow movement; *g* opening theme, Finale; *h* new thematic material introduced at the end of the development ('dedication'), Finale.

(a)   **Con fuoco**

(b)   (The Questions)

(c)

(d)

(e)   **Molto adagio**

cont. over/

Ex. 45. cont.

Such 'delights' and 'sport'—life's allurements—are scorned by a more agitated episode that follows (Ex. 45*d*) in which man, through 'distaste, discontent, nausea, and distress' is driven away from mental indolence to the strenuous mood of the opening. This mood initiates a development that is at once more tonally discursive, moving from G minor at its outset, through B flat, F minor, and on to G flat major—a beautiful tranquil memory of Milton's idle musings heard on clarinet and solo viola. From here the music gradually returns to the turbulent atmosphere of the opening, culminating in the recapitulation. The most remarkable feature of the restatement is undoubtedly the radiant coda which grows out of the final heroic statement of the main theme in the tonic major. This 'new phase of confidence and assurance' becomes subdued by a visionary calmness in which all thematic elements are recalled, transformed by quiet optimism.

The sheer grandeur of the first movement leaves the potent impression that the following movements are also to be cast on a similar scale. For this reason Parry undoubtedly considered that the original short *Intermezzo* formerly linking the first and slow movements was schematically redundant; hence it was dispensed with. The slow movement, 'Thinking on it', contrasts with the 'instinctive impulse' of the first movement, shifting to a reflective disposition. Structurally its sonata design has much in common with elements of the early Fantasie Sonata and Piano Concerto in the way it conflates second group and development, though the process of recapitulation is more standard in its procedure. The great strength of this movement, however, lies in its melodic pathos. Brooding, passionate, yearning, couched in rich diatonic sonorities, the main 'molto adagio' idea is one of Parry's most legendary (Ex. 45*e*). It was this type of thematic invention of which Jaeger talked and at which he believed Parry excelled. It also must have left a deep impression on Elgar who had heard it in 1889; indeed there are quite striking rhythmical and melodic similarities between the closing material of the first paragraph and the famous 'nobilmente' theme from the slow movement of Elgar's Second Symphony (Ex. 45*f*; also cf. Ex. 26*b*). From this meditative opening the music passes into a more restive, tonally fluid phase (again quite different from that of the original version) in which the discontent of the first movement is recalled as a prelude to a melodic subject symbolizing 'death'. As Parry described: 'The mental vitality that throbs within, like the unceasing pulse of the physical being, rebels against the idea of extinction; the self cries out against the shortness of the spell of individual consciousness poised betwixt two abysses.' In the more lavishly orchestrated recapitulation of the main theme, the second group interjects prematurely and more urgently. At the climax a full crystallization of the 'death' theme is heard before the agitation subsides, allowing the displaced melancholy voice of the solo violin to restore the contemplative atmosphere of the opening. This leads finally into a short coda in which the fragmented main theme with its distinctive diatonic progressions dissipates, 'vibrating in the memory'.

For the Scherzo, 'Playing on it', Parry decided to compose a completely new movement on a much larger scale than its A minor predecessor. In mood it looks back to the humour of the Greek incidental scores, and forward to the gaiety of 'Children's Pranks' in the delightful *Shulbrede Tunes*. In terms of construction the scheme is ostensibly tripartite, but the internal design is far from conventional. The opening paragraph is made up of three sections. The initial section, in G major, consists of two jaunty themes, the first bearing a distinct resemblance to a nursery rhyme. This gives way to a second episode in E flat of waltz-like character which eventually passes back to G major and a restatement of the opening material. The Trio, in C major, is distinguished by a bracing 'open-air' tune scored characteristically for horns and wind. This is briefly developed before it capitulates to a considerably modified restatement of the Scherzo. At this juncture the thematic order and tonal plan are appreciably altered and climax after a neat sidestep to E flat to incorporate a brief memory of the Trio. There then follows what Parry described as 'banter': a series of extrovert gestures and widely contrasting tempi as the movement tries to complete itself, one moment expeditiously, one moment calmly.

Of the three movements deriving from the original version, the Finale, 'Girt for it', is the most structurally reworked, and only one thematic component—the opening orchestral theme—was retained (Ex. 45g). The three thematic ideas of the exposition not only articulate its three important tonal stages (E major, C sharp minor, and G major), but also symbolize contrasting states of mind. The first represents man girded for the challenges of life, the second his sense of regret as he is impelled to forgo the comforts of domestic intimacy (as depicted by the third). The initial stages of the development derive from the first version, but they are soon superseded by more expansive treatment. The most radical departure in the movement, however, is yet to occur. As an apotheosis to the Symphony's overall programme, a new noble thematic idea (Ex. 45h), symbolizing 'dedication', is introduced, functioning as an interlude between development and recapitulation. Commencing in the stable tonality of C major it undergoes tonal development before arriving on the dominant of E. This return to the tonic is announced by a truncated affirmation of the new theme which gives way to the recapitulation. Seen in conventional sonata terms the recapitulation is unusual. Only the first expositional theme is deployed and through subsequent modification is deflected from E major to the dominant of F. This excursion to the Neopolitan ushers in an imposing restatement of 'dedication' which soon returns to the tonic. Finally, after a momentary reference back to the main theme of the first movement—the 'impulse' of the Symphony—the movement concludes with a last burst of energy.

After the Bournemouth performance of the Fourth Symphony, Parry shelved the work, though hoping that another opportunity might one day present itself for a hearing. That he believed in such a possibility is evidenced by the copious revisions he continued to make to the score. Revisions to the Scherzo, which included an arrangement for four hands, were made at intervals between January 1915 and September 1917. During this time Novello became interested in publishing the score and the slow movement went as far as the proof stage. But with the pressures of the war, publication did not take place in Parry's lifetime even though he evidently harboured hopes that it would. As late as 16 March 1918, he was trying over the slow movement and Scherzo with the College orchestra but the parts were defective and the experience depressed him. Eventually the task of editing the Symphony was undertaken by Emily Daymond and the score was published in 1921, though curiously without parts which undoubtedly acted as an obstacle to future performances.

Apart from a minor hymn tune *O Sylvan Prophet* written for S. Gregory Ould, the only other work to be published in 1910 was *Seven Part-songs for Male-voice Choir*. Many of them had been written much earlier. 'Orpheus', for example, was published separately by Novello in 1903 while the first three, 'Hang fear, cast away care' (Parry), 'Love wakes and weeps' (Scott), and 'The mad dog' (Goldsmith) were written between 1906 and 1907. Three of them, 'Hang fear', 'Orpheus', and 'An Analogy' were settings of Parry's own words, the last being taken from his early 'Sequence of Analogies' for Macmillan's Magazine in 1875. The whole set was dedicated to the Gloucester Orpheus Society of which the composer was President. The set has rarely if ever been performed since, though it is highly attractive, technically demanding, and extremely entertaining.

After the recovery of his health and spirits in 1909, 1910 proved to be an *annus mirabilis*. For the Leeds Festival in October he had revised *The Pied Piper* but what with exhaustive rehearsals for the performances of Vaughan Williams's *A Sea Symphony* and Stanford's new *Songs of the Fleet*, the chorus barely knew their parts. The rehearsal was, he wrote later, 'one of the most dreadful things I ever experienced',[17] but not wishing to offend Fricker, the chorus-master of the festival, he agreed to see it through. On the day of the performance he suffered a very bad heart attack and was unsure as to whether it would be safe to conduct. At the performance he insisted that Plunket Greene should be vigilant in case he collapsed on the rostrum, ready to beckon Stanford sitting with the score in the front row. As it happened, nothing untoward occurred.

A recurrence of his old heart problems early in the year was matched by a general relapse in Maude's health. On the advice of Beauchamp they spent the Easter and Christmas vacations in Menton but this was only partially effective. Maude's nervous condition soon led her to take regular doses of veronal, to which she soon became addicted. Her

---

[17] Diary, Memoranda, 1910.

behaviour changed; she became callous, quarrels intensified, and the atmosphere at home often became unendurable. For Maude the issue of suffrage had become an obsession and she was quite incapable of thinking or talking about anything else. Moreover, it made her completely indifferent to others. Apart from her emotionally estranged husband, whom she now barely understood, she also largely ignored her daughters and would on occasion speak of them (to Parry's horror) with an incomprehensible coldness. The effect on Dolly, happily married, settled, and devoted to her father, was negligible, but on Gwen, a more excitable character whose marriage was steadily deteriorating, it was more damaging. In the years that followed, Gwen's relationship with Plunket Greene rapidly disintegrated. Violent correspondence was followed by periods of conciliation and temporary amiability, but these grew shorter and scarcer until, in 1920, they finally went their separate ways. Owing to her mother's quixotic temperament and her animosity towards Plunket Greene, Gwen rarely communicated with Maude over the matter, and instead relied on her father's more rational judgement and compassion. Parry did all he could to rescue the marriage with little moral support from his wife, but he too realized towards the end of the war that separation was inevitable though he was spared the pain of witnessing it actually happen.

The estate at Highnam, which Maude had grown to dislike intensely, was also contributing its fair share of difficulties. Structural problems, the drains, the church spire and roof, and the decay of several of the tenants' dwellings put considerable pressure on the dwindling estate finances. Eels, the estate manager, did all he could to preserve the original beauty of the house inside and outside, but it was still necessary to make cuts in staff and equipment in order to maintain essentials. Yet while Highnam was in a state of atrophy, it was typical of Parry's munificent outlook to furnish the Gloucester Shire Hall with a sum of £1,500 in order to improve it for musical purposes. This consisted of enlarging the Hall, redecoration, and the provision of an extensive balcony ready for the Three Choirs Festival in September.

The death of Edward VII in May 1910 was another occurrence that overshadowed the year as a whole. Visits were made to Marlborough House and Buckingham Palace to sign the books of condolence and Parry attended the removal of the coffin from the Palace to Westminster Hall, and the funeral at Windsor where he rubbed shoulders with more international Heads of State than had ever been seen at such an occasion before. His College Address of September 1910 was entirely devoted to the King's memory:

We have lost our best and most loyal and most powerful friend. The King, who was the inventor and Founder of the College in days before most of you were born, was so true and liberal and large-hearted in his goodwill to the College that our circumstances can never be quite the same now he is gone from us. However gladly we may appreciate the proofs which his successor has already given of his sense of the responsibilities and opportunities of his great position, of his readiness to encourage and support work that is being worthily done, and his unselfish readiness to help forward anything which is for the good of his people, we must face the fact that the peculiarly personal interest which Edward VII took in its foundation cannot be expected to find a counterpart in the time to come.[18]

With the Coronation of George V planned for June 1911, Bridge requested, with the new King's fervent approval, a repeat performance of 'I was glad', but also asked if Parry would provide a setting of the Te Deum. Work began on the new commission in late January and was completed quickly, being finished by the beginning of March. Then began the time-consuming task of scoring the work for the customary large forces employed for the occasion. This took another two months.

Interrupting the preparations for the Coronation was one of the most important international musical events London had ever seen. Between 29 May and 3 June the International Musical Congress of the International Musical Society took place. Leading musicologists and heads of academies, conservatoires, and universities from four continents converged on London to deliver papers on a wide variety of subjects including history, church music, aesthetics, acoustics, notation, and musical instruments. Though internationalism was very much a watchword of the Congress, there was no hiding the fact that the occasion was also a shop window for British music. To this end a great deal of energy was expended to allow the fullest spectrum of indigenous compositional talent to be heard, an end for which Parry campaigned during the preliminary meetings in the year. His own contribution to the Congress, besides the usual formalities of speeches and courtesies, was a performance of the Symphonic Variations at the opening concert on 30 May and a paper on 'The Meaning of Ugliness in Art'—an attempt to articulate further his moral condemnation of superficial art brought about by commercialism, dilettantism, greed, and wanton lack of discrimination, the latter of which he blamed on society for treating the subject as negligible. The paper, which pulled no punches, was taken up avidly by the press and was published in full by the *Musical Times*.[19]

With such publicity Parry was disappointed that Macmillan was not able to publish *Style in Musical Art* in time for the Congress, though he might have been surprised to learn that Guido Adler was also publishing a similar historiographical study, *Der Stil in der Musik*, exploring the

[18] H. C. Colles (ed.), *College Addresses* (London, 1920), 57–8.
[19] See *Musical Times* (1 Aug. 1911), 507–11.

same ground. Parry's book was based on a tightly organized series of lectures given during his occupancy of the Heather Professorship at Oxford (the title being taken from his Inaugural Lecture at the university on 7 March 1900), though it should be added that much of the material for these lectures had already been drawn from those given at the Royal Institution and elsewhere. Ill health and resignation prevented him from completing the public lectures, but during 1909 and 1910 he set about rewriting them into a readable style, adding several new chapters and dispensing with others deemed unnecessary. The purpose of the book was an attempt to formulate a concept of style understood not only in terms of historical evolution (a theme already outlined in *The Evolution of the Art of Music*) but also within the sphere of wider philosophical principles. Although this entailed a largely impartial study of the technical demands and limitations of genres, the development of form, an examination of thematic evolution, and the question of texture, it is in the later discussions on the influence of audiences, methodical and conceptual antitheses (which lend a fascinating reflection of Parry's attitudes towards Classicism and Romanticism), realistic suggestion, and most didactic of all, quality, which increasingly reveal the strong moral stance of the author.

Soon after the Congress was over, rehearsals began in earnest for the Coronation. These moved to the Abbey two days before the great event in order to co-ordinate choreography and music, for since the previous Coronation, arrangements for processions and other details had been considerably elaborated. To Parry's consternation one of the major changes made was to the initial procession of the King and Queen which would completely undermine the basic musical scheme of 'I was glad'. Originally timed for six minutes, the procession was now expanded to over twenty, of which five were pauses between the Queen's entry and King's. 'Bridge had made me cut out what was between the shouts of the Westminster boys for Queen and King', he wrote irritably, 'so the situation became impossible. One could only shrug one's shoulders.'[20] The first main rehearsal proved to be a thoroughly confused fiasco as he recounted with a certain amusement in his diary:

Then the people for the general rehearsal came in, and they tried to fit the processional anthem. But they seemed to have no-one in authority—and started the procession and then stopped and began again. Bridge was fertile in expedients, but the whole scheme of the anthem went overboard. However, with various repetitions and bits of extemporization by Alcock it was finally more or less adjusted. We watched the general rehearsal with amusement. The Peers in their coronets looked extremely foolish and muddled hopelessly. The Duke of Norfolk occasionally bawled out instructions but we in the organ loft

[20] Diary, Memoranda, 20 June 1911.

couldn't hear what they were. They did a sort of mock abbreviated service, and some of the special functions, and then slowly dribbled out again—sticking fast apparently about nothing for full a quarter of an hour.[21]

At the Coronation itself on 23 June, Bridge unfortunately made a false start with the anthem and had to begin again, but with all the last minute changes and padding out with organ extemporization, he managed to time the end satisfactorily. As for the Te Deum, the choir and conductor were too exhausted to do it justice at the end of the service. Parry's Coronation celebrations almost came to a very unhappy end. After the ceremony and entertainments were over, he made for Littlehampton where the *Wanderer* was waiting to take him out to view the enormous fleet of warships assembled in the Channel. Unfortunately, however, the yacht ran aground heavily in the strong tide, was holed and nearly sank. Even worse, being full of water, they nearly steered into one of the warships, an accident which would have almost certainly proved fatal. It was therefore with great relief that yacht and crew limped back to port, tired but intact.

The Coronation Te Deum was given a more sympathetic hearing at the Worcester Festival on 12 September. For the performance Parry was able to give greater attention to detail (such as the contrast of Semi-Chorus and Full Choir) and to tempi which Bridge had rushed through rather perfunctorily in June. Since the shorter length of the work precluded any expansive symphonic development, Parry devised an elaborate scheme to unify the piece by integrating three old Church melodies which frequently lent a modal flavour to the harmony. The most prominent is 'St Ann' ('O God our help') which is heard in the short introduction. Besides permeating many of the accompanimental figures, this broad gesture frames both the first main section and the entire work, returning fittingly in the final stages as a response to the concluding words of the chorus 'let me never be confounded'. The two other principal themes are more elusive in their treatment. The 'Old Hundredth' ('All people that on earth do dwell'), for example, appears for the first time in diminution functioning as a ritornello (e.g. 'All the earth doth worship thee', and later in the relative minor, 'Heaven and earth are full of thy glory'). Further allusion is made to the tune in the descending scale of the second section ('The glorious company of the Apostles') but it is later in the work, with the anticipation of the return to the tonic ('And we worship thy name'), that the hymn tune emerges in its full majesty. The third melodic fragment, the Intonation to the Credo, is used only twice, first in augmentation to underpin the reference to 'The holy church', and later as a brief comment to the phrase 'Thou didst open the Kingdom of Heaven to all believers'.

[21] Ibid. 20 June 1911.

At the end of October news came that Lady Herbert had suffered two strokes and was not likely to live for more than another 24 hours. She died on 30 October in the early morning. Parry was taken up to see the body by his sister-in-law, Mary Herbert. '[P]oor Mama's body,' he mournfully recollected; 'Very distressing. Marble look of the face; very peaceful and horribly pathetic. Sisters' praying disturbed me.'[22] The funeral at Westminster Cathedral revived his pathological loathing for Romanism, but though he abhorred this side of his mother-in-law's existence, he had nevertheless softened towards her over the years. While Maude continued to dislike her mother thoroughly, with Parry there grew a certain affection which is evident from the letters he wrote to her. This feeling appears to have been mutual. Lady Herbert, for her part, returned a respect and fondness for the man she had attempted to dominate and patronize. Admiring the strength of character and single-mindedness which had brought success, fame, and the highest public accolades, she became one of his most fervent admirers, and took an interest in all his musical activities, albeit from a distance. For Parry the memories of her odious letter of 1870, forbidding his engagement to Maude, must have been vivid, and Lady Herbert's final warning of Maude's lack of interest in music must have rung loudly in his ears. Maude had indeed grown so indifferent to music and to her husband's creative compulsion that their relationship had inevitably cooled.

During a sailing trip to France in the summer of 1910, Parry promised his companion C. H. Lloyd that he would write him a set of chorale preludes. Once started he became fascinated by an idiom he had not touched for over thirty years. It was to be much like Brahms who, at the very end of his life, returned to the organ for the first time in almost forty years to write his own eleven Chorale Preludes, Op. 122. The Bachian tradition of Brahms's preludes, published posthumously in 1902, was undoubtedly a central impetus to Parry's own treatment of well-known tunes from hymns, psalms, or plainsong, though at times his more flamboyant approach moves more in the direction of his opulent contemporary Karg-Elert. During their composition in 1911 he submitted them to Lloyd, Parratt, and Stanford for criticism feeling unsure of their effect having been away from the instrument for so long. In December, the young and brilliant organist Douglas Fox played them over to him at the College and from this he was able to see whether any major changes were necessary. Four months later they were in the hands of Novello who agreed to publish them, with mottos from each hymn-text as an indication of the mood; Howells was to do the same in his Psalm Preludes a few years later. Within the limited textural confines of his

---

[22] Diary, 30 Oct. 1911.

organ style, Parry explores a significant range of sensibilities. 'Dundee' exudes the broad, diatonic confidence so prevalent in his choral works, while 'St Ann', the best of the animated movements, attempts to make full use of the possibilities of Romantic registration. Yet the most personal note is frequently sounded in the more contemplative preludes. 'Rockingham' ('Thither be all thy children led And may they all thy sweetness know'), better known for its words 'When I survey the wondrous cross', is a gentle study in lyricism in which the hymn-tune plays an elusive role as an inner part. Most beautiful of all is 'Christe Redemptor' where each phrase, soloed on the Great, is anticipated by gentle fantasias on the Swell.

The enthusiasm generated by the first set of Chorale Preludes encouraged him both to sketch three larger Fantasias, which were completed by the beginning of January 1912 (and played over by Fox at the end of March), and then to revise and publish his early Fantasia and Fugue in G major written originally between 1877 and 1878. The Fantasia was completely recomposed in 1882, but was subsequently shelved. When he exhumed the piece in November 1912 he wrote an entirely new Fugue. This version was published in 1913 and dedicated 'To my dear friend Walter Parratt'. Revisions of the Chorale Fantasias were, however, far more extensive than either the Preludes or the Fantasia and Fugue, for owing to the composer's general dissatisfaction with technical details, they were not published until 1915. From the end of 1913 they formed the subject of a correspondence with Walford Davies, the dedicatee of the first Fantasia on the *Old 100th*, who later helped with the registration:

Thank you ever so much for giving me the opportunity to hear 'The Old Hundredth'. It was a first rate lesson to me. It seemed to me that it was all right up to the place where the triplets begin in the semiquavers and then it got confused. I must sit tight over it and re-do a lot. The last line too which ought to make the final climax of sound was thin instead of big. It's the inner parts that did it, and they must come out. The mere massive statement of the final line in plain big chords will do much better. Your reading of it was most sympathetic to me. Your variations of time and plotting out of colour and sound were perfect.[23]

The stylistic treatment of the 'Old Hundredth' is strongly modelled on the Buxtehude tradition of quasi-improvisation and virtuosic display, though it is to the more intellectual, ornate works of Bach's few departures in the same genre (in particular the famous 'In dulci jubilo') that Parry's work most closely relates. The spirit of the third Fantasia (dedicated to Walter Alcock), another setting of 'St Ann', is similar, though its over-zealous contrapuntal texture becomes idiomatically

---

[23] Colles, *Walford Davies* (London, 1942), 68.

lumbering and technically ungrateful towards the end. Indeed, one often senses that the thinking behind much of the organ writing and registration was essentially orchestral, a feeling confirmed by the fact that Parry began an orchestration of the 'Old Hundredth' at a later date, though did not complete it. The central Fantasia, based on an old English tune 'When I survey the wondrous cross', is Parry's most serene work for the organ. In it he achieved a pathos similar to that of Brahms's autumnal polyphonic setting of 'O Welt ich muss dich lassen'. Originally it was composed in G minor and this was the version that Fox played through in 1912. But in 1914 he revised it thoroughly, recasting it in F minor. Reflecting the Baroque style of Boehm's intricate melodic embellishment (Ex. 46), Parry's thematic elaboration recurs as a yearning ritornello punctuating the freer episodes in which the un-ornamented hymn tune is given space to develop rhapsodically. So impressed was Finzi by the expressive intensity of this music, he was moved to rearrange it for strings, identifying the doleful ritornello with the plaintive timbre of a solo viola.

It was as if the momentum generated by the epic stature of the Fourth Symphony, the splendour of the Coronation Te Deum, and the disciplined intimacy of the organ works induced Parry to draw more deeply into the reserves of his creative imagination, for in 1912 he was to show that, in spite of increasing physical weakness, his compositional fecundity was capable of greater heights. Indeed the year was to be his

Ex. 46. Choral Fantasia No. 2, 'When I survey the wondrous cross' (1912–14), thematic elaboration of chorale theme.

most fertile period, though one which, with a public intrigued by the new voices of the 'Frankfurt Group', the quickly maturing styles of Holst and Vaughan Williams, and the challenging works of Elgar, Strauss, Schoenberg, and Mahler, went largely unnoticed.

A first indication of this high level of invention was the *Soliloquy from Browning's Saul* ('I believe it') written for the Browning Centenary in Westminster Abbey in May. Constructed entirely of a flowing *arioso* and held together by deft accompanimental reflections (strongly orchestral in conception), the *Soliloquy* has all the natural rhythmical accentuation and melodic poise demonstrated twenty years earlier in 'Through the ivory gate' (*English Lyrics* Set III), brought about, as Banfield has observed, by 'a grasp of technical restraint'.[24] With simplicity of texture, subtle diatonic colouring, and telling use of modulation, each nuance of Browning's words is subtly graded, and the tonal plan of third relationships is skilfully paced. Particularly telling is the move to E major which prefigures similar yearning passages in Gurney's songs, and the Neapolitan climax in the third section in G major ('A man like to me thou shalt love and be loved by for ever') is splendidly arresting, as is the subsequent recovery. A similar tonal procedure in the final section is also wonderfully enhanced by an ethereal cadence ('See the Christ stand'), and a poignant parting sigh from the organ.

During the composition of the Browning soliloquy between February and April, Parry was approached by Norman O'Neill, the director of music at the Haymarket Theatre, about the Keats–Shelley Festival, organized by the Keats–Shelley Memorial Association. Parry had been connected with the Association since 1906 when he had been invited to become a patron along with Elgar, Hardy, Colvin, and an enormous list of illustrious personages. The Association's initial aim had been to purchase the house in the Piazza di Spagna, Rome, where Keats had died. This successfully took place and the house rapidly became a place of pilgrimage for disciples of Keats and of Shelley (whose poem, 'Adonais', was inspired by the death of Keats). In March 1907 a concert at Stafford House was organized to bolster funds which included Parry's quartet 'Life of Life' from *Prometheus Unbound* and his part-song 'Music when soft voices die'. In order to complete the purchase of the house, the Committee decided to stage two Memorial Matinées at the Haymarket Theatre in June 1912 which would include poetic recitations and a wide variety of musical contributions. The musical part of the programme included the *Prelude to Adonais* by Bax, O'Neill's Dramatic Scena *La Belle Dame sans merci*, and a series of tableaux on 'St Agnes' Eve' accompanied by music specially written for the occasion by Coleridge

---

[24] Banfield, *Sensibility and English Song*, i. 25.

Taylor. Parry's contribution was a short ballet score, *Proserpine*, inspired both by the events of the ancient legend and Shelley's poem 'Song of Proserpine (whilst gathering flowers on the plain of Enna)'.

Composed in six days between 23 and 29 May, *Proserpine* was conceived as one scene in three orchestral numbers, *Prelude, Intermezzo*, and *Conclusion* linked by a setting of Shelley's poem for an unaccompanied female chorus of 'Unseen Spirits'. Parry's ballet (choreographed by Ina Pelly) has much in common with the pastoral delicacy and pellucid sensibility of Elgar's *Sanguine Fan* and shows a hitherto unrevealed side of his personality. Only perhaps in the hushed tenderness of the Intermezzo of *The Birds* or the slow minuet of the 'Lady Radnor' Suite does Parry come near to the translucent texture of the *Prelude*, and nowhere else in his orchestral music does one find such an evocative image of nature as depicted by the Wagnerian *Waldweben* with its wispish muted upper strings and strands of chattering woodwind. The ballet is undoubtedly one of the most transparent and sensitive examples of Parry's orchestration and has more to do with the French flair for pointillist timbres, belonging to the world of Delibes, Massenet, and Saint-Saëns. The finesse of the *Intermezzo* and last fleeting bars of the *Conclusion* with its crystalline string harmonics are especially delightful. Parry was made rudely aware at the rehearsals, however, that his fragile vision lay beyond the powers of a very inefficient orchestra and the two performances on 25 and 28 June were generally ragged. 'Proserpine mostly went well', he wrote after the second performance, 'but the band went all to pieces in the Introduction. I never heard such awful confusion. Band couldn't manage the cross rhythms in 6/8. Felt depressed after it.'[25]

Shortly after the Keats–Shelley Festival was over, he was saddened to hear of the death of his old friend Alma-Tadema whose funeral he attended at St Paul's on 5 July. Even more lamentable was the untimely death from pneumonia of Coleridge-Taylor in early September. For Parry his death was a tragedy equalling only that of Hurlstone in 1906 as was apparent by the tribute he wrote for the *Musical Times* the following month.[26]

His distress at the news of Coleridge-Taylor's death was mitigated only by the successful rehearsals at St Andrew's Hall of his new choral work for the Hereford Festival. In considering Robertson Sinclair's request for a work less esoteric in terms of literary content, Parry's imagination had immediately turned to the theme of the Nativity. With its mixture of joy, meditation, rapture, and innocence, it was a subject that had continually appealed to him from his youth, though the

---

[25] Diary, 28 June 1912.   [26] *Musical Times* (1 Oct. 1912), 638.

opportunity to write such a work had never presented itself until now. With Parry's established reputation for setting Milton, his friend William Hannam supposed that he might naturally gravitate towards Milton's 'On the morning of Christ's nativity', but in a letter of 16 October, shortly before the vocal score was obtainable in print, Parry observed: 'The Milton Ode has always appeared to me quite impracticable. The identical form of the stanzas tends to monotony.'[27] He may have found the monotony of the poem intractable, but he was also faced with the problem of dissection, for the 31 stanzas of Milton's Ode would have necessitated the time-consuming task of considerable reduction. By comparison, William Dunbar's lyric, 'Ode on the Nativity', with its strophic simplicity appeared eminently suitable for musical treatment. To some extent this suggested a design with which Parry had experimented in *The Lotos-Eaters*, but Dunbar's poem, with its subtly modified refrains, suggested a musical structure of a more challenging intellectual scope.

The choice of Dunbar, a poet who was generally unfamiliar to audiences at the beginning of this century, was unusual and perspicacious. The poem draws on the exultant words of Psalm 95, spoken at the Offertory of the first Mass on Christmas Day: 'Laetentur coeli, et exultet terra ante faciem domini: quoniam venit' ('Let the heavens rejoice, and let the earth be glad before the face of the Lord, because he cometh'). Dunbar also delights in a play on words as he relates 'The clear sun . . . surmounting Phoebus in the east' to the Son venerated in the introit of the Great Mass on Christmas Day, 'Et nobis Puer natus est'. These words are reiterated with deft modification in the refrains to each stanza, a familiar procedure in medieval religious lyrics. Furthermore, the summoning of the heavenly bodies, the elements, sinners, clergy, animals, and flowers (of which Mary is the Rose, the flower of flowers) suggests the influence of the Te Deum.

The simple poetic structure of Dunbar's lyric is clearly articulated in Parry's musical scheme, in which all stanzas, except for stanza 6, are well defined by contrasting tonalities (Ex. 47*a*). Recalling a similar technique used in the introduction to the *Te Deum* of 1900, Parry elusively incorporates a microcosm of the Ode's key scheme into the prelude (Ex. 47*b*) where we hear the tonalities of D major (stanza 2), F sharp major (stanza 3), and D flat major (stanza 4) form an oblique progression which eventually surfaces via F major (stanza 5) in the home key, B flat major (stanza 1 and the end of stanza 6).

Perhaps the most outstanding feature of the *Ode on the Nativity* is its thematic integration. The orchestral introduction and stanza 1 act as an

---

[27] Letter to William Hannam, 12 Oct. 1912, McUL.

Ex. 47. *Ode on the Nativity* (1912). *a* tonal and thematic plan; *b* opening of orchestral introduction, showing the Ode's key scheme in microcosm; *c* main theme of orchestral introduction showing figures 'x' and 'y'; *d* main theme of refrain; *e* secondary material, stanza 2; *f* combination of figures 'x' and 'y' and the refrain material, stanza 3; *g* further transformation in vocal material of stanza 5.

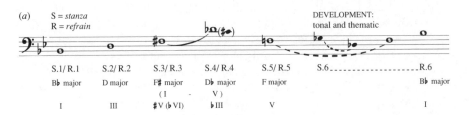

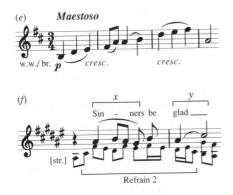

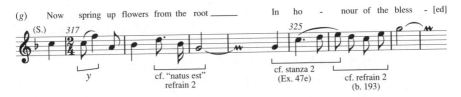

exposition of the work's seminal material. The gentle undulating figures ('x' and 'y') heard in the oboe's pastoral evocation at the opening emerge in a more fully blown form when B flat is announced (Ex. 47c). This material subsequently invades the Latin acclamation 'Rorate coeli desuper' of the first stanza sung by soprano soloist and chorus in antiphony and recurs as a form of punctuative ritornello. The function of the refrain 'Et nobis Puer natus est' in each stanza is to reaffirm the tonic in each case which is further emphasized by the presentation of a new thematic figure derived in part from the orchestral material at the end of the prelude (Ex. 47d). Stanza 2, for chorus alone, is articulated by a new secondary idea (Ex. 47e) which forms the basis of the vocal material (e.g. 'Archangels' bars 153–5 and 'To him give loving most and least' bars 178–81), while its refrain is the first of several variations on the polyphonic treatment essayed at the end of stanza 1. Stanza 3 is for soprano solo alone and continues to build on the material outlined above by reworking figures 'x' and 'y' in the vocal line supported by an accompaniment derived from the refrain material of stanza 2 (Ex. 47f). The latter material also provides the basis for a subtle variation in the refrain, complementing the textual modification 'Pro nobis Puer natus est'. The main body of stanza 4 for female voices alludes briefly to figure 'x' and to the opening of stanza 2, but its more florid moments stem principally from the melismatic ideas of the first refrain. This is concluded by a further variation (characterized by intensifying the imitation with stretto) of the refrain of stanza 2. The material in stanza 5 seems to be more freely moulded on its text than that of stanzas 2, 3, or 4, though on closer examination its figurations betray links with the first two stanzas and refrains (Ex. 47*g*). The last three lines of the stanza allude strongly to the opening material of stanza 2 ('Lay out your leaves lustily'), an idea stated more powerfully after the refrain as a majestic transition to the final stanza. The refrain of stanza 5 is closely linked to that of stanza 4 (paralleling the relationship of the refrains of stanzas 2 and 3) in the way it resumes the stretto treatment of the refrain theme now in an extended form and enlarged into eight-part polyphony.

Stanza 6 ('Sing heaven imperial'), initiated by one of the most arresting tonal divergences in all of Parry's choral music, forms much the most protracted musical structure of the Ode, for here the composer takes the opportunity to break loose from the comparatively stable, self-contained tonal structures of the previous five stanzas. In addition, the stanza is treated as a transitional and developmental paragraph in which, like the earlier Te Deum, both past thematic material and tonalities are recalled and reworked, while the refrain is used to restate both B flat (the home key of the work) and the material of stanza 1. This return is executed with particular skill in the way transformation after transformation of figure 'x' is gradually distilled to reveal the familar material of the opening bars, and the final climax is one of the most intense and ecstatic in British choral literature.

The *Ode on the Nativity* is without doubt one of Parry's supreme choral achievements. No other of his choral works (with perhaps the exception of *Blest Pair of Sirens*) displays such precision and formal tightness and nowhere else does he show such a facility for thematic homogeneity. Indeed the quintessence of the Ode is not simply the distinctive transformations that enunciate each stanza and refrain, but rather it is the greater subtlety of their organic development, integration, and absorption into an overall melodic style-unity that raises the piece on to a higher compositional plane. This is further enhanced by a disciplined handling of strophic form enriched by variation technique and procedures analogous to sonata practice, which *in toto* gave rise to an involuted canvas more symphonic than he had ever achieved before.

In many ways it was a marvel that Parry had been able to attend the Festival at Hereford, for Beauchamp had warned him in July that such action 'would be positively dangerous'.[28] During the course of the year his health continued to fluctuate. In April he underwent another operation for a cyst but showed extraordinary resilience in a swift recovery made possible to some degree by a wonderfully reviving

---

[28] Diary, 18 July 1912.

summer sailing trip to Ireland with Pearsall Smith and Walter Raleigh. It was to be a last view of the landscape he adored. He revisited old haunts: the picturesque bays of Glandore and Castlehaven; Crookhaven and the majesterial Bantry Bay; and most dear to him, the Great Skellig where he landed, taking newspapers to the lighthouse keepers who remembered him!

Returning to Rustington after such a voyage no longer held the same sense of anticipation. Maude's behaviour remained intolerable. She continued to take veronal in large doses: one moment she was buoyed up with enthusiasm for the suffrage movement, the next she was in the depths of despair, infirm, at times hysterical, and unbearable to live with. Maude, however, was only part of the problem. Stanford's conduct at the College had reached an all-time low. 'Spent the time at home looking up details of former rows with Stanford in my log', Parry recorded in his diary in January.[29] These memoranda reveal a perception of a man who had become increasingly egotistical, fractious, intensely argumentative, and jealous. In 1911 relations had worsened over the Coronation when an invitation for Stanford had not been forthcoming, and there had been problems at the Musical Congress when the Irishman complained bitterly that Elgar's Second Symphony had been given a disproportionate amount of rehearsal time. Another difficulty lay in the expiry of Stanford's tenure as conductor of the Leeds Festival which had been conceded reluctantly. When the Festival Committee put forward a policy of a joint-conductorship, he refused to take part, which left the way open for Nikisch, Allen, and Elgar. Parry refused to be dragged into the fray, but by February 1912 Stanford's behaviour had become so impossible that only formal business communications were feasible.

Privately Parry continued to be a piercing critic of Stanford's music. On 22 February he heard his Seventh Symphony (commissioned as part of the Philharmonic's Centenary celebrations) but found it rather 'mild conventional [and] Mendelssohnic—But not so interesting as Mendelssohn.'[30] Nevertheless, it appears that he was absorbed by the compactness of the work's symphonic design lasting less than twenty-five minutes, since for his own commission from the Philharmonic he began to consider the notion of a similarly compressed symphonic scheme of four connected movements. It was not until 3 September, however, that he was able to commence work on the Symphony. This was soon interrupted by the Hereford Festival and at the end of the month by another operation for a cyst in his groin. The anaesthetic left him overwhelmed with sickness which prevented any sustained work until the middle of October when he began to score the first three

[29] Ibid. 17 Jan. 1912.   [30] Ibid. 22 Feb. 1912.

movements. Composition of the finale had to wait until 7 November when, evidently seized with inspiration, he wrote it in just over week. The first performance of the Fifth Symphony '1912' took place on 5 December at Queen's Hall under the composer's direction and it made a deep impression on its audience. Balfour Gardiner, who had forged a reputation at his own concerts for music by members of the younger generation (such as Grainger, Scott, O'Neill, Bax, Holst, and Harty), was highly taken with the work and included it in his 1913 season. A third performance took place in Bournemouth on 17 April and, at the request of Henry Wood, it was given at Queen's Hall again on 1 November which, according to the composer, was 'A really wonderful performance. Warm and elastic.'[31] At the first of these performances the work was entitled simply 'Symphony in four linked movements in B minor 1912', a description which was superseded at the second Queen's Hall performance by the 'Fifth Symphony'. However, the autograph manuscript clearly bears the inscription *Symphonic Fantasia* in a different ink from the rest of the work which suggests that this was added some time later—a fact which appears to be borne out by Goodwin and Tabb's published score which bears the title 'Symphonic Fantasia in B minor "1912"' with 'Symphony' as a subtitle.

Schumann's Fourth Symphony (itself originally entitled *Symphonische Phantasie*) was undoubtedly the principal model on which Parry based his own work. His lengthy article on 'Symphony' (1883) for Grove's *Dictionary of Music and Musicians* clearly reveals his response to Schumann's symphony, most significantly by the following description:

The series of movements are as it were interlaced by their subject matter; and the result is that the whole gives the impression of a single and consistent musical poem. The way in which the subjects recur may suggest different explanations to different people, and hence it is dangerous to try and fix one in definite terms describing particular circumstances. But the important fact is that the work can be felt to represent in its entirety the history of a series of mental or emotional conditions such as may be grouped round one centre; in other words, the group of impressions which go to make the innermost core of a given story seems to be faithfully expressed in musical terms and in accordance with the laws which are indispensable to a work of art. The conflict of impulses and desires, the different phases of thought and emotion, and the triumph or failure of the different forces which seem to be represented, all give the impression of belonging to one personality, and of being perfectly consistent in their relation to one another.

Obviously one of the most attractive constructional features of Schumann's one-movement scheme was the element of incorporating four connected

---

[31] Diary, 1 Nov. 1913.

movements (i.e. the traditional constituents of a symphony—first-movement Allegro, slow movement, Scherzo, and Finale) into a tautly unified cyclic structure. Yet evidently another and perhaps the most persuasive element as Parry understood it was the so-called 'history of mental or emotional conditions such as may be grouped round one centre'. This 'centre' for Parry was 1912. Emulating the autobiographical scheme of his own Fourth Symphony, each movement of the work was allotted a title: 'Stress', 'Love', 'Play', and 'Now!', while the programme notes provided by the composer once again alluded to the symbolic significance of the main thematic strands.

The first movement, 'Stress', functions primarily as a large-scale exposition to the work in which all the important thematic and motivic ideas are introduced. Of these, two are seminal. The first, figure 'x' (Ex. 48*a*), which Parry labelled 'Brooding Thought', is heard at the very opening on lower strings. This leads to a second, more extended melody (Theme 1) played by the wind, symbolizing 'Tragedy' (Ex. 48*b*), which is constructed primarily on a three-note fragment, figure 'y'. Having stated these two ideas the movement works itself up into a dynamic 'allegro' where several additional themes are presented. The first of these (Theme 2), representing 'wrestling thought', is a rhythmically vigorous melody full of sequence and characteristic appoggiaturas (Ex. 48*c*). The tonality, an oblique B minor, gives way to F sharp minor which is articulated by a new subject, 'Revolt' (Theme 3—Ex. 48*d*). This material reaches a climax, after which we move on to a dominant pedal of D where a further fragment, figure 'z' (denoting 'Suffering and Distress'—Ex. 48*e*), is introduced. The dominant pedal encourages us to anticipate a move to D, and at first this appears to be confirmed by a lyrical outpouring in bar 56 with a new idea (Theme 4) constructed entirely from figures 'x' and 'z' (Ex. 48*f*). But it soon becomes clear that D major is only illusory as the submediant of a still operative F sharp minor whose dominant is reaffirmed in bar 59.

From a tonal point of view the development is extremely unusual in that it remains firmly anchored to expositional tonalities, breaking away decisively only in the last 28 bars. This has the effect of elongating the sense of exposition which, in the wider context of the Symphony, serves to balance the overall sense of recapitulation in the last movement. The content and process of thematic development are to a large extent determined by programmatic elements. At the development's outset a further melodic fragment is introduced representing 'Pity' (Ex. 48*g*). Although overwhelmed by a severe contrupuntal treatment of 'distress' (figure 'z') and climactic statement of 'revolt' (Theme 3), 'Pity' prevails as a dominant emotion. Musically, however, this also has the satisfactory effect of framing the development, an unusual device though one which

Ex. 48. Symphonic Fantasia, '1912' (1912). *a* 'Brooding thought' showing figure 'x', first movement ('Stress'); *b* 'Tragedy' showing figure 'y' (Theme 1), first movement; *c* 'Wrestling thought' (Theme 2), first movement; *d* 'Revolt' (Theme 3), first movement; *e* 'Suffering and distress' showing figure 'z', first movement; *f* Theme 4, first movement; *g* 'Pity', first movement; *h* 'Human love', opening theme of slow movement ('Love'); *i* 'Play', opening material of Scherzo ('Play'); *j* theme from the Trio; *k* 'Content and hopefulness', opening theme, Finale ('Now!'); *l* final restatement of Theme 1, Finale.

Parry would already have seen at work in the first movement of Elgar's First Symphony. The recapitulation is marked by the return to the tragic mood of Theme 1 clearly stated in B minor. Thus the two originally divided phrases of the exposition are brought together as a more continuous melody and the rhetorical ending of the second phrase is used as a transition to a final phrase restating figure 'z'. These 13 bars alone constitute the recapitulation of the first movement in which Parry distils and conflates elements of first- and second-group material. Such a truncated form of restatement deliberately leaves a sense of incompleteness which is only redressed by proceeding immediately with the next movement.

The slow movement, *Love*, represents the crystallization of the many tonal allusions to D major in the first movement. The canonic theme (Ex. 48*h*), symbolizing the healing power of human love and interaction, forms the main portion of a sophisticated ternary scheme. Of particular interest in this structure is the manner in which the principal second idea, based on figure 'x', is introduced in the tonic before it is heard more substantially in its new key, F major. Its subsequent lyrical and developmental extension stems from the numerous experimental slow movements in the Fantasie Sonata, Piano Concerto, and the revised Fourth Symphony. The recapitulation is comparatively more formal than the first movement in that Theme 5 is restated in full (the second idea is dispensed with). Yet although the movement is allowed to cadence into the tonic (unlike the first movement which used its final bars as a transition to D major), there is still a prevailing sense of incompleteness brought about by the gradual motivic 'deterioration' of thematic material which is then manipulated as a preparation for the Scherzo.

The playful Scherzo, in G major, is the most internally balanced structure of the Symphony, even though it too proves to be open-ended. Its apparently simple ternary design employs a scheme more closely allied to sonata principles in its outer sections (one which may well have derived from a similar experiment in the Scherzo of Brahms's Fourth Symphony). This is clearly exemplified by the move to the relative in the first section, which, in the restatement, is firmly rooted in the tonic. Thematically Parry continues to derive his material from the first movement, basing the main Scherzo idea on figure 'y' (Ex. 48*i*) and the contrapuntal secondary material on figure 'z'. The Trio, in C major, revealing Parry in alpine mood (curiously reminiscent of Mahler with its duet for horns), is constructed entirely from figure 'x' (Ex. 48*j*).

In a manner similar to the end of the second movement, the conclusion of the Scherzo is one of gradual thematic dissolution in anticipation of the Finale. A further parallel, however, can be drawn between this stage of the symphony and the corresponding stage of Schumann's Fourth Symphony in that both movements lead to an introduction. Of Schumann's introduction Parry stated:

The first subject of the first movement and the first of the last are connected by a strong characteristic figure, which is common to both of them. The persistent way in which this figure is used in the first movement has already been described. It is not maintained to the same extent in the last movement; but it makes a strong impression in its place there, partly by its appearing conspicuously in the accompaniment, and partly by the way it is led up to in the sort of intermezzo which connects the scherzo and the last movement, where it seems to be introduced at first as a sort of reminder of the beginning of the work, and as if suggesting the clue to its meaning and purpose.

Parry's introduction adheres to this basic description. In an 'intermezzo' reminiscent of Strauss's *Tod und Verklärung*, figure 'x' emerges and acts as a punctuation to a rhapsodic transfiguration of Theme 2 on solo strings and clarinet. In addition to being a 'reminder' of the work's opening, this transformation provides a foretaste of the first spacious theme of the finale (Ex. 48*k*—cf. Ex. 48*c*), a magnificent swirling melody in a radiant B major symbolizing 'content and hopefulness'. For the second group, a new more exuberant theme remotely related to Theme 1 is introduced in D major which powerfully recalls the tenacious role of that tonality throughout the symphony. Also its effect here is all the more pronounced in that it now acts as a third-related key (not the relative major) to the tonic, B major. In the ensuing short development Parry begins tentatively to gather in some of the threads of his cyclic design as material from the first movement is summoned. Predominant amongst this material was figure 'z' in much the same form as it occurred in the development of the first movement, a recurrence which was evidently intended to suggest a renewed crisis of 'distress'. Yet before this is allowed to gain any substantial momentum, we experience yet another truncated and transformed recapitulation in which, to use Parry's words, 'Hopefulness comes in a new guise'. The brevity of this recapitulation is this time resolved by further development as ideas from the first movement gather pace. The climax of this new developmental departure is articulated by the motive of 'Tragedy' (Theme 1) which in turn anticipates the grand programmatic and musical peroration of the work. The final restatement of Theme 1, nobly amplified in B major, is perhaps one of the most affecting moments in all Parry (Ex. 48*l*). Here 'Tragedy' is completely transformed, and 'the recognition of tragedy in the light of human love becomes the token of healing'. The movement, however, does not conclude at this point for the process of continual transformation (so quintessential to the symphony as a whole), spearheaded by renewed 'hopefulness', is only finally resolved in the massive cadence heard in the last bars of the work, in which all-pervasive but now transfigured 'Thought' (figure 'x') resounds triumphantly.

Although Parry's *Symphonic Fantasia* clearly bears the stamp of Schumann's Fourth Symphony, an overview of the piece suggests that other major structural influences were at work. The elongated recapitulation of the whole work, articulated by Theme 1 in the tonic major, is decidedly Lisztian, and brings to mind the sophisticated cyclic design of the Sonata in B minor. Yet even here there are noticeable differences of treatment. For example, Liszt's Finale acts as the omitted recapitulation of the first movement's interrupted sonata. Parry's Finale, on the other hand, attempts to be a movement in its own right (i.e. complete with exposition, development, and recapitulation) using material derived from that of the first movement. The addition of further development and the peroration of Theme 1 after these events would seem, at least in the context of cyclic unity, to explore a new evolutionary phase. The complex cyclic procedures essayed in Schoenberg's Quartet No. 1 in D minor, Op. 7 and the *Kammersymphonie*, Op. 9 show a fascinating affinity with the processes revealed in Parry's symphony, particularly in the manner in which material undergoes constant transformation. Certainly all Parry's restatements (including the Scherzo) follow this trend either through the use of new consequent material, new tonal developments, or through thematic transformation which is especially telling in the last movement, final recapitulation, and coda. It seems unlikely that Parry knew either of Schoenberg's works. It is remotely possible that he may have seen a score of the Quartet which had been published in 1907 by Birnbach, but a performance in London was not forthcoming until November 1913 when it was given by the Flonzalay Quartet. The *Kammersymphonie* was not published until 1912 and then not performed publicly in England until 1921. Nevertheless, even if he had no knowledge of these works, it is still remarkable (perhaps even more so) that the *Symphonic Fantasia* should show such a forward-looking attitude to modern structural procedures and exhibit such an advance on nineteenth-century techniques. For this reason alone it merits a firmer place in the canon of cyclic works, and perhaps more important still, it deserves to be more widely recognized as one of the finest and most assured utterances in British symphonic literature.

The three performances of the *Symphonic Fantasia* during 1913 were a measure of its relative success; it was in fact to be the last of his major works to receive such a degree of attention, though after its second performance at Queen's Hall it was not played again during Parry's lifetime and remained barely known until it was recorded by Sir Adrian Boult in 1980. For the composer the work accorded an unusual satisfaction and its quality of inspiration seemed to permeate the various works that were written in its wake. The first of these was an anthem, *God is our hope*, written for the 259th Anniversary of the Festival of the Sons of the Clergy at St Paul's Cathedral on 24 April 1913. Conceived for a large double choir, bass solo, and orchestra, its broad sweeping choral gestures recapture something of the polyphonic splendour of *Blest Pair of Sirens* combined with the simple yet expanded tonal scheme of *I was glad*. For the Three Choirs Festival in Gloucester he unearthed his Te

Deum in F which he revised extensively using the English text rather than the Latin. One section was also entirely rewritten. The original solo in A flat for bass and male chorus ('Salvum populum tuum') was replaced by one altogether more solemn in its neo-Bachian counterpoint for bass and full chorus. Its tonal behaviour is also different in that it commences in a plaintive C minor which only towards its end establishes A flat on a more positive note ('and lift them up for ever').

On a more intimate level, away from the grand scale of *God is our hope* and the Te Deum, was a set of piano pieces which had been occupying him on and off since the beginning of 1911. For some time he had been contemplating a musical expression of his deep affection for Shulbrede Priory and its inhabitants. Since Dolly and Arthur had moved there in 1902 the comfort and peace of the old building and its surrounding wooded countryside had brought intervals of relief and sympathy. It was the place where above all he felt loved and cherished—human emotions for which he longed were scant in his own home. In the *Shulbrede Tunes*, a series of ten miniatures, he attempted to depict both character and location, mood and atmosphere. When they were finally published in 1914 they generated a certain curiosity amongst pianists and critics as to who and what were pictured within the pages of the collection. In reply to a letter from W. A. Roberts, a Liverpool organist, Parry declared:

Shulbrede Priory is a romantic place among the hills and oakwoods near the Sussex border. It is the place where my daughter Mrs Ponsonby lives with her husband Arthur Ponsonby and her two children Elizabeth and Matthew. It is mainly the old ecclesiastical building of the fourteenth century [*Parry was wrong here—it was actually twelfth century*], with a vaulted hall and mysterious staircases and one splendid big room the 'Prior's Chamber', with high pitched roof and great oak beams across and a grand old fireplace; and some delightfully quaint Elizabethan frescoes. All the personally named tunes are portraits. 'Dolly' is Mrs Ponsonby; she had to have two tunes, as she has two distinct phases. Elizabeth is a lithe slip of a girl, very springy in her gait; Matthew a dear little boy of 10, of very enquiring turn of mind (that's why he begins with a question), and a serious side, and great interest in country life and animals. 'Father playmate' is all sorts of delightful things—a great companion to the children as well as a great politician and deeply interested in Art and Music as well. Of course it's a great place for children's pranks and also for bogies and sprites—and the garden, with the old monks' fishponds, is adorable. I am very glad you care to know about it, and thank you for your letter.[32]

The first piece, 'Shulbrede', is a robust animated piece which exudes a sense of activity and excitement, though we are also reminded in the closing bars of the extraordinary tranquillity induced by the gentle rural surroundings. 'Elizabeth' is a graceful song-like piece with a touch of

[32] Letter to W. A. Roberts, 21 May 1917, ShP.

caprice, while 'Matthew' with its ternary scheme, combines liveliness in its outer G major sections with a reflective central episode in E flat. 'Dolly' (No. 1), gentle and wistful, is eminently Schumannesque in figuration and tripping melody, while her other phase (No. 2) is a slow movement in D flat of great warmth and tenderness (Ex. 49a)—an expression surely of a deep empathy and personal intimacy. By contrast, in the numerous sides of 'Father playmate', his writing, his capacity for fun, his interest in history and the archaeology of his home, his love of discussion, politics, and art, are catalogued in a passacaglia structure of considerable pianistic difficulty that rounds off the collection. The children are depicted in another virtuoso display, 'Children's pranks'. Like 'Dolly' (No. 2) this piece craves the orchestra and its mixture of frolic tinged with melancholy shares an affinity with similar movements in Elgar's *Wand of Youth* Suites. 'Bogies and sprites that gambol by night', replete with distortions of 'Three blind mice' and melodramatic gestures, could be music for a shadow show. The garden, in which the composer delighted, is portrayed in a dainty pastorale ('In the garden— with the dew on the grass'), but the most evocative of all the descriptive pieces is 'Prior's Chamber by firelight', a slumberous nocturne that charms by its pulsating pedal points and long drowsy phrases (Ex. 49b).

Ex. 49. *Shulbrede Tunes* (1913). *a* opening of 'Dolly No. 2'; *b* opening of 'Prior's Chamber by firelight'.

At the end of March 1913, a telegram from Rome arrived announcing the sudden death of Lord Pembroke. Immediately Parry composed a short Elegy in A flat for organ which was played at the Earl's funeral at Wilton on 7 April. Soon afterwards Parry's health began to fail again. In mid-May he suffered a severe heart attack and was promptly banished from College by the Board for the rest of the term. During the summer he sailed up the Irish Sea to the Western Isles of Scotland, to Mull, Iona, and the Mull of Kintyre—old haunts he had not seen for almost twenty years. It was to be his last extensive maritime excursion on the *Wanderer*. After the Three Choirs Festival, in which the Te Deum was given a spirited performance in honour of the approaching 'Centenary of Peace between Great Britain and the United States', he underwent yet another operation this time on his throat. Recovery from this latest subjection to the surgeon's knife was less swift, and though he was able to deliver his address at the College, he was forced to send his apologies to Hannam at Leeds where his *Ode to Music* was to be conducted by Elgar. The rest of the Christmas term at the College proved to be a struggle. Pownall, his trusted Registrar, resigned for health problems, a position which was filled by Claude Aveling. Maude, who was desperately trying to wean herself off veronal, was in a dismal state of depression, and collapsed at Covent Garden during a performance of Rôze's *Joan of Arc*. Most distressing of all, however, was the dreadful news of Spencer Lyttelton's death on 5 December. Three days later Parry attended his old friend's memorial service at St Margaret's Westminster which he found extremely harrowing, and in the days that followed he could not dispel the memory. The last of his old Eton friends was gone and his loneliness seemed complete. Distraught, he wrote to Dolly:

That dear old Spencer is a most terrible loss. It has almost bowled me over. I took it for granted he would outlast me, and that some day, when my work was not so exacting, I should be able to enjoy the ancient friendship to the full. One never thinks of some things till too late; and I remember with pain how, when he would sometimes come into my room here when I was busy and sit down and talk, I used to get restive, when I ought to have been glad to get any opportunity to talk with him. And so one lets one's chances slip irreparably. And really I depended on him so much. I never lost the feeling of his being the older boy at Eton, and with the ardent friendship was mixed up a sort of gratitude.[33]

The shadow of Spencer's death was only part of a much greater shadow that hung over him. The absorbing issues of Women's Suffrage and Home Rule for Ireland which he had continued to support, paled into significance with the much more serious threat to peace that was terrorizing Europe. Two Balkan Wars had left that part of eastern

[33] Letter to Dorothea Ponsonby, 10 Dec. 1913, ShP.

Europe in a state of flux and instability, while the major European powers were gripped inexorably by the arms race. The uncertainty of the future appeared menacing.

The chaos of international politics seemed to be mirrored by the extraordinary diversity and novelty that the London concert scene was experiencing. On the one hand there were the first English performances of *Parsifal* conducted by Bodanzky at Covent Garden which attracted enormous audiences. On the other hand there was a fever for Russian operas at Drury Lane under Thomas Beecham. Rimsky-Korsakov's *Ivan the Terrible* and *Le Coq d'or*, Mussorgsky's *Boris Godunov* and *Khovanshchina*, and Borodin's *Prince Igor* generated considerable enthusiasm, not least for the memorable performances by Chaliapin. Parry was greatly taken with this unfamilar repertoire and with the two newly introduced ballet scores by Stravinsky, *Le Rossignol* and *Petroushka*. 'It really is a marvellous piece from every point of view', he wrote of *Petroushka*; 'Stravinski's [sic] wild fancy, the story, the dancing—all wonderful.'[34] Indigenous talent was also well represented by the first performance of Vaughan Williams's 'London' Symphony on 27 March at Queen's Hall which he found 'full of interest and thought'.[35] More attention, however, was focused on the visit to London in March by Scriabin who was the soloist in his own Piano Concerto in F sharp and a participant in *Prometheus* conducted by Wood. The effect on Parry of *Prometheus*, with its harmonic modernisms, was undoubtedly mitigated by the sensation of the concert year—Schoenberg's visit to London to conduct his *Fünf Orchesterstücke*. The reaction to these pieces in September 1912, when Wood had conducted them at a Promenade Concert, had been one of shock and bewilderment, hence it was with a renewed inquisitiveness provoked by such articles as Newman's 'A propos of Schoenberg's Five Orchestral Pieces' that the capital's musical public flocked to Queen's Hall on 17 January 1914 to revive or modify their perceptions. Parry had not been at the notorious Promenade Concert so he was eager to hear the pieces for himself. His impressions were decidedly unfavourable. The violence and discord of Schoenberg's expressionism and pantonal language induced him to renounce the music as an 'elaboration of noises which reminded me of the Nursery when children play with toy instruments. But I noticed the band applauded and it surprised me. There was much applause at the end.'[36] He was more impressed, perhaps understandably, by the progressive chromatic tonal style of *Verklärte Nacht*, which had been avidly taken up by several London chamber ensembles, including one at the College. But the progressivist tendencies of Schoenberg's experiments puzzled him as did

---

[34] Diary, 20 July 1914.   [35] Ibid. 27 Mar. 1914.   [36] Ibid. 17 Jan. 1914.

the music of Mahler (whose Seventh Symphony he had heard on 18 January 1913) and Scriabin, and he was similarly perplexed by new developments in the visual arts such as Post-Impressionism and Futurism which he eventually concluded were 'the results of artistic indigestion'.[37]

During the week of 18–24 February Parry's incidental music to Aristophanes' *Acharnians* was produced by the OUDS in the New Theatre. The invitation to supply the music had come from Cyril Bailey in November 1912 and though some of the chorus material was written during the spring of 1913, he was only able to make serious headway after his unexpected exile from the College in May. There were some difficulties and misunderstandings in working with Bailey, not least because the stress of work and constant amendments kept him ill and short-tempered.

Though not the most distinguished of Aristophanes' comedies, the play's continued appeals for peace had a very poignant message for the times. Its talk of wars, alliances, invasion scares, 'jingoists', and peace delegations had a significance that all who performed in the production could appreciate. During the composition and production of the *Acharnians* Parry sincerely believed that talk of war with Germany lacked foundation, and he sought to parody those (the 'Blue-Funkers') who were whipping up panic and hysteria in government and elsewhere. The Overture, a medley of popular tunes from the street and music-hall, programmatically enact such a sentiment. Scare-mongering is symbolized by 'An 'orrible tale we have to tell' which predominates and is buoyed up with a distortion of military frenzy and posturing represented by strains of 'Rule Britannia', 'The British Grenadiers', and 'We don't want to fight, but by jingo if we do'. Dicaepolis, a peasant who strives for peace, emerges to Schumann's 'Merry Peasant', but he is submerged by militarism. Lamachus, the shoddy military hero whom Dicaepolis derides, is depicted by a pompous, swaggering tune which Parry no doubt intended to parody the big themes of Elgar's 'Pomp and Circumstance' Marches (what Parry called in his programme notes 'A Parody of some Patriotic Effusions'). The *entente cordiale* is similarly parodied by a grand climactic conflation of the National Anthem and the Marseillaise, which contrasts with the paranoia over German spies and infiltration portrayed by elusive reference to 'Die Wacht am Rhein'. Vying for position in all of this is the simple answer to the scares—'O dear, what can the matter be'. During the course of the play other references also appear, particularly in the lengthy 'Parabasis' (No. 8). The Waltz from *Der Rosenkavalier*, a work which Parry had heard for the

---

[37] Marginal note to a draft lecture on 'Modernisms' for the Easter Term, 1915.

first time in February 1913, appears to exaggerate the 'Smooth-Tongued Cajoleries of Foreigners', while the heedless atmosphere of 'Popular Indifference' is captured by ragtime themes. At the end of the 'Parabasis' he could also not resist having a jibe at Debussian modernities as he explained to Bailey:

My elaborate joke at the end is at your disposal to cut out or not. The young boys of these days following Debussy have developed an inordinate passion for consecutive fifths [*one feels sure here that such a comment was aimed with tongue in cheek at Vaughan Williams*], so the occasion is suitable to remind folk that that is exactly what their primitive forefathers did, and I have introduced a hideous bit of 'organizing', quite correct, and the tune is the plain song of 'Tu Patris sempiternus es Filius'—after all you are the sons of your fathers! Don't be shocked at the profanity.[38]

This modernistic parody was also taken to further extremes in the first of two instrumental numbers, 'Ancient Grudges' which is saturated with consecutives, while the discomfort of the bound informer (No. 12) is illustrated by a few bars of bitonality.

In the main the performances were undertaken by Allen or Boult. Parry felt only strong enough to conduct the afternoon and evening performances on 21 February, and then he only directed the Overture and 'The little pigs' minuet'. These two numbers were revised and augmented with additional wind and brass for the Bournemouth Municipal Orchestra's 'coming of age' celebrations in May. At their performance on 21 May the composer was acutely conscious of the audience's reticence especially at the meaning of the Overture. It was 'as if they were afraid it wasn't quite proper!' he noted somewhat defiantly in his diary afterwards.[39]

Yet the irony and incredulity of the escalating international situation was that Britain would be dragged into a terrible struggle. Discussion with Arthur at Shulbrede, which examined the possibility that Britain might remain neutral, soon began to turn ominously pessimistic as the probability of outright conflict loomed. After the fateful assassination of Archduke Franz Ferdinand on 28 June in Sarajevo, Parry looked on with desperation as the polarized alliances declared war on each other. So it was that on 4 August Parry had to suffer the terrible reality that Britain was now at war with Germany and that the hopes of a lasting peace expressed in the *Acharnians* had been hopelessly dashed. What he did not realize, amongst the talk of a war 'over by Christmas', was that he would not see an end to the terrifying conflagration into which Europe had launched itself.

[38] Charles L. Graves, *Hubert Parry* (London, 1926), ii. 271.
[39] Diary, 21 May 1914.

16

War, Sadness, and Death

NEWS of the outbreak of war reached Parry while he was planning a trip to Norway and Sweden with Pearsall Smith and Raleigh. Already the day before war was declared, a rude reminder of the difficulties he would have to encounter occurred in the Solent when a navy launch restrained them from penetrating too far into mined waters. The *Wanderer* had quite obliviously been avoiding 'strange-looking buoys' for some time. On 4 August they tried to sail out of the Solent but were sent back by a government tug, the *Ajax*, after three shots had been fired across their bow. For a while sailing was entirely restricted to the Solent which was full of passenger ships transporting troops to Belgium. Eventually they were given clearance to cruise as far as Dartmouth, but nothing further afield was permitted by the authorities. By the beginning of September he decided to return to Littlehampton, frustrated that he could not even make for Ireland.

Very soon the war made itself felt in all aspects of Parry's life. Zeppelins were seen over Littlehampton. German firms, which included many of the most reputable music publishers, were vilified, though he defended Augener with alacrity when Stanford was seen to be leading the attack against a firm which was acknowledged by the Board of Trade to be British. He volunteered his services for Clara Butt's Relief Fund along with Elgar, Mackenzie, Cliffe, Squire, and Cowen, and agreed readily to assist Vaughan Williams, Walford Davies, Fox Strangways, and Colles in their efforts to provide work for native professional musicians whom the War had deprived of work. The so-called Music in Wartime Committee issued a circular of its aims in November, and within weeks it was giving concerts in schools, hospitals, and camps, as well as providing funds to keep ailing choral societies going. On the domestic front, Moulder, his chauffeur, volunteered for the forces and was at once employed as an army driver. More worrying, however, was the announcement in October that all Germans between the ages of 15 and 45 were to be interned. This would directly affect Parry's trusted factotum, George Schlichenmeyer, who had lived in England for twenty years. Travelling with George to Rustington was impossible as the police, ever ready to label any German as a spy, would have seized him. To prevent his arrest, Parry immediately set about obtaining naturalization papers for him, and appealed on George's behalf to the Home Secretary. His entreaties fell on deaf ears; Schlichenmeyer's naturalization was refused, and he was eventually interned in a camp at Tytherington, not far from Gloucester.

For Parry the war with Germany also signified a blow of more personal artistic import. Germany's fall from grace he paralleled with that of Lucifer from heaven with the result that his perception of aesthetic truth took a severe pounding. He was at a loss to understand how a nation so pre-eminent for its contribution to artistic ideology and creativity should at once be responsible for the outbreak of a conflict more widespread than the world had ever witnessed before. In his Christmas-term address to the College students, whose male population was already being depleted by those volunteering for the front, he made plain his attitude to the war. Germany's behaviour, seen through its invasion of France and neutral Belgium, had been infamous. A nation renowned for its philosophers, artists, and musicians had been perverted by hate, by a so-called philosophy of 'bitter spite' expressed by Nietzsche. But allied with his disgust was an incredulity combined with a profound sense of betrayal that a nation of artistic heroes, who had taught him everything and to whose mast he had nailed his true colours, could be capable of such carnage:

I have my own confession to make. For I have been a quarter of a century and more a pro-Teuton. I owed too much to their music and their philosophers and authors of former times to believe it possible that the nation at large could be imbued with the teaching of a few advocates of mere brutal violence and material aggression; with the extravagance of those who talked about super-morality; with the ruthless implications of their insistence that the State is power, and nothing but power, and has no concern with honour, right, justice, or fair play.[1]

Reluctantly Parry believed that the war against Germany was justified and joined the general political consensus throughout the country that the invasion of Belgium was a *casus belli*. On the other side of the English Channel events were accelerating into the catastrophe of the First Battle of Ypres, and in Parry's mind there was no doubt as to who should shoulder the blame. His address caught the tone of this conviction:

We know now that it is arrogance run mad. We know it is the hideous militarism of the Prussians that has poisoned the wells of the spirit throughout Germany—that it has poisoned them by cynical manipulation of the Press, and all the channels through which enlightenment can flow to the millions, for nearly half a century—by actually preventing their government-controlled newspapers from publishing truth, by cultivating the arts of false suggestion,

[1] Sir Hubert Parry, ed. Colles, *College Addresses* (London, 1920), 222.

and by holding up to general worship the fetish formula of 'Blood and Iron,' which has been their bane! We know now that if we cannot scotch the war-fiend the world will not be worth living in. We know too that we must be prepared for tremendous sacrifices, for sufferings, for losses, for terrible blows and anxieties. And we must learn to look them steadfastly and coolly in the face.[2]

This speech was made not long after the German Army had been repulsed at the Battle of the Marne, though it had become clear that Europe was in for a protracted war of attrition as both sides were digging in.

Parry was one who could see the writing on the wall. As patriotic fervour for national glory swept the nation, hosts of young men queued to enlist. On returning to the College in September Parry soon became aware that the faces of a number of promising students were missing, amongst them E. J. Moeran. Others too were eager to join up. Gurney could barely wait, and Arthur Benjamin, regarded by many as a star pupil, enlisted before a letter from his mother in Brisbane could reach the Director begging him to make the gifted Australian change his mind. Parry's reply to Benjamin's mother was equally concerned that someone of such prodigious talent should not be treated 'on the same footing as the millions who have no exceptional promise of a special kind. As I have pointed out to him, people who have special gifts may benefit the country and humanity at large in a higher way than those who offer themselves as mere unspecialised individuals in the fighting hosts.'[3] He was also disturbed to learn that other past students of the College were taking the same course of action such as Butterworth, R. O. Morris, Geoffrey Toye, Fox, Dyson, Bliss, Farrar, and Vaughan Williams who were all keen 'to do their bit' at the front. Among the most talented that remained behind of this generation, there was only Howells.

Another major musical casualty caused by the outbreak of war was the indefinite postponement of the country's major provincial festivals. During the spring Parry had been engaged in a considerable revision of *The Vision of Life* much to the chagrin of Novello who foresaw additional expenditure in publishing a new vocal score. But when war was announced, Norwich was one of the first to cancel, and so all hope of ever hearing it again evaporated. The Brighton Festival, however, courageously decided to go ahead in November which led Parry to turn his attention more urgently to a commission from the Festival Committee for an orchestral work. Having held back in case of cancellation, he worked feverishly on a symphonic poem in two connected movements entitled *From Death to Life* which he wrote and completed in October. 'Death, arm-in-arm with Fate, walks ever in our

[2] Ibid. 222–3.
[3] Charles L. Graves, *Hubert Parry* (London, 1926), ii. 69.

midst, while Life unceasingly protests, grieves, deplores, defies, despairs and finally triumphs spritually.'[4] Such was the summary of the work, familiarly philosophical, characteristically aspiratory; and yet this time the 'programme' had a new and more immediate reality inspired by the terrible events that were touching the lives of every citizen.

The first of the two movements, subtitled 'Lament', essays a sonata structure in B flat minor full of dark, brooding ideas that look back to the mournful threnody of the unperformed *Elegy for Brahms*. Central to the movement is the idea of 'Death' infused with an 'inscrutable mystery' (Ex. 50a). As a human comment on death comes a secondary thematic strand symbolising 'Lament' (Ex. 50b) which 'shudders into silence' as 'Death' reasserts itself. Moving to the relative, D flat major, the cor anglais and oboe sing out what Parry termed the 'personal' motif ('the clinging to loved ones') of undoubted intimate significance within the circumstances of his own family relationships, but also for those who had been parted by the international crisis (Ex. 50c). The turbulence of the development, like those of the first movements of the Fourth Symphony and *Symphonic Fantasia*, symbolizes mental protest, though in this context the struggle is placed in the additional perspective of death's tyranny. In the recapitulation the ideas of 'Death' and 'Lament' return with increased solemnity and richness, but the last thoughts are of a personal nature, for it is the memory of loved ones that lingers. The second movement, 'Consolation', is a stately sonata rondo whose recurring slow-step march theme in the tonic major is evolved from the 'personal' motif (Ex. 50d). This was to represent 'Life' in all its earnestness and joy. But this idea was intended not only to express a fundamental spiritual optimism, but also in its muscular diatonicism and melodic simplicity, Parry wished to capture an 'English directness of expression'. The exuberance of this splendidly vigorous paragraph results in a more animated idea in the wind characterized by dotted rhythms expressing 'the courage and confidence in facing life's responsibilities' which in turn leads to a second group in the dominant (F major). The second group consists of two buoyant ideas. The first heard on massed strings exudes a sense of *élan vital* ('confidence') which frames one of increased ebullience in D flat (Ex. 50e) conveying 'the selfless gaiety of companionship that faces the King of Terrors with a smile on its lips.' After a restatement of the rondo march theme, the second principal episode develops the ideas of 'confidence' and 'optimism' which again intensify into a mood of insistent protest against the 'ruthlessness of fatality'. At this point of climax 'Death' and 'Lament' rear their heads in a brief reflective interlude. But though this acts as a

---

[4] This and all ensuing quotations are taken from the programme notes written for the Brighton Festival and the Royal Philharmonic Society (where they were revised) by F. Gilbert Webb.

Ex. 50. *From Death to Life* (1914). *a* 'Death'; *b* 'Lament'; *c* 'Personal' motif ('the clinging to loved ones'); *d* 'Life'; *e* 'Selfless gaeity'.

reminder that 'Death' is for ever with us, it is to the natural revitalizing forces of 'Life' that man should look, a sentiment conveyed by the exultant recapitulation of the rondo theme together with references to 'selfless gaiety' and a triumphant coda affirming the sentiments of 'confidence' and 'responsibility'.

The performance at Brighton was moderately successful though 'rather scratchy'.[5] Five days later Parry was approached by Percy Pitt of the Royal Philharmonic Society who wanted to include it in the new

[5] Letter to Dorothea Ponsonby, 17 Nov. 1914, ShP.

season's programme. Revision took place early in January 1915 in which the coda of the second movement was modified, the forces of piccolo and organ were added, and the titles of the two movements were replaced by 'Via Mortis' and 'Via Vitae' respectively. At the Queen's Hall performance on 18 March, *From Death to Life* seemed out of place sandwiched between Vaughan Williams's scintillating *Wasps* Overture on the one hand and Elgar's *Carillon* and bracing Second Symphony on the other. The critics, while recognizing that it contained some fine music, also acknowledged that its pensive introversion was lost on an audience requiring a moral escape from the horrors of carnage. Parry would not hear it played again. It was to be his last major orchestral composition and one that belonged to the same inspirational vintage as the *Symphonic Fantasia*, not perhaps so much for its structural imagination which is largely conservative, but for the rare quality of its thematic invention.

After Christmas Parry was filled with an overwhelming sadness that he might not see Highnam for some time to come. With the reports of the war becoming increasingly serious—the alarming loss of life and the German blockade—his services were more regularly required for Music in Wartime and the Professional Classes Relief Committees who were soon to amalgamate. He had hoped that Highnam could be utilized as accommodation for the wounded, but its old-fashioned sanitary arrangements would have necessitated extensive reconstruction which was impossible to implement effectively. So far the grave reality of multiple casualties sustained in the horrors of trench warfare had hardly touched the College, but in April the death of Frank Pownall's son at Gallipoli was to shatter its superficial tranquillity. Within days the death of Aveling's nephew was announced which upset Parry to the point where he almost broke down in his address to the students. His anger at German atrocities intensified when he heard of the appalling tragedy of the *Lusitania*, torpedoed off the Irish coast on 8 May, a ship he had seen during his last visit to Ireland in 1912 adorning the harbour at Queenstown. In May Zeppelins repeatedly bombed London smashing homes and killing civilians. No longer was war the exclusive affair of the armed forces.

There seemed little escape from the constant assault of bad news. The situation regarding Gwen's marriage appeared hopeless but at least there was talk of an amicable settlement. At Shulbrede he found himself, much to his regret, in passionate controversy with Arthur over the war. In helping to found the Union of Democratic Control, a dissenting organization arguing the case for neutrality, Ponsonby had courageously adopted a maverick political stance questioning the validity of Britain's role in the conflict. This had led to accusations from all sides (quite erroneously) of his being pro-German: from his constituency, his friends, and perhaps most hurtful of all, his family. Even his father-in-law harboured doubts, and for the first time in their relationship, arguments were less amicable in disagreement.

With little prospect of a voyage on the *Wanderer* in August, Parry decided to throw caution to the wind by visiting Canada and the United States. He did so knowing that there were considerable risks involved. The indiscriminate torpedoing of allied and American shipping by German submarines would have deterred many from making such a trip, but he was determined to escape the grey existence the war had imposed on him, at least for a while. With Allen as companion he crossed the Atlantic from Liverpool on the *Corsican*. They toured Quebec, enjoyed the Montgomery Falls and steamed up the Saquenay River. In Montreal he met the organist of the Cathedral, Arthur Egg, and made arrangements to visit Prescott, Toronto, and the Niagara Falls. At the end of August they travelled down the Hudson River to New York where they savoured views from the skyscrapers and investigated the renowned Public Library. From there they made for Boston spending time at the Harvard Observatory. The return crossing from New York was on the *St Paul*. It was a nervous few days. Boats were lowered on both sides ready for 'eventualities' and long arms were fixed on both sides of the ship to project light on to the American flags painted on the vessel. Mercifully the voyage was uneventful, though the following year Parry recognized his good fortune when he heard of the liner *Sussex* and the gifted Spanish composer and virtuoso pianist, Enrique Granados, who went down in her on 24 March 1916.

With the cancellation of virtually all the nation's major festivals, Parry's participation in concert life dwindled to almost nothing. Without such demands, which for the last twenty-five years had been common routine, he found himself with more time to devote to composition and writing. Moreover, there were no longer the nagging anxieties of deadlines to meet, proofs to read, and rehearsal schedules to agree. During late 1914 and the whole of 1915 he spent much of his time in the completion of miniatures. Three of them were in answer to requests from colleagues. One was an elaborate and extended five-part madrigal, a setting of Keats's 'La belle dame sans merci', for Daniel Wilberforce Rootham's 50th anniversary as conductor of the Bristol Madrigal Society on 14 January 1915. This institution he remembered with fondness from his youth for the Elizabethan and Jacobean madrigals performed in Bristol, and for the tradition of antiquarian English part-song instigated by the Society's founder, Robert Lucas Pearsall. A second request was a setting of Mary Hamilton's *A Hymn for Aviators* for Clara Butt's Red Cross Concert at the Albert Hall on 13 May, a piece he came to loathe but felt obliged to submit for publication purely for the war effort.

Finally, for the Royal Choral Society's annual Christmas Concert at the Albert Hall he wrote a carol 'When Christ was born of Mary free' (Harleian MS) which Bridge conducted on 18 December.

In addition to the provision of new musical works, Parry also found time to initiate a literary project that had been on his mind for many years. In March 1913 Macmillan had asked him to write another historical text book, but Parry had turned down the invitation. He believed that he could not improve upon *The Evolution of the Art of Music*, considered that his age was against him, and in any case he wished to devote himself to a more important project. During the 1890s when he had been intoxicated with the challenging works of Zola, Gissing, Hardy, and Ibsen, he had also been powerfully drawn to evolutionary studies of social behaviour by Lecky and Kidd. Kidd's *Social Evolution* had especially impressed him in its considerations of human progress, history, the role of religious beliefs in social evolution, modern socialism, and a rationale for change. The thrust and organization of Kidd's book inspired Parry to plan a thesis along similar evolutionary lines, but emphasizing two factors on which he had laid great store during his own creative life. These were 'Instinct' and 'Character', watchwords familiar to all those who had come into close contact with him as friends or pupils. In many ways the book was the result of years of gestation, from the enquiring days of the 'Essay and Discussion Club' when he had first developed a love for philosophy, psychology, and anthropology. In the 1880s and 1890s he had filled notebook after notebook, sometimes hastily jotting down simple observations of human nature; at other times discussing elemental moral artistic questions at length. Such thinking had subsequently surfaced in his musicological writings and lectures, but Parry had constantly felt the need to expand his theories beyond the concerns of music. Consequently he soon found that, in exploring and elucidating the manifestations of 'Instinct'—the essential force determining the survival of the race—together with the powerful controlling forces of religion, creative 'excitement', and morality, he confronted an argument at once too large and involuted for the purposes of a single book. Yet he felt inexorably compelled to define and justify ideas which might function as an abstract backdrop to *The Evolution of the Art of Music* and to *Style in Musical Art*, and which of itself would represent a philosophical *apologia* of his life's work.

Over the past three years the sheer physical exertion of composition had been lessened to a considerable extent by the assistance of Emily Daymond, one of his very first pupils at the College. She had remained totally devoted to him, had written to him often from her home in Eastbourne, and had done much to ease the burden of proof-reading, copying, and checking. Her letters, addressed to her 'dear old

Pedagogue', reveal an ardour bordering on adoration, and the work she did in cataloguing, editing, and arranging her mentor's works after his death testify to this. During the war years, especially the holidays, she was almost part of the family at Rustington or Highnam, a presence not always entirely appreciated by Maude who resented the attention given by the younger woman to her husband. Arthur too, while not resenting her close attention, felt that at times her unselfishness seemed almost aggressive.[6] When seeking a diversion from work, Parry and Daymond would frequently go for cycle rides (petrol being scarce for the car) in the surrounding country, and there can be no doubt that, besides her valuable and faithful service, he enjoyed her lively company. Her help was particularly appreciated in the preparation of a second set of Chorale Preludes for organ which he wrote mostly during the spring and summer of 1915. The first set had proved so popular that Novello had requested, at his convenience, another collection. Just as with his previous works for organ, Parry sought advice over registration and idiomatic technicalities, this time from Walford Davies and Harold Darke who was then assistant to Davies at the Temple Church. Darke included three of the new preludes, still in manuscript, in a recital at St James's, Paddington in November, and continued afterwards to be a noted exponent of Parry's music. Of the more energetic preludes 'St Thomas' is the most successfully worked out though it suffers occasionally from being too congested, a fault which was partially redressed after consultation with Darke. Notwithstanding this failing, the key scheme is well thought out and the sudden change of direction to the flat submediant before the presentation of the chorale's last line is particularly magnificent. 'Croft's 136th', a great favourite of the composer, is also well composed though on a simpler tonal basis than 'St Thomas'. Its one weakness, however, lies in the quasi-improvisational clichés of the last two pages. A similar shortcoming also afflicts the cadenza-like opening of the final prelude, 'Hanover', whose ensuing thick orchestral textures are reminiscent of the third Chorale Fantasia 'St Ann'. The remaining four preludes are all of a slow, contemplative nature. Parry was deeply attached to 'Martyrdom', which was played at his funeral along with 'Croft's 136th'. Its diatonic innocence, which develops, blossoms, and subsides towards the flat mediant, is particularly compelling, as is the euphonious coda. 'St Mary', similar in conception to 'Christe Redemptor' with its mellifluous fantasias, is too long and tonally undistinguished, a feeling which fails to be offset by the one affecting move to the tonic major in the last nine bars. Amongst the most poetic of all Parry's preludes is 'St Cross', a mournful threnody characterized by the sighing appoggiaturas of the

---

[6] Diary of Arthur Ponsonby, 20 Aug. 1917.

introduction and the elegiac vein of the closing bars. 'Eventide' is conceived on a similar structural footing though its accompanying material is inspirationally dull and rhythmically stilted by comparison.

Although Parry devoted a considerable amount of time and effort to the second set of Chorale Preludes, his overriding preoccupation in 1915 was the long-standing desire to complete a set of substantial *a cappella* motets comparable in stature to those by Brahms (particularly Opp. 109 and 110) and Reger. In 1906 Parratt had asked him if he would write a motet for a special memorial service at the Royal Mausoleum at Frogmore on 22 January, 1907. The outcome was a setting of John Gibson Lockhart's 'There is an old belief'. After the performance at Windsor the motet was shelved until 1913, when he subjected it to extensive revision. The result encouraged him to write a further three motets, 'My soul there is a country', 'I know my soul hath power to know all things', and 'Never weather beaten sail'. According to Emily Daymond, who witnessed their gradual evolution, drafts of the four motets were complete by September 1913 when she heard them at Highnam. Soon afterwards, at the College, Parry heard the Choral Class sing through Stanford's *Three Motets*, Op. 135 and was impressed by their fluency and textural imagination. This experience increased his resolve to perfect the four motets already substantially composed. 'Never weather beaten sail' reached its final form in June 1914, and 'I know my soul hath power' in August. The manuscripts of 'My soul there is a country' and 'There is an old belief' are undated, though the extensive quantity of sketches suggest that these two pieces caused greater problems and were therefore completed later, probably in early 1915 after the exertions of *From Death to Life* were over. This would also appear to be confirmed by an informal 'sing-through' of the four motets by Emily Daymond and a small choir at the RCM on 24 March 1915. These were later tried over in the Chapel of New College, Oxford with the help of Allen. Preparation of the Chorale Preludes necessitated putting the motets to one side until the autumn of 1915 when he conceived of two further works. Howells begged him to consider a setting of Raleigh's 'Even such is time', but instead he followed Dunhill's recommendation and set Donne's 'At the round earth's imagined corners'. This, along with a monumental setting of Psalm 39 ('Lord, let me know mine end') for double choir, brought the set to a conclusion. Both were completed in December 1915.

During the composition of the motets, particularly the last two, Parry's heart condition began to deteriorate to the point where he could not suppress attacks with his usual strength of will. While exerting himself on the estate at Highnam, bereft of farmhands that had gone off to the war, he rapidly became exhausted and would sometimes suffer as many as three attacks per day. Some of these seemed strangely and ominously virulent and he began to be haunted by a feeling that death might claim him at any moment. Consequently the valedictory sentiments of the motets, collectively entitled *Songs of Farewell*, began to take on a more personal significance. On 27 February 1918, Parry wrote to Howells and expressed the intuitive certainty that he had come to the last milestone of his life and that he would not survive man's commonly allotted span of existence. His mind, according to Howells, was more than ever upon the *Songs of Farewell* for he knew then that this magnificent codicil was his spiritually unorthodox farewell to a world in turmoil and distress.

With the exception of Psalm 39, the motets were first performed by the Bach Choir under Allen at the College on 22 May 1916. The performance thrilled the composer who poured out his enthusiasm in a letter to Allen two days later:

I never was so hugely fortunate in all my life. I never heard such real interpretation. You somehow got to the inside of the motets to an extent I never came across before. You even seemed to influence the very colour of the voices. And it really did fill me with unusual joy to hear the certainty with which you hit upon the very utmost I wanted—Phrasing and gradation and all! I was most deeply grateful. And the way they responded to you was marvellous. The beloved old Choir surpassed themselves. I have owed them much gratitude on many occasions but never more than then. I felt they were ungrudgingly giving of their very best, and were really sympathetic.[7]

Darke, Allen, Dolly, Arthur, and Gwen were profoundly moved, as was the entire audience who encored 'There is an old belief'. 'Lord, let me know mine end' was performed in the chapel of New College, Oxford by the Oxford Bach Choir, again under the baton of Allen, on 17 June 1917. 'They sang "Lord let me know mine end" beautifully. The first time I had heard it. It seemed to come off all right', Parry wrote in his diary shortly afterwards. Sadly, he never heard the motets sung as an entire set. They were eventually heard altogether at a Memorial Concert at Exeter College, Oxford on 23 February 1919, sung by the combined choirs of New College and Christ Church and members of the Oxford Bach Choir once more under Allen's direction.

The Songs of Farewell commence with two motets in four parts. The first, 'My soul there is a country' from the poem 'Peace' by the seventeenth-century metaphysical poet, Henry Vaughan, is perhaps the best known and most accessible. Motivically concentrated and metrically flexible, it is superbly constructed. In a language of consummate diatonic simplicity it is extraordinary to observe the aptness and concision in the

<hr/>

[7] Letter to Sir Hugh Allen, 24 May 1916, RCM (Dept. of Portraits).

variation of moods. These follow in quick succession unified by the metrical symbolism of longing (in 3/4) and, quintessentially, peace (in 6/8). Most memorable, however, is the strikingly oblique statement of the opening which is highlighted by the succession of two-chord progressions and the rising intervals of the soprano (Ex. 51a). Both these elements are extended to the three affirmatory phrases of the final bars ('Thy God, Thy life, Thy cure'), which are subtly anticipated by the incorporation of the rising intervals as a counterpoint in the previous polyphonic episode ('One who never changes'). The final progressions of 'My soul there is a country', an example of striking juxtapositions of root position harmonies, bear witness to Parry's diatonic resourcefulness. This feature is intrinsic to the second motet, 'I know my soul hath power to know all things', a setting of Sir John Davies's lengthy didactic poem 'Nosce Teipsum'. Texturally the motet is uniformly homophonic throughout, achieving potency and momentum through the use of tonally fluid harmony of disciplined intensity, most notably those accompanying the last affecting attestation via the Neapolitan ('I know myself a Man, which is proud and yet a wretched thing'). 'Never weather beaten sail', quiet and self-possessed in its restrained rapture, increases the vocal forces to five parts. Consistent with Thomas Campion's melodious lute-song, Parry adopted an overtly lyrical style of counterpoint within a strophic design that employs deft means of variation both

Ex. 51. *Songs of Farewell. a.* opening phrase of 'My soul there is a country' (?1915); *b* concluding bars of 'At the round earth's imagined corners' (1915).

in the verses and the refrains. The solemnity of 'There is an old belief' with its rich six-part polyphony recalls the sombre atmosphere of the part-song 'Sorrow and Pain'. After an opening section full of sumptuous dissonances, a brief interlude quotes the plain-song intonation of the Credo appropriate to the text 'That creed I fain would keep'. In the final paragraph ('Eternal be the sleep') where diatonic dissonance is powerfully exploited, Parry reveals his long-standing indebtedness to the English cathedral music of S. S. Wesley and Stainer. The more protracted structures of the last two motets rely on a series of contrasting episodes. 'At the round earth's imagined corners', a seven-part setting of one of John Donne's *Divine Meditations*, impressively depicts the triumphs and horrors of the Last Judgement. Amongst the vivid portrayal of angel trumpets and human catastrophe, Parry included one of his most visionary passages ('And you whose eyes shall behold God') sung by the upper voices. This sets the scene for the concluding penitential paragraph containing some of the composer's most impeccable counterpoint, while perhaps the greatest pathos is reserved for the poignant cadence (Ex. 51*b*). In the final motet, for double choir, the text dwells on the subject of the transitoriness of life and man's vanity, an idea which punctuates the piece at two important junctures ('and verily every man living is altogether vanity'). Besides this one significant unifying feature the ambitious canvas maintains variety with masterly manipulation of counterpoint, homophony, and antiphonal exchange. Much of the motet is doleful in mood, but the central section ('Take thy plague away from me') is more violent and animated, reaching an anguished climax before subsiding in resignation and self-abandonment. As in the previous motet, the most emotional utterances appear at the end. There is a sublime poise about the submissive passage 'When thou with rebukes' and the pleading tone of 'Hear my prayer O Lord'. But central to the whole of Parry's spiritual philosophy is the confession 'For I am a stranger with Thee and a sojourner' which is complemented by the still more profoundly moving, hushed tranquillity of the final supplication 'O spare me a little before I go hence'. These few pages of music belong to the highest echelons of Romantic *a cappella* music.

The winter of 1915 brought ferocious storms and gales which had a ruinous effect on the estate at Highnam. Over one hundred of the best elms were blown down and in March 1916 Eels reported the additional loss of old cedars, firs, and many valued coniferous trees in the Pinetum. This natural disaster seemed bad enough, but the sense of loss was exacerbated by the later demands of the War Office to fell more trees for the provision of rifle butts.

The war events of the last part of 1915 were a depressing confirmation of the military deadlock in Flanders and northern France. More than 100 College students had now volunteered and no fewer than 16 existing scholars were at the Front or preparing to go there. Parry's addresses to the remaining students reflect a preoccupation with comradeship, selflessness, individual bravery, and duty. Moreover, hc felt determined to emphasize that musicians were as ready and able to defend their country as any other profession. But he nevertheless fretted constantly about the safety of those risking their lives:

I am not sure indeed that there is not some risk of their being too rash and needlessly exposing lives which really have rather an exceptional value. Musicians are liable to be lifted off their feet into the higher plane of fervent enthusiasm, which makes personal considerations of little moment; and we know one or two who in such a state of mind would expose themselves to a fearful death without any concern at all.

One of the cruellest things in warfare is the uncertainty of it all. It is the merest chance who falls and who survives, except that those who are endowed with the finest qualities are likeliest to expose themselves to danger.[8]

This unsettling fear soon became a terrible reality. On 1 July 1916 the Battle of the Somme was launched with frightening casualties. In the first day alone 60,000 British troops were mown down in a bloodbath unrivalled by anything else in history. Reports came that Arthur Bliss had been injured and was being returned to England. But more terrible was the devastating news that Butterworth had been killed at Pozières on 5 August. Writing to Butterworth's father, Parry declared:

I felt your tragic loss very much; and ours—for your son was one of those we looked forward to doing something individual and of fine quality—The sacrifice there has been of rare and irreplaceable gifts in this indiscriminate carnage is dreadful. The reckless fates seem to have taken some of our very choicest natures.[9]

In addition to the death of Butterworth, there were other deaths at home and abroad that saddened him. Frank Pownall, his lifelong friend from his days at Exeter College, died on 26 January, having never really recovered from the death of his son in the war. In February he attended the funeral of Sir George Martin, the organist of St Paul's, who had been one of his first colleagues at the newly founded Royal College of Music. Then, in August, he was informed of the premature death of Hamish MacCunn who had been suffering from a long and painful illness. But perhaps most poignant was the communication he received at the beginning of 1917 of Richter's death. Through the misfortunes of war, Richter had been forced to sever his relationship with a country he had

[8] Parry, *College Addresses*, 246–7.
[9] Letter to Sir Alexander Butterworth, 9 Jan. 1918. Bod. MS Eng. Misc. c.453.

served for thirty-two years and relinquish all the honours that had been bestowed upon him. In letters to his daughter, Mrs Sydney Loeb, still living in England, he continually expressed a high regard for his English colleagues:

Give my love to my friends and all the artists who worked with me, when you meet them. They are with me in my waking hours and in my dreams, and my thoughts of them are always good and pleasurable. With thankfulness I think of the hours I spent with them. They were the happiest of my artistic life.[10]

For Parry such a tribute was the stuff of memories of better times—of pioneering orchestral standards and new repertoire—all of which had now been besmirched by the artificial divisions of war.

In 1916 The Year Book Press published *Kookoorookoo and Other Songs*, a collection of settings of Christina Rossetti's poetry designed primarily for schoolchildren. Parry was one of the thirteen composers asked to contribute and he chose to set 'Brown and furry', 'The peacock has a score of eyes', and 'The wind has such a rainy sound'.[11] He also wrote a part-song 'I know an Irish Lass', a poem which had caught his eye in the *Westminster Gazette* in February and which he set at once, though it was never performed or published. Kipling's publishers asked him to set 'For all we have and are' but he felt out of sympathy with its sentiments and though the music was written he decided to withdraw it from publication. On a similar more fatefully significant tack, he was asked by Robert Bridges in March if he would set the opening verses of Blake's 'Milton' for 'Fight for Right',[12] an organization founded by General Sir Francis Younghusband to counteract German propaganda and to circulate some of its own about the justice of an Allied victory. Bridges was insistent that it should be 'suitable, simple music to Blake's stanzas—music that an audience could take up and join in.'[13] At first Parry was not altogether sure of his commitment to the cause of 'Fight for Right', but not wanting to disappoint either Bridges or Walford Davies, he agreed. 'And did those feet in ancient time' was written down on 10 March and shown to Davies the following day at the College. It was an occasion Davies clearly remembered:

Sir Hubert Parry gave me the manuscript of this setting of Blake's 'Jerusalem' one memorable morning in 1916 . . . We looked at it long together in his room at the Royal College of Music, and I recall vividly his unwonted happiness over it.

[10] Obituary of Hans Richter, *Musical Times* (1 Jan. 1917), 22.
[11] The other twelve who contributed were Dunhill, Buck, Silver, Charles Wood, Stanford, Parratt, Tovey, Frederick Bridge, Mackenzie, Alcock, Lloyd, and Davies. The collection consists in total of 26 songs.
[12] Bridges also suggested that if Parry could not take on the task, then Butterworth might try his hand, but by then the younger man had gone to the front.
[13] Letter from Bridges, n.d. [? Mar. 1916]—see Graves, *Hubert Parry*, ii. 92.

One momentary act of his should perhaps be told here. He ceased to speak, and put his finger on the note D in the second stanza where the words 'O clouds unfold' break his rhythm. I do not think any word passed about it, yet he made it perfectly clear that this was the one note and one moment of the song which he treasured . . . I copyrighted it in the composer's name and published it in 1916. We needed it for the men at that time . . . I know Dr Bridges specifically wanted every one of us to sing it, and this is happily coming true.[14]

'And did those feet in ancient time' (or 'Jerusalem', its published title) was performed at a meeting of 'Fight for Right' on 28 March at Queen's Hall where it was sung by a choir of 300 volunteers from the principal choral societies and choirs of London under the direction of Walford Davies. The unison song, with its stirring melody, subtle phraseology, and robust harmony was an instant success. The version sung at Queen's Hall was one for choir and organ and it was this that was initially published by Curwen, though with the suggestion that a soloist should take the first verse and 'all available voices' take the second. However, it was soon requested that Parry make an orchestral arrangement of the accompaniment which he did in November for the purposes of large-scale concerts and gatherings. Though this accompaniment was frequently used during the composer's lifetime and in the years directly after his death, it fell into obscurity when Elgar, who much admired the tune, re-orchestrated it for the large orchestra of the Leeds Festival in 1922. The typically greater opulence of Elgar's arrangement soon became favoured by conductors and it is this version that has largely survived, particularly through the Last Night of the Proms. Parry's orchestration is characteristically more sober and was intended for a smaller band given the circumstances for which it was arranged. Nevertheless, it has a distinctive quality which gives complete prominence to the tune without the distractions of Elgar's dynamic embellishments. For this reason alone, it seems a pity that it should have been almost totally ignored.

The appeal generated by 'Jerusalem' bolstered the cause of 'Fight for Right'; they were proud of their new song. Soon Parry found himself being approached by other organizations requesting similar unison settings for patriotic purposes. In August 1916 James Frazer, the renowned social anthropologist and supporter of 'Fight for Right', asked if Parry might set 'Pour un chiffon de papier' by Lieutenant Paul Loyson, but he declined. Evidently he felt unhappy about both the purpose and sentiment of the piece. As is clear from the cynicism of *The Acharnians*, he intensely disliked jingoism and the half-truths of propaganda machines. Supporting 'Fight for Right' unsettled him; blatant, unthinking patriotism made him uncomfortable. In consequence in

[14] Letter from Sir Walford Davies to *The Times* (27 Aug. 1927).

May 1917 he decided to write to Sir Francis Younghusband withdrawing his support for an organization with whose causes he could no longer wholeheartedly identify. 'Jerusalem' continued to be lustily sung the length and breadth of the country and the sound of massed unison voices in the second verse always excited him. But he was more gratified when the song was taken up by the Women's Movement in 1917. On 17 March he conducted 'Jerusalem' for the ladies of the Albert Hall Choir at a Women's Demonstration meeting which proved to be providential, for the following year Mrs Fawcett asked if it could be sung as part of a Suffrage Demonstration concert on 13 March 1918. After the meeting Mrs Fawcett wrote an effusive letter to Parry suggesting that 'Jerusalem' ought to become the Women Voters' Hymn. Parry was delighted. 'Thank you for what you say about the "Jerusalem" song. I wish indeed it might become the Women Voters' hymn, as you suggest. People seem to enjoy singing it. And having the vote ought to diffuse a good deal of joy too. So they would combine happily.'[15] It was an association that was set to endure after the war and after women obtained voting rights, for it became the national song for the Women's Institutes.

One of the events that made the headlines in early June 1916 was the major sea battle at Jutland. Though Britain remained ruler of the waves, she received a bloody nose in the process, and many lives were lost. After news of the battle had been digested, Allen lost no time in arranging a concert to 'commemorate the officers and men of His Majesty's Fleet and of the Mercantile Marine who [had] fallen in the war, and to celebrate the achievements of the Empire at sea.' It also seemed a perfect opportunity to revive the well-tried collaboration between Parry and Bridges. Both expressed themselves interested. Bridges completed a suitable sea-poem in June and sent it off to Parry immediately. Occupied with the revisions of the Scherzo of the Fourth Symphony, a new piano work for Emily Daymond, as well as with a deluge of wartime committee work and College examinations, he did not start work for another two months. During interludes from August haymaking at Highnam he meditated on Bridges' words, but the music was not sketched until early September when he was at Rustington with Maude.

The Chivalry of the Sea (or *Naval Ode*, a title Bridges preferred) was performed by the Bach Choir on 12 December at Queen's Hall in a programme including Stanford's *Songs of the Fleet* and Vaughan Williams's *A Sea Symphony*. Allen conducted valiantly but the choir, under strength and under-rehearsed, were below par and the orchestra lost their place towards the end. Even during rehearsals Parry felt thoroughly dejected and disconsolate about the Ode, and the bad

[15] Graves, *Hubert Parry*, ii. 93.

performance did nothing to improve his impressions. Allen did his best to reassure him:

When I wrote to you it was in no sense from a desire that you should say nice things to me but purely because I felt that if you were disappointed with the Ode it might have been my fault. I don't at all agree with you about the impression the Ode makes. I found it to stand the best of all tests, intimate knowledge, triumphantly, and I am quite happy in my own mind that it does all come off, and the more so because it is on the broad simple lines which are entirely essential for a poem of that length and width of range.[16]

The Ode received two further performances in London in 1917, the first on 28 April with the Royal Choral Society under the composer's direction, and the second at the Albert Hall on 24 November—a performance which coincided with the London première of Elgar's *Spirit of England*.

Though *The Chivalry of the Sea* speaks of patriotism and the roaming 'heart of Britain', Parry wanted its message to be one primarily of selfless bravery rather than one of 'King and country'. After the devastation of the Allied offensives at Verdun and the Somme and the U-Boat successes in the Atlantic, he had no stomach for the seemingly brazen patriotic gestures of Elgar's trilogy which he dismissed as sentimental. The loss of life seemed too incalculable to dwell on the immutability and greatness of the Empire. For this reason alone he felt that audiences would not respond to his new work, and for the most part he was right. In the Ode Parry was seized by the tragedy of the lonely, unrecorded graves such as that of the poem's dedicatee Charles Fisher, an Oxford student who went down with the *Invincible* at Jutland. In the dark sonorities of the opening orchestral prelude and the subdued atmosphere of the conclusion ('The wide warring waters under the starry skies') we are transported to the lament of *From Death to Life*. But whereas the symphonic poem was given an injection of optimism in its second half, the Naval Ode betrays a more entrenched distress where hope, battered by the protracted conflict, seems more remote. Scored for five-part chorus and orchestra the work is full of splendid choral climaxes such as the bracing 'and a great glory at heart', but is tempered by the grieving of 'Idly our tears arise' which belongs more to the intimate emotions of the *Songs of Farewell*.

The overwhelming despondency of *The Chivalry of the Sea* summarized the gloom that clouded every aspect of the composer's outlook. College life never seemed more desolate as he received visit after visit from students in uniform and demoralizing reports from the front. Benjamin was a changed man, Dyson's nerves were broken, and the young Eugene

---

[16] Letter from Hugh Allen, 26 Dec. 1916, ShP.

Goossens was distraught with the death of his brother. In October 1916 Parry went to the Philharmonic Hall to see some of the war films and was shocked by their graphic images. Here at last he could see for himself the hell into which the flower of a generation had launched itself. 'Dreadfully vivid', he recollected in his diary; 'The varieties of artillery most interesting. The trenches sometimes sickening. Advances; dead bodies; operating stations. Vast numbers of prisoners. Running in with hands up and under guard. Nightmare altogether.'[17] In February 1917 he had a long visit from Fox who had been sent home temporarily with trench fever. The brilliant organist returned to the front later in the year but was so badly wounded in his right arm that amputation was necessary just above the elbow. When Parry learnt of the tragedy from A. H. Peppin, Fox's great friend at Rugby School, he was beside himself with grief:

Thank you for your letter about this truly horrible tragedy. I don't think anything that has happened in this atrocious war has so impressed me with the very malignity of cruelty as the utter destruction of that dear boy's splendid gifts. I can't help thinking of the thirst that will come to him to use his rare powers of interpretation and be utterly debarred. It is devilish . . . I know you will feel it very keenly . . . I can hardly bear to think of him in connection with music any more.[18]

On 16 January 1918, Fox paid Parry a visit and stayed to lunch. It was a gruelling experience, not so much for Fox, who had apparently accepted his plight with admirable stoicism, but for Parry who was deeply moved and found it difficult to express himself, so overcome was he with compassion. Fox's predicament was a cruel blow, but there were others at the College whose lot seemed even more calamitous. News had filtered through in September 1917 that Gurney had been gassed during the horrific slaughter at Passchendaele. Eagerly Parry awaited further news of the young composer's recovery from Howells and from Marion Scott. Eventually, in June 1918 he received a letter from Gurney announcing that he intended to commit suicide. Reports soon came from Marion Scott that nothing serious had ensued,[19] but nevertheless it was perfectly clear that the gifted Gloucester scholar was entering a phase of severe mental instability from which he would never rally.

Such harrowing experiences as these only served to emphasize that the tragedy of this European conflict was both comprehensive and personal. With the war dragging on into a fourth year it seemed that his innate sense of mission, his belief in the visionary purpose of the College, and the results of his life's vocation had been so savagely undermined that a

---

[17] Diary, 4 Oct. 1916.
[18] Winifred Fox, *Douglas Fox: A Chronicle* (Bristol, 1976), 26.
[19] See also M. Hurd, *The Ordeal of Ivor Gurney* (Oxford, 1984), 124.

new start would have to be made, and that he, as likely as not, would not be a part of it. Additions to the student population were dwindling to almost nothing, and many of those who had gone to the front had either been killed or maimed. By the middle of 1917 his patience with the Germans had all but run out. London was beset with bombing raids, the boom of guns, flying shrapnel, destruction to buildings, and the loss of civilian life. Such belligerence disgusted him. In July he wrote to Dolly angrily declaring his abhorrence of German militarism and the havoc it had wreaked:

It's not my personal feelings that are concerned but the fact that this hideous madness is causing the slaughter of numbers of splendid young men who are quite irreplaceable. The horrible indiscriminateness of it! And it is all owing to militarism and the vile fury of forceful domination which is the German creed. They are all sodden with it. The peasant[s] and clerks are not innocent. They all gloat over the killing of children and women in the raids, and the vile doings of the submarines. The reason why we cannot get at Hindenberg and Tirpitz and Reventlow is that the peasants and clerks have allowed themselves to be hoaxed into arming and massing in their millions to prevent our getting at them. No doubt they are grumbling over there, but it's only talk. When they really do something it will be time enough to talk about peace. I hate and loathe war as much as you do, but to try to break off now when militarism is absolutely in possession of Germany is merely to leave those who advocate it in the position to make it override justice and truth and honest living throughout the world. The absolutely needful thing is to get done with it; and with such a necessity before us if poor peasants and clerks combine to prevent it, it is inevitable to treat them to such experiences as will make them wiser. Germany has challenged the world to submit to her ideas. She is the representative of reckless force. Whether she is all to blame in this war is not the question. She it is who still advocates mad and reckless bloodshed in order to establish her fiendish theory. The longer it lasts the more fiendish [it] proves to be.[20]

It was a fearsome diatribe and one that was intended to meet Arthur's and Dolly's wholehearted opposition to the war. But though made in a fit of disgust, no doubt in reaction to the constant bombardment of bad news, he nevertheless retained a powerful sense of forgiveness towards the enemy. Early on in the war he begged the students at the College to 'show none of that same arrogance which has caused it to be the most poisonous emblem in the whole universe, but display our victorious joy with modesty, and even with chivalrous courtesy to our enemies.'[21] Throughout the war he held firmly to this principle and chastised those who talked of recriminations when victory loomed on the horizon.

Besides the strains of the war and its effect on the College, there was one other aspect of Parry's life there which came to a head during 1916

[20] Letter to Dorothea Ponsonby, 26 July 1917, ShP.
[21] Parry, *College Addresses*, 226.

and 1917. In the years immediately prior to the war Parry's relationship with Stanford was already in serious decline. The intensity of altercations between them steadily grew with the result that periods of subsequent healing took longer and were initiated with greater difficulty. At the heart of the problem was Stanford's behaviour which Parry found utterly repellent. In Parry's eyes the Irishman was arrogant, considered himself indispensable, was at times aggressively overbearing in the performance of his own music, and, worst of all, was less than conscientious regarding his teaching responsibilities. Matters began to erupt at the end of 1915 when it came to Parry's notice that Stanford had been using the hour allotted for a wind ensemble to try over one of his compositions for string quartet. Parry was infuriated and decided to confront his colleague. On 8 January, 1916 Stanford was summoned to the Director's office:

He [Stanford] began with his complaints about Aveling and James. I led him onto the subject of his false entries on the 'professors slips' to his charging for lessons he had not given because he was talking in other professors' rooms when he ought to have been giving them, and to his having a *string* quartet to play his own compositions which he charged for as an hour's *wind* ensemble, and a few more things of the kind
. . . He concluded by saying 'I always believe in being straight. I am straight'— which I did not endorse, thinking the exact opposite. It was a tiring hour.[22]

After this stormy confrontation, relations between the two men were, perhaps inevitably, pitched into a downward spiral. Parry became more and more impatient, Stanford more and more indignant. On 20 June 1916, during a meeting of the Associated Board, Stanford's manner was so exasperating that discussion was impossible; 'I should have flown into violence!', wrote the Director in a moment of frenzied rage. In December Stanford attempted to defend his conduct in a long fractious letter. At first Parry, weary of the incessant quarrelling, felt disposed to lay it aside. But in the end he did reply and declared that their turbulent friendship of the last forty years was irrevocably spent:

I read the first page of your letter, and think that is sufficient. I do not believe in quarrelling. It seems to me pure waste of time and labour—But I will take the opportunity to say a few words about the relations which your attitude towards me in the last 20 years has brought about. I always gladly and heartily acknowledge the wonderful generosity and kindness with which you treated me in early days. I owed you more than it is possible to put into words. There is hardly anyone I can think of who helped me so much. It is a delightful memory to look back to—They were great days and joyful days. But alas you are quite a different person now. As your old friend Arthur Coleridge said to me 'you must have your quarrel'. And in spite of everything I could do to humour you and shut my eyes to your growing ill will you forced a quarrel upon me. I did not

[22] Diary, 8 Jan. 1916.

take part in it, but you had your [quarrel]; and ever since I have been enduring with all the patience I could muster your constant use of any thing available as a handle to represent things in an injurious light . . . So by degrees it has come about that the delightful relations of the Cambridge days have been destroyed. To what an extent can be gauged by two incidents. Near the end of Christmas term 1915 I went into the office to speak to Perry and found you and Cairns James there. I went straight up to you and held out my hand. You turned your back and walked out, before the clerks and boys. On May 25 of this year we were invited with several representative musicians to Courtnege's rooms at the Shaftesbury to discuss ways of helping poor MacCunn. I came in late, and shook hands with them all and came up to you and held out my hand, and you, before all of them, refused it. To talk of friendship after such behaviour is ridiculous. To me it is final. As long as I am Director of the College and you a Professor of it, I shall continue to treat you with all the consideration due to a member of the staff; if either of us cease to be in either of those positions I shall feel no longer bound to keep to myself the reasons why our early friendship came to an end.

Only as a forlorn hope I would ask if you thought it possible to reconsider your ways of behaving to your fellowmen—your habit of making accusations against them and quarrelling and treating them offensively—then perhaps you might then become something more like what you were thirty years ago![23]

When Stanford received the letter he was at once overwhelmed with regret, and, unable to face his old friend, hastily sent his wife to Kensington Square as an intermediary. Parry related the event clearly in his diary:

After tea Lady Stanford made her appearance and a letter from C.V.S. It was very plucky of her, and she behaved very well. I told her it was impossible to discuss a man with his wife. But she stuck to it. She brought a very slippery and tortuous letter from C.V.S. Evading the issues as usual. We got hot now and then, but in the end she induced me to write a letter for her to take. I couldn't climb down much, but she thought it would do and went off after an hour's discussion, and presently the bell rang and she came back with C.V.S. who advanced with his hand out. His face with something more of his old expression, and I made the best of it.[24]

Plunket Greene, in his biography of Stanford, talks positively of this reconciliation, as if all the rancour and mistrust dissipated after their meeting, but it seems from later diary entries—Stanford's relationships with the Harrison sisters and with Cecil Forsyth—that Parry's scepticism persisted to the end.

At the close of 1917 Parry's health again began to collapse. All who knew him saw that a great change had come over his overtly ebullient, charming personality. Now he was weary, often silent, and deeply pensive as he watched the war enter another year. The defeat of the

[23] Letter [draft] to Sir Charles V. Stanford, [Dec.] 1916, ShP.
[24] Diary, 3 Jan. 1917.

Russian army on the Eastern Front seemed ominous as did the rise of a new political force in the guise of the Bolsheviks. With the introduction of conscription, the presence of young male students at the College all but evaporated and it became virtually impossible to hold such normal parts of the curriculum as choral classes. A terrible reminder of the human toll of war was the memorial to the 'Seven Divisions' who fought at Mons and Ypres which took place at the Albert Hall on 15 December. Among the items in the programme were Elgar's *Cockaigne* Overture, Vaughan Williams's *Toward the Unknown Region*, Howells's *Elegy for Strings*, Stanford's song with chorus 'Farewell', Somervell's Ode 'To the Vanguard 1914', and Parry's 'There is an old belief':

Huge gathering very impressive. Long rows of khaki in the boxes. The scheme of the concert was unfortunately misconceived, as it was mainly in the mournful [key] of regret for those who had fallen, whereas the soldiers were not concerned for that but were in an exuberant state ready for triumphant exhilaration at coming together again with a sense of honour. They bore it meekly. But it was oppressive. Choir sang well especially 'There is an old belief'. But naturally there was no enthusiasm for such things! It would have been better in church. Arthur Balfour read 'Praise famous men' and Lord Derby the lists of officers and regiments, which latter was punctuated with shouts of applause throughout.[25]

The Christmas festivities were marked initially by the performance at the Royal Choral Society's Carol Concert on 22 December of two new carols, 'I sing the birth' and 'Welcome Yule' conducted by Bridge. At Highnam he was pressed to cut down more trees and it broke his heart when Government orders arrived compelling him to fell his favourite larch plantation and the chestnut grove. 'The place looks bald already', he wrote in a cry of anguish to Plunket Greene; 'What it will be when they have accomplished all their fell designs is too tragic to think of.'[26] Highnam seemed too dispiriting a place to spend Christmas; besides, Maude was ill, so deranged with the effects of veronal that she could neither make the journey nor tolerate the cold of the house. At Rustington he, too, suddenly became ill. It was his heart again, and his doctors were worried as to whether he would pull through. He was confined to bed for ten days and recovered sufficiently to return to London on 4 January, but without Maude who was forbidden to move.

1918 saw only a handful of smaller pieces come to fruition. In January he wrote a memorial hymn, 'Hush for amid our tears', for Littleton at Novello, and in taking charge of the music for Mrs Fawcett's Demonstration meeting at Queen's Hall, he scored an arrangement of Purcell's chorus 'Soul of the World' (from the 'Ode to St Cecilia', 1692)

[25] Ibid. 15 Dec. 1917.   [26] Graves, *Hubert Parry*, ii. 86.

which he conducted along with parts of the 'Lady Radnor' Suite and 'Jerusalem'. 'Jerusalem' having become so nationally popular, Gilbert Murray and Ernest Walker asked if he might set John of Gaunt's famous speech from Act II of *Richard II* ('This royal throne of kings, this sceptred island'). 'Not very suitable,' he wrote sceptically, 'but I had to make the best of it.'[27] Just as with 'Jerusalem' he had been reticent about the composition of a song with barefaced patriotic intentions. The song, entitled 'England', was dispatched to Walker who was pleased with the result, and Parry was then urged to score it which he did between 7 and 9 June. 'England' followed the trend of 'Jerusalem' as a sturdy unison setting. Allen gave its first performance in Oxford in 1918, but it never caught on to the same extent as its famous predecessor, though Sir Adrian Boult remained one of its firmest advocates. As well as 'England' Edward Arnold published three further school songs, 'Neptune's Empire' (Campion), 'The wind and the leaves' (Cooper), and 'Song of the nights' (Cornwall), which were written for Dunhill's collection of *School Songs*. But perhaps the most substantial publication was *Hands across the Centuries*, a suite for piano written and dedicated to Emily Daymond. The Suite was begun in 1916 and as its original title 'Da vivis rediviva' suggests, it was an attempt to breathe a 'contemporary' air into the Baroque keyboard genre. Originally the composer had designs on an athletic Toccata at the beginning but he eventually opted for a more dignified Prelude. The sober mood of this movement set the tone for 'The Passionate Allemande', 'The Wistful Courante', and 'Quasi Sarabande'. By way of contrast, the last three movements, 'Gavotte and Musette', 'Quasi Minuetto', and 'The Whirling Jig' (originally entitled 'The Devil's Jig') are animated and lighthearted. This at first gave the composer the idea of calling it *The Topsy Turvy Suite* 'because the first movements are so solemn, and the last so infernally cheerful',[28] but he was finally more persuaded by the nostalgic link with the past.

27 February 1918 marked his 70th birthday. His room at the College was filled with flowers and there were accolades from colleagues and members of the press. A few days later, on 4 March, he was treated to a fine performance of the Symphonic Variations by Adrian Boult. Having had some doubts as to the conductor's interpretative powers he wrote to Boult the following day: 'I am much beholden to you for a surprisingly good performance of those ancient variations. They all bucked up splendidly and put their backs into it, and deserve my hearty thanks. I congratulate you on the good hold you have on the performers and the insight and spirit of your interpretations . . .'.[29] It was the last major public performance of his music he would ever hear.

---

[27] Diary, 2 June 1918.   [28] Emily Daymond's catalogue of Parry's works, 32, ShP.
[29] Letter to Adrian Boult, 5 Mar. 1918, BL Add. MS 60499.

By the beginning of January 1918 Parry was close to the completion of his book, *Instinct and Character* which had occupied him on and off since 1915. It had been a long and difficult haul. Though constantly fascinated by the issues of human behavioural evolution and their numerous manifestations, he had found the explanation of his arguments hard to put into words. Arthur, always his close confidant during the book's development, admired the fertility of thought and philosophy but was unsure of its organization and over-amplification. Parry was sensitive to his son-in-law's criticisms and, as the book approached its conclusion, began to sense with a cold dread that it was a failure. Yet still he entertained the hope that Macmillan might publish it. On 30 May he wrote to the publisher with whom he had had dealings since the early days of the Musical Dictionary:

I am almost ashamed to confess, in these days, that I have been at work for some years on a book which is not ostensibly connected with music. It is [a] sort of apologia which I could not resist the craving to make, in connection with my having devoted my life mostly to art, which so many people think to be merely self-indulgence. Indirectly the book has a close connection with music, as one of the main objects is to deal with the spiritual and material influences in life, which in these times have become so urgent. If I was not at least egotistical enough to feel that the subjects it deals with are so peculiarly urgent I should be content to let it remain unprinted, as an attempt to clarify my own mind by thinking out the things which have presented themselves in my particular sphere of work—But the line that has presented itself to me is rather different from what I am accustomed to hear around me and I believe very much in the usefulness of having many points of view, so I dare to think it may be useful. It works out to something like the same conclusion as Kidd's Social Evolution, but by a very different road—and the matter of the road seems to me to affect the conclusions and what will follow from them. But at any rate your having Kidd's book makes me hope you might favourably consider mine. I am fully aware of the difficulties of the moment, in scarcity of paper and so forth, but I should much prefer it to be brought out in a handy and unpretentious form—like the copy I have recently seen of Kidd's book—and have no feeling about sumptuousness or spaciousness—At all events I hope you may feel inclined to look at it, and help me to my natural desire to see it someday in print. I have called it 'Instinct and Character' . . .[30]

On 4 June he lunched with Macmillan and left the manuscript of *Instinct and Character* with 'little or no hope that he would undertake it'.[31] He was right not to hope. On 14 June a letter came declining the book. Demoralized by the rejection he wrote to Dolly:

A very depressing blow! I don't yet know what I shall do further. I am trying to reconcile myself to never seeing it in print, in the view that it has been useful to

[30] Letter to Macmillan, 30 May 1918, BL Add. MS 55239.   [31] Diary, 4 June 1918.

me to think it all out fully. And as the scheme works out so completely it will be of service in connection with things I may have to write and say about music.[32]

As for his relations with Macmillan and the publishing house, he was saddened but not embittered:

I am thoroughly appreciative of the great service you have done the College in the past, and the likelihood of your doing many more in the future, so I think it will be better if the subject of my book is never again mentioned between us. Only I am aware you must have had to pay someone a fee for reading it, and I am unwilling to put you to expense—so if you will allow me I will gladly repay the amount.[33]

Macmillan's refusal largely overshadowed the end of the summer term at College which enjoyed the presence of Hamilton Harty who came to examine both the composition students and the orchestra. After the term was over Parry was a guest of the King and Queen at Buckingham Palace and went to Mackenzie's Testimonial Concert at Queen's Hall in celebration of the Scotsman's thirty-year Principalship of the Royal Academy of Music. Then he went in some haste to Gloucestershire where he first met George Schlichenmeyer who took him to the quarries at Tytherington. Having satisfied himself that his factotum was in good health he inspected the estate at Highnam with Eels, broken-hearted at the untended garden deliberately abandoned because of the war. It was the last time he would ever see his beloved Gloucestershire home. Briefly he returned to London and then made for Rustington to wile away the summer months. He enjoyed the company of his neighbours, the Johnstons and the Rackhams. Feeling redundant he made an impulsive visit to the Office of Agriculture in early August to see if they could offer him a month's work. There was talk of him accompanying agricultural inspectors, but the officials seemed unconvinced and so he left. Days later reports circulated of the big Allied advance against Germany and Turkey. At last the tide was turning and the end of the war seemed a real possibility.

Much of August was spent idly with Emily Daymond cycling around the countryside of southern Sussex visiting Arundel and Highdown Hill. During the evenings at Rustington he could not tear himself away from *Instinct and Character* and resolved to write a summary of the book perhaps in the hope that a shorter version might yet attract a publisher. He visited Shulbrede for a few days, and was, according to Arthur, splendidly happy in the Priory's enchanting surroundings. He seemed fit and well, his mind as ever sharp and clear. But the next time Arthur was to see his father-in-law, he was to be shocked by the sight of a man,

[32] Letter to Dorothea Ponsonby, 14 June 1918, ShP.
[33] Letter to Macmillan, 20 June 1918, BL Add. MS 55239.

drawn, delirious, and wracked with pain. On 6 September Parry and Emily had gone out cycling. On the return journey, as Parry recounted, 'Emily, overhasty, bustled along all the way to Littlehampton Common. I was by that time very tired. At dinner I chaffed her about it and she took violent offence and sulked all dinner and went to bed directly after.'[34] The following morning a large protuberance was found in his groin which the doctor thought might have been caused by a pinch between truss and saddle of the bicycle. Parry was ordered to bed and could only manage the occasional walk round the garden. The doctor's anxieties were justified. In June he had undergone the latest of a series of operations for cysts, the last of which had been delayed by work pressures. It had taken some time to remove the badly suppurating cyst and there must have been some danger even then to the weakened old man. This new protuberance, however, was more serious and it soon became evident that his blood had been poisoned. Dolly and Gwen were telegraphed and came swiftly to Rustington with Arthur close on their heels. Cultures of the patient's blood were made into a vaccine in the hope of reviving him, but even though he seemed to rally for a time, it was evident that his days were numbered. 'It is all too terrible to see him suffering and prostrate to be helpless and see him gradually sinking,' Arthur recollected in his diary. 'Lady M[aude] very difficult like a child but beginning to realise what it means. D[olly] is in a terrible state the blow will hurt her fearfully. He means so much to her and the whole idea of his splendid life coming to an end is almost impossible to grasp.'[35] It seemed an ironic end for a man who had no doubt expected to die from the heart problems that had harassed him all his life. His agony and delirium dragged on until he died on the evening of 7 October, a month before Armistice and the peace he had longed for. An account of those harrowing last days was recorded by his son-in-law:

CHHP died on Oct 7. I do not think I can go through the days in recollection. The whole three weeks were day by day as painful as they well could be. Waiting for death is a grim occupation. One has to eat and sleep and go on with all the little petty affairs of life just the same. One seeks refuge in books and some small activities trying to help and feeling all the while utterly helpless. The tiptoeing whispering consulting discussing symptoms anatomical and medical details the characters of the nurses, waiting, watching, one moment buoyed up by hope the next utterly without hope. Snatched intervals of reading, Metchinkoff's 'The Nature of Man', A Life of Swift, Walton's Life of Donne, Lecky's Rise of Rationalism. Attempts at distraction, forced hilarity, scares that the end was near, hope for a few hours again, witnessing pain, discomfort, struggle, delirium, longing for the end—not yet, not yet—howling westerly gales, sheets of rain, still the heavy breath going on, less consciousness, no

---

[34] Diary, 6 Sept. 1918. [35] Diary of Arthur Ponsonby, 28 Sept. 1918.

words, lifeless staring eyes—not yet—a little October sunshine, the sun setting through the poplars, the wind dropping—come up, you had better come up—breathing slower—would there be another, yes, yes and still another on again for a little—slower, slower—the last one silence—what a tremendous silence. And then, the chirping song of a bird at the window—a bird who had followed him when he moved to another room and had sung to him in the morning . . .[36]

Letters of condolence were thick and plentiful as were the public tributes and obituaries. The funeral took place at St Paul's Cathedral on 16 October. It was presided over by the Archbishop of Canterbury and attended by representatives of the King, the Prince of Wales, and Queen Alexandra. The building was packed with mourners. Stanford, Elgar, Mackenzie, Cowen, Lloyd, Bridge, and Parratt were there as were representatives of all the many and varied institutions and organizations with which he had been associated. The Universities of Cambridge, Oxford, London, and Trinity College, Dublin were represented as were the Royal Academy of Music and the Guildhall School of Music. Then there were representatives of the Handel Society, the Bach Choir, the Musical Association, the Royal Choral Society, the Royal Geographical Society, the Literary Society, and the Royal Academy of Art. Other societies were also present including the Professional Classes War Relief Council (which had absorbed Music in Wartime), the Oxford University Dramatic Society, and the Royal Yacht Squadron. The coffin was borne by nine Etonians led, symbolically, by the Keeper of the Field. Walford Davies conducted the choirs of St Paul's and the Temple Church who sang Croft's funeral sentences as the processions moved up the Nave. After the lesson the Bach Choir, conducted by Allen, sang 'There is an old belief'; it was the high point of the service. The conclusion, normally marked by the oppressive tones of a Funeral March, was instead transformed by the sounds of the composer's Chorale Preludes, amongst them 'Martyrdom', 'Ye boundless realms of joy', and 'St Ann' played by Alcock, Ley, Gray, Atkins, Parratt, and Davies. 'Some felt God's presence', Arthur wrote afterwards; 'I felt *his* presence the great noble soul pervading everything the wonderful inspiring influence which will dwell on and on after we are all dead'.[37]

In November the College paid its own tribute with a Memorial Concert in which Stanford conducted Parry's as yet unperformed *Elegy for Brahms*. The news of the Director's death was especially crushing to the Irishman, for he no doubt sensed that the rift between them had had precious little time to heal. In 1918 Stanford had been hard pressed to finish his Magnificat in B flat for unaccompanied double choir. His intention was to dedicate it to his colleague but death intervened.

---

[36] Diary of Arthur Ponsonby, 12 Oct. 1918.   [37] Ibid. 19 Oct. 1918.

Consequently the dedication was made posthumously in the knowledge of a denied reconciliation as is implied by the Latin inscription 'Huic operi quod mors vetuit ne Carolo Huberto Hastings Parry vivo traderem nomen illius moerens praescribo' ('This work which his death prevented me from handing Charles Hubert Hastings Parry in life, I dedicate to his name in grief'). Exeter College, Oxford, paid its own respects with a concert on 23 February 1919 which included all the *Songs of Farewell*, the slow movement of the 'English' Symphony, extracts from the 'Lady Radnor' Suite, and movements from *Hands across the Centuries* orchestrated by G. M. Sims.

For Dolly and Arthur the weeks after the funeral service were filled with tributes and reminiscences, but these were tarnished by more unpalatable experiences. Maude continued to be awkward and unpredictable. Arthur found her presence especially trying and reflected on the burden she must have been to her husband while he was alive:

With all his outward buoyancy and apparent cheerfulness, he was terribly lonely and always had been. His wife never cared for his music never shared his life was no companion and with her funny arrested development and self-centred smallness of vision was no help or comfort to him at all. His devotion to her was pathetic and yet it always seemed as if he were unaware that he could never win her. She hampered him, irritated him, bullied him was a drain on him, prevented many people from seeing him who wanted to and even made it difficult for us to see him as living with her was too trying. This gave him the note of melancholy which came out in his music.[38]

To be fair to Lady Maude, however, Arthur did his utmost to illuminate her positive points and to imagine the attraction which Parry had once felt so keenly:

She had been most lovely in her youth and in spite of her utter carelessness with regard to her appearance she remained a very beautiful woman with exceptional and very aristocratic charm and a delightful sense of humour. They married young and he had loved her with such intensity that whatever transformations she might have undergone that wonderful memory enforced his loyalty to her and bound his affection to her forever. Only once or twice was he sharply angry with me and that was because, in my impatience I suppose, I had been inconsiderate to her. He always took her side to the extent of believing some of her extravagant fancies. But for himself deep down unseen by any mortal eye his disillusionment which followed the early brilliance must have been poignant and the constant effort to adapt himself, seldom very successfully, to her curious caprices and her perversity must have been terribly wearing . . . Difficult and trying as she was in many ways she had certain unique characteristics. Her charm was unfailing, her laugh was lovely and even in her old age someone described her as 'wondrously beautiful'. She was very amusing and at different

[38] Ibid. 24 Oct. 1918.

times Jack Gordon (Stanmore), Louis Mallet, Sir Harry Johnston, Francis of Teck, and others much appreciated her exceptional form of fun. No-one less snobbish has ever been created. In her car with the dentist's wife, the cook and manservant and child and her latest young girlfriend she enjoyed herself more than with her sister Lady Ripon or any society people whom she loathed passionately. Her clothes were beyond belief torn and bedraggled but she drove in a Rolls Royce, she saved the coals on the fire and bought very expensive bits of furniture. She argued the Free Trade case well and was a keen suffragist but would talk absolute nonsense by the hour. She was quite unaccountable. Her likes and dislikes were extreme. We discovered a Russian ancestor of hers who seems to have had precisely the same characteristics down to the impossible clothes. She hated her mother Lady Herbert she adored her brothers George Pembroke and Michael Herbert. She would sit playing games with the servants but was furious if anyone called her Lady Parry [*since this title was incorrect, the correct form being Lady Maude Parry*]. The nearer you were to her, the more difficult, unreasonable and capricious she became. The degree this reached with her husband nobody will ever know.[39]

Though she had been 'ill' all her life, Maude did not die until 1933, though the last few years were dogged by a series of strokes which steadily incapacitated her. As Arthur commented: 'Mercifully H[ubert] P[arry] was spared the watching of cruel decay which overcame her in the last years of her life.'[40]

Perhaps the most distressing event that took place immediately after Parry's death was the vacating of Highnam. The deep rift that had never healed between Parry and Ernest Gambier Parry came home to roost in November when it was necessary to collect up all papers, correspondences, manuscripts, and other belongings so that Ernest could move in as soon as possible. In August 1915 Ernest's wife, Evelyn, had written to Parry before his trip to Canada and the USA expressing the hope of a belated reconciliation. 'I would give all I possess', she wrote, 'to bring you two together, but that will never be in this world, so it only remains to accept the fact, deplorable altho' it is.'[41] At that time Ernest's mental state was still unstable. He suffered a continuous series of nervous breakdowns and fretted constantly about the estate at Highnam. As trees were felled to assist the war effort he grew angry and wrote further injurious letters to his half-brother with misconceptions of Parry's intentions over the timber on the estate. Arthur was furious at Ernest's insensitivity and denounced him as a 'sentimental self-pitying cantankerous unforgiving religious recluse who by his letters must have been to CHHP a perpetual thorn in the flesh.'[42]

[39] A. Ponsonby, 'Brief Glimpses: Hubert Parry' (unpub., c.1938), ShP.
[40] Ibid.
[41] Letter from Evelyn Gambier Parry, 6 Aug. 1915, ShP.
[42] Diary of Arthur Ponsonby, 1–3 Nov. 1918.

Dolly was distraught at the loss of her father and felt bereft for many years, as did Arthur. She in particular remained a staunch advocate of his music and would fiercely repudiate those who misinterpreted or misconstrued his true character. With regard to the latter, one particular *bête noir* was Arnold Bax. In his autobiography *Farewell My Youth*, Bax drew a picture of a Victorian man of convention, the conservative squire, a sportsman, and a churchman. Worse still, however, was the acceptance of Bax's impression by others which eventually resulted in Dolly writing a forthright letter to the *Musical Times* in 1948 to crush the 'fantastic legend about her father':

As I knew him for forty years, I give the facts. My father was the most naturally unconventional man I have known. He was a Radical, with a very strong bias against Conservatism—he writes somewhere that he found himself continually in a minority of one, and reduced to silence by the champions of Conservatism. He was a free-thinker and did not go to my christening. He never shot, not because he was against blood-sports, but felt out of touch and ill at ease in the company of those who enjoyed shooting parties. His friends, apart from his schoolfriends, were mostly in the artistic and literary world—the Burne Joneses, William Morris, de Morgan, Robert Bridges, and many obscure and struggling musicians. He was an ascetic and spent nothing on himself. The puritanical vein in him is considered by some to spoil his music, as tending to lack of colour. Far from its being an advantage to be the son of a Gloucestershire squire, my father's early life was a fight against prejudice. His father thought music unsuitable as a profession, and the critics of music in the mid-nineteenth century showed no mercy to anyone they considered privileged. My father was sensitive, and suffered from bouts of deep depression.

The extraordinary misinterpretation of him that exists should not persist.[43]

Gwen's reaction to her father's death was rather different. After the war and her separation from Plunket Greene her outlook on life changed. Having happily embraced agnosticism while her father was alive, she became obsessively religious in the 1920s largely under the influence of her uncle, Baron Friedrich von Hügel. She converted to Roman Catholicism and spent the last years of her mother's life trying to draw her into the fold. Had it not been for Dolly's vigilance she might have succeeded. In 1930 Dent published *Two Witnesses*, 'a personal recollection of Hubert Parry and Friedrich von Hügel'. It was, as Arthur somewhat angrily put it, a book in which she 'used her father as a peg on which to hang mild self disparagement and egotism and washy religious platitudes',[44] while beneath the façade trying to reconcile her actions with her father's absolute detestation of the religious persuasion she had entered.

[43] *Musical Times* (May 1956), 263. This was written in response to Peter J. Pirie's article 'Crippled Splendour: Elgar and Mahler', *Musical Times* (Feb. 1956), 70–1.
[44] R. A. Jones, *Arthur Ponsonby* (London, 1989), 196.

Emily Daymond undertook the editing of those completed works which, because of the war, had not achieved print. Named after his yacht, the Toccata and Fugue in G major and E minor, the *Wanderer*, was written in November 1912 and was tried over by Fox and Parratt at the College. The composer had evidently been dissatisfied with the Toccata since two versions of it exist. It was published by Novello in 1921 and first performed in a recital at Westminster Abbey by one of Parry's last pupils, George Thalben Ball. In addition to the piano suite *Hands across the Centuries* which Parry dedicated to Daymond, he also wrote another suite for her, this time for string orchestra. The bulk of the English Suite dates from 1914 and 1915 though some movements were written much earlier. The 'Pastoral', dates from about 1890 appearing in a different key (B flat) as a piano piece and also as a piece for violin. The 'Sarabande' is also earlier and includes a quotation from the 'Lullaby' of the *Twelve Short Pieces* Set I No. 4 for violin and piano written in 1894. This was probably the date of the movement's composition and it may well have been a rejected movement for the 'Lady Radnor' Suite which dates from the same year. The last of the movements to be written (sometime between 1916 and 1917) was the 'Air'—originally entitled 'Intermezzo' by the composer but altered by Daymond 'to match the other names'.[45] Similarly the 'Caprice' and the last movement 'Frolic' were chosen and given titles by the editor since the composer had not decided on any definite names, nor had he settled on any definitive last movement. The movements of the English Suite are generally larger in scope than those of the 'Lady Radnor', and the harmonic language is more capricious, particularly in the jocular 'Caprice' and 'Frolic'. The 'Air' attempts to recapture the serenity of the earlier Suite's 'Slow Minuet' but never quite achieves its sensuous intimacy. 'In Minuet Style' is distinguished by particularly imaginative string writing and a colourful mixture of tonality and modality. Most distinctive of all is the stately Elgarian 'Sarabande' with its broad diatonicism and liberal dissonance. After two semi-private performances under Allen's direction, one at a College Orchestral Concert, and the other at the Bach Choir's Parry Concert on 10 May 1921, the Suite was given its first fully public hearing on 22 October 1922 at a Promenade Concert under Henry Wood.

At the request of the composer's executors two further volumes of *English Lyrics* were published by Novello in 1920 under the editorship of Emily Daymond, Harry Plunket Greene, and Charles Wood. Of the fifteen songs only five or six carried a firm indication that the composer wished to publish them, though from evidence found among his papers

[45] Emily Daymond's catalogue of Parry's works, 34, ShP.

the editors were satisfied that Parry intended to assemble two more sets. Of the eight songs in Set XI four were by Alfred Perceval Graves who featured in Set VI. At least two of these settings date from 1912 when the composer had been corresponding with the author over a projected new set of songs. Several of the songs dwell on the recurrent theme of lost love, 'What part of dread eternity' (the text probably by Parry), 'Why art thou slow' (Massinger), 'If I might ride on puissant wing' (Sturgis), and most autobiographically pertinent, 'The faithful lover' (Graves) which seems to parallel almost exactly the hopeless battle Parry fought for Maude's love. Set XII contains not only the last complete setting Parry ever made ('The sound of hidden music' signed on his birthday, 27 February 1918) but also a number of much earlier settings. By the nature of the early handwriting, 'Rosaline' dates from his first maturity, and the style of harmonic language suggests an affinity with the first two volumes of *English Lyrics* of the early 1880s. Herrick's 'To Blossoms' was attempted as far back as 1877, and further versions were made in 1879 and 1881. But it was not until 1917 that he convinced himself that he had mastered the poem's metrical problems. 'O world! O life! O time!' (Shelley) was also written in numerous versions, the first dating from 1870. It was almost included in Set X of the *English Lyrics* but was finally left out after Agnes Nicholls preferred Rossetti's 'My heart is like a singing bird'. The dates of two of the most striking songs are less certain but they probably derive from the war years. The overtly eschatological 'When the sun's great orb' (Warner), while by no means musically successful, is nevertheless an intriguing and extrovert attempt at the style of dialogue first essayed in 'Through the ivory gate' (*English Lyrics* Set III). Bold accompanimental textures are combined with shades of Wagnerian declamation to portray the tumult of Armageddon, though it must be said that some of the dramatic gestures (such as the tired diminished sevenths of 'hell's fury') seriously undermine the song's impact. By contrast, 'Dream Pedlary' (Beddoes) is reflective, harmonically subtle, gently lyrical with a shade of melancholy and must rank as one of Parry's most exquisite miniatures.

As for *Instinct and Character*, the task of editing and revising the rejected manuscript fell to Arthur Ponsonby who, after the war, paid for his opposition to the military solution by losing his seat in parliament. Between 1919 and 1921 he set about the rearrangement of the various sections adding new headings and titles to assist the reader, and included as the book's conclusion the poem of 'The Vision of Life'—in many ways the summation of Parry's ethical exploits. The book was submitted to the Clarendon Press but the response mirrored that of Macmillan. Sir Walter Raleigh was consulted over the matter but he along with others admitted that many of its arguments were too vulnerable to the new philosophical and psychological theories of post-war Europe. Arthur was downcast but not surprised. *Instinct and Character* was, he later confessed, 'cram full of the shrewdest and most sagacious judgements and the most illuminating opinions. But it was too abundant and tangled in its own amplitude.'[46]

In 1922, as the result of appeals by the Parry Memorial Committee, a tablet was designed by Emery Walker, inscribed by Robert Bridges, and placed in Gloucester Cathedral. A score of the Symphonic Fantasia '1912' was also published. Bournemouth erected its own memorial in the Winter Gardens, and the College's gesture was to open the Parry Room Library in 1921. But perhaps the most touching token of his friends' esteem was a collection of organ miniatures, *For the Little Organ Book*, a title taken from the original heading of Parry's own piece which begins the set. It was published by Novello in 1924.[47]

After the First World War Parry's music suffered a considerable decline, with no more than a handful of choral works remaining in the repertoire. Post-war Britain was hungry for new artistic ideals and was, for the most part, happy to ignore the paradigms of its Victorian and Edwardian forefathers. Some were disposed to accuse Parry and his contemporaries of having prevented the one central talent, Elgar, from realizing success earlier than he did. In this respect Shaw, perhaps more than anyone, was most outspoken, and pointed the finger at the former Director of the Royal College as the leader of a 'little clique of musicians' who had resented the rise of talent outside their priveliged society.[48] Elgar's fierce defence of Parry's role in his rise to fame stands as a forceful rebuttal against Shaw's somewhat dogmatic assertions. However, Shaw's reaction epitomized the widespread reaction felt by the post-war generation against much that had been achieved by the late Victorians and Edwardians. Others were prepared to go even further, and Ernest Newman was happy to denounce Parry as a composer 'who never was'. Such a condemnation was symptomatic of an age which looked to new artistic and aesthetic criteria. As R. O. Morris remarked, the musical world in 1920 had 'erected a process into a principle, and harmonic research [had] become the starting point from which nearly all our young composers set out to conquer new worlds. Parry could not conceivably be the vogue today.'[49]

    [46] Ponsonby, 'Brief Glimpses: Hubert Parry'.
    [47] *For the Little Organ Book* included 13 pieces in all with contributions by Stanford, Brewer, Gray, Macpherson, Atkins, (Frank) Bridge, Darke, Wood, Alcock, Thalben Ball, Ley, and Walford Davies.
    [48] G. B. Shaw, 'Sir Edward Elgar', *Music and Letters*, 1 (Mar. 1920), 10.
    [49] R. O. Morris, 'Hubert Parry', ibid. 97.

Nevertheless, Parry's spiritual legacy lived on in the works of the succeeding generations. This manifested itself most fundamentally in the sense of creative 'morality' that remained an intrinsic feature of British composition for many years. It is perhaps most markedly exemplified in the appropriation and continuance of the diatonic style in which Parry's position is seminal. Vaughan Williams was an obvious recipient as is clear from the pages of *Toward the Unknown Region*, the *Sea Symphony*, and the *Serenade to Music*, and the songs of Gurney show a similar indebtedness. The ceremonial music of composers such as Bliss is another clear demonstration as is the church music of Howells. Passages such as 'By the waters of Babylon' from Walton's *Belshazzar's Feast* display a passing acknowledgment of this tradition, but of all the younger generation it was Gerald Finzi who appropriated and perpetuated the stylistic features of Parry's music, a fact borne out by the diatonic appoggiaturas and falling sevenths of *Dies Natalis*, the elusive simplicity of *In terra pax*, and the spacious choral sonorities of *Intimations of Immortality*. Not surprisingly it was Finzi who remained Parry's most staunch advocate during the 1940s and 50s when the popularity of such music had reached its lowest ebb. 'Hubert Parry: A Revaluation' is a testimony of the younger man's devotion and conviction to the artistic integrity of his mentor.[50]

Seventy years on, our assessment of Parry the man and (primarily) the composer is rapidly shifting as we view his accomplishments in a wider perspective. His personality, as with many Victorians, was far from simple; indeed at times it seems impenetrably complex and mysterious. In Parry it is a question of reconciling the contradictions. In one sense he was undoubtedly a radical, a Victorian idealist, even a political rebel; but, as a figure of the establishment, he was also an advocate of tradition and was in many ways essentially conservative and restrained. He was attracted to hedonism but at the same time chose to offset this penchant for pleasure with a puritanical ardour. Moreover, to compound these apparent paradoxes, he was profoundly religious and yet he developed a pathological revulsion of organized religion. This conundrum says much not only about Parry as a composer but about the influence he exerted on British musical sensibility in general, a sensibility which has invariably revealed itself to be capable of passionate yearning and unorthodoxy yet imbued with a natural reserve, a tempered respect for technique, and a propensity for moderation. Most complex of all, however, was Parry's perception of the composer's role within society which did more than anything else to instil into the creative musical psyche of this country a profound sense of public duty combined with a personal morality.

[50] This article was taken from a BBC broadcast on the Third Programme which was later published in the *Music Maker* (Summer 1949), 4–8.

Sincerity, character, and responsibility were the mainstays of his teaching as were his example and his motivation as a composer. 'A great artistic personality,' he declared, 'is the concentrated essence of the highest human qualities of its time, the choice flower of the best nurtured garden of the soul, the manifestation of all the best tendencies, efforts, and aspirations of the finest natures, who seek after the ideals of human life, and the true happiness of mankind.'[51] This was Parry's credo, and he did his utmost to live it in life as well as in music.

[51] Notebook, ShP.

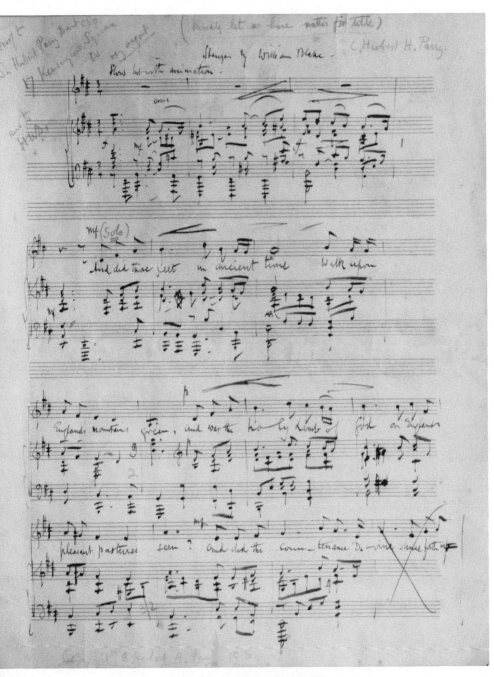

The first page of *Jerusalem* (1916)

APPENDIX I

HUBERT PARRY came from a large family. His father, Thomas Gambier Parry, married twice; the first genealogical tree is intended to clarify the lineage of his first marriage (to Anna Maria Isabella Fynes Clinton—the progeny of which were called simply 'Parry') and his second marriage (to Ethelinda Lear—the progeny of which were called 'Gambier Parry'). The tree should also make clear the Majendie connection, the relationship of Thomas Gambier Parry's wives, and close relationship of the two families of children. The second genealogical tree is one showing the lineage of Maude Herbert.

All those who figure prominently in the book appear in bold type.

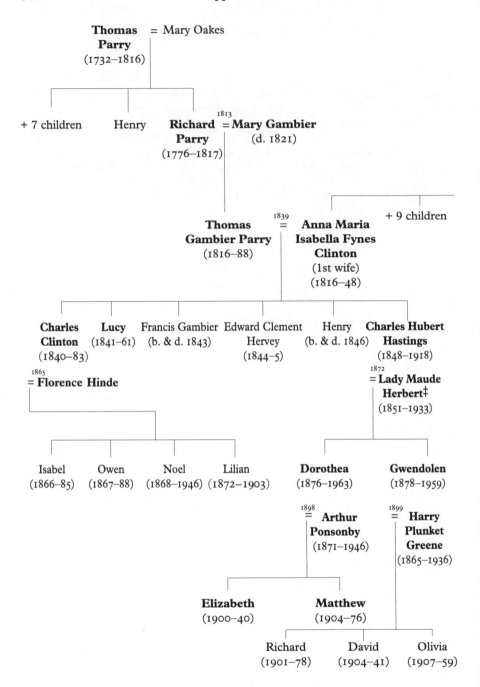

Thomas Parry (1732–1816) = Mary Oakes

+ 7 children | Henry | Richard Parry (1776–1817) =[1813] Mary Gambier (d. 1821)

+ 9 children

Thomas Gambier Parry (1816–88) =[1839] Anna Maria Isabella Fynes Clinton (1st wife) (1816–48)

Charles Clinton (1840–83) =[1865] Florence Hinde

Lucy (1841–61)

Francis Gambier (b. & d. 1843)

Edward Clement Hervey (1844–5)

Henry (b. & d. 1846)

Charles Hubert Hastings (1848–1918) =[1872] Lady Maude Herbert‡ (1851–1933)

Isabel (1866–85) Owen (1867–88) Noel (1868–1946) Lilian (1872–1903)

Dorothea (1876–1963) =[1898] Arthur Ponsonby (1871–1946)

Gwendolen (1878–1959) =[1899] Harry Plunket Greene (1865–1936)

Elizabeth (1900–40) Matthew (1904–76)

Richard (1901–78) David (1904–41) Olivia (1907–59)

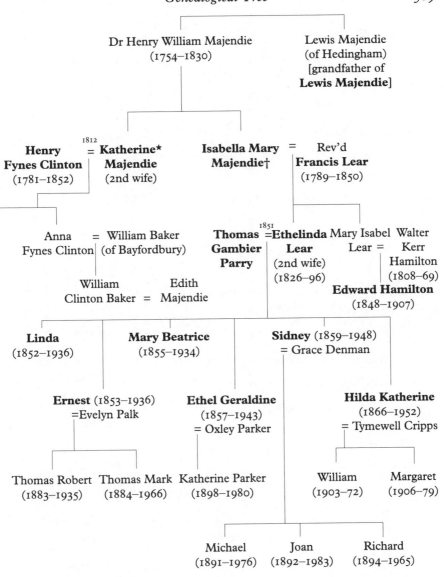

Dr Henry William Majendie
(1754–1830)

Lewis Majendie
(of Hedingham)
[grandfather of
Lewis Majendie]

**Henry
Fynes Clinton**
(1781–1852)

1812
= **Katherine*
Majendie**
(2nd wife)

**Isabella Mary
Majendie†**

=

Rev'd
Francis Lear
(1789–1850)

Anna
Fynes Clinton

= William Baker
(of Bayfordbury)

**Thomas
Gambier
Parry**

1851
=**Ethelinda
Lear**
(2nd wife)
(1826–96)

Mary Isabel
Lear

=

Walter
Kerr
Hamilton
(1808–69)

William
Clinton Baker

=

Edith
Majendie

Edward Hamilton
(1848–1907)

Linda
(1852–1936)

Mary Beatrice
(1855–1934)

Sidney (1859–1948)
= Grace Denman

Ernest (1853–1936)
=Evelyn Palk

Ethel Geraldine
(1857–1943)
= Oxley Parker

Hilda Katherine
(1866–1952)
= Tymewell Cripps

Thomas Robert
(1883–1935)

Thomas Mark
(1884–1966)

Katherine Parker
(1898–1980)

William
(1903–72)

Margaret
(1906–79)

Michael
(1891–1976)

Joan
(1892–1983)

Richard
(1894–1965)

* (3rd daughter)
† (5th daughter)
‡ see Herbert family tree

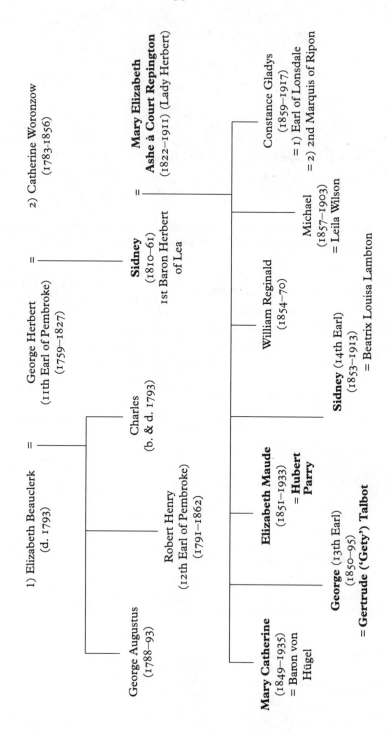

APPENDIX 2

HUBERT PARRY: LIST OF WORKS

MUSICAL works are listed in the following order of categories, broadly adhering to the format used in vol. ii of J. C. Dibble, 'The Music of Hubert Parry: A Critical and Analytical Study' (Doctoral thesis, Southampton University, 1986): A. Choral Works; B. Church Music; C. Opera; D. Theatre Music; E. Symphonies; F. Concertos; G. Orchestral Works; H. Chamber Works; I. Piano Solo; J. Organ Solo; K. Part-songs/Carols; L. Unison Songs; M. Solo Songs; N. Arrangements and Copies; O. Books; P. Articles and Public Lectures.

Opus numbers were attached by Parry only to a few early works but these appear to have no real significance in any sense. Hence they have been dropped from the present listing.

At the end of each entry an abbreviated reference to the location of the autograph manuscript (Aut.) has been included.

A. Choral Works

Published only in vocal score except where 'full score' is indicated. With the exception of the anthem *Hear my words ye people* of 1894 which has accompaniment for organ, brass, and timpani, a normal orchestra is used. Unless otherwise stated, the first performances listed below were conducted by the composer. Dates of first performances are given along with subsequent revisions. In addition to the location of the autograph manuscripts, the autographs of the vocal scores (v.s.) used by the printers have also been included.

O Lord, Thou hast cast us out (words: Bible), cantata, pub. Lamborn Cock, 1867; Eton College, 8 Dec. 1867.

Scenes from Shelley's 'Prometheus Unbound' (words: Shelley), dramatic cantata, pub. Novello, 1880; Three Choirs (Gloucester) Festival, 7 Sept. 1880. Rev. 1881 and 1885. Aut. RCM; v.s. (almost complete) Bod.

The Contention of Ajax and Ulysses: The Glories of Our Blood and State (words: J. Shirley), ode, pub. Novello, 1885 (full score rev. 1908 and 1914, pub. 1914); Three Choirs (Gloucester) Festival, 4 Sept. 1883. Rev. 1908 and 1914. Aut. RCM; v.s. Bod.

At a Solemn Music: Blest Pair of Sirens (words: Milton), ode, pub. Novello, 1887; St James's Hall, 17 May 1887, cond. Stanford. German trans. Josephson; Italian trans. Visetti. Aut. TCC (Wren Library); v.s. (incomplete) Bod.

Judith or *The Regeneration of Manasseh* (words: composer and Apocrypha), oratorio, pub. Novello, 1888; Birmingham Festival, 29 Aug. 1888, cond. Richter. Aut. RCM.

Ode on St Cecilia's Day (words: Pope), ode, pub. Novello, 1889; Leeds Festival, 11 Oct. 1889 Aut. Bod.

L'Allegro ed Il Penseroso (words: Milton), cantata, pub. Novello, 1890; Norwich Festival, 15 Oct. 1890. Rev. 1909. Aut. RCM; v.s. Bod.

Eton (words: Swinburne), ode, pub. Novello, 1891; Eton College, 28 June 1891. Aut. Eton College Library; v.s. (incomplete) Bod.

De Profundis (words: Psalm 130), pub. Novello, 1891; Three Choirs (Hereford) Festival, 10 Sept. 1891. Aut. ShP. v.s. (incomplete) Bod.

The Lotos-Eaters (words: Tennyson), choric song, pub. Novello, 1892; Cambridge, 13 June 1892. Aut. RCM; v.s. (incomplete) Bod.

Job (words: composer and Bible), oratorio, pub. Novello, 1892 (full score 1898); Three Choirs (Gloucester) Festival, 8 Sept. 1892. Aut. RCM; also BPL; v.s. (almost complete) Bod.

Hear my words ye people (words: Bible), anthem, pub. Novello, 1894; Salisbury Cathedral, 10 May 1894. Aut. RCM.

King Saul (words: composer and Bible), oratorio, pub. Novello, 1894; Birmingham Festival, 3 Oct. 1894. Aut. RCM; v.s. (incomplete) Bod.

Invocation to Music (words: Bridges), ode, pub. Novello, 1895; Leeds Festival, 2 Oct. 1895. Aut. RCM; v.s. (almost complete) Bod.

Magnificat (words: liturgical), pub. Novello, 1897; Three Choirs (Hereford) Festival, 15 Sept. 1897. Aut. BL; v.s. (almost complete) Bod.

A Song of Darkness and Light (words: Bridges), pub. Novello, 1898; Three Choirs (Gloucester) Festival, 15 Sept. 1898. Aut. RCM; v.s. Bod.

Thanksgiving Te Deum (words: liturgical), pub. Novello (Latin) 1900, (English) 1913; Latin version, Three Choirs (Hereford) Festival, 11 Sept. 1900; English (rev.) version, Three Choirs (Gloucester) Festival, 11 Sept. 1913. Aut. RCM; v.s. Bod.

Ode to Music (words: A. C. Benson), ode, pub. Novello 1901; RCM, 13 June 1901. Aut. RCM; v.s. (incomplete) Bod.

I was glad (words: Psalm 122), coronation anthem, pub. Novello, 1902, and rev. version 1911; Coronation of Edward VII, Westminster Abbey, 9 Aug. 1902, cond. Bridge; rev. version, Coronation of George V, Westminster Abbey, 23 June 1911, cond. Bridge. Aut. (rev. version 1911) RCM; v.s. Bod.; see also RCM Novello Collection for score (in copyist's hand) of original version 1902.

War and Peace (words: composer and A. C. Benson), symphonic ode, pub. Novello, 1903; Albert Hall, 30 Apr. 1903. Aut. Bod.; v.s. (almost complete) Bod.

Voces Clamantium (words: composer and Bible), motet, pub. Novello, 1903; Three Choirs (Hereford) Festival, 10 Sept. 1903. Aut. RCM; v.s. (almost complete) Bod.

The love that casteth out fear (words: composer and Bible), sinfonia sacra, pub. Novello, 1904; Three Choirs (Gloucester) Festival, 7 Sept. 1904. Aut. RCM; v.s. (almost complete) Bod.

The Pied Piper of Hamelin (words: Browning), cantata, pub. Novello, 1905 (full score 1906); Norwich Festival, 26 Oct. 1905. Rev. 1910. Aut. RCM; v.s. (incomplete) Bod.

The Soul's Ransom: A Psalm of the Poor (words: composer and Bible), sinfonia sacra, pub. Novello, 1906; Three Choirs (Hereford) Festival, 12 Sept. 1906. Aut. Bod; v.s. Bod.

The Vision of Life (words: composer), symphonic poem, pub. Novello 1907; Cardiff Festival, 26 Sept. 1907. Rev. for Norwich Festival, 1914 but unperformed after postponement: pub. Novello, 1914 Aut. RCM; v.s. (almost complete) Bod.

Beyond these voices there is peace (words: composer and Bible), motet, pub. Novello, 1908; Three Choirs (Worcester) Festival, 9 Sept. 1908. Aut. RCM; v.s. (incomplete) Bod.

Eton Memorial Ode (words: R. Bridges), ode, pub. Novello, 1908; Eton College, 18 Nov. 1908. Aut. Eton College Library; v.s. (incomplete) Bod.

Coronation Te Deum (words: liturgical), pub. Novello 1911; Coronation of George V, Westminster Abbey, 23 June 1911, cond. Bridge. Aut. RCM; v.s. Bod.

Ode on the Nativity (words: Dunbar), ode, pub. Novello, 1912; Three Choirs (Hereford) Festival, 12 Sept. 1912. Aut. RCM; v.s. (incomplete) Bod.

God is our hope (words: Psalm 46), pub. Novello, 1913; St Paul's Cathedral, 24 Apr. 1913. Aut. RCM; v.s. (almost complete) Bod.

The Chivalry of the Sea (words: Bridges), naval ode, pub. Novello, 1916; Albert Hall, 12 Dec. 1916, cond. Allen. Aut. Bod.; v.s. (almost complete) Bod.

B. Church Music

Date of composition is given where not immediately followed by publication. The *Songs of Farewell* have been included here for convenience, though they were not conceived specifically as liturgical works. Unless otherwise stated, extant autographs of works written before 1873 are to be found in manuscript books at Shulbrede Priory. Copies of some of the earliest compositions were made by Emily Daymond in her so-called *Eton Books* now in the Bodleian, Oxford (Bod. MS Mus. d.229).

i. *Canticles*

    Te Deum in B flat, ?1864. Aut. Bod.
    Magnificat and Nunc Dimittis in A, 1864 (unpub.)
    Te Deum and Benedictus in D, pub. Novello, 1868
    Communion, Morning, and Evening Services in D, pub. Novello, 1869. Aut. Evening Service, ORHG.
    Te Deum in E flat, 1873 (unpub.)
    Evening Service in D, 1881; pub. Stainer and Bell (ed. J. Dibble) 1984. Aut. Bod.
    Four-part Grace before a City Dinner (Benedictus), 1897 (unpub.). Aut. ShP.

ii. *Anthems*

    'In my distress', 1863 (unpub.)
    'Fear thou not', 1864 (unpub.). Aut. ORHG
    'O sing unto the Lord a new song', 1864 (unpub.). Aut. ORHG
    'Blessed is he', pub. Novello 1865
    'Prevent us O Lord', pub. Novello 1865; pub. Oxford University Press 1944. Aut. ORHG
    'Why boastest thou thyself', 1865 (unpub.). Aut. ORHG
    'Kyrie eleison' (Fugue a8), 1867 (unpub.)
    'Lobet den Herren', 1867 (unpub.)
    'Blessed are they who dwell in thy house', 1870 (unpub.)
    'Lord I have loved the habitation of thy house', 1870 (unpub.)

iii. *Motets*

(Aut. all in Bod.)
'My soul there is a country', pub. 1916
'I know my soul hath power to know all things', pub. 1916
'Never weather beaten sail', pub. 1916
'There is an old belief', pub. 1916
'At the round earth's imagined corners', pub. 1917
'Lord, let me know mine end', pub. 1917

iv. *Hymns*

'Praise God from whom all blessings flow' (chorale), 1864–5 (unpub.)
147 (Westminster Abbey Hymn Book), pub. 1898
297 (Westminster Abbey Hymn Book), pub. 1898
'The morning the bright and the beautiful', pub. [?]
'The spring's sweet influence', pub. [?]
'God of all created things', pub. 1902
'Freshwater', pub. 1903
'Rustington', pub. 1904
'Amberley', pub. 1904
'Gaudium celeste', pub. 1904
'Intercessor', pub. 1904
'Infantium laudes', pub. 1904
'Richmond', pub. 1904
'Clinton', pub. 1904
'In age and feebleness', pub. 1904
'The day of resurrection', pub. 1904
'Angmering', pub. 1904
'O sylvan prophet', pub. 1910
'Laudate Dominum', pub. 1915
'Hush for amid our tears', pub. 1918

Unpublished hymn tunes which are not possible to date are:
'He is risen'
'Lead kindly light'
'Lord when we bend'
'Of all the thoughts of God'
'St Agatha'
'The Happy morn is come/There is a book'
'Through the day'
'Veni creator'

v. *Miscellaneous*

'Praise God in his holiness', for bass and organ, 1906, unpub.; Hurstbourne
Priory, 19 May 1906. Aut. ShP.
'Soliloquy from Browning's *Saul*' ('I believe it') for bass and organ, unpub.;
Westminster Abbey, 7 May 1912. Aut. Bod.

C. Opera

Guenever (text: Una Taylor; German trans.: Althaus), completed 1886 for Carl Rosa Opera Company. After refusal heavily revised 1886, but remained unperformed. MS v.s. (incomplete) RCM.

D. Theatre Music

Published only in vocal score. Dates of first performances given and revisions. Unless otherwise stated, the first performances listed below were conducted by the composer. In addition to the location of the autograph manuscripts, the autographs of the vocal scores used by the printers have also been included.

The Birds (Aristophanes), incidental music, pub. Stanley Lucas, 1885; rev. version pub. CUP, 1903; Cambridge Amateur Dramatic Club, 27 Nov. 1883, cond. Stanford. Rev. version 24 Nov. 1903. Aut. RCM.

The Frogs (Aristophanes), incidental music, pub. Breitkopf und Härtel, 1892; OUDS, 24 Feb. 1892. Rev. version for OUDS, 19 Feb. 1909. Aut. RCM; v.s. Bod.

Hypatia (Stuart Ogilvie), incidental music, unpub.; Haymarket Theatre, 2 Jan. 1893. Also performed as a suite of five movements (Overture; Entr'acte; Street Scene; Second Entr'acte; Orestes' March) for the Philharmonic Society; St James's Hall, 9 Mar. 1893. Aut. RCM.

A Repentance (Pearl Mary Teresa Craigie—'John Oliver Hobbes'), incidental music, unpub.; St James's Theatre, 28 Feb. 1899. Aut. RCM.

Agamemnon (Aeschylus), incidental music, pub. Novello, 1900; Cambridge Amateur Dramatic Club, 16 Nov. 1900. Aut. RCM; v.s. (almost complete) Bod.

The Clouds (Aristophanes), incidental music, pub. Breitkopf und Härtel, 1905; OUDS, 1 Mar. 1905. Aut. RCM; v.s. Bod.

Proserpine (Shelley), ballet, unpub.; Haymarket Theatre, 25 June 1912. Aut. RCM; see also Bod. for part-song for female voices.

The Acharnians (Aristophanes), incidental music, pub. Breitkopf and Härtel; OUDS, 21 Feb. 1914. Aut. RCM; v.s. Bod.

E. Symphonies

Date of composition is given where not immediately followed by publication. Dates of first performances given along with revisions.

Symphony No. 1 in G major, 1880–2, unpub.; Birmingham Festival, 31 Aug. 1882. Aut. Bod.

Symphony No. 2 in F major, 'The Cambridge', pub. Novello, 1906; Cambridge, 12 June 1883, cond. Stanford; rev. for Richter, St James's Hall, 6 June 1887; rev. version with finale, St James Hall, 30 May 1895. Aut. RCM.

Symphony No. 3 in C major, 'The English', pub. Novello, 1907; St James's Hall, 23 May 1889; rev. for Leeds Subscription Concerts 30 Jan. 1895, with addition of trombones; revised extensively in 1902 for Bournemouth (18 Dec.). Aut. RCM.

Symphony No. 4 in E minor, first version, unpub.; St James's Hall, 1 July 1889; cond. Richter. Aut. RCM; second version, 'Finding the Way', pub. Novello (full score only), 1921; Queen's Hall, 10 Feb. 1910. Aut. RCM.
Symphonic Fantasia (Symphony No. 5), '1912', pub. Goodwin & Tabb, 1922; Queen's Hall, 5 Dec. 1912. Aut. RCM.

F. Concertos

Date of composition is given where not immediately followed by publication. First performances also included.

Concerto for Piano and Orchestra in F sharp major, 1878–80, unpub.; Crystal Palace, 3 Apr. 1880, cond. Manns, soloist Dannreuther; rev. Oct. 1895. Aut. RCM.

G. Orchestral Works

Date of composition is given where not immediately followed by publication. First performances also included along with revisions.

Allegretto Scherzando in E flat, 1867, unpub. Aut. RCM.
Intermezzo Religioso, unpub.; Three Choirs (Gloucester) Festival, 3 Sept. 1868. Aut. RCM.
Overture, *Vivien*, 1873 [lost].
Concertstück in G minor, 1877, unpub. Aut. RCM.
Overture, *Guillem de Cabestanh*, unpub.; Crystal Palace, 15 Mar. 1879, cond. Manns. Aut. RCM.
Suite Moderne (Suite Symphonique), unpub.; Three Choirs (Gloucester) Festival, 9 Sept. 1886. Rev. 1892. Aut. RCM.
Overture to an Unwritten Tragedy, pub. Novello, 1906; Three Choirs (Worcester) Festival, 13 Sept. 1893. Rev. 1897 and again 1905. Aut. RCM.
'Lady Radnor' Suite for strings, pub. Novello, 1902 (also pub. by Novello for piano solo, 1905, and for violin and piano, 1915); St James's Hall, 29 June 1894, cond. Lady Radnor. Autograph of string version missing. Version for small orchestra Aut. RCM.
Elegy for Brahms, 1897, unpub.; RCM, 9 Nov. 1918, cond. Stanford. Aut. RCM.
Symphonic Variations in E minor, pub. Novello, 1897; St James's Hall, 3 June 1897. Aut. RCM.
Symphonic poem in two connected movements, *From Death to Life*, unpub.; Brighton Festival, 12 Nov. 1914. Aut. RCM.
An English Suite for strings, 1890–1918, pub. Novello, 1921 (also pub. by Novello for piano solo, 1923); Promenade Concert, 20 Oct. 1922, cond. Henry Wood. Aut. RHBNC.
Foolish Fantasia ('To finish the frolic if it will do') for wind band, date unknown, unpub. Aut. RCM.

H. Chamber Music

Date of composition is given where not immediately followed by publication.

Three movements for violin and piano in D, 1863, unpub.
String Quartet in G minor, 1867, unpub. Aut. Bod.
Two duettinos for cello and piano, 1868, unpub.
Short trios in F for violin, viola, and piano, 1868, unpub. Aut. Bod.
String Quartet in C, 1868, unpub. Aut. Bod.
Six pieces ('Freundschaftslieder') for Violin and Piano, 1872, unpub. Aut. (incomplete) ShP.
Sonata in D minor for violin and piano, 1875, unpub. Aut. Bod.
Nonet for wind in B flat, 1877, unpub. Aut. RCM.
Piano Trio in E minor, pub. Breitkopf und Härtel, 1879; 12 Orme Square, Bayswater, 31 Jan. 1878. Aut. (incomplete) Bod.
Fantasie Sonate in H moll in einem Satz für Violine und Klavier, 1878, unpub.; 12 Orme Square, Bayswater, 30 Jan. 1879. Aut. Bod.
Piano Quartet in A flat, pub. Novello, 1884; 12 Orme Square, Bayswater, 13 Feb. 1879. Aut. (incomplete) Bod.
String Quartet in G, unpub.; 12 Orme Square, Bayswater, 26 Feb. 1880. See pp. xv–xvi.
Sonata for Cello and Piano in A, pub. Novello, 1883; 12 Orme Square, Bayswater, 12 Feb. 1880. Aut. Bod.
String Quintet in E flat, pub. Novello (score only), 1909; 12 Orme Square, Bayswater, 18 May. 1884. Revised 1896 and again in 1902. Aut. Bod.
Piano Trio in B minor, pub. Novello, 1884; 12 Orme Square, Bayswater, 25 Nov. 1884. Aut. (incomplete) Bod.
Partita in D minor for Violin and Piano (revision of Suite for Violin and Piano 1877), pub. as 'Partita' by Czerny, later Chanot 1890; 12 Orme Square, Bayswater, 2 Dec. 1886. Aut. Bod.
Sonata for Violin and Piano in D, unpub.; 12 Orme Square, Bayswater, 14 Feb. 1889. Rev. 1894. Aut. Bod.
Piano Trio in G, unpub.; 12 Orme Square, Bayswater, 13 Feb. 1890. Aut. Bod.
Twelve Short Pieces for Violin and Piano, pub. Novello, 1895. Aut. Bod.
Piece in G for Violin and Piano, 1896, unpub. Aut. Bod.
Romance in F for Violin and Piano, pub. Teague and Bell, Winchester, 1896. Aut. Bod.
Suite for Violin and Piano in D, pub. Novello, 1907. Aut. Bod.
Suite for Violin and Piano in F, pub. Novello, 1907. Aut. (incomplete) Bod.

I. Piano Solo

Date of composition is given where not immediately followed by publication.

Little Piano Piece (variations), 1862, unpub. ShP.
Piano Piece in G minor, 1865, unpub. Aut. Bod.
Fugue in C minor, 1865, unpub. Aut. Bod.

Fugue in E flat, 1865, unpub. Aut. Bod.
Fugue in F, 1865, unpub. Aut. ORHG.
Fugue in E minor, 1865, unpub. Aut. ORHG.
Andante non troppo in B flat, 1865, unpub. Aut. ORHG.
Overture in B minor for Piano Duet, unpub.; Eton College, 9 Dec. 1865. Aut. Bod.
Sonata in F minor for Piano Duet, 1865, unpub. Aut. (incomplete) ORHG.
Andante in C, 1867, unpub.
Sonnets and Songs Without Words Set I, 1868; pub. Lamborn Cock, 1869.
Three miniatures, 1868, unpub. Aut. Bod.
Sonnets and Songs Without Words Set II, 1867–75; pub. Lamborn Cock, 1875. Aut. (incomplete) Bod.
'A Little Forget-me-not'—Lento delicatissimente in B flat, 1870, unpub. Aut. ORHG.
Seven *Charakterbilder*, pub. Augener 1872.
Two Short Pieces in C and F, ?1873, unpub.
Variations on an Air by Bach, 1873–5, unpub.; Hotel de Provence, Cannes, 9 Mar. 1877; first English performance, 4 Carlton Gardens (home of Arthur Balfour), 1 Apr. 1879. Aut. Bod.
Großes Duo in E minor for Two Pianos, 1875–7, pub. Breitkopf und Härtel, 1877; 12 Orme Square, Bayswater, 11 Apr. 1878. Aut. (incomplete) Bod.
Sonata No. 1 in F, pub. Lamborn Cock, 1877. Aut. (incomplete) Bod.
Sonnets and Songs Without Words Set III, 1870–7, pub. Lamborn Cock, 1877. Aut. Bod.
Sonata No. 2 in A, 1876–7, pub. Stanley Lucas, 1878 (repr. Augener, 1903). Aut. (incomplete) Bod.
Theme and Nineteen Variations, 1878, pub. Stanley Lucas, 1885; 12 Orme Square, Bayswater, 10 Feb. 1885. Aut. missing.
Characteristic Popular Tunes of the British Isles for Piano Duet (2 books: (i) English and Welsh; (ii) Scotch and Irish), 1885, pub. Stanley Lucas, 1885 (repr. Augener, 1901). Aut. (incomplete) Bod.
'Cosy', pub. *Girl's Own Paper*, 1892 (see Five Miniatures, below). Aut. Bod.
Shulbrede Tunes, pub. Augener, 1914. Aut. ShP.
'Sleepy' ?1917, (see 'Five Miniatures', below). Aut. Bod.
Suite, 'Hands across the Centuries', pub. Augener, 1918. Aut. BL.
Five Miniatures (incorporating 'Cosy' and 'Sleepy'), pub. Curwen, 1926. Aut. Bod.

J. Organ Solo

Date of composition is given where not immediately followed by publication.

Four-part Fugue in G (Grand fugue with three subjects), unpub.; St George's Chapel, Windsor, 22 Feb. 1865. Aut. Bod.
Chorale Preludes Set I, pub. Novello, 1912. Aut. RCM.
Fantasia and Fugue in G, initially composed 1877. New Fantasia composed 1882; new Fugue composed 1912; pub. Novello, 1913. Aut. Bod.

Elegy in A flat, pub. privately Novello, 1913; for general circulation, 1922; Wilton, 7 Apr. 1913 (for the funeral of 14th Earl of Pembroke). Aut. ShP.

Three Chorale Fantasias, pub. Novello, 1915. Aut. RCM and ShP.

Chorale Preludes Set II, pub. Novello 1916. Aut. RCM.

Toccata and Fugue in G, 'The Wanderer', 1912–18, pub. Novello, 1921. Aut. Bod.

'For the Little Organ Book', date unknown, incorporated into a publication of short organ pieces by Parry's contemporaries in memory of the composer, pub. Novello, 1924.

K. *Part-songs/Carols*

Date of composition is given where not immediately followed by publication. Numbers of parts (e.g. *a*5) are included as are dedications.

'Tell me where is fancy bred' (Shakespeare), 1864, unpub. Aut. ShP.

'Take, O take those lips away' (Shakespeare), TTBB, unpub.; Eton College, 9 Dec. 1865. Aut. ORHG.

'Persicos odi' (Horace), 1865, unpub. Aut. ShP.

'Fair daffodils' (Herrick), madrigal *a*5, pub. Lamborn Cock, 1866. Aut. ORHG and RCO.

'Oft in the stilly night' (Moore), 1866, unpub. Aut. Eton College Library and RCM.

'Dost thou idly ask' (W. C. Bryant), 1867, unpub. Aut. ORHG.

'Pure spirit; oh where art thou now' (composer?), 1867, unpub. Aut. ORHG.

'There lived a sage' (composer), 1869, unpub. Aut. RCM.

'He is coming' (Gladstone), carol, pub. Novello, 1874.

Three Trios for Female Voices, pub. Lamborn Cock, 1875; ded. 'The Miss Liddells': (i) 'To night' (Hamilton Aidé); (ii) 'To Diana' (Ben Jonson); (iii) 'Take, O take those lips away' (Shakespeare).

Six Lyrics from an Elizabethan Song Book, pub. Novello, 1897; ded the Hon. Spencer Lyttleton CB. Aut. (incomplete) Bod.: (i) 'Follow your saint' (Campion), *a*4; (ii) 'Love is a sickness' (S. Daniel), *a*4; (iii) 'Turn all thy thoughts to eyes' (Campion), *a*4; (iv) 'Whether men do laugh or weep' (from an Elizabethan Song Book), *a*4; (v) 'The sea hath many a thousand sands (from an Elizabethan Song Book), *a*4; (vi) 'Tell me, O love' (from an Elizabethan Song Book), *a*6.

Six Modern Lyrics, pub. Novello, 1897; ded. Magpie Madrigal Society. Aut. (incomplete) Bod.: (i) 'How sweet the answer' (Moore), *a*4; (ii) 'Since thou, O fondest and truest' (Bridges), *a*4; (iii) 'If I had but two little wings' (Coleridge), *a*4; (iv) 'There rolls the deep' (Tennyson), *a*4; (v) 'What voice of gladness' (Bridges), *a*4; (vi) 'Music, when soft voices die' (Shelley), *a*4.

Eight Four-part Songs, pub. Novello, 1898; ded. Walter Parratt. Aut. (incomplete) Bod.: (i) 'Phillis' (from an Elizabethan Song Book); (ii) 'O Love, they wrong thee much' (from an Elizabethan Song Book); (iii) 'At her fair hands' (Robert Jones); (iv) 'Home of my heart' (Arthur Benson); (v) 'You gentle nymphs' (from an Elizabethan Song Book); (vi) 'Come, pretty wag'

(M. Pierson); (vii) 'Ye thrilled me once' (Bridges); (viii) 'Better music ne'er was known' (Beaumont and Fletcher).

'Who can dwell with greatness' (Dobson), *a*5, pub. Macmillan, 1900 as part of a volume entitled 'Choral Songs by various writers and composers in honour of Her Majesty Queen Victoria' compiled by Walter Parratt. Aut. Bod.

'In praise of song' (composer?), *a*8, pub. Novello, 1904. Aut. Bod.

Six Part-songs, pub. Novello, 1909; ded. Lionel Benson. Aut. (incomplete) Bod.: (i) 'In a harbour grene' (R. Wever), *a*4; (ii) 'Sweet day, so cool' (Herbert), *a*4; (iii) 'Sorrow and pain' (Lady C. Elliot), *a*6; (iv) 'Wrong not, sweet Empress' (Sir W. Raleigh), *a*4; (v) 'Prithee, why?' (Sir J. Suckling), *a*4; (vi) 'My delight and thy delight' (Bridges), *a*4.

Seven Part-songs for Male-voice Choir, pub. Novello, 1910, scored for ATB; ded. Gloucester Orpheus Society. Aut. (incomplete) Bod.: (i) 'Hang fear, cast away care' (composer); (ii) 'Love wakes and weeps' (Scott); (iii) 'The mad dog' (Goldsmith); (iv) 'That very wise man, old Aesop' (Dickens); (v) 'Orpheus' (composer); (vi) 'Out upon it!' (Sir J. Suckling); (vii) 'An Analogy' (composer).

'La belle dame sans merci' (Keats), madrigal *a*5, 1914–15, lithographed for private circulation; pub. Broude Brothers, New York, 1979 (ed. P. M. Young); ded. D. W. Rootham and the Madrigal Society of Bristol. Aut. Bod.

'When Christ was born of Mary free' (Harleian MS), carol, pub. Novello, 1915.

Two Carols, pub. Novello, 1917. Aut. Bod.: (i) 'I sing the birth'; (ii) 'Welcome, Yule' (15th century carol).

'I know an Irish lass', ? 1916, unpub.

L. Unison Songs

Date of composition is given where not immediately followed by publication.

'Rock-a-bye', pub. Novello, 1893 (children's Souvenir Song Book). Aut. Bod.

'Land to the leeward ho!' (Margaret Preston), pub. Novello, 1895. Aut. Bod.

'The best school of all' (Henry Newbolt), 1908, pub. Year Book Press 1916. Aut. Bod.

Four Unison Songs, pub. Year Book Press, 1909. Aut. (incomplete) Bod.: (i) 'The owl' (Tennyson); (ii) 'A contented mind' (Sylvester); (iii) 'Sorrow and Song' (Hedderwick) (iv) 'The mistletoe' ('Father Prout').

School Songs, pub. Year Book Press, 1911. Aut. Bod and RCM: (i) 'The way to succeed' (N. Macleod), *a*2; (ii) 'Hie away' (Scott), *a*3; (iii) 'Dreams' (C. F. Alexander), *a*3.

Three Unison Songs, pub. Year Book Press, 1913. Aut. Bod and RCM: (i) 'You'll get there' ('The Trent Otter'); (ii) 'Goodnight' (A. M. Champneys); (iii) Ripple on (A. M. Champneys).

School Songs, pub. Year Book Press, 1914. Aut. Bod.: (i) 'The fairies' (A. M. Champneys), *a*2 in places but optional; (ii) 'The Brown Burns of the Border' (W. H. Ogilvie), *a*3.

'Come join the merry chorus' (Horace Smith), pub. Year Book Press, 1915. Aut. Bod.

'A Hymn for Aviators' (Mary C. D. Hamilton), pub. Year Book Press, 1915 (also pub. Boosey in four-part hymn version). Aut. Bod.

'Three songs for "Kookoorookoo"' (Christina Rossetti), pub. Year Book Press, 1916. Aut. (incomplete) Bod.: (i) 'Brown and furry'; (ii) 'The Peacock'; (iii) 'The wind has such a rainy sound'.
'Jerusalem' (Blake), pub. Curwen 1916 in vocal and full score. Aut. ShP and RCM.
'For all we have and are' (Kipling), 1916, unpub. Aut. Bod.
Three School Songs, pub. Edward Arnold 1918. Aut. Bod.: (i) 'Neptune's empire' (Campion); (ii) 'The wind and the leaves' (Cooper), *a*2; (iii) 'Song of the nights' (Barry Cornwall), *a*2.
'England' (Shakespeare), pub. Year Book Press, 1919 (also full score). Aut. Bod. and RCM.

M. Solo Songs

Date of composition is given where not immediately followed by publication. Dedications given. Unless otherwise stated all autograph manuscripts are located in the Bodleian, Oxford.

'Fair is my love' (Spenser), 1864, unpub. Aut. Bod and ShP.
'When stars are in the quiet skies (Bulwer-Lytton), 1865, unpub. Aut. ShP and ORHG.
'Why does azure deck the sky' (Moore), 1865, pub. Lamborn Cock, 1866; ded. F. Cecil Ricardo.
'Love not me' (anon.), 1865, unpub. Aut. ShP and ORHG.
'Autumn' (Hood), 1865–6, pub. Lamborn Cock, 1867; also scored for high voice and orchestra 1867; ded. Lewis Majendie. Aut. Bod and ShP.
'When the grey skies are flushed with rosy streaks', ? 1866, unpub. Aut. ShP.
'Love the Tyrant' (composer), 1866, unpub.
'Angel hosts, sweet love, befriend thee' (Lord Francis Hervey), 1866, pub. Lamborn Cock, 1867; ded. the Hon. Spencer Lyttleton.
'Go lovely rose' (Waller), 1866, unpub. Aut. ORHG.
'Sleep, my love, untouched by sorrow', 1867, unpub.
'Dainty form, so firm and slight', 1868, unpub.
'An epigram' ('Fairest dreams may be forgotten') (? composer), 1869, unpub.
'Ah! woe is me! poor silver wing!', 1869, unpub.
Three Odes of Anacreon (trans. T. Moore), 1869–78, pub. Augener, 1880. Aut. missing: (i) 'Away, away, you men of rules'; (ii) 'Fill me, boy, as deep a draught' (also with orchestra 1891 Aut. RCM); (iii) 'Golden hues of life are fled'.
'The river of life' (Lord Pembroke), pub. Lamborn Cock, 1870; ded. Lady Maude Herbert. Aut. ShP.
'Not unavailing' ('The flower of purest whiteness'), ? 1872, unpub.
Three Songs, pub. Lamborn Cock, 1873: (i) 'The poet's song' (Tennyson); ded. Lady Alexandrina Murray; (ii) 'More fond than cushat dove' (Thomas Ingoldsby); ded. 'to his wife'; (iii) 'Music [when soft voices die]' (Shelley); ded. 'to his wife'.
'An evening cloud' (John Wilson), 1873, unpub.
'A shadow' ('What lack the valleys') (Adelaide Proctor), 1873, unpub.

A Garland of Shakespearian and Other Old-Fashioned Songs, pub. Lamborn Cock, 1874; repr. by Boosey, 1880–1: (i) 'Love's Perjuries' ('On a day, alack the day') (Shakespeare); (ii) 'A Spring Song' ('It was a lover') (Shakespeare); (iii) 'A Contrast' ('The merry bird sits in the tree') (anon.); (iv) 'Concerning Love' ('Love is a sickness') (S. Daniel); (v) 'A Sea Dirge' ('Full fathom five') (Shakespeare); (vi) 'Merry Margaret' (Skelton).

Four Sonnets (Shakespeare, trans. into German by Friedrich Bodenstedt), 1873–82, pub. Stanley Lucas, 1887; repr. Augener, 1904; ded. Hugh Montgomery. Aut. PRONI: (i) 'When in disgrace'; (ii) 'Farewell, thou art too dear'; (iii) 'Shall I compare thee'; (iv) 'When to the sessions'.

'Twilight' (Lord Pembroke), 1874, pub. Lamborn Cock, 1875.

'Sonnet' ('If thou survive') (Shakespeare), 1874, unpub. Aut. Bod. and PRONI.

'Absence, hear my protestation' (John Hoskins), 1881, unpub.

'And wilt thou leave me thus?' (Sir Thomas Wyatt), 1881, unpub.

'My passion you regard with scorn' ? 1881, unpub.

'I arise from dreams of thee' (Shelley), 1883, unpub.

English Lyrics Set I, 1881–5, pub. Stanley Lucas, 1885; repr. Novello: (i) 'My true love hath my heart' (Sir Philip Sidney); ded. 'to my wife'. Aut. Bod. and RCM; (ii) 'Good night' (Shelley); ded. Mrs Arthur Lyell. Aut. RCM and NYPL; (iii) 'Where shall the lover rest' (Scott); ded. Miss Anna Williams. Aut. RCM; (iv) 'Willow, willow, willow' (anon.); ded. 'to my wife'.

English Lyrics Set II (all texts by Shakespeare), 1874–85, pub. Stanley Lucas, 1886; repr. Novello: (i) 'O mistress mine', Aut. ShP; (ii) 'Take, O take those lips away'; (iii) 'No longer mourn for me' (Sonnet LXXI); (iv) 'Blow, blow thou winter wind', Aut. ShP; (v) 'When icicles hang by the wall'.

'The maid of Elsinore' (Harold Boulton), pub. Leadenhall Press, 1891 in H. Boulton (ed.), 'Twelve New Songs by British Composers'; repr. Novello.

English Lyrics Set III, pub. Novello, 1895: (i) 'To Lucasta' (Lovelace); (ii) 'If thou would'st ease thine heart' (Beddoes); (iii) 'To Althea' (Lovelace); (iv) 'Why so pale and wan' (Suckling); (v) 'Through the ivory gate' (Sturgis); (vi) 'Of all the torments' (attrib. William Walsh).

English Lyrics Set IV, 1885–96, pub. Novello, 1896: (i) 'Thine eyes still shined for me' (Emerson); ded. 'to Dolly'. Aut. ShP; (ii) 'When lovers meet again' (L. E. Mitchell); ded. 'to Maude'; (iii) 'When we two parted' (Byron); ded. 'to Gwen'. Aut. ShP; (iv) 'Weep you no more' (anon.); ded. Mrs Robert Benson; (v) 'There be none of Beauty's daughters' (Byron); ded. Evelyn de Vesci; (vi) 'Bright star' (Keats); ded. Robert Benson.

'The north wind' ('Fresh from his fastnesses') for bass and orchestra (W. E. Henley), 1899, unpub. Aut. RCM.

'Von edler Art' ('Noble of air') (from a Nuremberg song book, 1549, trans. Paul England), 1900, pub. Boosey, 1906.

'The soldier's tent' for baritone and orchestra (from 'The Bard of Dimbovitza', English version by Alma Strettell and Carmen Sylva), 1900, pub. Novello, 1901 only in v.s.; ded. 'to Mrs Harry Plunket Greene'. Aut. RCM.

English Lyrics Set V, 1876–1901, pub. Novello, 1902; ded. 'to my sister Hilda': (i) 'A stray nymph of Dian' (Sturgis); (ii) 'Proud Maisie' (Scott); (iii) 'Crabbed age and youth' (Shakespeare); (iv) 'Lay a garland' (Beaumont and Fletcher); (v)

'Love and laughter' (Arthur Butler). Aut. ShP; (vi) 'A girl to her glass' (Sturgis). Aut. ShP; (vii) 'A Welsh lullaby' ('Ceirog', trans. E. O. Jones).
English Lyrics Set VI, pub. Novello, 1903: (i) 'When comes my Gwen' ('Mynydogg', trans. E. O. Jones); ded. H[arry] P[lunket] G[reene] and G[wen] P[lunket] G[reene]. Aut. RCM; (ii) 'And yet I love her till I die' (anon.); ded. E. M[aude] P[arry]; (iii) 'Love is a bable' (anon.); (iv) 'A lover's garland' (Greek, trans. Alfred Perceval Graves); (v) 'At the hour the long day ends' (Greek, trans. Alfred Perceval Graves). Aut. ShP; (vi) 'Under the greenwood tree' (Shakespeare).
'Newfoundland' (first setting) (Sir Cavendish Boyle), pub. Novello, 1904.
'Fear no more the heat o' the sun' (Shakespeare), pub. Ditson, Boston, USA, 1905.
'The Laird of Cockpen' for baritone (Lady Nairn), 1906, pub. Novello, 1907. Aut. ShP.
English Lyrics Set VII, 1888–1906, pub. Novello, 1907: (i) 'On a time the amorous Silvy' (anon.); ded. 'to Dolly'; (ii) 'Follow a shadow' (Ben Jonson). (iii) 'Ye little birds' (attrib. Thomas Heywood); ded. 'To Harry'; (iv) Sonnet CIX ('O never say that I was false of heart') (Shakespeare); ded. 'to my wife'. Aut. Bod. and ShP; (v) 'Julia' (Herrick); (vi) 'Sleep' (Sturgis); ded. 'to my wife'.
English Lyrics Set VIII, c.1904–6, pub. Novello, 1907: (i) 'Whence' (Sturgis); ded. 'to Dolly'; (ii) 'Nightfall in winter' (L. E. Mitchell); ded. 'to Gwen'. Aut. ShP; (iii) 'Marian' (Meredith); ded. 'to Dolly'; (iv) 'Dirge in woods' (Meredith); ded. N[orah] D[awnay]; (v) 'Looking backward' (Sturgis); ded. 'to my wife'; (vi) 'Grapes' (Sturgis).
English Lyrics Set IX (to poems of Mary Coleridge), 1908, pub. Novello, 1909; ded. Arthur Duke Coleridge: (i) 'Three aspects'; (ii) 'A fairy town (St Andrews)'; (iii) 'The witches' wood'. Aut. Bod. and ShP; (iv) 'Whether I live'; (v) 'Armida's garden'; (vi) 'The maiden'; (vii) 'There'.
English Lyrics Set X, 1909, pub. Novello, 1918 ded. Agnes Hamilton Harty: (i) 'My heart is like a singing bird' (C. Rossetti); (ii) 'Gone were but the winter cold' (Allan Cunningham); (iii) 'A moment of farewell' (Sturgis) Aut. ShP; (iv) 'The child and the twilight' (L. E. Mitchell). Aut. ShP; (v) 'From a city window' (L. E. Mitchell); (vi) 'The ungentle guest' ('One silent night of late') (Herrick). Aut. ShP.
English Lyrics Set XI, 1910–18, pub. Novello, 1920, Emily Daymond, Harry Plunket Greene, Charles Wood (eds.): (i) 'One golden thread' (Julia Chatterton); (ii) 'What part of dread eternity' (? composer); (iii) 'The spirit of the spring' (Alfred Perceval Graves). Aut. ShP; (iv) 'The blackbird' (Alfred Perceval Graves); (v) 'The faithful lover' (Alfred Perceval Graves); (vi) 'If I might ride on puissant wing' (Sturgis); (vii) 'Why art thou slow' (Philip Massinger); (viii) 'She is my love' (Alfred Perceval Graves). Aut. ShP.
English Lyrics Set XII, various dates (some very early), pub. Novello, 1920;, Emily Daymond, Harry Plunket Greene, Charles Wood (eds.): (i) 'When the dew is falling' (Julia Chatterton); (ii) 'To blossoms' (Herrick); (iii) 'Rosaline' (Thomas Lodge). Aut. ShP; (iv) 'Resurrection' ('When the sun's great orb') (H. Warner); 'written for Miss Alice Elieson'; (v) 'Dream pedlary' (Beddoes); (vi)

'A lament' ('O world! O life! O time!') (Shelley); (vii) 'The sound of hidden music' (Julia Chatterton).

The following unpublished songs were completed but their dates are unknown:

'Arise!' (H. Warner)
'As thro' the land at eve we went' (Tennyson)
'Bitter sweet' ('He leapt to arms') (Newbolt)
'The day of life' (Hamilton Aidé)
'Does the road wind upwards' (? C. Rossetti)
'Her eyes the glow-worm lend thee' (Herrick)
'High on the throne of golden light'
'Hollow and vast starr'd skies are o'er us'
'I feed a flame within' (? Dryden)
'Miss Agnes had two or three dolls'
'The moon has cast her soft pale light'
'My soul is like a bird, singing in fair weather' (with orchestra)
'Newfoundland' (second setting—probably 1904) (Sir Cavendish Boyle)
'One day I was watching a boat' (possibly 1865) Aut. ORHG
'She thought by heaven's high wall that she did stray'
'Sweet violets'
'Tired are mine eyes of the world'
'Vergiss mein nicht' (also arr. for piano, organ, or violin and piano)
'Weep not over poets wrong'
'Welcome, sweet treasure'
'When I was a maid nor of lovers afraid' (? James Kenney)
'Where Claribel low-lieth' for high voice, strings and two horns (Tennyson)
'The woods are clothed with violets'
'Ye flowering banks of bonny Doon' (Burns)

N. Arrangements and Copies

Arrangement of Suite in E minor by William Boyce for string orchestra (additional viola part by Parry), pub. Joseph Williams, 1892; St James's Hall, 29 June 1894.
Copy of Brahms's Serenade in A, Op. 16, copied Mount Merrion, Dublin, Ireland, 1874. Aut. Bod.
'Soul of the World' by Henry Purcell (From 'Hail, bright Cecilia', 1692), arranged with additional orchestration; Queen's Hall, Suffrage Demonstration Concert, 13 Mar. 1918. Aut. RCM.

O. Books

Studies of the Great Composers, pub. George Routledge & Sons Ltd., 1887; first appeared as a series of articles in *Every Girl's Magazine*. Aut. ShP.
The Art of Music, pub. Kegan Paul, Trench, Trübner & Co. Ltd., 1893; later enlarged and repub. as *The Evolution of the Art of Music*, 1896. Aut. Bod.

Summary of Music History (full title: *Summary of the History and Development of Medieval and Modern European Music*), pub. Novello, 1893; 2nd edn., 1904. Aut. ShP.

The Music of the Seventeenth Century (*Oxford History of Music*, iii), pub. Oxford University Press, 1902. Aut. ShP.

Johann Sebastian Bach, pub. G. P. Putnam's Sons, 1910. Aut. ShP.

Style in Musical Art, pub. Macmillan & Co. Ltd., 1911. Aut. ShP.

'Instinct and Character', unpub. *c*.1915–18, foreword by Arthur Ponsonby; typescripts lodged in BL, RCM, Bod., and ShP.

College Addresses, H. C. Colles (ed.), pub. Macmillan & Co. Ltd., 1920.

P. Articles and Public Lectures

Articles for *A Dictionary of Music and Musicians* (*A.D. 1450–1889*), edited by Sir George Grove DCL, pub. Macmillan & Co., 1890: Arrangement; Alberti Bass; Bass; Basso Continuo; Basso ostinato; Beats; Benedicite; Benedictus; Cadence; Cadenza; Cantata; Cantate Domino; Canticle; Cantoris; Chamber Music; Chladni; Chorale; Chord; Chromatic; Classical; Close; Coda; Codetta; Comma; Communion Service; Compass; Composition; Concord; Consecutive; Consonance; Construction; Contrapuntal; Contrary Motion; Countersubject; Credo; Creed; Alfred Day; Dance Rhythm; Decani; Degree; Deus Misereatur; Development; Diapason; Diatonic; Diesis; Diminished Intervals; Diminution; Discord; Dissonance; Dominant; Episodes; Exposition; Fantasia; Fermata; Fifth; Figure; Figured Bass; Form; Fourth; French Sixth; Fundamental Bass; German Sixth; Gloria; Ground Bass; Harmony; Harmony Metamorphosis; Imperfect Cadence; Interval; Introduction; Italian Sixth; Jubilate; Key; Kirchen Cantaten; Leading Note; Leitmotif; Licence; Liedform; Lyric; Major; Measure; Melody; Minor; Mixed Cadence; Modulation; Motion; Natural; Neapolitan Sixth; Ninth; Octave; Passage; Passing Notes; Percussion; Perfect; Period; Phrase; Plagal Cadence; Preparation; Progression; Relation; Resolution; Retardation; Root; Second; Sequence; Seventh; Sixth; Sonata; Sonatina; Subdominant; Submediant; Suite; Supertonic; Suspension; Symphony; Third; Tonality; Transition; Triad; Tune; Unison; Variations; Working-out.

'A Lecture on the Science of Sound', Town Hall, Chertsey, 7 Sept. 1875.

'Early Italian Sixteenth-century Music', Royal Institution, 21 Nov. 1889.

'Characteristics of Early English Secular Choral Music', Masonic Hall, Birmingham (Birmingham Musical Guild), 7 Feb. 1890.

'Evolution in Music', Royal Institution, 28 Feb. 1890.

'The Position of Lully, Purcell, and Scarlatti in the History of Opera', Royal Institution, 12, 19 and 26 Feb. 1891.

'Expression and Design in Music', Royal Institution, 21 and 28 Jan., 4 and 11 Feb. 1893.

'Realism and Idealism in Art', Royal Institution, 1, 8, and 15 Feb. 1896.

'Neglected By-ways in Music', Royal Institution, 20 and 27 Jan., 3 Feb. 1900.

'Style in Musical Art', an inaugural lecture at the University of Oxford, 7 Mar. 1900.

'How Modern Song Grew up', lecture given at Reading University College, 9 Nov. 1910; (see text in *Musical Times* (1 Jan. 1911), 11–15).

'The Meaning of Ugliness in Art', International Musical Congress of the International Musical Society, London, 30 May 1911.

BIBLIOGRAPHY

SOURCES of major musical and biographical reference, together with books and articles yielding important social background, are listed here. However, I have not attempted to present a comprehensive bibliography of Sir Hubert Parry and his works; many books merely regurgitating secondary or anecdotal material have been omitted.

The general alphabetical listing is by author. Files of the *Illustrated London News*, *Musical Times*, *The Times*, *Pall Mall Gazette*, *Athenaeum*, *Fortnightly Review*, *Monthly Musical Record*, *Musical Herald*, *Musical Opinion*, *Musical Standard*, and *Music Student* proved invaluable throughout.

All titles were published in London except where otherwise stated.

ABDY, J., and GERE, C., *The Souls* (1984).

ABRAHAM, G. (ed.), *The New Oxford History of Music*, ix, *Romanticism 1830–1890*, (Oxford, 1990).

BACHE, CONSTANCE, *Brother Musicians: Reminiscences of Edward and Walter Bache* (1901).

BAILEY, C., 'Sir Hubert Parry and OUDS', *Oxford Magazine* (25 Oct. 1918), 24–5.

BANFIELD, S., 'British Chamber Music at the Turn of the Century', *Musical Times* (Mar. 1974), 211–13.

—— 'Renaissance Men', *Listener* (12 Jan. 1984), 32.

—— *Sensibility and English Song* (Cambridge, 1985).

BARNETT, J. F., *Musical Reminiscences and Impressions* (1906).

BARSHAM, E., 'Parry's Manuscripts: A Rediscovery', *Musical Times* (Feb. 1960), 86–7.

BAYLIS, S., 'The Lady Radnor of Parry's Suite', *Strad* (Oct. 1939), 251–2.

BEECHEY, G., 'Parry and his organ music', *Musical Times* (Oct. 1968), 956–8; (Nov. 1968), 1057–9.

BENTLEY, J., *Ritualism and Politics in Victorian Britain* (1978).

BLOM, E., *Music in England* (1942).

BLUME, F., *Classic and Romantic Music* (1972).

BOUGHTON, R., 'Modern British Song Writers: II. Parry', *Music Student* (May 1913), 39–40.

BRENT-SMITH, A., 'Charles Hubert Hastings Parry', *Music and Letters*, 7/3 (July 1926), 221–8.

BRIDGE, SIR F., *A Westminster Pilgrim* (1918).

BUMPUS, J. S., *A History of English Cathedral Music, 1549–1889* (1908).

CARLEY, L., *Delius: A Life in Letters*, i. (1983); ii. (Aldershot, 1988).

CHADWICK, OWEN, *The Victorian Church* (2 vols.; 1966–70).

CHARLTON, P., *John Stainer* (1984).

COLERIDGE-TAYLOR, A., with YOUNG, P. M. *The Heritage of Samuel Coleridge-Taylor* (1979).

COLLES, H. C., *The Growth of Music* (Oxford, 1916).

—— 'Sir Hubert Parry', *Music Student* (Mar. 1916), 177–8.

—— (ed.), *Grove's Dictionary of Music and Musicians*, 3rd edn. (5 vols.; 1927).

—— *Oxford History of Music*, vii. (Oxford, 1934).

—— *Walford Davies: A Biography* (1942).

—— 'Parry as a Song-writer', *Essays and Lectures* (Oxford, 1945), 55–75.

CUNNINGHAM A., and JARDINE, N., *Romanticism and the Sciences* (Cambridge, 1990).

DARKE, H., 'Memories of Parry', *RCM Magazine* (Christmas Term 1968), 77–8.

DAYMOND, EMILY, 'Hubert Parry: A Catalogue of Works', [MS], ShP.

—— 'On an Early Manuscript Book of Sir Hubert Parry's', *RCM Magazine* (Summer Term 1924), 75–9.

—— *Catalogue* for the 3rd edn. of *Grove's Dictionary of Music and Musicians*, ed. H. C. Colles (1927).

DEMUTH, NORMAN, *Musical Trends in the Twentieth Century* (1952).

DENT, E. J., 'Parry's Prometheus Unbound', *Cambridge Review* (8 June 1927), 488.

DIBBLE, J. C., 'Structure and Tonality in Parry's Chamber Music', *Journal of the British Music Society*, 3 (1981), 13–23.

—— 'The RCM Novello Library', *Musical Times* (Feb. 1983), 99–101.

—— 'Parry and English Diatonic Dissonance', *Journal of the British Music Society*, 5 (1983), 58–71.

—— 'Parry and Elgar: A New Perspective', *Musical Times* (Nov. 1984), 639–43.

—— 'Under a Bushel', *Listener* (10 Oct. 1985), 35.

—— 'Inner Loneliness', *Listener* (19 Mar. 1987), 31.

DICKINSON, A. E. F., 'The Neglected Parry', *Musical Times* (Apr. 1949).

—— *Vaughan Williams* (1963).

ELGAR, E., *A Future for English Music and Other Lectures*, ed. Percy M. Young (1968).

ELVEY, Lady, *The Life and Reminiscences of Sir George Elvey Knt* (1894).

FINZI, G., 'Hubert Parry: A Revaluation', *Music Maker*, 5 (Summer 1949), 4–8.

FOSTER, MYLES BIRKET, *History of the Philharmonic Society* (1912).

FOX, WINIFRED, *Douglas Fox: A Chronicle* (Bristol, 1976).

GAMBIER PARRY, E., *Annals of an Eton House* (1907).

GANZ, WILHELM, *Memories of a Musician* (1913).

GATENS, W. J., *Victorian Cathedral Music in Theory and Practice* (Cambridge, 1986).

GLASSTONE, VICTOR, *Victorian and Edwardian Theatres* (1975).

GOMME, G. L., *London in the Reign of Victoria* (1898).

GRAVES, CHARLES L., *Sir George Grove, C.B.* (1903).

—— *Hubert Parry* (2 vols.; 1926).

GREENE, G., *Two Witnesses* (1930).

GREENE, H. PLUNKET, *Charles Villiers Stanford* (1935).

GRIERSON, M., *Donald Francis Tovey* (Oxford, 1952).

GROVE, G. (ed.), *A Dictionary of Music and Musicians (A.D. 1450–1889)* (1879–89).

HADOW, W. H., 'Parry', *Proceedings of the Royal Musical Association* (1918–19), 135–47; also published in *Collected Essays* (Oxford, 1928), 148–61.
—— 'Parry's Music', *Musical Herald* (July 1919), 220–1.
HAVERGAL, FRANCIS T., *Memorials of Revd Sir Frederick Arthur Gore Ouseley Bart.* (1889).
HAWEIS, Revd. H. R., *Music and Morals* (1871).
HOGARTH, GEORGE, *The Philharmonic Society of London* (1862).
HONOR, HUGH, *Romanticism* (1979).
HOWELLS, H., 'Hubert Parry', *RCM Magazine* (Christmas Term 1968), 19–23.
HOWES, FRANK, *The English Musical Renaissance* (1966).
HUEFFER, FRANCIS, *The Troubadours* (1878).
—— *Half a Century of Music in England 1837–1887* (1889).
HURD, M., *The Ordeal of Ivor Gurney* (Oxford, 1984).
JACKSON, H., *The Eighteen Nineties: A Review of Art and Ideas at the Close of the 19th Century* (1913 and 1976).
JACOBS, A., *Arthur Sullivan* (Oxford, 1986).
JONES, R. A., *Arthur Ponsonby* (1989).
KEATING, P., *The Haunted Study* (1989).
KENNEDY, M., *Portrait of Elgar*, rev. and enlarged edn. (Oxford, 1982).
LAURENCE, D. H. (ed.) *Shaw's Music* (1981).
LEGGE, R. H., 'Charles Hubert Hastings Parry', *Musical Times* (Nov. 1918), 489–91; obituary followed by 'The Funeral', 491–2.
LUCE, K. H., 'Parry's Chorale Preludes', *Music Student* (Aug. 1918), 456.
LYSONS, Revd. D., AMOTT, J., LEE WILLIAMS, C., GODWIN CHANCE, H., *Origins and Progress of the Meeting of the Three Choirs of Gloucester, Worcester, and Hereford and of the Charity connected with it, commenced by the Revd Daniel Lysons, carried on to 1864 by John Amott (organist of Gloucester Cathedral), and continued to 1894 by C. Lee Williams and H. Godwin Chance* (Gloucester, 1895).
MACFARREN, GEORGE A., *Addresses and Lectures* (1888).
MACKENZIE, A. C., 'Hubert Hastings Parry: His Place among British composers', *Proceedings of the Royal Institution of Great Britain*, 22 (1922), 542–9.
—— *A Musician's Narrative* (1927).
MACKERNESS, E. D., *A Social History of English Music* (1964).
MACLEAN, C., 'Hubert Parry's Latest Work', *Zeitschrift der Internationalen Musikgesellschaft* (Leipzig), 4 (1903), 673–80.
MACNAUGHT, W., 'Hubert Parry 1848–1918', *Musical Times* (Feb. 1948), 41–2.
MCVEAGH, D., *Edward Elgar: His Life and Music* (1955).
MAITLAND, J. A. FULLER., 'Mr C. Hubert Parry's "Scenes from Prometheus Unbound"', *Monthly Musical Record* (Aug. 1881), 153–4.
—— *English Music in the Nineteenth Century* (1902).
—— *The Music of Parry and Stanford* (Cambridge, 1934).
MOORE, G., *Singer and Accompanist*, (1953).
MOORE, J. NORTHROP, *Edward Elgar: A Creative Life* (Oxford, 1984).
—— *Elgar and his Publishers* (2 vols.; Oxford, 1987).
—— *Edward Elgar: The Windflower Letters* (Oxford, 1989).

MOORE, J. NORTHROP. *Edward Elgar: Letters of a Lifetime* (Oxford, 1990).

MORRIS, R. O., 'Hubert Parry', *Music and Letters* (Mar. 1920), 94–103.

MULLEN, R., and MUNSON, J., *Victoria: Portrait of a Queen* (1987).

NEAD, L., *Myths of Sexuality* (Oxford, 1988).

NEWELL, H. G., *William Yeates Hurlstone* (1936).

NEWMAN, E., 'Hubert Parry', *Sunday Times* (4 and 11 Apr. 1926).

PARRY, C. Hubert H., *Studies of the Great Composers* (1887).

—— *The Art of Music* (1893); also revised as *The Evolution of the Art of Music* (1896).

—— *Summary of Music History* (1893).

—— *The Music of the Seventeenth Century*, Oxford History of Music, iii (Oxford, 1902).

—— *Johann Sebastian Bach* (New York and London, 1910).

—— *Style in Musical Art* (1911).

PEMBLE, J., *The Mediterranean Passion* (Oxford, 1987).

PONSONBY, A., 'On Instinct and Character', *Times Literary Supplement* (23 Mar. 1922), 195–6.

PONSONBY, D., 'Pages from the Notebooks of Hubert Parry', *Music and Letters* (Oct. 1920), 318–29.

PRAZ, MARIO, *The Romantic Agony* (1933).

QUENNELL, P., *Romantic England* (1970).

RAINBOW, BERNARR, *The Choral Revival in the Anglican Church* (1970).

RICHARDS, JOHN MORGAN, *The Life of John Oliver Hobbes* (1911).

RIPPIN, J. W., 'George Butterworth, 1885–1916', *Musical Times* (1966), 680–2; 769–71.

RUSKIN, J., *The Queen of the Air* (1869).

—— *Ruskin on Music*, ed. A. M. Wakefield (1894).

SCHOLES, P., *The Mirror of Music, 1844–1944: A Century of Musical Life in Britain as Reflected in the Pages of the 'Musical Times'* (2 vols.; 1947).

SHAW, G. B., *The Perfect Wagnerite* (1898).

SHAW, H. WATKINS, *The Three Choirs Festival* (Worcester, 1954).

SHINN, F. G., 'King Edward the Seventh and the Founding of the Royal College of Music', *RCM Magazine*, 6/3 (Summer 1910).

STANFORD, C. V., *Studies and Memories* (1908).

—— *Pages from an Unwritten Diary* (1914).

—— *Interludes, Records, and Reflections* (1922).

STANFORD, DONALD E. (ed.), *The Selected Letters of Robert Bridges* (Delaware, 1984).

STERNDALE BENNETT, J. R., *The Life of Sir William Sterndale Bennett* (Cambridge, 1907).

SUTCLIFFE SMITH, J., *The Story of Music in Birmingham* (Birmingham, 1945).

TEMPERLEY, N. (ed.), *The Romantic Age 1800–1914*, The Blackwell History of Music in Britain, v. (Oxford, 1988).

THOMPSON, F. M. L., *English Landed Society in the Nineteenth Century* (1963).

THOMSON, D., *England in the Nineteenth Century* (1950).

TOVEY, D., and PARRATT, G., *Walter Parratt* (1941).

TOVEY, D. F., *Essays in Musical Analysis*, ii, iv, and v (Oxford, 1937).

TREVELYAN, G. M., *English Social History* (1942).
VAUGHAN WILLIAMS, R., 'Parry' (obituary), *Music Student* (Nov. 1918), 79.
—— *National Music and Other Essays*, 2nd edn. (Oxford, 1987).
WALKER, E., *A History of Music in England* (Oxford, 1907), 3rd edn. enlarged and rev. by J. A. Westrup (Oxford, 1952).
—— 'Parry's Shulbrede Tunes', *Monthly Musical Record* (Nov. 1935), 151–2.
WALVIN, J., *Victorian Values* (1987).
WEBB, F. G., 'The Words of Sir Hubert Parry', *Musical Times* (Nov. 1918), 492–4.
WHEELER, M., *Death and the Future Life in Victorian Literature and Theology* (Cambridge, 1990).
WHITTAKER, W. G., 'A Neglected Masterpiece', *Musical Times* (Dec. 1938), 898–9.
WHITTALL, A., *Romantic Music* (1987).
WICKHAM, C. T., *The Story of Twyford School* (Winchester, 1909).
WICKHAM, R. G., *Shades of the Prison-House* (Winchester, 1986).
WILLEBY, C., *Masters of English Music* (1893).
WOOD, HENRY J., *My Life of Music* (1938).
YOUNG, P. M., *Sir Arthur Sullivan* (1971).
—— *George Grove* (1980).

List of Documentary Sources

Extensive use has been made of Parry's diaries (ShP) which begin in 1864 and end a month before his death in September 1918. At present the diary for 1887 has not been found, though fortunately Dorothea Ponsonby made a copy of numerous select entries which have been used in this study. The diaries of Mrs Isabella Mary Lear (ShP), Charles Clinton Parry (ShP), Thomas Gambier Parry (ORHG), and Arthur Ponsonby (ShP) also proved invaluable as did the following sources of letters:

BL MSS 40730, 41570, 41638, 41639, 42233, 46252, 46253, 48341, 48621, 55239, 60499, D.123.f. (p. 92), Egerton 3090, 3305, Loan 48 13/26, BLUL MS 361/185–190, Bod. MS Eng. Letters, BUL DM47, DM56, DM433, CUL 6218, 6463, 6259, 4403, 7481, Fz/MC, HWRO 705:445 5247/8, McUL, RCO, RCM Add. MS 4764 RAWC W.19/6, Add. 17/2014–16, PPVIC.21774 (1897), RUL 1399/2/2, ShP, TCC MS.R.2.48, and in the possession of Sylvia Loeb, Michael Darke, and Robert Lowry.

INDEX OF WORKS

NB. Numbers underlined are those that pertain to music examples.

INDEX